M. PURBHOO   CHRISTINE A. HEANEY

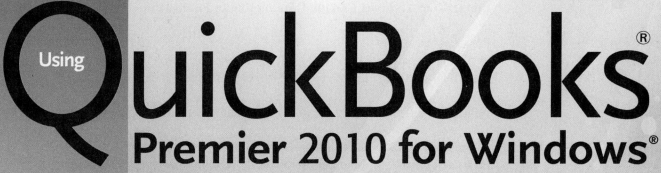

Using **QuickBooks**®
Premier 2010 for Windows®

D1298943

Pearson Canada
Toronto

Library and Archives Canada Cataloguing in Publication

Purbhoo, Mary, 1949–
    Using QuickBooks Premier 2010 for Windows / M. Purbhoo, Christine A. Heaney. —
QuickBooks Pro 2007 update ed. / 2007 updates by Christine Heaney

ISBN 978-0-321-68718-0 (trade ed.). — ISBN 978-0-321-68719-7 (college ed.)

1. QuickBooks. 2. Small business—Accounting—Computer programs. 3. Small
business—Finance—Computer programs. 4. Accounting--Computer programs. I.
Heaney, Christine, 1961– II. Title.

HF5679.P885 2010   657'.9042028553   C2010-901659-9

This edition is also published as Teach Yourself QuickBooks Premier 2010 for Windows.

ISBN 978-0-321-68719-7 (college)
ISBN 978-0-321-68718-0 (trade)

Vice-President, Editorial Director: Gary Bennett
Editor-in-Chief and Acquisitions Editor: Nicole Lukach
Marketing Manager: Cas Shields
Developmental Editor: Christina Lee
Project Manager: Lila Campbell
Production Editor: Susan Adlam
Copy Editor: Marg Bukta
Compositor: Debbie Kumpf
Art Director: Julia Hall
Cover and Interior Designer: Anthony Leung
Cover Image: ShutterStock Images

1 2 3 4 5   14 13 12 11 10

Printed and bound in United States of America.

CONTENTS

CD-ROM Chapters

PREFACE

Using QuickBooks® Premier 2010 for Windows® is the second edition of the QuickBooks series. This textbook is an introduction to QuickBooks, where we have covered the basic and most commonly used features of the QuickBooks program.

The biggest challenge in writing this textbook was presented by the QuickBooks program itself — the program is very flexible and offers many different ways of completing each type of transaction. Our efforts to present keystroke instructions in a simple, straightforward way, meant making choices about the method we describe as the main one. In most cases, we present some alternative keystrokes when we introduce a new feature. We expect that users will choose the methods they prefer for opening forms and completing them. As long as the information entered on the form is correct, the end result is the same.

In Chapter 1, we provide an introduction and overview of the program using a practice company data set with which you can experiment safely without damaging any other data files. This chapter also covers the basics of the Help features in the program, and we expect that you will draw on these as needed as you work through the exercises. Chapter 2 provides an overview of sales taxes —GST, PST and HST. Feedback from instructors has told us that this is an important chapter.

To teach the software, we have created 12 company simulations (Chapters 13 and 14 are found on the CD that accompanies this textbook) with realistic transactions or source documents so that as you learn the program you are also completing realistic business accounting activities. At the end of each chapter or simulation, you will be able to generate a set of meaningful business reports from these transactions.

To create meaningful reports, you must enter a variety of transactions — no business has only sales or only purchases. Therefore, we have organized topics by the features the company in the chapter might use, beginning with a very simple cash transaction business (cash sales and cash purchases) that generates basic business reports. To this we add more features in each chapter so that the chapters build progressively in both number of features and complexity of the business. Each chapter continues to use, and build on, the types of transactions introduced earlier. This approach provides practice, reinforces earlier topics and makes the simulations more realistic.

To get you started immediately, we provide data files already set up and ready for transactions. Setting up a new company is more complex than most accounting transactions, so we introduce them later, progressing from a very simple business to a more complex setup. Even for the setup exercises, we provide data files that are ready for transactions so that you can complete the transactions for additional practice before attempting the setup of new data files.

The first time a feature is introduced in the textbook, we provide simple-to-follow step-by-step keystroke instructions with a large number of screen shots that guide you through the transactions. Chapters that introduce new transactions also include complete instructions for generating the reports related to those transactions.

After covering the very basic cash business in Chapter 3, the second company, in Chapter 4, introduces the General Journal but still makes cash sales and cash purchases. Because of frequent requests from instructors to introduce company setups early on in the text, in Chapter 5 we show the setup for a simple non-profit organization that completes only cash and General Journal transactions. We also set up the taxes for the non-profit to track the 2.5% eligible GST and the 2.5% ineligible GST.

Then we add Accounts Payable (Chapter 6) and Accounts Receivable (Chapter 7) transactions. More advanced features within the areas covered up to Chapter 7 are introduced in the next two chapters — discounts , estimates and purchase orders in Chapter 8, and banking, account reconciliation and sales tax remittance in Chapter 9. In Chapter 10, the second setup chapter, you learn how to set up all the features that you have used in the previous chapters. Payroll, including payroll tax remittance, is covered in Chapter 11 and inventory is covered in Chapter 12. Chapter 13 (found on the CD included with the textbook) is the final keystroke setup chapter that includes setting up the payroll and inventory features. Chapter 14 (found on the CD included with the textbook) is a comprehensive practice chapter that you set up on your own. This chapter includes all the elements covered in the text for a final review.

Using This Book

The accounting applications in this textbook were prepared using QuickBooks Premier 2010 software published by Intuit Canada. You must have installed the QuickBooks Premier 2010 program that is available as a download with this textbook or another licensed copy of QuickBooks Premier to work through the applications in this textbook.

You must also have a hard disk and CD-ROM drive or a network system with Windows installed. Network users should work with their site administrator to ensure program and data access.

To review accounting principles, you should have a standard accounting text. We provide some accounting principles in the text and in the Review of Basic Accounting on the Data CD, but these are not intended to replace the breadth and depth of most standard accounting texts.

Instructors can access the Instructor Solutions on the Pearson catalogue at http://vig.pearsoned.ca which includes all the transactions completed for all applications together with the required reports. These solution files must be accessed using QuickBooks Premier 2010.

Updating QuickBooks

From time to time, Intuit releases updates for its products. Updates contain updated payroll tax tables as well as any program fixes. At the time of creating the data files on the Data CD, Release 4 was available and all company files on the CD that accompany this textbook have been created with this release. Release 4 accommodates the new HST tax in British Columbia and Ontario. When you install the QuickBooks software available as a download with this textbook, Release 5 will have become available. Release 5, or the current release, must be installed either automatically through the QuickBooks installation or manually downloaded from the Intuit website. Instructions to use the automatic download feature in QuickBooks are described on page 16 in Chapter 1.

To confirm that you have the R5 or later upgrade installed, press F2 on your keyboard to display the Product Information screen. In the top left hand corner of the screen you will see: Product QuickBooks Premier Edition 2010 Release R5P (or later). R5P was the latest release at the time of writing this textbook so you may have a higher Release number. If you have R1P, R2P, R3P, or R4P, you must update QuickBooks before continuing. The company files in this textbook require that the latest Release be installed.

Manually Download the QuickBooks Update

Although QuickBooks should automatically download the latest release, some software programs installed on your computer may stop the installation. If you receive an error message when updating QuickBooks using the Update QuickBooks screen, you can manually download the QuickBooks update. At the time of writing this textbook the update can be downloaded by performing the following steps:

a) **Visit http://support.intuit.ca/quickbooks/**

b) **Click** the **Product Updates link** under the Today's Hot Topics heading on the right hand side of the screen

c) **Click QuickBooks 2010** under the QuickBooks product updates heading

d) Refer to the instructions on the screen to manually install the product update

e) **Click** the **file** under the EasyStart/Pro/Premier/Industry specific heading under the Install the manual update heading and install per instructions

What if I Don't Upgrade QuickBooks to the Latest Release?

As indicated, it is important that you upgrade your QuickBooks software to the latest release. These releases include updated payroll tax tables as well as any fixes required in the software. If you install the software in the textbook and do not upgrade it to the latest release, the following message will be displayed when you open a company file supplied on the Data CD:

Figure Preface-I

Although you can still use the file if you receive this message, Intuit recommends that you upgrade to the latest release. Refer to the instructions under the Updating the Program heading on page 15 in Chapter 1 to learn how to update QuickBooks.

INTUIT SUPPORT WEBSITE

If you have any problems while using QuickBooks, visit http://support.intuit.ca/quickbooks/ and enter the problem you are having in the search box for detailed information.

Restoring Files from Different Updates

If you do not update your software to Release 4 or higher, you will receive the following message when you restore a company file and select Yes to replace the existing file:

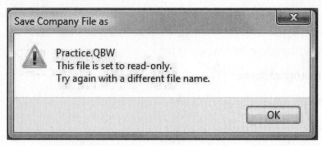

Figure Preface-2

If you receive this message, you must either rename the file, thus creating a new file and not replacing the existing file, or remove the read-only property from the existing file before continuing. To remove the read-only property from the existing file:

    a) **Close** the **message** shown in Figure Preface-2

    b) **Right click** on the **filename** you are trying to use in the Save Company File as window

    c) **Select Properties**

    d) **Click** the **box** beside the Read Only option to turn this option off

    e) **Click Save**

    f) **Click Yes** to replace the existing data file

    If the file already exists, the following message will be displayed asking you to confirm deletion of the data file:

Figure Preface-3

The Data CD

The data files are ready to use immediately. No passwords have been added to any of the files. You can install the data files easily because the Data CD should open automatically. The installation procedure on the CD will copy the files to your hard disk. The Data CD also includes Chapters 13 and 14 of the textbook, the Source Document file, a ReadMe file, a PDF file of the Review of Basic Accounting, an Accounting Cycle Tutorial, and a link to the Acrobat Reader program if you do not have it installed already on your computer. You need Acrobat Reader installed in order to read PDF files.

Installing the Data Files to Your Hard Disk Drive

    1. **Insert** the **Data CD** into your CD-ROM Drive

       If the CD does not open immediately:

       a) **Choose** the **Windows Start menu**

       b) **Click Run**

       c) **Click Browse** and find the CD Drive from the Look in drop-down list

       d) **Click** the **CD drive** to open it

e) **Click Start.exe**

f) **Click Open** to return to the Run window (Start.exe will be displayed in the Open field)

g) **Click OK**

2. The Data CD home page window should be displayed

   Choose to install the data files, open Chapters 13 or 14, access the Source Document file, view the ReadMe file, open the Review of Basic Accounting file or Accounting Cycle Tutorial, or click the link to install Acrobat reader from the Adobe website (required to open the Review of Basic Accounting file).

3. To install the data files:

   a) **Click Data Files for Exercises** in the Text in the left sidebar menu

   b) **Click** the **Install Data Files button**

   The data files are copied to a Data folder and a Setup folder on your hard drive and located within a new data folder called QkBkData in Drive C. The files are ready to work within QuickBooks.

4. **Close**   the **Data CD window**

Copying Selected Data Files from the Data CD

To copy a single file or multiple files from the CD to your working folder using the Copy and Paste commands in Windows Explorer perform the following steps. In the following steps we will select the Data folder. You can also select the Setup folder.

1. **Insert**   the **Data CD** into the CD-ROM Drive

2. **Right click**   on the **Start button**

3. **Choose**   **Explore**

4. **Click**   **Computer** in the Folders list

5. **Click**   **D: (or the drive letter for your CD drive)** to view the folders on the CD

6. **Click**   **Data** to view the individual data files and folders. (Files and folders will be listed on the right side of the Folders list). You can copy the entire data set at once, or one or more files.

   To select all files for copying:

   a) **Click Bookroom**, the first file in the list to select it

   b) **Press** (shift) and **click Tours**, the last file in the list (or choose the Edit menu and click Select All)

   To select a single file for copying:

   a) **Click Chelsea.qbw** or the file you want to copy

7. Copy the selected files by performing the following steps

   a) **Choose** the **Organize menu** (Edit menu if you are using XP) and click Copy; or

   b) **Press** (ctrl) **+ C**

   c) All selected files are copied to the Windows Clipboard

8. **Click**   **Drive C:** and scroll looking for the QkBkData folder

9. **Click**   **QkBkData**, the folder created from the CD installation; or if you would prefer to create a new folder for your data files:

a) **Right click** the **folder or drive** where you want to create the new folder

b) **Select New** from the menu and then Folder

c) **Type** a **name** for the new folder

10. To paste the selected files to the QkBkData folder or

a) **Select** the **Organize menu** (Select the Edit menu if you're using Windows XP)

b) **Select Paste**

c) Replace the existing file(s) with the new one if you are asked

Setting the Computer's Date Format

The date format that you use in QuickBooks is determined by your Windows operating system and not by QuickBooks. The dates used in this textbook are in month/day/year format.

Determine which format your computer is in (you may have to do this before every session if you are working in a lab) by looking in the Regional Settings section of the Control Panel. If you begin to enter transactions without checking the date format of the computer, you may find that you have posted transactions to the wrong fiscal period.

If your computer is not set up in the month/day/year format, you have two choices:

1. You can enter the dates used in the textbook in the same format as your computer. Remember to change each date in the textbook to the format of your computer's date format or your data will not be accurate.

2. You can change your computer's date format. To change the format in Windows XP or Windows Vista®, do the following:

Windows XP

1. **Click** the **Start button** on the taskbar
2. **Click** on **Control Panel**
3. **Double click** on **Regional and Language Options**
4. **Click** on the **Customize button**
5. **Click** on the **Date tab**
6. **Click** on the **drop-down arrow** beside Short date format
7. **Select** one of the **styles** where the month is the first choice (**M, MM = month**)
8. **Click** on the **drop-down arrow** beside Long date format
9. **Select** one of the **styles** where the month is the first choice (**MMMM = month**)
10. **Click OK** to save the changes
11. **Click OK** to exit the Regional and Language Options window
12. **Close** the **Control Panel**

Windows Vista

1. **Click** the **Start button** on the taskbar
2. **Click** on **Control Panel**
3. **Click** on **Classic View** (if it is not already selected)
4. **Double click** on **Regional and Language Options**
5. **Click** on the **Formats tab** (this is the default tab and may already be displayed)
6. **Click** on the **Customize this format button**
7. **Click** on the **Date tab**
8. **Type mm/dd/yyyy** in the Short date field
9. **Click** on the **drop-down arrow** beside the Long date field

10. **Select** one of the **styles** where the month is the first choice (**MMMM = month**)
11. **Click OK** to save the changes
12. **Click OK** to exit the Regional and Language Options window
13. **Close** the **Control Panel**

Working through the Applications

Setup applications are introduced early in the text. Advanced users should have no difficulty working through the applications in the order given and may even choose to skip some applications. However, at a minimum, we recommend working through all of the step-by-step instructions in each chapter so you become familiar with all the journals before starting the more comprehensive applications.

Order of Applications

There is an alternative order for working through the applications or chapters in the workbook. All the chapters with step-by-step instructions for transactions may be completed first and the setup chapters (Chapters 5, 10 and 13) later. Transactions for these three setup chapters may be completed before you complete the setup to provide additional practice entering transactions, to familiarize yourself with the file structure for the companies, and to make the setups easier to complete. The company files for these chapters with the setup instructions completed can be found on the CD under the Setup folder. Chapter 14 is the last chapter, and we do not provide step-by-step instructions or a setup data file for it. This chapter is intended as a challenging comprehensive practice exercise. Chapters 13 and 14 are not included in the textbook, but can be found on the CD that accompanies the textbook.

Keystroke Instruction Style

We have incorporated different paragraph styles for different kinds of statements in the text to help you identify the instructions that you must follow to complete the transactions correctly and view the screens that we present. These different styles are illustrated below:

1. **Press**   `tab` to advance to the Date field (Keystroke command line — command word is bold face and the object of the command, what you press, is in colour. Keystrokes are numbered and spaced apart.)

2. **Type**   **Spread the Word** (Command line with text you type in colour)

Regular text is presented in normal paragraphs like this one. Key words are shown in colour to make it easy to identify the topics covered in the text. The text also uses Notes and Warnings that contain information and caution. The shaded boxes contain information that you may need while working with transactions.

Source Documents

Source documents are incorporated throughout the text. Some source documents are displayed for information purposes and will be marked with an SD Instructions heading. The step-by-step instructions to enter the source document follow it. Note that if you complete a source document on your own that contains step-by-step instructions, you will end up entering the source document twice and the print screens in the text will not match yours.

Other source documents are listed for you to try on your own allowing you to have more practice entering transactions. Beside each source document or list of source documents, you will find an SD Practice heading describing what you are supposed to do.

If you have used this text in the past and would prefer to skip the step-by-step instructions and work only with a list of source documents, refer to the CD in the back of the textbook for the source documents file. You can print the complete list of source documents for the chapter you are currently working on.

Dates

Transaction Dates

When you open a QuickBooks company file, the default transaction date will either be your current computer date or the last entered date, depending on how your preferences are set up. When you open forms in QuickBooks, do not compare your dates to the ones displayed in the textbook. The dates in the textbook reflect the date the author created the print screen. The dates of the completed transaction should match those in the textbook.

On Reports

In the top left-hand corner of most reports, you will see a date and time stamp. Do not compare your date and time stamp to the ones shown in the textbook. The dates in the textbook reflect the date the author created the print screen.

Sample Files

> **Notes**
> The payroll information and calculations in each chapter do not reflect current payroll information. Do not use the figures calculated in the payrolls in your company file.

The data files for Chapters 11, 12, 13 and 14 have been converted to a sample file so that you can enter payroll information for dates outside of the current payroll tax table period. This is important for learning purposes. No matter what QuickBooks tax table you have installed, the payroll information in the print screens in the textbook will be the same as yours as long as you use the sample file. The sample data file is set up so that Dec. 15, 2007 is the current date displayed when entering forms. You will override this date and use dates in 2012 as you are working in each chapter.

Acknowledgements

Updating the textbook from version 2005 to version 2010 has been quite a monumental task that could not have been accomplished without a lot of help. First, I'd like to thank Mary Purbhoo for giving me the opportunity to update the textbook. Many thanks to Marg Bukta who did a complete and thorough job during the copy edit process, suggesting necessary, although at times, very time-consuming, changes and Susan Adlam, the Production Editor, who provided editorial assistance and kept us all on track. Also, thank you to Christina Lee, Developmental Editor, and Lila Campbell, Project Manager, for their continued support.

Many thanks to Debbie Baker-Longley from Mohawk College who agreed to review the textbook, not once, but twice, during an extremely busy time in her life.

And finally, to my family, John, Jamie and Mandy. Thank you again for your patience, support and understanding.

Part One
Getting Started

CHAPTER ONE

Getting Started: Introduction to

QuickBooks

Objectives

After completing this chapter, you should be able to:

- *download and install* the QuickBooks program
- *use* the QuickBooks data files on the Data CD
- *access* QuickBooks data files
- *register* QuickBooks
- *update* QuickBooks
- *understand* the QuickBooks Home page
- *understand* QuickBooks Centres
- *use* QuickBooks lists
- *use* QuickBooks keyboard shortcuts
- *change* QuickBooks preference settings
- *access* Help, Live Community, and Support
- *back up* and *verify* a data file
- *restore* a data file from a backup
- *finish* a QuickBooks work session

Getting Started

Data Files

Notes
The instructions in this chapter for installing the program, starting the program, and copying files refer to Windows Vista® procedures. If you are using a different version of Windows, please refer to Windows and QuickBooks Help for assistance with these procedures.

The **data files** on the Data CD were prepared using the Windows Vista® operating system and QuickBooks Premier Edition 2010 by Intuit. Subsequent versions of the software may have changes in screens or keystrokes.

The instructions in this workbook have been written for a stand-alone PC, with a hard drive and a CD-ROM drive. Microsoft Windows should be correctly installed on your hard drive. Your printers should be installed and accessible through the Windows operating system. Refer to Windows Help and manuals for assistance with these procedures.

This workbook reflects the author's approach to working with QuickBooks. There are alternative approaches to setting up company accounts and to working with QuickBooks. Refer to QuickBooks and Windows Help and manuals for further details.

All company files for each chapter have been set up in advance so you can begin entering transactions immediately. For chapters that require you to create the company data files from scratch, a setup company file has been created for you and can be found in a Setup folder on the CD, so you can complete the transactions or source documents without working through the company setup if required.

QUICKBOOKS COMPANY FILES

COMPANY NAME	FOLDER\FILENAME	CHAPTER	
Practice	Data\Practice.qbw	1	
Chelsea's Chocolates	Data\Chelsea.qbw	3	
Bob's Bookroom	Data\Bookroom.qbw	4	
River Run	Setup\River.qbw	5	See Notes
Just a Buck	Data\Buck.qbw	6	
Malin's Makeovers	Data\Malin.qbw	7	
Terrific Tours	Data\Tours.qbw	8	
Curly's Cabinets	Data\Curly.qbw	9	
Darya's Dance Studio	Setup\Darya.qbw	10	See Notes
Scotts' Total Concept	Data\Scott.qbw	11	
Sparkles	Data\Sparkles.qbw	12	
Contre le Vent	Setup\Vent-start.qbw	13	See Notes
	Setup\Vent-data.qbw	13	See Notes
Melody Music Centre	Setup\Melody.qbw	14	See Notes

OTHER FILES ON THE DATA CD

Ch. 13 Contre le Vent: Payroll & Inventory Setup
Ch. 14 Melody Music Centre: Practice Application
Source Documents
ReadMe file
Review of Basic Accounting
Accounting Cycle Tutorial

As you work through this textbook, the businesses and the chapters become more complex, with each chapter introducing new features or setups. Each chapter also includes the features covered in previous chapters for review. This progression is shown in the following chart:

CH	COMPANY NAME	TOPIC NO.*	NEW TOPICS**	ALL TOPICS***
3	Chelsea's Chocolates	1	Cash sales and purchases	1
4	Bob's Bookroom	2	General Journal	1 + 2
5	River Run	3	Set up a cash only business	2 + 3
6	Just a Buck	4	Basic vendor transactions	2 + 4
7	Malin's Makeovers	5	Basic customer transactions	4 + 5
8	Terrific Tours	6	Advanced customer and vendor transactions	5 + 6
9	Curly's Cabinets	7	Credit cards and bank reconciliation	6 + 7
10	Darya's Dance Studio	8	Setup for complete customer and vendor transactions	7 + 8
11	Scotts' Total Concept	9	Payroll	7 + 9
12	Sparkles	10	Inventory	9 + 10
13	Contre le Vent****	11	Comprehensive setup with payroll and inventory	10 + 11
14	Melody Music Centre****	12	Comprehensive setup practice exercise	12

NOTES

*   Topic No. is the number used for the new topics covered in a chapter for reference in the All Topics column.

**   Step-by-step instructions are provided throughout each chapter for new topics. You are required to set up company files from scratch for River Run (Chapter 5), Darya's Dance Studio (Chapter 10), Contre le Vent (Chapter 13), and Melody Music Centre (Chapter 14). As discussed earlier, you can use the company data files in the Setup folder for each of these companies if you prefer to work through the transactions and not complete the company setup.

***   These numbers indicate that each chapter includes the topics and features that are explained in the previous chapters, except for the company setup. For example: Scotts' Total Concept (7 + 9) introduces payroll (9) as a new topic and includes cash sales and purchases, general journal transactions, advanced customer and vendor transactions, and credit cards (all the topics in 7), but setup is not required.

**** Chapters 13 and 14 are now found on the CD that accompanies this text.

Notes
The Setup folder has data files for chapters that require you to set up the company file before working through the transactions. Three of these files — River, Darya, and Vent-data — are complete setup files that allow you to proceed with entering source document transactions.
The other two data files — Vent-start and Melody — are starter sample files that allow you to set up the data file and use the payroll features.

Notes
After you install the data files on the CD, they can be found within the C:\QkBkData folder.

Notes
The Data CD also includes a brief review of basic accounting principles. The file is in PDF and you need to have Acrobat Reader installed in order to read the file. If you do not have Acrobat Reader, you can install it from the Adobe website using the link on the Data CD.

Notes
No keystroke instructions are provided for Melody Music Centre in Chapter 14, found on the CD that accompanies this textbook.

⚠ WARNING!
Do not download and install the QuickBooks program until you are ready to begin working on the exercises in the textbook. The program will remain valid and accessible for 13 months after you activate it.

Notes
The time it takes to download the QuickBooks program will depend on your internet connection

Installing QuickBooks

1. **Start** your **computer** and **turn off** or **close** all other **applications** and files. You should be in the Windows desktop.

2. Refer to the card in the inside cover of the textbook.

3. If you agree with the terms and conditions and understand that opening the card means that once opened you cannot return the textbook, open the package to obtain the website information.

4. As soon as you go to the QuickBooks student download website indicated on the card, you'll receive the following screen:

Figure 1-1

5. **Click** **Save** to save the file to your computer

6. **Select** **Desktop** (or you can select a different folder on your hard drive)

7. **Click** **Save**

8. The following screen will be displayed after the download is complete:

Figure 1-2

9. **Click** **Run** and the following warning will be displayed:

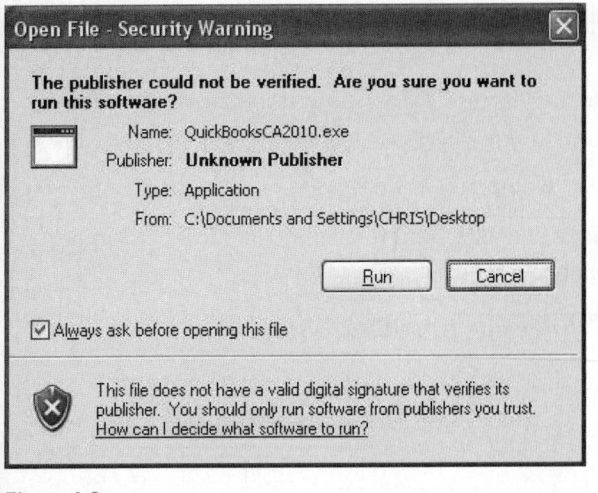

Figure 1-3

10. **Click** **Run**

11. You will see the following welcome screen:

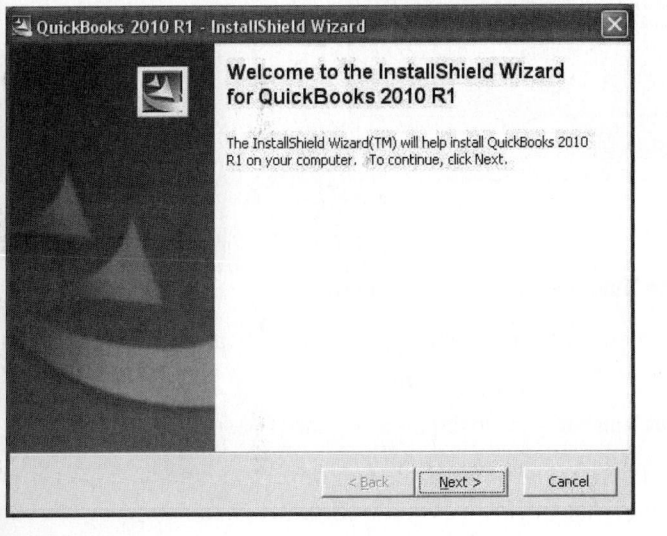

Figure 1-4

12. **Click** **Next** to begin. The Licence Agreement screen is displayed:

Notes
   If you do not accept the licence agreement, the installation procedure will be cancelled.

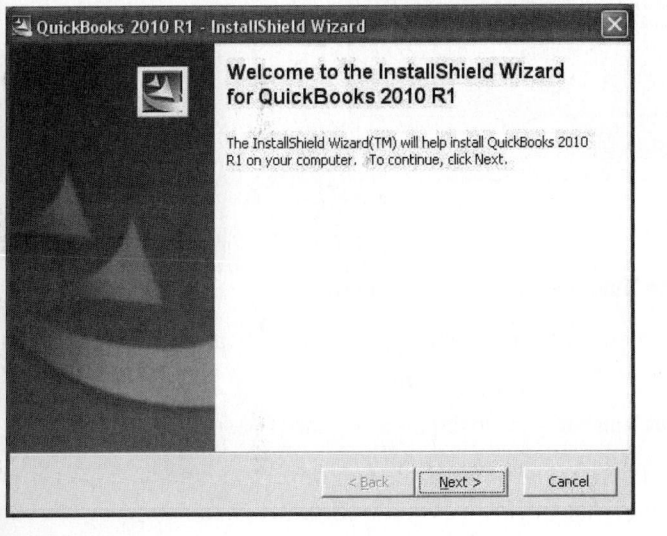

Figure 1-5

13. **Read**	the **License Agreement** (you will have to use the scroll bar to read the entire agreement)
14. **Click**	the **button beside** the *I accept the terms in the license agreement* option if you agree to the terms of the licence agreement
15. **Click**	**Next** to display the Number of Users screen
16. **Accept**	the **One user default** and **click Next** to display the Licence Number and Product Number screen:

Figure 1-6

17. **Enter**	the **License Number** (located on the card)

Do not enter the dash between numbers. The program automatically advances to the next entry box.

18. **Enter**	the **Product Number** (also located on the card)
19. **Click**	**Next**. If you entered an incorrect licence or product number, you will see a warning that the License and/or Product Numbers you entered are invalid. If you receive this warning, click OK and try entering them again.
20. **Click**	**Next** to view the QuickBooks Installation screen:

Figure 1-7

You can install QuickBooks Premier Edition 2010 to the default folder, or select a different folder by clicking on the Change button.

21. **Click**   **Next**

22. The next screen asks if you want to use Google Desktop to search QuickBooks

23. **Select**   **Yes** (**select No** if you do not want to use Google Desktop)

24. **Click**   **Next** to view the Ready to Install QuickBooks screen

You can use the Back button at any time to make any necessary corrections.

25. **Click**   the **Install button** when you're ready to begin the QuickBooks installation

QuickBooks will display various screens during the installation procedure.

26. **Click**   **Finish** when the QuickBooks Installation Complete screen is displayed

Using the CD Data Files

Many of the chapters in this textbook begin with a QuickBooks company file that has already been created for you. These QuickBooks company files are found on the Data CD that accompanies this textbook. Before you can use the company files in QuickBooks, you must copy them from the Data CD to your hard drive. QuickBooks cannot open the files on the CD because they are read-only files; therefore, you cannot work with the files directly from the CD. If you try to open the QuickBooks files from the CD you will see the following warning:

Warning

QuickBooks cannot open this file because it exists as a Read-Only file. Please make the file Read-Writable and then try opening it again.

OK

Figure 1-8

After copying the data files to your computer, store the original CD in a safe place. If you install the data files on the CD, your files will be placed in the QkBkData folder below Drive C.

Installing Data Files to Your Hard Drive

We have set up the Data CD so that it will open automatically. When you choose the button to install the data files, the files will be copied directly to your hard drive and the read-only attributes will be removed in a single step. To do this:

1. **Insert**   the **Data CD** into your CD-ROM drive and the Data CD should open immediately (follow the instructions below if it does not open)

If the CD does not open immediately, follow these instructions if you are using Windows Vista (ask your instructor for instructions if you are not using Windows Vista):

a) **Choose** the **Windows Start menu** on the taskbar

b) ~~Type run in the Start Search field~~

c) **Click Browse** and browse for the **CD Drive**

d) **Click** the **CD drive** to open it

e) **Click Start.exe**

f) **Click Open** to return to the **Run window**. Start.exe will be displayed in the **Open** field

g) **Click OK**

When the Data CD home page is displayed, you can choose to install the data files, to view Chapters 13 and 14, the Source Document file, or the ReadMe file, to open the Review of Basic Accounting file (PDF format) or to install Acrobat reader (required to open the Review of Basic Accounting file).

2.	**Click**	**Data & Setup Files**
3.	**Click**	**INSTALL Data & Setup Files button**

After you install the data files, they can be found on your hard drive in a new QkBkData folder in drive C. A data and setup folder will be created below the QkBkData folder. The data files in these folders are now ready to be used and can be opened directly in QuickBooks.

4.	**Close**	the **Data CD window**

Copying Data Files from the CD

If a single data file becomes unreadable or if you want to start a chapter over again, you can copy a single file from the CD to your working folder.

1.	**Insert**	the **Data CD** into the CD-ROM drive
2.	**Right click**	the **Start button** on the task bar
3.	**Click**	**Explore**
4.	**Click**	**Computer** in the Folders list
5.	**Right click**	**Drive D:** (or the drive letter for your CD drive) on the right-hand side of the screen
6.	**Click**	**Explore**
7.	**Double click**	the **Data folder** or the **Setup folder** to view the individual data files
8.	**Copy**	the **entire data folder** at once, or **copy** only **one or more files in the Data or Setup folders** to your hard drive
9.	**Right click**	an **entire folder** or a **specific data file** and **click Copy**
10.	**Browse**	for the **QkBkData folder** (created when you originally installed the files from the Data CD) or **select** a **different folder** if you are storing your company data files in a different folder
11.	**Right click**	the folder and **click Paste**

Starting QuickBooks and Accessing Data Files

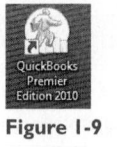

Figure 1-9

1. To start the QuickBooks program:

   a) **Click** the **QuickBooks Premier Edition 2010 icon** on the Desktop if you installed the shortcut; or

   b) **Choose Start**, then **All Programs**, **click QuickBooks**, and then **click QuickBooks Premier Edition 2010**

2. The first screen that will be displayed when you open QuickBooks Premier 2010 after downloading it from the student website for the first time is the QuickBooks Update Service screen:

Figure 1-10

   This screen will allow you to update your QuickBooks program with the latest product update. At the time of updating this portion of the text, the latest product update is R5. Depending on when you are installing the QuickBooks program, the product update may be higher than 5. You must upgrade your software to the latest release in order to use this textbook.

3. **Click**   **Install Now** and the following screen will be displayed:

Figure 1-11

4. **Click**   **Yes**

The QuickBooks update will be installed.

5. The following screen will be displayed when the upgrade has finished installing:

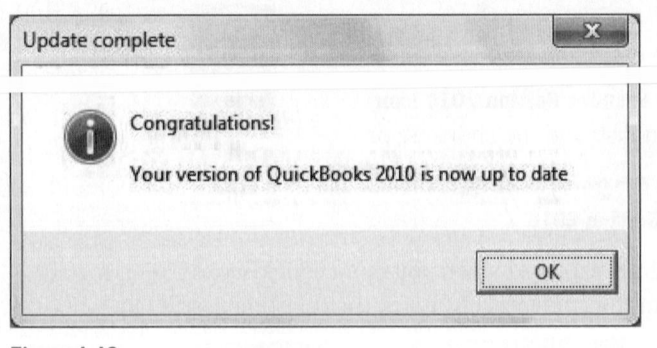

Figure 1-12

6. Click   OK

7. The QuickBooks registration screen will be displayed:

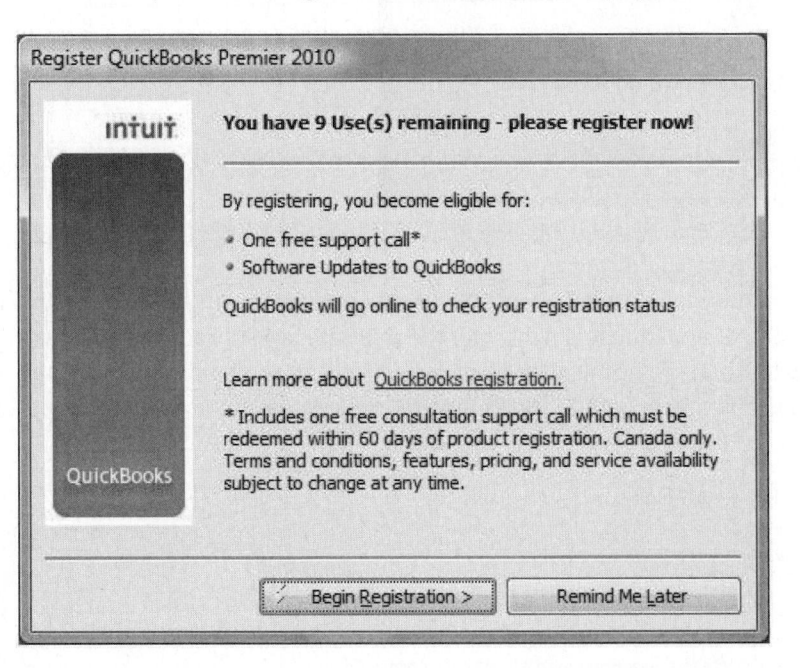

Figure 1-13

Notes
You must be connected to the Internet to download updates.

You can use QuickBooks 10 times before you must register it with Intuit. You can click the *Begin Registration* button to register immediately, or click the *Remind Me Later* button to register later.

You should click the Begin Registration button to register your QuickBooks program. You will need to fill in the information on the Product Information form as well as the information on a second screen asking about your purchase. After you answer the information on these two forms, a QuickBooks registration card will be displayed which you can print and keep for your records.

8. After you click the Begin Registration button and register your software, or click the Remind Me Later button, QuickBooks will open with the Practice Company available in the 2010 software displayed:

Figure 1-14

9. **Choose** **File** from the menu, and then **click Close Company**

10. The No Company Open window is displayed:

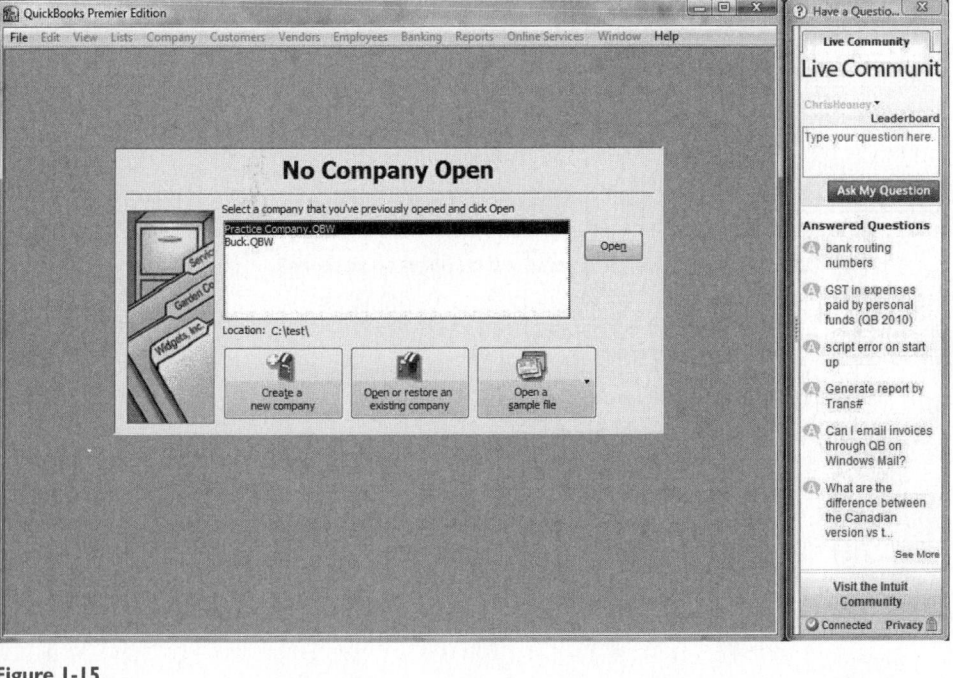

Figure 1-15

The next time you start QuickBooks, the company data file you previously worked with will open automatically (unless you choose Close Company from the File menu before exiting QuickBooks).

11. Click   a) the **Open or restore an existing company button**:

 or

Open or restore an existing company

Figure 1-16

b) **choose** the **File menu** and **click** **Open or Restore Company**

File
New Company...
Open or Restore Company...
Open Previous Company ▶
Save Copy or Backup...
Close Company
Switch to Multi-user Mode
Remote Access
Utilities ▶
Accountant's Copy ▶
Print ...   Ctrl+P
Save as PDF...
Print Forms ▶
Printer Setup...
Send Forms...
Exit   Alt+F4

Figure 1-17

to display the **Open or Restore Company screen**:

Open or Restore Company

What type of file do you want to open or restore?

○ **Open a company file**
 • Open a regular company file (.qbw)

○ **Restore a backup copy**
 • Restore a backup file (.qbb)
 • Restore files from the QuickBooks Online Backup service

○ **Restore a portable file**
 • Re-create a company file that was stored as a portable file (.qbm)

Back   Next   Finish   Help   Cancel

Figure 1-18

The option you select on this screen depends on how the company data file that you want to open was saved. You can determine how the file was saved by the extension of the file name:

FILE TYPE	FILE EXTENSION	SELECT
QuickBooks company file	.qbw	Open a company file
QuickBooks backup file	.qbb	Restore a backup copy
QuickBooks portable file	.qbm	Restore a portable file

Notes
All company files on the Data CD are QuickBooks company files.

12. Click   **Open a Company file** and **click Next**

Use this window to browse for the QuickBooks data that you copied onto your hard drive. If you used the install option on the CD, the data files can be found in the data or setup folder within the QkBkData folder on drive C.

Notes
The default starting file location when you open a company is the Company Files folder inside the QuickBooks program folder.

13. Click   the **drop-down arrow** in the Look In field and **click Drive C**

14. Double click   the **QkBkData folder** and then the **data folder** to view the files in the data folder as shown:

Notes
If you used a different location for the data files, browse for that folder in the Look in field.

Open a Company

Look in:	QkBkData

Recent Places
Desktop
Chris
Computer
Network

Name	Date modif...	Type	Size
Bookroom.QBW			
Buck.QBW			
Chelsea.QBW			
Curly.QBW			
Malin.QBW			
Practice.QBW			
Scott.QBW			
Sparkles.QBW			
Tours.QBW			

File name: Practice Company.QBW

Files of type: QuickBooks Files (*.QBW,*.QBA)

Open   Cancel   Help

☐ Open file in multi-user mode

Figure 1-19

15. Highlight   the **company file** that you want to open and **click** the **Open button** or **double click** the **company file** to open it automatically

The data files on the CD that accompany the textbook have been created with R4

you open a company file on the data CD for the first time, you will receive the following message:

Figure 1-20

16. Click   **Yes**

If another update is released by Intuit, you will receive a message indicating that a new QuickBooks Release is available. Refer to the "What if I don't upgrade QuickBooks to the latest release?" heading under the "Updating QuickBooks" heading on page xi of the Preface.

Program Maintenance

Registering the Program

As we discussed during the installation of QuickBooks, you can use the program only 10 times until you must register it. If you did not register your program after installation, a screen will be displayed each time you open QuickBooks reminding you of the number of remaining times you can use the program before you must register it.

1. Click   **Begin Registration**

2. After filling in your contact information and answering some questions, your QuickBooks program is automatically registered over the Internet

To view your product and licence information at any time, choose the Help menu and click My License Information.

⚠️ **WARNING!**
The program that is available with this book includes payroll activation for 13 months after registration, but you must still download the latest updates to use the payroll features.

Updating the Program

When you first opened QuickBooks, you were prompted with a message to download the latest product update. If you did not do it then, you must do it before proceeding. Updates fix problems in the software, incorporate new features, and contain updated payroll taxes. You must download updates regularly if you want to use the Payroll features of the program. This ensures that you have the latest tax tables available for the program. The QuickBooks program that is available as a download with this textbook contains the Payroll Service and is available for 13 months. The Company files in this textbook require that Release 4 or later be installed; however, the most recent product update will be available when you download the QuickBooks program.

The automatic update feature is automatically turned on when you install QuickBooks. To view this option:

1. **Choose** the **Help menu** and **click Update QuickBooks**:

Figure 1-21

Notes
An ongoing company must be signed up for the QuickBooks Payroll Service with Intuit before the payroll features in the program can be used, unless you are working with a QuickBooks sample company.

Notes
The program is set to download updates automatically whenever you are connected to the Internet.

To turn off the automatic updates option, choose the Options tab and click the No button beside Automatic Update. Click Yes from this same screen to turn automatic updates back on.

As you can see, this screen indicates that the automatic update feature is turned on. With this feature selected, QuickBooks is updated automatically without any effort on your part. If this screen indicates that the automatic option is turned off, you can select it on the Options tab and if you choose to manually update QuickBooks, you can do so from the Update Now tab.

Although QuickBooks should automatically download the latest upgrade, some software programs installed on your computer may stop the installation. If you receive an error message when updating QuickBooks using the Update QuickBooks screen, you can manually download the QuickBooks update. Follow the instructions under the "Manually download the QuickBooks update" heading found in the Preface under the "Updating QuickBooks" heading on page x.

2. **Click**   **Close** to exit the Update QuickBooks window

The QuickBooks Home Page

When you first open a company file in QuickBooks, the Home page is displayed as shown here:

Figure 1-22

Each area on the QuickBooks Home page shown in Figure 1-22 has been numbered and is described below:

1. **QuickBooks Title Bar**: contains the control button at the far left, displays the company name, QuickBooks edition, and the usual Windows sizing icons on the right. The ☒ in the title bar can be used to close QuickBooks. If you click the ☒ in the title bar, a warning will be displayed asking if you want to exit QuickBooks.

2. **Main Menu**: is displayed directly below the title bar. Many activities in QuickBooks can be accessed from more than one location in the program, but all activities are available from the main menu. The usual Windows sizing icons are displayed on the main menu and affect the current open window. The ☒ in the main menu can be used to close the current open window.

3. **Icon Bar**: the Icon bar provides quick and easy access to some of the most commonly used QuickBooks activities and functions. Although QuickBooks sets the icons on the Icon bar by default when you

Notes
Customizing the Icon bar is covered in Chapter 3.

create a new company, you can customize the Icon bar to include only the icons that represent the tasks you use on a regular basis. If the icons on the Icon bar cannot all be displayed, click the double arrow on the far right-hand side of the Icon bar to view a list of the icons that are not displayed.

4. Vendors section: The Vendors section of the Home page shows the workflow arrows for business tasks specific to vendors. You can click on an icon to open the form and you can click on the Vendors button on the far left-hand side of the screen to open the Vendor Centre. The Vendor Centre will be discussed in more detail in Chapter 6.

5. Customers section: The Customers section of the Home page shows the work flow arrows for business tasks specific to customers. You can click on an icon to open the form and you can click on the Customers button on the far left-hand side of the screen to open the Customer Centre. The Customer Centre will be discussed in more detail in Chapter 7.

6. Employees section: The Employees section of the Home page shows the work flow arrows for business tasks specific to employees. You can click on an icon to open the form and you can click on the Employees button on the far left-hand side of the screen to open the Employee Centre. The Employee Centre will be discussed in more detail in Chapters 11 and 13, the latter of which is found on the Student CD-ROM.

7. Company section: The Company section of the Home page provides quick access to the Chart of Accounts and the Items list.

8. Banking section: The Banking section of the Home page provides quick access to all banking related functions such as recording customer deposits, reconciling accounts, writing cheques, using the cheque register, printing cheques, and entering credit card charges.

9. QuickBooks Coach: The QuickBooks Coach provides detailed information of the workflows available in each section of the Home page, as well as access to a tutorial. To open the QuickBooks Coach click the Show Coach Tips button and when you're finished with it, click the Hide Coach Tips button. You can view the tutorial by clicking on the View Tutorial button.

10. Account Balances: This section displays each bank and credit card account and its current balance.

11. Learn About Services: This section displays information about payroll, supplies, and other services you can purchase from Intuit or third-party vendors.

12. Reminders & Alerts: Use this section to view reminders that you have set up in QuickBooks, such as a list of outstanding invoices or cheques that need to be printed. In this section, you may also find alerts that have been sent from Intuit.

13. Live Community/ Help: This pane contains two tabs: Live Community and Help. The Live Community tab allows you to ask or answer questions in the QuickBooks community while working directly in QuickBooks. The Help tab is context-sensitive and allows you to review relevant search topics or use the search feature. You can close the Live Community/Help pane at anytime by clicking on the ⊠ in the top right-hand corner. The easiest way to bring back the Live Community/Help pane, is to press F1.

QuickBooks Centres

QuickBooks organizes specific functions in Centres. There are five Centres in QuickBooks: the Customer Centre, the Vendor Centre, the Employee Centre, the Online Banking Centre, and the Report Centre. In this chapter, we will look at the Vendor Centre and the Report Centre to learn how Centres are used.

The Vendor Centre

1. **Open** the **Vendor Centre** using one of the following options:

   a) **Click** the **Vendors button** in the Vendors section of the Home page; or

   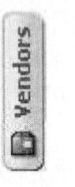

   Figure 1-23

   b) **Choose** the **Vendors menu**; or

   Figure 1-24

   c) **Click** the **Vendor Centre icon** on the Icon bar:

   Figure 1-25

2. The Vendor Centre will be displayed as shown:

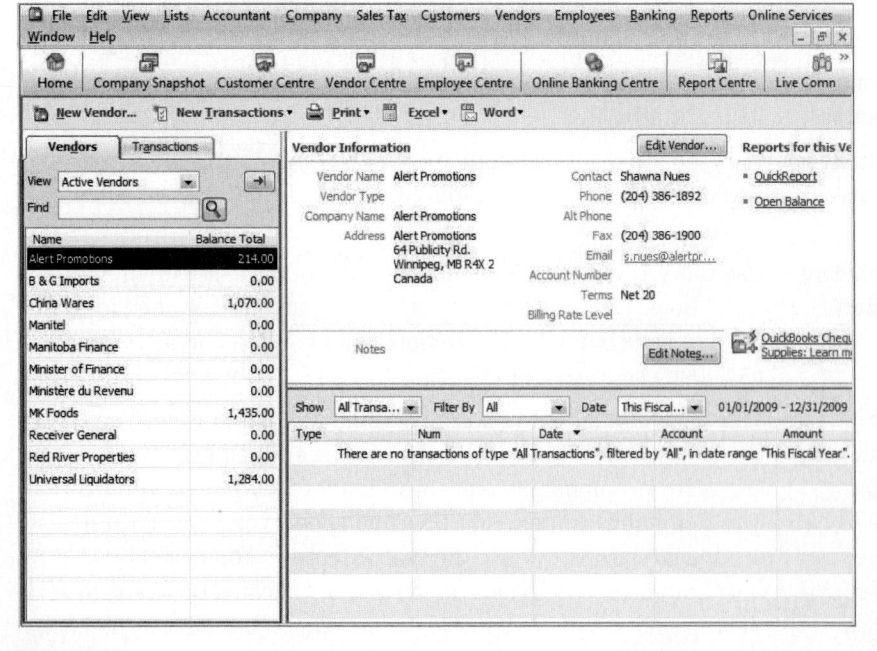

Figure 1-26

The Vendor Centre contains all the information about your vendors and their transactions. On the left-hand side of the screen, you'll see two tabs: Vendors and Transactions.

When you click the Vendors tab, the vendor list is displayed on the left-hand side of the screen, which displays each vendor's name and balance total. You can sort the vendor list by vendor name or balance total and in ascending or descending order by clicking on the list headings.

When you highlight a vendor in the list (there is always a vendor highlighted by default), their vendor information is displayed in the top right portion of the screen, allowing you to quickly view the vendor address information. Click the Edit Vendor button to access the vendor record where you can make changes to it, click the QuickReport or Open Balance button to print reports for the vendor, or use the Edit Notes button to add notes to the vendor record. The transaction details for the vendor are listed in the bottom right portion of the screen. You can use the headings across the top of the transaction details to select which type of transaction you'd like to view and filter the transactions by a date range.

You can use the buttons across the top of the screen to add a new vendor, enter new transactions, print vendor information, export information to Excel®, or print Word documents. The highlighted vendor will automatically be selected when you choose one of these options.

When you click on the Transactions tab, a list of transaction types is displayed. When you click on one of the transaction types, a list of all transactions for all vendors will be displayed based on the criteria selected in the Filter By and Date fields.

The Report Centre

The Report Centre deals only with reports, and most QuickBooks reports are accessible from it. Although it offers most of the same reports as the Reports menu, it has the advantage of showing a sample report and a brief description of what you can learn about your company from the report.

1. Open the **Report Centre** using one of the following options:

   a) **Choose** the **Reports menu**; or

Reports
Report Centre
Company Snapshot
Memorized Reports ▶
Process Multiple Reports
Company & Financial ▶
Sales Tax ▶
Customers & Receivables ▶
Sales ▶
Jobs, Time & Mileage ▶
Vendors & Payables ▶
Banking ▶
Accountant & Taxes ▶
Budgets & Forecasts ▶
List ▶
Custom Summary Report
Custom Transaction Detail Report
QuickReport   Ctrl+Q
Transaction History
Transaction Journal

Figure 1-27

b) **Click** the **Report Centre icon** on the Icon bar; or

Figure 1-28

2. The Report Centre will be displayed as shown:

Reports		▤ Memorized	⇄ Preferences	▢ Learning

Company & Financial
Find out how well your company is doing financially.

Company & Financial		
Sales Tax	**Profit & Loss (income statement)**	
Customers & Receivables	☐ Standard	How much money did my company make or lose over a specific period of time? More...
Sales	☐ Detail	What are the year-to-date transactions (and totals) for each income and expense account, so I can determine what contributed to my company's net profit? More...
Jobs, Time & Mileage		
Vendors & Payables	☐ YTD Comparison	How do my income and expenses for a recent period of time compare to the entire fiscal year to date? More...
Employees & Payroll	☐ Prev Year Comparison	Is my company making more money now than for the same period a year ago? More...
Banking	☐ By Job	How much money is my company making or losing on each job? More...
Accountant & Taxes	☐ By Class	How much money did my company make or lose on each business segment that is tracked through QuickBooks classes? More...
Budgets & Forecasts	☐ Unclassified	How much money did my company make or lose that is not tracked through QuickBooks classes? More...
List		

Income & Expenses

☐ Income by Customer Summary — What is the gross profit (sales minus cost of goods sold) received from each customer? More...

☐ Income by Customer Detail — What is the gross profit (sales minus cost of goods sold), broken down by transaction, received from each customer? More...

☐ Expenses by Vendor Summary — What are my company's total expenses for each vendor? More...

☐ Expenses by Vendor Detail — What are my company's total expenses, per transaction, for each vendor? More...

☐ Income & Expense Graph — How does my company's income compare to expenses? What are the largest sources of income and expenses? More...

Balance Sheet & Net Worth

Figure 1-29

Various headings are listed down the left-hand side of the screen. As you click on a heading, the reports available for that heading are displayed to the right.

3. **Click** the **different headings** to view the reports available for that heading:

Each report has the following information available:

a. An icon to the left of the report name is used to display a sample of the report by simply hovering your mouse over the icon

b. The report name is represented by a link that can be clicked to open the report

c. To the right of the report name is a question that will be answered by the report

d. The More button can be used to open QuickBooks help to obtain detailed in formation about the report

Notes
Modifying reports is covered in Chapter 4.

When you open a report, you can select a predefined date range from the Dates drop-down list or enter a range of dates. To begin the customization of a report, you use the Modify Report button. Once you have entered your report settings, the updated report should automatically display on the screen; however, you may have to press `tab` or click the Refresh button to update it. You can select Print to print the report, or select Export to save the report as an Excel spreadsheet.

You can Modify reports by adding or omitting information, by changing font style and sizes, and by sorting and filtering the reports to reorganize or select certain criteria to include in the report. Once you have customized a report, you can memorize the report settings so that you do not have to re-enter them the next time you want to print the same report.

QuickBooks Lists

The QuickBooks Centres contain their respective lists. You will find the Customers & Jobs list in the Customer Centre, the Vendors list in the Vendor Centre, and the Employees list in the Employee Centre. There are other lists found in list windows that are also available in QuickBooks. To view the lists in list windows:

1. **Click**   the **Lists menu**

Lists	
Chart of Accounts	Ctrl+A
Item List	
Fixed Asset Item List	
Price Level List	
Sales Tax Code List	
Other Names List	
Customer & Vendor Profile Lists	▶
Templates	
Memorized Transaction List	Ctrl+T

Figure 1-30

All the list menus, other than the QuickBooks Centre lists, can be found in this menu and some of them can also be found in other related menus. Lists are central to the way QuickBooks works, and we will work with many different lists as we work through the chapters in this textbook. All QuickBooks list windows include the same three buttons with menu options relevant to the open list. Some lists contain additional buttons. To see this, let's open the Chart of Accounts.

2. **Click**   **Chart of Accounts** to view the Chart of Accounts:

Chart of Accounts			
Name	⚡	Type	Balance Total
◆ Employee Advances		Other Current Asset	0.00
◆ Accumulated Depreciation		Fixed Asset	0.00
◆ Buildings and Improvements		Fixed Asset	0.00
◆ Furniture and Equipment		Fixed Asset	0.00
◆ Leasehold Improvements		Fixed Asset	0.00
◆ Vehicles		Fixed Asset	0.00
◆ Accounts Payable		Accounts Payable	0.00
◆ GST/HST Payable		Other Current Liabi...	0.00
◆ GST/QST Payable		Other Current Liabi...	0.00
◆ Payroll Liabilities		Other Current Liabi...	0.00
◆ PST Payable (ON)		Other Current Liabi...	0.00
◆ Worker's Comp Premiums - Admin		Other Current Liabi...	0.00
◆ Opening Balance Equity		Equity	0.00
◆ Owners Draw		Equity	0.00
◆ Owners Equity		Equity	
◆ Accounting Services Income		Income	
◆ Bookkeeping Services Income		Income	
◆ Consulting Income		Income	
◆ Payroll Services Income		Income	
◆ Tax Preparation Services Income		Income	
◆ Contracted Services		Cost of Goods Sold	
◆ Merchant Account Fees		Cost of Goods Sold	

| Account ▼ | Activities ▼ | Reports ▼ | ☐ Include inactive |

Figure 1-31

Let's review the different buttons available on the list:

3. Click   the **Account button** (this button's name is always indicative of the list) to view the menu available with this button:

Figure 1-32

4. Click   the **Activities button** (this button's name is the same in each list) to view the menu available with this button:

Figure 1-33

5. **Click**   the **Reports button** (this button's name is the same in each list) to view the menu available with this button:

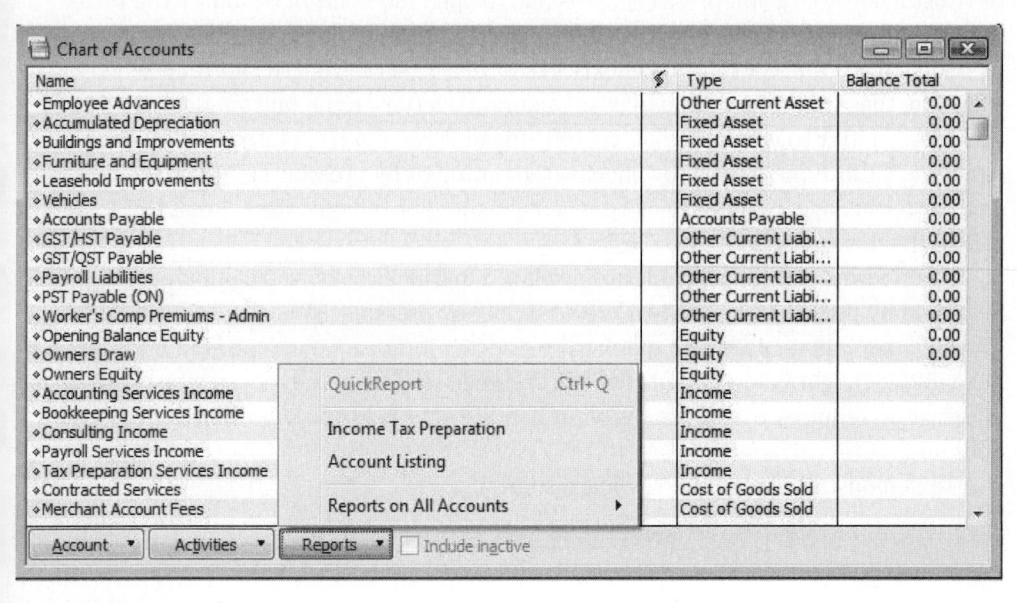

Figure 1-34

Other lists contain an Excel button which allows you to import and export information from the list to and from Microsoft Excel.

6. **Click**   [X] to close the Chart of Accounts list

Using QuickBooks Keyboard Shortcuts

All Windows-based software applications are designed to be used with a mouse. However, there may be times when you would prefer to use keyboard commands to work with a program because they are faster. There are also times when you need to know the alternatives to using a mouse, especially when the mouse doesn't work. It is not necessary to memorize all the keyboard commands.

A few basic principles will help you understand how they work, and over time you will use the ones that help you work most efficiently. Some commands are common to more than one Windows-based software program. For example, $ctrl$ + **C** (press and hold the Control key while you press the letter "c" is commonly used as the copy command and $ctrl$ + **V** as the paste command. Any selected text or image will be copied or pasted. alt + **<F4>** is a common shortcut for closing a window or program. Many QuickBooks functions can be accessed in more than one way — from the Home page icons, QuickBooks Centres, the main menu, list menus, the icon bar, and keyboard shortcuts.

To use the keyboard shortcuts and activate the underlined letters in the main menu, press the alt key. With the underlined letters displayed, click an underlined letter in a menu item name to open the menu. Once the menu is open, use the up and down arrow keys ▲ ▼ to move up and down through the menu, or the left and right arrow keys ◀ ▶ to move back and forth to other menus. Some menu choices have direct keyboard alternatives or shortcuts. If the menu item has an underlined letter, pressing alt together with the underlined letter will access that option directly. For example, alt + **F** (press alt, and while holding down alt, press the letter "**F**") accesses the File menu. Then pressing "**O**" (the underlined letter for Open) will give you the dialogue box for opening a new file.

Notes
Keyboard shortcuts are also available for many functions.

Notes
Keyboard shortcuts are not case sensitive. You do not need to hold down the $shift$ key even if the underlined letter is upper case.

Some of the most common QuickBooks functions have their own keyboard shortcuts other than the ones discussed. For example, to open an invoice you press (ctrl) + **I**; to open the Customer Centre you press (ctrl) + **J**, and to open the Chart of Accounts you press (ctrl) + **A**. These shortcuts are displayed beside the items in their respective menus.

Some icons and buttons in QuickBooks have a direct keyboard shortcut. When available, these shortcuts appear as an underlined letter on the button. Press (alt) + the underlined letter to enter the button's command. For example, on the Invoice form, you can Save & Close the invoice by clicking the button or by pressing (alt) + **a**, the underlined letter in Save. To choose or open a highlighted or selected item, press (enter). To cancel the menu display, press (esc).

When forms with input fields are displayed in QuickBooks, you can move to the next field by pressing (tab) or to a previous field by pressing (shift) and (tab) together. The (tab) key can be used as a quick way to accept input, advance the cursor to the next field, and highlight field contents for editing purposes. Using the mouse while you input information requires you to remove your hands from the keyboard, while the (tab) key does not.

To demonstrate using the keyboard shortcuts:

1. From the Home page, **press** the (alt) key (to activate the underlined letters in the menu)

Each item in the main menu should now have a letter underlined in its name. By pressing the (alt) key, you can view which letters must be selected in order to open a menu item.

Notes

The (alt) key acts as a toggle to turn on and off the underlined letters in the menu.

2. **Press**   **u** to open the Customers menu ("u" is the underlined letter in "Customers")

Each menu item in the Customers menu also has an underlined letter in its name. Selecting a letter will open the form.

3. **Press**   **y** to open the Receive Payments form (you could also have used the down arrow key to access the Receive Payments option)

The buttons on the bottom of the form also contain underlined letters. When you enter a customer payment in the Receive Payments window, you can press (alt) + **a** to select Save & Close, or press (alt) + **S** to select Save & New.

4. **Press**   (esc) to close the Receive Payments form

When you open a menu, some of the items in the menu also have shortcuts displayed to the right of their name. These shortcuts are usually memorized and used for quick access. Let's take a look at this.

5. Press   `alt` **+ U** to open the Customers menu:

Customers	
Customer Centre	Ctrl+J
Create Estimates	
Create Sales Orders	
Create Invoices	Ctrl+I
Enter Sales Receipts	
Enter Statement Charges	
Create Statements...	
Assess Finance Charges	
Receive Payments	
Create Credit Memos/Refunds	
Enter Time	▶
Item List	
Change Item Prices	

Figure 1-35

On this menu, both the Customer Centre and the Create Invoices options have specific keyboard shortcuts. To open the Customer Centre and the Create Invoices form:

6. Press   `ctrl` **+ J** to open the Customer Centre

7. Press   `esc` to close the Customer Centre

8. Press   `ctrl` **+ I** to open the Create Invoices form

9. Press   `esc` to close the Create Invoices form

QuickBooks Preferences

In this chapter, we will provide only an introduction to the preference settings. You won't need to change any preferences for the files we have set up but you may want to adjust some of them. In this chapter, we will show you the preference settings that do not affect how the program works. We will cover the preferences for other modules in detail later as we use them in creating new company data files.

1. Choose   the **Edit menu** and **click Preferences**:

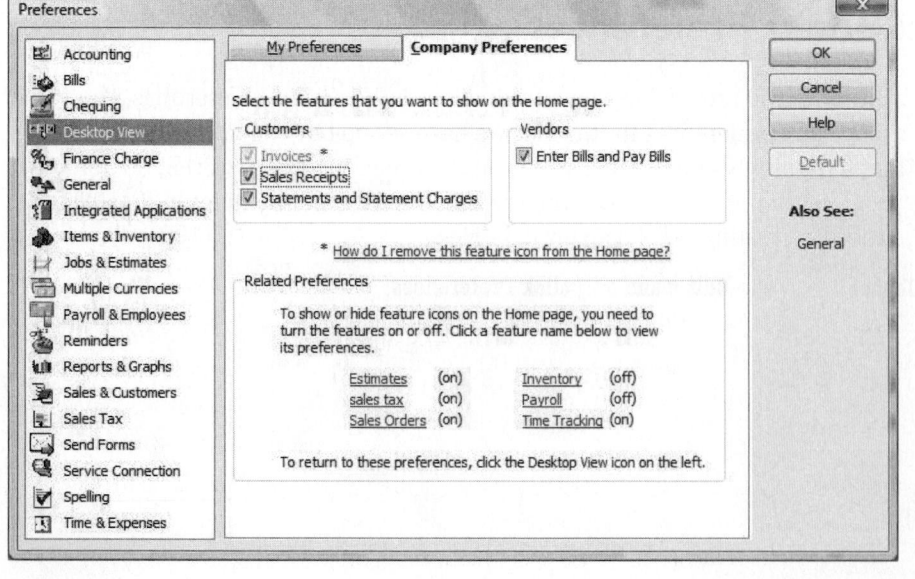

Figure 1-36

2. Click   the **Desktop View** heading on the left-hand side of the screen and **click** the **My Preferences tab** to view the window shown above if necessary

    Preferences are divided into two tabs: Company preferences that can only be changed by the administrator of the company file, such as whether or not specific QuickBooks features are used; and My Preferences that influence how you work with the program and can be modified by all users to suit their own personal preferences. On the My Preferences tab for the desktop view heading, you can allow the simultaneous display of multiple open windows or just one window, save the desktop when you close the file, show the Home page when opening a company file, show the Coach window and features, show Live Community and Help, and change the colour scheme used in QuickBooks. You can also access the Windows settings for Display and Sounds. The Help button will explain each option on the Preferences window.

3. Click   the **Company Preferences tab**:

Figure 1-37

    The preferences on the Company Preferences tab can only be changed by the Administrator of the company file and affect all users of the system when you are working in a multi-user environment. If you are working in a single-user environment, then you will be the Administrator of the company file and can make the necessary changes on the Company Preferences tab.

In the Desktop View heading, you can select the features you want to show on the Home page, such as Sales Receipts, Statements and Statement Charges, and Enter Bills and Pay Bills. If you don't use these features, you can turn them off so you don't clutter the Home page with icons you don't use. You can also use this tab to turn on or off Estimates, Sales Tax, Sales Orders, Inventory, Payroll, and Time Tracking. The Help button will explain each option on the current Preferences window.

4. Click   the **General heading** and **click** the **My Preferences tab**:

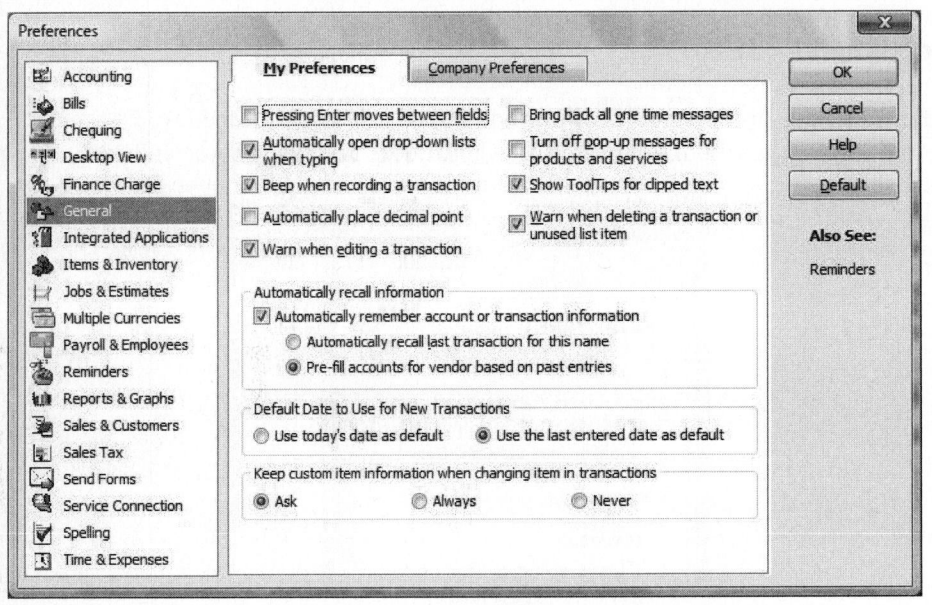

Figure 1-38

On this tab there are a number of preferences you can select, such as Beep when recording a transaction, Warn when editing a transaction, Warn when deleting a transaction or unused list item, and the Default Date to use for New Transactions.

5. Click   **Help** and **read** the **explanation for each preference**

6. Click   the **Company Preferences tab**:

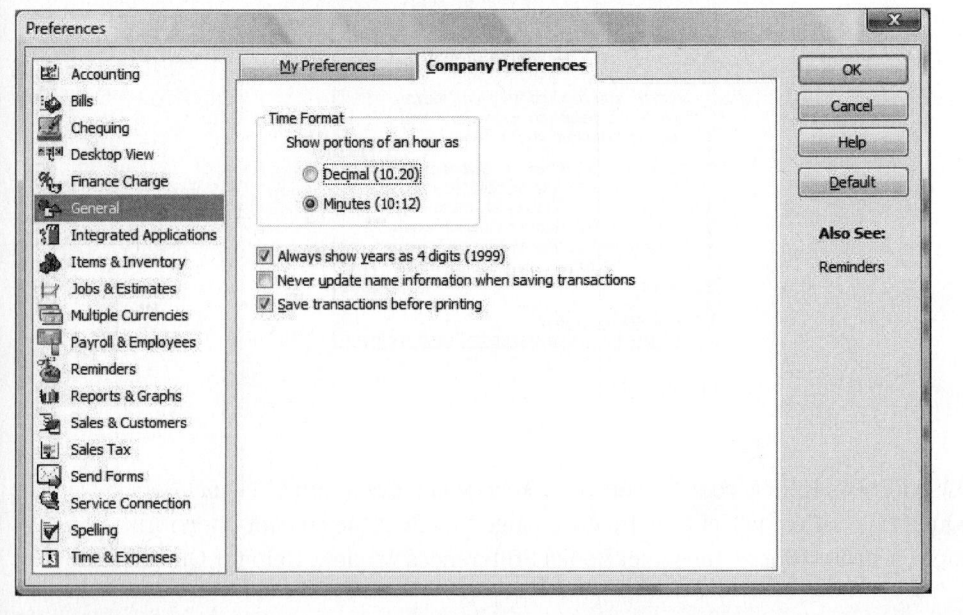

Figure 1-39

Use this tab to determine the date and time format, to indicate whether name information changed on forms should be updated in the QuickBooks record, and to save transactions before printing.

8. Do not save the changes you make

9. Close the **Preferences window** when you have finished

Notes
You can reset the changes back to the default by clicking Default.

Accessing Help in QuickBooks

QuickBooks Help

QuickBooks Help is displayed in its own window pane together with the Live Community to the right of the QuickBooks desktop. The QuickBooks Help pane is shown here:

Figure 1-40

QuickBooks Help is context-sensitive, so as you move around in QuickBooks, the QuickBooks Help will automatically change to reflect the current open form. For example, when you open the QuickBooks Preferences window, Help for QuickBooks

Preferences is displayed. However, as you move from one preference heading to another, you may have to click the Help button to update the information for the current preference heading.

With the Help window displayed on the screen, you can click the Relevant Topics tab in the upper section of the screen to view relevant topics for the current screen selected. Click on any of the relevant topics to view the help information in the bottom of the screen. Alternatively, you can click the Search tab and enter a help topic.

You can access Help using one of the following options:

a.   **Click Help** ⌐ⓘ Help ⌐ on the Icon bar; or

Figure 1-41

b.   **Choose** the **Help menu** and **click QuickBooks Help**; or

Figure 1-42

c.   **Press F1** (the keyboard shortcut)

1. Click   the **Help icon** on the Icon bar (if the Live Community and Help pane is not currently displayed)

2. Click   the **Create Invoices icon** on the Customer section of the Home page to open the Create Invoices form

3. Click   the **Relevant Topics tab** (if necessary) to view the help topics relevant to creating invoices. Notice the topics are all about invoices because you have the Create Invoices form open

4. Click   a **topic** to view the information in the bottom of the Help pane

5. **Click**   the **Search tab**

6. **Type**   **Vendor Payments** and **press** (enter)

Even though you are currently on the Create Invoices form, help topics about Vendor Payments are displayed.

7. **Click**   a **topic** to view the help information

8. **Click**   [X] to close the Help window pane

Live Community

QuickBooks Live Community is displayed in its own window pane together with QuickBooks Help to the right of the QuickBooks desktop. The Live Community portion is shown here:

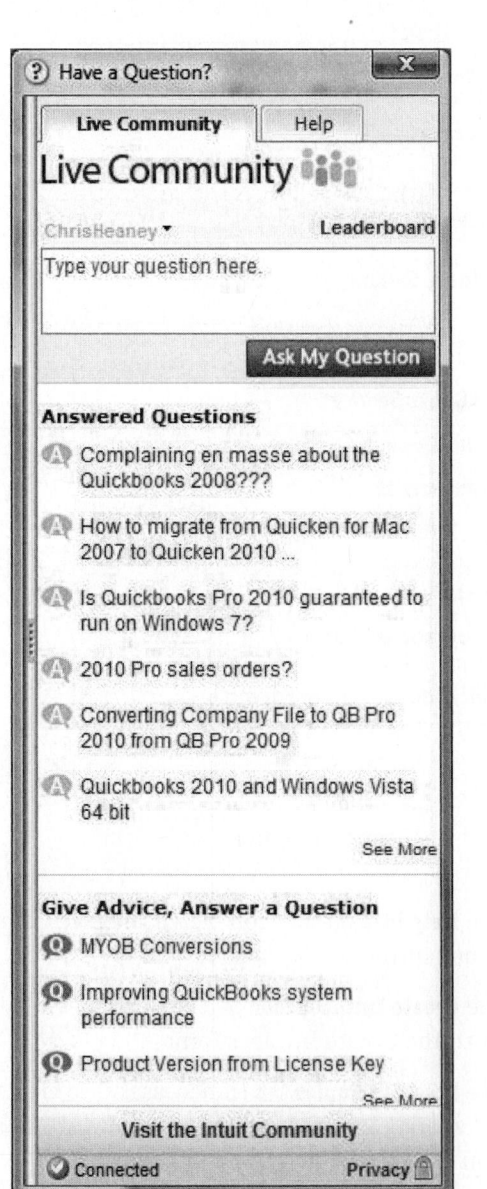

Figure 1-43

If you have an Internet connection, you can use Live Community to receive answers directly from the QuickBooks Community from within QuickBooks. As you learned earlier, the Live Community is displayed in the same window as Help: Help is displayed on the screen and so is the Live Community.

To access the Live Community:

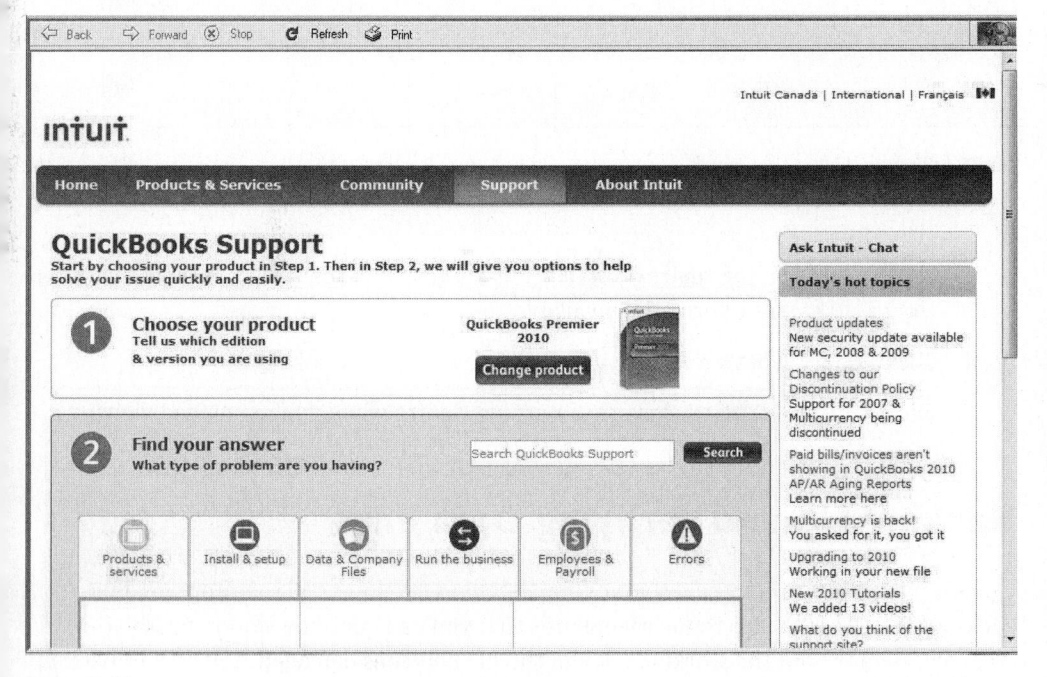

a. **Click** the **Live Community button** on the Icon bar (if it is displayed on the icon bar); or

Figure 1-44

b. **Press** any of the **options** that open QuickBooks help; or

c. **Click** the **Live Community tab** if necessary to display the Live Community pane:

With the Live Community displayed, enter your question in the box and click the Ask My Question button. You can also click the Visit Intuit Community link at the bottom of the Live Community pane to access more information from the QuickBooks community.

Support

You can access QuickBooks Support from the Help menu. You need an Internet connection to use this feature. To access QuickBooks support:

1. **Choose**   **Help** from the menu

2. **Click**   **Support** to open the QuickBooks Support webpage:

Figure 1-45

3. Take some time to review the information found on the QuickBooks Support webpage

The Learning Centre

The Learning Centre includes a number of resources to help you get started using QuickBooks.

To access the Learning Centre:

1. Choose   **Help** from the menu

2. Click   **Learning Centre**:

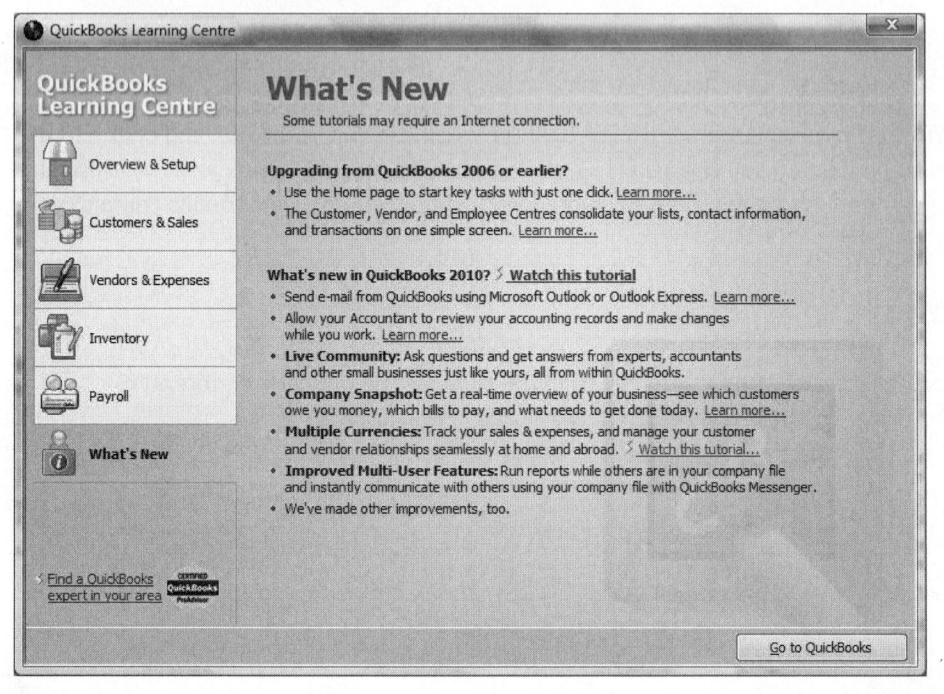

Figure 1-46

3. Click   on the **topics** down the left-hand side of the screen to view the different information available

4. Click   **What's New** to learn what's new in QuickBooks 2010

5. Click   ![X] to close the Learning Centre when you're finished viewing it

Backing Up and Verifying Data Files

QuickBooks automatically saves your company file as you work in the program, but backing up your data files regularly ensures that you can continue working with your company data even if the working copy of the file becomes damaged. You should back up to a separate drive whenever possible for even greater security. We will demonstrate the backup procedure to a USB drive.

To back up the QuickBooks company file currently open:

1. Choose   **File** from the menu

2. Click   **Save Copy or Backup** to open the Save Copy or Backup screen:

Figure 1-47

3. **Click** **Backup Copy** (the default) and **click Next**:

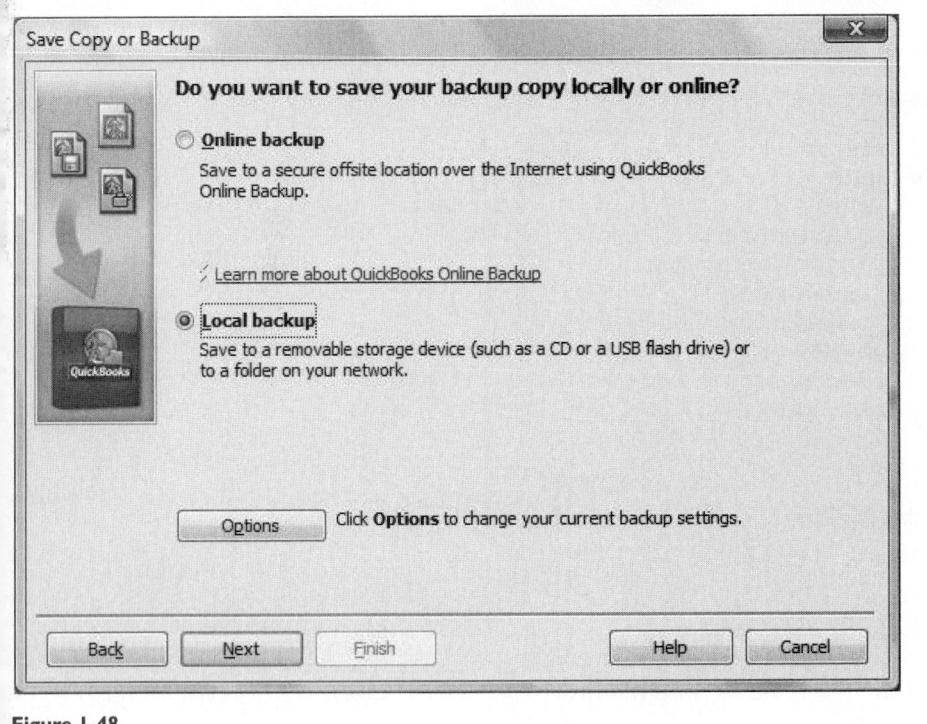

Figure 1-48

Use this screen to indicate whether you want to save your backup locally or online.

4. **Accept** **Local Backup** (this is the default) and **click Options**:

Figure 1-49

The Backup Options screen is used to set the backup options.

5. Click   **Browse** to display the Browse for Folder screen:

Figure 1-50

6. Select   your **USB drive**

7. Click   **OK** to close the Browse for Folder screen

The next time you back up this company file, this drive will automatically be displayed in the Browse field.

Add the date and time to the backup file name so it is very easy to identify when the backup file was created. When you limit the number of backups in the folder, you'll be prompted to delete the oldest backup from the folder when you reach the number entered in this field. You can decide to delete the oldest backup or choose not to.

We want to verify the data file each time we make a backup. Although this step will slow down the backup process, data file errors can be detected during this process. We can then choose to rebuild the data file to correct the errors or to restore the file from an earlier backup. We will also set the program to remind us to make a backup when the company file is closed every 4 times.

Notes
You can also verify your data at any time by choosing the File menu, then choosing Utilities and Verify Data. Notice that the option to Rebuild Data is located here as well.

8. **Click**   **Complete Verification** as the verify option (this should be selected as the default)

9. **Accept**   the default to be reminded to back up the company file when it is closed every 4 times

10. **Click**   **OK** to close the Backup Options screen

11. **Click**   **Next** on the Save Copy or Backup screen to view the next backup screen:

Figure 1-51

12. **Click**   **Finish**

When the backup is complete, you will see the following message:

Figure 1-52

Notice that the file name contains the date and time when the backup was created and the file name ends with a.QBB extension.

13. Click   **OK** to return to the company file

Scheduling Automatic Backups

QuickBooks allows you to schedule automatic backups so the data file is backed up regularly either when you close the data file, or on some other schedule.

1. Choose   **File menu** and **click Save Copy or Backup** to open the Backup screen

2. Select   **Backup copy** and **click Next**

3. Select   **Local backup** and **click Next**

4. The following screen allows you to choose the backup schedule options:

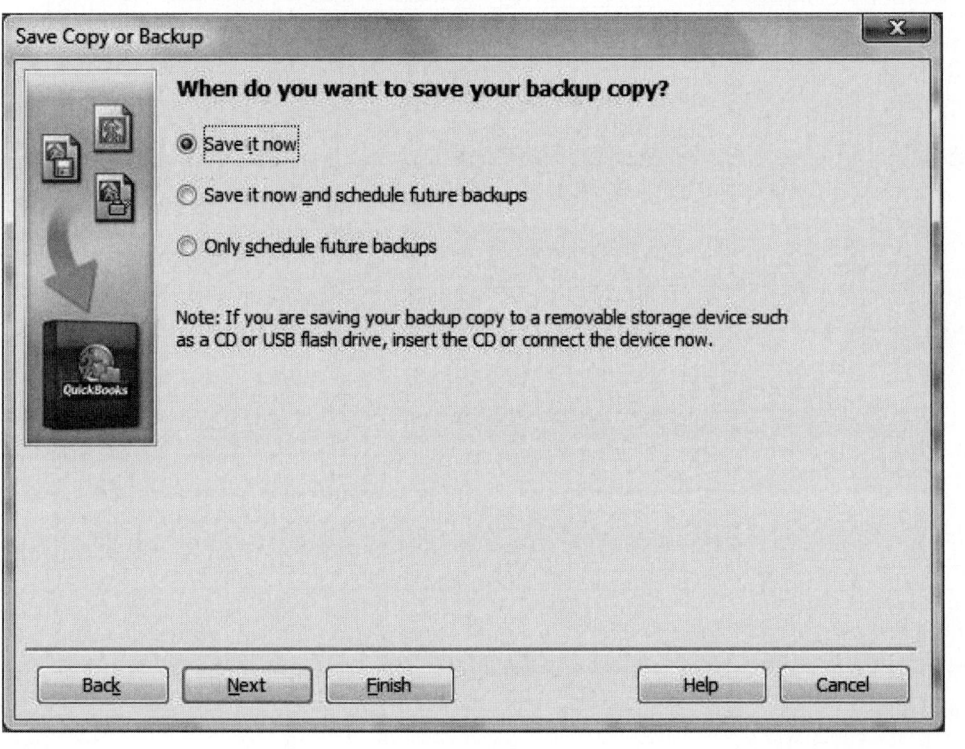

Figure 1-53

You can choose to create a backup now, create a backup now and schedule future backups, or only schedule future backups. Since we just completed a backup, we'll choose to only schedule future backups.

5. Click   the **Only schedule future backups** option and **click Next**:

Figure 1-54

You can select to have the data file backup automatically when you close the program by selecting the *Save backup copy automatically when I close my company file every ___ times* option and entering a number in the field.

6. Click   the **box** beside the *Save backup copy automatically when I close my company file every ___ times* option

The number field will become available. Every 3 times is entered as the default frequency. If you want to back up each time you close the file, enter 1 to replace the 3 as the default frequency.

7. Enter   **the number you want** in the *every ___ times* field

8. Click   the **Options button** and **enter** the **location** of the backup. Modify any of the other information found on this screen

9. Click   **OK** to close the Backup Options window after you have selected the appropriate options

You can also schedule automatic backups. Companies frequently back up their data at night when the computers are not being used by employees. To use this feature, you must, of course, leave your computer on, and the data file being backed up must not be open or in use.

10. Click   **New** to open the Schedule Backup screen:

Schedule Backup

Describe the backup task you want to schedule:

Description _____

Location _____ [Browse...]

☐ Number of backup copies to keep [3]

Select the time and day you want to save the backup:

Start time [01 ▼] : [00 ▼] [AM ▼]

Run this task every [1 ▼] weeks on:

☐ Monday ☐ Tuesday ☐ Wednesday
☐ Thursday ☐ Friday ☐ Saturday
☐ Sunday [Store Password...]

[OK] [Cancel] [Help]

Figure 1-55

You must enter a description or name for the backup routine, a location for the backup file, the number of backups to keep before they are replaced by more current files, and how often you want to perform a backup. To back up the data file daily, you would choose 1 in the Run this task every __ weeks on field, and click each weekday name. You must enter the Windows password for the automatic backup to work.

11. **Type**   **Daily Backup** in the description field

12. **Click**   **Browse** to browse for the drive and folder you will use to save your backup file

13. **Choose**   **1** in the *Run this task every __ weeks on* field

14. **Click**   in the **box** beside each weekday name

15. **Click**   **OK** to save the schedule

16. You will be prompted to enter the Windows password:

Store Windows Password

Enter your Windows username and password.

QuickBooks stores this information for you so that the backup can run at the scheduled time.

Username: [Chris]

Password: [_____]

[OK] [Cancel] [Help]

Figure 1-56

You must enter the Windows password required to unlock your computer so the QuickBooks backup can run at the scheduled time.

17. **Click** **OK** and you'll be returned to the Backup screen where the new backup schedule is listed:

Save Copy or Backup

When do you want to backup your company file?

Back up automatically:

☑ Save backup copy automatically when I close my company file every 3 times

Click **Options** to view or change where the automatic backup copies will be saved.   [Options]

Back up on a schedule:

Click **New** to schedule regular backups of your company file.

Description	Backup Location	Status	Next Backup
Daily Backup	J:\	New	12/10/2009

[New...] [Edit...] [Remove]

[Back] [Next] [Finish]   [Help] [Cancel]

Figure 1-57

Restoring a File from a Backup

If your data files have become damaged, or if for some other reason you need to return to an earlier version of the data files, you can restore a file from its backup.

1. **Choose** the **File menu** and **click Open or Restore Company** to open the Open or Restore Company window:

Open or Restore Company

What type of file do you want to open or restore?

◉ **Open a company file**
  • Open a regular company file (.qbw)

◯ **Restore a backup copy**
  • Restore a backup file (.qbb)
  • Restore files from the QuickBooks Online Backup service

◯ **Restore a portable file**
  • Re-create a company file that was stored as a portable file (.qbm)

[Back] [Next] [Finish]   [Help] [Cancel]

Figure 1-58

> **Notes**
> The No Company Open window also includes an Open or restore an existing company button that starts the Restore Company Backup wizard.

2. **Click**   **Restore a backup copy** and **click Next**:

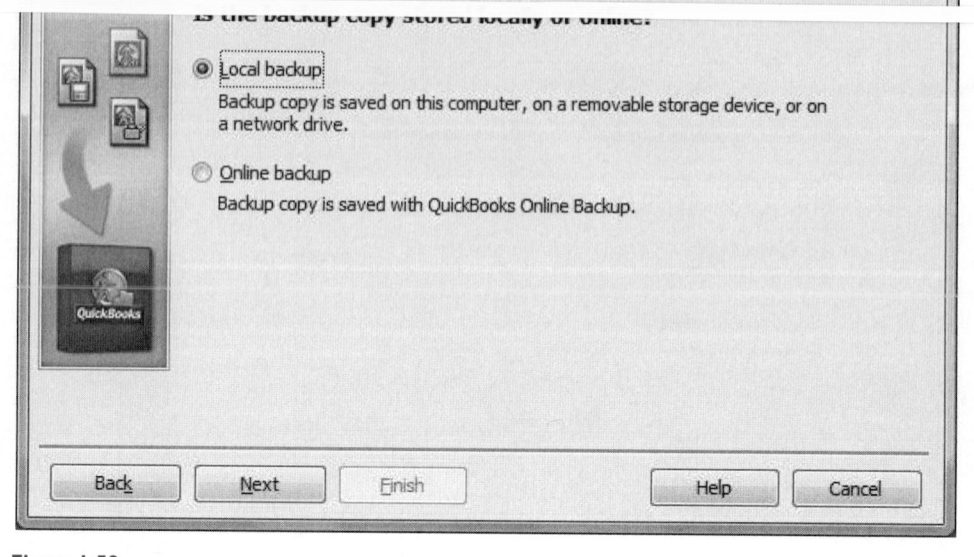

Figure 1-59

Use this screen to indicate whether your backup was saved locally or online.

3. **Click**   **Local backup** and **click Next**:

Notes
  Your file may be displayed differently depending on the view you have selected to display your files. In Figure 1-60, files are set to display by Medium Icons.

Figure 1-60

4. **Use**   the **Look in: field** to browse for the backup file if necessary

5. **Highlight**   the **file** and **click Open**:

Figure 1-61

This screen indicates that you must choose the location where you want to restore your backup file and gives you information about overwriting your existing company file.

6. **Click**   **Next**

On this screen, select the location where you want to restore the backup file. The default is the original file name and location of the file you are restoring.

7. **Click**   the **drop-down arrow** in the Save in field to select the drive and folder where you want to restore the backup file

8. **Click**   **Save**

If you are replacing an existing data file, you will be asked to confirm that you want to replace it:

Figure 1-62

You must confirm that you are replacing the existing file. You can still make changes by clicking No to return to the Restore Company Backup window.

9. Click   **Yes** (if you are going to replace the existing file)

If you receive a message that this file is set to read only, please refer to page xi of the Preface under the "Restoring Files from Different Updates" heading under the Updating QuickBooks heading.

If the file already exists, and is not set to read only, the following message will be displayed asking you to confirm deletion of the data file:

Figure 1-63

a) **Type yes** in the confirmation if you want to permanently delete the existing file

10. You will receive the following message after you restore your file regardless of whether you created a new file or replaced an existing file:

Figure 1-64

11. Click   **OK**

Finishing Your Session

When you have finished entering all your accounting data in a work session, or just want to take a break, you should close the data file and QuickBooks program. If you close the company file, you will see the No Company Open screen (page 12) the next time you start QuickBooks; otherwise, the last data file you worked with will open automatically. You may want to close the company file if you work with many different company files so that you can choose a different company file the next time you start QuickBooks, or if you are unsure which data file you used most recently. If you work with the data for the same company each time, you won't want to close the company each time you finish your session. To close the company file:

1. Choose   the **File menu** and **click Close Company**

2. The No Company Open window will be displayed

3. Click   ☒ on the program title bar or choose the File menu and click Exit to close QuickBooks

GST, HST, and PST

Objectives

After completing this chapter, you should be able to:

- *understand* the terms relevant to the federal Goods and Services Tax (GST)
- *understand* the different methods of calculating the GST
- *understand* Harmonized Sales Tax (HST) in relation to GST
- *understand* how to file for GST or HST remittances or refunds
- *understand* other provincial sales taxes in relation to GST

General Tax Information

Definition of GST

The Goods and Services Tax (GST) is levied by the federal government at the rate of 5 percent on most goods and services in Canada. Retailers pay the GST to their wholesalers and vendors but are allowed to deduct any GST they pay from the GST they collect from customers. Retailers remit the difference, GST owing, to the Receiver General for Canada or claim a refund with monthly or quarterly returns.

Notes
Provinces may, or may not, include GST in the price on which they calculate Provincial Sales Tax (PST). Provincial tax rates vary from province to province. (See page 47.)

GST Registration

Any business with annual sales exceeding $30,000.00 per year must register for GST collection and must collect GST on all applicable sales. Registration is optional for most smaller businesses. Businesses that are not registered for GST do not charge GST on sales to their customers, but they also cannot recover the GST they pay on business-related purchases.

Notes
GST collected on sales is reduced by the GST on sales returns.

Collecting the GST

The business must collect GST for those goods and services sold that are not zero rated or tax exempt. The business must remit GST at regular intervals, filing GST returns monthly, quarterly, or annually and paying installments, depending on annual income and GST owing.

Zero-Rated Goods and Services

Zero-rated goods and services are those on which the tax rate is zero. These goods include basic groceries, prescribed medical devices, prescribed drugs, exported goods and services, agricultural products, and fish products. A business selling only zero-rated goods and services does not collect GST on sales, but it can still claim a refund for GST it pays for purchases.

Tax-Exempt Goods and Services

Tax-exempt goods and services are those on which tax is not collected. These goods and services include health care, dental care, daycare services, and rents on residences. Most educational and financial services are also included in this group. These businesses are not able to claim refunds for GST paid for business purchases related to selling tax-exempt goods and services.

Paying the GST

Notes
The input tax credit is reduced by the amount of GST for purchases returned.

A business must pay GST for purchases made specifically for business purposes, unless the goods or services purchased are zero rated or tax exempt. The business can use the GST paid as an input tax credit by subtracting the amount of GST paid from the amount of GST collected and remitting GST owing or claiming a refund. GST amounts paid on purchases for personal use do not qualify as input tax credits.

Bank and Financial Institution Services

Most bank products and services are not taxable. Exceptions include safety deposit box rentals, custodial and safekeeping services, personalized cheques, self-administered registered savings plan fees, payroll services, rentals of night depository, rentals of credit card imprinters, and reconciliation of cheques. Banks remit the full amount of GST they collect from customers. Because most bank services are not taxable, banks cannot claim input tax credits for GST they pay on business-related purchases.

GST on Imported and Exported Goods

Notes
Visitors to Canada can request a refund for GST paid on goods purchased in Canada that they are taking home with them. They cannot claim a refund for GST paid on goods and services they consumed in Canada, such as entertainment and dining.

GST is not charged on exported goods. Customers in other countries who import goods from Canada do not pay GST. However, businesses in Canada must pay GST on the items they import or purchase from other countries. The GST is collected by the Canada Revenue Agency (CRA) when the goods enter Canada based on the purchase price (plus import duty) and current exchange rates. Businesses must pay this GST and other import duties before the goods are released to them.

Administering the GST

The federal government has approved different methods of administering the GST; the regular method is most commonly used.

The Regular Method

The regular method of administering the GST requires the business to keep track of GST paid for all goods and services purchased from vendors (less returns) and of GST collected for all goods and services sold to customers (less returns). It then deducts the GST paid from the GST collected and files for a refund or remits the balance owing to the Receiver General on a monthly or quarterly basis.

Accounting Examples Using the Regular Method (without PST)

SALES INVOICE

Sold goods to customer for $200.00 plus $10.00 GST (5%). Invoice total, $210.00.

Date	Particulars	Debit	Credit
02/15	Accounts Receivable	$210.00	
	GST Charged on Sales		$ 10.00
	Revenue from Sales		200.00

PURCHASE INVOICE

Purchased supplies from vendor for $300.00 plus $15.00 GST (5%). Invoice total, $315.00

Date	Particulars	Debit	Credit
02/15	Supplies	$300.00	
	GST Paid on Purchases	15.00	
	Accounts Payable		$315.00

The GST owing is further reduced by any GST adjustments — for example, GST that applies to bad debts that are written off. If the debt is later recovered, the GST liability is also restored as an input tax credit adjustment.

Other Methods of Calculating GST

Certain small businesses may be eligible to use simpler methods of calculating their GST refunds and remittances that do not require them to keep a separate record for GST on each individual purchase or sale. The simplified accounting method, the streamlined accounting method and the quick method are examples of these alternatives.

Notes
GST Paid on Purchases is a contra-liability account because it normally has a debit balance while most liability accounts have a credit balance. Therefore, GST Paid on Purchases reduces the total GST liability to the Receiver General.

Notes
Under the Quick Method, the GST remittance or refund amount is based on a flat rate percentage of total sales, including GST. The remittance rate varies for different types of businesses. GST paid on purchases of capital is an input tax credit to reduce the amount owing (or increase the refund). These alternative methods of calculating GST are not used in the applications in this workbook.

Calculating GST Refunds or Remittances

The following example uses the regular method for a retailer who is filing quarterly.

Quarterly Total Sales (excluding GST)	$50,000.00	
Quarterly Total Qualifying Purchases	29,700.00	
5% GST Charged on Sales		$2,500.00
Less: 5% GST Paid on Purchases:		
Cash Register (cost $1,000.00)	50.00	
Inventory (cost $25,000.00)	1,250.00	
Supplies (cost $500.00)	25.00	
Payroll Services (cost $200.00)	10.00	
Store Lease (cost $3,000.00)	150.00	
Total GST Paid		− 1,485.00
GST Remittance		$1,015.00

GST Remittances and Refunds

The business must file returns that summarize the amount of GST it has collected and the amount of GST it has paid. CRA may require reports monthly, quarterly, or yearly, depending on total sales. Yearly reports usually require quarterly installments.

GST Collected on Sales	>	GST Paid on Purchases	=	GST Owing
GST Collected on Sales	<	GST Paid on Purchases	=	GST Refund

> **Notes**
> The rules concerning the GST may change periodically. For example, in the 2006 federal budget, the GST rate changed from 7 percent to 6 percent. In the 2007 federal budget, the rate was reduced again to 5 percent. Always refer to current guidelines.

Accounting Examples for Remittances

Usually, a business will make GST remittances since sales usually exceed expenses — the business operates at a profit. The following example shows how the GST accounts are cleared and a liability (*Accounts Payable*) is set up to remit GST owing to the Receiver General for Canada. In this case, the usual one, the Receiver General becomes a vendor for the business so that the liability can be entered and the payment made.

Date	Particulars	Debit	Credit
03/31	GST Charged on Sales	$2,500.00	
	GST Paid on Purchases		$1,485.00
	A/P - Receiver General		1,015.00
03/31	A/P - Receiver General	1,015.00	
	Cash in Bank		1,015.00

Accounting Examples for Refunds

The example below shows how the GST accounts are cleared and a current asset account (*Accounts Receivable*) is set up for a GST refund from the Receiver General for Canada. In this case, the Receiver General owes money to the business; that is, it acts like a customer, so a customer record is set up to record and collect the refund.

Date	Particulars	Debit	Credit
03/31	GST Charged on Sales	$1,500.00	
	A/R - Receiver General	500.00	
	GST Paid on Purchases		$2,000.00
04/15	Cash in Bank	500.00	
	A/R - Receiver General		500.00

Harmonized Sales Tax (HST)

Five provinces have adopted the HST method of taxing goods and services: British Columbia, Ontario, New Brunswick, Nova Scotia, and Newfoundland and Labrador. When HST applies, the GST and provincial taxes are harmonized at a single rate. In all provinces, five percent of the HST rate is the federal portion, or GST, while the remainder is the provincial portion. Provincial retail sales tax rates vary from one province to another, so the HST rates also vary. In British Columbia, the HST rate is 12 percent (5 percent federal and 7 percent provincial); in Ontario, New Brunswick, and Newfoundland and Labrador, the HST rate in 2010 is 13 percent (5 percent federal and 8 percent provincial), and in Nova Scotia, the HST rate is 15 percent (5 percent federal and 10 percent provincial). The HST replaces the former separate GST and PST and, unlike those separate taxes, it is administered entirely at the federal level. This removes some administrative work both from the provincial Ministries of Finance and from the businesses that charge taxes to their customers. They have only one tax to calculate and remit.

The full 12, 13, or 15 percent Harmonized Sales Tax (HST) operates much like the basic GST: HST is applied at each level of sale, resale, and manufacturing; has the same business registration requirement of annual sales exceeding $30,000.00; is applied to the same base of goods and services; and is collected the same way. HST returns and remittances are also calculated the same way as GST returns and remittances. The business remits any excess of HST collected over HST paid for its business expenses, or claims a refund when HST paid exceeds the HST collected from customers.

The following example illustrates the application in Ontario (or New Brunswick, Newfoundland and Labrador) where the HST rate is 13 percent.

> **Notes**
> Prices shown to a customer may have the HST included (tax-inclusive pricing), but they must show either the amount of HST included in the price or the HST rate.

An Ontario business sold goods on account for $565.00, including HST at 13% ($500.00 base price).

HST = (0.13 × 500.00) = $ 65.00
Total amount of invoice = $565.00

Date	Particulars	Debit	Credit
02/15	Accounts Receivable	$565.00	
	HST Charged on Sales		$ 65.00
	Revenue from Sales		500.00

A single remittance for the full 13 percent is made to the Receiver General; the provincial portion of the HST is not tracked or collected separately by the business. The following examples show the journal entries for an HST remittance and an HST refund.

Remittance: A British Columbia business calculates and pays HST owing.		
Date	Particulars	Debit	Credit
03/31	HST Charged on Sales		
	A/P - Receiver General		$2,500.00
	HST Paid on Purchases		3,500.00
04/15	A/P - Receiver General	2,500.00	
	Cash in Bank		2,500.00

Refund: A British Columbia business qualifies and applies for an HST refund.		
Date	Particulars	Debit	Credit
03/31	HST Charged on Sales	$3,000.00	
	A/R - Receiver General	1,500.00	
	HST Paid on Purchases		$4,500.00
04/15	Cash in Bank	1,500.00	
	A/R - Receiver General		1,500.00

Goods and Services Exempt for HST

Under the HST method, all items that are exempt for GST or are zero rated are also exempt for HST or are zero rated for HST. In addition, each province has decided that some items will be exempt for HST and subject only to GST. For example, books and children's clothing are exempt for HST but not for GST. For these goods, the customer pays only the 5 percent GST portion of the tax. At the retail level, for these special items a separate tax code for GST only is applied. When the business files its HST return, it will remit the HST collected plus the GST collected, less the amounts of GST plus HST paid on qualifying business-related purchases on a single return.

The following example shows these calculations for a book seller who also sells music CDs in British Columbia. HST at the rate of 12 percent (includng a provincial portion of 7 percent) applies to the sale of CDs while GST at the rate of 5 percent applies to the sale of books.

Notes
Instead of applying different tax rates, retailers who sell PST-exempt goods may also charge the full HST rate and provide an immediate point-of-sale rebate for the customer for the provincial portion. They will then claim an adjustment for the rebate amount on their HST return to reduce the amount remitted. The net amount of the two methods is the same.

	Debit	Credit
Quarterly Total Sales (excluding taxes):	$92,000.00	
Quarterly Total Qualifying Purchases (excluding taxes):	$52,000.00	
HST Charged on Sales (12% x 41,000.00)	$4,920.00	
GST Charged on Sales (5% x 51,000.00)	2,550.00	
Total GST/HST collected		7,470.00
Less: GST Paid on Purchase of books for resale (5% x 21,000.00)	1,050.00	
HST Paid on other Purchases (12% x 31,000.00)	3,720.00	
Total HST Credits		− 4,770.00
HST Remittance		$2,700.00

GST and Other Provincial (Retail) Sales Taxes

The rules governing Provincial Sales Tax (PST) vary from province to province in terms of the tax rate, the goods and services that are taxed, and whether PST is applied to the GST as well as to the base purchase price (that is, whether GST is taxable). The following examples assume that the item sold has both GST and PST applied.

Although GST is applied at each level of sale, resale, and manufacturing, PST is a retail sales tax and, therefore, is paid only by the final consumer of a product or service. Therefore, it is generally referred to as a Retail Sales Tax by the provincial governments and the terms RST and PST are equivalent. Thus, a business purchasing inventory to sell to customers will not pay PST on these purchases. When the same business buys supplies or services for its use in conducting business, it must pay PST because it has become the final consumer of these goods or services.

PST applies only to sales within a province, not to sales to customers in a different province or in a different country. HST and GST do apply to interprovincial sales.

Alberta, the Northwest Territories, Yukon, and Nunavut

Alberta, the Northwest Territories, Yukon, and Nunavut do not have Provincial Sales Taxes. Customers in these regions pay only the 5 percent GST on their purchases. Thus, the examples provided earlier without PST illustrate the application of GST for these regions.

PST in Manitoba and Saskatchewan

These two prairie provinces apply PST to the base price of the sale, the amount without GST included. In Manitoba, the retail sales tax rate is 7 percent; in Saskatchewan, the rate is 5 percent. The following example illustrates the application in Manitoba.

A Manitoba business sold goods on account for $500.00 GST charged is 5% and PST charged is 7%.

GST   = (0.05×500.00) = $25.00
PST in Manitoba   = (0.07×500.00) = $35.00
Total amount of invoice = $500.00 + $25.00 + $35.00 = $560.00

Date	Particulars	Debit	Credit
02/15	Accounts Receivable	$560.00	
	GST Charged on Sales		$ 25.00
	PST Payable		35.00
	Revenue from Sales		500.00

The full amount of PST collected on sales is remitted to the provincial Minister of Finance (less any applicable sales tax compensation).

Quebec Sales Tax (QST)

Provincial sales tax in Quebec (QST) is also combined with the GST. The provincial tax rate is applied to a broader base of goods and services than PST in other provinces, like the base that has GST applied. The QST is calculated on the base amount of the sale plus the GST. That is, QST is applied to GST — a piggy-backed tax or a tax on a tax.

Notes
If a business purchases inventory for resale but later uses the inventory within the business instead, it must remit PST on this internal transaction. The business has become the final consumer of the products.

Notes
Quebec was the first province to introduce a Harmonized Sales Tax. It differs from the model in the Atlantic provinces in that the GST and QST components are both administered by the provincial government. QST is covered in Chapter 13.

A Quebec business sold goods on account for $500.00. GST charged is 5% and QST charged is 7.5%.

GST = (0.05 × 500) = $25.00
QST = (0.075 × 525) = $39.38
Total amount of invoice = $500.00 + $25.00 + $37.38 = $564.38

Date	Particulars	Debit	Credit
02/15	Accounts Receivable	$564.38	
	GST Charged on Sales		$ 25.00
	QST Charged on Sales		39.38
	Revenue from Sales		500.00

QST and GST are calculated separately but both are remitted to the Ministre du Revenu du Québec. Because the QST is also refundable, businesses can deduct the QST they pay on their purchases from the QST they collect on sales as they do their GST paid. The QST paid on a few items or services — QST on some telecommunication services and insurance — is not refundable. Therefore, QST paid must be designated as refundable or non-refundable at the time of the purchase and when the purchase is recorded.

PST in Prince Edward Island

Prince Edward Island's PST is applied to the base sale price plus GST. However, unlike Quebec, some items have only GST applied, and some have both GST and PST applied.

A PEI business sold goods on account for $500.00. GST charged is 5% and PST charged is 10%.

GST = (0.05 × 500.00) = $25.00
PST = (0.10 × 525.00) = $52.50
Total amount of invoice = $500.00 + $25.00 + $52.50 = $577.50

Date	Particulars	Debit	Credit
02/15	Accounts Receivable	$577.50	
	GST Charged on Sales		$ 25.00
	PST Payable		52.50
	Revenue from Sales		500.00

The full amount of PST collected on sales is remitted to the provincial Minister of Finance (less 3 percent sales tax compensation).

Part Two
Applications

Objectives

After completing this chapter, you should be able to:

- *write* cheques to vendors for purchases
- *enter* sales receipts to customers
- *customize* QuickBooks forms
- *add* an icon to the Icon bar
- *add* new vendors and customers
- *correct* cheques and receipts before recording
- *review* transaction journals after recording transactions
- *edit* sales receipts and cheques after recording
- *display* and *print* reports
- *display* and *print* graphs

Company Information

Company Profile

Notes
Chelsea's Chocolates
350 Godiva Ave.
Victoria, BC V7H 3L8
Tel: (250) 286-6199
Fax: (250) 288-6387
E-mail: ct@chelseas.com
Web: www.chelseas.com
Business No.: 448 399 844

Chelsea's Chocolates, located in Victoria, British Columbia, is a sole proprietorship owned and operated by Chelsea Truffles. After finishing high school in Victoria, Chelsea pursued her dream. She studied at one of Belgium's culinary schools specializing in candy and apprenticed with several famous Belgian chocolatiers to build her experience. Then she returned to Victoria to start her own business, initially selling chocolate truffles from her home, gradually expanding her business and finally opening her own store. She has maintained several of her Belgian contacts and still imports all her chocolate and cocoa ingredients directly from Belgium.

Chelsea operates a cash business — all customers pay at the time of the sale, mostly in cash. A few customers who place large or special orders pay by cheque. All vendors who supply the store require payment immediately on receipt of merchandise, and Chelsea always pays by cheque so that she will have a complete record of her business transactions.

Her store is busiest in advance of major holiday seasons — chocolates are favourite gifts for Easter and Christmas — and she caters to special occasions for all religions. Originals, the major craft show in early April and late November, precedes some of these major holidays, and Chelsea is usually very successful at both shows, selling chocolates directly to customers and discussing special orders for future business. She has just purchased a large inventory of candy ingredients to prepare candy for the November craft show.

Over time, Chelsea acquired the capital equipment needed for her business, including the stove tops for making chocolates, refrigerators for food supplies and customized refrigerated display shelves to keep the prepared candy fresh while on display. She keeps a minimum inventory on hand so that candy ingredients such as butter, cream, nuts, dried fruits and marzipan are always fresh. She uses a variety of sugars to flavour the candy and also keeps these as regular inventory items. Her non-food inventory includes packaging materials, such as waxed tissue paper, paper and plastic bags, boxes in all sizes, decorative gift tins and supplies of plastic and vinyl gloves for serving customers.

Chelsea pays monthly rent for store space that includes heat and hydro. Her rent is higher than average for the store space to cover her above-average usage of hydro. She also pays rent for her booth at the Originals craft show.

On November 1, Chelsea's Chocolates is ready to use QuickBooks for accounting transactions after using the following information to convert the accounting records to QuickBooks:

- Chart of Accounts
- Trial Balance
- List of Vendors, Customers, and Items
- Accounting Procedures

Chart of Accounts

Chelsea's Chocolates

ASSETS
Bank
    Bank Chequing
    Bank Savings

Current Assets
    Inventory:Chocolate
    Inventory:Other Candy Ingredients
    Inventory:Packaging Material
    Supplies

Fixed Assets
    Automobile
    Candy Making Equipment
    Computer/Cash Register
    Display Cabinets & Shelves
    Range/Ovens
    Refrigerators

LIABILITIES
Current Liabilities
    HST Payable

Long Term Liabilities
    Long Term Loan

EQUITY
    Capital, Chelsea Truffles
    Retained Earnings

INCOME
    Revenue from Candy Sales
    Revenue from Interest

EXPENSE
Cost of Goods Sold
    Cost of Candy Ingredients

Expenses
    Advertising
    Insurance
    Maintenance and Repairs
    Packaging Materials Used
    Rental Expense
    Supplies Expense
    Utilities

Notes
We have changed the name of the GST/HST Payable account to HST Payable.

Chelsea's Chocolates

AS AT OCTOBER 31, 2012

	Debits	Credits
Bank Chequing	$ 29,200.00	
Bank Savings	18,580.00	
Inventory:Chocolate	5,150.00	
Inventory:Other Candy Ingredients	3,450.00	
Inventory:Packaging Material	600.00	
Supplies	1,500.00	
Automobile	14,000.00	
Candy Making Equipment	5,000.00	
Computer/Cash Register	4,500.00	
Display Cabinets & Shelves	3,800.00	
Range/Ovens	3,300.00	
Refrigerators	26,000.00	
HST Payable	$ 450.00	
Long Term Loan		$ 24,000.00
Capital, Chelsea Truffles		57,940.00
Revenue from Candy Sales		88,500.00
Revenue from Interest		2,000.00
Cost of Candy Ingredients	8,300.00	
Advertising	2,100.00	
Insurance	1,700.00	
Packaging Materials Used	3,900.00	
Rental Expense	34,000.00	
Supplies Expense	1,710.00	
Utilities	5,200.00	
	$172,440.00	$172,440.00

Chelsea's Chocolates

VENDORS

Belgian's Finest
Covers
Fournier's Fine Foods
Minister of Finance (BC)
NuTel
Originals (Craft Show)
Receiver General for Canada
Suite Properties
SuperSacs

CUSTOMERS

Craft Show Customers
Store Customers

ITEMS

Candy Sold in Store
Craft Show Sales
Special Orders

Accounting Procedures

Taxes: HST

Chelsea's Chocolates pays 12 percent HST on all goods and services that it buys, including the imported products, and charges HST on all sales and services. HST collected from customers is recorded as a liability in the *HST Payable* account. HST paid to vendors is recorded in the *HST Payable* account as a decrease in liability to the Canada Revenue Agency. The report is filed with the Receiver General for Canada by the last day of the month for the previous quarter, either including the balance owing or requesting a refund. *HST Payable* shows a debit balance because Chelsea has recently submitted a return and payment and has made a large number of purchases to prepare for the craft show.

Customer and Vendor Account Terms

Most customers pay in cash. Cash received from customers is deposited immediately and is recorded in the *Bank Chequing* account. It is not held for later deposit. Some special order customers pay for their purchases by cheque.

All vendors demand payment on receipt of merchandise. All payments are made by cheque.

Cost of Goods Sold

Most food items and supplies are used shortly after purchase so these amounts are entered directly as expenses rather than as assets. At the end of the fiscal year, adjusting entries are made for unused food inventory that is available for future periods. This amount is debited to the appropriate asset account and the expense account is reduced.

Instructions

1. Using the Chart of Accounts, Trial Balance, and other information, record entries for the source documents for November 2012 using QuickBooks. You will find the source documents marked with an SD beside them and listed as you work through the chapter. The procedures for entering each new type of transaction are outlined in step-by-step instructions in the chapter. Additional source documents will be provided, allowing you to have more practice entering transactions. If you have used this textbook in the past and would prefer to skip the step-by-step instructions and work only with a list of source documents, refer to the CD in the back of the textbook for the list of source documents for this chapter.

2. After you have finished making your entries, print the reports and graphs for November 2012 indicated on the following printing form.

Notes
We realize that in the classroom, printing facilities may be limited. Your instructor will tell you which reports to print and which ones to display.
Instructions for reports begin on page 83.

REPORTS FOR NOVEMBER 2012		Accountant & Taxes		GRAPHS	
Company & Financial		☑	Trial Balance from Nov. 1 to Nov. 30	☑	Income and Expense
☑	Balance Sheet Standard: Nov. 30	☑	General Ledger from Nov. 1 to Nov. 30	☑	Net Worth
☑	Profit & Loss Standard (Income Statement) from Nov. 1 to Nov. 30	☑	Journal from Nov. 1 to Nov. 30		

Entering Transactions in QuickBooks

Entering transactions in QuickBooks involves entering information on different types of forms. Many of those look like the regular forms that a business uses every day — cheque registers, journal ledgers, customer and vendor invoices, cheques and so on. Other than in a journal entry, you do not need to enter debit and credit amounts. QuickBooks creates the debit and credit entries for the journal behind the scene so you see them only when you look at the journal reports. In many cases, you do not even need to add the account because the account is preselected as a default for the item or transaction. Intuitive, non-accounting terms are generally used.

Command words are in bold black type; the object of the command is shown in colour.

Opening Data Files

1. **Open**   **Chelsea.qbw** or Chelsea, the data file for Chelsea's Chocolates using the instructions for accessing a data file in Chapter 1, page 9.

2. **Click**   **OK** to **close** the **Learning Centre window** if it is displayed

3. **Close**   the **QuickBooks Coach** window if necessary

4. **Click**   the **Close button** 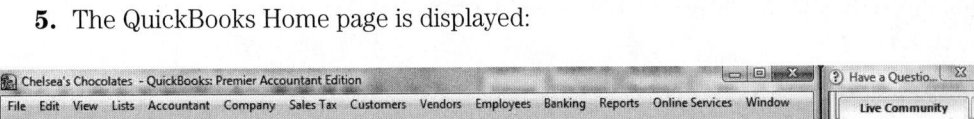 and **click OK** in the dialogue box to close the **Live Community** and **Help window**

5. The QuickBooks Home page is displayed:

Figure 3-1

> **Notes**
> Your computer setup may not show the file extension.qbw.

> **Notes**
> Keystroke instructions that you must use are shown in highlighted text in indented paragraphs like the one beside this note, starting with Open.

> **Notes**
> If you want to keep the Live Community and Help window open, please feel free to do so.
> If you close it, you can open it again at any time by clicking Help on the Icon bar.

Cash Purchases: Writing Cheques

The first transaction that we will enter in this company file is a purchase that was paid by cheque. Refer to the following source document as we work through the steps to enter it:

SD1: Cash Purchase Invoice #BF-3367

Dated November 1, 2012

From Belgian's Finest, $450.00 for cocoa, dark chocolate, and cocoa butter, ingredients for chocolate candy. Food is zero rated for HST. Wrote cheque #235 to pay invoice in full.

Chelsea pays for all purchases immediately by cheque. This combines the steps of entering an invoice followed by a payment.

You can access the form for writing cheques in different ways.

We will begin from the Banking section of the Home page shown below:

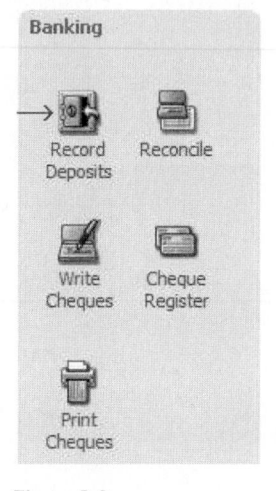

Figure 3-2

The Banking section of the Home page is the starting point for all activities involving the bank accounts. Paying for purchases that have not been entered first as vendor bills, involves writing cheques.

1. **Open** the **Write Cheques form** using one of the following options:

   a) **Click** the **Write Cheques icon** on the Icon bar; or

   b) **Press** ⌨ctrl + **W**, the keyboard shortcut; or

   c) **Choose** the **Banking menu** and **click Write Cheques**

SD Instructions
Refer to the following source document and then follow the step-by-step instructions to enter it.

Notes
When payments are made on account, invoices are recorded first and payments are recorded later.

2. The Write Cheques form will be displayed as shown:

Figure 3-3

The Write Cheques form opens for the *Bank Chequing* account, the account selected in the Bank Account field. The form includes an upper cheque portion and a lower invoice form for the details of the purchase. Together they provide a complete record of the purchase.

The initial default date for transactions is always your current computer date, so we need to change it for this transaction. Once you begin to enter transactions, the last date used will appear as the default until you close and re-open the company data file.

3. Press ⬚tab to advance to the date field

4. Type **11/01/12**

5. Click the **drop-down arrow in the Pay to the Order of field** to view the company's list of vendors:

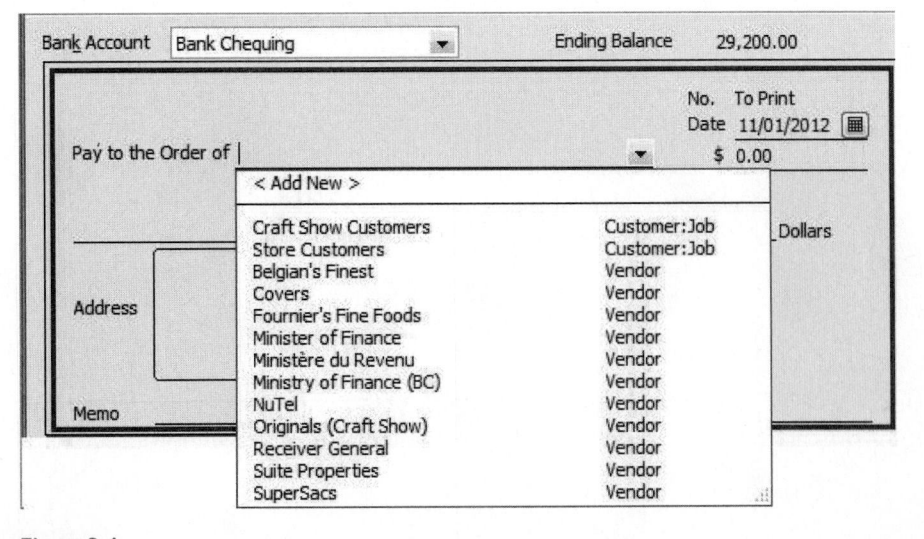

Figure 3-4

Notice that this is a list of all payees — all vendors, customers, employees, or others such as the owner and tax agencies — because you can write a cheque to any of these payees.

6. Click   **Belgian's Finest**

7. Click   **the Account field** to display the drop-down arrow

8. Click   the **drop-down arrow** in the Account field to view the following list of accounts:

Automobile	Fixed Asset
Candy Making Equipment	Fixed Asset
Computer/Cash Register	Fixed Asset
Display Cabinets & Shelves	Fixed Asset
Range/Ovens	Fixed Asset
Refrigerators	Fixed Asset
HST Payable	Other Current Liability
Long Term Loan	Long Term Liability
Capital, Chelsea Truffles	Equity
Retained Earnings	Equity
Revenue from Candy Sales	Income
Revenue from Interest	Income
Cost of Candy Ingredients	Cost of Goods Sold
Advertising	Expense
Insurance	Expense
Maintenance and Repairs	Expense
Packaging Materials Used	Expense
Rental Expense	Expense
Supplies Expense	Expense
Utilities	Expense

Figure 3-5

> **Notes**
> If you need to see additional accounts, you can scroll up the list to view the asset accounts.

Accounts are listed in order by type — Income Statement accounts follow Balance Sheet accounts. Expense accounts are frequently used for vendor purchases, so the account list shows them first. Most candy ingredients purchased are used immediately so the expenses associated with sales are entered directly as the cost of sales. Costs are not tracked separately because it is difficult to record the cost of each candy sold.

9. Click   **Cost of Candy Ingredients**

10. Press   (tab) to advance to the Tax field

11. Click   the **drop-down arrow** in the Tax field to view the tax codes available for purchases:

> **Notes**
> Adjusting entries are made at the end of a business period for supplies on hand that can be carried forward to the next period.

< Add New >		
H	HST	Taxable
Z	Zero Rated	Taxable
E	Tax Exempt	Non-taxable

Figure 3-6

The tax codes available include: HST, Zero Rated, and Tax Exempt.

12. Click   **Z - Zero Rated**

13. Press   (tab) to advance to the Amount field — the amount of the purchase before taxes

Do not type dollar signs when you enter amounts. For whole numbers, you do not need to enter the decimals.

14. **Type**   450

15. **Press**   (tab) to advance to the Memo field so you can enter a description for the purchase

16. **Type**   Cocoa and other chocolate ingredients

If additional items were purchased from the vendor, enter them on the following lines of the form by repeating the steps for the first purchase.

We still need to add the vendor's invoice number to include it in the journal records.

17. **Click**   the **Memo field** in the cheque portion, below the Address text box

18. **Type**   **Inv BF-3367**

19. **Click**   the **To be printed check box** below the cheque area to remove the checkmark

When you deselect the To be printed check box, the To Print entry beside the No. field in the top right-hand corner of the cheque portion of the window changes to 1, the first cheque number as shown in the updated form below:

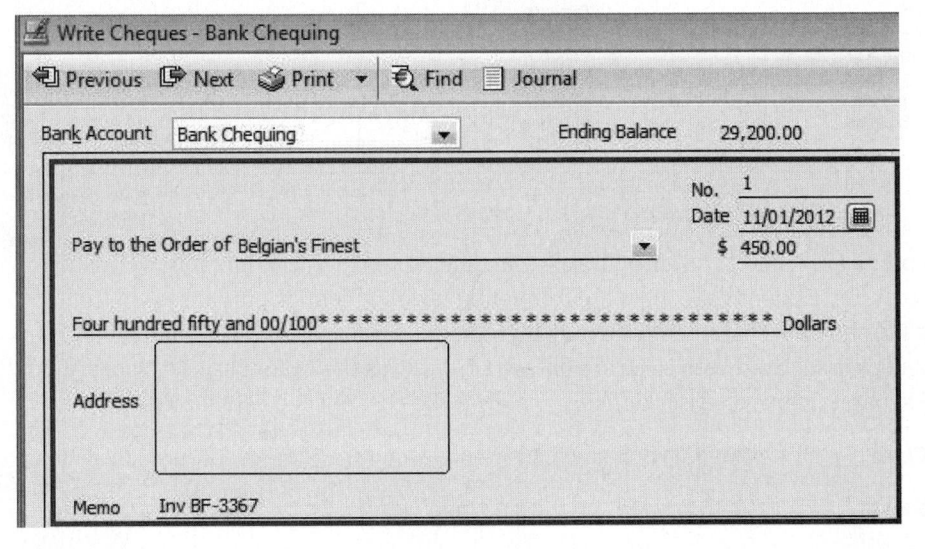

Figure 3-7

We need to enter a beginning cheque number to start the automatic numbering sequence for cheques. The first cheque we are writing is number 235. Once you enter a cheque number, QuickBooks will update the subsequent cheque numbers automatically.

20. **Double click** **1 in the No. field** in the cheque portion of the window

21. **Type**   **235**

We have set up the company data files to use the *Bank Chequing* account as the default account for cheques. You can select a different account by clicking in the drop-down arrow in the Bank Account field in the upper left section of the window. All accounts defined as bank accounts will be available for selection. For this transaction, the default account is correct.

Your completed transaction should look like the one that follows:

Figure 3-8

22. Review the **transaction** and **make corrections** if necessary

CORRECTING CHEQUES OR CASH PURCHASES

Click a field to return to the error. Press (tab) to move forward from one field to the next. Highlight the incorrect information. With the incorrect information highlighted, type the correct information to replace it. After changing an invoice amount, press (tab) and click the Recalculate button at the bottom of the form if necessary to update the amount in the cheque portion of the form.

If you want to start the transaction over, you can *click* the **Clear button** in the lower right-hand corner of the Write Cheques form. The transaction information will be removed, leaving you with a blank Write Cheques form.

In the next step, we will preview the transaction journal for this transaction so leave the Write Cheques form open. The Save & Close button will save the transaction and close the form, while the Save & New button will save the transaction and leave the form open.

23. Click **Save & New** or **press** (alt) + **S** (the underlined letter on the Save & New button) to save the transaction and open a blank cheque form

24. As shown below, the cheque number is automatically updated to 236 after we saved the initial entry:

> ### WARNING!
> When you change a cheque amount, you must click the Recalculate button to update the cheque portion of the form.

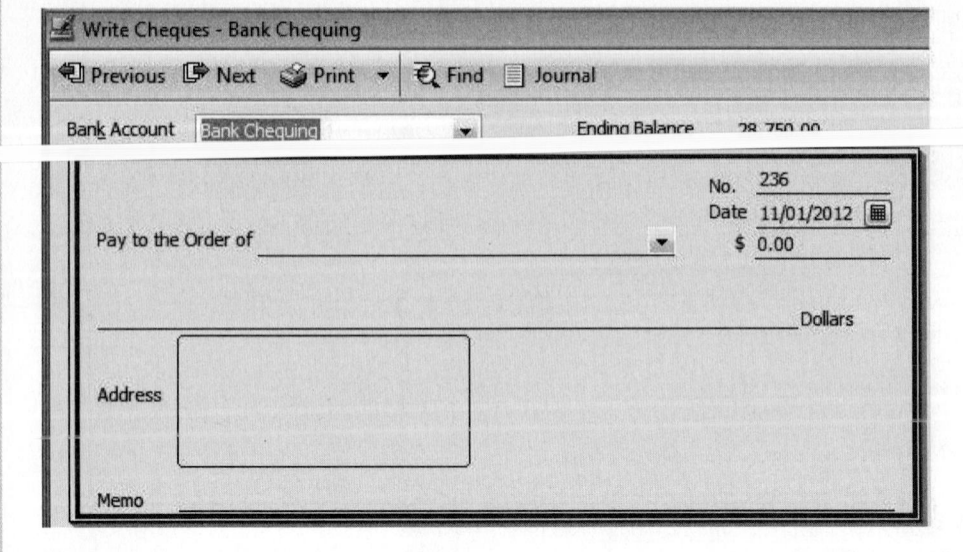

Figure 3-9

The bank account ending balance is also updated by the cheque we entered.

Reviewing the Transaction Journal Report

To view the journal entry created by the transaction, we can look at the transaction journal report. You can view the transaction journal report created by the transaction from the Write Cheques form after recording the entry and when the saved transaction is displayed on the screen. Therefore, we need to display the transaction again before we can display the transaction journal report.

A blank Write Cheques form should be displayed on the screen.

1. Click the **Previous button** [Previous] to display cheque #235 in the Write Cheques form:

2. Press [ctrl] + **Y** to display the Transaction Journal report:

7:25 AM				Chelsea's Chocolates				
02/26/10				**Transaction Journal**				
				All Transactions				
Type	Date	Num	Name	Item	Item Description	Account	Sales Price	Amount
► Cheque	11/01/2012	235	Belgian's Finest			Bank Chequing		–450.00 ◄
			Belgian's Finest			Cost of Candy Ingredients	450.00	450.00
			Receiver General	HST (ITC) Zero Rated	HST on Zero Rated...	HST Payable	0.0%	0.00
								0.00
TOTAL								0.00

Figure 3-10

QuickBooks automatically creates a journal entry each time you complete a transaction by debiting and crediting the appropriate accounts. The *Bank Chequing* account is credited for the transaction, reducing the bank account balance, and the *Cost of Candy Ingredients* account, the expense account, has been debited or increased for the amount of the purchase. The *HST Payable* amount is zero because we chose Z as the tax code — (zero-rated HST 0%). When you choose tax exempt as the code, there is no entry for *HST Payable*.

Notes
In previous versions of QuickBooks, a journal icon was available on the icon bar of a form that could be used to display the Transaction Journal report. This button is no longer available on forms, so we must use the [ctrl] + **Y** shortcut to access the Transaction Journal report.

Notes
The columns in the Transactions Journal reports in this chapter have been adjusted to fit within the textbook; therefore, you will have additional columns in your reports.

Notes
Throughout the textbook, we have customized the Transaction Journal reports by hiding unused columns on the report. Refer to page 90 for more information on modifying reports.

3.	**Click**	to close the Transaction Journal report

3. **Click**   [x] to close the Transaction Journal report

4. **Click**   **No** when asked to memorize the report if you made any changes to the report

5. **Click**   the **Next button** [↪ Next] on the Write Cheques icon bar or **press** (alt) + **N** to close the cheque for Belgian's Finest and open a blank chequing form

The second transaction that we will enter is a purchase and cheque for Super Sacs. Refer to the following source document as we work through the steps to enter it:

SD2: Cash Purchase Invoice #SS-1197

Dated November 1, 2012

From SuperSacs, $540.00 plus $64.80 HST for plastic carrier bags imprinted with logos for store and Originals craft show. Purchase invoice total $604.80. Wrote cheque #236 to pay invoice in full.

6. **Click**   the **drop-down arrow** in the Pay to Order of field to view the list of vendors

7. **Click**   **SuperSacs**

8. **Type**   **11/01/12** as the date

9. **Type**   **Inv SS-1197** in the Memo field

10. **Click**   the **Account field** to display the drop-down arrow

11. **Click**   the **drop-down arrow** to view the list of accounts

12. **Choose**   **Packaging Materials Used** as the account

13. **Choose**   **Tax Code HST** (HST 12%) as the tax code so that taxes will be automatically calculated and included in the invoice total

14. **Enter**   **540** as the amount

15. **Press**   (tab) to advance to the **memo field**

16. **Type**   **Plastic bags for store and Originals Craft Show**

17. **Click**   **Save & Close** or **press** (alt) + **a** to close the Write Cheques form

Entering Sales Receipts

Chelsea's Chocolates is a cash business. Customers do not have accounts and always pay for purchases immediately. Most of the sales are for very small amounts that would involve a large number of entries. Therefore, we have chosen to show the sales as bi-weekly summaries of total sales for the period. The entries for smaller individual sales would be entered in exactly the same way as the ones we show. Cash receipts are always deposited immediately to the *Bank Chequing* account.

The next transaction that we will enter is a sales receipt. Refer to the following source document as we work through the steps to enter it:

SD3: Sales Receipt #2092

Dated November 1, 2012

To store customers, $870.00 plus $104.40 HST for chocolate sold in store in past three days. All customers paid cash for their purchases. Sales total $974.40 was deposited to the Bank Chequing account.

SD Practice
Continue to develop your skills by entering the following source document(s).

SD Instructions
Refer to the following source document and then follow the step-by-step instructions to enter it.

Notes
  Some QuickBooks func-
tions can be hidden on the
Home page depending on the
options selected in QuickBooks
Preferences. We will learn how
to customize Preferences in
Chapter 5.

Because Chelsea accepts only immediate payment for all sales, most of the transaction functions in the Customer section of the Home page are not used. We have customized the Home page to make it more suitable for Chelsea's Chocolates. Some of the icons, such as Estimates and Sales Orders, have been removed because they are not needed. These types of transactions will be covered in later chapters.

Two icons in the Customer section of the Home page can be used to enter sales: Invoices and Sales Receipts. However, because customers pay immediately and do not have accounts set up with the chocolatier, sales are entered as sales receipts rather than as invoices. We are bypassing the invoice entry step just as we bypassed the bill entry step for purchases.

We will enter the sales receipt by selecting the Create Sales Receipts icon from the Customers section of the Home page.

1. To access the Create Sales Receipt form:

 a) **Click** the **Create Sales Receipts icon** in the Customers section of the Home page as shown; or

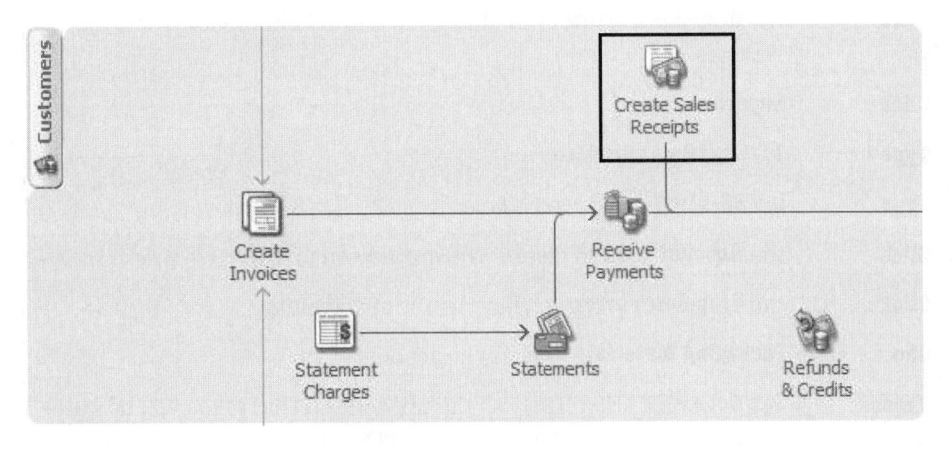

Figure 3-11

 b) **Choose** the **Customers menu** and **click Enter Sales Receipts**

2. The Enter Sales Receipt form will be displayed as shown:

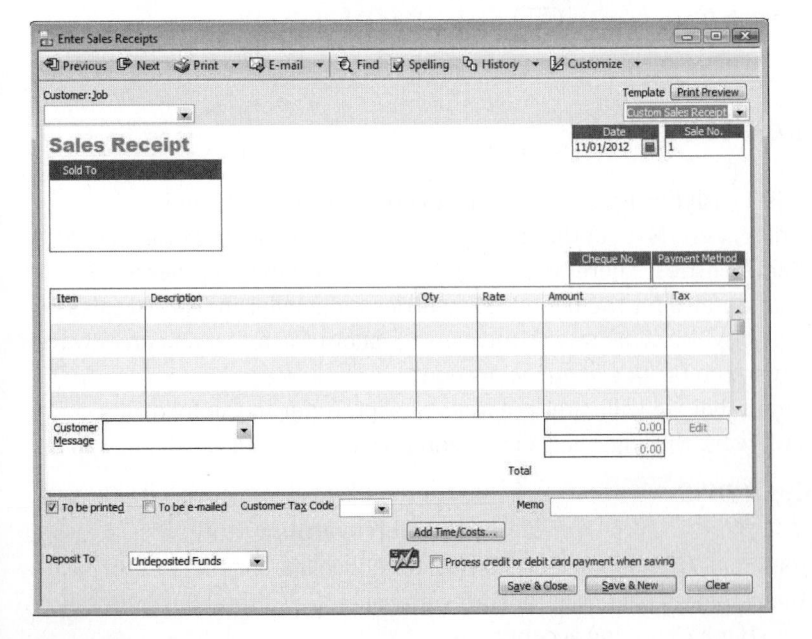

Figure 3-12

The Sales Receipts form looks just like a sales invoice; however, unlike an invoice, when you enter a sales receipt, you enter both the invoice information and the payment information together on the form. The form includes some columns that we do not need. We will customize the form after completing the sales entry.

The customer name field is always named Customer:Job in QuickBooks because companies may work on more than one job at once for a customer. You may want to track these jobs separately. When you add a customer, you can also add a job name, and you can add new jobs for existing customers.

3. Click the **drop-down arrow in the Customer:Job field** to view the list of customers:

< Add New >	
Craft Show Customers	Customer:Job
Store Customers	Customer:Job

Figure 3-13

We have created two summary level customers that will separate the sales in the store from the sales at the Originals craft show.

4. Click **Store Customers** to add the name to the invoice

For each customer, we have entered a default method of payment in their customer record. All store and craft show customers pay cash, so this is the default method of payment selected. The sale number is updated automatically by the program. Because no sales have been entered yet, 1 appears as the default starting number. We need to change it.

5. Press ⌨ *tab* to advance to the **date field**

6. Type **11/01/12**

7. Press ⌨ *tab* to advance to the **Sale No. field**

8. Type **2092**

9. Click the **drop-down arrow** in the **Payment Method field** to view the payment method options:

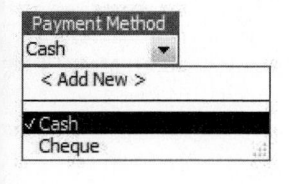

Figure 3-14

Only cash and cheque, two immediate payment methods, are listed because account terms are not offered and credit cards are not accepted. Cash is selected because it is the default payment method for store customers. If you need to change the payment method for the sales receipt you can choose it from the drop-down list.

10. Click **Cash**

11. Press ⌨ *tab* to advance to the **Item field**

Notes
Although you do not need to select a customer to complete a sales receipt, choosing a customer allows more detailed reporting because several reports can be prepared by customer.

Choosing a customer also allows the automatic entry of additional information for the customer, such as the method of payment and payment terms.

Items in QuickBooks

Notes

We will use different kinds of items in later chapters and learn how to create items when we complete a company setup in Chapter 5.

Items are central to QuickBooks. Sales forms can be completed only by selling items. Items may be created for services, inventory that is tracked, store merchandise that is sold but not tracked as individual items, and even items that are purchased but not sold, such as regular supplies. Beginning in QuickBooks version 2008, taxes are also set up as items.

Items are linked directly to accounts — revenue accounts for items that are sold and expense or asset accounts for purchases. Tax codes are also set up as part of the item record. Prices for items may be set up in the data files as defaults, or they can be omitted from the item records and entered on the sales invoices or receipts.

12. Click the **drop-down arrow in the Item field** to view the items created for the store:

Item		
< Add New >		
Candy Sold in Store	Non-inventory Part	
Craft Show Sales	Non-inventory Part	
Special Orders	Non-inventory Part	
GST Zero Rated	Sales Tax Item	GST on Zero Rated sales
HST	Sales Tax Item	HST on sales
HST Adjustments	Sales Tax Item	HST Adjustments on sales (Line 104)
HST Zero Rated	Sales Tax Item	HST on Zero Rated sales

Figure 3-15

We have set up three items for the store to record sales in the store, sales at the craft show and sales from special or customized orders. Inventory is not tracked and no prices are entered because items are individually priced.

13. Click **Candy Sold in Store** to select this item

14. Press ⸤tab⸥ to advance to the **Description field**

Notice that tax code H is added automatically in the last column for this item. You can select another tax code from the list by clicking on the drop-down arrow in the Tax field and selecting a different tax code if needed.

15. Type **sale of chocolates**

16. Double click **0.00** in the **Rate field** to highlight it

17. Type **870**

18. Press ⸤tab⸥ to update the invoice with the tax amounts

19. Click **OK** if you receive the price level message

In QuickBooks Premier, you can add custom pricing for customers and jobs by creating price level lists. We will not be using the price level feature.

You can enter the sale of additional items on the sales receipt by adding more item detail lines. To do so, repeat the steps described for the first item.

Next, we will choose a comment for the sales receipt. Again, you can create a list of predefined comments for the company to choose from, or create a new comment when entering the transaction.

20. Click the **drop-down arrow in the Customer Message field** to view the list of predefined comments:

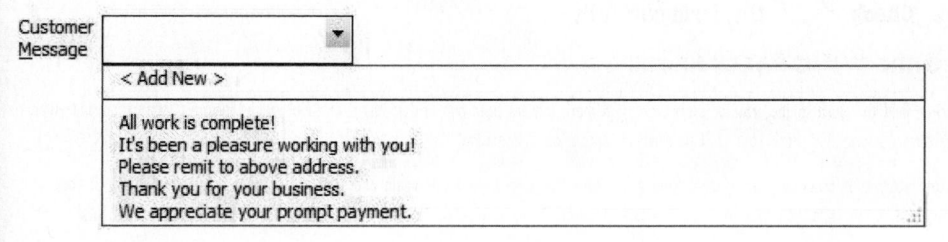

Customer
Message

| < Add New > |
| All work is complete! |
| It's been a pleasure working with you! |
| Please remit to above address. |
| Thank you for your business. |
| We appreciate your prompt payment. |

Figure 3-16

| 21. | **Click** | **Thank you for your business.** to add that comment to the invoice |
| 22. | **Click** | the **To be printed check box** in the lower left-hand corner of the form to remove the checkmark |

If you want to print each invoice, leave the *To be printed* option checked. Depending on how the preferences for the QuickBooks reminders are set up, you may be reminded to print the invoice in the Reminders list. Printing invoices is covered in Chapter 7.

The final option that we need to change concerns the deposit of the sales receipts. The two options that control how deposits are recorded are located in the lower left-hand corner of the Enter Sales Receipts form. By default, the cash receipt will be grouped with other undeposited funds and recorded as a debit entry for the *Undeposited Funds* account. This step would be followed by a separate transaction that deposits the funds to the bank account. Instead, we will record the deposit to the bank account directly. In Chapter 7, you will learn the procedure for grouping undeposited funds and then making a deposit later.

| 23. | **Click** | the **drop-down arrow** in the Deposit To field |
| 24. | **Choose** | **Bank Chequing** |

The *Bank Chequing* account will remain selected as the default account to deposit funds into for future sales receipts so you will not have to change it again unless you need to select a different account.

25. The transaction is now complete and should look like the one that follows:

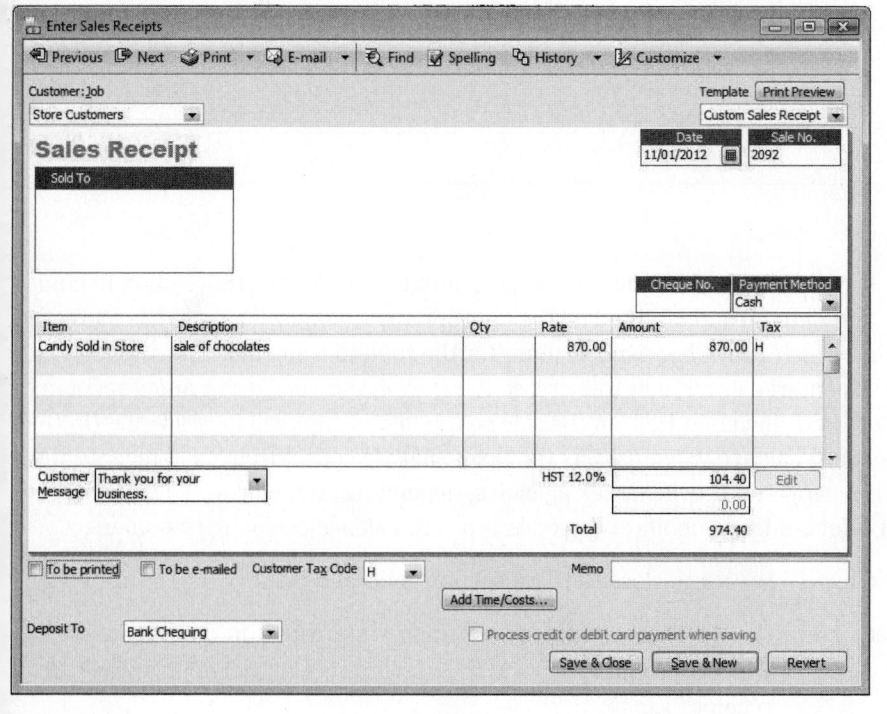

Figure 3-17

> **Notes**
> We assume that in most cases when you are practising, you will not want to print all the invoices.

26. Check   the **form** carefully

The next transaction is also a sales receipt so we will leave the Enter Sales Receipts form open.

27. Click   **Save & New** or **press** ⬚alt⬚ + **S** to open a new blank sales receipt form

Before entering the next sale, however, we will review the Transaction Journal report for the sale we just completed.

Reviewing the Transaction Journal Report

The procedure for reviewing a Transaction Journal report for a sales receipt is the same procedure we used to display the Transaction Journal report for the cheque we entered earlier. We use the Previous button on the Sales Receipts form to display the transaction on the screen and then press ⬚ctrl⬚ + **Y** to view the Transaction Journal report.

1. Click   ⬚◀ Previous⬚ on the Enter Sales Receipts icon bar:

Clicking the Previous button displays the transaction you entered most recently according to the transaction date.

2. Press   ⬚ctrl⬚ + **Y** to view the Transaction Journal report:

7:51 AM				Chelsea's Chocolates				
02/26/10				**Transaction Journal**				
				All Transactions				
Date	Num	Name	Memo	Item	Item Description	Account	Sales Price	Amount
▶ 11/01/2012	2092	Store Customers				Bank Chequing		974.40 ◀
		Store Customers	Sale of Choc...	Candy Sold in Store		Revenue from Can...	870.00	-870.00
		Receiver General	HST on sales	HST	HST on sales	HST Payable	12.0%	-104.40
								0.00
								0.00

Figure 3-18

Again, QuickBooks has created the proper journal entry for the transaction behind the scenes and debited and credited all the appropriate accounts. The sale has increased the balance for the *Bank Chequing* account for the total sale amount. The sale amount net of taxes is entered as a credit to increase the *Revenue from Candy Sales* account. The tax code, HST, included HST on the sale so the tax amount will increase the *HST Payable* account balance. We must pay the taxes that we collect from customers to the appropriate federal and provincial tax agencies, depending on the province that we are in. The net effect of these debits and credits is a zero balance owing by customers.

3. Click   ⬚X⬚ to close the Transaction Journal report

4. Click   the **No** when prompted to memorize the report in the Receipts window or **press** ⬚alt⬚ + **N** to close the receipt and open a blank receipt form

Customizing QuickBooks Forms

We will now customize the Sales Receipt form to best reflect the items we sell to customers. We will be entering a large number of sales receipts so we will modify the Sales Receipt form by removing columns that we do not need and then we will add a Sales Receipts icon to the Icon bar for quick access to the Sales Receipt form.

Customizing the Sales Form

1. **Click**   the **Customize button** ![Customize] in the Sales Receipt icon bar to open the Basic Customization window:

> **Notes**
> If you try to modify a default template that is supplied with QuickBooks, you will be asked to first make a copy of the template before you can modify it.

Figure 3-19

    The Custom Sales Receipt is the selected template (displayed in the top left-hand corner of the window) and it is the one we want to edit.

    On the Basic Customization screen, you can change the colour scheme, change the font for various headings, and add or exclude company and transaction information from the selected template.

2. **Click**   the **Additional Customization button** [Additional Customization...] to open the Additional Customization window:

Figure 3-20

You can edit many areas of the sales receipt form by selecting the appropriate tab. We want to edit the form by removing the columns that do not apply to Chelsea's Chocolates.

3. Click the **Columns tab**:

Figure 3-21

The available columns of the form are all listed. They can be included on the Screen, on the Print form or both. A ✓ indicates the column is included. Only three columns are mandatory and must be displayed on the screen — Item, Amount, and Tax Code — and the checkmarks for these columns under the screen heading are dimmed because they cannot be changed. You can change the order of the items on the forms and you can also change the title displayed for each item.

We do not need Rate or Quantity displayed on our screen or printed form so we will remove them.

4. **Click**   the **Screen column for Quantity** to remove the ✓

5. **Click**   the **Screen column for Rate** to remove the ✓

6. **Click**   the **Print column for Quantity** to remove the ✓

7. **Click**   the **Print column for Rate** to remove the ✓

8. **Click**   **OK** to save the changes

9. **Click**   **OK** to exit the Basic Customization screen and return to the revised form:

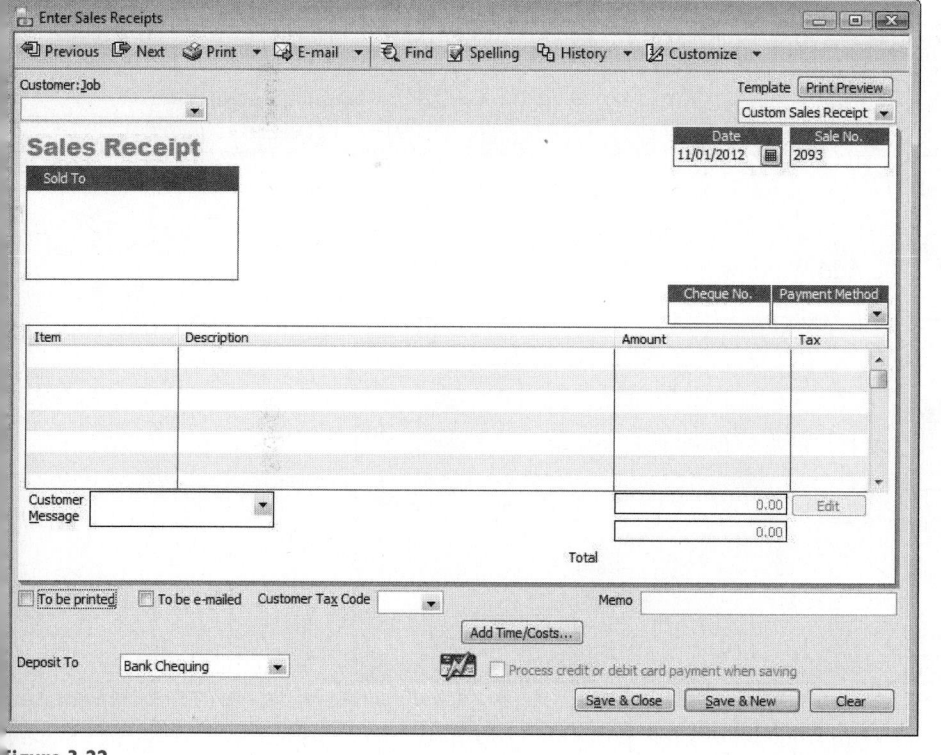

Figure 3-22

Compare the differences between the form displayed in Figure 3-22 (after the modification) to the form displayed in Figure 3-17 (before the modification).

Adding an Icon to the Icon Bar

When a form is open, you can add an icon for it directly to the Icon bar for easy access.

1. **Display**   the **Enter Sales Receipt form** from the previous exercise (open it if it is not displayed)

2. **Choose**   the **View menu** and **click Add "Enter Sales Receipts" to Icon Bar** as shown:

Notes
You can also add an icon to the Icon bar without opening a form first by selecting the View menu, then Customize Icon bar, and then selecting the item you want to add.

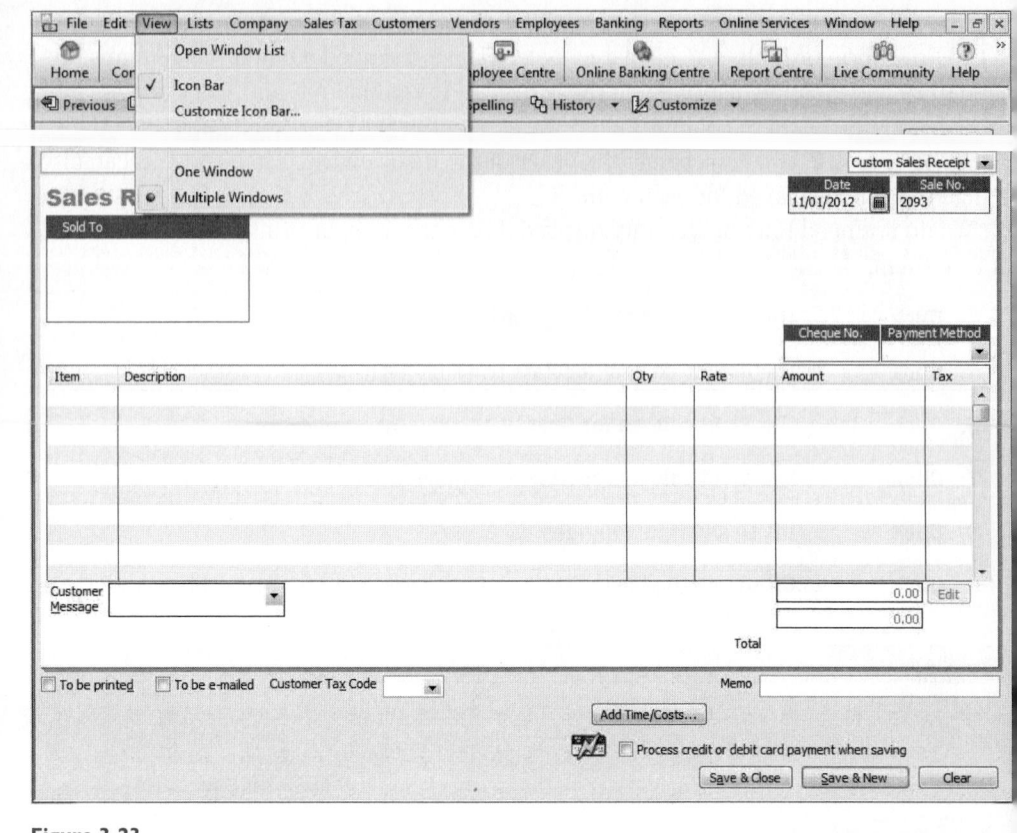

Figure 3-23

3. The Add Window to Icon Bar dialogue window opens:

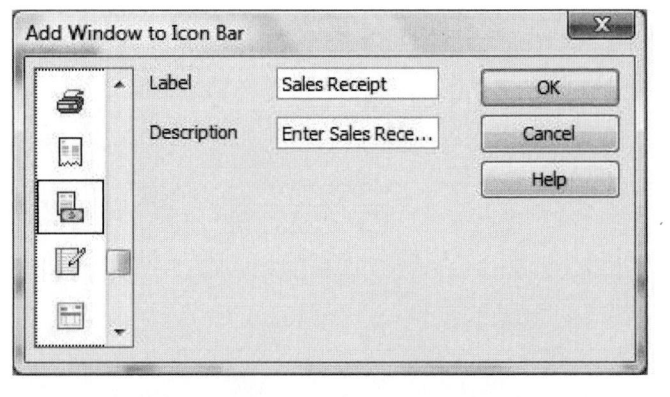

Figure 3-24

An Icon image, a Label, and a Description are suggested for the new icon. You can accept these or change them. We will accept the label and description but choose an invoice icon in a different colour from the one for invoices already displayed on the bar.

4. Click the **orange/red coloured Invoice icon**

5. Click **OK** to return to the program and you'll see that Sales Receipt has been added to the far right-hand side of the Icon bar:

> **Notes**
> You can also change the location or order of icons on the Icon bar. Choose Customize Icon Bar from the View menu to view the changes that you can make.

Figure 3-25

As you work through the remaining transactions for this company, the changes you made to the Sales Receipt form and the Icon bar will remain in effect for this company data file unless you change them again.

Source Document

Now that you have learned some of the new concepts introduced in this chapter, enter the following source document. You may need to refer to the instructions in this chapter for additional information:

SD4: **Sales Receipt #2093**   **Dated November 5, 2012**

To store customers, $990.00 plus $118.80 HST for chocolate sold in the store in the past three days. All customers paid cash for their purchases. Sales total $1,108.80 was deposited to the Bank Chequing account.

SD Practice
Continue to develop your skills by entering the following source document(s).

Adding New List Items

Most businesses have the need to add new records for customers, vendors, or accounts after they set up the company files. QuickBooks allows users to add these new accounts on the fly, while entering transactions.

Adding New Vendors

The next purchase is from a vendor whose name is not yet in the company data files; therefore, we must add the name. We can do this directly from the Write Cheques input form. Refer to the following source document as we work through the steps to enter it:

SD5: **Cash Purchase Invoice #SW-444**   **Dated November 5, 2012**

From Spread the Word (use Quick Add for new vendor), $980.00 plus $117.60 HST for posters to be placed in the store to advertise upcoming Originals craft show, business cards for use at craft show, and promotional flyers with discount coupons attached for craft show customers to use in the store after the craft show. Purchase invoice totalled $1,097.60. Wrote cheque #237 to pay invoice in full.

SD Instructions
Refer to the following source document and then follow the step-by-step instructions to enter it.

1. **Click**   Write Cheques   to open the Write Cheques form

The cheque number is correct because the program updates it automatically. If necessary, it can be changed.

The date on the blank Write Cheques form should be 11/01/12. If you have a different date, it is because you either changed it since you completed the previous cheque entry, or you closed the QuickBooks data file and your current computer date is now displayed.

Notes
Remember that you can also open the Write Cheques form by choosing the Banking menu and clicking Write Cheques or by using the keyboard shortcut $ctrl$ + **W**.

2. **Double click** the **date field** and **type 11/05/12** if necessary

3. **Click**   the **Pay to the Order of field**

4. **Type**   **Spread the Word**

Notice that as you type the vendor name, the vendor list is displayed.

5. **Press** tab to view the following message:

Figure 3-26

This message gives you three different options. Choosing **Quick Add** allows you to add only the vendor's name to the list of vendors. You can add the remaining vendor details later if necessary. **Set Up** allows you to create a complete record for the new vendor by opening all the vendor record fields, and **Cancel** allows you to return to the cheque without creating a record if you have typed the vendor name incorrectly or selected the wrong vendor. We will add only the vendor's name. We will set up a complete vendor record in Chapter 6.

6. **Click**   **Quick Add** or press ⏎ to continue:

Figure 3-27

You must indicate what type of name you are creating. Remember that you can write cheques to any payee so several name types are listed. Because this is a cheque, QuickBooks selects Vendor as the default name type and this is correct.

7. **Click**   **OK** or press ⏎ to proceed

8. **Click**   the **Memo field** below the vendor address box

9. **Type**   **SW-444** - the invoice number

10. **Click**   the **drop-down arrow in the Account field** to view the account list

11. **Choose**   **Advertising** from the list of accounts

12. **Click**   the **drop-down arrow in the Tax field** to display the tax codes list

13. **Choose**   **H** (HST)

14. **Double click** **0.00 in the Amount field**

15. **Type**   **980**

16. **Press**   ⇥ to advance to the Memo field

17. **Type**   **posters to advertise craft show**

18. **Review**   the **transaction** and **make corrections** if necessary before saving the entry

The next transaction is a sales receipt so we should close the cheque window.

19. Click   **Save & Close** to return to the Home page

Adding New Customers

Just as we can add vendors while entering transactions, we can add new customers on the fly from any Customer:Job field.

When you enter the next source document, sales receipt #2094, you will see that the customer named in the transaction is not on the customer list. We must add the customer. Refer to the following source document as we work through the steps to enter it:

SD Instructions
Refer to the following source document and then follow the step-by-step instructions to enter it.

SD6:   **Sales Receipt #2094**   **Dated November 5, 2012**

To Swete Touth (use Quick Add for new customer), $520.00 plus $62.40 HST for special order of theme chocolate decorations for anniversary party. Sales total $582.40 was paid by cheque #599 and deposited to the Bank Chequing account.

1. Click   the **Create Sales Receipt icon**   [Create Sales Receipts]   on the Icon bar — the icon we added in a previous exercise

2. Enter   **11/06/12** as the transaction date in the Date field

3. Click   the **Customer:Job field**

4. Type   **Swete Touth**

5. Press   (tab) to see the following message:

Notes
Remember that you can also access the Enter Sales Receipts form from the Customer Centre or from the Customer menu.

Notes
A colon separates a customer name from a job name and cannot be used as part of the customer name.

Customer:Job Not Found

?   Swete Touth is not in the Customer:Job list.

[Quick Add]   [Set Up]   [Cancel]

Figure 3-28

This screen gives you the same three options that we saw for vendors: choosing **Quick Add** allows you to add only the customer's name and add the other record details later if necessary; **Set Up** allows you to create a complete customer record and **Cancel** allows you to return to the form without creating a record if you have typed incorrectly. For now, we will add only the customer's name. We will set up a complete customer record in Chapter 7.

6. Click   **Quick Add** or **press** (enter) to return to the Enter Sales Receipts form

Notice that the payment method is not selected because we did not set up a complete customer record that includes this information.

7. Click   the **drop-down arrow in the Payment Method field** and **choose** **Cheque**

8. Type   **599 in the Cheque No. field**

9. Enter   the rest of the **transaction details. Choose** **Special Orders** as the Item, **add a description for the sale**, **enter 520** as the amount, **choose H** as the tax code if this is not entered as the default, and **choose** a **Customer Message**

10. Click   **Save & Close** to close the Enter Sales Receipts form

Source Document

Now that you have learned some of the new concepts introduced in this chapter, enter the following source document. You may need to refer to the instructions in this chapter for additional information:

SD Practice
Continue to develop your skills by entering the following source document(s).

SD7:   **Cash Purchase Invoice #C-784**   **Dated November 6, 2012**

From Covers, $610.00 plus $73.20 HST for paper bags, foils, and boxes of various sizes for packaging chocolates purchased by customers. Purchase invoice totalled $683.20. Wrote cheque #238 to pay invoice in full.

Correcting Entries after Recording

WARNING!
The audit trail is always on while working in QuickBooks and records all business transactions for a company. Using the audit trail, an auditor can confirm which records have been modified and that records have not been altered dishonestly.

Correcting entries after saving them is very simple in QuickBooks. You can find the transaction and display it on the form on which it was entered, make any necessary corrections, and then save the transaction again. The procedure is essentially the same for correcting all kinds of transactions.

Audit Trail

Notes
Beginning with Quick-Books version 2008, the audit trail is "always on," which means that it cannot be turned off. You will find all transactions that have been added, deleted, and modified in the audit trail. If you have users set up in your QuickBooks company file, you will be able to tell which user made the changes.

When you make changes in accounting records, you must leave a complete record of all changes so that an auditor will know that all changes were entered honestly. Pencils and erasers are not allowed in accounting. In a manual accounting system, you would make a correction by completing a reversing entry and then entering the correct entry to provide a complete audit trail. As soon as you save the changes to a transaction that you saved before, QuickBooks will save both entries because of the built-in audit trail. The original entry and the correction will be included in the Audit Trail Report. The audit trail is always on while you are working in QuickBooks and cannot be turned off.

Correcting Purchase Entries after Recording

The purchase from Spread the Word for advertising was entered with an incorrect amount so we need to correct it. The transaction was entered as a cheque, so we will open the Write Cheques form to find the cheque and correct it. Refer to the following source document as we work through the steps to enter it:

SD Instructions
Refer to the following source document and then follow the step-by-step instructions to enter it.

SD8:   **Memo #1**   **Dated November 7, 2012**

From Owner: Cheque #237 to pay purchase invoice #SW-444 from Spread the Word was entered incorrectly. The correct invoice amount was $995.00 plus $119.40 HST. The purchase invoice totalled $1,114.40. Edit cheque #237 to make the correction.

1. **Press**   `ctrl` **+ W** to open the Write Cheques form

Notes
You may use one of the other methods to open the Write Cheques form. See page 57.

There are two methods of opening the transaction that has the error. If the transaction you need was entered recently, you can use the Previous and Next icons on the forms icon bar to scroll through the transactions. Each form also has a Find tool to assist you in finding the form that you want to view or correct. If you have a large number of transactions of the same type, it is faster to use the Find tool to access the transaction you want to correct. Using the Find tool will be covered in a later chapter.

We have entered only three cheques so we can scroll through all the cheques using the Previous icon.

2. Click 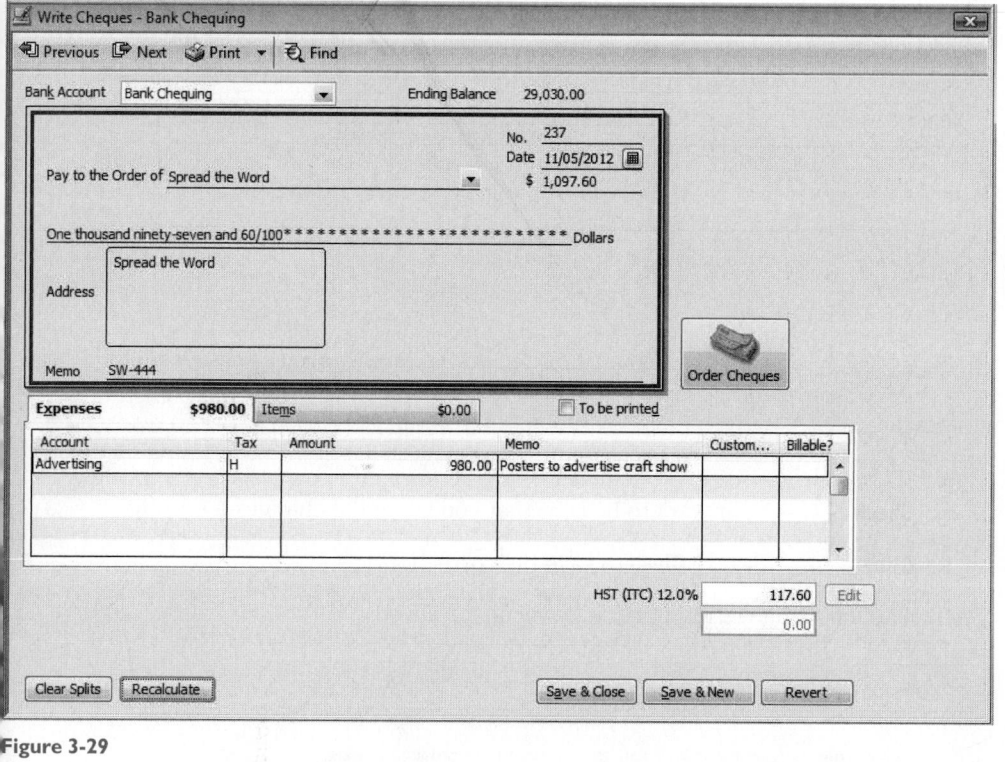 Previous on the Write Cheques icon bar

The last cheque we entered, cheque #238 to Covers, appears on the screen. This is not the one we need.

3. Click Previous on the icon bar again. Cheque #237 to Spread the Word is displayed:

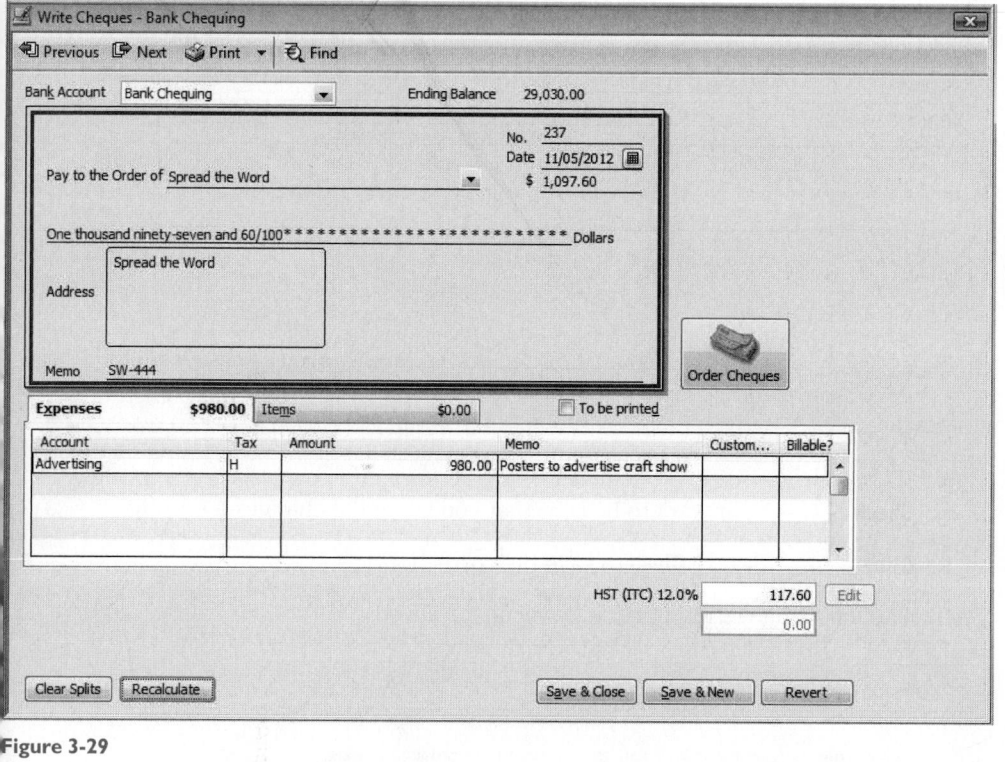

Write Cheques - Bank Chequing

Previous | Next | Print ▼ | Find

Bank Account | Bank Chequing ▼ | Ending Balance | 29,030.00

No. 237
Date 11/05/2012

Pay to the Order of Spread the Word ▼ | $ 1,097.60

One thousand ninety-seven and 60/100* Dollars

Spread the Word
Address

Memo SW-444

Order Cheques

| Expenses | $980.00 | Items | $0.00 | | To be printed |

Account	Tax	Amount	Memo	Custom...	Billable?
Advertising	H	980.00	Posters to advertise craft show		

HST (ITC) 12.0% | 117.60 | Edit
0.00

Clear Splits | Recalculate | Save & Close | Save & New | Revert

Figure 3-29

With the transaction displayed on the screen, you can delete it or void it. The delete and void options are available from the Edit menu or on the shortcut menu displayed by right clicking in the transaction. The menu options change to match the window that is currently open, so the menu options for this window appear as Delete Cheque and Void Cheque. Both actions will change all amounts for the transaction to zero. Voiding a cheque will leave a record of the transaction in QuickBooks while deleting it will not.

Notice that the Clear button from the original cheque form has been replaced by Revert. If you make a change to the transaction and do not want to save it, choosing Revert will restore the recorded transaction and you can begin the edit process again or close the form.

4. Double click **980.00** in the Amount field

5. Type **995**

6. Press (tab) to enter the amount and update the taxes

Notice that the amount in the cheque portion has not yet changed. Currently, it is $1,097.60.

7. Click the **Recalculate button** in the lower left-hand corner of the cheque window to complete the revision and update all amounts as shown:

Notes
Deleted entries are also listed in the Audit Trail Report.

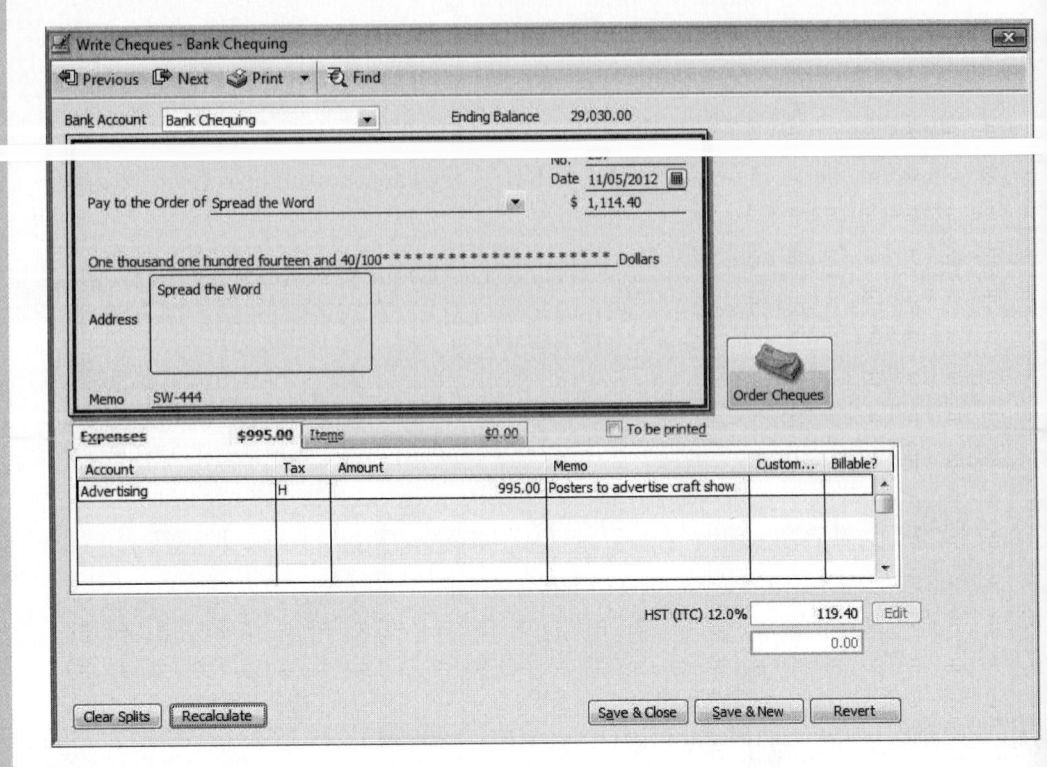

Figure 3-30

8. Check your **work** to be sure that you made the changes correctly

9. Click **Save & Close** to save the correction

10. The following warning message will be displayed:

Figure 3-31

> **Notes**
> To turn on this QuickBooks preference, Select Edit from the menu and then Preferences. Select the General heading on the left-hand side of the screen. On the My Preferences tab, select the **Warn when editing a transaction** option.

We have turned on the *Warn when editing a transaction option* in QuickBooks preferences so that changes are not made to recorded entries accidentally. Choosing **No** will clear the form without saving the changes. Choosing **Cancel** will leave the form open for further changes. Choosing **Yes** will save the changes, and the new revised form will replace the previous one.

11. Click **Yes** to save the changes and **close** the **Write Cheques form**

Correcting Sales Receipts after Recording

Correcting sales receipts or invoices is similar to correcting cheques. You access the completed sales receipt on the Enter Sales Receipts form, make the changes, and save the revised form. There is no need to make a reversing journal entry.

For this next source document, we need to correct the amount on sales receipt #2092. Refer to the following source document as we work through the steps to enter it:

SD9:   **Memo #2 Dated**   **November 7, 2012**

From Owner: Sales receipt #2092 was entered incorrectly. The actual sales total amount was $910.00 plus $109.20 HST for chocolate sold in the store. Sales total $1,019.20. Edit the sales receipt to make the correction.

1. **Click**   the **Sales Receipt icon** Sales Receipt on the icon bar that you added in a previous exercise

2. **Click**   🔁 Previous **on the Sales Receipt icon bar**. You should see receipt #2094

3. **Click**   🔁 Previous on the icon bar two more times until you reach receipt #2092

4. **Double click** **870.00 in the Amount field** to highlight it

5. **Type**   910

6. **Press**   ⌨ *tab* to update the taxes and total amount

If you make a mistake, you can click Revert to restore the original recorded receipt without saving any changes. You can then begin the edit process again. For practice, you can click Revert and then make the correction again.

Your corrected receipt should look like the one shown here:

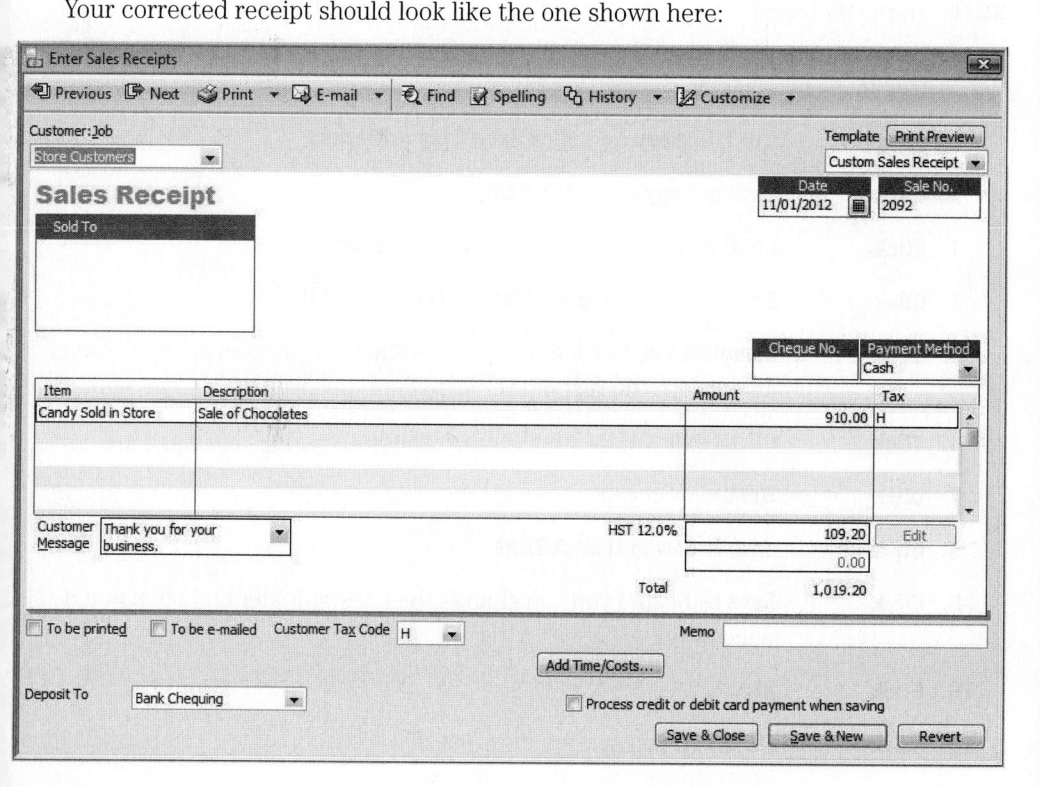

Figure 3-32

7. **Check**   your work carefully and make additional corrections if necessary

8. **Click**   **Save & Close** to record the correction and close the Enter Sales Receipts form

Because you have made changes, the program asks you to confirm that you want to save the changes:

SD Instructions
Refer to the following source document and then follow the step-by-step instructions to enter it.

Notes
Remember that you can also choose the Customers menu and click Enter Sales Receipts, or click the Create Sales Receipts icon in the Customers section of the Home page to open the Sales Receipts form.

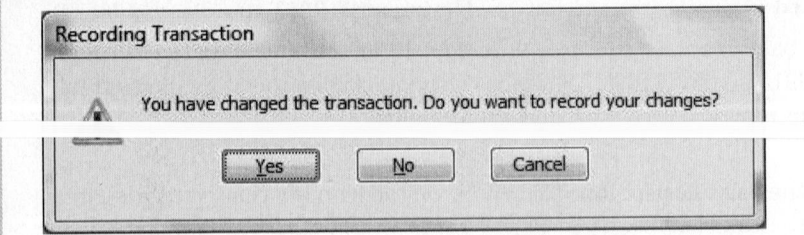

Figure 3-33

9. **Click**   **Yes** to record the changed sales receipt and continue

Backing Up and Verifying Your Data File

Now that we have completed one week of transactions, we should back up the data file. Refer to Chapter 1, page 32 for complete instructions on backing up a data file if you need further assistance. Refer to the following source document as we work through the steps to enter it:

Refer to Chapter 1, page 32 for complete instructions on backing up a data file

📄 **SD Instructions**
Refer to the following source document and then follow the step-by-step instructions to enter it.

SD10: Memo #3 Dated   November 7, 2012

From Owner: Back up and verify the data file. Continue to back up and verify on a weekly basis.

1. **Choose**   the **File menu** and **click Save Copy or Backup**

2. **Click**   **Backup Copy** and **click Next**

3. **Click**   **Local Backup** and **click** the **Options button**

4. **Click**   **Browse** and **choose a folder** for the backup file

5. **Click**   **Complete Verification** (it should already be selected as the default) and accept the rest of the defaults on this screen

6. **Click**   **OK** to exit the Backup Options window

7. **Click**   **Next**

8. **Click**   **Save it now** and **click Next**

9. **Click**   **Save** to begin (you can change the backup folder and file name if necessary)

10. **Click**   **Finish**

11. **Click**   **OK** when you see the message that a backup of the company file has been saved

Source Documents

Now that you have learned some new concepts taught in this chapter, continue to develop your skills by entering the following source documents in QuickBooks. Use the information in this chapter as a guide if necessary:

📄 **SD Practice**
Continue to develop your skills by entering the following source document(s).

SD11: Sales Receipt #2095   Dated November 9, 2012

To store customers, $960.00 plus $115.20 HST for chocolate sold in the store in the past three days. All customers paid cash for their purchases. Sales totalling $1,075.20 were deposited to the Bank Chequing account.

SD12: Sales Receipt #2096   **Dated November 12, 2012**

To store customers, $1,075.00 plus $129.00 HST for chocolate sold in the store in the past three days. All customers paid cash for their purchases. Sales totalling $1,204.00 were deposited to the Bank Chequing account.

SD13: Cash Purchase Invoice #SP-11-06   **Dated November 13, 2012**

From Suite Properties, $3,400.00 plus $408.00 HST for monthly store rent. Purchase invoice totalled $3,808.00. Wrote cheque #239 to pay invoice in full.

SD14: Cash Purchase Invoice #PPC-44998   **Dated November 15, 2012**

From Pacific Power Corp. (use Quick Add to set up new vendor), $480.00 plus $57.60 HST for monthly hydro expense. Purchase invoice totalled $537.60. Wrote cheque #240 to pay invoice in full.

SD15: Sales Receipt #2097   **Dated November 15, 2012**

To Originals craft show customers, $2,045.00 plus $245.40 HST for chocolate sold at Originals show in first three days. All customers paid cash for their purchases. Sales totalling $2,290.40 were deposited to the Bank Chequing account.

SD16: Sales Receipt #2098   **Dated November 15, 2012**

To store customers, $560.00 plus $67.20 HST for chocolate sold in store in past three days. All customers paid cash for their purchases. Sales totalling $627.20 were deposited to the Bank Chequing account.

SD17: Sales Receipt #2099   **Dated November 18, 2012**

To Originals craft show customers, $1,930.00 plus $231.60 HST for chocolate sold at Originals show in past three days of the show. All customers paid cash for their purchases. Sales totalling $2,161.60 were deposited to the Bank Chequing account.

SD18: Sales Receipt #2100   **Dated November 19, 2012**

To store customers, $995.00 plus $119.40 HST for chocolate sold in the store in the past three days. All customers paid cash for their purchases. Sales totalling $1,114.40 were deposited to the Bank Chequing account.

SD19: Cash Purchase Invoice #FFF-216   **Dated November 20, 2012**

From Fournier's Fine Foods, $910.00 for sugar, cream, nuts, and other food ingredients for making chocolates. Food is zero rated for tax purposes. Purchase invoice totalled $910.00. Wrote cheque #241 to pay invoice in full.

SD20: Cash Purchase Invoice #NT-9023   **Dated November 21, 2012**

From NuTel, $180.00 plus $21.60 HST for telephone, cell phone, and Internet service for one month. Purchase invoice totalled $201.60. Wrote cheque #242 to pay invoice in full. Choose the Utilities account.

SD21: Sales Receipt #2101   **Dated November 22, 2012**

To Originals craft show customers, $1,675.00 plus $201.00 HST for chocolate sold at Originals show in the past three days. All customers paid cash for their purchases. Sales totalling $1,876.00 were deposited to the Bank Chequing account.

SD22: Sales Receipt #2102   **Dated November 22, 2012**

To store customers, $1,180.00 plus $141.60 HST for chocolate sold in the store in past three days. All customers paid cash for their purchases. Sales totalling $1,321.60 were deposited to the Bank Chequing account.

SD23: Sales Receipt #2103   **Dated November 25, 2012**

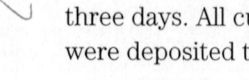

To store customers, $1,660.00 plus $199.20 HST for chocolate sold in store in past three days. All customers paid cash for their purchases. Sales totalling $1,859.20 were deposited to the Bank Chequing account.

SD24: Sales Receipt #2104   **Dated November 25, 2012**

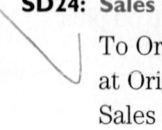

To Originals craft show customers, $1,990.00 plus $238.80 HST for chocolate sold at Originals show in past three days. All customers paid cash for their purchases. Sales totalling $2,228.80 were deposited to the Bank Chequing account.

SD25: Cash Purchase Invoice #GW-1649   **Dated November 25, 2012**

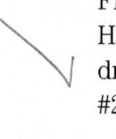

From GlassWorks (use Quick Add for the new vendor), $550.00 plus $66.00 HST to replace glass and repair display cabinet frames in the store. A customer dropped box and cracked glass. Purchase invoice totalled $616.00. Wrote cheque #243 to pay invoice in full.

SD26: Sales Receipt #2105   **Dated November 29, 2012**

To store customers, $1,485.00 plus $178.20 HST for chocolate sold in the store in the past three days. All customers paid cash for their purchases. Sales totalling $1,663.20 were deposited to the Bank Chequing account.

SD27: Sales Receipt #2106   **Dated November 30, 2012**

To Originals craft show customers, $4,350.00 plus $522.00 HST for chocolate sold at Originals show in the final three days of the show. All customers paid cash for their purchases. Sales totalling $4,872.00 were deposited to the Bank Chequing account.

SD28: Sales Receipt #2107   **Dated November 30, 2012**

To Birdsall Book Club (use Quick Add for the new customer), $1,310.00 plus $157.20 HST for special order of theme chocolate decorations for 40th anniversary celebration. Sales total of $1,467.20 was paid by cheque #104 and deposited to the Bank Chequing account.

SD29: Cash Purchase Invoice #O-2009   **Dated November 30, 2012**

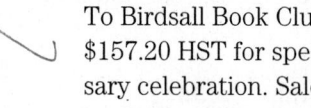

From Originals (Craft Show), $3,000.00 plus $360.00 HST for booth rental at craft show. Purchase invoice totalled $3,360.00. Wrote cheque #244 to pay the invoice in full.

SD30: Cash Purchase Invoice #AP-3883   **Dated November 30, 2012**

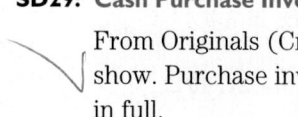

From Ads Plus (use Quick Add for the new vendor), $1,250.00 plus $150.00 HST for advertising, posters, brochures, and business cards for store. Purchase invoice totalled $1,400.00. Wrote cheque #245 to pay the invoice in full.

SD31: Cash Purchase Invoice #CP-1649   **Dated November 30, 2012**

From Car Protectors (use Quick Add for the new vendor), $185.00 plus $22.20 HST for business automobile insurance. Purchase invoice totalled $207.20. Wrote cheque #246 to pay the invoice in full.

Reports

For the last source document, you will need to learn how to print the Income Statement, verify the Sales Receipts amount, and adjust any errors. Refer to the following source document as we work through the steps to perform the various steps:

SD32: Memo # 4

SD Instructions
Refer to the following source document and then follow the step-by-step instructions to enter it.

Dated November 30, 2012

From Owner: Display the Income Statement and verify the sales receipt amounts. Correct the final sales entry for craft show sales (#2106). The correct revenue amount was $2,350.00 plus $282.00 HST. Sales total of $2,632.00 was deposited to the Bank Chequing account.

QuickBooks offers a wide range of reports for companies. We will not cover all the reports in any one chapter. Instead, we will focus on the reports most relevant to the company in the chapter. There are many similarities in the way you display, modify, and print various reports, so once we cover the basics, you should be able to use the rest on your own. In this chapter, we will display five basic reports: the Journal, the Income Statement (Profit & Loss), the Balance Sheet, the Trial Balance, and the Audit Trail.

Reports can be accessed in a variety of ways: from the Reports menu, from the Report Centre, and from the Reports button on List windows within a list window (like the Chart of Accounts list). The list windows include only the reports that relate directly to that list. For example, from the Chart of Accounts list window, you can display reports related to the Chart of Accounts. When you click the Reports button, you can see the reports that are available. These are the QuickReport for the selected account, the Income Tax Preparation report, the Account Listing, as well as some reports that affect all accounts, like the Profit & Loss or Balance Sheet. Other list windows also have a Reports button with related reports.

The Report Centre is a useful tool for accessing reports when you are learning the program because it includes all reports and shows a sample report with a brief description of the report. To access the Report Centre,

1. **Click** the **Report Centre icon** on the Icon bar as shown: `Report Centre`

You can also access the Report Centre as well as individual reports, from the Reports menu.

The Report Centre lists reports by the same categories used in the Reports menu. Generally, the reports within each category are the same as the ones on the Reports menu submenus. An advantage to using the Report Centre is the sample report that shows what your report will look like, and what the contents of the reports will show. The list of Company & Financial reports is shown initially. You can see that many of the reports in this category are variations of the Income Statement. Since the Balance Sheet is also displayed, we will begin there.

In general, to see any report or graph in any of the report categories or groupings:

a) **Choose** the **report category** from the left-hand side of the screen

b) **Hover** your **mouse** over the icon to the left of the report name to display the sample report

c) **Click** the **report name** to display the report

d) **Enter** the **dates** for your report and make any other necessary modifications

Income Statement (Profit & Loss Statement)

The Income Statement shows how much income a business has earned after taking

period you choose. In QuickBooks, the Income Statement is named the Profit & Loss Report. You can see the report as a summary (standard), in detail with all transactions listed individually, in comparative format that shows two different income periods, for individual customers and jobs, and so on. In this chapter, we will cover the standard or summary reports. In the next chapter, we will examine other reports that deal with all accounts.

The report dates can be changed after you display the report on the screen. Your computer's calendar date is the default date used for reports. Since the company files in this textbook have been created for the year 2012, you can use the custom date filter to enter the required dates or simply enter the required dates in the From and To date fields.

> **Notes**
> Depending on your current calendar date, your default report dates will be different from the ones shown in the textbook.

2.	**Click**	the **Company & Financial** heading on the left-hand side of the screen
3.	**Hover**	**your mouse pointer** over the icon beside the Standard report under the Profit & Loss heading
4.	**Click**	on the **Standard report link** to open the report
5.	**Click**	on the **drop-down arrow beside the Dates field**
6.	**Scroll down**	the **list of dates** and **select Custom**
7.	**Press**	`tab` to advance to the From date field and **enter 11/01/2012**
8.	**Press**	`tab` to advance to the To date field and **enter 11/30/2012**
9.	**Press**	`tab` or **click** on the **Refresh button** to display the updated amounts

> **Notes**
> Of course, if you complete this chapter in November 2012, you will see data for your current month and won't have to change the dates for the report.

> **Notes**
> The report dates in the upper left corner of your reports will be different from the ones shown in the textbook because your current calendar date will be different from ours.

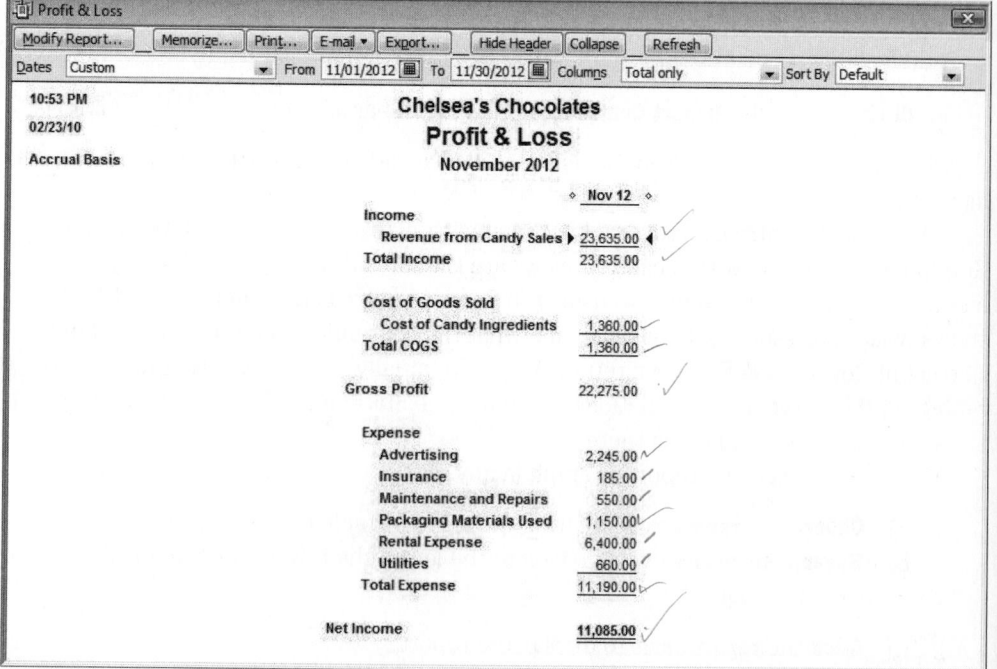

Figure 3-34

For each account, the total income or expense for the period we selected is shown. Gross Profit — total revenue minus the cost of goods sold — is reported separately from

Net Income. The revenue amount appears to be suspiciously high. We can zoom in to see the details of this amount.

The dates drop-down list shows the entry Custom because we entered our own range of dates. When you are using current calendar dates for your company, you can choose a date range from the drop-down list.

Zooming In for More Detail

The Income Statement from the previous exercise should still be open on the screen. If not, please open it.

A magnifying glass icon appears in reports that you display whenever you are able to drill down to view more details for an amount or a transaction. If you hold the mouse over different parts of the report, the magnifying glass will appear, and double clicking will display the additional information or report.

1. **Double click**   the **amount** for Revenue from Candy Sales to view the Transaction Detail By Account report for this account:

Figure 3-35

The last sales receipt for the craft show sales was entered incorrectly. The amount should be $2,350.00, not $4,350.00. We can drill down directly to the Sales Receipt transaction from here to make the correction.

2. **Double click**   **Sales receipt #2106** (you can click anywhere on the line) to drill down to the transaction

3. **Double click**   the amount **4,350.00**

4. **Type**   **2350**

5. **Press**   tab to update the tax amounts. The HST should now be $282.00

6. **Click**   **Save & Close**

7. **Click**   **Yes** when asked if you want to save the changed transaction

You will return to the Transaction Detail By Account Report. Notice that the report has changed to include the correction we made.

8. **Click** 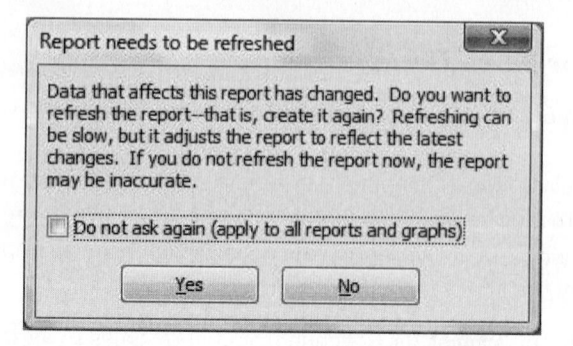 to close the Transaction Detail By Account Report and return to the Profit & Loss Statement. You will see this warning message.

Report needs to be refreshed

Data that affects this report has changed. Do you want to refresh the report—that is, create it again? Refreshing can be slow, but it adjusts the report to reflect the latest changes. If you do not refresh the report now, the report may be inaccurate.

☐ Do not ask again (apply to all reports and graphs)

Yes   No

Figure 3-36

9. **Click** the **Do not ask again check box** so that all reports and graphs will be refreshed or updated automatically when we make a change

10. **Click** **Yes** to update the report

You will return to the Profit & Loss Report. Notice that this report has also changed to include the correction we made.

11. **Click** 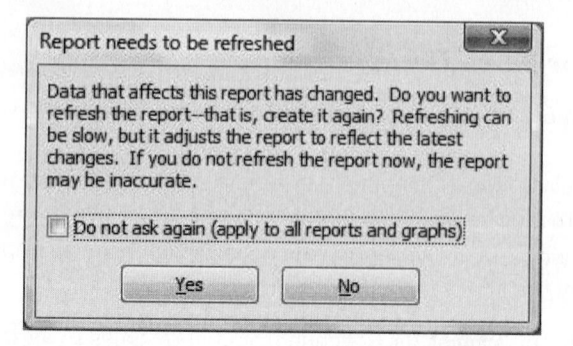 to close the Profit & Loss Report and return to the Report Centre

12. You will see the following message:

Memorize Report

⚠ You have modified the settings for this report. Adding this report to the Memorized Report List will save these settings for future use.

Would you like to memorize this report?

☐ Do not display this message in the future

Yes   No   Cancel

Figure 3-37

Since you have modified the report settings, you can create a memorized report so you can access the report with these new settings in the future. We will learn how to create memorized reports in a later lesson.

13. **Click** the **Do not display this message in the future check box**

14. **Click** **No** when asked to create a memorized report

Displaying Profit & Loss Reports from the Reports Menu

1. **Choose** the **Reports menu**

2. **Click** **Company & Financial**

3. **Click** **Profit & Loss Standard**

Notes
You cannot view a sample report when you select reports from the Report menu.

Depending on your system date, there may be no information displayed on the report because there is no data for the date range displayed by default. We need to change the dates in the report first.

In the dates field, the date range *This Month To Date* is displayed. When you are using current calendar dates for your company, you can choose a date range from the drop-down list. Because we have not used the current calendar dates, we need to customize the date range by modifying the From and the To date fields.

4. **Double click**   the **date in the From field**

5. **Type**   **11/01/12**

6. **Press**   (tab) to advance to the To date field

7. **Type**   **11/30/12**

8. **Click**   the **Refresh button** or **press** (tab) to update the report

9. **Click**   [X] to close the Income Statement when you have finished viewing it

We will access the remaining reports from the Report Centre.

Balance Sheet

The Balance Sheet is also listed with the Company & Financial reports. This report shows the financial state of the company at a particular point in time. The balances for all asset, liability, and equity accounts are shown for a selected date. In QuickBooks, you can display the Balance Sheet for any date that the company was active.

1. **Click**   the **Report Centre icon** in the Icon bar

2. **Click**   the **Company & Financial heading** on the left-hand side of the screen (it may already be selected because this is the default)

3. **Hover**   your **mouse pointer** over the icon to the left of the Standard report under the Balance Sheet & Net Worth heading

4. **Click**   the **Standard report link**

The Balance Sheet will be displayed. We need to change the report date because there is no data for the current date.

5. **Press**   (tab) **to advance to the As of date field** and **enter 11/30/12**

6. **Press**   (tab) **to refresh** the report:

Notes
To display the Balance Sheet from the Reports menu, choose the Reports menu, then choose Company & Financial, and then click Balance Sheet Standard. With the Balance Sheet displayed on the screen, you can drill down to the transaction details as you did for the Profit & Loss Report. You can view the Transaction Detail Report when you double click an amount. When you double click a line in the Transaction Detail Report you can drill down to the original transaction.

Figure 3-38

7. **Click** to close the Balance Sheet when you have finished viewing it

Trial Balance Report

The Trial Balance shows the account balances for both Balance Sheet and Income Statement accounts at a specific date in two columns of debit and credit balances.

As you have seen, you can access all reports from the Report Centre. However, the Trial Balance Report is not found in the Company & Financial heading, so we need to choose a different report group. The Trial Balance and the next two reports we will look at are found within the Accountant & Taxes heading.

For the following exercise, you need to have the Report Centre open.

Notes
To access the Trial Balance from the Reports menu, choose the Reports menu, then choose Accountant & Taxes and then click Trial Balance.

1. **Click**   the **Company & Financial** heading on the left-hand side of the screen to view the list of reports found in this heading

2. **Click**   the **Accountant & Taxes** heading to change the list of reports:

3. **Click**   the **Trial Balance** link under the Account Activity heading

We need to change the report dates because there is no data for the current month.

4. **Press**   `tab` to advance to the **date** in the **From** field

5. **Type**   **11/01/12**

6. **Press**   `tab` to advance to the **date** in the **To** field

7. **Type**   **11/30/12**

8. **Press**   `tab` to refresh the report:

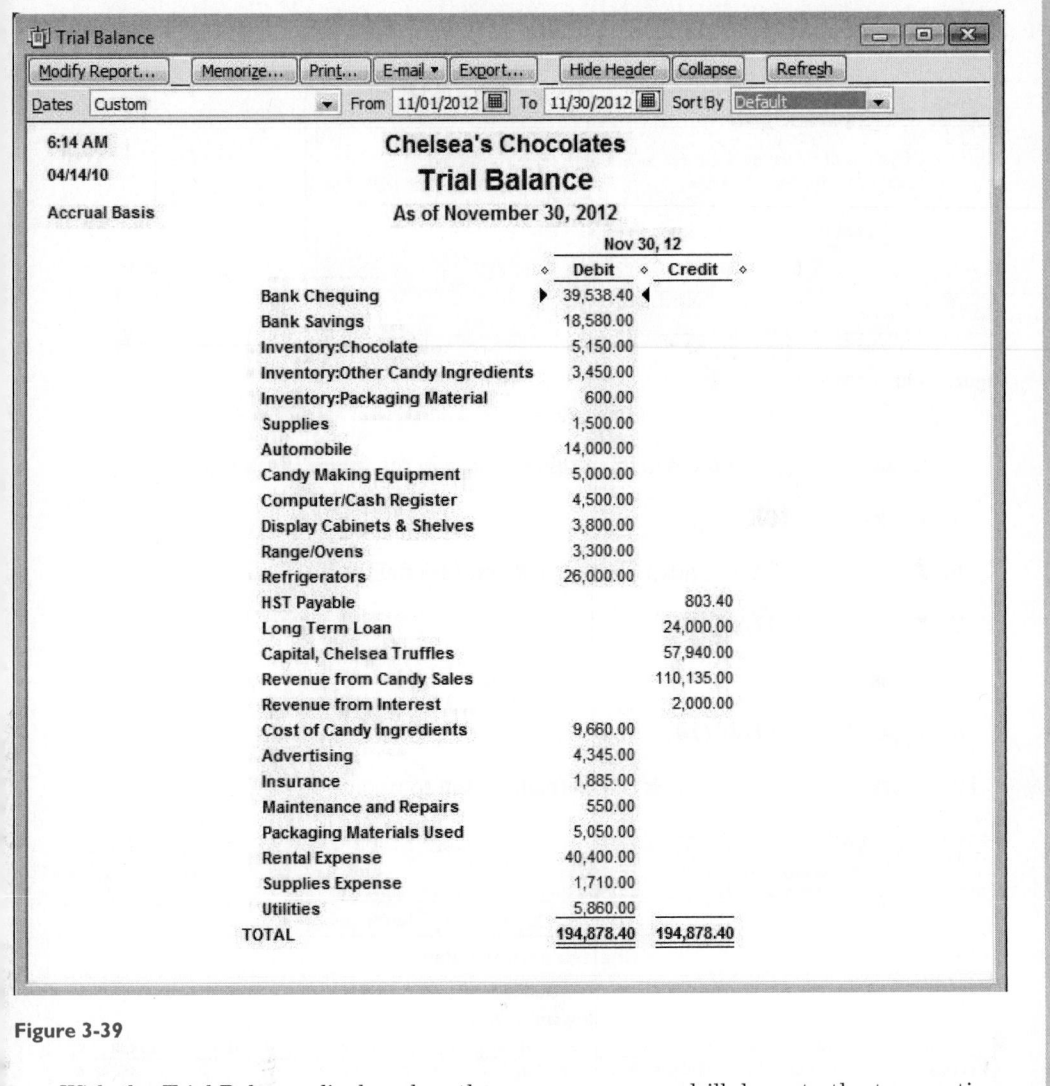

Figure 3-39

With the Trial Balance displayed on the screen, you can drill down to the transaction details as you did for the Profit & Loss Report and the Balance Sheet. You can view the Transaction Detail Report when you double click an amount. When you double click a line in the Transaction Detail Report you can drill down to the original transaction.

9. **Click** [X] to close the Trial Balance when you have finished viewing it

Journal Report

The Journal Report shows all transactions that have taken place within the range of dates you enter for the report. Transactions are displayed in traditional accounting journal format as debit and credit entries.

We need to modify the default dates to include the dates for the transactions we entered, that is, November 1, 2012, to November 30, 2012.

For the following exercise, you need to have the Report Centre open.

1. **Click** the **Accountant & Taxes heading** on the left-hand side of the Report Centre

2. **Click** **Journal** under the Account Activity heading

3. You will see the following warning:

Notes
There are also journal entries for October 31, 2012, but these entries were created for the data file setup.

Notes
To access the Journal report from the Reports menu, choose The Reports menu, then choose Accountant & Taxes and then click Journal.

Figure 3-40

4. **Click**   the **Do not display this message in the future check box**

5. **Click**   **OK**

6. **Press**   ⌧tab to advance to the **From date field**

7. **Type**   **11/01/12**

8. **Press**   ⌧tab to advance to the **To date field**

9. **Type**   **11/30/12**

10. **Press**   ⌧tab or **click** the **Refresh button** to update the report:

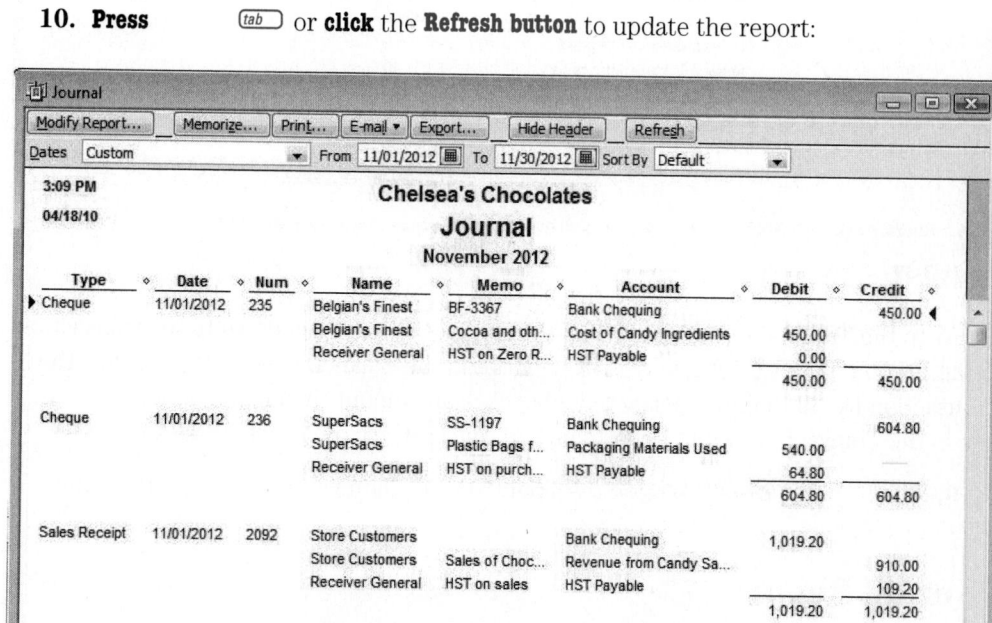

Figure 3-41

Modifying Reports

When you view a report on the screen, it may not fit the window size you are using. Frequently, a report includes columns that are empty or not needed. Resizing the columns will also help to fit the printed report on a page.

1. **Click** ⬜ to maximize the window to full-screen size

We will now modify the report so that it does not include information we do not want in the final report. We do not need the transaction number because these numbers include the historical setup transactions that you did not enter. We can drag a column heading to make the column narrower or to remove the entire column. Dragging to the right will make the column wider.

2. **Drag** the diamond ◇ beside Trans #

Trans # ◇
▶   2

in the column heading to the left as far as possible

The column is removed (it's actually hidden) from the report. Since the Debit and Credit columns are wider than needed, and the Account column is too narrow to fit the entire account name, we will change the width of these columns.

3. **Drag** the column heading diamond for both the Debit and Credit columns to the left a small amount to make the columns narrower

4. **Drag** the column heading diamond for Account to the right a small amount to make this column wider

5. **Change** the size of other columns that do not fit the contents or are wider than needed

6. **Close** the report when you have finished modifying it

7. Do not memorize the report if you are prompted

Audit Trail Report

The Audit Trail Report shows the journal transactions with additional information — the date that the transaction was modified most recently. Beginning in QuickBooks 2008, the audit trail is "always on," which means that it cannot be turned off. You will find all transactions that have been added, deleted, and modified in the audit trail.

The Accountant & Taxes heading should still be selected in the Report Centre.

1. **Click** the **icon to the left of the Audit Trail** under the Account Activity heading to display a sample report

Audit Report dates are linked to the current calendar date because they show the date and time that the entry was recorded.

2. **Click** the **Audit Trail link** to open the report

3. **Click** the **drop-down arrow in the Date Entered/Last Modified field**

4. **Click** **This Fiscal Year** to display the report:

Notes
When you drag the diamond to the left as far as you can, the column disappears.

Notes
The Audit Trail Report is based on the date the transactions were entered rather than the dates of the transactions. The dates in the Enter/Last Modified column will be different on your report.
Your Audit Trail may be different from the one displayed depending on the changes you have made in your company file.

Notes
To access the report from the Reports menu, choose Accountant & Taxes, and then click Audit Trail.

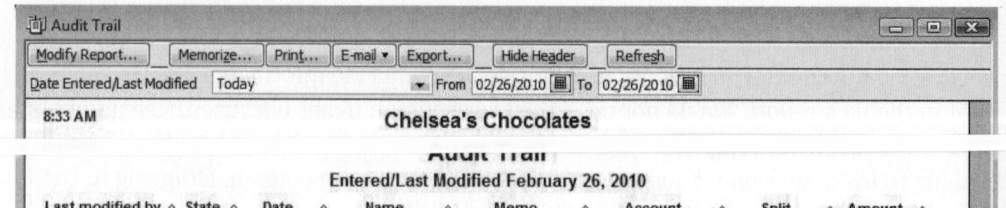

Figure 3-42

The Audit Trail Report is similar to the Journal Report. It shows each accounting transaction that was entered. The audit trail shows the current journal entry (marked as Latest) for a transaction as well as any previous journal entries (marked as Prior) for the same transaction. Deleted entries are marked as deleted. The calendar date and time are entered for each transaction.

5. Close   **the report** when you have finished viewing it

Graphs

You can also display graphs easily in QuickBooks in the same way that you display reports: from the Report Centre or from the Reports menu. Sometimes information is easier to understand when we look at it in a different format, and graphs offer this opportunity.

Income and Expense Graph

We can display the Profit & Loss Report information as a graph. This graph is accessed from the Company & Financial report group.

The Report Centre should still be open from the previous exercise.

1. Click   the **Company & Financial heading** on the left-hand side of the screen to change the list of reports

2. Click   **Income and Expense Graph** under the Income and Expenses heading

3. Click   the **Dates button**

4. Press   (tab) to advance to the **From date**

5. Type   **11/01/12**

6. Press   (tab) to advance to the **To date**

7. Type   **11/30/12**

8. Click   **OK** to update and display the graph:

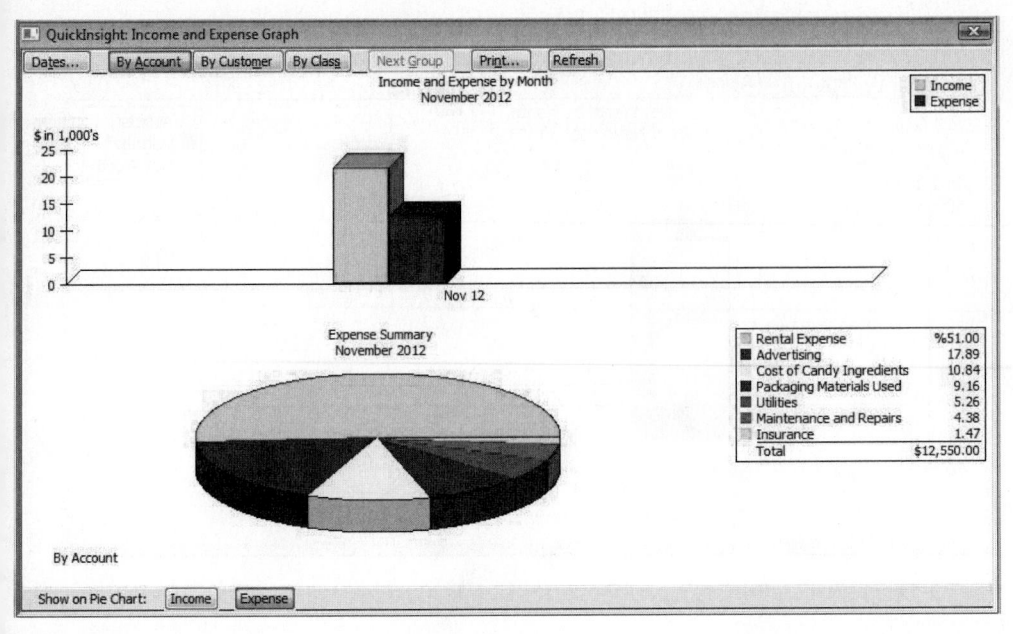

Figure 3-43

The display shows two graphs: the bar chart of total income and expense amounts for the month and the pie chart of expenses for the month. The summary key on the right shows individual expense accounts, their percentage of total expenses, and the total amount. You can zoom in on more detail from graphs, just as you do for reports.

Double click either the Income or Expense bar of the graph to show, in a pie chart, how that single amount is broken down. Double click a part of the detail pie chart to see a bar chart for the amount. Double click the bar chart to see the transaction details. Double click a transaction detail line to drill down to the current transaction.

Double click any part of the Expense pie chart to show a bar chart for that amount. Double click the bar chart to view the transactions for that account. Double click any transaction to drill down to the current transaction.

9. **Click**   on the **graph** to display the information described above

10. **Close**   the **graph** when you have finished viewing it to return to the Report Centre

Net Worth Graph

The Net Worth graph is the pictorial equivalent of the Balance Sheet — it shows the financial position at a selected point in time.

1. **Click**   **Net Worth Graph** in the Company & Financial heading under the Balance Sheet & Net Worth section. You may need to scroll down the list to see this graph

2. **Click**   the **Dates button**

3. **Press**   (tab) to advance to the **From date**

4. **Type**   **11/01/12**

5. **Press**   (tab) to advance to the **To date**

6. **Type**   **11/30/12**

7. **Click**   **OK** to update and display the graph:

> **Notes**
> To access the graph from the Reports menu, choose Company & Financial and click Net Worth Graph.

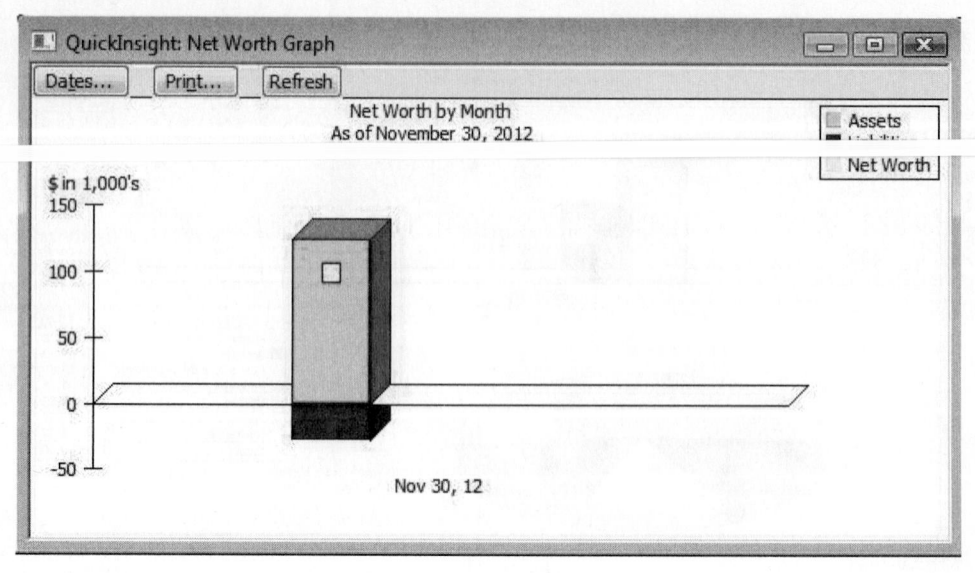

Figure 3-44

The bar graph shows assets above the line, liabilities below the line, and net worth, the difference between them, as a point on the asset portion. Again, you can zoom in on more detail from graphs.

Double click any portion of the graph to show, in a pie chart, how that single amount is broken down. Double click a part of the detail pie chart to see a bar chart for the amount and then double click that bar chart to see the transaction details. Double click a transaction detail line to see the original entry for it.

8. **Double click**   the **graph** to display the information described above

9. **Close**   the **graph** when you have finished to return to the Report Centre

Printing Reports and Graphs

Notes
We understand that in the classroom, printing facilities may be limited. Your instructor will tell you which reports to print and which ones to display.

Notes
To display the Profit & Loss Standard Report from the Reports menu:
• Choose Company & Financial and click Profit & Loss Standard.
• Enter 11/01/2012 in the From date field and 11/30/2012 in the To date field

You can print any report that you can display. The instructions that follow apply to printing any report so we will not repeat them for all reports. We will work with the Standard Profit & Loss Statement.

1. **Display**   the **Profit & Loss Standard Report for Nov. 1–Nov. 30, 2012**. (Refer to page 84 for instructions if necessary)

2. **Click**   the **Print button** in the report window. You will see the following Print Reports dialogue box:

Figure 3-45

This Settings tab allows you to select the printer you are using, the number of copies, the pages you want to print, and the page orientation (portrait or landscape — upright or sideways on the page. You can also choose whether to allow the program to apply "smart" page breaks (such as starting a new page between sections), to print in colour, or to shrink the report so that it fits on a single page. If you have a very wide report, you may prefer to print in landscape orientation.

The remaining control options are more advanced and the default settings are usually appropriate. You can access other settings from the Options button and scrolling through the various tabs. You should review these settings but you do not need to change them.

3. Click the **Margins tab** to view the options for changing the page margins:

Notes
The Options button will show printer options that are specific to your own printer.

Figure 3-46

Notes
The default margins at 0.50 inches may be too small to allow for three-hole punching or binding.

From this window you can change the side, top, and bottom margins to suit your printer's capabilities or your desired report appearance. The default margins may be set for the limits of your printer.

4. Change the **margins** to suit your printing needs

You can click Cancel to close a settings window without making any changes

Notes
You should preview the report before printing to see whether you need to make additional changes to the report options.

5. Click the **Preview button** to view what the report will look like when you print it

6. Click **Close** to close the preview. The Printer Settings window will open where you can make additional printer adjustments before printing

7. Click the **Print button** to begin printing

8. Close the **displayed report**

9. Close the **Report Centre**

Finishing Your Session

1. Back up the **company data file**

2. Close the **Company file**

3. Close the **QuickBooks program**

CHAPTER EIGHT

Objectives

After completing this chapter, you should be able to:

- **enter** journal transactions in the account register
- **enter** transactions in the General Journal
- **create** new General Ledger accounts
- **edit** General Journal entries before recording
- **review** General Journal entries after recording transactions
- **correct** General Journal entries after recording
- **use** the QuickBooks calculator in journal entries
- **display** and **print** General Ledger reports
- **modify** and **memorize** reports

Company Information

Company Profile

Bob's Bookroom, located in St. John's, Newfoundland, is a sole proprietorship owned and operated by Bob Bestseller. The store sells used books and heavyweight canvas book bags with the store name and logo. Bob encourages his customers to re-use the book bags each time they visit in order to reduce plastic waste as one small environmentally friendly step.

Bob Bestseller obtains books from various sources. He buys books back from customers and, by offering fair prices, he maintains a steady supply. He also makes the rounds of private garage sales on Saturday and Sunday mornings throughout the spring and summer, plus church and charity sales, to collect books to sell. And he buys remainders of out-of-print books from publishers. Often these are hard-cover books that have had paperback editions released.

> **Notes**
> Bob's Bookroom
> 222 Dickens Rd.
> St. John's, NL A1E 2B7
> Tel: (709) 755-5766
> Fax: (709) 755-6996
> E-mail: BB@bookroom.com
> Web: www.bookroom.com
> Business No.: 138 745 309

Experience has taught Bob which books customers will usually buy — new books, bestsellers, cookbooks, and gardening books are especially popular. The books must be in good condition. By concentrating his purchases on these types of books, he achieves the high turnover he needs to remain profitable.

He does not track books individually as inventory items, except for the mental picture he carries in his head of his current stock. The books in the store are shelved alphabetically and organized in the categories found in most other bookstores.

The store has a few regular vendors for cleaning, office supplies, telephone service, and rent. None offers discounts. The business also has a small bank loan used to buy books and Bob will occasionally take out another loan when a good source of books becomes available.

The bookstore has very few capital or fixed assets but does include a sitting room area with comfortable sofas and chairs in front of a fireplace. Customers relax here while they browse through the books before purchasing. The store has a good supply of repeat customers who are mostly known to the owner. Most customers pay in cash, but a few regulars are allowed to pay by cheque.

The bookstore is located in a busy section of downtown St. John's in rented space. Store rent includes heat, hydro, and water service, leaving telephone service as the only additional utilities expense.

In Newfoundland, 13 percent HST is charged and paid on all goods and services, except zero-rated and tax-exempt items. Therefore, customers pay the HST when they buy the books and bags, and Bob pays the HST on all purchases.

On June 1, the bookstore is ready to use QuickBooks for accounting transactions after converting all the accounting records to QuickBooks using the following:

- Chart of Accounts
- Trial Balance
- List of Vendors, Customers, and Items
- Accounting Procedures

Notes
We have changed the name of the GST/HST Payable account to HST Payable.

Chart of Accounts

Bob's Bookroom

ASSETS
Bank
  Bank Chequing
  Bank Savings

Current Assets
  Book Bag Inventory
  Book Inventory
  Office Supplies
  Plastic Bags
  Prepaid Advertising
  Prepaid Insurance
  Prepaid Rent

Fixed Assets
  Automobile:Cost
  Automobile:Depreciation
  Computer Equipment:Cost
  Computer Equipment:Depreciation
  Store Furniture and Fixtures:Cost
  Store Furniture and Fixtures:Depreciation

LIABILITIES
Current Liabilities
  Bank Loan
  HST Payable

Long Term Liabilities
  Long Term Loan

EQUITY
  Capital, Bob Bestseller
  Retained Earnings

INCOME
  Revenue from Interest
  Revenue from Sales

EXPENSE
Cost of Goods Sold
  Cost of Bags Sold
  Cost of Books Sold

Expense
  Advertising
  Insurance Expense
  Interest Expense
  Maintenance and Repairs
  Office Supplies Used
  Plastic Bags Used
  Rental Expense
  Telephone

Trial Balance

Bob's Bookroom

	Debits	Credits
Bank Chequing	$ 14,350.00	
Bank Savings	29,580.00	
Book Bag Inventory	3,600.00	
Book Inventory	51,800.00	
Office Supplies	420.00	
Plastic Bags	380.00	
Prepaid Advertising	3,600.00	
Prepaid Insurance	2,500.00	
Prepaid Rent	3,400.00	
Automobile:Cost	18,000.00	
Automobile:Depreciation		$ 2,700.00
Computer Equipment:Cost	8,000.00	
Computer Equipment:Depreciation		1,200.00
Store Furniture and Fixtures:Cost	30,000.00	
Store Furniture and Fixtures:Depreciation		1,500.00
Bank Loan		8,500.00
HST Payable		3,600.00
Long Term Loan		45,000.00
Capital, Bob Bestseller		65,660.00
Revenue from Interest		180.00
Revenue from Sales		96,800.00
Cost of Bags Sold	2,250.00	
Cost of Books Sold	41,200.00	
Advertising	790.00	
Insurance Expense	6,250.00	
Interest Expense	1,125.00	
Maintenance and Repairs	2,200.00	
Office Supplies Used	380.00	
Plastic Bags Used	205.00	
Rental Expense	4,250.00	
Telephone	860.00	
	$225,140.00	$225,140.00

Vendor, Customer, and Item Lists

Bob's Bookroom

VENDORS

Canvas Crafts
Office Essentials
Receiver General
Signal Communications
Signals

CUSTOMERS

Cash Customers

ITEMS

Book Bags
Books

Accounting Procedures

Taxes: HST

Notes

Refer to Chapter 2 for details on sales taxes.

Bob's Bookroom pays 13 percent HST on all goods and services that it buys and charges 13 percent HST on all sales. It uses the regular method for remittance of the tax. HST collected from customers is recorded as a liability in the *HST Payable* account. HST paid to vendors is recorded in the *HST Payable* account as a decrease in the liability to the Canada Revenue Agency. The report is filed with the Receiver General for Canada by the last day of the month for the previous quarter, either including the balance owing or requesting a refund.

In Newfoundland, PST is included in the 13 percent HST and is not calculated or remitted separately.

Customer and Vendor Account Terms

All customers pay in cash. Cash received from customers is deposited immediately and is recorded in the Bank Chequing account and not held for later deposit. Cash sales are summarized to minimize the number of individual transactions you need to enter.

All vendors demand payment on receipt of merchandise. All payments are made by cheque.

Cost of Goods Sold

At the end of each month, the books, bags, and supplies remaining in inventory are counted to determine the cost of sales and supplies used in the month. Adjusting journal entries are completed to reduce the asset accounts and increase the relevant expense accounts.

Instructions

1. Using the Chart of Accounts, Trial Balance, and other information, you will record entries for source documents for June 2012 using QuickBooks. You will find the source documents marked with an SD beside them and listed as you work through the chapter. The procedures for entering each new type of transaction are outlined in step-by-step instructions in the chapter. Additional source documents will be provided, allowing you to have more practice entering transactions. If you have used this textbook in the past and would prefer to skip the step-by-step instructions and work only with a list of source documents, refer to the CD in the back of the textbook for the list of source documents for this chapter.

2. After you have finished making your entries, you will print the reports and graphs for June 2012 listed on the following printing form. Instructions on how to print the reports begin on page 123.

REPORTS FOR JUNE 2012

Lists
- ☑ Account Listing

Company & Financial
- ☑ Balance Sheet Detail: June 30
- ☑ Profit & Loss Detail (Income Statement) from June 1 to June 30

Accountant & Taxes
- ☑ Trial Balance from June 1 to June 30
- ☑ General Ledger from June 1 to June 30
- ☑ Journal from June 1 to June 30
- ☑ Transaction List by Date from June 1 to June 30
- ☐ Transaction Detail by Account

Other
- ☐ Custom Summary Report
- ☐ Custom Transaction Detail Report
- ☑ Transaction History
- ☑ Transaction Journal

GRAPHS
- ☐ Income and Expense
- ☐ Net Worth

General Journal Entries

Transactions that do not involve selling or buying products or services are entered in the General Journal. They do not involve customers, vendors, or employees and are often adjusting entries that must be completed at the end of a fiscal period — month, quarter, year — such as supplies used during the period, prepaid assets that have expired, adjustments for bad debts, depreciation, and so on. Bank account transactions, such as receiving a loan or making a loan payment, also are usually entered in the General Journal.

In QuickBooks, you can enter these types of transactions in the General Journal or the Accounts Register. The final journal entry will be the same for both methods, and we will demonstrate both methods in this chapter.

Entering Transactions in the Account Register

The first transaction that we need to enter is the deposit of a bank loan to the chequing bank account. This transaction is a regular General Journal entry that we will enter in the account register. You can use the account register to enter transactions for any Balance Sheet account except the Retained Earnings account. Refer to the following source document as we work through the steps to enter it:

SD1: **Bank Credit Memo #CM-8902**

Dated June 1, 2012

From Literary Credit Union, a $5,000.00 short term loan at 6 percent interest approved for large book purchase. Amount deposited to the Bank Chequing account.

1. **Open** the files for Bob's Bookroom. You can access account registers from the Chart of Accounts. To access the Chart of Accounts:

   a) **Press** ctrl + **A**; or

   b) **Choose** the **company menu** and then click **Chart of Accounts**; or

   c) **Choose** the **Lists menu** and then click **Chart of Accounts**; or

   d) **Click** the **Chart of Accounts icon** in the Company section of the Home page

2. **Open** the **Chart of Accounts** using one of the methods listed above:

> **Notes**
> General Journal entries are usually entered in the Make General Journal Entries form rather than in the account register, but we want to illustrate both methods. We will enter the second transaction in the Make General Journal Entries form.

> **SD Instructions**
> Refer to the following source document and then follow the step-by-step instructions to enter it.

Figure 4-1

Notes
Account numbers are used in Chapter 9.

All accounts created for the company are listed in alphabetic order within their type. Bob's Bookroom does not use account numbers. First the Balance Sheet accounts are displayed (assets, liabilities and equities), followed by Income Statement accounts (revenue followed by expenses). Balance Sheet accounts show the account balance while Income Statement accounts do not. You can enter journal transactions for the Balance Sheet accounts, except the Retained Earnings account, from this window. From the **Account button** menu at the bottom of the window you can add new accounts, edit accounts, and delete accounts. From the **Activities button** you can select the accounting activity you want to complete, and from the **Reports button** you can select a report related to the Chart of Accounts.

Notes
The Activities button menu includes such tasks as Writing Cheques, Making General Journal Entries, and Using the Register.

3. **Double click** **Bank Chequing** in the Chart of Accounts to open its register:

Notes
Double clicking a Balance Sheet account (other than the Retained Earnings account) will open the register for that account. Double clicking an Income Statement account will open a QuickReport for the account that lists the transactions for the selected period.

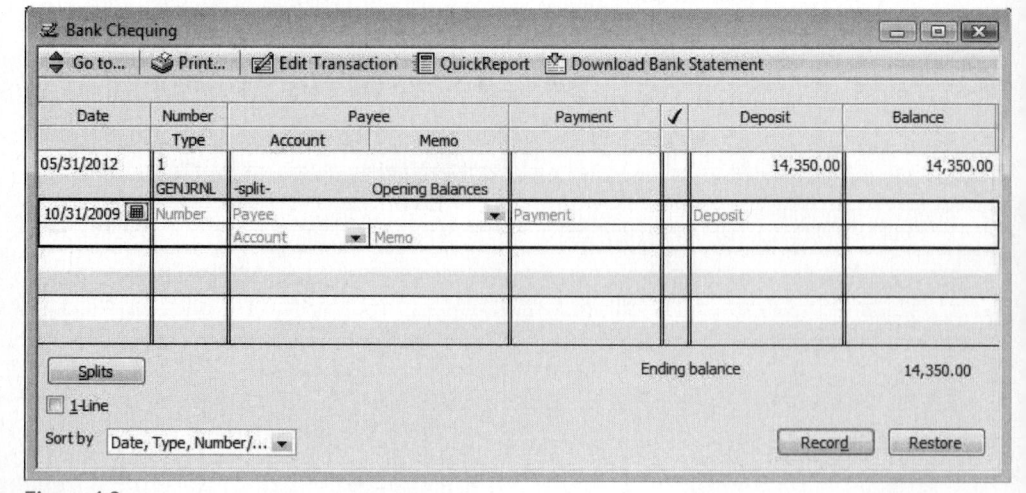

Figure 4-2

Accessing the Account Register

You can also access an account register in a number of other ways:

a. **Select** the **account** from the Chart of Accounts and then:

    i) **Click** the **Activities button** and **click Use Register**; or

    ii) **Press** `ctrl` **+ R**; or

    iii) **Right click** and **select Use Register**

b. From anywhere in QuickBooks:

    i) **Choose Banking** from the menu and then **click Use Register**; or

    ii) **Press** `ctrl` **+ R**

Either of these methods will display the Use Register window where you need to click the drop-down arrow and select the Balance Sheet account you want to use:

Figure 4-3

Notes
If you want to use an expense account or a revenue account (Income Statement account) in a register transaction, start the transaction from the Balance Sheet account of the transaction or use the General Journal as shown in the next source document transaction.

Entering the Account Register Transaction

We have selected the default option to show two lines for each transaction — the 1-Line option is not selected. The labels in the two heading lines show the contents of the field. The first line has the Date, Number, Payee, Payment amount, cleared (✓) column, Deposit amount, and Balance. Line 2 shows the Exchange Rate (if applicable), Type of transaction, Account, and Memo.

The date is highlighted, with the current calendar date entered as the default. Once you begin to enter transactions, the last date used will appear as the default until you close and re-open the data file.

Notes
If additional journal entry lines are required, you can choose Splits to open a journal-like window for the transaction, allowing you to enter additional lines.

4. Type   06/01/12

5. Press   `tab` to advance to the **Number field**

6. Press   `del` to remove the **default entry**. (This is the next cheque number, a common choice for a bank account number entry)

Payee appears in dimmed type to indicate that this field would contain the name of an employee or vendor, if that was appropriate for the entry. There is no payee for this transaction. The Payee entry is removed when you delete the cheque number.

7. Press   `tab` to advance to the **Payee field**

We are making a deposit to the bank account so we must skip the Payment column and enter the amount in the Deposit column.

8. Press   `tab` to advance to the **Deposit column**

9. Type   5000

10. Press   `tab` to advance to the **Account field** (on the second line of the entry)

Notice that QuickBooks has entered DEP (deposit) as the type of transaction.

Now we must enter the second account for the transaction. The primary account for the first part of the transaction is the account whose register we are working in — the Bank Chequing account.

11. Click the **drop-down arrow** in the Account field to view the list of accounts:

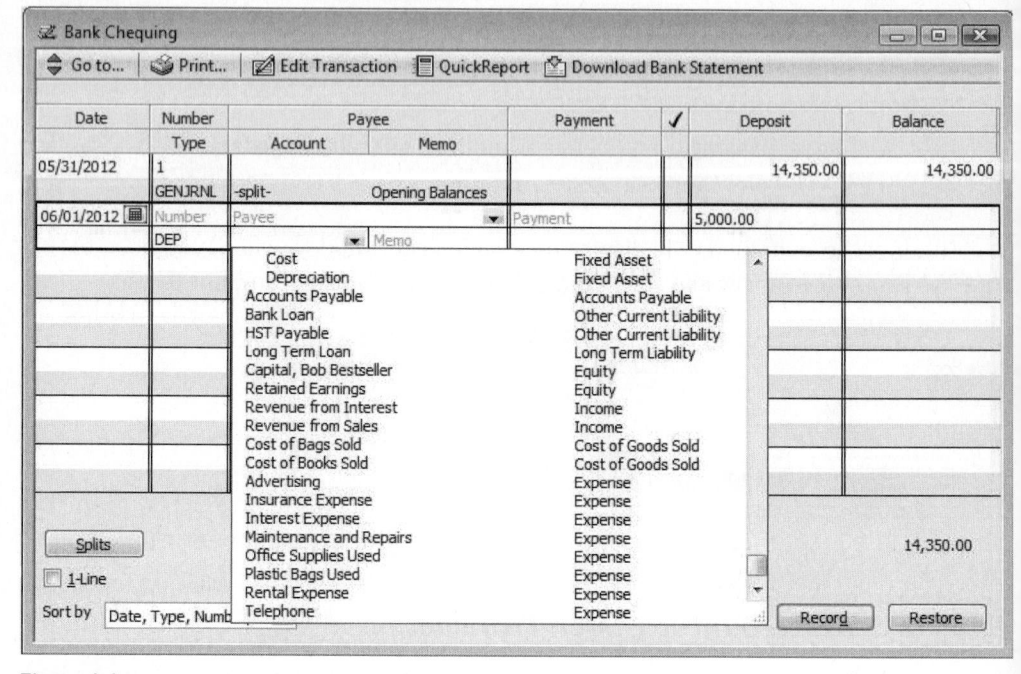

Figure 4-4

Accounts are listed in the same order as the accounts in the Chart of Accounts on page 98. *Bank Loan*, the account we need, may not be in view. Use the scroll bar to scroll up or down the list of accounts until *Bank Loan* is displayed in the list.

12. Click **Bank Loan** and it is added to the register

As soon as you selected the account, the entry was recognized as a transfer rather than a deposit and the transaction type is changed automatically. You cannot change the transaction type.

The Memo field is used for a comment, description, or source document number that helps to identify the transaction. You can type up to 60 characters in the Memo field.

13. Press ⌜tab⌟ to advance to the Memo field

14. Type **Short term loan @ 6%**

You can add the Bank Credit Memo number and bank name to the description in the Memo field.

15. The completed transaction is shown:

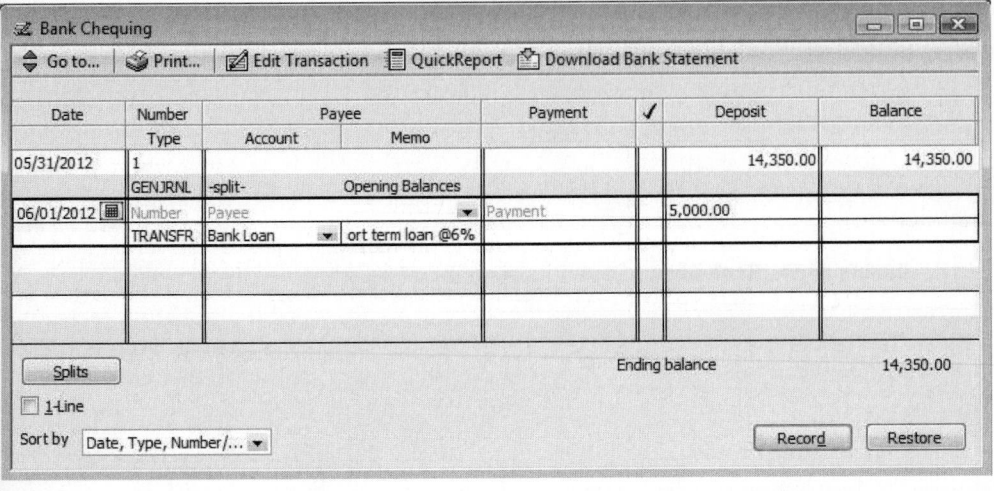

Figure 4-5

Before recording the transaction, you should review your work and make corrections if needed.

Correcting the Journal Transaction

You can make corrections on the screen before saving a transaction in QuickBooks. The concept of making corrections is the same for all journals and forms. The procedure is similar to editing text in other Windows programs.

CORRECTING REGISTER TRANSACTIONS BEFORE RECORDING

Click the field that contains the error. Press (tab) to move forward from one field to the next. Highlight the incorrect information and then type the correct information to replace it. Press (tab) if necessary to advance to the next field.

To correct an account selection, click the drop-down arrow in the Account field and click the correct account.

CORRECTING REGISTER TRANSACTIONS AFTER RECORDING

To make corrections after recording, open the Register for the account and make the necessary changes just as you did before saving the transaction. Click Record to save the changes. Click Yes when you are prompted to save the changes.

When you are certain that the information is correct, you can record the entry.

16. Click the **Record button** to save the transaction and update the register account balance as shown:

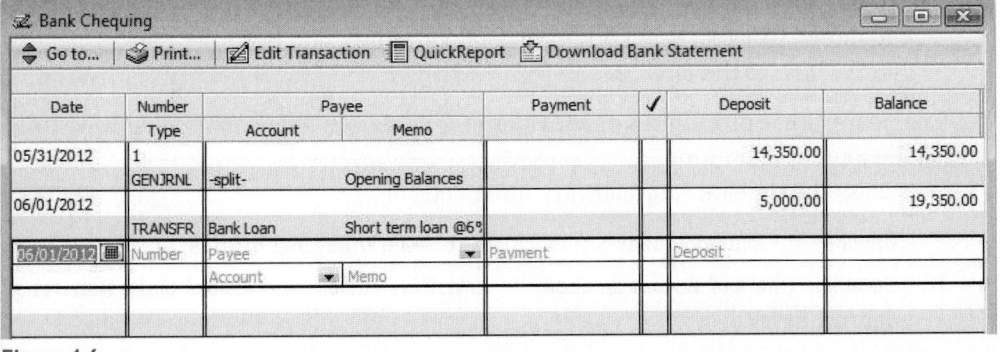

Figure 4-6

The Balance for the bank account is increased by $5,000.00; the amount of the loan deposit. Notice the bank account balance is now $19,350.00.

17. Click in the Bank Chequing register window to close it and return to the Chart of Accounts

Notice the *Bank Account* and *Bank Loan* balances have been updated by the transaction.

18. Double click Bank Loan to open its account register:

Date	Ref	Payee		Increase	✓	Decrease	Balance
	Type	Account	Memo				
05/31/2012	1			8,500.00			8,500.00
	GENJRNL	Bank Chequing [split Opening Balances					
06/01/2012				5,000.00			13,500.00
	TRANSFR	Bank Chequing	Short term loan @6%				
06/01/2012	Ref	Payee		Increase		Decrease	
		Account	Memo				

Figure 4-7

You can see that the same transaction appears in the *Bank Loan* register. Notice that the transaction has been added automatically to this ledger as an increase in the account. To record the bank loan deposit, we could have started the transaction from the *Bank Loan* register, entered the amount in the Increase column, and selected *Bank Chequing* as the offsetting account.

We will close both the register window and the Chart of Accounts window; however, you can choose to keep them open if you want.

19. Click in the Bank Loan Register window

20. Click in the Chart of Accounts window to return to the Home page

Entering Transactions in the General Journal

Accessing the General Journal

For the next transaction, we will use the General Journal to enter the transaction. Refer to the following source document as we work through the steps to enter it:

 SD Instructions
Refer to the following source document and then follow the step-by-step instructions to enter it.

SD2: Memo #6-1

Dated June 1, 2012

From Owner: The owner withdrew $250.00 cash to buy birthday gifts for his twin daughters. Create a new Equity account: Drawings, Bob Bestseller. Add a General Journal icon to the Icon bar.

Like many other procedures or activities in QuickBooks, there are several ways to access the journal entry form.

To access the General Journal Entry form, you can:

a) **Choose** the **Company menu** and **click Make General Journal Entries**; or

b) **Open** the **Chart of Accounts**, **click** the **Activities button**, and **choose Make General Journal Entries**; or

c) **Open** the **Chart of Accounts**, **right click** on an **account**, and **select Make General Journal Entries**

Notes
There is no keyboard shortcut or icon on the Icon bar for General Journal entries. We will customize the icon bar by adding a General Journal icon.

Entering Transactions

We will open the General Journal Entry form from the Company menu.

1. **Choose** the **Company menu** and **click General Journal Entries**

You will see the following message about automatic journal entry numbers:

Figure 4-8

The numbering applies only to journal entries, not to other kinds of transactions. All transactions are assigned a transaction number, and journal entries are included in this numbering too.

2. **Click**   the **Do not display this message in the future** check box

3. **Click**   **OK** to close the message and open the journal entry form:

Figure 4-9

General Journal transactions are entered as traditional accounting entries with debit and credit amounts. The *Drawings, Bob Bestseller* equity account will be debited (increased) and *Bank Chequing* will be credited (decreased). Refer to "A Review of Basic Accounting" on the Data CD-ROM if you want to review debits, credits, and accounting principles.

It is easier to complete General Journal entries using the Make General Journal Entries form than it is to use the Register. You can complete multiple or split transactions, and you have full access to all ledger accounts.

4.	**Enter**	**06/01/12** as the date if this is not the default date for the current general journal entry
5.	**Click**	the **account field**
6.	**Click**	the ~~drop~~ ~~~~~~~~~~~~~~~~~~ ~~Account field to access the account list~~

The account we need is not on the list so we need to create it.

Adding New General Ledger Accounts

QuickBooks allows you to add General Ledger accounts from any general ledger account field on the fly, while entering a transaction, just as it allows adding new vendors and customers.

7.	**Press**	(esc) to close the account list
8.	**Type**	**Drawings, Bob Bestseller** in the account field
9.	**Press**	(tab) and the following message is displayed:

Figure 4-10

Because the account name is not found in the Chart of Accounts, you have the option to create it. If you have typed an incorrect account name, you can choose Cancel. Quick Add is not an option for accounts because the program must know what type of account is being created in order to place it correctly in the financial statements.

10.	**Click**	**Set Up** or **press** (enter) to continue
11.	The Add New Account form will be displayed:	

Figure 4-11

On this screen, you must choose the **Account Type** for the new account. If you're not sure what Account Type to select, click each Account Type to view a list of sample accounts for that type on the right-hand side of the screen.

The account type determines the position of the account in the Chart of Accounts and Balance Sheet or Income Statement. The type also determines the column headings in the account register and whether the opening balance is a credit or debit amount.

Depending on which form you are creating the new account from, the account type may already be selected for you. The suggested **default type** will be based on the type of transaction you are entering. When entering an account from the Make General Journal Entries form, the Account Type is left blank.

Drawings is an Equity account so we need to choose Equity as the account type.

Notes
Most of the account types are self-explanatory. We will tell you what type to use when you create a new account. Account types are explained in greater detail in Chapter 5.

Notes
If you create a new account while entering a purchase, Expense is the default type selected.

12. Choose   the **Equity button** as shown here:

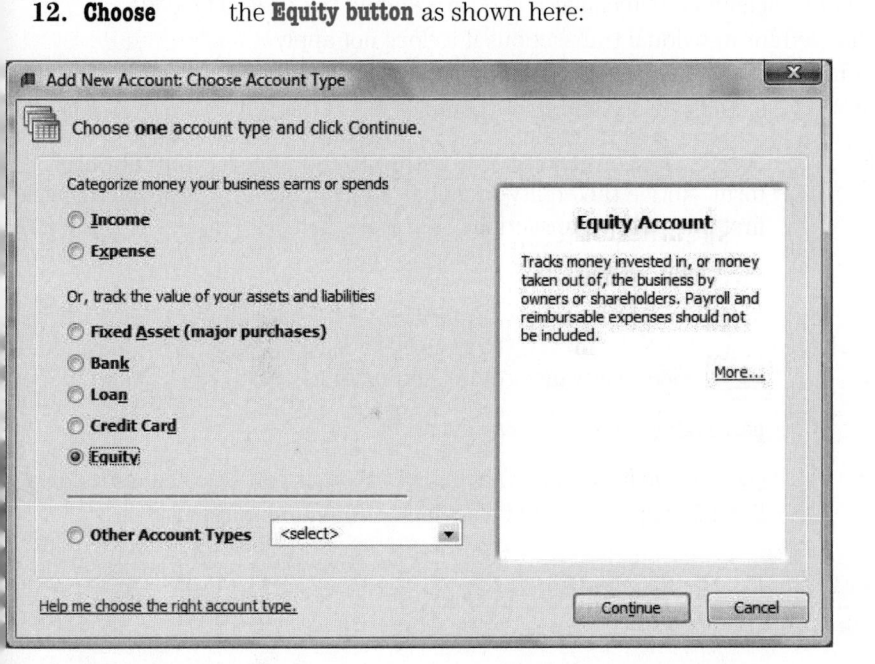

Figure 4-12

13. Click   **Continue** to display the second screen of the Add New Account form:

Figure 4-13

Notice the account name we originally typed in the Account field in the Make General Journal Entries window is entered in the Account Name field.

Most of the information on the Add New Account form is optional. If the account is part of a group of accounts under a subheading, you can select the account of which it is a subaccount. For example, you might group several bank accounts together as subaccounts under a parent account named Bank. Or you might group a capital asset with its accumulated depreciation account, as we have done for Bob's Bookroom. We used subaccounts for the fixed asset accounts. A colon in the name indicates a parent and subaccount connection so you cannot use a colon in the account name.

The description you add will become part of the reports and could be helpful if several accounts have similar names. You can add even further information in the Note field. For Expense accounts, you can also choose a default tax code. The code can always be changed for individual transactions if it does not apply.

This is a new account, so there is no opening balance. The remaining fields are optional. We do not need them so the form is complete.

14. **Click**   **Save & Close** or **press** (enter) to return to the General Journal Entry form. Notice the equity account you just entered is displayed on the first line in the transaction

15. **Click**   the **Debit column**

16. **Type**   **250**

17. **Press**   (tab) twice to advance to the Memo field

18. **Type**   **personal: cash for birthday gifts**

19. **Press**   (tab) to the second journal line. As soon as you advance to the next line of the journal, the balancing credit amount appears:

Account	Debit	Credit	Memo	Name	Tax Item	Billable?
Drawings, Bob Bestseller	250.00		personal: cash for b...			
		250.00				
Totals	250.00	250.00				

Figure 4-14

20. **Click**   the **drop-down arrow in the Account field** in the second line

Notice that the balancing credit amount, $250.00, is automatically entered as the default for the next part of the transaction. If you add several journal lines, this amount

WARNING!

Colons are not allowed as part of an account name because QuickBooks uses the colon to indicate parent and subaccount relationships.

Notes

As soon as you advance to the next line of the journal, the balancing credit amount appears.

If the second line of the transaction is another debit amount, just click the Debit column and type the correct amount. The credit entry will be removed from the second line automatically and will be displayed when you move down to the third line in the transaction.

changes continually to keep the transaction in balance as you add other amounts. The amount is correct and it is a credit entry, so we do not need to change it.

21. Click   **Bank Chequing** to add the second account to the journal

22. Click   the **Memo field**

23. Type   **Memo 6-1** to replace the current memo entry

QuickBooks Premier Edition automatically adds the first memo comment to each journal line; however, you can override it as we did for this source document. We will also add Owner to the entry so that the journal report will include this information.

24. Press   `tab` to advance to the Name field

25. Type   **Owner**

26. Press   `enter` or **press** `tab`

27. Choose   **Quick Add** when prompted that Owner is not in the Name list

28. Choose   **Other** as the type for the name and **click OK** to return to the completed journal, as shown:

Figure 4-15

29. Review   the **transaction** and **make corrections** if necessary

CORRECTING JOURNAL TRANSACTIONS BEFORE RECORDING

Click in the field that contains the error. Highlight the incorrect information and then type the correct information to replace it. Press `tab` if necessary to advance to the next field.

To correct an account selection, click the drop-down arrow in the Account field, and select the correct account.

To clear the transaction on the screen and begin again, click the Clear button.

Notes
The Other payee type is used for payees who do not supply or buy goods and services.

Notes
Some of the columns have been widened to display all of the information in the journal entry.

Adding a General Journal Icon

Before closing the Make General Journal Entries form, we will add an icon for it on the Icon bar for easy access because we will be using this form frequently in this chapter.

1. **Choose**   the **View menu** and **click "Add Make General Journal Entries" To Icon Bar**

2. **Choose**   ⊞ as the icon or another icon suitable for the journal. Scroll down the icon list if necessary. You can accept the label and description

3. **Click**   **OK**

4. **Click**   **Save & Close** to save the Journal Entry and return to the Home page

Source Documents

Now that you have learned some of the new concepts taught in this chapter, continue to develop your skills by entering the following source documents in QuickBooks using the Sales Receipts, Write Cheques, and Make General Journal Entries forms. Use the information in this chapter as a guide if necessary. You may also need to refer to information in Chapter 3 to complete some of the source documents.

SD3: Cash Purchase Invoice #CC-201   **Dated June 1, 2012**

From Canvas Crafts, $440.00 plus $57.20 HST for printed canvas book bags. Purchase invoice totalled $497.20. Wrote cheque #436 to pay invoice in full. Remember to click the To be printed box so that cheques will not be listed later for printing.

SD4: Cash Purchase Invoice #BCH-211   **Dated June 1, 2012**

From Book Clearing House (use Quick Add for the new vendor), $4,200.00 plus $546.00 HST for remaindered books. Purchase invoice totalled $4,746.00 Wrote cheque #437 to pay invoice in full.

SD5: Sales Receipt #615   **Dated June 4, 2012**

Sold to Shelley Byron (use Quick Add for the new customer), $270.00 plus $35.10 HST for books and $20.00 plus $2.60 HST for canvas book bags. Sales total of $327.70 was paid in full by cheque #138 and deposited to the Bank Chequing account. Remember to click the To be printed box so that sales receipts will not be listed later for printing.

SD6: Memo #6-2   **Dated June 5, 2012**

From Owner: Add the Sales Receipt icon to the Icon tool bar and customize the Sales Receipt Journal by removing the Quantity and Rate columns.

SD7: Cash Purchase Invoice #S-444   **Dated June 5, 2012**

From Signals, $750.00 plus $97.50 HST for designing ads to run in a local newspaper. Purchase invoice totalled $847.50. Wrote cheque #438 to pay invoice in full.

SD8: Memo #6-3   **Dated June 5, 2012**

From Owner: Owner withdrew $150.00 cash to buy decorations and cake for daughters' birthday party.

SD9: Sales Receipt #616   **Dated June 7, 2012**

Sales to cash customers in past week, $4,490.00 plus 583.70 HST for books and $260 plus 33.80 HST for book bags. All customers paid cash for their purchases. Sales totalling $5,367.50 were deposited to the Bank Chequing account.

SD Practice
Continue to develop your skills by entering the following source document(s).

Notes
When a publisher discontinues a book, the remaining stock is often sold at a discount to bookstores as remainders. Often, hardcover books are remaindered when the paperback version is released.

Correcting General Journal Entries after Recording

Correcting General Journal entries is similar to correcting sales and cheques. After displaying the incorrect entry on the screen, you can make the changes you need and save the new transaction. QuickBooks will keep a record of the changes you have made to the original entry in the audit trail.

Most transactions completed in the Register can also be corrected from the General Journal window because they have resulted in a normal journal entry. However, there are some exceptions. Transfers of funds, like our first loan deposit, do not appear in the General Journal so they must be corrected in the Register or in the Transfer Funds window (found in the Banking menu). For this reason, we prefer to use the Make General Journal Entries form to enter journal entries. Transactions entered in other forms can also be edited in the Register window although it is generally easier to correct a transaction in the same form you used to create the original entry.

The entry we need to change is memo #6-3, the one we entered most recently. Refer to the following source document as we work through the steps to enter it:

SD10: Memo #6-4

Dated June 7, 2012

From Owner: Memo #6-3 was entered incorrectly. The amount withdrawn for personal reasons was $180.00. Edit the journal entry for memo #6-3 to make the correction.

SD Instructions
Refer to the following source document and then follow the step-by-step instructions to enter it.

1. **Click** | General Journal | the icon you created, or **choose** the **Company menu** and **click Make General Journal Entries** to open the Make General Journal Entries form

2. **Click** the **Previous button** | Previous | to view the entry for memo #6-3 on the screen

3. **Double click** the **Debit field** to highlight it

4. **Type** 180

5. **Press** (tab). Notice that the credit amount is not changed automatically

6. **Click** the **Credit field** and then **double click** to highlight **the amount**

7. **Type** 180. **Press** (tab) to enter the amount.

Click the Revert button at any time if you need to cancel the changes.

8. Review your work carefully. The corrected journal entry should be displayed as shown:

WARNING!
If you click the third line of the journal entry before you change the credit amount, QuickBooks will try to add a debit line equal to $70.00 to balance the entry. Delete this extra amount if it appears.

Figure 4-16

    9. Click   **Save & New** to leave the Make General Journal Entry form open for the next transaction

  10. You will see the warning confirmation message that appears each time you record changes to a transaction:

Figure 4-17

  11. Click   **Yes** to save the corrected entry

Creating New Expense Accounts

The next transaction uses a new Expense account. Each account type in QuickBooks has a different input form with fields to match the type of account. Refer to the following source document as we work through the steps to enter it:

SD Instructions
Refer to the following source document and then follow the step-by-step instructions to enter it.

SD11: Bank Debit Memo #DM-3771

                                      Dated June 7, 2012

    From Literary Credit Union: For monthly bank service charges, $25.00 was withdrawn from the Bank Chequing account. Create a new Expense account: Bank Charges (leave tax code blank).

    1. You should still be in the Make General Journal Entries window. The date should also be correct from the previous entry

2.	**Check**	that **06/07/12 is entered as the date**. Enter this date if necessary
3.	**Click**	the **Account field**
4.	**Type**	**Bank Charges**
5.	**Press**	(tab)

QuickBooks will try to match your entry with an existing account, so *Bank Chequing* will appear in the Account field until you type a unique sequence of letters.

| 6. | **Click** | **Set Up** when the Add New Account message is displayed |
| 7. | **Choose** | **Expense** as the Account Type: |

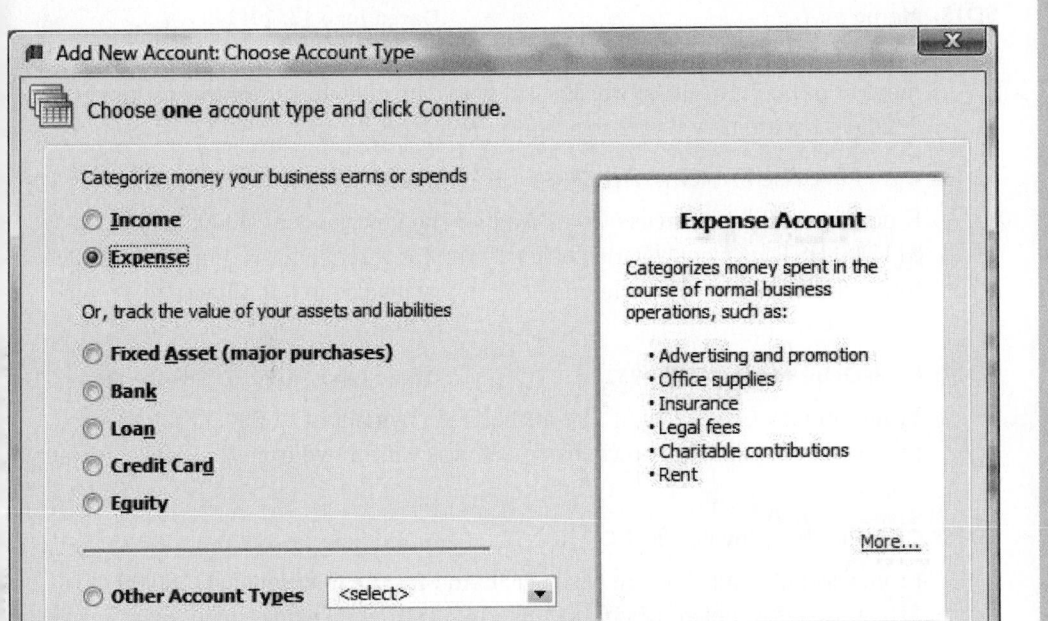

Figure 4-18

| 8. | **Click** | **Continue** |

The form is complete. The default is no tax so the default tax code entry is correct. We don't need to add a description because the name is unique and complete.

| 9. | **Click** | **Save & Close** to return to the journal entry window |
| 10. | **Complete** | the **journal entry**, **review** it, and then **save** it |

Source Documents

Continue to develop your skills by entering the following source documents in QuickBooks. Use the information in this chapter as a guide if necessary. You may also need to refer to information in Chapter 3 to complete some of the source documents.

SD12: **Bank Debit Memo #DM-3779**   **Dated June 7, 2012**

From Literary Credit Union: For interest on long term loan, $180.00 was withdrawn from the Bank Chequing account.

⚠ WARNING!
When you type Bank Charges, QuickBooks will try to enter the Bank Chequing account because the initial letters match that account. Keep typing until you replace the default entry.

On pages 120-121, we show how selecting the Add New Account option from the Account List avoids this problem.

📄 Notes
If you enter the transaction for service charges from the Bank Chequing account ledger, enter the amount in the Payment column.

Open the Chart of Accounts (press (ctrl) + **A**) and double click Bank Chequing, the asset account, to open the ledger. You cannot record transactions from an expense account ledger.

Enter the debit memo number in the Number field.

📄 Notes
Banks use the terms *debit* and *credit* in the opposite way that accountants use the terms. A debit for the bank (the bank receives a payment for bank charges or interest from you) is a bank account credit for you (you have incurred an expense). Money deposited to your bank account, such as interest received or sales deposits (your debit), is a credit for the bank (they owe that money to you).

📄 SD Practice
Continue to develop your skills by entering the following source document(s).

SD13: Memo #6-5   Dated June 7, 2012

From Owner: Paid $280.00 in cash to various customers for books during the week. No HST was included in the purchase because the customers were not registered to collect HST. Use the General Journal for this transaction and choose Cash Customers in the Name field.

SD14: Sales Receipt #617   Dated June 9, 2012

Sold to Chaucer Shakespeare (use Quick Add for the new customer), $860.00 plus $111.80 HST for books and $40.00 for book bags plus $5.20 HST. Sales total of $1,017.00 was paid by cheque #684 and deposited to the Bank Chequing account.

SD15: Memo #6-6   Dated June 12, 2012

From Owner: Water entered the store from an open window and damaged a number of books in the store. The value of damaged inventory was estimated at $620.00. Create new Expense account: Inventory Losses.

SD16: Cash Purchase Invoice #SHN-3095   Dated June 13, 2012

From Signal Hill News (use Quick Add for the new vendor), $900.00 plus $117.00 HST for weekly series of ads to run for three months. Purchase invoice totalled $1,017.00. Wrote cheque #439 to pay invoice in full. Charge to Prepaid Advertising.

SD17: Bank Debit Memo #DM-4982   Dated June 14, 2012

From Literary Credit Union: Pre-authorized payment of $1,500.00 to reduce principal owing on short-term bank loan was withdrawn from the Bank Chequing account.

SD18: Cash Purchase Invoice #OAC-718   Dated June 14, 2012

From Oswald's Auto Centre (use Quick Add for the new vendor), $80.00 plus $10.40 HST for fuel and $110.00 plus $14.30 HST for regular maintenance service of business automobile. Purchase invoice totalled $214.70. Wrote cheque #440 to pay invoice in full. Create new Expense account: Vehicle Maintenance (choose H as the default tax code).

SD19: Sales Receipt #618   Dated June 14, 2012

Sales to cash customers in past week, $6,200.00 plus $806.00 HST for books and $300.00 plus $39.00 HST for book bags. All customers paid cash for their purchases. Sales totalling $7,345.00 were deposited to the Bank Chequing account.

SD20: Cash Purchase Invoice #SC-98998   Dated June 15, 2012

From Signal Communications, $210.00 plus $27.30 HST for monthly telephone bill, including Internet and mobile phone charges. Purchase invoice totalled $237.30. Wrote cheque #441 to pay invoice in full.

SD21: Memo #6-7   Dated June 15, 2012

From Owner: Another small batch of water-damaged books was found. The value of damaged inventory was revised to $750.00. Edit memo #6-6 to make the correction.

SD22: Memo #6-8   Dated June 15, 2012

From Owner: Paid $380.00 in cash to various customers for books during the week. No HST was included in the purchases because the customers were not registered to collect HST.

SD23: Sales Receipt #619   **Dated June 18, 2012**

Sold to Austen Bronte (use Quick Add for the new customer), $530.00 plus $68.90 HST for books and $40.00 plus $5.20 HST for canvas book bags. Sales total $644.10 paid in full by cheque #6102 and deposited to the Bank Chequing account.

SD24: Cash Purchase Invoice #OE-216   **Dated June 20, 2012**

From Office Essentials, $240.00 plus $31.20 HST for printer cartridges, paper, and invoice forms. Purchase invoice totalled $271.20. Wrote cheque #442 to pay invoice in full.

SD25: Sales Receipt #620   **Dated June 21, 2012**

Sales to cash customers in past week, $5,900.00 plus $767.00 HST for books and $420.00 plus $54.60 HST for book bags. All customers paid cash for their purchases. Sales totalling $7,141.60 deposited to the Bank Chequing account.

SD26: Bank Debit Memo #DM-5118   **Dated June 21, 2012**

From Literary Credit Union: For interest on short-term bank loan, $45.00 was withdrawn from the Bank Chequing account.

SD27: Cash Purchase Invoice #KCMS-455   **Dated June 21, 2012**

From Keep Clean Maintenance Services (use Quick Add for the new vendor), $440.00 plus $57.20 HST for contracted store cleaning service for one month. Purchase invoice totalled $497.20. Wrote cheque #443 to pay invoice in full.

SD28: Memo #6-9   **Dated June 22, 2012**

From Owner: Paid $445.00 in cash to various customers for books during the week. No HST was included in the purchase because the customers were not registered to collect HST.

SD29: Sales Receipt #621   **Dated June 25, 2012**

Sold to Atwood Ondaatje (use Quick Add for the new customer), $380.00 plus $49.40 HST for books and $20.00 plus $2.60 HST for canvas book bag. Sales totalling $452.00 were paid in full by cheque #249 and deposited to the Bank Chequing account.

SD30: Cash Purchase Invoice #MU-1649   **Dated June 26, 2012**

From Memorial University (use Quick Add for the new vendor), $1,250.00 plus $162.50 HST for used books. Purchase invoice total $1,412.50. Wrote cheque #444 to pay invoice in full.

SD31: Cash Purchase Invoice #OAC-1020   **Dated June 28, 2012**

From Oswald's Auto Centre, $70.00 plus $9.10 HST for fuel for business automobile. Purchase invoice totalled $79.10. Wrote cheque #445 to pay invoice in full.

SD32 Sales Receipt #622   **Dated June 29, 2012**

Sales to cash customers in past week, $6,900.00 plus $897.00 HST for books and $360.00 plus $46.80 HST for book bags. All customers paid cash for their purchases. Sales totalling $8,203.80 were deposited to the Bank Chequing account.

SD33: Memo #6-10   **Dated June 30, 2012**

From Owner: Paid $310.00 in cash to various customers for books during the week. No HST was included in the purchase because the customers were not registered to collect HST.

Compound Journal Entries

All the General Journal entries so far have involved a single debit and matching credit amount. When we complete end-of-period adjustments, we frequently need to make a compound entry, like the one in memo #6-11. Refer to the following source document as we work through the steps to enter it:

SD34: Memo #6-11

SD Instructions
Refer to the following source document and then follow the step-by-step instructions to enter it.

Dated June 30, 2012

Complete an adjusting entry for the inventory and supplies used during the month.

Books	$11,900.00
Canvas Bags	500.00
Paper and Plastic Bags	245.00
Office Supplies	140.00

We will follow traditional accounting practice and enter all the debit amounts first.

1. **Open** the **Make Journal Entries form** if it is not open already
2. **Enter** **06/30/12** as the date if this date does not appear by default from the previous transaction entered
3. **Choose** **Cost of Books Sold** as the first account
4. **Press** (tab) to advance to the Debit field
5. **Type** **11900**
6. **Enter** an **appropriate comment** in the Memo field
7. **Choose** **Cost of Bags Sold** as the second account

The amount $11,900.00 appears as the default amount in the Credit field for the account. We need to enter another debit amount for the second cost account.

8. **Press** (tab) field to advance to the Debit field
9. **Type** **500**
10. Now amounts appear in both the Debit and Credit fields as shown:

Notes
You can complete these adjustments as four separate journal entries if you want.

Figure 4-19

11. **Press**	(tab)	to enter the debit amount and remove the default credit entry
12. **Choose**	**Plastic Bags Used** as the third account

The credit amount is updated to $12,400.00 because this amount will now balance the journal entry; however, we have more debit amounts to enter.

13. **Press**	(tab)	to advance to the Debit field
14. **Type**	**245**	
15. **Choose**	**Office Supplies Used** in the Account field on the next line	
16. **Press**	(tab)	to advance to the Debit field
17. **Type**	**140**	
18. **Choose**	**Book Inventory** as the next account	

The total of all debit amounts appears as the default credit amount as shown here:

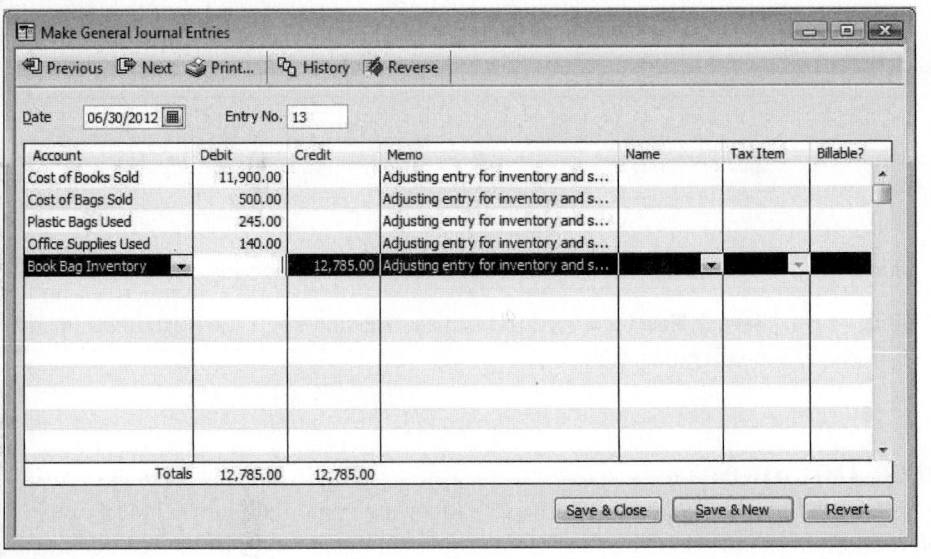

Figure 4-20

19. **Press**	(tab)	to advance to the Credit field and **select** the **default entry**
20. **Type**	**11900**	
21. **Choose**	**Book Bag Inventory** as the next Account	

Notice that the default credit amount has been decreased by the $11,900.00 we entered for *Book Inventory*.

22. **Press**	(tab)	to advance to the Credit field
23. **Type**	**500**	
24. **Choose**	**Plastic Bags** as the next Account	

The default credit amount is reduced again.

25. **Press**	(tab)	to advance to the Credit field
26. **Type**	**245**	

27. Choose   **Office Supplies** as the final account

28. The remaining credit default amount of $140.00 correctly matches the entry for this account so we can accept it to complete the entry as shown:

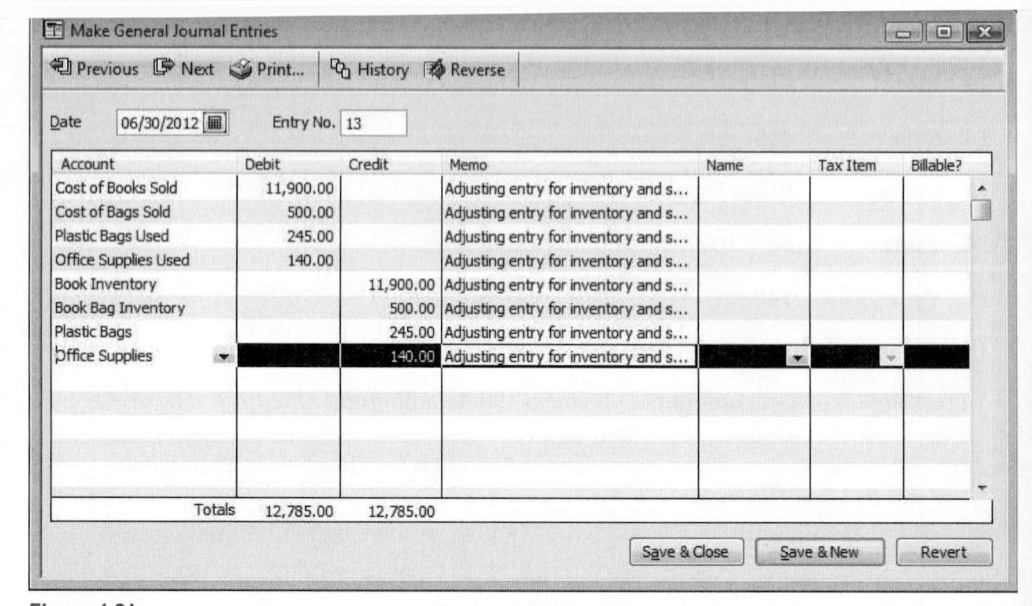

Figure 4-21

29. Check   your **entry** carefully and **make corrections** if needed

30. Click   **Save & New** to record the transaction and keep the form open for the next transaction

Source Documents

Continue to develop your skills by entering the following compound journal entry. Use the information in the previous transaction as a guide if necessary. The source document is as follows:

SD Practice
Continue to develop your skills by entering the following source document(s).

SD35: Memo #6-12   **Dated June 30, 2012**

From Owner: Enter the adjustments for prepaid expenses expired.

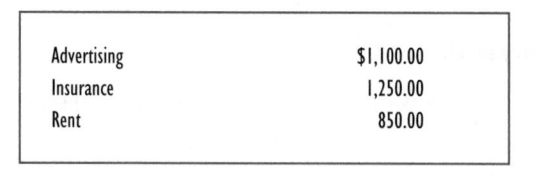

Advertising	$1,100.00
Insurance	1,250.00
Rent	850.00

Using the Add New Account Option

The final source document in this chapter requires a new depreciation account. Refer to the following source document as we work through the steps to enter it:

SD36: Memo #6-13

SD Instructions
Refer to the following source document and then follow the step-by-step instructions to enter it.

Dated June 30, 2012

From Owner: Complete an adjusting entry for six months of depreciation on fixed assets. Create a new Expense account: Depreciation Expenses (leave the tax code blank). Use the calculator to calculate the total depreciation amount.

AAutomobile	$2,295.00
Computer Equipment	1,020.00
Store Furniture and Fixtures	1,425.00

Although the source document requires a new depreciation account, depreciation is already used as an account name for the subaccounts for fixed assets. This will make it difficult to add the account by typing the name in the Account field, because QuickBooks will try to use the Computer Equipment:Depreciation account. In addition, we will enter the amount for depreciation as a single total amount for all assets, and we will use the built-in calculator to find the correct amount.

The date should be correct from the previous entry.

1. **Enter**   **06/30/12** as the date if necessary

2. **Click**   the **drop-down arrow in the Account field** to open the list of accounts as shown:

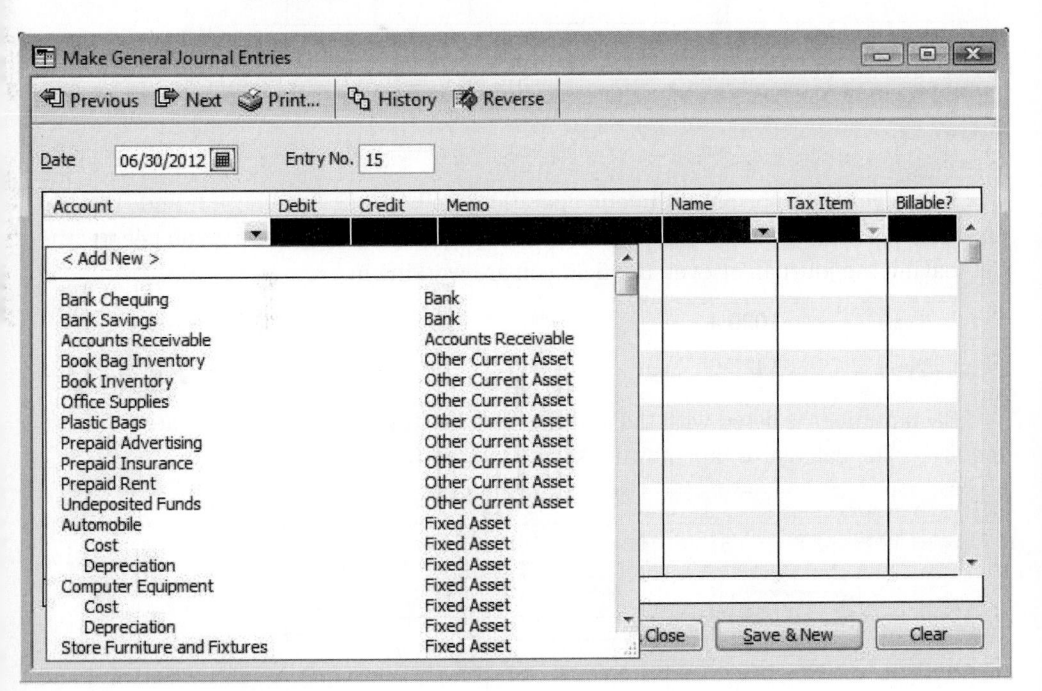

Figure 4-22

Notice that the first item on the list is the option to add a new account.

3. **Click**   **<Add New>** to open the new account form

4. **Choose**   **Expense** as the Account Type

5. **Press**   **Continue**

6. **Type**   **Depreciation Expense** as the Account Name

7. **Click**   **Save & Close** to return to the Journal

Notes
Choose Add New Account from the Account list to add the Depreciation Expense account.

Using the QuickBooks Calculator

Following the usual accounting practice, we will enter the debit part of the transaction first. Therefore, we must calculate the total amount for *Depreciation Expense*. We will use the built-in QuickBooks calculator to do the addition for us.

8. Click   the **Debit field**

9. Type   **2295**

10. Press   **+** (the plus sign) to open the calculator tape as shown:

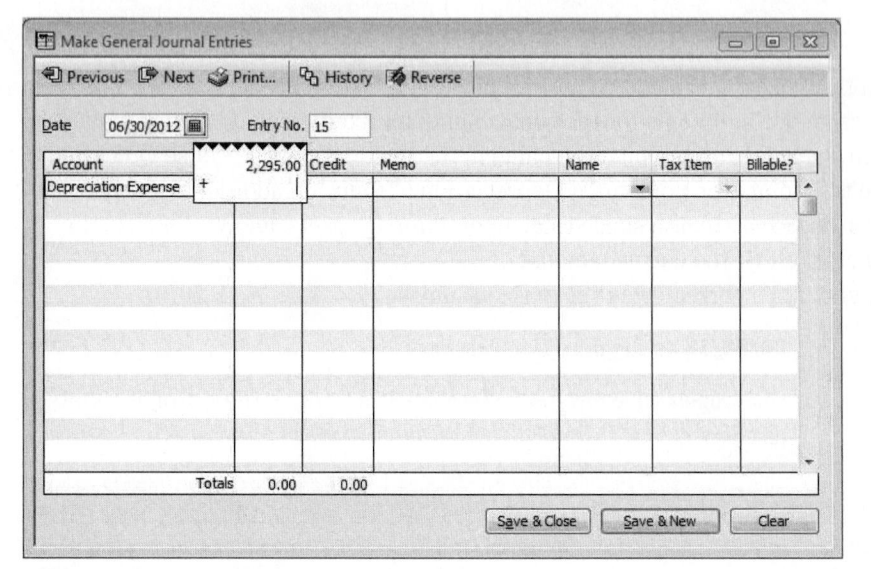

Figure 4-23

Whenever you type an arithmetic operation symbol character (+, −, *, and /) in an amount field, the calculator opens so you can complete the calculations you need without leaving the journal, or even the field you are working in.

11. Type   **1020 +**

12. Type   **1425**

Each number is listed with the addition sign beside it to show the operation required. The calculator tape now looks like the one below

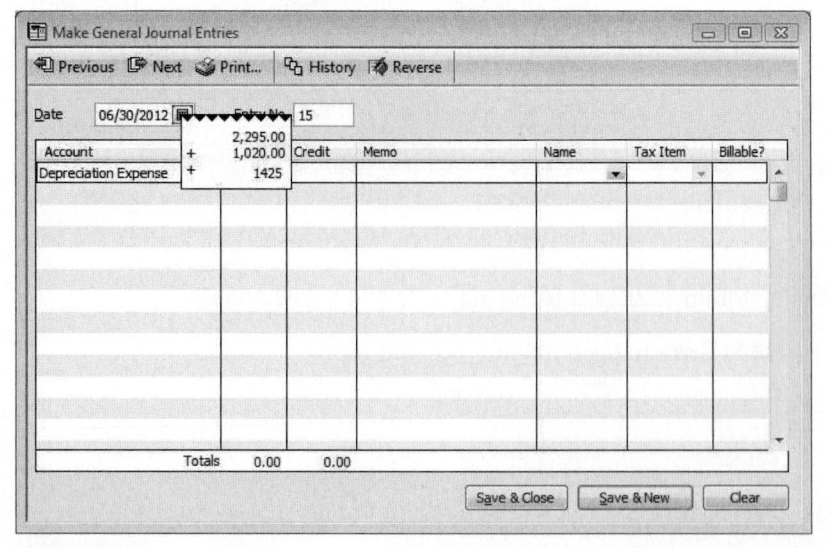

Figure 4-24

13.	**Press**	(enter) to add the total to the journal
14.	**Click**	the **Memo field** and **type total depreciation**
15.	**Enter**	the **three asset accounts, amounts, and memos for the transaction**. (Choose **Depreciation** under **Automobile**, **Computer Equipment**, and **Store Furniture and Fixtures** to select the correct asset accounts)
16.	**Review**	your **work** and **make corrections** if necessary
17.	**Click**	**Save & Close** to return to the QuickBooks Home page. You will see the following message:

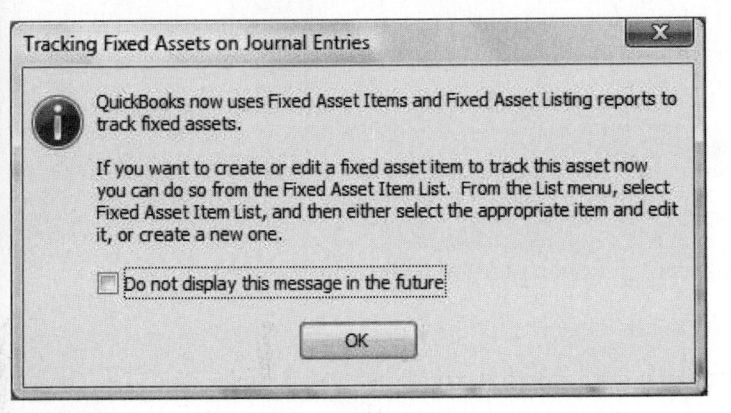

Figure 4-25

We are not using QuickBooks to track fixed assets.

18.	**Click**	the **Do not display this message in the future check box**
19.	**Click**	**OK** to continue

General Reports

QuickBooks has a large number of reports built in, and all of these can be customized or modified to suit your individual business needs. Many of the reports include similar details so you can arrive at the final report in more than one way.

In this chapter, we will show the detail version of the Profit & Loss Statement and the Balance Sheet reports. In addition, we will view the remaining reports that relate to all accounts: the General Ledger Report, the Transaction Detail Report by Account, and the Transaction List by Date. We will also cover the Chart of Accounts or Account Listing and some custom and transaction reports in this chapter. We will also show how to customize these reports by changing the headers and removing and adding details.

Many reports can be accessed from the Chart of Accounts so we will start there.

1.	**Click**	[Chart of Accounts] in the Company section of the Home page or **press** (ctrl) + **A** to open the Chart of Accounts

The Reports button menu in the Chart of Accounts window is shown selected:

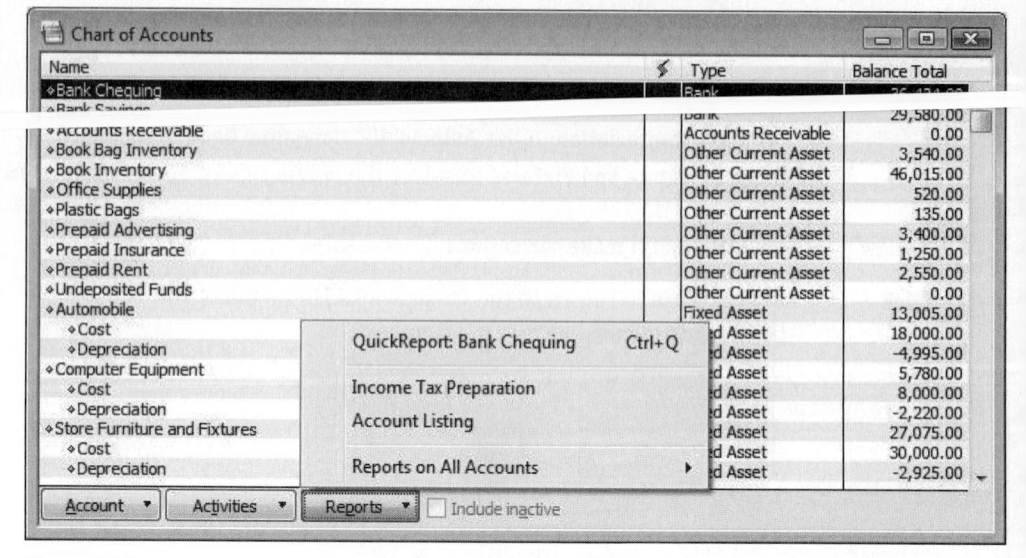

Figure 4-26

Other list windows also have a Reports button with reports related to that list.

The Chart of Accounts (Account Listing)

The Chart of Accounts or Account Listing provides a list of all General Ledger accounts and their current account balances. There is no Date field — the current calendar date is shown — but the report always shows the latest account balances.

1. Choose the **Reports button** (at the bottom of the Chart of Accounts window) and **click Account Listing** to open the report:

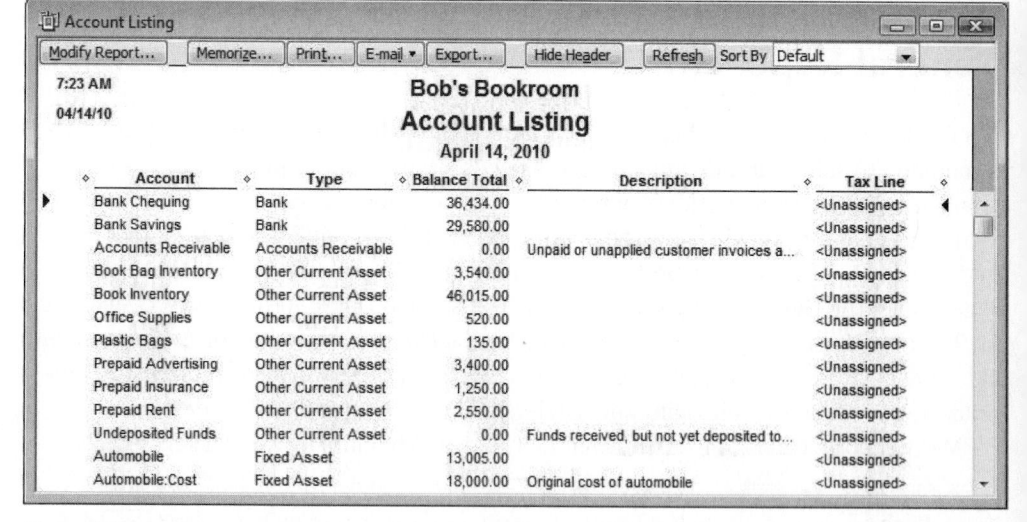

Figure 4-27

The report shows the current calendar date in the report heading. All accounts are included with their name, account type, description (if one was included in the record), current balance and tax line (if one was assigned). Account balances are displayed for Balance Sheet accounts except the Retained Earnings account.

Notes

To access the report from the Reports menu:
- Choose the Reports menu, then choose List and click Account Listing; or
- Choose the Reports menu, then choose Accountant & Taxes and click Account Listing

Notes

We first prepared this report on April 14, 2010, so this date is displayed in the heading of the report. The date on your reports will reflect your current computer date.

Notes

To access the Account Listing from the Report Centre:
- Click the Report Centre icon on the Icon bar, then choose the List heading on the left-hand side of the screen, and click Account Listing under the Listing heading; or
- Click the Report Centre icon on the Icon bar, then choose the Accountant & Taxes heading on the left-hand side of the screen, and click Account Listing under the Listing heading

Modifying Reports

We have not assigned a tax line to accounts for Bob's Bookroom so we will modify the report to omit this information.

1. Click   the **Modify Report button** (on the upper left-hand corner of the Icon bar in the report window) to open the Modify Report window:

Figure 4-28

The Modify Report window opens with the Display tab shown. From this window, we can choose the details that we want to add to or remove from the report. Each detail is listed in a separate column so you can choose the columns for the report. Columns with a ✓ beside the name are on the report. Clicking any column name will add a ✓ if one is not there and remove it if it is present. From this window you can also enter sorting criteria for the report: default, account, type, balance total, description, or tax line, and you can show any of these in ascending or descending order.

We want to remove the empty Tax Line column.

2. Click   **Tax Line under the Columns heading**. The ✓ is removed

3. Click   **OK** to return to the report and view the results

4. Click   the **Modify Report button** again so that we can make further changes

Click **Revert** at any time to cancel your changes and to return to the default selections and format. The Revert button applies only to the changes made on the tab screen that is open.

Filtering Reports

Filtering Reports involves setting criteria for what you will include in the report. For example, you might want to create a list of all Asset accounts that have balances less than $1,000.00. Or you might want to report only Ex~~~~~

| 5. **Click** | the **Filters tab** to view the filters available: |

Figure 4-29

Different reports have different filters available. For each filter named, a different input field appears for entering your selections. You cannot use the same filter more than once, but you can apply more than one filter. For example, you can choose Current Asset as the account Type for the first filter and Balance > 1,000.00 as the second filter to show only Asset accounts that have a balance greater than $1,000.00.

6. **Click**	**Name Contains** in the list of filters
7. **Type**	**Depreciation** in the text box and **press** (tab) to add the filter to the list of current filter choices
8. **Click**	**OK** to view the list of active accumulated depreciation asset accounts and the depreciation expense account in the Account Listing report
9. **Click**	the **Modify Report button** and **click** the **Filters tab** again
10. **Click**	**each filter** in turn and **watch** the changes to the **selection field**
11. **Click**	the **Revert button** to remove the filters
12. **Click**	**Account in the Filter list**. An Account field with a drop-down arrow is displayed
13. **Click**	**All Fixed Assets** in the drop-down list

Currently, the active status filter is selected and set to Active and the Account filter is set to All fixed assets.

> **Notes**
> You need to press (tab) to enter the Name Contains filter so that the program will know when you have finished typing the text that serves as the filter. When you select a filter from a drop-down list, the filter is added to the choices immediately.

If you want to change the report filter, click a Filter in the Current Filter Choices and click Remove Selected Filter to remove the filter from the Current Choices list, or click Revert to remove all filters.

14. **Click**   **OK** to view the list of active fixed asset accounts in the Account Listing report

15. **Click**   the **Modify Report button** and **click** the **Filters tab** again

Changing Report Headers and Footers

Headers and footers in the report affect the appearance but not the data in the report. Again, you can modify the information contained in these parts of the report. We will change the report title to Fixed Assets and Depreciation to match our revised list. We will also change the report date (subtitle) and remove the date and time prepared. Then we will add our own names to the report footer for reference.

1. **Click**   the **Header/Footer tab**:

Figure 4-30

2. **Highlight**   **Account Listing** in the **Report Title text field** to select the title

3. **Type**   **Fixed Assets and Depreciation**

4. **Highlight**   the **date** in the **Subtitle field**

5. **Type**   **June 30, 2012**

6. **Click**   the **Date Prepared check box** to remove the ✓

7. **Click**   the **Time Prepared check box** to remove the ✓

8. **Click**   the **text field for the Extra Footer line**

9. **Type**   **Prepared by <add your own name>**

10. **Click**   **OK** to see the revised report

Review the changes that you made to the report. The footers are not displayed on-screen; however, they are displayed when the report is printed.

Changing Report Fonts and Numbers

You can alter the appearance of the report in other ways too. You can change the font (type face or appearance of the letters) and size for different parts of the report. You can also change the way numbers are presented in the report. We will show negative numbers in red for this report.

1. **Click**   the **Modify Report button** again so that we can make further changes (assuming the Account Listing report is still displayed on the screen)

2. **Click**   the **Fonts & Numbers tab**:

Notes
Notice the underlined letters in the options that indicate keyboard shortcuts. Press `alt` plus the underlined letter to make the selection.

Figure 4-31

You can change the font and size for each part of the report separately. The text displayed for the word, Example, displayed in the middle of the screen, shows you the current style selected for the highlighted option.

3. **Click**   an **entry on the Change Font For list**

4. **Click**   the **Change Font button** to open the Font dialogue box

5. **Choose**   the **font, style, size, effects, and colour** for the item

Click Revert in the Font & Numbers tab screen at any time to change the style back to the default settings.

6. **Click**   **OK** to save the changes

7. **Click**   **No** to change all related fonts when prompted

You can also choose a preferred style for numbers in the chart. Negative numbers may be displayed in black or bright red type, in parentheses (brackets), or with a minus sign before or after. All numbers may be shown as dollar amounts only, omitting the cents, or in thousands of dollars. This last feature is useful for companies that have very large amounts and want to make their summary reports more readable.

Notes
If no printer is set up, you will see a pop-up message suggesting that a printer be set up.

We will change the appearance of negative numbers.

8.	**Click**	**In Parentheses**. The number example to the right changes to match your selection
9.	**Click**	**In Bright Red** to change the number example again
10.	**Click**	**OK** to view the revised report

We no longer need the account type in the report because the report includes only one type. We can remove the column from the report by selecting the appropriate option on the Display tab, as we did for the Tax Line column, or we can drag the account type column marker to the left directly on the report until the column is completely removed from the report, as we did in the previous chapter.

11.	**Click**	the **Modify Reports** button to open the Display tab screen
12.	**Click**	**Type in the Columns list** to remove the ✓
13.	**Click**	**OK** to view the final report
14.	**Click**	the **Print button** and then **click Preview**. Your report should look like the one that follows:

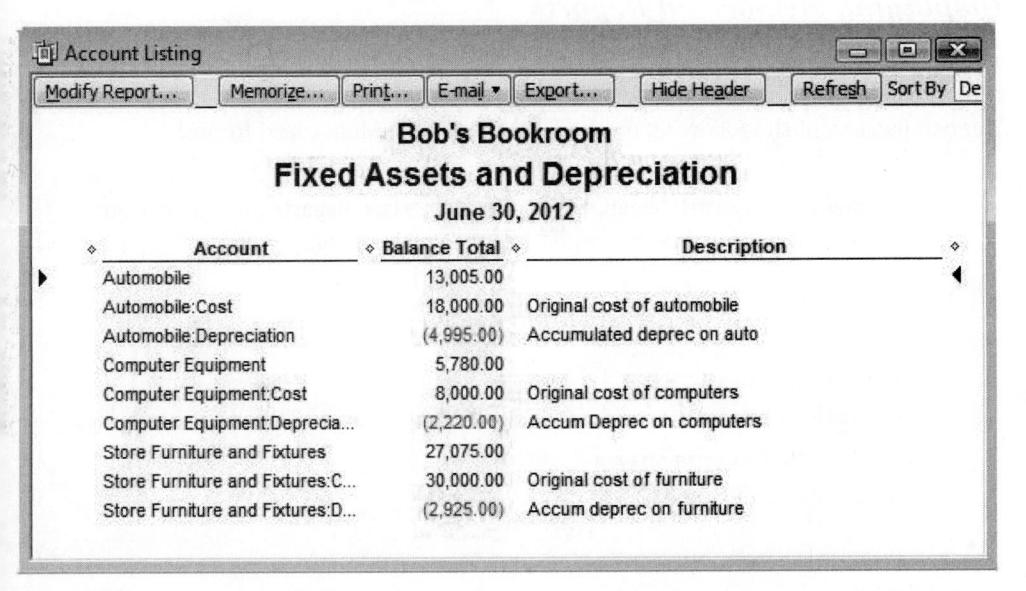

Figure 4-32

15.	**Click**	**Print** to begin printing or **click Close** to return to the Print Reports dialogue box
16.	**Click**	**Cancel** to close the Print Reports dialogue box and return to the Account Listing report

Memorizing Reports

We have made a number of changes to the report, so we should save the report under a new name to make it available later with the modifications.

1.	**Click**	the **Memorize button** in the report display screen to open the Memorize Report dialogue box:

Figure 4-33

The suggested name for the report is the revised report title. You can accept this or enter a different name. The memorized report will be found on the Memorized Reports list, either within one of the existing report groups or on its own. We will accept the name. We will also place the report on its own in the list rather than in a group.

2. **Click**   **OK**

3. **Close**   the **report**

Displaying Memorized Reports

You will now be able to access the report you just memorized, and any other memorized reports from the Reports menu or from the Memorized Report link in the Report Centre. You can use any of the following methods to display the Memorized Report:

    a.   **Choose** the **Reports menu,** then **click Memorized Reports** and the various memorized reports and report groups will be displayed as shown; or

Reports	
Report Centre	
Company Snapshot	
Memorized Reports ▶	Memorized Report List
Process Multiple Reports	Accountant ▶
Financial Statement Designer	Banking ▶
Company & Financial ▶	Company ▶
Sales Tax ▶	Customers ▶
Customers & Receivables ▶	Employees ▶
Sales ▶	Fixed Assets and Depreciation
Jobs, Time & Mileage ▶	Nonprofit ▶
Vendors & Payables ▶	Vendors ▶

Figure 4-34

b. **Choose** the **Reports menu, click Memorized Reports**, and then **click Memorized Report List** to view the new report added to the Memorized Report List; or

Figure 4-35

c. **Click** the **Report Centre icon** from the Icon bar and **click** the **Memorized link** in the top right-hand corner of the Report Centre to display the Memorized Transaction List as shown in Figure 4-35

The Fixed Assets and Depreciation report is displayed by itself on the menu in Figure 4-34 and in Figure 4-35 because we did not add it to a group when we memorized it. The menu options with right arrows in Figure 4-34 indicate that they are a group that contain memorized reports, and the headings in Figure 4-35 indicate they are a group.

Profit & Loss Statement (Income Statement) YTD Comparison

This Income Statement Report allows you to compare a selected period with a previous period of the same length, either in the same year or in a previous year.

To access the report from the Reports menu, see the margin notes.

1. **Click**   the **Report Centre Icon** on the Icon bar to open the Report Centre for the remaining reports

2. **Choose**   the **Company & Financial heading** on the left-hand side of the screen and then **click YTD Comparison** under the **Profit & Loss (Income Statement) heading**

3. **Enter**   **06/01/12** as the **From date** for the report

4. **Enter**   **06/30/12** as the **To date**

5. **Press**   ⌨ *tab* or **click** the **Refresh button** to update the report:

Notes
To access the report from the Reports menu:
• Choose the Reports menu, then choose Company & Financial, and click Profit & Loss YTD Comparison to open the report
  • Enter 06/01/12 as the From date for the report
  • Enter 06/30/12 as the To date
• Press *tab* or click the Refresh button to update the report

Figure 4-36

The current, selected period is compared with the year-to-date totals. To include a separate column for the year prior to the selected period, you can modify the report.

6. Click   the **Modify Report button** to display the Modify Report Dialogue box, which opens on the Display tab:

Figure 4-37

You can add columns for a previous period (of the same length as the date range you entered), for year-to-date amounts, and for amounts for the previous year, if you have them. You can also add columns for percentages of the total row, column, income, or expense amounts if you want. When you add a previous period, you can include the dollar amount or percentage change from period to period.

Another option is to display columns by total, by day, by week, or by some other criterion you select from the Display columns by drop-down list.

We will add two columns to the report.

7.	**Click**	**Previous Period** to add a ✓
8.	**Click**	**% of YTD** under the Year-To-Date heading
9.	**Click**	**OK** to view the revised report
10.	**Close**	the **report** when finished. Do not save the changes

Notes
The May column is actually the total for the period from January 1 to May 31. This total comes from the summary historical data that was entered for May 31st to set up the company files.

Detail and Transaction Reports

In the previous chapter, we saw standard reports that showed the total amounts for the selected period. We will now look at more detailed reports that include listings for individual transactions. The reports that follow show similar kinds of information for different groups of accounts.

Profit & Loss Statement (Income Statement) Detail

This report shows a Profit & Loss Statement with the individual transactions that made up the income and expenses for the selected period.

To access the report from the Reports menu, see the margin notes.

| 1. | **Click** | the **Report Centre icon** on the Icon bar to open the Report Centre |
| 2. | **Choose** | the **Company & Financial** heading on the left-hand side of the screen and **click Detail** under the **Profit & Loss (Income Statement) heading** |

We need to set the report dates.

3.	**Enter**	**06/01/12** as the **From date** for the report
4.	**Enter**	**06/30/12** as the **To date**
5.	**Press**	⟨tab⟩ or **click Refresh** to update the report:

Notes
To access the report from the Reports menu:
• Choose the Reports menu, then choose Company & Financial, and click Profit & Loss Detail
• Change the report dates because there is no data for the current month
• Enter 06/01/12 as the From date for the report
• Enter 06/30/12 as the To date
• Press ⟨tab⟩ or click Refresh to update the report

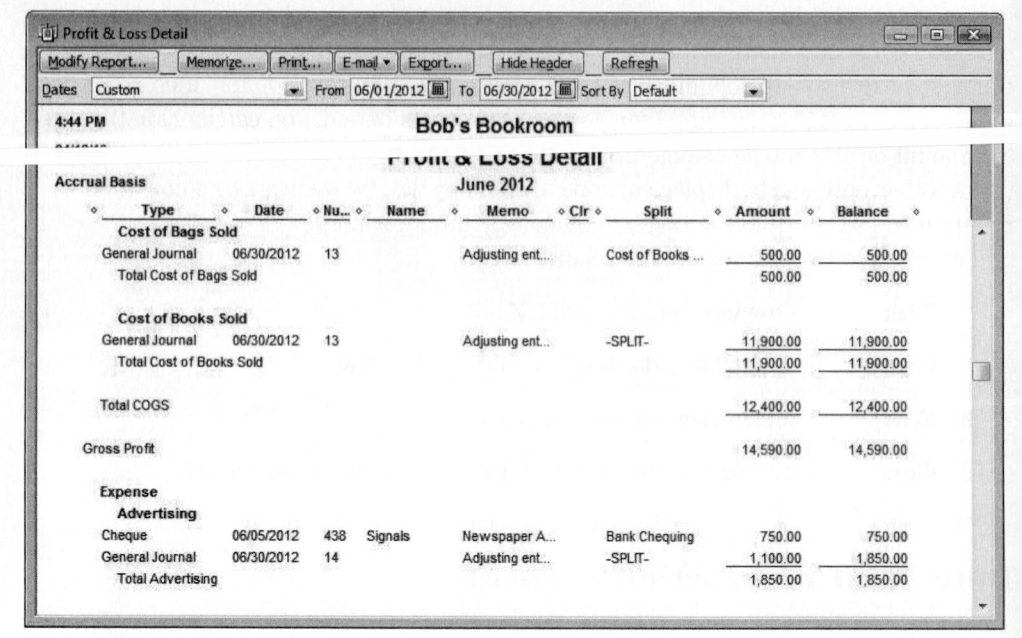

Figure 4-38

We have shown the Cost of Goods and part of the Expenses section of the statement. The report shows each transaction for each account for the income period selected. The more detailed reports can help to identify individual items that may be unreasonably high or low for a period, and may point to errors in data entry or to the need for analysis of company costs.

Double click any part of a transaction to drill down to the original transaction entry. When you drill down to the transaction, you can make any necessary corrections. When you return to the report, it will be updated with the changes you made to the transaction. Double click a total amount in the report to view the transaction detail report for that total.

6. Close the **report** when you have finished reviewing it. Do not save the changes

Balance Sheet Detail Report

Just as the Income Statement was available in a detailed version, so is the Balance Sheet. Again the individual transactions that make up the balances for all Balance Sheet accounts are shown on the Balance Sheet Detail report.

1. Open the **Report Centre** if it is not already displayed from the previous exercise

2. Choose the **Company & Financial heading** on the left-hand side of the screen and **click Detail** under the **Balance Sheet & Net Worth heading**

3. Enter **06/01/12** as the **From date**

4. Enter **06/30/12** as the **To date**

5. Press [tab] or **click Refresh** to update the report:

Notes
To access the Balance Sheet Detail Report from the Reports menu:
- Choose the Reports menu, then choose Company & Financial, and click Balance Sheet Detail
  - Enter 06/30/12 as the To date
- Press [tab] or click the Refresh button to update the report

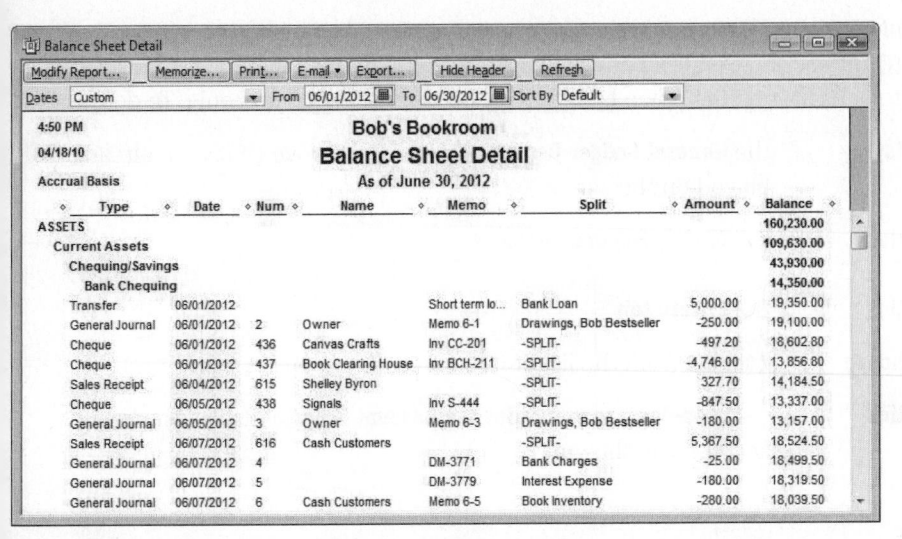

Figure 4-39

    This form of the Balance Sheet shows the totals for asset subgroups (Current Assets and Chequing/Savings) at the top of each section of the report, followed by the listing of transactions for each account.

    Double click any transaction detail to view the original entry. Double clicking on a General Journal entry will open the Register for the account.

    6. Close   the **report** when finished

General Ledger Report

The General Ledger Report shows all accounting transactions for a selected period in order by accounts. All accounts will be included in the report.

    1. Open   the **Report Centre** if it is not already displayed from the previous exercise

    2. Choose   the **Accountant & Taxes heading** on the left-hand side of the screen and **click General Ledger** under the **Account Activity heading**

    3. Enter   **06/01/12 as the From date** for the report

    4. Enter   **06/30/12 as the To date**

    5. Press   ⟨tab⟩ to **click Refresh** and update the report

Some transactions for the Bank Chequing account are shown here:

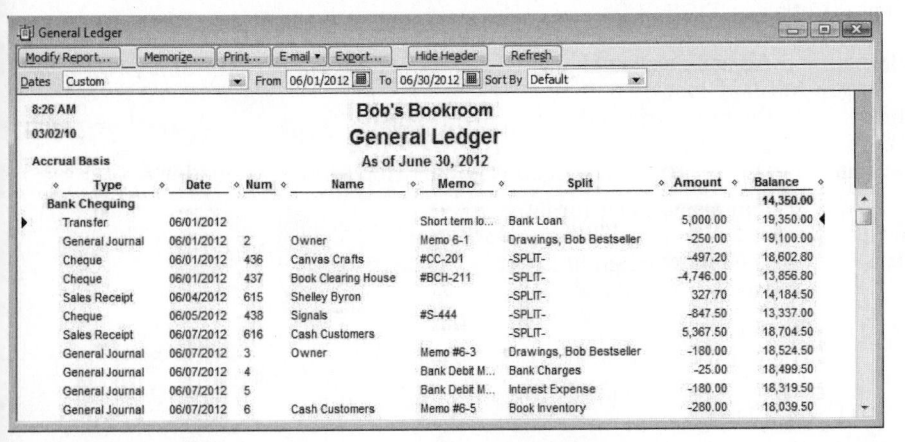

Figure 4-40

Notes
To access the General Ledger Report from the Reports menu:
- Choose the Reports menu, then choose Accountant & Taxes, and click General Ledger to open the report
  - Enter 06/01/12 as the From date for the report.
  - Enter 06/30/12 as the To date
- Press ⟨tab⟩ or click the Refresh button to view the report

Double click any transaction detail to view the original entry.

You might use the General Ledger Report to compare the company records with a bank statement for reconciliation by reporting on the bank accounts only. To do this:

1. **Display** the **General Ledger Report** as instructed above (if it's not already displayed on the screen)

Notes
We modify the General Ledger Report in Chapter 9 to prepare for bank reconciliation.

2. **Click** the **Modify Report button**

3. **Click** the **Filters tab**

4. **Choose** **Account** from the list of filters

5. **Click** the **drop-down arrow under the Account field** to display the list of accounts as shown:

Figure 4-41

You can select a group of accounts from the list or scroll down the list to select an individual account.

6. **Click** **All bank accounts**

7. **Click** **OK** to return to the modified report

8. **Rename** this **report** Bank Account Ledger Report on the Header/Footer tab and **memorize** it for later use

9. **Close** the **report** when finished

Transaction Detail by Account Report

The Transaction Detail by Account Report also shows the transactions that have been entered for each account.

Notes
To access the Transaction Detail by Account Report from the Reports menu:
- Choose the Reports menu, then choose Accountant & Taxes and click Transaction Detail by Account
- Accept any warning messages
- Enter 06/01/12 as the From date for the report
- Enter 06/30/12 as the To date
- Press (tab) or click the Refresh button to update the report

1. **Open**   the **Report Centre** if it is not already displayed from the previous exercise

2. **Choose**   the **Accountant & Taxes heading** on the left-hand side of the screen and **click Transaction Detail By Account** under the **Account Activity heading**

3. **Click**   the **Do not display this message in the future** check box if you receive the warning message about Collapsing and Expanding Transactions

4. **Click**   **OK** to continue

5. **Enter**   **06/01/12 as the From date** for the report

6. **Enter**   **06/30/12 as the To date**

7. **Press**   (tab) or **click Refresh** to update the report

The report does not include the opening balances for the accounts that were entered on May 31, 2012, so many of the Balance Sheet accounts have negative balances. We can change the start date for the report to show the opening balances as well.

8. **Enter**   **05/31/12 as the From date** for the report and **press** (tab) twice or **click** the **Refresh** button to update the report

The transactions for the *Book Bag Inventory* and *Book Inventory* accounts are shown here:

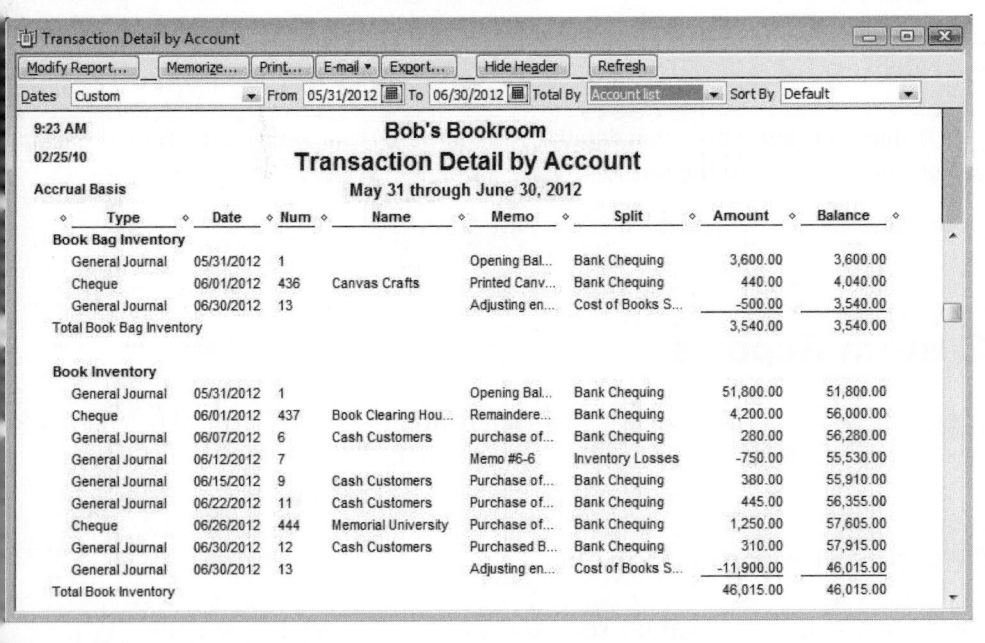

Figure 4-42

Double click any transaction detail to drill down to the original entry. Double clicking journal entries will open the register for the account.

9. **Close**   the **report** when you have finished viewing it

Transaction List by Date Report

The Transaction List by Date Report also shows all transactions that have been entered during the selected periods.

To access the Transaction List by Date Report from the Reports menu:
- Choose the Reports menu, then choose Accountant & Taxes and click Transaction List by Date to open the report
  - Enter 06/01/2012 as the From date for the report
  - Enter 06/30/2012 as the To date
  - Press (tab) or click Refresh to view the report

1. **Open**   the **Report Centre** if it is not already displayed from the previous exercise

2. **Choose**   the **Accountant & Taxes heading** on the left-hand side of the screen and **click Transaction List by Date** under the **Account Activity heading**

3. **Enter**   **06/01/12 as the From date** for the report

4. **Enter**   **06/30/12 as the To date**

5. **Press**   (tab) or **click** the **Refresh button** to view the report:

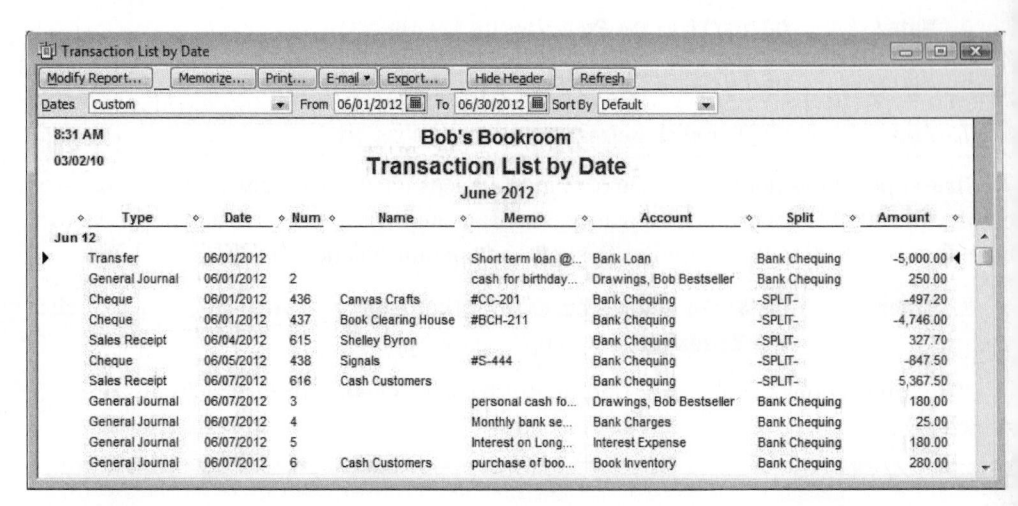

Figure 4-43

   Double click any transaction detail to drill down to the original entry. Double clicking journal entries will open the register for the account.

6. **Close**   the **report** when you have finished

Custom Reports

The two custom reports are similar to other reports but they are intended to be modified to suit your own needs. They are not available from the Report Centre.

Custom Summary Report

The Custom Summary Report is a standard Income Statement; however, it can be used to create customized income statements for your business.

1. **Choose**   the **Reports menu** and **click Custom Summary Report**

   The report opens in the background and the Modify Report window opens in front so that you can make your changes before viewing the report:

Figure 4-44

The modification options are almost the same as those for the Profit & Loss Standard Report. The option to select different criteria for rows has been added, allowing you to customize an income statement to show the bottom line profitability for the item you select.

We need to enter the dates for our report because the current month-to-date setting is not appropriate.

2. **Enter**   06/01/12 as the From date

3. **Enter**   06/30/12 as the To date

4. **Click**   OK to view the report:

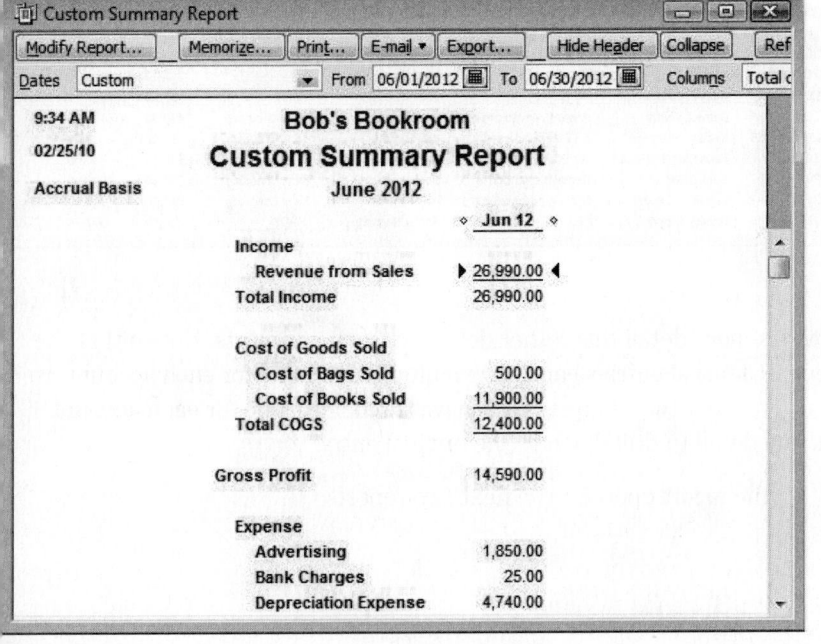

Figure 4-45

Without any modifications made on the Display tab, this report is a standard Income Statement.

Double click any amount to drill down to the original transaction details for that amount. Double click any transaction detail to see the original form.

5. **Close** the **report** when you have finished viewing it. Do not memorize the report

Custom Transaction Detail Report

The Custom Transaction Detail Report includes a list of all transactions during the selected period. It differs from other transaction lists by providing a separate report line for each account used in the transaction.

1. **Choose** the **Reports menu** and **click Custom Transaction Detail Report**, or **open** the **Chart of Accounts window, click** the **Reports button, choose Report On All Accounts**, then **choose Other**, and **click Custom Transaction Detail Report**

The report opens in the background and the Modify Report window opens in front so that you can make your changes before viewing the report.

2. **Enter** **06/01/12 as the From date** for the report

3. **Enter** **06/30/12 as the To date**

4. **Click** **OK** to view the report:

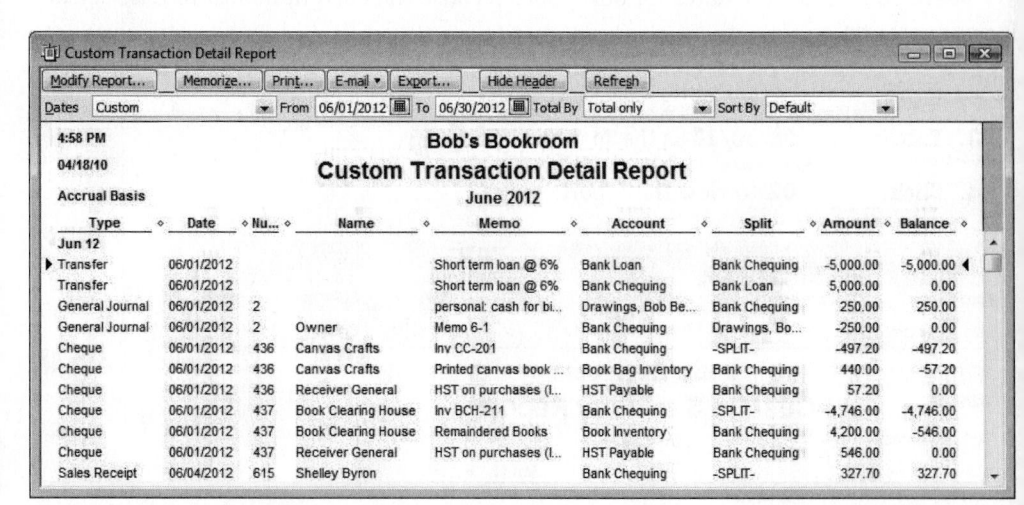

Figure 4-46

This list provides more detail than other detail transaction reports. Notice that the Transfer and General Journal entries each have multiple lines, one for each account used in the transaction. The next two cheques each have three lines, one for each account.

Double click any detail to drill down to the original entry.

5. **Leave** the **report** open for the next two reports

Transaction Reports

The final two reports we will cover in this chapter are reports for individual transactions. To view these reports, you must first open another report that shows transaction details and select a transaction in the report. You will then be able to go to another level for the selected transaction. We will work from the Custom Transaction Detail Report that should still be open.

Transaction History Report

1. **Display** the **Custom Transaction Detail Report** for June 2012 if you have closed it. (Refer to the previous page for details on accessing this report)

The Transaction History Report shows all transactions that are linked to the transaction you select. For example, if you choose an invoice, the report will show payments related to that invoice.

2. **Click** **any transaction detail line** for the Sales Receipt to Shelley Byron on the Custom Transaction Detail Report to drill down to the transaction

3. **Choose** the **Reports menu** and **click Transaction History** to view the transaction history for the open transaction:

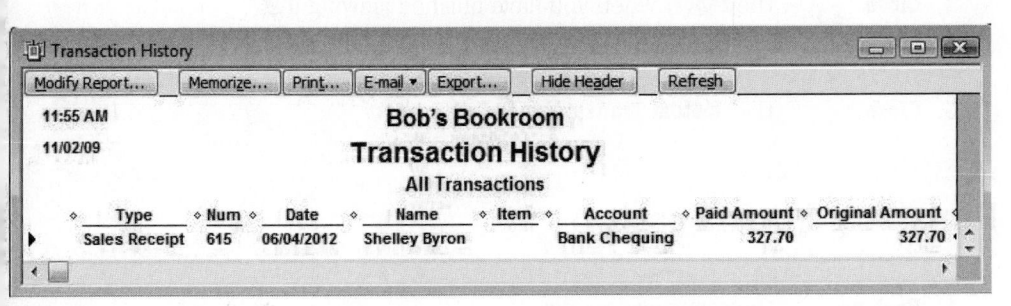

Figure 4-47

The single line for the report indicates that no other transactions are linked to this one. This is as we expected because customers do not have accounts in this company, and, therefore, invoices and customer payments are not recorded separately. The original amount of the transaction is fully paid. You can modify this report just like any other report.

Double click any detail to drill down to the original transaction.

4. **Close** the **report** when you have finished viewing it to return to the Custom Transaction Detail Report

Transaction Journal Report

The final report shows the journal entry for a single transaction. To use this report, you must have selected a transaction in another report to view the journal.

1. **Click** the **Sales Receipt for Shelley Byron** on the Custom Transaction Detail Report to drill down to the original transaction

2. Choose   the **Reports menu** and **click Transaction Journal** to view the journal entry for the open transaction:

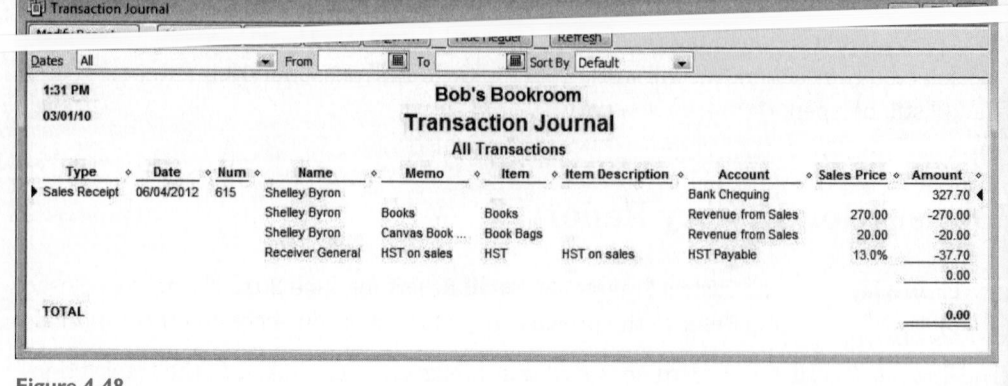

Figure 4-48

The report is the same one that we see when we display a transaction on the screen and press `ctrl` + **Y**. You can use the Reports menu as an alternative way of accessing this report in a transaction window. You can also double click a transaction in a report to view the original entry and then press `ctrl` + **Y**. The same report shown in Figure 4-48 would be displayed by `ctrl` + **Y**.

3. Close   the **report** when you have finished viewing it

4. Close   the **Sales Receipt to Shelley Byron**

5. Close   the **Custom Transaction Detail Report**

Finishing Your Session

1. Back up   the **company data file**

2. Close   the **Company file**

3. Close   the **QuickBooks program**

Notes
We dragged the Class and Transaction # column heading markers to the left to remove these columns and changed the size of some of the other columns so the report in Figure 4-48 would fit in the window.

Notes
You can close all open QuickBooks windows at one time by choosing Window from the menu and then Close All.

River Run

Objectives

After completing this chapter, you should be able to:

- **set up** new company files from manual accounting records
- **create** a Chart of Accounts
- **understand** and **use** different account types
- **enter** opening balances for accounts
- **create** customer records
- **create** vendor records
- **customize** QuickBooks preferences for a company
- **create** items
- **edit** and delete accounts
- **make** accounts and vendors inactive
- **define** a new sales tax
- **delete** default payment terms and methods
- **edit** customer messages

Company Information

Company Profile

River Run is a charitable foundation created to raise money for environmental clean-up and restoration, focusing on rivers, waterfronts, and the surrounding parks. This run will be held for the second time in Winnipeg, Manitoba, and the foundation hopes to extend the event to other Manitoba communities in the near future.

The run covers a total distance of 20 kilometres — 10 kilometres in one direction on one side of the river and 10 kilometres return on the other side. The run begins and ends at a registration and information site in Kildonan Park on Main Street beside the Red River. Runners follow the path beside the river where possible, moving out to the street for short distances when there are breaks in the path. Emergency stations are set

Notes
River Run
100 Portage Avenue
Winnipeg, MB R3C 3X2
Tel: (204) 837-4733
Fax: (204) 837-1811
E-mail: admin@riverrun.
com
Web: www.riverrun.com
Business No.: 933566211

Notes
The Business Number is the CRA (Canada Revenue Agency) number for the company that applies to all federal returns. It is also the GST/HST number for the business and, for non-profits if applicable, the charitable tax number.

up at bridges to allow staff, supplies, and participants to cross over if necessary. Food and drinks are available at these stations, as well as at other points along the route. All runners receive a t-shirt and cap for sun protection at the start of the run and bottled water along the route. Spectators can buy t-shirts, caps, and snacks and beverages to

Revenues are generated from participants' (runners') registration fees, from sponsors of runners, and from photos of the runners (before and after the run) sold to participants. Runners may register individually or in teams of up to four persons. Individual runners pay $25.00 to participate, and teams of up to four persons pay $80.00 per team.

The event is registered as a charity and does not charge any taxes. Like any regular business, the foundation pays 5 percent GST and 7 percent PST on taxable purchases. However, as a registered charity, the event is eligible for a rebate of 50 percent of GST paid, and it files for these refunds once a year before closing the books for the fiscal period.

A self-employed event manager, Charity Spiritus, organizes the event and is paid monthly on a contractual basis. The rest of the work is completed by a large crew of volunteers.

At the beginning of January 2012, the event manager is ready to set up the accounting records in QuickBooks using the following:

- Chart of Accounts
- Post-closing Trial Balance
- Vendor List
- Customer List
- Item List
- Accounting Procedures

Notes
We have changed the name of the GST/HST Payable account to GST Payable. You will do this in the edit accounts section of this course.

Chart of Accounts

River Run

ASSETS
Bank
    Bank - Chequing
    Cash on Hand
Other Current Assets
    Food Supplies
    Office and Computer Supplies
    T-shirts and Caps
Fixed Assets
    Computers/Digital Equipment [P]
        Cost [S]
        Depreciation [S]

LIABILITIES
Other Current Liabilities
    Bank Loan
    GST Payable

EQUITY
    Accumulated Surplus
    Retained Earnings

INCOME
    Revenue from Donations
    Revenue from Registrations
    Revenue from Sales

EXPENSE
Cost of Goods Sold
    Cost of Food and Drinks
    Cost of T-shirts and Caps

EXPENSES
    Depreciation Expense
    Non-refundable GST Expense
    Office & Computer Supplies Used
    Office Rent
    Printing and Copying
    Publicity and Promotion
    Telephone Expense
    Wage Contract Expenses

KEY
[P] Parent account
[S] Subaccount

Post-closing Trial Balance

River Run

AS AT JANUARY 1, 2012

	Debits	Credits
Bank - Chequing	$15,540.00	
Cash on Hand	480.00	
Office and Computer Supplies	210.00	
Computers/Digital Equipment:Cost	4,500.00	
Computers/Digital Equipment:Depreciation		$ 1,820.00
Bank Loan		11,000.00
Accumulated Surplus		7,910.00
	$20,730.00	$20,730.00

Vendor Information

River Run

Vendor Name	Terms
Bell Canada	due on receipt
Receiver General	
Receiver General - Non-Taxable	
RoofOver Properties Inc.	due on receipt
Sobey's Food Mart	due on receipt
Staples	due on receipt
Wear Ads	due on receipt
Winnipeg Free Press	due on receipt

Customer Information

River Run

Customer Name	Preferred Method of Payment	Terms
Donors	cash	due on receipt
Runners	cash	due on receipt

Item List

River Run

Item	Type	Price	Tax Code	Account
SERVICES ITEMS				
Photos	Service	$10.00	E	Revenue from Sales
Single Registration	Service	$25.00	E	Revenue from Registrations
Sponsorship	Service	varies	E	Revenue from Donations
Team Registration	Service	$80.00	E	Revenue from Registrations
NON-INVENTORY PART ITEMS				
Caps	Non-inventory part	$15.00	E	Revenue from Sales
Snacks and Beverages	Non-inventory part	varies	E	Revenue from Sales
T-shirts	Non-inventory part	$20.00	E	Revenue from Sales

Accounting Procedures

Taxes: GST and PST

Registered charities have two options with respect to the GST. Like regular for-profit businesses, they can register to apply the GST, charge GST on all sales and membership fees, and claim all GST paid as input tax credits to reduce the liability to the Receiver General. The second option, used by River Run, does not require registration or collection of GST but permits a partial rebate of GST paid. Periodically, the charity submits an application for refunds, listing the total of all GST paid toward its operating expenses. Fifty percent of this amount is eligible for the rebate. Therefore, River Run records GST paid on all purchases and debits these amounts to *Non-refundable GST Expense*. The rebate application is for 50 percent of this amount, leaving 50 percent as an expense. *GST Refund Receivable* is debited to record the rebate request until the refund is received and deposited.

Bank Accounts and Deposits

The proceeds from registrations and from the sale of merchandise are entered into the bank account. All cheques and cash are deposited on receipt. The *Bank - Chequing* account is used for all cheques to suppliers and to cover operating and administrative expenses and merchandise — beverages, snacks, t-shirts, caps, and supplies. During the event, the *Cash on Hand* account is used for expenses incurred by the volunteer staff. Transfers are made from the *Bank - Chequing* account to *Cash on Hand* by writing cheques to the event manager.

Cheques are hand printed at the time of the transaction and not printed through the program.

Account Terms

All customers, participants, sponsors, and spectators pay cash. All purchases are paid by cheque at the time of purchase. No accounts are set up with vendors for delayed payment.

Supplies

Supplies left at the end of the event are counted and adjusting entries are prepared. Leftovers that cannot be used for the following year's run are donated to other registered charitable organizations.

Instructions

1. Using the Chart of Accounts, the Trial Balance, and other information, set up the company files for River Run. Detailed instructions for the setup follow.

2. Record entries for the source documents from January to June, 2012, using QuickBooks. The source documents begin on page 210 following the instructions for setup. If you prefer to complete the source documents without setting up the company file, you can start with the data file Setup\River in your QkBkData folder.

3. After you have finished making your entries, print the reports and graphs for 2012 marked on the following printing form.

Creating a New Company

When you create new company files in QuickBooks, you can complete the setup step-by-step-yourself, or you can complete the QuickBooks EasyStep Interview. We will choose to bypass the Interview so that you can see all the steps separately and their locations in the program. This way, you will be able to easily correct or modify settings later if needed. Although we are bypassing the EasyStep Interview, there are a few screens that must be entered in the EasyStep Interview in order to create and save the company file before you can begin working in QuickBooks.

The EasyStep Interview screens include a great deal of information that helps you make the correct choices for your business during the setup. You should read all these screens carefully before advancing to the next screen. Frequently, they also allow you to read extra information on a specific topic.

Setting up a new company involves the following steps:

1. Creating a data file
2. Adding accounts
3. Adding any required special taxes
4. Adding opening account balances
5. Creating vendor and customer records
6. Creating items
7. Choosing preferences to customize settings for all aspects of the program
8. Printing reports to check your setup data
9. Backing up your data file

Creating a Data File

You can create new companies from the File menu when another company file is open, or when no company is open. We will close any open companies before beginning.

1. **Start** the **QuickBooks** program. If a company file opens automatically, **choose** the **File menu** and **click Close Company**

2. The No Company Open window is displayed:

> **Notes**
> You may want to complete the setup for River Run a second time using the EasyStep Interview.

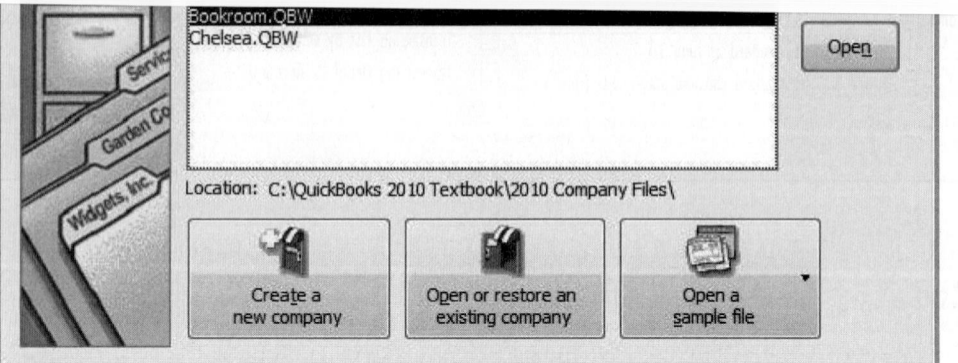

Figure 5-1

No Company Open

Select a company that you've previously opened and click Open

Bookroom.QBW
Chelsea.QBW

Open

Location: C:\QuickBooks 2010 Textbook\2010 Company Files\

Create a
new company

Open or restore an
existing company

Open a
sample file

You will see this window when you are using the program for the first time or whenever you have closed the company you were last working with. The company files you worked with most recently are listed. You can open one of the listed files or choose another option from the buttons below the list. One of these options is to create a new company.

3. **Click** the **Create A New Company button**:

Figure 5-2

4. The Welcome screen for the EasyStep Interview appears:

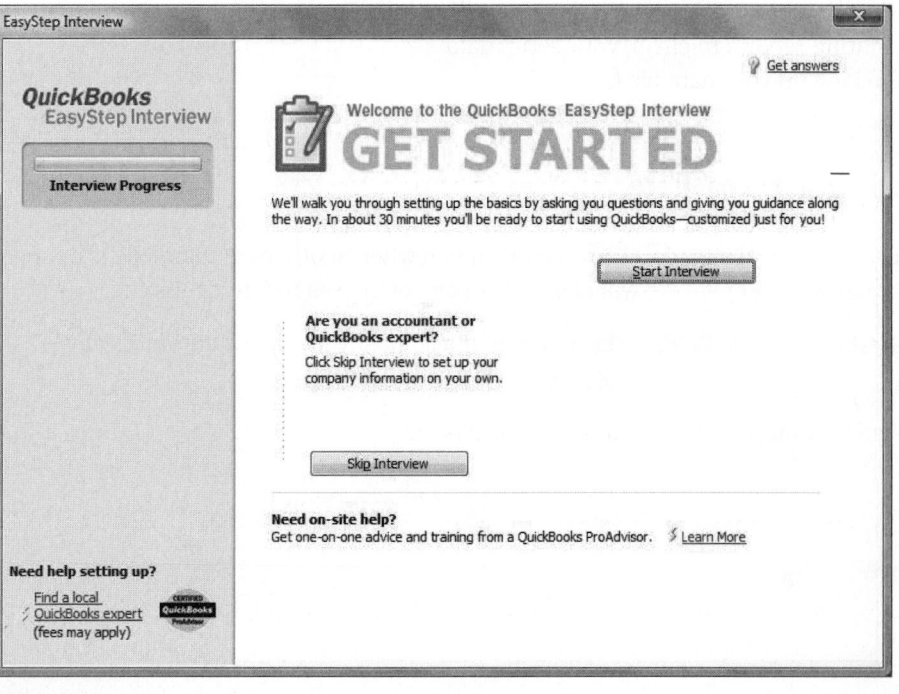

Figure 5-3

Setting up a QuickBooks company file begins with the EasyStep Interview. If you choose the **Start Interview** button, you will go through a number of screens answering questions about your company and completing much of the required company setup. If you select the **Skip Interview** button, you will be asked only a few questions about your company and you will need to enter information about your company in QuickBooks before you begin entering transactions. No matter which option you select, at any time you can click the **Back** button to go back to previous screens to change your answers and you can click the **Next** button to advance to the next screen. Some screens contain required information and you cannot advance to the next screen until you complete the required information. You should always check your answers before moving to the next screen. Some information in the EasyStep Interview cannot be changed once it is selected. When you are entering information that cannot be changed later, you will receive a message warning you of this. Check your answers very carefully if you receive a warning message.

As mentioned, you can skip the EasyStep Interview after completing some of the company information and complete the setup from scratch. That is the approach we will use while creating the company file in this chapter. Once you have seen all the setup screens and steps this way, you will be able to easily use the EasyStep Interview on your own. It merely breaks down the setup into more steps with more instructions and screens.

We will enter some necessary company information and then leave the EasyStep Interview and begin the manual setup process.

5. **Click**   **Skip Interview** Skip Interview to open the Company information window:

> **Notes**
> When you use the EasyStep Interview, you can leave at any time by clicking the Leave button and then enter the remaining details on your own in your QuickBooks company file. However, if you leave the EasyStep Interview before you reach the step of entering a file name, your new company file will not be created.

> **Notes:**
> If you click the Start Interview button, you will receive different screens as you work through this exercise. If this happens to you, click the back button until you return to this screen where you can select the Skip Interview button.

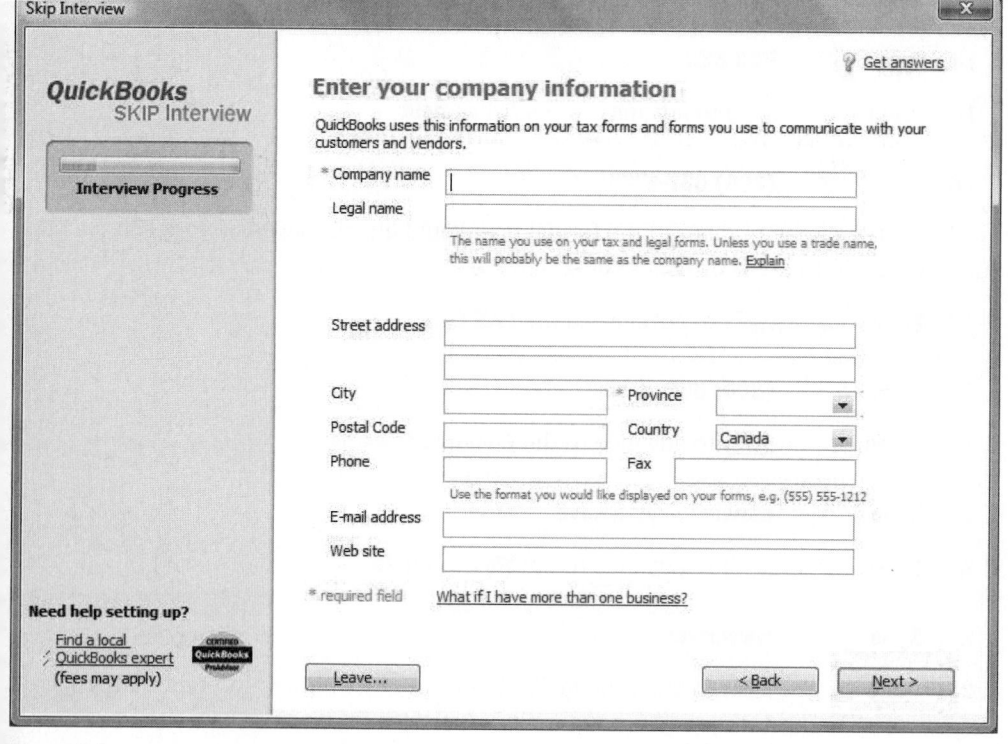

Figure 5-4

This screen is used to enter the company name and address information. Notice that the Company name field and the Province field have asterisks beside them indicating that they are required fields and must be entered before you can continue. If you choose not to enter the rest of the address information on this screen, it can be entered on the

Company Information screen when you open QuickBooks by choosing the Company menu and then Company Information. You can also use the Company Information screen to add or change company information details later.

by which customers know you. This is also the name that will appear in the title bar of your QuickBooks desktop window. The second name is the legal name of the business, the one you use with Canada Revenue Agency and on all financial reports. The two names may be the same, as they are for River Run.

6. **Type**   **River Run**

7. **Press**   `tab`

The name is automatically copied to the Legal name field

8. **Press**   `tab` to advance to the **Street address field**

The information you enter here should be the legal address for the business. The cursor is on the Street address line.

9. **Type**   **100 Portage Avenue**

10. **Press**   `tab` to advance to the **City field**

11. **Type**   **Winnipeg**

12. **Press**   `tab`

13. **Click** the **drop-down arrow** in the Province field and **choose MB**

The Province is used by QuickBooks to create a default set of sales taxes.

14. **Type**   **R3C 3X2**

15. **Press**   `tab` to advance to the **Phone field**

16. **Type**   **(204) 837-4733**

Enter the phone number in the format you would like displayed on forms. It is not automatically formatted by QuickBooks.

17. **Press**   `tab` to advance to the **FAX field**

18. **Type**   **(204) 837-1811**

19. **Press**   `tab` to advance to the **E-mail address field**

20. **Type**   **admin@riverrun.com**

21. **Press**   `tab` to advance to the **Web site field**

22. **Type**   **www.riverrun.com**

23. **Click**   **Next** to open the next window in the EasyStep Interview where you indicate how your company is organized:

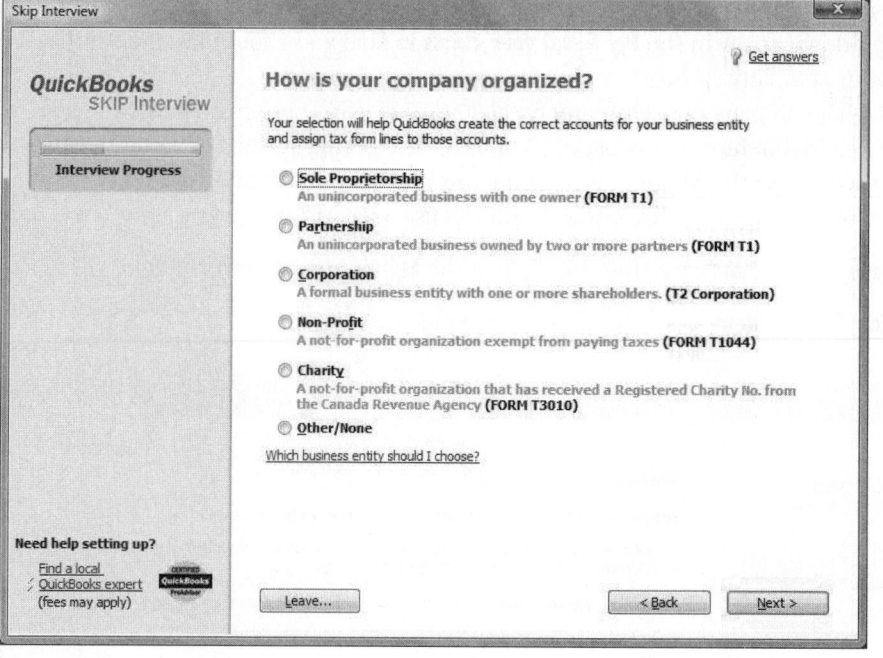

Figure 5-5

This screen asks you to select your business entity. Your selection will help QuickBooks determine which tax forms will be used to report taxes for your company. Choosing the correct form will allow you to use QuickBooks to help prepare the income tax form at the end of the year. If the business is incorporated, you should choose Corporation. If the business is a sole proprietorship that combines personal and business income tax in a single return, you should choose Sole Proprietorship. If you are uncertain, you can choose Other.

24. **Click**   the **button** beside Charity

25. **Click**   **Next** to open the next window in the EasyStep Interview where the company's fiscal year is defined next:

Figure 5-6

January is entered as the default for the month your fiscal year starts. You can click on the drop-down arrow in the **My fiscal year starts in** field and choose the month that matches your company records.

~~Although a company may have any fiscal start date, CRA prefers businesses, espe~~ cially sole proprietorships, to choose a 12-month fiscal period starting in January. Some businesses also close their books more frequently and choose a shorter fiscal period for internal reporting purposes. River Run begins its fiscal year in January.

26. Leave   **January** as the selection in the My fiscal year starts in field

27. Click   **Next** to see the selection of industry types:

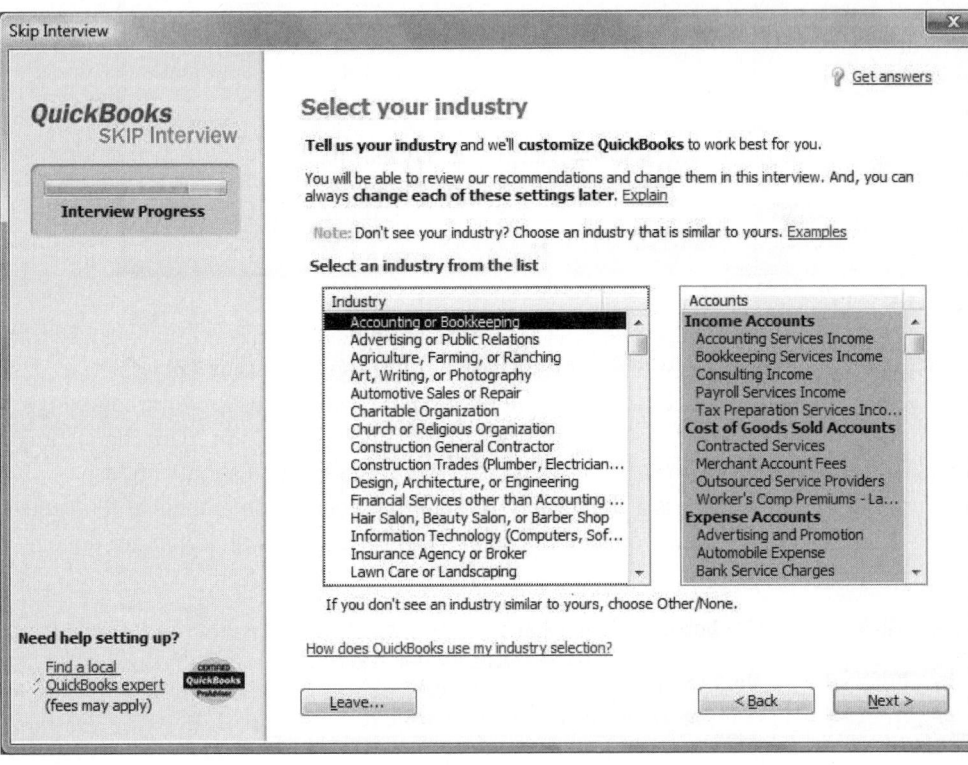

Figure 5-7

You can choose an industry type for the company from the list on the left-hand side of the screen. QuickBooks uses this information to set up other defaults and a set of accounts for the company file. As you select an industry type, the default Chart of Accounts for that industry type will be displayed in the column on the right. When you set up your company file, you will be able to modify the default Chart of Accounts.

QuickBooks also uses the industry type to recommend features that best suit your industry, such as using estimates, managing inventory, creating income and expense categories, and turning on sales orders. You can easily change any of the settings that QuickBooks selects in the Preferences window when you open the company file in QuickBooks. You can access the Preferences window in QuickBooks by selecting Edit from the menu and then Preferences.

We want to create our own Chart of Accounts for this company because it is a small set, so we will choose Other/None as the industry type.

28. Choose   **Other/None** from the list of industry types

29. Click   **Next** to continue to the Create your company file window:

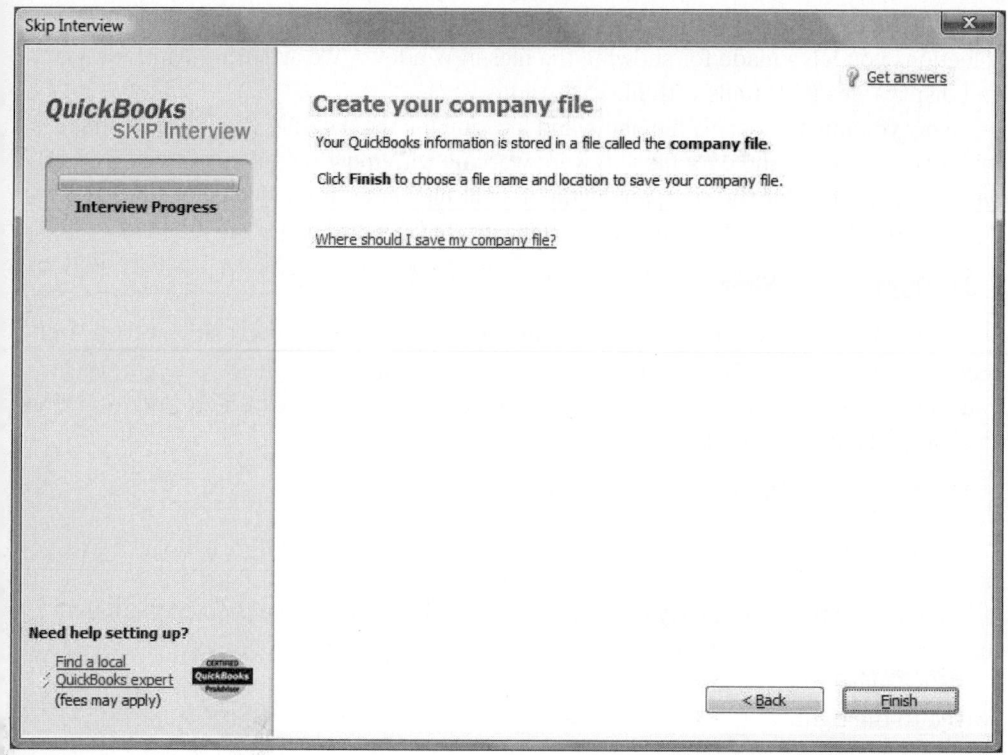

Figure 5-8

This screen indicates that you will be choosing a filename and location for your company file when you click Finish. If you are not sure where to store your files, click the **Where should I save my company file? link** for more information.

30. Click **Finish** to continue to the Filename window

Figure 5-9

Notes
Showing file extensions is a Windows file management setting that you can choose.

Notes
We generally use short file names to ensure that the entire name will always appear on your display lists, regardless of which Windows program or display options you use.

The Filename window displayed will depend on your version of Windows and the selections you have made for showing the files in Windows. We are using Windows Vista and display files by Details with file extensions.

Now you must choose a file name and location for the data files. By default, the folder that contains the data file you were working with most recently is selected and the name you entered for the company is the default file name. You can change both of these if you want. The default file name is already selected. We will name the file River.

31. Type   River

QuickBooks will add the appropriate file extension for you so that the program will recognize the data file. Do not change the file extension. Change the location of the file if you want by selecting another location from the Save in field. Click the drop-down arrow to change the drive or folder.

32. Click   Save

Be patient while QuickBooks creates the file based on the information you have provided.

If you selected an industry type, QuickBooks will create a Chart of Accounts that may be suitable for the business. You can modify this list later if you want.

The QuickBooks Home page opens with the Live Community and Help pane displayed to the right.

Figure 5-10

Notes
You can open the Live Community and Help pane at any time by clicking the Help or Live Community icon on the Icon bar.

The Live Community and Help pane can be closed at any time.

33. Click   the "x" in the top right-hand corner of the Live Community and Help pane to close it

34. Click   OK when prompted with the message that Live Community will be opened the next time you start QuickBooks

When you create a new company file in QuickBooks, default settings and a Chart of Accounts are created based on the industry type you selected in the EasyStep Interview. Tax information for the province you selected in the company address is also created.

When setting up this company, we selected the Other/None industry type so a very basic Chart of Accounts has been created. Before we start working in QuickBooks, we must modify the defaults or preferences to suit our business and then create the Chart of Accounts, vendor, customer, and item records. We also need to enter opening account balances to add the historical information.

Creating the Chart of Accounts

The first step in setting up a new company is creating new accounts. It is not necessary to create all the accounts before entering transactions in QuickBooks because they can be added to the Chart of Accounts at any time or they can be added in any account field on the fly during transaction entry when you need them. However, by creating accounts first, we can easily choose the accounts we need as defaults for other setup steps, and we can monitor the creation of the accounts in a logical order. Before we can create the new accounts, we should set some of the preferences that will influence how the accounts are set up.

Setting Preferences

Preferences in QuickBooks influence how the program works and looks. Some of the preferences are personal — you choose how you like to work with the program on the My Preferences tab screens. For example, you can define the rules for Spell Check or have the program beep when you enter transactions. Other preferences that relate to the way the company operates are located on the Company Preferences tab screens. For example, a business may or may not prepare sales estimates and purchase orders. By eliminating the unused icons, the program is easier to use. Some of these preferences should be set before you work with a module while others can be changed at any time. Some aspects of the program have only personal preferences and some have only company preferences.

When you use the complete EasyStep Interview, you also set many of these preferences. However, each interview screen usually controls a single preference question and is followed by one or more input screens. When you use the Preferences screens, you can make several selections from a single input window.

We will begin by setting some general preferences for the program. We will change the preferences for individual modules later. Preferences are set from the main menu in the desktop window. This menu is always available, and preferences can be changed at any time if the needs of the business change.

General Preferences

1. **Choose**   the **Edit menu** and **click Preferences**

2. **Click**   the **General heading** on the left-hand side of the screen and, if necessary, **click** the **My Preferences tab**

The My Preferences tab for the General Preferences is displayed as shown:

Figure 5-11

The icons for preference topics or areas are listed alphabetically on the left-hand side of the screen. While accessing any of the Preferences windows, click the Help button on the right-hand side of the screen for more detailed information.

3. Click   Help to see explanations of the options for each set of preferences

You can leave the Help window open until you have finished setting all preferences. Just click the Help button again after you choose the next preference heading or area to update the Help topic information.

Since the General preferences do not affect the financial aspects of the program, you should decide for yourself how you want to interact with the program and choose your settings. From this screen you can choose to:

- press (enter) to move between fields. Otherwise pressing (enter) is like choosing OK, Record or Save & New, whichever button is highlighted
- automatically open drop-down lists when typing
- turn on or off the beep (sound) when recording transactions
- automatically add a decimal point to numbers. Thus, 4950 becomes 49.50 but 49 becomes 0.49. This option requires you to add trailing zeros for whole numbers
- warn when editing a transaction. Always leave this option selected
- bring back all one-time messages that were turned off when you selected "Do not display this message again." You can select this option later to restore the messages that you turned off
- turn off pop-up messages for products and services
- show ToolTips for clipped text
- warn when deleting a transaction or unused list item. Always leave this option selected
- automatically recall account or transaction information by selecting to recall the last transaction for the person entered on the transaction or by pre-filling accounts for vendors based on past transactions
- choose the current date or last transaction date as the default date for new transactions

To select or deselect preferences, click in the check box beside the preference to select it (which will add a ✓ indicating that the preference is selected) or click in the box that contains a checkmark (which will remove the ✓ indicating that the preference is deselected).

4. Click the **checkmark beside Beep when recording a transaction** to turn this preference off

We will use the default settings for the rest of the General preferences on the My Preferences tab.

5. Click the **Company Preferences tab**:

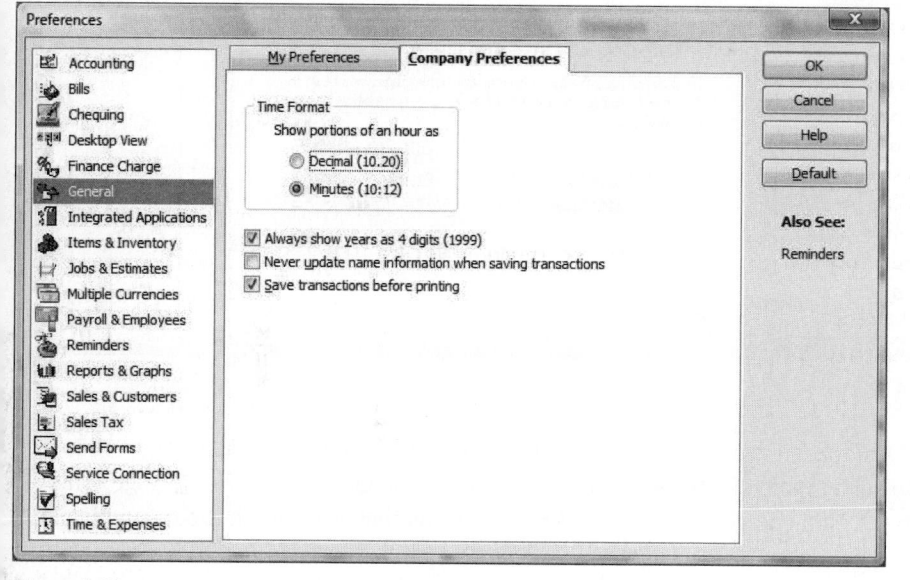

Figure 5-12

The General company preferences relate to how dates and times are entered and displayed in the program, if information updated in transactions should be updated when saving transactions and if transactions should be saved before printing. The four-digit year format ensures that you are working with 2000 dates instead of 1900 dates. The *Never update name information when saving transactions* option is not selected, so the default setting allows you to update customer and vendor record details from invoice and form windows. The final option will save your transactions before you print them.

We will use the default settings for the General preferences on the Company Preferences tab.

Desktop View Preferences

6. Click the **Desktop View** heading on the left-hand side of the screen to view the Desktop View preferences

Because we have made changes to the General preferences, the following warning message appears:

Figure 5-13

> **Notes**
> Only the administrator of the company file can change the preferences on the Company Preferences tab for all preference headings. Other users cannot change these settings. If the file has one user, that user is the administrator.

> **Notes**
> Most two-digit year entries with low numbers are automatically converted to years beyond 2000, whereas high numbers are automatically interpreted as 1900s. Because early versions of Windows do not make this conversion correctly, showing the year as four digits helps ensure that you enter dates correctly.

7. Click   **Yes** to save the General preferences changes

The following company preferences are displayed for Desktop View:

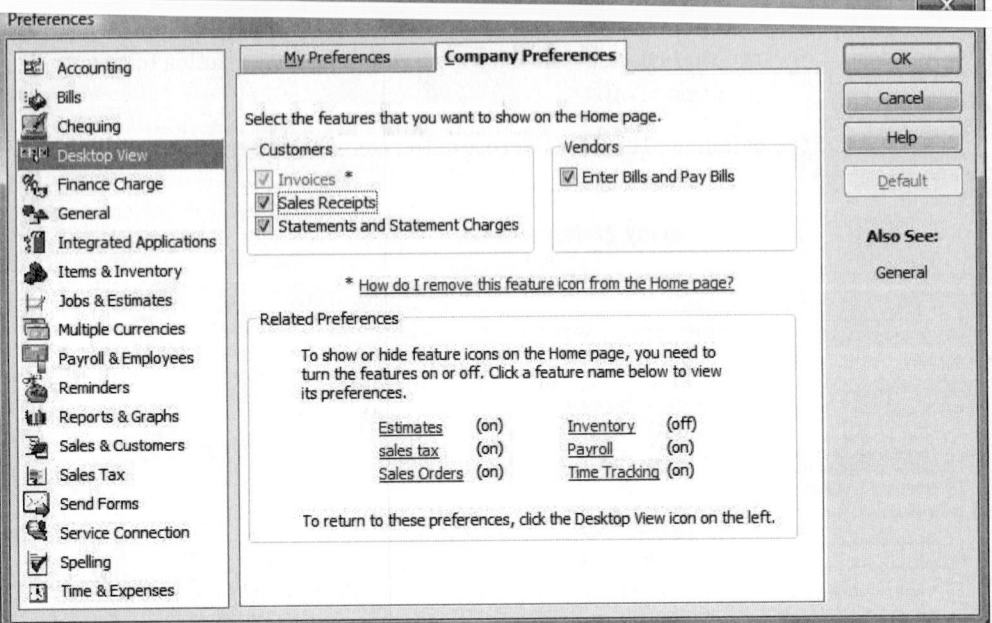

Figure 5-14

The Desktop View preferences on the Company Preferences tab allow the administrator to select which features will be displayed on the QuickBooks Home page. This cleans up the Home page by displaying only the icons that are used in the company file. From this window, you can easily turn off Sales Receipts, Statements and Statement Charges, Enter Bills and Pay Bills. You can also use this window to turn off related preferences. As you select or deselect the related preferences, the appropriate preference window will open allowing you to turn the preference on or off.

We will not be changing any of the Desktop View Company preferences.

8. Click   the **My Preferences tab**:

Figure 5-15

The default settings here are to open one window at a time while working in QuickBooks, to save the last desktop you worked in so that all the windows you had open when you exited the program will open the next time you open the data file, and to show the Home page, QuickBooks Coach, and Live Community when opening a company file. You can also choose the colour scheme for the forms in the program and access the Windows display and sounds settings. Most of the options are self-explanatory but the Help button provides additional information if needed.

We have not changed these default settings but you may choose to do so.

Reminders Preferences

9. Click   the **Reminders** heading on the left-hand side of the screen

If you made any changes to the Desktop View preferences, you'll need to click yes to accept them before moving to the Reminders preferences.

10. Click   **Yes** to save the Desktop View preferences if needed

The following preferences are displayed on the My Preferences tab for Reminders:

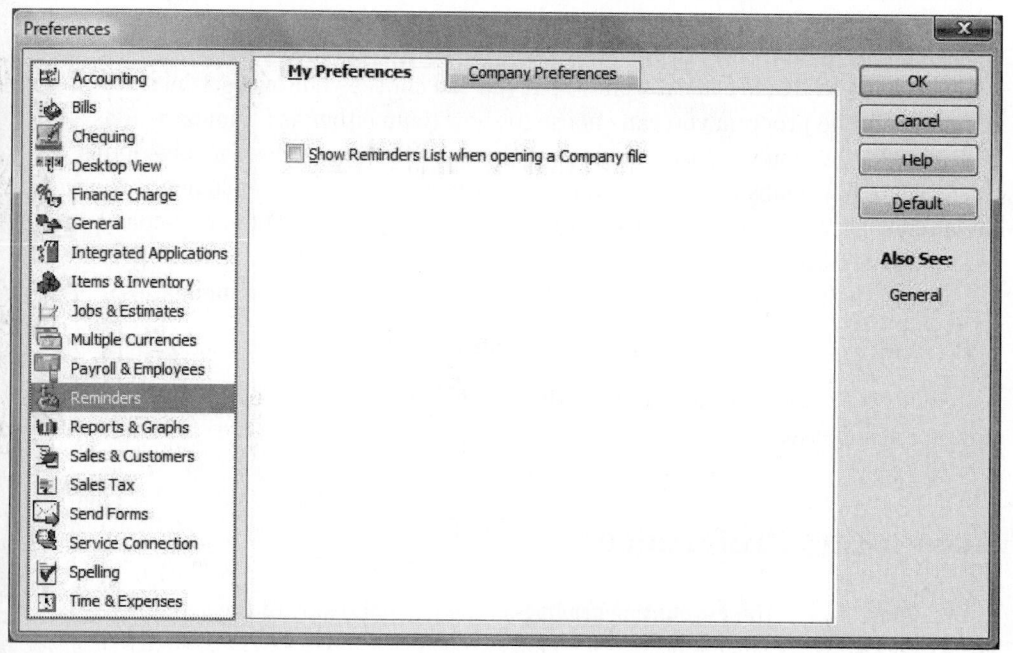

Figure 5-16

The default setting here is to not show reminders when opening the company file.

11. Click   the **Company Preferences tab**:

Notes
Reminders are linked to the current calendar dates so we are not able to use them for the data files in the textbook.

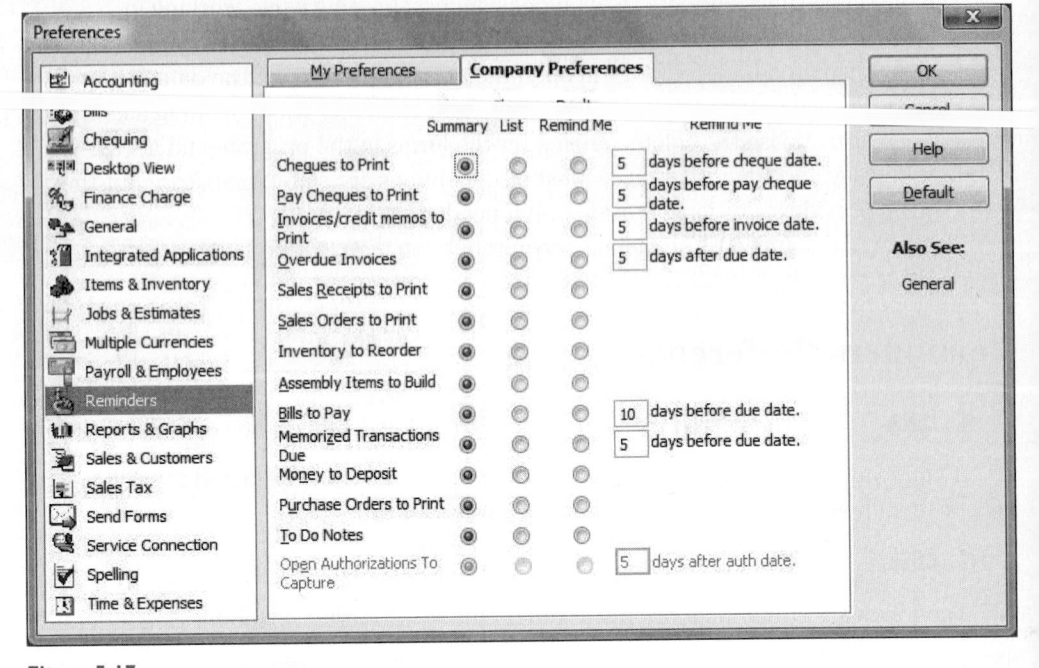

Figure 5-17

This window displays a list from which you can choose your own settings. If you use reminders in the program you can choose to show them either as a summary or as a list, indicate whether you want to be reminded about the item, and then for some items you can indicate how many days before the item is due the reminder should appear on the Reminders list We have not changed any of these settings for any of our company data files in this textbook. Use the Help button to provide more detail if needed.

We are not using reminders so we do not show reminder lists or summaries.

12. Click   **Don't Remind Me** for each feature

Before we set up the Accounts for the data file, we should define the preference settings for accounting.

Accounting Preferences

13. Click   the **Accounting heading** on the left-hand side of the screen

Since you made changes to the Reminders preferences, you'll need to click yes to accept them before moving to the Accounting preferences.

14. Click   **Yes** to save the changes to the Reminder preferences

15. Click   the **My Preferences tab** for the Accounting preferences:

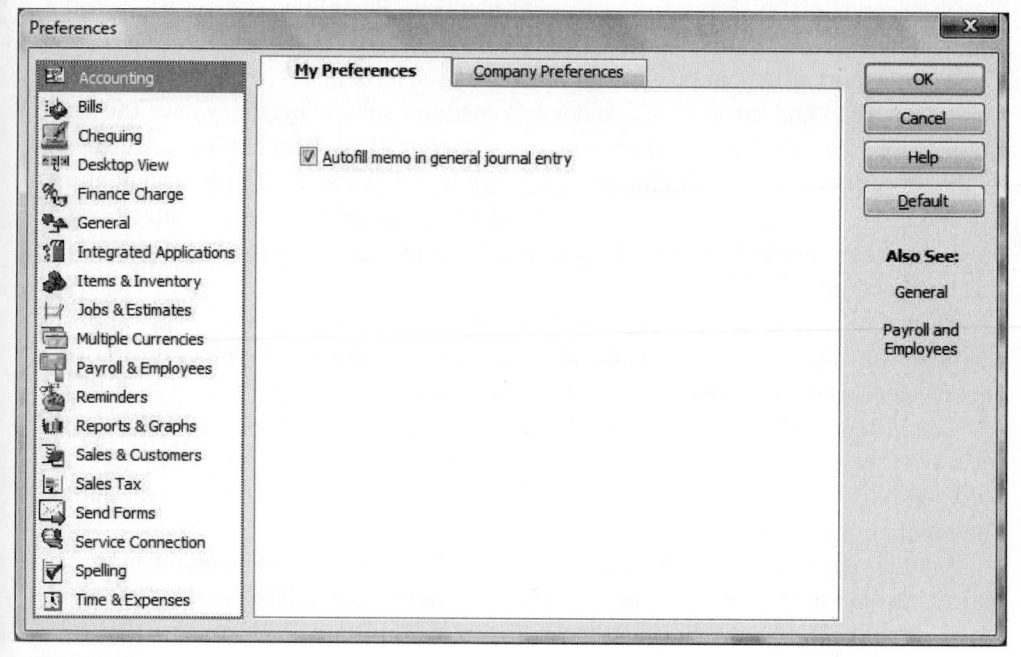

Figure 5-18

The default setting here is to automatically have the memo field that you enter in the first line of a general journal entry appear automatically in subsequent lines.

We have not changed the default setting but you may choose to do so.

16. **Click** the **Company Preferences tab**:

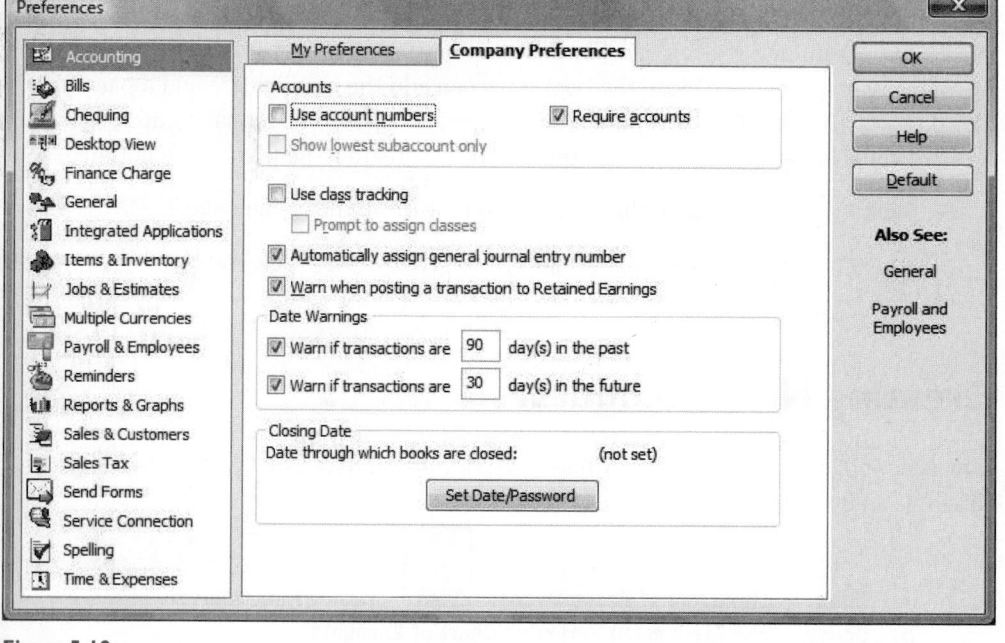

Figure 5-19

One of the preferences that affects accounts is the option to use account numbers. In our early applications, we are not using account numbers. Accounts are listed in alphabetic order within their account type. When account numbers are used, the accounts are listed in numeric order within their account type. Although you can use any numbering system you want, it is best to use a logical sequence of account numbers. The default program setting is not to use account numbers. River Run does not use account numbers.

We will show all accounts — parent as well as subaccounts — in the account lists to make it easier to find the account ~~...~~ ~~Sometimes subaccounts may have the same~~ name — for example, *Depreciation* may apply to more than one fixed asset. We will also require accounts — you must choose an account in the Account field when you enter a transaction. When accounts are not required, the program uses the *Uncategorized Income* account or the *Uncategorized Expense* account as the default when you do not enter an account.

We will not use class tracking, which lets you assign transactions to classes. For example, you could use class tracking to define income and expense transactions by department, location, or any meaningful breakdown for your business.

QuickBooks will automatically assign journal entry numbers to journal entries. You have the option to be warned when we post transactions to the Retained Earnings account and when transactions are entered 90 days in the past or 30 days in the future. The number of days entered in these fields can also be modified.

Since the transactions in this textbook are in the year 2012 and are likely more than 30 days in the future in relation to your current computer date, we will turn off the *Warn if transactions are 30 days in the future* option so we do not receive a warning message each time we enter a transaction. In a work environment, you should keep this option selected to ensure proper dates are entered on your transactions.

17. **Click**   the **check box** beside the Warn if transactions are 30 days in the future option to turn this off

In previous versions of QuickBooks, you could indicate on this screen whether you wanted QuickBooks to track all edited and deleted transactions through the audit trail. Beginning with QuickBooks 2008, the audit trail is always on and cannot be turned off. In accounting practice, you must show a complete record of all transactions, and changes must be apparent and recorded.

When we are ready to close the books, we can add the closing date and a password. The password for this field prevents unauthorized changes to historical records.

We will change the necessary preferences after creating the Chart of Accounts.

18. **Click**   OK to save the changes and return to the Home page

If you were not automatically returned to the Home page, click the Home icon on the Icon bar.

Creating New Accounts

New accounts are added from the Chart of Accounts window. The Chart of Accounts window can be accessed in a number of ways:

a) **Click**   the **Chart of Accounts icon** on the Home page; or
b) **Choose**   the **Lists menu** and **click Chart of Accounts**; or
c) **Press**   `ctrl` **+ A**, the keyboard shortcut

1. **Open**   the **Chart of Accounts** by using one of the methods listed above.

When you set up this company file in the EasyStep Interview, you selected that your company was a charity and you selected the Other/None option as the industry type. Even though you selected Other/None, QuickBooks creates the following basic accounts in the Chart of Accounts:

In the left margin:

Notes
Journal Entry numbers are not assigned to other types of transactions although transaction numbers are assigned to all entries.

Notes
In accounting practice, pencils and erasers are not allowed because these could cover up any unauthorized changes to the data.

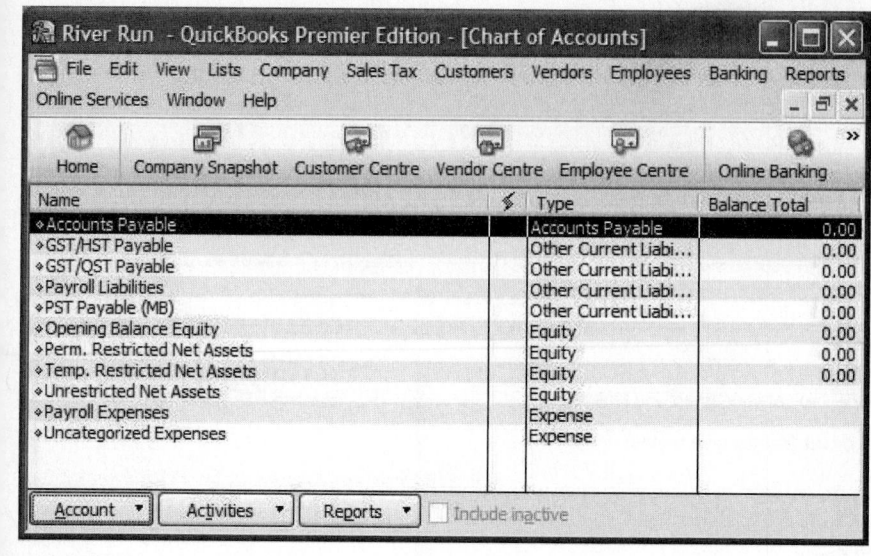

Figure 5-20

Notes
The accounts listed in the Chart of Accounts were added automatically by QuickBooks when you selected the Other/None Industry Type in the EasyStep Interview.

The *Accounts Payable* account tracks what your company owes to its vendors. The tax accounts are set up based on the province you entered for the company address in the EasyStep Interview. The payroll liabilities account is used to track liabilities incurred for payroll taxes and other employee deductions. The *Opening Balance Equity* account is the net worth of a company, and this account is used as the offsetting account when entering opening balances. *The Perm. Restricted Net Assets, Temp. Restricted Net Assets* and *Unrestricted Net Assets* accounts are automatically set up by QuickBooks to record donations and contributions. The *Payroll Expense* account is automatically added to your chart of accounts if payroll is turned on (it is automatically turned on in QuickBooks Premier Student and School edition). Finally, the *Uncategorized Expenses* account is used when you enter opening balances for your vendors.

2. **Click**   the **Account button** (at the bottom of the Chart of Accounts window) to view the pop-up menu and **click New** as shown:

Notes
You can use the keyboard shortcut (ctrl) + **N** to open the Add New Account window

Figure 5-21

Entering Bank Accounts

The Add New Account entry screen will open where you select the account type:

Figure 5-22

Use this screen to select the account type. You can select Income, Expense, Fixed Asset, Bank, Loan, Credit Card, Equity, or click on the Other Account Types option and select from Accounts Receivable, Other Current Asset, Other Asset, Accounts Payable, Other Current Liability, Long Term Liability, Cost of Goods Sold, Other Income, and Other Expense.

As you select an account type, the box on the right-hand side of the screen will display examples of accounts for the selected account type.

As we saw in the previous chapter, the input fields on the New Account form vary with the account type. The first account we need to create is a bank account

3. Click   the **Bank button**

Notice the right-hand side of the screen displays examples of accounts that can be entered using this account type.

4. Click   **Continue** to go to the next page of the Add New Account window:

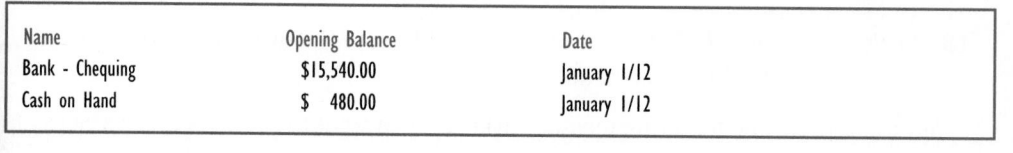

Figure 5-23

Because we chose not to use account numbers, the account name field appears without a number field. The account is not a subaccount so you can leave this field blank. We will use subaccounts for the fixed asset accounts. The description is optional. Sometimes you will want to distinguish accounts that are very similar by including the purpose of the account or a longer account name in the description field. Many of the other fields relate specifically to bank accounts. We are not using online banking so we do not need to add the bank account number and we will not be exporting our tax information to tax preparation software so we do not need to select a tax line mapping option. Also, we are not using pre-printed cheques so we can leave those fields blank as well.

We do need to add the opening account balance. We will enter the balance as of January 1, 2012, the day we begin to use the program for current transactions.

Name	Opening Balance	Date
Bank - Chequing	$15,540.00	January 1/12
Cash on Hand	$ 480.00	January 1/12

We need to enter two bank accounts:

5. Type   **Bank - Chequing** in the Account Name field

6. Click   the **Enter Opening Balance button** to display the Enter Opening Balance window:

Notes
When you choose to use account numbers, the New Account forms include a field for the account number.

Notes
Remember we cannot use colons in account names. Colons are reserved for subaccounts and are added automatically by the program.

Enter Opening Balance: Bank Account

Enter the ending date and balance from the last bank statement you received before your QuickBooks start date.

ℹ️ **Attention:** If this account **did not** have a balance before your QuickBooks start date, click **Cancel** and use a transaction to put money in this account. Example transactions

Statement Ending Balance

Statement Ending Date

OK   Cancel   Help

Figure 5-24

For bank accounts, you must use this screen to enter the ending date and balance from the last bank statement you received before your QuickBooks start date.

7. Type   **15540** in the Statement Ending Balance field

8. Press   `tab`

9. Type   **01/01/12** in the Statement Ending Date field

10. Press   `tab`

Because we will use the same opening balance date for all accounts, you do not have to type it each time. You can copy it and then paste it to the remaining accounts.

11. Double click **01/01/2012** in the Statement Ending Date and **press** `ctrl` + **C** to copy the date to the Windows Clipboard

When you enter the next account, you can press `ctrl` + **V** in the date field to paste the date.

12. Click   **OK** to close the **Enter Opening Balance** window and return to the Add New Account window

If you omit a year in the date field, the program enters the current calendar year from your computer system.

To save the new account, you can click Save & Close to save the account and close the Add New Account form or click Save & New to save the account and open a blank Add New Account form. Before creating more accounts, we will view the changes that QuickBooks has made to the file.

13. Click   **Save & Close** to save the account, close the form, and return to the Chart of Accounts

You will receive the following message asking if you want to set up online services:

Set Up Online Services

Set up online services to save time.

Your financial institution may offer account statement downloads and other online banking services for this account.

Do you want to set up online services for this account if these services are available?

If yes, all open QuickBooks windows will be closed temporarily.

Yes   No

Figure 5-25

We will not be setting up Online Services for this company file.

14. Click   **No** and you are returned to the Chart of Accounts:

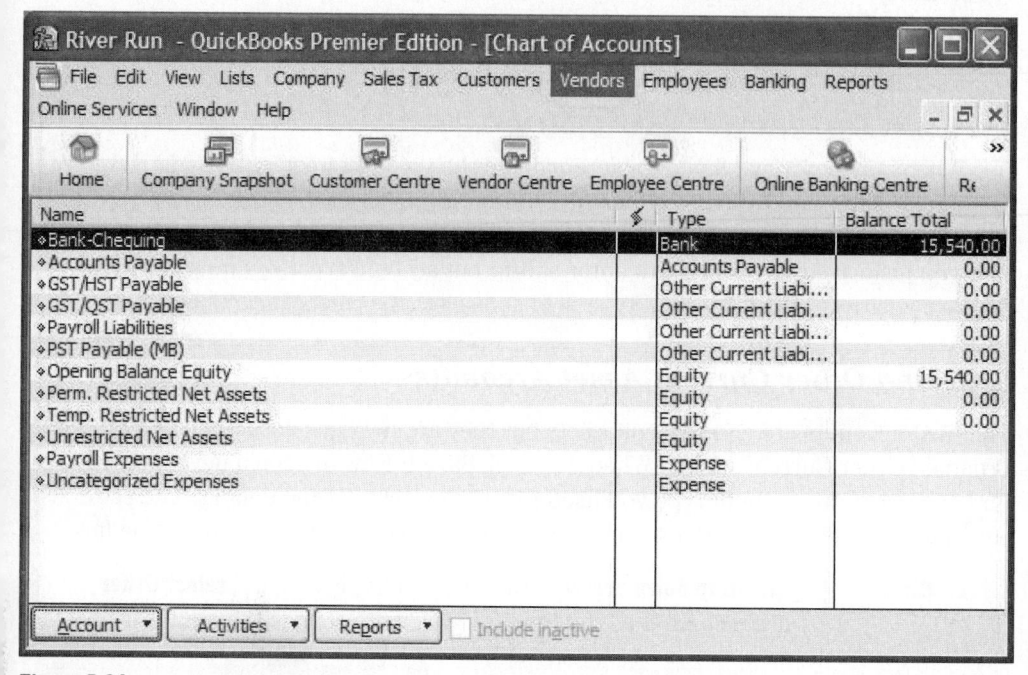

Figure 5-26

Notice that the program has added $15,540.00 to the *Bank - Chequing* account and to the *Opening Balance Equity* account. All account opening balances are treated as journal entries with the entry to *Opening Balance Equity* as the second part of the transaction. We will rename this account later.

15. Double click   the **Opening Balance Equity account** to view the journal entry in the register:

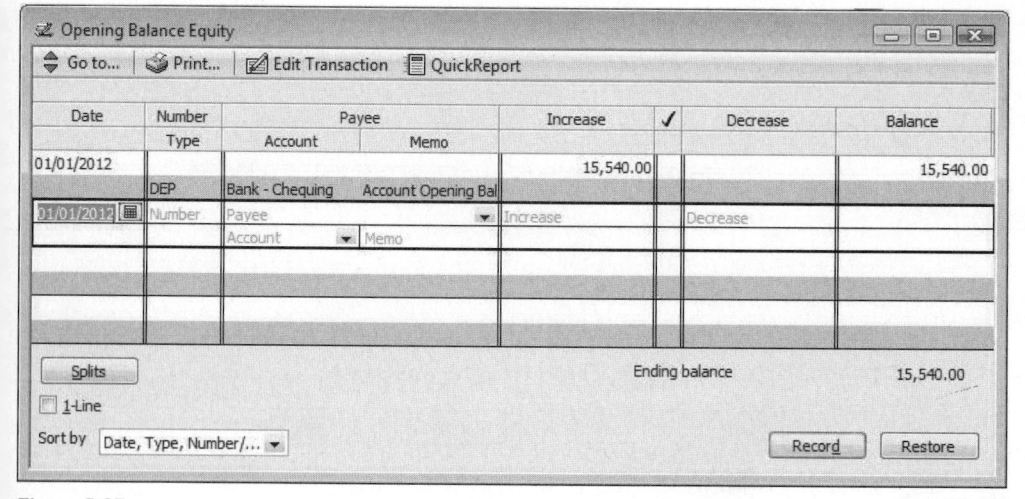

Figure 5-27

16. Close   the **register** to return to the Chart of Accounts

17. Press   [ctrl] + **N** to open the Add New Account window to enter the next account

Notes
River Run does not use
Accounts Receivable accounts
~~because all transactions are cash~~
transactions.

18. **Create** the **Cash on Hand account**. Refer to the Post-closing Trial Balance on page 145

19. ~~Enter~~ the account name, statement ending balance, and statement ending date or **press** (ctrl) **+ V** to use the date that we copied onto the clipboard

20. **Click** **Save & New** or **press** (alt) **+ N** to save the account and open a blank Add New Account form

When you click Save & New, you remain on the second screen of the Add New Account window and bypass the first screen where you select the account type. QuickBooks assumes that you want to add another account for the same account type that you just saved. If you want to enter a different account type, you must click the drop-down arrow in the Account Type field and select the correct account type.

Entering Other Current Asset Accounts

The next accounts are also current assets but they are not bank accounts. This group is named Other Current Assets. When you click Save & New to open a new account form, the previous account type you used remains selected as the default. The previous account type we used was Bank, so it is currently displayed in the Account Type field.

1. **Click** the **drop-down arrow** in the Account Type field and **select Other Current Asset** as the type (or type o) to change the input form:

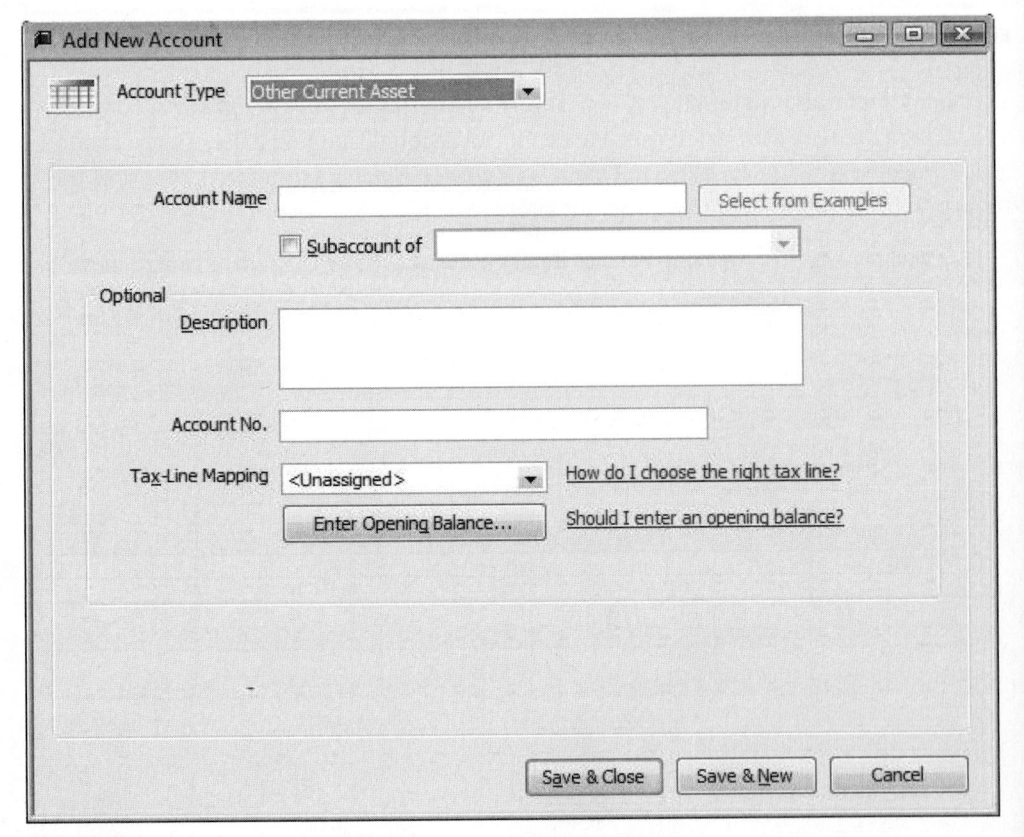

Figure 5-28

Notice that the fields that apply only to bank accounts, such as the cheque information, are not included on the input form for this account type. Notice that the Enter Opening Balance button is available. For this group of accounts you must enter the account name, and enter the opening balance and date if you have historical data to enter. The remaining fields, including the description, are optional.

The three Other Current Asset accounts that we must enter are listed here:

Name	Opening Balance	Date
Office and Computer Supplies	$210.00	January 1/12
Food Supplies	0.00	January 1/12
T-shirts and Caps	0.00	January 1/12

2. Type   **Office and Computer Supplies** in the Account Name field

3. Click   the **Enter Opening Balance** button to display the Enter Opening Balance window:

Enter Opening Balance: Other Current Asset Account

Enter the balance this account had on the day before your QuickBooks start date.

Attention: If this account **did not** have a balance before your QuickBooks start date, click **Cancel** and use a transaction to put money in this account. Example transactions

Opening Balance [　　　　] as of [　　　　] 🔲

OK   Cancel   Help

Figure 5-29

4. Type   **210** in the Opening Balance field

5. Press   `tab` to advance to the **as of date field**

6. Type   **01/01/12** or **press** `ctrl` **+ V** if you copied the date to the clipboard

7. Click   **OK** to close the **Enter Opening Balance** screen and return to the Add New Account window

8. Click   **Save & New** or **press** `alt` **+ N**

For the next two accounts, the opening balance is zero so we need to enter only the account name, not the opening balance or the date.

9. Enter   the two **Other Current Asset account names** shown above and then **click Save & New or press** `alt` **+ N**

Entering Fixed Asset Accounts

The next group of assets are fixed assets. These appear as the last assets on the Balance Sheet because they are the least liquid — they take longest to be converted to cash. River Run's fixed assets are grouped into parent (heading) and subaccounts for each type of asset. This allows us to see the net asset value or subtotal (cost minus accumulated depreciation) as the parent account balance.

Notice that Other Current Asset is still selected as the account type.

1. Click   the **drop-down arrow** in the Account Type field and **select Fixed Asset** as the type (or type f) to change the input form:

Notes
Fixed asset is the only account type that begins with F, so entering F while your cursor is in the Account Type field will select this account type.

Figure 5-30

Instead of a Bank Account Number field, fixed assets allow you to add a note. Otherwise, the form is the same as that for Other Current Assets.

For parent accounts, you must enter only the account name. For subaccounts you must enter the name, the opening balance and date if applicable; indicate that the account is a subaccount; and choose the parent account from the list. The other fields are optional. For parent accounts, the balance is calculated automatically by the program as the sum of the subaccount balances.

Depreciation accounts are contra-asset accounts. Their credit balances are entered as negative amounts, so they reduce the total asset value.

The complete list of fixed assets is presented in the following chart:

Name	Subaccount of	Description	Opening Balance	Date
Computers/Digital Equipment [Parent account]				
Cost	Computers/Digital Equipment	Original cost of computers	$4,500.00	January 1/12
Depreciation	Computers/Digital Equipment	Accum deprec on computers	$−1,820.00	January 1/12

2. Type   **Computers/Digital Equipment** in the Account Name field

You do not define an account as a parent account. QuickBooks defines it automatically when you identify a subaccount for it. QuickBooks also calculates its opening balance as the sum of all its subaccount balances.

3. Click   **Save & New** or **press** **alt** **+ N**

4. Type   **Cost** as the next Account Name

5. Click   the **Subaccount of checkbox**

6. Click   the **drop-down arrow** in the Subaccount of field

Notes
QuickBooks has some helpful shortcuts on the Account input form too. From the Account Name field, press *tab* to advance to the Subaccount option box. Press the Space bar to select the subaccount option. Press *tab* to move to the Subaccount name field. Assuming that the parent account is already entered, you can type its first letter, in this case type C, and press *tab* to continue. Computers is the first account on the Chart of Accounts beginning with the letter C so it is entered as the default.

7. **Choose**	**Computers/Digital Equipment**	
8. **Press**	(tab) to advance to the **Description field**	
9. **Type**	**Original cost of computers**	
10. **Click**	the **Enter Opening Balance button**	
11. **Type**	**4500** in the Opening Balance field	
12. **Press**	(tab)	
13. **Press**	(ctrl) + **V** to paste the date (or type 01/01/12)	
14. **Click**	**OK**	
15. **Click**	**Save & New** or **press** (alt) + **N**	
16. **Type**	**Depreciation** as the next Account Name	
17. **Click**	the **Subaccount of checkbox**	
18. **Click**	the **drop-down arrow** in the Subaccount of field	
19. **Choose**	**Computers/Digital Equipment**	
20. **Press**	(tab) to advance to the **Description field**	
21. **Type**	**Accum deprec on computers**	
22. **Click**	the **Enter Opening Balance button**	

Depreciation accounts are contra-asset accounts. They have a credit balance instead of a debit balance, which is normal for asset accounts. They reduce the total asset value on the Balance Sheet. Therefore, you must enter a negative opening balance amount (add a minus sign) to create a credit balance for these accounts.

23. **Type**	**−1820**	
24. **Press**	(tab)	
25. **Press**	(ctrl) + **V** to paste the date from the clipboard (or type 01/01/12)	
26. **Click**	**OK**	
27. **Click**	**Save & New** or **press** (alt) + **N** after adding **Depreciation**	

River Run has no accounts of the Other Asset type.

Entering Other Current Liability Accounts

The next group of accounts are the Liability accounts. As with assets, there are several types of liability accounts. *Accounts Payable* is the first type of QuickBooks liability account — it appears before other liability accounts on the Balance Sheet. QuickBooks automatically created an Accounts Payable account when the company file was originally set up using the EasyStep Interview. River Run has no Accounts Payable accounts or Credit Card accounts so we will have to delete the Accounts Payable account later.

The next type of account we will enter is Other Current Liability. *Fixed Asset* is still selected as the account type since it was the last account type that was entered.

QuickBooks has already created four accounts in the Other Current Liabilities section of the chart of accounts — *GST/HST Payable, GST/QST Payable, Payroll Liabilities,* and *PST Payable (MB).* The tax accounts are created automatically by QuickBooks, depending on the province selected when setting up your company file. Some of these accounts are not needed or they do not have the correct account name as used in our chart of accounts. Throughout this chapter, we will work with each account, either making it inactive or renaming it.

We need to make one other current liability account, the *Bank Loan* account:

1. **Click**   the **drop-down arrow** in the Account Type field

2. **Choose**   Other Current Liability as the account type (~~~~~~~~~~~~~~ til Other Current Liability is displayed)

This form has the same input fields as the Other Current Asset type. Refer to page 168 for assistance if needed.

3. **Enter**   **Bank Loan** as the account name, **11 000** as the opening balance, and **01/01/12** in the as of date field

4. **Click**   **OK**

5. **Click**   **Save & New** or **press** (alt) + **N**

Entering Equity Accounts

There are no other Liability accounts so we are now ready to look at the group of Equity or capital accounts. QuickBooks has already created an equity account, the *Opening Balance Equity* account. We will be renaming the *Opening Balance Equity* account to *Accumulated Surplus*. We will edit this account later to match the Equity accounts in our Chart of Accounts on page 144.

Entering Income Accounts

After adding all the Balance Sheet accounts, we must create Income Statement accounts. River Run has only regular income accounts.

1. **Click**   the **drop-down arrow** beside Account Type and **choose Income** (or type i) to change the form:

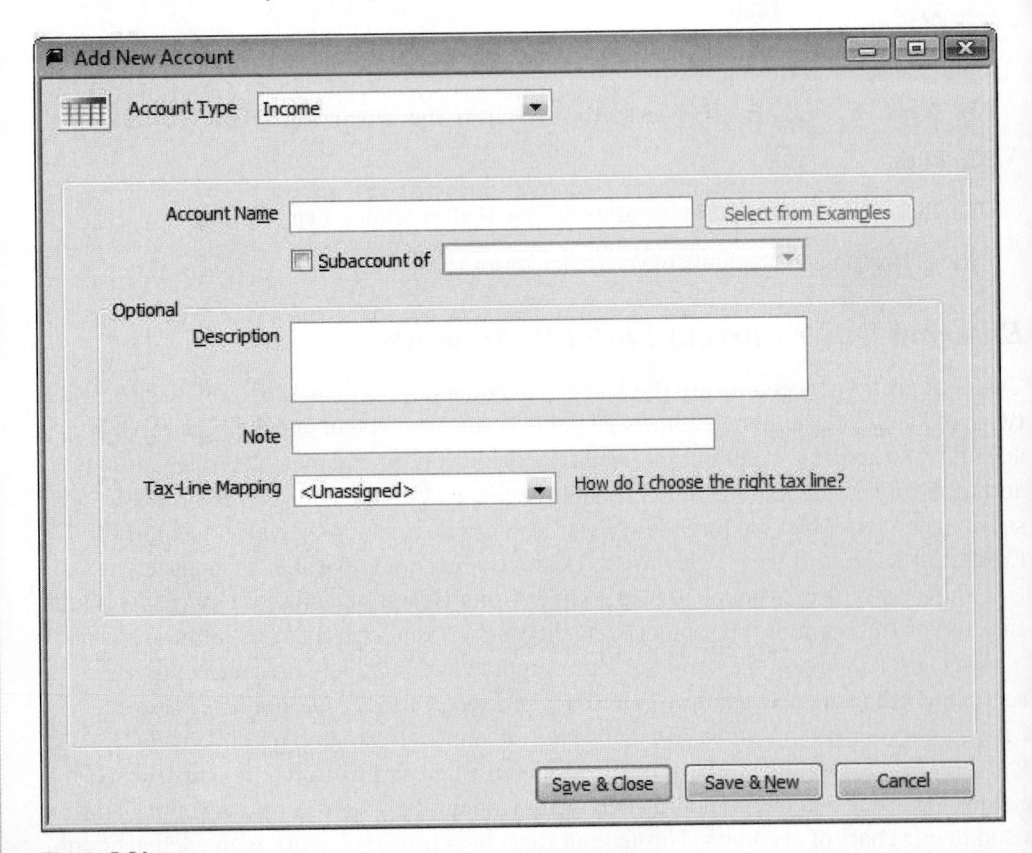

Figure 5-31

The form for income accounts has no opening balance field. The balance is generated automatically from the transactions for the account. When you have historical balances to enter, the opening balances for income accounts are added through a ledger entry for the *Opening Balance Equity* account (decreasing equity balance). All income accounts for River Run have a zero balance because the books have been closed.

Notes
Our income and expense account balances are all zero because we are entering post-closing amounts at the start of a new fiscal period.

We will enter opening income and expense account balances for Darya's Dance Studio in Chapter 10.

2. **Type**   **Revenue from Donations**

3. **Click**   **Save & New** or **press** (alt) **+N**

4. **Create**   the **remaining two income accounts**: Revenue from Registrations and Revenue from Sales

Entering Cost of Goods Sold Accounts

QuickBooks has two types of expense accounts: Cost of Goods Sold and Expenses. Cost of Goods Sold appears separately on the Income Statement to arrive at the Gross Profit. Other expenses are then included to determine Net Income. Cost of Goods Sold applies to retail businesses that buy merchandise to resell. River Run resells T-shirts and caps as part of its fundraising campaign, so it has costs related to this merchandise. At the time of the run, food and drinks are also sold to spectators and these related costs will also be tracked.

1. **Click**   **Save & New** or **press** (alt) **+ N** and **choose Cost of Goods Sold** as the account type (or type c) to change the form:

Figure 5-32

The Cost of Goods Sold account form is similar to the Income account form, but it has an additional field for the sales tax code. Many expenses are associated with taxable purchases so entering the sales tax code with the account will save some data entry time when entering transactions. Of course, you can edit the sales tax code if necessary for individual purchases.

When River Run purchases items for sale, it enters the goods as inventory. The cost of goods sold is entered later as an adjustment to the asset account so no tax code is required.

Like income accounts, the Cost of Goods Sold account opening balance is generated by the program as the sum of all transactions for the account. Our opening account balances are zero.

2. Press   `tab` to advance to the **Account Name field**

3. Type   **Cost of Food and Drinks**

4. Click   **Save & New** or **press** `alt` **+ N**

5. Type   **Cost of T-shirts and Caps**

Entering Expense Accounts

We are now ready to enter the final group of accounts — the Expense accounts.

1. Click   **Save & New** or **press** `alt` **+ N** and **choose Expense** as the account type (or type e) to change the form

The Expense account form is the same as the one for Cost of Goods Sold. Expense accounts for River Run are listed in the following chart:

Name	Tax Code
Depreciation Expense	(blank)
Office & Computer Supplies Used	(blank)
Office Rent	G
Printing and Copying	S
Publicity and Promotion	G
Telephone Expense	S
Wage Contract Expenses	(blank)

You can add sales tax codes to expense accounts so the default tax for each account is displayed automatically when entering a bill. We have to make some changes to the taxes to accommodate the non-refundable GST for our charity, so we will leave the tax codes blank for now.

2. Press   `tab` to advance to the **Name field**

3. Type   **Depreciation Expense**

4. Click   **Save & New**

5. Type   **Office & Computer Supplies Used**

6. Click   **Save & New**

For Office Rent, you must also enter a sales tax code. Business rent has GST applied.

7. Type   **Office Rent**

QuickBooks has created a default set of sales tax codes that apply to businesses in the province we selected when we set up our company file. If necessary, you can change the default sales tax code when you enter a transaction. The codes are correct for River Run. In a later chapter, we will learn how to add and modify sales tax codes.

8. Enter   the **remaining expense accounts**

After adding the Wage Contract Expenses account:

Notes
Depending on the account type selected in the Account Type field, the Equity type may be displayed the first time you type the letter "e". To move to the Expense type, type "e" again.

9. **Click**   **Save & Close** instead of Save & New to save the account and close the Add New Account form

Notes
The other account types are not used by River Run.

You will return to the Chart of Accounts. You should notice several changes. All the new accounts you created have been added with balances if you entered one for them.

There are still some accounts listed on the Chart of Accounts that we do not need, such as some of the tax codes, the *Accounts Payable* account, and payroll accounts. We will be working with these accounts later in this chapter.

Notes
The equity balances may not be correct if there are income and expense account balances, or if you entered an incorrect amount for any account.

In addition, the *Opening Balance Equity* account balance has changed. Every time you entered an opening account balance, the program added an offsetting amount to the *Opening Balance Equity* account. If the account you created had a debit balance, the *Opening Balance Equity* account was credited by the same amount. If you added a credit balance, a debit amount was entered for *Opening Balance Equity*. This ensures that the Trial Balance remains balanced. The final account balance should be $7,910.00 if you entered all amounts correctly. We will rename the *Opening Balance Equity* account to *Accumulated Surplus* later in this chapter.

10. **Compare**   the **Chart of Accounts** displayed on the screen with the one on page 144 and **mark** the **accounts that require corrections. Ignore** the **tax accounts** for now.

We will now make the necessary corrections to the Chart of Accounts.

Deleting Accounts

The Chart of Accounts includes the following accounts, other than the tax accounts, that are not needed. (we will be working with the tax accounts later in this chapter):

> Accounts Payable
>
> Payroll Liabilities* (cannot be deleted because it is used on a payroll item)
>
> Perm. Restricted Net Assets
>
> Temp. Restricted Net Assets
>
> Unrestricted Net Assets
>
> Payroll Expenses* (cannot be deleted because it is used on a payroll item)
>
> Uncategorized Expenses

Notes
You also cannot delete any account that has a balance or has been used in journal transactions.

The accounts with an asterisk beside them cannot be deleted from the Chart of Accounts. Accounts cannot be deleted if they are used by other items in QuickBooks. Both the *Payroll Liabilities* and the *Payroll Expenses* accounts are used on a payroll item and cannot be deleted. In order to remove them from the Chart of Accounts, we will learn how to make them inactive or hide them later in this chapter.

1. **Click**   **Accounts Payable** to select it

2. **Press**   ctrl + **D** (or **choose** the **Account** button and **click Delete**)

You will see the following warning message:

Figure 5-33

3.	**Click**	**OK**
4.	**Click**	**Perm. Restricted Net Assets** to select it
5.	**Press**	ctrl + **D** (or **choose** the **Account** button and **click Delete**)
6.	**Click**	**OK**
7.	**Continue deleting**	the rest of the accounts in the list (other than the ones with an asterisk beside their name)
8.	**Click**	**OK** to return to the Chart of Accounts when you have finished deleting the accounts

Making Accounts Inactive

There may be accounts that you don't need in the Chart of Accounts but they cannot be deleted. For example, you cannot delete accounts that are linked to other items, have balances, or have been used in transactions. If an account meets any one of these criteria, then the account must be made inactive (or hidden).

The Chart of Accounts includes the following accounts that we do not need but cannot be deleted:

> Payroll Liabilities
>
> Payroll Expenses
>
> GST/QST Payable
>
> PST Payable (MB)

We'll try to delete the first account so you can see the type of message displayed when an account cannot be deleted:

1.	**Click**	**Payroll Liabilities** and **press** ctrl + **D**
2.	The following warning is displayed:	

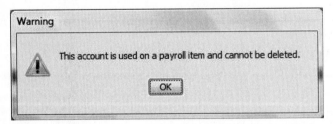

Figure 5-34

The account is used on a payroll item and cannot be deleted. You could delete the payroll item for which the account is used and then delete the account or just make the account inactive (or hide it), which will allow you to make it active again in the future if you find you need to use it.

3.	**Click**	**OK**
4.	**Right click**	**Payroll Liabilities** and **click Make Account Inactive**

The account is removed from the Chart of Accounts.

5.	**Make**	the **Payroll Expenses, GST/QST Payable and PST Payable (MB) accounts inactive**

Notes
To make an inactive account active, click on the Include Inactive check box found at the bottom of the screen. Inactive accounts will be displayed with an X to the left of their name. Click on the X to remove the inactive status and make the account active. Click the Include Inactive checkbox to remove the inactive column from the list.

Warning

⚠ This account is used on a payroll item and cannot be deleted.

OK

Editing Accounts

When you review the Chart of Accounts, you may find that some of the accounts were entered incorrectly. You can easily correct an account number or name at this stage by opening the account record. To correct an opening balance or date, you must change the amount in the register for the account. As soon as you save a new account, the Opening Balance button is no longer available in the record; however, it is replaced with a Change Opening Balance button that will open the account register, allowing you to make changes to the opening balance.

Editing Account Names

Two accounts automatically created by QuickBooks do not match the accounts on our Chart of Accounts. We need to edit the account names as shown in the following chart:

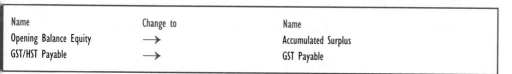

Name	Change to		Name
Opening Balance Equity	→		Accumulated Surplus
GST/HST Payable	→		GST Payable

WARNING!
Do not double click the account as this will open the register for the account, not the account form.

1. **Open**   the **Chart of Accounts**, if it is not still open from the previous exercise

2. **Click**   **Opening Balance Equity**

3. **Press**   ⌷ctrl⌷ + **E** (or **choose** the **Account** button and **click Edit**)

The Edit Account form appears for the selected account:

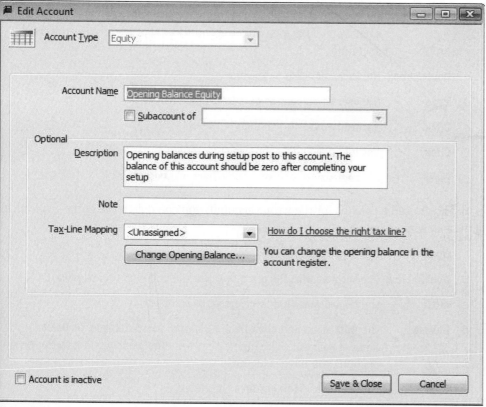

Figure 5-35

Notice that the Opening Balance button has been replaced with the Change Opening Balance button. Clicking on this button would open the account register where you can update the balances entered for the Opening Balance Equity account. Since this account is the offsetting account for all opening balances entered, you would have to change the individual transactions in the register.

The account type is dimmed. You cannot change the type if the account has been used in journal entries or if the account is linked to another function. The *Opening Balance Equity* account has been used in several journal transactions — one for each account opening balance we added — so its type cannot be changed. The account name is highlighted so we can change it.

4.	**Type**	**Accumulated Surplus** to replace Opening Balance Equity as the Account Name
5.	**Click**	**Save & Close** to save the changes and return to the Chart of Accounts
6.	**Edit**	**the GST/HST Payable account**
7.	**Click**	**Save & Close** to save the changes and return to the Chart of Accounts
8.	**Close**	out of the **Chart of Accounts** to return to the Home page

Editing Opening Balances and Dates

Notes

Opening balances and dates can be edited for an account directly from its register. All Balance Sheet accounts have registers, except the Retained Earnings account.

As soon as you save a new account with its opening balance, the opening balance field is closed. To edit the balance, or the opening balance date, you must edit the entry in the account register.

If you find that you entered an incorrect opening amount or date for an account perform the following steps:

a)	**Open**	the **Chart of Accounts**
b)	**Double click**	the **account with the error** to open the account's register (this is only available for Balance Sheet accounts except the Retained Earnings account)
c)	**Double click**	the **incorrect date or amount**
d)	**Type**	the **correct amount or date** to replace it
e)	**Click**	**Record** to save the change
f)	**Click**	**Yes** when asked to confirm the change
g)	**Close**	the **register** to return to the Chart of Accounts

If you entered a balance for the wrong account, you can delete the entry by performing the following steps:

a)	**Open**	the **Chart of Accounts**
b)	**Double click**	the **account with the error** to open the account's register
c)	**Click**	the **transaction that is incorrect** to select it
d)	**Choose**	the **Edit menu** and **click Delete Deposit, Delete Cheque,** or **Delete General Journal.** (The menu item will change according to the type of account you have selected)
e)	**Click**	**OK** when asked to confirm the deletion
f)	**Close**	the **register** to return to the Chart of Accounts
g)	**Close**	the **Chart of Accounts**

Sales Taxes

Changing Tax Preferences

The settings for sales taxes can be found on the Company Preferences tab of the Sales Tax heading in QuickBooks preferences.

1. **Choose**   the **Edit menu** and **click Preferences**

2. **Click**   the **Sales Tax heading** on the left-hand side of the screen. There are no personal preferences on the My Preferences tab for sales taxes

3. **Click**   the **Company Preferences tab** to view the screen we need:

Figure 5-36

The first question on the form — Do you charge sales tax? — is preset to Yes. If no taxes are charged or tracked, you can choose No and the remaining options will be dimmed and unavailable. All prices can be recorded with taxes included.

Use this screen to determine if you want QuickBooks to use the sales tax codes entered in customer and vendor records instead of the sales tax codes assigned to items when entering transactions. You can also determine how sales taxes will be displayed on forms. You can select to display the amount on forms to include tax and/or you can select to display only one sales tax total on forms instead of separate provincial and federal tax amounts. You can save time when entering items by selecting the default tax code to be used for new taxable and non-taxable items.

River Run is not registered for GST or PST. As a registered charity, however, River Run is eligible for a rebate of 50 percent of all GST paid on purchases. Therefore, we do need to set up the GST so that GST paid can be tracked. The request for a rebate is filed annually.

4. **Click**   **Yes** beside the question **Do you charge sales tax?**

5. **Click**   **OK** to close the **Company Preferences window** and return to the **Home page**

Defining a New Sales Tax

When you set up a company file, QuickBooks automatically sets up a list of common sales tax codes, sales tax agencies, and sales tax liability accounts based on the province selected for your company. If your company charges the standard taxes for your province, then you can use these tax codes without making changes. However, if you have other taxes that you need to set up such as a tire tax or a hotel tax, or if you have a variation on the standard taxes, you need to manually add additional vendors, tax items, tax groups, and tax codes.

River Run does not require registration or collection of GST but receives a partial rebate of GST paid. The charity submits an application for refunds annually, listing the total of all GST paid toward its operating expenses. Fifty percent of this amount is eligible for the rebate. Therefore, River Run records GST paid on all purchases and debits these amounts to the *Non-refundable GST Expense* account. The rebate application is for 50 percent of this amount, leaving 50 percent as an expense. *GST Refund Receivable* is debited to record the rebate request until the refund is received and deposited.

When setting up new a new tax to track GST at 2.5 percent eligible and 2.5 percent ineligible, there are five steps that need to be followed:

1. **Create**   a **Sales Tax Agency vendor** to track the ineligible GST portion

2. **Create**   two sales tax items — one for **GST @ 2.5% eligible** and one for **GST @ 2.5% ineligible**

3. **Create**   a **sales tax group**

4. **Create**   a **sales tax code**

5. **Assign**   the **sales tax code to your expense accounts**

Create a Sales Tax Agency Vendor to Track the Ineligible GST Portion

The GST is remitted to the Receiver General, which is automatically set up by QuickBooks at the current rate of 5 percent. In order to set up the GST to keep track of the GST rate of 2.5 percent refundable and 2.5 percent non-refundable, we must first set up a sales tax agency vendor to track the non-refundable GST that cannot be claimed as an input tax credit on your GST return.

1. **Click**   the **Vendor Centre icon** on the Home page

Notice that there is a vendor called Receiver General. This vendor keeps track of the 5 percent GST that can be claimed as an input tax credit on your GST return.

2. **Click**   the **New Vendor button**

3. **Type**   **Receiver General Non-Taxable** in the Vendor Name field

4. **Click**   the **Vendor is a Sales Tax Agency check box** on the right-hand side of the screen

5. **Click**   the **Tax Agency Info tab**

6. **Click**   on the **drop-down arrow** beside the **Tax Return field**

7. **Select**   **GST/HST Return**

8. **Type**   **GST Non-refundable** in the **Tax Label field**

9. **Click**   the **Track tax on purchases separately to checkbox**

10. **Type**   **Non-refundable GST Expense** and **press** (enter)

11. **Click**   **Setup** in the **Account Not Found** message

12. **Click**   **Save & Close**

13. The Tax Agency Info tab for the vendor should contain the following information:

Figure 5-37

14. **Click**   **OK**

The Receiver General Non-Taxable should now be displayed in the Vendor list.

15. **Close**   the **Vendor Centre**

Create Sales Tax Items

Next, we have to create two sales tax items that make up the 5 percent GST Tax rate. One item will track the GST @ 2.5 percent that is claimable on the GST Return, while the other will track the portion of GST @ 2.5 percent that is not claimable on the GST Return.

1. **Choose**   **Lists** and **click Item List**

The items that are currently listed on the item list are tax items that were set up automatically by QuickBooks when you set up the company file. You also use the item list to add items that you buy and sell. We'll add items that we sell a little later in the chapter.

First, we'll enter the tax item that will track the 2.5 percent of GST that is claimable on the GST Return.

2. Click the **Item button** and **click New**

3. Choose **Sales Tax Item** as the Type (we'll talk more about item types later)

4. Type **GST Eligible 2.5%** in the Sales Tax Name field

5. Press [tab]

The sales tax name is automatically entered in the description field.

6. Press [tab] to advance to the **Tax Rate (%) or Amt field**

7. Type **2.5%** (make sure you type the percent sign)

8. Click the **drop-down arrow** under the **Tax Agency field**

9. Select **Receiver General**

10. Click the **drop-down list beside the Sales Tax Return Line**

11. Select Line 106 Input Tax Credits (ITCs)

12. The completed tax item should appear as shown:

Figure 5-38

13. Click **OK**

If the Spell Check window is displayed, use it to check your work.

Next, we'll enter the tax item that will track the 2.5 percent of GST that is not claimable on the GST Return.

1. Click the **Item button** and **click New**

2. Choose **Sales Tax Item** as the Type

3. Type **GST Ineligible 2.5%** in the **Sales Tax Name field**

4. Press [tab]

The sales tax name is automatically entered in the description field.

5. Press [tab] to advance to the **Tax Rate (%) or Amt field**

6. **Type**	**2.5%** (make sure you type the percent sign)
7. **Click**	the **drop-down arrow** under the **Tax Agency field**

The following selection is very important and is what differentiates the GST from being eligible or ineligible.

8. **Select**	**Receiver General Non-Taxable**
9. **Click**	the **drop-down arrow** beside the **Sales Tax Return Line**
10. **Select**	**Line 106 Input Tax Credits (ITCs)**

11. The completed tax item should appear as shown:

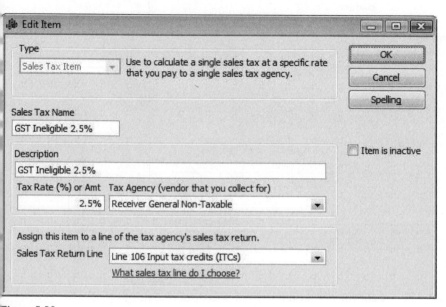

Figure 5-39

12. **Click**	**OK**

If the Spell Check window is displayed, use it to check your work.

Create a Sales Tax Group

A sales tax group must be created that contains the two GST tax items that you just added. Sales tax groups are used to group sales tax items that are needed on individual sales or purchase transactions.

After you create a sales tax group, you assign it to a sales tax code. When you enter a bill from a vendor that contains GST only, you select the sales tax code to use on the bill.

1. **Choose**	**Lists** and **click Item List**, if you are not already on the Item list from the previous exercise
2. **Click**	the **Item button** and **click New**
3. **Choose**	**Sales Tax Group** as the Type
4. **Type**	**GST Eligible/Ineligible** in the **Group Name/Number field**
5. **Press**	(tab) **to advance** to the **Tax Item column**
6. **Click**	the **drop-down arrow** in the **Tax Item field**
7. **Select**	**GST Eligible 2.5%**

Notes
Enter an easily identifiable name as the group name.

Notice the information entered on the screen. You can view the Rate, Tax Agency, and Description for the selected Tax Item.

8. Click   the **drop-down arrow** on the second line under the **Tax Item field**

9. Select   **GST Ineligible 2.5%**

10. The Sales Tax Group should be displayed as shown:

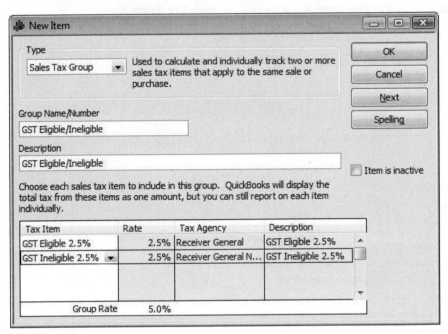

Figure 5-40

11. Click   **OK** if the Spell Check window is displayed

River Run also purchases items from vendors that contain both GST (2.5 percent eligible and 2.5 percent ineligible) and PST. Therefore, we need to create one more sales tax group that will contain all three taxes.

The item list must be open to perform the following steps:

1. Click   the **Item button** and **click New**

2. Choose   **Sales Tax Group** as the Type

3. Type   **GST Eligible/Ineligible and PST** in the Group Name/Number field

4. Press   `tab` to advance to the **Tax Item column**

5. Click   the **drop-down arrow** in the **Tax Item field**

6. Select   **GST Eligible 2.5%** on the first line

7. Select   **GST Ineligible 2.5%** on the second line

8. Select   **PST (MB) on purchases** on the third line

9. The Sales Tax Group should be displayed as shown:

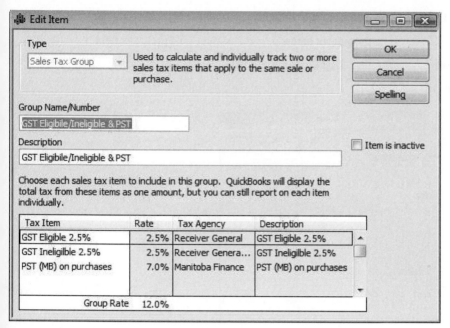

Figure 5-41

10. **Click**   **OK** to save the new Sales Tax Group and return to the Item list

11. **Close**   the **Item list**

Create a Sales Tax Code

Next, we have to add sales tax codes and assign the sales tax groups we just created to them.

1. **Choose**   **Lists** and **click Sales Tax Code List** to display the Sales Tax Code list:

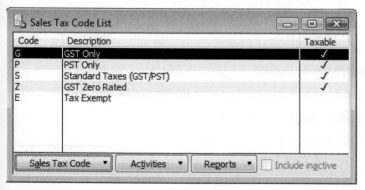

Figure 5-42

These are the default sales tax codes created by QuickBooks. Sales Tax Codes are used to determine the taxes calculated when entering customer sales transactions and vendor bills.

2. **Click**   the **Sales Tax Code button** and **click New**

3. **Type**   **GEI** in the Sales Tax Code field (this can be a maximum of any 3 characters that you want to use to describe the sales tax code)

4. **Press**   ⌨ tab ⌨ to advance to the description field

5. **Type**   **GST Eligible/Ineligible**

Notes
You can use any 3 characters you want to create your sales tax code.

6. **Click**   the **button beside Taxable**

7. **Click**   the **drop-down arrow** in the **Tax Item for Purchases field**

8. **Select**   the **GST Eligible/Ineligible** Sales Tax Group

9. The GEI sales tax code should be displayed as follows:

Figure 5-43

10. **Click OK**

11. **Click** the **Sales Tax Code button** and **click New**

We need to create another sales tax code that not only includes the eligible and ineligible GST but must also include PST. Consider a bill from a vendor that contains both GST and PST. We want to track the GST correctly (2.5 percent eligible and 2.5 percent ineligible), but we also need to include PST. The only way to do this is to create another sales tax code that includes all 3 sales tax items.

12. **Type**   **GP** in the **Sales Tax Code field** (this can be a maximum of any 3 characters that you want to use to describe the sales tax code)

13. **Press**   [tab] to advance to the **description field**

14. **Type**   **GST Eligible/Ineligible and PST**

15. **Click**   the **button beside Taxable**

16. **Click**   the **drop-down arrow** in the **Tax Item for Purchases field**

17. **Click**   **GST Eligible/Ineligible & PST** Sales Tax Group

18. The GP sales tax code should be displayed as follows:

Figure 5-44

19. **Click**   **OK**

20. **Close**   the **Sales Tax Code** list

Assigning Sales Tax Codes to Expense Accounts

The last step when setting up taxes is to assign sales tax codes to accounts. When we set up the expense accounts earlier, if the sales tax codes were set up correctly, we could have assigned the sales tax codes at that time. Now that the sales tax codes have been set up correctly, we will go back and assign the sales tax codes to the expense accounts.

We will edit the accounts from the Chart of Accounts window.

1. **Choose**   **Company** and then **click Chart of Accounts**

2. **Right click**   **Office Rent** and **click Edit Account**

3. **Click**   the **drop-down arrow** in the **Sales Tax Code field**

4. **Click**   **GEI**

When we receive a bill for rent, we are charged GST only. We will use the GEI sales tax code because it has been set up to track 2.5 percent of the GST as eligible and the other 2.5 percent of the GST as ineligible.

5. **Click**   **Save & Close** or `alt` + **A**

6. **Add**   the following sales tax codes to the following accounts:

Name	Tax Code
Printing and Copying	GP
Publicity and Promotion	GEI
Telephone Expense	GP

7. **Close**   the **Chart of Accounts**

Creating Customer Accounts

As we have seen in earlier chapters, customer records can be entered from any customer field in the program. Although we could use this approach to add customers as needed, it is more efficient to start with a list of existing customers. Even though we will create only skeletal customer records, we will create the records at the start so that we can add the payment terms and method of payment as defaults.

As with many other activities in QuickBooks, customers can be added in many ways. Other than starting in a Customer:Job field on a form, all other methods begin from the Customers & Jobs list. This list can be viewed in the Customer Centre, which can be accessed in several ways:

a)   **Click**   the **Customer Centre icon** on the Icon bar; or

Figure 5-45

> **Notes**
> The G sales tax code has been set up automatically by QuickBooks to track 5 percent of the GST as eligible.

> **Notes**
> The GEI sales tax code has been set up to track 2.5 percent of the GST as eligible and the other 2.5 percent as ineligible.

> **Notes**
> The GP sales tax code has been set up to track 2.5 percent of the GST as eligible and the other 2.5 percent ineligible and includes PST @ 7 percent.

> **Notes**
> The S code is set up automatically by QuickBooks to track 5 percent of the GST as eligible and includes PST @ 7 percent.

b) **Click** the **Customers icon** in the Customers section of the Home page; or

Figure 5-46

c) **Click** the **Customers menu** and **select Customer Centre**; or

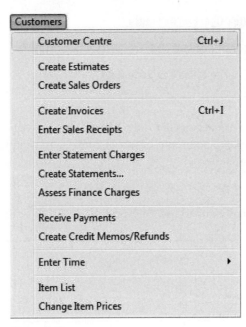

Figure 5-47

d) **Press** (ctrl) **+ J**

1. Open the **Customers & Jobs list** using one of the options listed above

You will notice that there are no customers on the Customers & Jobs list because we have not yet created them.

2. Click the **New Customer & Job button** to view the menu and **click New Customer** as shown here or **press** (ctrl) **+ N:**

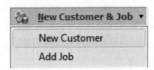

Figure 5-48

Notes
The keyboard shortcut commands for creating, editing, and deleting a record are the
~~same for~~ ~~making it easy~~
to remember and use these shortcuts.

Pressing (ctrl) **+ N** will open a new form in the current list once the list is displayed on the screen. The other keyboard ~~shortcuts~~ ~~are the same~~ from one list to another. To edit a record, click (ctrl) **+ E;** and to delete a record, click (ctrl) **+ D**.

A blank customer record form opens:

Figure 5-49

The cursor is in the Customer Name field where you add the customer's name.

3. Type   **Donors**

The date in the *as of* field on this form applies only to customers with outstanding invoices, so you do not need to change it.

Since this customer record will be used for all donors and not a specific donor, the address and contact information will be left blank.

4. Click   the **Additional Info tab** to access the next group of customer record fields

On this screen, we need to add only the customer terms.

5. Click   the **Terms list arrow** to view the default payment terms:

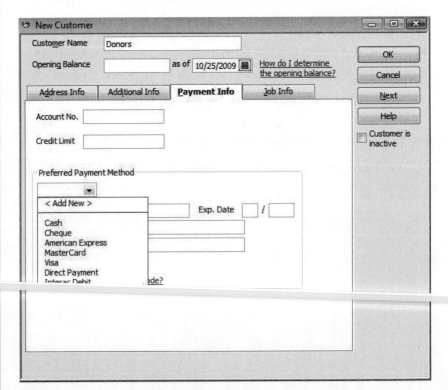

Figure 5-50

River Run accepts only cash from its participants and sponsors. Later, we will delete the terms that we do not use.

6. Click **Due on receipt** to add the term to the customer record

7. Click the **Payment Info tab** to view the next group of customer details

8. Click the **Preferred Payment Method list arrow** to view the options:

Figure 5-51

Again, these payment methods were created automatically by the program, and we will edit the list later. All customers pay cash.

9. Click   Cash

The fourth tab, Job Info, allows you to organize the work done for customers according to specific jobs. This allows you to track the work done for customers in a more detailed way. When jobs are set up, you can choose the Customer and Job from the Customers & Jobs list. Customer jobs do not apply to River Run.

CORRECTING CUSTOMER RECORDS

Before Saving the Record

To correct a record while you are creating it, just return to the field that has the error, highlight the incorrect details, and type the correction. Click the Address Info tab and Additional Info tab to return to those screens for checking your work. If the terms are incorrect, select the correct terms from the list to replace the incorrect ones.

After Saving the Record

If you need to make corrections or changes later, open the Customers & Jobs List. Click the customer name to select it. With the customer selected, there are a number of ways to open the customer record for editing. You can right click the customer name and select Edit: Customer:Job, you can double click the customer name, you can select Edit from the menu, and then select Edit Customer:Job, or you can use the keyboard shortcut ⌖ ctrl ⌗ + E. With the customer record open, find the incorrect details and type the correction. Click OK to save the changes and return to the Customer:Job List.

---

10. Check   your work carefully

11. Click   ⌖ alt ⌗ + N or click Next to save the record and open a new input form

12. Enter   the name, terms, and method of payment for Runners, the second customer record. Refer to page 145 for details

13. Click   OK to save the last customer record and return to the Customer Centre

Your new customers are displayed in the Customers & Jobs list on the left-hand side of the screen.

14. Close   the Customer Centre

Creating Vendor Records

As with many other activities in QuickBooks, vendors can be added in many ways. Other than starting in a Vendor field on a form, all other methods begin from the Vendor list found in the Vendor Centre. This list can only be viewed in the Vendor Centre, which can be accessed in several ways:

a) **Click**   the **Vendor Centre icon** on the Icon bar; or

Figure 5-52

b) **Click**   the **Vendors icon** in the Vendors section of the Home page:

Figure 5-53

or

c) **Click** the **Vendors menu** and **select Vendor Centre**:

Figure 5-54

The Vendors section of the Home page has the minimum number of icons displayed because we have not indicated that we want to use inventory and purchase orders:

Figure 5-55

We will examine the preferences later to see if any others need to be changed. They do not affect the entry of new vendor records.

1. Open the **Vendor list** by using one of the options listed above

QuickBooks has created records for Manitoba Finance, Ministère du Revenu, and the Receiver General, the tax agencies for the collection of sales taxes. You cannot remove these records, even if you do not collect taxes. We will make the Ministère du Revenu and Manitoba Finance records inactive so they will not appear on our lists.

2. Click the **New Vendor button** or **press** $ctrl$ + **N**:

Figure 5-56

Notes
The keyboard shortcuts that apply to the Customer List also apply to the Vendor List.

A blank vendor record form opens:

Figure 5-57

All vendors require immediate payment, so we will create only partial records for vendors that contain names and payment terms.

The cursor is in the Vendor Name field where you add the vendor's name.

3. Type   **Bell Canada**

As in customer records, the date in the *as of* field on the vendor form applies only to vendors with outstanding bills, so you do not need to change it.

4. Click   the **Additional Info tab** to access the remaining vendor record fields

5. Click   the **Terms list arrow** to view the predefined list of terms:

Figure 5-58

All vendors demand payment on receipt of goods or invoice.

6. Click   **Due on receipt**

7. Check   **your work** carefully

CORRECTING VENDOR RECORDS

Before Saving the Record

To correct a record while you are creating it, just return to the field that has the error, highlight the incorrect details, and type the correction. Click the Address Info tab and Additional Info tab to return to those screens to check your work. If the terms are incorrect, select the correct terms from the list.

After Saving the Record

If you need to make corrections or changes later, open the Vendors List. Click the vendor name to select it. With the vendor selected, there are a number of ways to open the vendor record for editing. You can right click on the vendor name and select Edit Vendor, you can double click on the vendor name, you can select Edit from the menu and then Edit Vendor, or you can use the keyboard shortcut (ctrl) + E. With the vendor record open, highlight the incorrect details and type the correction. Click OK to save the changes and return to the Vendors List.

---

8. Click   **Next** or **press** (alt) + **N** to save the record and open a new blank vendor input form

9. Enter   the **remaining vendor records** on page 145. **Enter** the **name** and **choose** **Due on receipt** from the Terms list

10. Click   **OK** to save the last new vendor and return to the Vendor List (**Click** **Cancel** if you have a blank vendor form open)

Making a Vendor Record Inactive

The Ministère du Revenu and the Manitoba Finance records are not used by River Run, but we cannot delete them because they are tax agencies. We can, however, make the records inactive so they will not be displayed on the vendors list for selection when we are writing cheques.

1. Right Click   **Ministère du Revenu** on the **Vendor List window**

2. Click   **Make Vendor Inactive** or **choose** the **Edit menu** and **click Make Vendor Inactive**

If you need to show the inactive vendor records, click the drop-down arrow in the View field and select All Vendors to show all active and inactive vendors.

Notes

Before you can make a record active again, it must be displayed in the vendor list.

The inactive records have an X beside them as shown:

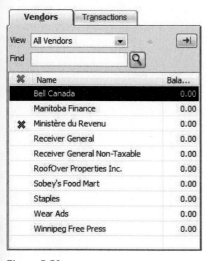

Figure 5-59

Once inactive records are displayed in the list, you can select a record and make it active. One way to do this is to click the vendor name in the vendors list and then right click and select Make Vendor Active or choose the Edit menu and click Make Vendor Active. Alternatively, when all vendors are displayed, clicking on the "X" in the inactive column to the left of the vendor name will make the vendor active. If there is no "X" in the inactive column, clicking in the column will add an "X" and make the record inactive.

3. **Click**   the **inactive column beside Manitoba Finance** to add an "X" to the column and make the vendor inactive

4. **Close**   the **Vendor Centre**

Creating Items

We have seen that QuickBooks processes all sales by selling items. Revenue accounts are linked to items. Therefore, you must create items to use the program. You cannot access revenue accounts from any of the customer sales forms.

Perhaps because items are central to the way the program operates, you can add records for items from many different places. Just like customers and vendors, you can add items on the fly from any Item field in a form. You can also set up records for items from the Item List that you can access in several ways. To open the Item List:

a)   **Choose** the **Lists menu** and **click Item List:**

Figure 5-60

b)   **Choose**   the **Sales Tax menu** and **click Item List**; or

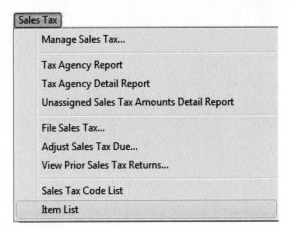

Figure 5-61

c)   **Choose**   the **Customers menu** and **click Item List**; or

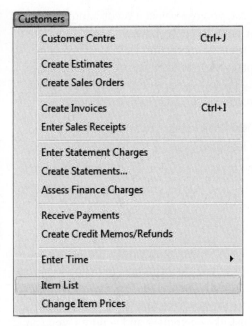

Figure 5-62

d)   **Choose**   the **Vendors menu** and **click Item List**; or

e) **Choose** the **Items and Services icon** on the Home page:

Items &
Services

Figure 5-64

1. **Open** the **Item List** by using one of the options listed above:

Figure 5-65

2. **Click** the **Item button** and **click New** as shown, or **press** ⌃ + **N**:

Figure 5-66

Notes
Again, we can use the same keyboard shortcuts for the Item List as we did for the Customers & Jobs List and the Vendors List.

The New Item form opens:

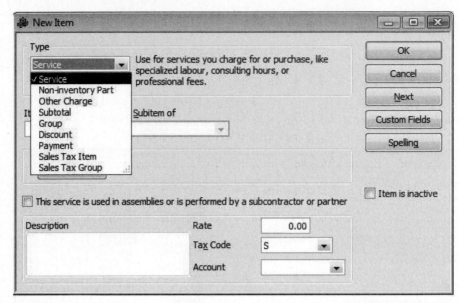

Figure 5-67

Creating Service Items

The Type list is displayed immediately when the new form is opened, and Service is selected. It is the type that we need for most of the items for River Run. The description to the right of the selected item type appears to assist you in selecting the correct item type. We will explain other types of items when we use them.

3. **Click**   **each type in turn** and read the description

4. **Select**   **Service** from the drop-down list

Service items are not purchased, held in stock or tracked as inventory. They are associated only with an income account for income tracking. For each service, you can indicate the item name and/or number, description, default price (rate), tax code, and account. You can change the tax code and price for individual sales, but you cannot change the income account.

You can also set up services under headings by creating a parent item with subitems, just as you do for accounts, but this setup is optional. If the service is used in assemblies or provided by a subcontractor or partner, you can also select that option in the item record.

Item numbers are not used by River Run so the list will appear in alphabetical order on item selection lists in the Item fields on sales and purchase forms.

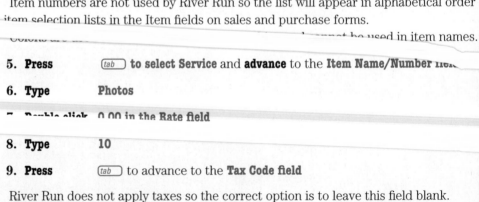

5. **Press**   [tab] to select **Service** and **advance** to the **Item Name/Number** box

6. **Type**   **Photos**

7. **Double click** 0.00 in the **Rate field**

8. **Type**   **10**

9. **Press**   [tab] to advance to the **Tax Code field**

River Run does not apply taxes so the correct option is to leave this field blank.

Notes

Inventory items cannot be created until you turn on the *Inventory and Purchase Orders are active* preference. River Run does not have inventory items, so we will not be turning this preference on in this company file.

Notes

You can create service items, non-inventory items (like supplies), other charges (like delivery charges or setup fees), subtotals, groups of items, discounts, payments, sales tax items and sales tax groups.

10. **Highlight**	the **Tax Code** field and **press** (del)
11. **Press**	(tab) to advance to the **Account field**
12. **Click**	the **drop-down arrow** in the **Account field**
13. **Select**	**Revenue from Sales**

If the account is not on the list, type the account name in the account field and press (tab) to open the option to add the account. Click Set Up to open the New Account screen. Income will be selected correctly as the account type for services.

CORRECTING ITEM RECORDS

Before Saving the Record

To correct a record while you are creating it, return to the field that has the error, highlight the incorrect details, and type the correction.

After Saving the Record

If you need to make corrections or changes later, open the Item List. Click the item name to select it, then click the Item button and choose Edit Item to open the record for editing. Highlight the incorrect details and type the correction. Click OK to save the changes and return to the Item List.

| 14. **Click** | **Next** or **press** (alt) + **N** to save the item and open a blank New Item screen |

Notice that the tax code and account number selected in the previous entry are the defaults for this new item (this only applies if you selected the Next button on the screen and did not close the item window and then opened a new window).

15. **Enter**	the **remaining service items** on page 145
16. **Leave blank**	the **Rate field** for Sponsorships
17. **Click**	**Next** after entering Team Registration

Creating Non-inventory Part Items

The remaining items are inventory items that we do not track individually.

| 1. **Click** | the **drop-down arrow in the Type field** |
| 2. **Choose** | **Non-inventory Part** from the type list to modify the form: |

Figure 5-68

> **Notes**
> You could choose Service as the type for all items for River Run because it has all the fields we need: name, account, and tax code.

> **Notes**
> Even though food, t-shirts, and caps are inventory items, they are not tracked individually so we enter them as Non-inventory Parts.

3. **Read** the **Non-inventory Part description** on the input form

This type is used for inventory that is not tracked — either items that you sell, items that you make and sell, or items that you buy as supplies. It is also used for items that are reserved for specific customer jobs and charged back to the customer. It has the input fields that we need and the same ones we used for service items: item name, price, tax code, and account. We need to delete the default tax code, and add the name, price, and account.

4. **Press** [tab] to advance to the Item Name/Number field

5. **Type** **Caps**

6. **Double click** **0.00** in the Rate field

7. **Type** **15**

8. **Remove** the **tax code** in the Tax Code field

9. **Click** the **drop-down arrow** in the Account field

10. **Select** **Revenue from Sales**

11. **Click** **Next**

Notice that the Non-inventory Part remains selected in the Type field

12. **Enter** the remaining two items on page 145. **Enter** the **Price for T-shirts**. **Leave the Price field for Snacks and Beverages** and **the tax code field blank**, and **choose Revenue from Sales** in the Account field for both items

13. **Click** **OK** to save the item and close the New Item form

14. **Close** the **Item List**

Changing Preferences

We are now ready to change the remaining QuickBooks preference settings. This involves setting some more defaults and turning off features that we are not using in order to streamline the appearance of the Home page.

1. **Click** the **Edit menu** and **click Preferences** to open the preference window you worked with previously

Changing Preferences for Chequing

Preferences for chequing can be set for personal and company details.

Changing Personal Preferences for Chequing

2. **Click** the **Chequing heading** on the left-hand side of the screen to display the cheque preferences

3. Click the **My Preferences tab** if necessary:

Figure 5-69

From this screen you can choose a default account for writing cheques, paying bills, and making deposits. River Run uses the *Bank - Chequing* account for all these purposes. You must indicate that you want to set a default account for each action, and then choose the account. You can change these defaults at any time.

4. Click **Open the Write Cheques** or its check box to add a ✓

5. Choose **Bank - Chequing** from the account drop-down list

6. Click the **check box for Open the Pay Bills and Open the Make Deposits Preferences** and **choose Bank - Chequing** as the default account for both

Changing Company Preferences for Chequing

1. Click the **Company Preferences tab**:

Figure 5-70

The company preferences affect all users and can be changed only by the administrator of the account. The options are:

- **include** the account name (or item) as well as the other information on the voucher part of a cheque
- **change** the cheque date to the current date instead of the transaction date
- **display** the cheque in French instead of English
- **start** with the cursor in the payee or vendor field instead of the account field on forms
- **warn** if the cheque number is a duplicate
- automatically **add** the vendor account number if there is one in the vendor record
- automatically **open** payroll cheques with the selected default account

The warning about duplicate numbers is on by default, and you should leave it on. The remaining options do not apply to River Run. We are not using payroll so we do not need to add accounts for these options. Do not change cheque dates for the exercises in this book so that your answers will match the ones we provide. For the other settings you can choose your own preferences.

Changing Preferences for Jobs & Estimates

River Run does not give estimates, so we can turn off this feature.

1. Click   the **Jobs & Estimates** heading on the left-hand side of the screen and **click Yes** to save the previous changes. The company preferences screen opens:

Figure 5-71

This screen allows you to indicate whether the business uses estimates for customer jobs or services and to assign names to the different stages of a job in progress. Progress invoicing is also enabled from this screen. Progress invoicing allows you to invoice customers regularly for work in progress. Again, a warning about duplicate estimate numbers is switched on as the default, and you should use this warning. Estimates and progress invoicing do not apply to River Run.

Estimates and progress invoicing appear as questions on the form. We will answer No to the question Do You Create Estimates? This will remove the Estimates icon from the Customers section of the Home page. The option for progress invoicing will become unavailable because it no longer applies.

2. **Click**   **No** for the question Do You Create Estimates?

There are no personal preferences for jobs and estimates.

Changing Preferences for Reports & Graphs

Report preferences can be set for individual and company levels.

1. **Click**   the **Reports & Graphs** heading on the left-hand side of the screen and **click Yes** to save the previous changes

2. **Click**   **OK** when told that QuickBooks must close all open windows to apply the change

You will see the company preferences for Reports and Graphs:

> **Notes**
> QuickBooks will close all QuickBooks windows that you have open in the background before it can make the changes to the Jobs & Estimates settings.

Figure 5-72

River Run uses the accrual basis for summary reports so this setting is correct. We want to use account names only in reports because we have not used descriptions for all accounts. If you want, you can add both name and descriptions to reports. Aging periods do not apply because all transactions are cash and no account terms are offered. In other data files, we age reports from the transaction date.

The Format button allows us to choose a standard format for reports — what headings to include, date format, fonts, etc., and the Classify Cash button allows us to decide how accounts should be classified for cash flow reports.

We will change the report format from this window so that the changes will apply to all our reports. Later, you can still modify individual reports if you want. We will add our own name to the report, remove the time from the report and remove the basis because all reports are accrual based. We will change the format for negative numbers.

3. **Click**   the **Format button** to open the report formatting screens

4.	**Click**	the **Time Prepared and Report Basis options** to remove the ✓
5.	**Click**	in the **Subtitle field**
6.	**Type**	**Report prepared by {your name}**
7.	**Click**	the **Fonts & Numbers tab**
8.	**Click**	the **In Parentheses and In Bright Red for Show Negative Numbers options**
9.	**Choose**	**other standard format settings** for the report if you want
10.	**Click**	**OK** to save the format changes

Changing Personal Preferences for Reports & Graphs

1.	**Click**	the **My Preferences tab** to view the personal preferences screen:

Figure 5-73

From this screen, you can decide whether to display the Modify Report window automatically when you select a report. You can also choose whether reports should be refreshed automatically when you make a change to any of the settings. Graphs can be drawn in two or three dimensions and with or without patterns.

2.	**Click**	**Refresh Automatically** for the Reports and Graphs option
3.	**Change**	**other settings** to suit the way you want to work with the program

Changing Preferences for Sales & Customers

Some of the options for Sales & Customers relate to features that we do not need. They are initially turned on by default.

1.	**Click**	the **Sales & Customers heading** on the left-hand side of the screen to open the Sales & Customers preferences
2.	**Click**	**Yes** to save changes to the reports and graphs preferences

3. The My Preferences tab for the Sales & Customers preferences is displayed:

Figure 5-74

River Run does not bill customers for time and costs, so you can leave the Ask what to do option selected.

4. Click the **Company Preferences tab**:

Figure 5-75

Many of these settings refer to businesses that sell inventory. We can skip these fields. Shipping does not apply to River Run, nor do pricing levels. The option to automatically assign payments to invoices does not apply to cash transactions. Sales orders should be turned off so the icons for it are removed from the Home page. Duplicate numbers should prompt a warning. Zero amounts should not be included on forms so these default settings are correct.

5.	**Click**	the **Use Price Levels** option to remove the ✓
6.	**Click**	the **Enable Sales Orders** option to remove the ✓ and dim its related options

Changing Time Tracking Preferences

QuickBooks allows you to keep track of the time that employees spend on specific jobs for specific customers. River Run does not use time tracking so we should turn it off.

1.	**Click**	the **Time & Expenses** heading on the left-hand side of the screen to access the Time & Expenses preferences
2.	**Click**	**Yes** to save the changes for Sales & Customers

3. The company preferences screen is displayed:

Notes
If other windows are open, you will be told that QuickBooks must close them to apply the Sales & Customers changes (or the Time Tracking changes below). Click OK to accept the warning. If the windows are still closed from a previous change you made, you will not see the message.

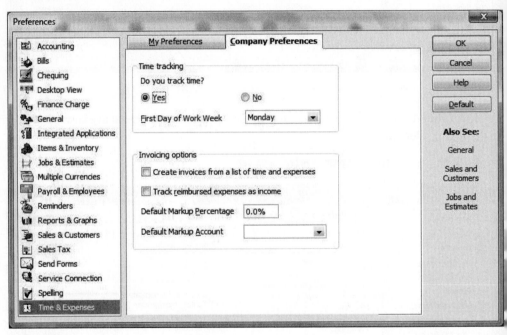

Figure 5-76

4.	**Click**	**No** for the question Do You Track Time?

Changing Spelling Preferences

The final preferences we will examine relate to the QuickBooks spell checking feature.

1.	**Click**	the **Spelling heading** on the left-hand side of the screen
2.	**Click**	**Yes** to save the changes made to the Time & Expenses preferences

There are no Company Preferences for Spelling.

3. **Click**   the **My Preferences tab**:

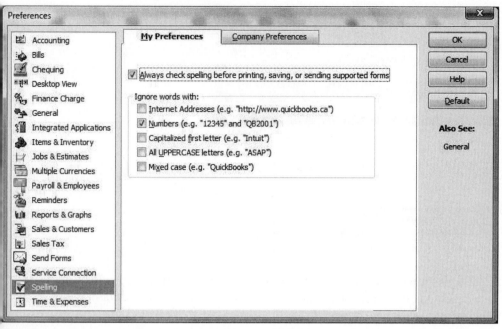

Figure 5-77

The spelling feature is initially turned on. When you use the spelling feature, you should limit the words that the program will check for you. The spelling preferences has a list of word types that are most likely to generate incorrect spelling messages. You can choose to exclude all or some of these word types. For example, in this text and in most businesses, many names will be considered incorrectly spelled words. Therefore, excluding words with initial caps is a good idea.

4. **Select**   the **spelling preferences** you want

5. **Click**   **OK** to save all your changes

Other Preferences

The initial default settings for the remaining preferences are correct so we do not need to change any of the settings for them. We will modify some of these preferences in later setup applications.

Editing Lists

When we chose terms and payment methods for vendors and customers, we saw that QuickBooks created a number of selections automatically. We do not need all these settings so we should delete the extra ones.

Editing Terms

1. **Choose** the **Lists menu**, then **choose Customer & Vendor Profile Lists**, and **click Terms List**

The Terms List will open:

Figure 5-78

This list is just like any other list in QuickBooks. From this window, you can create new terms, edit or delete terms, make terms inactive, display a number of reports, etc. The keyboard shortcut commands are the same as for other lists.

Most of these terms are not needed so we will delete them. The only one we need to keep is Due on receipt, the term that applies to cash transactions.

2. **Click** **1% 10 Net 30** if this is not already selected

3. **Click** the **Terms button** and **click Delete Terms** or **press** ⌨ctrl + **D** to view the warning message

4. **Click** **OK** to authorize the deletion

5. **Delete** the **remaining terms except Due on receipt**

6. **Close** the **Terms List**

Editing Payment Methods

1. **Choose** the **Lists menu**, then **choose Customer & Vendor Profile Lists,** and **click Payment Method List**

The Payment Methods List will open:

Figure 5-79

We can delete most of the methods on the list. We want to keep Cash and Cheque.

2. **Click** **American Express**

3. **Click** the **Payment Method button** and **click Delete Payment Method** or **press** ⌨ctrl + **D** to view the warning message

4. **Click**	**OK** to authorize the deletion
5. **Repeat**	the **above steps** to **delete MasterCard, Visa, Direct Payment, and Interac Debit**
6. **Close**	the **Payment Method List**

Editing Customer Messages

1. **Choose**	the **Lists menu**, then **choose Customer & Vendor Profile Lists**, and **click Customer Message List**

The Customer Message List will open:

Figure 5-80

We can delete most of the messages on this list because they are not appropriate for River Run. We will keep one message: "Thank you for your business," and edit it to make it suitable for the charity.

2. **Click**	**Thank you for your business**
3. **Click**	the **Customer Message button** and **click Edit Customer Message** or **press** *ctrl* **+ E** to open the editing screen:

Figure 5-81

The message appears and is highlighted for editing. We will modify the message to "Thank you for your donation. Ask to be placed on our mailing list."

4. **Double click**	**business**, the last word in the current message
5. **Type**	**donation. Ask to be placed on our mailing list.**
6. **Click**	**OK** to save the revised message and return to the list
7. **Click**	**All work is complete!**
8. **Click**	the **Customer Message button** and **click Delete Customer Message** or **press** *ctrl* **+ D** to view the warning message

Notes
Or choose the Edit menu and click Delete Customer Message.

9. **Click**   **OK** to authorize the deletion

10. **Delete**   **all other customer messages except the one we changed**

11. **Close**   the **Customer Message List**

Checking the Setup

The final step before entering transactions is to make a final check of all the information you entered to verify the accuracy of your work. Although you can make corrections at any time, you should attempt to have a data file that is error free.

Notes
Refer to page 88 for help with displaying the Trial Balance and page 124 for help with displaying the Account Listing.

1. **Print or display**   the **Account Listing and Trial Balance dated January 1, 2012**

2. **Review**   the **Customer List, Vendor List, and Item List**

Your reports and lists should match the ones on pages 144–145.

Source Documents

Now that you have set up the company, you are ready to begin entering source documents. You may need to refer to previous chapters for additional information.

When entering the following source documents, be sure to use the sales tax codes that we set up earlier in this chapter to track 2.5 percent of GST as eligible and 2.5 percent of GST as ineligible.

January 1 – January 31, 2012

SD Practice
Continue to develop your skills by entering the following source document(s).

SD1:   **Cash Purchase Invoice #ROP-06-01**   **Dated January 2, 2012**

From RoofOver Properties, $1,800.00 plus $90.00 GST for office rent for six months. Invoice total of $1,890.00 paid by cheque #188. Create new Other Current Asset account: Prepaid Rent. Remember to click To Be Printed to change the selection.

SD2:   **Cash Purchase Invoice #WFP-2252**   **Dated January 10, 2012**

From the Winnipeg Free Press, $1,500.00 plus $75.00 GST for weekly ads publicizing the event to appear in the local newspaper for five months. Invoice total of $1,575.00 paid by cheque #189. Create new Other Current Asset account: Prepaid Advertising.

SD3:   **Cash Purchase Invoice #S-9976**   **Dated January 15, 2012**

From Staples, $160.00 plus $8.00 GST and $11.20 PST for printing registration and sponsorship pledge forms for participants and sponsors. Invoice total of $179.20 paid by cheque #190.

SD4:   **Cash Purchase Invoice #BC-10116**   **Dated January 20, 2012**

From Bell Canada, $50.00 plus $2.50 GST and $3.50 PST for telephone service for one month. Invoice total of $56.00 paid by cheque #191.

SD5:   **Memo #1**   **Dated January 28, 2012**

Pay Charity Spiritus, the event manager (use Quick Add and choose Other as the type of payee), $2,000.00 monthly contract wages. Issue cheque #192 in full payment. Use the Write Cheques form to pay event manager contract fee.

February 1 – March 31, 2012

SD6: **Funds Raised Form #1**   **Dated February 6, 2012**

Cash and cheques received for early registrations from runners.
16 Single registrations @ $25.00 $400.00
11 Team registrations @ $80.00 $880.00
Total $1,280.00 deposited to Bank - Chequing account.
Remember to click To be printed and Deposit To in order to change the
selections. Add Sales Receipt icon to the Icon bar.

Notes
Enter funds raised as sales receipts. Remember: you can add a Sales Receipt icon to the Icon bar.

SD7: **Memo #2**   **Dated February 28, 2012**

Pay Charity Spiritus, the event manager, $2,000.00 monthly wages as per con-
tract. Issue cheque #193 in full payment. Use the Write Cheques form to pay
event manager contract fee.

SD8: **Funds Raised Form #2**   **Dated March 15, 2012**

Cash and cheques received for early registrations from runners.
28 Single registrations @ $25.00 $700.00
8 Team registrations @ $80.00 $640.00
Total $1,340.00 deposited to Bank - Chequing account.

SD9: **Cash Purchase Invoice #BC-17910**   **Dated March 20, 2012**

From Bell Canada, $90.00 plus $4.50 GST and $6.30 PST for telephone service for
two months. Invoice total of $100.80 paid by cheque #194.

SD10: **Memo #3**   **Dated March 31, 2012**

Pay Charity Spiritus $2,000.00 monthly wages as per contract. Issue cheque #195
in full payment.

April 1 – April 30, 2012

SD11: **Funds Raised Form #3**   **Dated April 6, 2012**

Cash and cheques received for early registrations from runners.
38 Single registrations @ $25.00 $950.00
16 Team registrations @ $80.00 $1,280.00
Total $2,230.00 deposited to Bank - Chequing account.

SD12: **Cash Purchase Invoice #WA-4200**   **Dated April 14, 2012**

From Wear Ads, $2,500.00 plus $125.00 GST and $175.00 PST for t-shirts for par-
ticipants, volunteers, and fundraising. T-shirts are printed with event and sponsor
logos. Invoice total of $2,800.00 paid by cheque #196.

SD13: **Cash Purchase Invoice #KP-5306**   **Dated April 15, 2012**

From Kopy Plus (use Quick Add for the new Vendor), $500.00 plus $25.00 GST
and $35.00 PST for printing environmental conservation information leaflets for
participants and spectators. Invoice total of $560.00 paid by cheque #197.

SD14: **Cash Purchase Invoice #WA-4232**   **Dated April 24, 2012**

From Wear Ads, $2,400.00 plus $120.00 GST and $168.00 PST for printed caps
for participants, volunteers, and fundraising. Invoice total of $2,688.00 paid by
cheque #198.

SD15: **Memo #4**   **Dated April 30, 2012**

Pay Charity Spiritus $2,000.00 monthly wages as per contract. Issue cheque #199
in full payment.

May 1 – May 31, 2012

Notes
Choose Cash on Hand as the bank account for the purchase from Stitsky's.

SD16: Cash Purchase Invoice #S-18299 Dated May 1, 2012

From Stitsky's (use Quick Add for new vendor), $40.00 plus $2.00 GST and $2.80 PST for safety pins to pin number tags on runner participants for identification. Invoice total of $44.80 paid from Cash on Hand. (Use Office and Computer Supplies account.)

SD17: Funds Raised Form #4 Dated May 2, 2012

Cash and cheques received from runners.

52	Single registrations @ $25.00	$1,300.00
22	Team registrations @ $80.00	$1,760.00

Total $3,060.00 deposited to Bank - Chequing account.

SD18: Funds Raised Form #5 Dated May 2, 2012

Cash and cheques received from donors deposited to Bank - Chequing account. Sponsorships $4,800.00

SD19: Cash Purchase Invoice #S-14322 Dated May 3, 2012

From Staples, $250.00 plus $12.50 GST and $17.50 PST for photo paper and colour printer cartridges. Invoice total of $280.00 paid by cheque #200.

SD20: Cash Purchase Invoice #QAS-4632 Dated May 3, 2012

From Quarts Arts Supplies (use Quick Add for new vendor), $190.00 plus $9.50 GST and $13.30 PST for bristol board and paint supplies to make signs to place along running route. Invoice total of $212.80 paid by cheque #201. (Use Office and Computer Supplies account.)

SD21: Cash Purchase Invoice #SFM-3990 Dated May 12, 2012

Sobey's Food Mart, $1,800.00 for zero-rated food and beverages for participants and spectators during event, and $800.00 plus $40.00 GST and $56.00 PST for taxable snack foods. Invoice total of $2,696.00 paid by cheque #202.

SD22: Memo #5 Dated May 18, 2012

From Event Manager: Issue cheque #203 for $1,500.00 to Charity Spiritus to transfer funds to Cash on Hand for miscellaneous expenses during event.

Notes
Remember that you can add a General Journal icon to the Icon bar.

SD23: Memo #6 Dated May 18, 2012

From Event Manager: Give t-shirt and cap to each volunteer. The cost of t-shirts given out is $240.00. The cost of caps is $210.00. Reduce T-shirt and Caps asset account and increase Cost of T-shirts and Caps expense account.

SD24: Funds Raised Form #6 Dated May 20, 2012

Cash and cheques received from runners on day of event.

64	Single registrations @ $25.00	$1,600.00
14	Team registrations @ $80.00	$1,120.00
730	Photos sold to participants	$7,300.00

Total $10,020.00 deposited to Bank - Chequing account.

SD25: Funds Raised Form #7 Dated May 20, 2012

Cash and cheques received from donors deposited to Bank - Chequing account. Sponsorships $8,200.00

SD26: Cash Purchase Invoice #SFM-4821 Dated May 20, 2012

Sobey's Food Mart, $400.00 for zero-rated food and beverages for participants and spectators during event, and $200.00 plus $10.00 GST and $14.00 PST for taxable food items. Invoice total of $624.00 paid from Cash on Hand.

SD27: Memo #7   **Dated May 20, 2012**

From Event Manager: Give t-shirt and cap to each participant. The cost of t-shirts given out is $880.00. The cost of caps is $835.00. Reduce T-shirt and Caps asset account and increase Cost of T-shirts and Caps expense account.

SD28: Funds Raised Form #8   **Dated May 20, 2012**

Cash and cheques received from event Spectators. Use Quick Add for new customer — Spectators.
180	T-shirts @ $20.00 sold to spectators	$3,600.00
186	Caps @ $15.00 sold to spectators	$2,790.00
	Snacks and beverages sold to spectators	$5,280.00

Total $11,670.00 deposited to Bank - Chequing account.

SD29: Cash Purchase Invoice #PPH-34982   **Dated May 20, 2012**

From Papa's Pizza House (use Quick Add for new Vendor), $270.00 plus $13.50 GST and $18.90 PST for pizza and soft drinks for volunteers. Invoice total is $302.40. Paid from Cash on Hand. Create new Expense account: General Expenses. Choose S as the tax code.

SD30: Cash Purchase Invoice #BC-30837   **Dated May 20, 2012**

From Bell Canada, $90.00 plus $4.50 GST and $6.30 PST for telephone service for two months. Invoice total of $100.80 paid by cheque #204.

SD31: Cash Purchase Invoice #S-21110   **Dated May 30, 2012**

From Staples, $140.00 plus $7.00 GST and $9.80 PST for printing receipt forms for participants and sponsors. Invoice total of $156.80 paid by cheque #205.

SD32: Memo #8   **Dated May 31, 2012**

Pay Charity Spiritus $2,000.00 monthly wages as per contract. Issue cheque #206 in full payment.

June 1 – June 30, 2012

SD33: Funds Raised Form #9   **Dated June 2, 2012**

Cash and cheques received from sponsors.
Sponsorships $45,460.00
Total $45,460.00 deposited to Bank - Chequing account.

SD34: Funds Raised Form #10   **Dated June 9, 2012**

Cash and cheques received from sponsors.
Sponsorships $9,560.00
Total $9,560.00 deposited to Bank - Chequing account.

SD35: Memo #9   **Dated June 13, 2012**

From Event Manager: Issue cheque #207 for $500.00 to Charity Spiritus to transfer funds to Cash on Hand to purchase postage for mailing charitable donation receipts.

SD36: Cash Purchase Invoice #CP-2   **Dated June 15, 2012**

From Canada Post (use Quick Add for new Vendor), $500.00 plus $25.00 GST for postage to mail receipts. Invoice total $525.00. Paid from Cash on Hand. Create new Expense account: Postage. Use tax code GEI.

SD37: Memo #10   **Dated June 15, 2012**

From Event Manager: Display the Trial Balance to determine amounts for the GST rebate and adjusting entries. Apply for GST rebate of $287.00. Create new Other Current Asset account: GST Refund Receivable.

Notes
Use the General Journal to record the GST rebate application.

SD38: Bank Debit Memo #TDCT-5218   **Dated June 20, 2012**

From TD-Canada Trust, withdraw $11,330.00 from chequing account to repay loan for $11,000.00 plus $330.00 interest. Create new Expense account: Interest Expense.

SD39: Cash Purchase Invoice #BC-36464   **Dated June 20, 2012**

From Bell Canada, $50.00 plus $2.50 GST and $3.50 PST for final month of telephone service. Invoice total of $56.00 paid by cheque #208.

SD40: Memo #11   **Dated June 30, 2012**

Pay Charity Spiritus $2,000.00 monthly wages as per contract. Issue cheque #209 in full payment.

SD41: Bank Debit Memo #TDCT-5881   **Dated June 30, 2012**

From TD-Canada Trust, $42.50 in accumulated bank charges for cheques and statement preparation. Create new Expense account: Bank Charges.

Notes
Use the General Journal to record the deposit of balance of Cash on Hand. You can also use the Transfer Funds form in the Banking menu, but we have not yet covered it in this text.

SD42: Memo #12   **Dated June 30, 2012**

From Event Manager: Transfer $983.80, balance of Cash on Hand to Bank - Chequing account.

SD43: Memo #13   **Dated June 30, 2012**

From Event Manager: Small quantities of supplies were left at the end of the tournament. Leftover food supplies and t-shirts have been donated to women's shelters; craft and some office supplies have been donated to the University's daycare centre. Reduce the following asset accounts and increase the corresponding expense accounts to reflect supplies used during tournament:
Reduce T-shirts and Caps and increase Cost of T-shirts and Caps by $3,078.00.
Reduce Food Supplies and increase Cost of Food and Snacks by $3,270.00.
Reduce Office & Computer Supplies and increase Office & Computer Supplies Used by $503.00.

SD44: Memo #14   **Dated June 30, 2012**

From Event Manager: Enter adjustment for prepaid expenses:
Charge $1,800.00 to Office Rent for Prepaid Rent expired.
Charge $1,500.00 to Publicity and Promotion for Prepaid Advertising expired.

SD45: Memo #15   **Dated June 30, 2012**

From Event Manager: Enter $800.00 as depreciation on computer equipment. (Click OK to close the message about fixed assets.)

SD46: Memo #16   **Dated June 30, 2012**

Received cheque #488129 for $287.00 from the Receiver General for GST rebate. Enter the receipt in the General Journal and deposit the refund to Bank - Chequing account.

Finishing Your Session

1. **Back up**   the **company data file**

2. **Close**   the **Company file**

3. **Close**   the **QuickBooks program**

51 Just a Buck

Objectives

After completing this chapter, you should be able to:

- **enter** bills from vendors for purchases
- **enter** payments to vendors
- **edit** vendor transactions before recording
- **create** complete new vendor records
- **review** vendor transactions after recording transactions
- **memorize** recurring transactions
- **find** previously recorded transactions
- **use** memorized transactions
- **edit** memorized transactions
- **enter** receipts for multiple items
- **correct** bills after recording
- **correct** payments after recording
- **print** cheques
- **display** and **print** vendor reports and graphs

Company Information

Company Profile

Just a Buck, located in a busy suburban mall in Winnipeg, Manitoba, is a typical dollar store in terms of the products it sells. However, Luanne (Lu) Nees, the owner, made a decision when starting the business that no item would ever cost more than one dollar. Items that cost less than one dollar are even sold in packages so that the total is always one dollar. This pricing decision makes Just a Buck different from some dollar stores that carry a wider price range of low-cost merchandise.

Notes
Just a Buck
Store 3499, Red Deer Mall
Winnipeg, MB R4T 6C4
Tel: (204) 453-4992
Fax: (204) 453-5882
E-mail: ln@justabuck.com
Web: www.justabuck.com
Business No.: 586 566 490

The store accepts only cash from customers; cheques, credit cards, and debit cards are not accepted, making the sale transactions straightforward.

Nees has accounts set up with vendors, and she writes cheques to pay for the goods she buys. Invoices arrive with the merchandise and payment terms vary. Currently, no vendors offer discounts for early payments.

Just a Buck sells both taxable and non-taxable items. The store sells a few canned goods and dried and packaged foods that are non-perishable — these food items are non-taxable. All other store merchandise is taxable and both PST and GST apply. Taxable merchandise includes foods such as candy, chocolate bars, and soft drinks. All non-food items sold in the store, the largest portion of the store's inventory, are taxable. The products are quite varied, including house and kitchenware items (dinnerware, mugs, glasses, cutlery, glass and plastic storage containers, vases) paper products (cards, stationery, wrapping paper, gift bags, decorations), toys (balloons, party favours, small games, toys) and office supplies (pens, paper clips, staplers, tape, sticky note pads, paper, envelopes, glue).

To facilitate tax reporting and entering merchandise sales, the inventory is divided into taxable and non-taxable food items, and other taxable merchandise. Just a Buck pays only GST on its taxable inventory purchases — items that it will sell — because these items are resold and only the final customer pays PST. However, the store pays both GST and PST on other business-related purchases.

The store has very few non-inventory assets other than some store display shelves and computer equipment. The monthly rent for the store includes all utilities except telephone.

At the end of March 2012, Luanne Nees converted her accounting records to QuickBooks. On April 1, the files are ready for data entry in QuickBooks. To convert the records, Nees used the following information:

- Chart of Accounts
- Trial Balance
- Vendor List
- List of Customers and Items
- Accounting Procedures

Chart of Accounts

Just a Buck

ASSETS
Bank
    Bank Chequing
    Bank Savings
Other Current Assets
    Inventory:Food
    Inventory:Merchandise
    Prepaid Insurance
    Supplies
Fixed Assets
    Computer/Cash Register
    Display Cabinets & Shelves

LIABILITIES
Accounts Payable
    Accounts Payable
Other Current Liabilities
    Bank Loan
    GST Payable
    PST Payable (MB)

EQUITY
    Capital, Luanne Nees
    Drawings, Luanne Nees
    Retained Earnings

INCOME
    Revenue from Interest
    Revenue from Sales

EXPENSE
Cost of Goods Sold
    Cost of Goods Sold
Expense
    Advertising and Promotion
    Insurance Expense
    Interest Expense
    Rental Expense
    Supplies Used
    Telephone Expense

Just a Buck

AS AT MARCH 31, 2012

	Debits	Credits
Bank Chequing	$ 31,450.00	
Bank Savings	48,690.00	
Inventory:Food	1,800.00	
Inventory:Merchandise	9,400.00	
Prepaid Insurance	6,900.00	
Supplies	550.00	
Computer/Cash Register	6,300.00	
Display Cabinets & Shelves	11,200.00	
Accounts Payable		$ 4,003.00
Bank Loan		14,000.00
GST Payable		407.00
PST Payable (MB)		780.00
Capital, Luanne Nees		86,940.00
Drawings, Luanne Nees	6,000.00	
Revenue from Interest		420.00
Revenue from Sales		41,900.00
Cost of Goods Sold	7,800.00	
Advertising and Promotion	1,500.00	
Insurance Expense	6,900.00	
Interest Expense	420.00	
Rental Expense	9,000.00	
Supplies Used	180.00	
Telephone Expense	360.00	
	$148,450.00	$148,450.00

Vendor Information

Just a Buck

Vendor Name (Contact)	Address	Phone No. / Fax No.	E-mail / Business No.	Terms / Credit Limit
Alert Promotions (Shawna Nues)	64 Publicity Rd. Winnipeg, MB R4X 2P8	Tel: (204) 386-1892 Fax: (204) 386-1900	s.nues@alertpromo.com 453 774 883	net 20 $6,000.00
B & G Imports	450 Red Deer Path Winnipeg, MB R3B 8G6	Tel: (204) 577-6875 Fax: (204) 577-9012	bg@bgimports.com 126 355 472	net 15 $5,000.00
China Wares (Crystal Bowles)	510 Corelle Blvd. Winnipeg, MB R2L 7V4	Tel: (204) 386-3377 Fax: (204) 386-8100	CBowles@chinawares.com 283 453 591	net 20 $5,000.00
Manitel (Oral Speaker)	19 Converse Ave. Winnipeg, MB R2P 6R1	Tel: (204) 577-3481 Fax: (204) 577-3927		net 10 $500.00
Manitoba Finance	125 Fiscal Way Winnipeg, MB R3J 6M9	Tel: (204) 577-0811 Fax: (204) 577-0283		23rd of month
MK Foods (Mario Kapinski)	1500 Caloric Rd. Winnipeg, MB R4F 6G1	Tel: (204) 387-4500 Fax: (204) 387-5003	MKapinski@mkfoods.ca 488 181 503	net 30 $4,000.00
Receiver General	200 Governors Rd. Winnipeg, MB R2K 8B2	Tel: (204) 384-6186 Fax: (204) 384-5813		end of month
Red River Properties (Red Rivers)	999 Towers Rd. Winnipeg, MB R3C 4D6	Tel: (204) 578-4880 Fax: (204) 578-2833	rr@rrp.com 723 456 199	due on receipt
Universal Liquidators (Leff Tovers)	900 Algone Ave. Winnipeg, MB R3N 8F3	Tel: (204) 386-1990 Fax: (204) 386-2736	lt@getridofit.com 725 912 273	net 10 $4,000.00

Outstanding Vendor Transactions

Just a Buck

Vendor Name	Date	Terms	Due Date	Invoice No./ Cheque No.	Amount	Balance Owing
Alert Promotions	03/20/12	net 20	04/9/12	AP-4992	$ 214.00	$ 214.00
China Wares	03/26/12	net 20	04/15/12	CW-3400	$1,070.00	$1,070.00
MK Foods	03/5/12	net 30	04/4/12	MKF-59902	$ 935.00	
	03/25/12	net 30	04/24/12	MKF-68230	500.00	$1,435.00
Universal Liquidators	03/27/12	net 10	04/6/12	UL-4002	$1,284.00	$1,284.00
				Grand Total		$4,003.00

Customer and Item Lists

Just a Buck

CUSTOMERS

Cash Customers

ITEMS

Food - Non-taxable
Food - Taxable
Merchandise

Accounting Procedures

Taxes: GST and PST

Just a Buck pays GST on all goods and services that it buys, except the food items that are zero rated. The store charges GST and PST on the sale of all items except the food items that are zero rated. It uses the regular method for remittance of the GST. GST collected from customers is recorded as a liability in the *GST Payable* account. GST paid to vendors is recorded in the *GST Payable* account as a decrease in the liability to the Canada Revenue Agency. The report is filed with the Receiver General for Canada by the last day of the month for the previous quarter, either including the balance owing or requesting a refund.

In Manitoba, PST at the rate of 7 percent is calculated on the base amount of the invoice, which does not include the GST. In this application, PST is applied to all taxable food and merchandise sold by Just a Buck.

Account Terms

All customers pay cash at the time of the sale. Cash received from customers is deposited to the *Bank Chequing* account immediately; it is not held for later deposit.

Accounts are set up with some vendors, and payment terms range from net 30 days to payment due on receipt of goods. However, presently, no vendors offer discounts. All payments are made by cheque.

Items Sold in Store

Separate items were created for taxable and non-taxable food items because they have different tax codes. When food items are purchased, they are combined in the

Inventory:Food asset account. All other items are grouped as Merchandise items for both sales and purchases.

Cost of Goods Sold

The owner counts inventory on a monthly basis to determine the cost of goods sold, and adjusting entries for this inventory are completed at the end of each month.

Instructions

1. Using the Chart of Accounts, the Trial Balance, and other information, you will record entries for source documents for April 2012 using QuickBooks. You will find the source documents marked with an SD beside them and listed as you work through the chapter. The procedures for entering each new type of transaction are outlined in step-by-step instructions in the chapter. Additional source documents will be provided allowing you to have more practice entering transactions. If you have used this textbook in the past and would prefer to skip the step-by-step instructions and work only with a list of source documents, refer to the CD in the back of the textbook for the list of source documents for this chapter.

2. After you have finished making your entries, print the reports and graphs for April 2012 as indicated on the following printing form.

Notes
Instructions for Vendors and Payables begin on page 257.

REPORTS FOR APRIL 2012	Accountant & Taxes	Vendor
Lists	☑ Trial Balance from Apr. 1 to Apr. 30	☑ Accounts Payable Aging at Apr. 30
☐ Account Listing	☐ General Ledger	☑ Vendor Balance
☐ Vendor Phone List	☑ Journal from Apr. 1 to Apr. 30	☑ Unpaid Bills at Apr. 30
☐ Vendor Contact List	☐ Transaction List by Date	☑ Transaction List by Vendor — Apr. 1 to Apr. 30
	☐ Transaction Detail by Account	
Company & Financial		**GRAPHS**
☑ Balance Sheet Standard at Apr. 30	**Other**	☐ Income and Expense
☑ Profit & Loss Standard (Income Statement) from Apr. 1 to Apr. 30	☐ Custom Summary Report	☐ Net Worth
	☐ Custom Transaction Detail Report	☑ Accounts Payable at Apr. 30
☐ Expenses by Vendor	☐ Transaction History	
	☐ Transaction Journal	

Entering a Bill for Purchases

Entering bills for merchandise purchased on account is similar to entering cheques for purchases. However, instead of entering cash purchases and paying the vendors as soon as you purchase the item using the Write Cheques feature as you learned in Chapter 3, you enter the bill and then pay the bill at a later time, thus creating two transactions in QuickBooks.

Using the instructions on page 9,

1. **Open**   **the data file** for Just a Buck. The QuickBooks Home page appears

Notes
Vendor invoices are referred to as Bills in QuickBooks. Invoices and Bills are used interchangeably throughout this chapter.

The first transaction is a purchase invoice (referred to as a Bill in QuickBooks). Refer to the following source document as we work through the steps to enter it:

SD Instructions
Refer to the following source document and then follow the step-by-step instructions to enter it.

SD1: Purchase Invoice #BGI-2118

Dated April 2, 2012

From B & G Imports, $825.40 plus $41.27 GST for paper products (merchandise inventory). Invoice totals $866.67. Terms: Net 15.

Vendor transactions can be entered from three different areas in QuickBooks:

a. The Vendors section of the Home page:

Notes
We have hidden the icons for vendor functions that are not used by Just a Buck in the Items & Inventory heading of QuickBooks preferences. These functions will be used in later chapters.

Figure 6-1

The Vendors section of the Home page is organized like a flow chart that indicates the usual sequence of transactions. For example, after entering bills, the next step is to pay them. We have turned off the items and inventory features that are not used by Just a Buck, so the icons for them are removed from this company file.

From this window, you can also pay sales taxes by using the Manage Sales Tax icon (the Receiver General and Manitoba Finance are listed as vendors for the company), and access the Vendor Centre by clicking on the Vendors icon.

b. The Vendors menu:

Notes
To access the Items & Inventory preferences, choose the Edit menu, click Preferences and then click the Items & Inventory icon.

Figure 6-2

You can use the Vendors menu to access the Vendor Centre, enter bills, pay bills, and access the item list.

c.   The Vendor Centre:

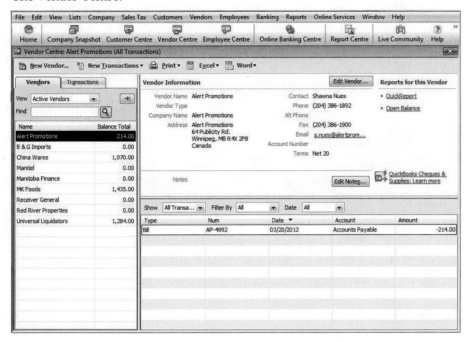

Figure 6-3

The Vendor Centre contains more information and it requires more explanation. On the left-hand side of the screen, you'll see two tabs: a Vendors and a Transactions tab.

When you click on the Vendors tab, the vendor list is displayed on the left-hand side of the screen, which displays each vendor's name and the total outstanding balance. You can sort the vendor list by vendor name or balance total and by ascending or descending order by clicking on the list headings.

When you highlight a vendor in the list, the vendor information is displayed in the top right portion of the screen, allowing you to quickly view the vendor address information, click on the Edit Vendor button to access the vendor record where you can make changes to it, click on the QuickReport or Open Balance button to print reports for the vendor, or use the Edit Notes button to add notes to the vendor record. The transaction details for the vendor are listed in the bottom right portion of the screen. You can use the headings across the top of the transaction details to select which type of transactions you'd like to view and filter them by a date range.

You can use the buttons across the top of the screen to add a new vendor, enter new transactions, print vendor information, export information to Excel, or print Word documents. The highlighted vendor will automatically be selected when you choose one of these options.

When you click on the Transactions tab, a list of transaction types is displayed. When you click on one of the transaction types, a list of all transactions for all vendors will be displayed based on the criteria selected in the Filter By and Date fields.

As we work through this chapter, we will use various methods to access the vendor transactions.

2. **Click**   the **Enter Bills icon**   to open the Enter Bills form:

Figure 6-4

> **Notes**
> The date displayed on the Enter Bills form when you first open it will reflect your current computer's date.

Notice that this invoice form resembles the Write Cheques window but the cheque details are missing. Completing the invoice is also similar to writing cheques for cash purchases. The selection box for Bill Received is checked, and in this example this setting is correct.

> **Notes**
> If merchandise arrives before the invoice, you can uncheck this box and mark the bill received at that time. See Chapter 8.

3. **Click** the **drop-down arrow in the Vendor field** to view the list of vendors in the vendor list:

Figure 6-5

Unlike the Write Cheques Pay to the Order of list that includes all possible payees, the Enter Bills form shows only vendors entered in the vendor list.

4. Click   **B & G Imports**

5. Press   `tab`

The vendor's payment terms, net 15 days, are added to the form, and the due date has changed to reflect these terms. The date is highlighted with the current calendar date entered as the default. As in the previous chapter, once we enter transactions, the last date used will appear as the default until the current calendar date changes or you close the company data file.

6. Type   **04/02/12**

7. Press   `tab` to enter the transaction date and revise the due date. It is now 15 days past the transaction date as shown in the following cheque portion of the form:

Figure 6-6

The next steps are the same as they are when writing cheques. We need to add the invoice number from the vendor so that this will be added to the journal records. Then we will enter the account, tax code, and memo.

8. Type   **BGI-2118** in the Ref. No. field

9. Click   the **Account field** to display the drop-down arrow

10. Click   the **drop-down arrow in the Account field** to view the list of accounts available in the Chart of Accounts

As usual for purchases, the list displays all the expense accounts. If you have a lot of expense accounts, the list begins at the expense accounts. If you have a small number of expense accounts, the list displays other accounts together with the expense accounts. We need to choose an asset account for the purchase.

11. Click   the **up scroll arrow** ▲ to view the asset accounts

12. Click   **Merchandise** under the Inventory subheading to select the account

13. Press   `tab` to advance to the Tax field

14. Click   the **drop-down arrow in the Tax field** to view the tax codes available for purchases

Businesses do not pay PST on items that are purchased for resale. Only GST applies to these purchases, so the tax code G (GST Only) is needed.

15. Click   **G (GST Only)** to select the code

> **Notes**
> The amount due field in the cheque portion of the form will be updated when we enter expense accounts in the account portion of the form.

16. Press   (tab) to advance to the Amount field — the amount of the purchase before taxes

17. Type   **825.40**

18. Press   (tab) to advance to the Memo field so you can enter a description for the purchase

19. Type   **assorted paper inventory products**

Notice that the total invoice amount is updated in the Amount Due field in the cheque portion of the form.

Enter additional items, if there are any, in the same way. Click the account field on the second line, choose the account, enter the tax, amount, memo, and so on.

20. Your completed transaction should look like the one shown here:

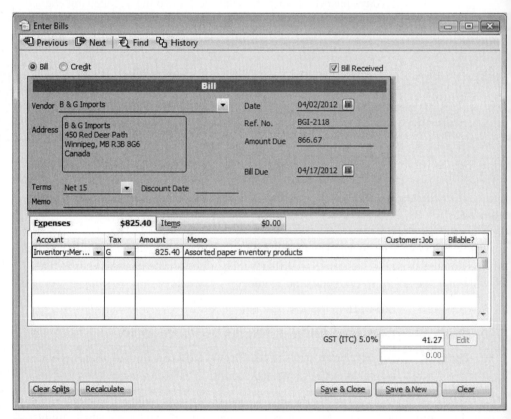

Figure 6-7

CORRECTING PURCHASE INVOICES OR BILLS BEFORE RECORDING

Click the field that contains the error. You can press (tab) to move forward from one field to the next. Highlight the incorrect information and type the correct information in the field. Press (tab) if necessary to update the information.

If the incorrect information was selected from a list, click the drop-down arrow again and select the correct item. If you select a different account, you must re-enter the tax code. If you change the amount, press (tab) to update the taxes and totals. Click the Recalculate button at the bottom of the Enter Bills form if necessary to update the totals.

Click the Clear button to start again.

Notes
If you discover an error in the transaction later, you can still make corrections. See page 244.

21. Check   your **work** carefully before recording the purchase so you won't need to make corrections later

We want to review the transaction journal so we should save the entry without closing the Enter Bills form.

22. Click   **Save & New** or **press** `alt` **+ S** to save the transaction

Reviewing the Transaction

To begin this exercise, a blank Bill should be displayed on the Enter Bills form from the previous exercise.

1. Click   the **Previous button** ⬅ Previous or **press** `alt` **+ P** to view the bill we just completed

2. Press   `ctrl` **+ Y** to view the Transaction Journal report:

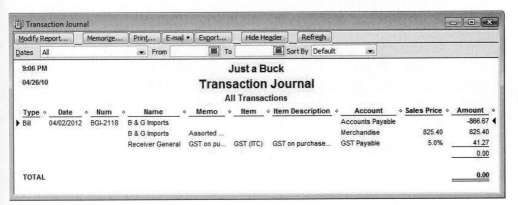

Figure 6-8

The only account we entered on the Bills form was the *Inventory:Merchandise* account. QuickBooks has debited this account for the purchase. In addition, QuickBooks has automatically debited the *GST Payable* account to reduce the liability to the Receiver General and increased (credited) the *Accounts Payable* account for the full amount of the purchase. The account for the vendor, B & G Imports, has also been increased as we will see when we display the vendor reports later in the chapter.

3. Click   ☒ when you have finished viewing the report to close the Transaction Journal report and return to the Bill from B & G Imports

The next transaction that we are going to enter is a bill payment so we should close the Enter Bills form.

4. Click   ☒ to close the Enter Bills form and return to the QuickBooks Home page

Paying Bills

The second transaction that we are going to enter is a cheque paid to MK Foods for items purchased before the starting date, that is, before the files were converted to QuickBooks. Refer to the following source document as we work through the steps to enter it:

SD2: Cheque Copy #197

Dated April 2, 2012

To MK Foods, $1,035.00 in payment of account. Reference invoices #MKF-59902 and #MKF-68230.

> **Notes**
> We have deleted the transaction number and class columns from the transaction journal report and re-sized some of the other columns by dragging the column heading markers to the desired location in order to display all the important details on the screen. Most of the Transaction Journal reports throughout the textbook have been modified to fit on the page.

> **SD Instructions**
> Refer to the following source document and then follow the step-by-step instructions to enter it.

In this transaction, two bills are being paid with one cheque. The first invoice is fully paid and the second one is partially paid. Bills are paid after purchases are recorded.

QuickBooks distinguishes between paying a bill listed as an Accounts Payable and paying for a cash purchase. When you are paying an outstanding Accounts Payable bill —working with vendor accounts — you are "paying bills." When you make cash purchases that are paid by cheque you are "writing cheques."

If you try to pay outstanding vendor bills from the Write Cheques window, you will see the following warning when you choose the vendor:

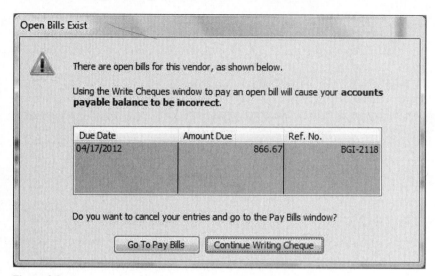

Figure 6-9

The Write Cheques form should be used only for cash purchases — when items are received and paid for immediately. If you select the Write Cheques icon, select a vendor and the Open Bills Exist window is displayed as shown above, click **Go To Pay Bills** to open the Pay Bills window where you can enter the payment to the vendor. Alternatively, you can click **Continue Writing Cheque** to continue writing a cheque to the vendor in the Write Cheques window — ignoring the warning message.

Vendor bills are paid on the Pay Bills window, which can be accessed through the Vendor section of the Home page, the Vendors menu, or the Vendor Centre.

The Vendor section of the Home page shows the flow of business activities and in which order they should be performed. As you can see, the Vendors section of the Home page indicates that Vendor bills are paid after the Vendor bills have been entered:

Figure 6-10

1. **Click**   the **Pay Bills icon** to open this window, or **choose** the **Vendors menu** and **click Pay Bills**:

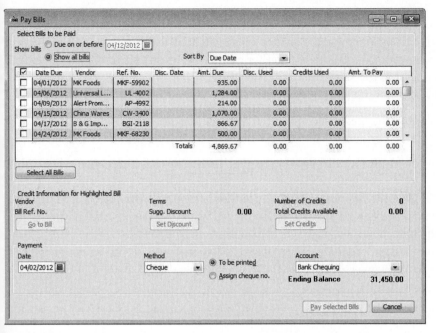

Figure 6-11

The default setting for selecting bills to be paid is to show all bills. With this option selected, all outstanding vendor bills are displayed. Notice that the total amount due displayed at the bottom of the Amt. Due column is $4,869.67. You can also select bills to be paid that are due on or before a specific date. To demonstrate this:

2. Click   the **button beside the Due on or before field**

3. Type   **04/12/12** in the Date field (if necessary)

Notice that some of the vendor bills have been removed from the list. With this option selected, notice the total amount due has changed to $2,433.00. The bills displayed have a due date of April 12, 2012, or earlier.

To show invoices due within a shorter period, type an earlier date in the Select bills to be paid due on or before date field. To show more bills, enter a later date in this date field or leave the Show all bills option selected.

We are making a payment toward both bills from MK Foods. Currently, only one of these bills is displayed on the screen.

4. Click   the **button beside Show all bills**

Both bills from MK Foods are now included on the list as the first and last entries. You will have to scroll down the list to view the second bill. You can change the order of the bills on the screen by selecting a different option in the Sort By field. The default order is by the date that bills are due, a logical choice because bills due first are generally paid before those due later.

5. Click   the **drop-down arrow in the Sort By field** to view the sort options:

Figure 6-12

Notes
If you change the order in the Sort By field, your new selection becomes the default the next time you open the Pay Bills form.

Notes
When an invoice is selected for payment, the Go To Bill button is available. Clicking this button will open the invoice so you can review it or make corrections.

6. **Click**   **Vendor**

Sorting the list by Vendor will place the bills in alphabetic order by vendor name. Bills for the same vendor will appear together on the list. When you are paying several bills for one vendor at the same time, you may prefer to sort the bills by vendor. The two MK Foods invoices now appear together in the list.

7. **Click**   the box to the left of the **first bill from MK Foods** to select it for payment

A ✓ (checkmark) is now displayed in the box indicating that it has been selected for payment.

The full invoice amount is automatically entered in the Amt. To Pay column. You can accept this amount or enter a smaller amount if you want to make a partial payment. We can accept the full amount because this invoice is being paid in full.

The payment cheque includes $100.00 as a partial payment for the second invoice so we need to select this invoice as well and then change the default amount in the Amt. To Pay column.

8. **Click**   the **box to the left of the second bill** from MK Foods to select it for payment

A ✓ (checkmark) will be displayed in the box indicating that it has been selected for payment.

9. **Double click** **500.00** in the Amt. To Pay column to select the amount

10. **Type**   **100** to enter a partial payment

11. **Press**   ⌨ *tab* to update the totals as shown:

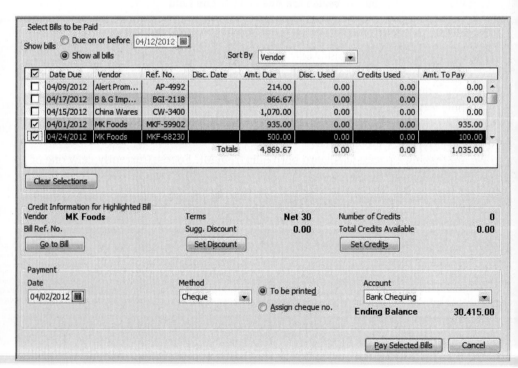

Figure 6-13

Notice that the Ending Balance for *Bank Chequing* is updated to include the payment you are entering.

We are now ready to make the necessary selections on the bottom portion of the screen. The Payment Date should be correct from the previous transaction, unless you have closed the program.

12. **Confirm** that the **date** in the Payment Date field at the bottom of the form is 04/02/2012. If necessary, **type 04/02/12**

Cheque is correctly selected as the method of payment, and the default bank account for the payment is correct. These selections are set as default Chequing Preferences for the company data file. If you need to select a different account, you can click on the drop-down arrow in the account field and choose from the list of Bank accounts.

Writing Cheques Manually

We want to prepare the cheque manually and assign the cheque number. If we do not uncheck the to be printed option, the cheque will be added to the list of cheques to be printed (see page 238). You can assign cheque numbers when you print the cheques.

1. **Click** the **button beside the Assign cheque no.** option

The to be printed option is no longer selected.

2. **Click** **Pay Selected Bills** or **press** (alt) **+ P** to continue. The Assign Cheque Numbers screen is displayed:

Figure 6-14

Numbers are assigned automatically or manually, based on the selection on this screen. You can accept the next default cheque number and allow QuickBooks to assign it automatically, or you can manually enter cheque numbers for each cheque in the list. When you are paying bills from several vendors at once, you might need to change the numbering sequence to match the numbers on the cheques because you may not have prepared the cheques in the same order as the list in this window.

We need to enter the first cheque number to begin the automatic numbering sequence. Even though we are preparing the cheques manually, we want the numbers to match the ones in the QuickBooks file.

3. **Click** the **Cheque No.** field

4. **Type** 197

If you are not ready to assign cheque numbers yet, you can choose Cancel to return to the Pay Bills window.

5. Click OK to display the Payment Summary screen:

Figure 6-15

You can click [Pay More Bills] to return to the Pay Bills window and pay more bills or you can click [Done] to close the window.

6. Click [Pay More Bills] to return to the Pay Bills window

Notice that the first invoice from MK Foods has been removed from the list and the amount due for the second invoice has been reduced by the partial payment of $100.00. The original invoice was $500.00 and the amount due is now $400.00. Before proceeding, we will add a Pay Bills icon to the Icon bar.

Adding a Pay Bills Icon to the Icon Bar

When a form is displayed on the screen, an icon for it can be easily added to the Icon bar.

1. Choose the **View menu** and **click Add "Pay Bills" To The Icon Bar**

Select a new icon to be placed on the Icon bar and accept the default label and description. (We chose the icon that resembles a dollar bill.)

2. Click OK to return to the Pay Bills form

Reviewing the Transaction

We have already saved the payment entry but we want to review the Transaction Journal report. The Pay Bills form does not have a tool bar. Once a cheque has been written, it must be viewed from the Write Cheques form, just like the cheques we entered for Chelsea's Chocolates in Chapter 3.

1. Click [X] to close the Pay Bills form

2. Click the **Cheque icon** [Cheque] on the Icon bar to open the Write Cheques form, or **choose** the **Banking menu** and **click Write Cheques**, or **click** the

Write Cheques icon 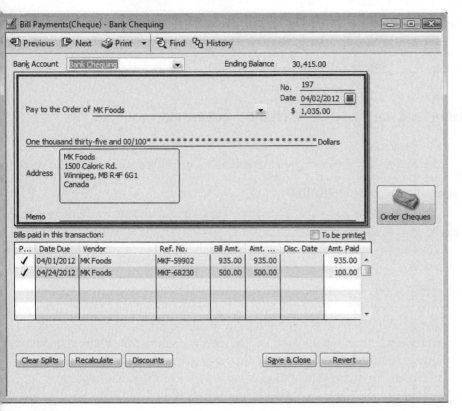 on the Banking section of the Home page

3. **Click** Previous or **press** *alt* + **P** to view the cheque we just wrote:

Figure 6-16

> **Notes**
> Notice that the Write Cheques form title has changed to Bill Payments (Cheque) because we are reviewing a cheque that was issued to pay bills.

> **Notes**
> If you discover an error in the transaction you can make corrections to it. See page 241.

This cheque form is different from the ones we saw for Chelsea's Chocolates because this cheque was issued to pay vendor bills. Therefore, the reference or stub portion of the form includes the invoices paid by the cheque instead of the account and item purchased with the cheque. Those items appear on the invoice and were entered on the Enter Bills form.

4. **Press** *ctrl* + **Y** to view the Transaction Journal report:

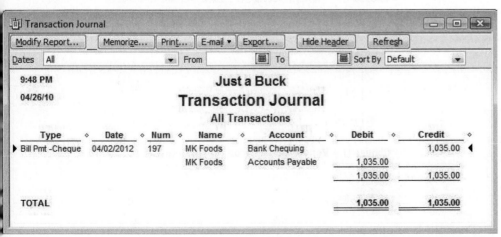

Figure 6-17

> **Notes**
> The report has been modified to accommodate all important columns.

Although we did not enter any accounts for the bill payment, QuickBooks created a complete journal entry for the transaction. The *Accounts Payable* account has been debited to reduce the total amount owing to the vendor and the *Bank Chequing* account has been credited or reduced by the amount of the payment. The account for the vendor, MK Foods, has also been reduced as we will see when we display the vendor reports later in the chapter.

5. **Click**   [X] to close the Journal Transaction report and return to the Cheque for MK Foods

6. **Click**   [X] to close the Bill Payments (Cheque) window

Adding a Complete Vendor Record

For the next transaction, we will be setting up a new vendor and entering a purchase invoice. Refer to the following source document as we work through the steps to enter it:

SD3: Purchase Invoice #BB-451

Dated April 2, 2012

From Bulk Bargains (set up the new vendor), $600.00 plus $30.00 GST for inventory merchandise to be sold in store. Purchase invoice totals $630.00. Terms: Net 25 days.

In previous chapters, we added new vendor records by choosing Quick Add after typing a new name on a form. From the Vendor field in the Enter Bills or Write Cheques form, we can also add complete vendor details by choosing Set Up when prompted instead of Quick Add. Choosing the Setup option allows us to include address details and payment terms so that this information will appear on cheques or invoices. You can also add vendors directly from the Vendor List, as we did for River Run in Chapter 5.

The Vendor List can only be accessed from the Vendor Centre.

1. **Select**   **one of the following methods** to open the Vendor Centre:

      a) **Click** the **Vendors icon** in the Vendors section of the Home page; or

      b) **Choose** the **Vendors menu** and **click Vendor Centre**; or

      c) **Choose** the **Vendor Centre icon** on the Icon bar

From the Vendor Centre, you can create, edit and delete vendor records, make an unused vendor record inactive so it does not appear in vendor lists, find transactions involving the vendor, print lists and so on.

SD Instructions
Refer to the following source document and then follow the step-by-step instructions to enter it.

Notes
Bulk Bargains
Contact: Max Cheipe
500 Risquer Blvd.
Winnipeg, MB R3R 7H8
Phone: (204) 459-4990
Fax: (204) 459-6889
Alt. Contact: Asst. Manager
E-mail: mc@bbargains.com
Terms: Net 25
Credit Limit: $3,000.00
Business No.: 345 668 299

2. Click the **New Vendor button** at the top of the Vendor List or **right click** in the **Vendor list** and **click New Vendor**, or **press** (ctrl) + **N** to open the New Vendor form:

New Vendor	
Vendor Name	[ ]
Opening Balance	[ ] as of 11/29/2009 ▦ How do I determine the opening balance?

OK
Cancel
Next
Help

☐ Vendor is inactive
☐ Vendor is a Sales Tax Agency

Address Info | Additional Info | Account Prefill

Company Name [ ]   Contact [ ]
Mr./Ms./... [ ]   Phone [ ]
First Name [ ] M.I. [ ]   FAX [ ]
Last Name [ ]   Alt. Phone [ ]
    Alt. Contact [ ]
Name and Address [ ]   E-mail [ ]
    Cc [ ]

    Print on Cheque as
[Address Details]   [ ]

Figure 6-18

The cursor is in the Vendor Name field where you add the name of the vendor.

3. Type **Bulk Bargains**

There is no opening balance because this is a new vendor. The current date displayed on this form will be the current system date on your computer. The Opening Balance field and as of fields apply only to historical or opening balance invoices.

4. Click the **Company Name field**

5. Type **Bulk Bargains**

6. Press (tab) twice to advance to the First Name field

7. Type **Max**

8. Press (tab) twice to advance to the Last Name field

9. Type **Cheipe**

10. Press (tab)

The company name and contact name appear in the Address text area and the name we entered is added to the Contact field. You can enter a different name in the Contact field if necessary. The cursor advances to the Address text box.

Notes
QuickBooks allows you to add historical information (before the Start date) after you start using the program for accounting transactions.
We entered all historical data before entering the current transactions because it is easier to find and correct errors.

Notes
You might want to remove the contact name from the Address field if the name should not appear on address labels.

11.	**Press**	(enter) to move to the blank line below Max Cheipe
12.	**Type**	**500 Risquer Blvd.**
13.	**Press**	(enter)
14.	**Type**	**Winnipeg, MB**
15.	**Press**	(enter)
16.	**Type**	**R3R 7H8**
17.	**Press**	(tab)

There are no more lines for address information, and the Address Details button is selected. You could have used the Address Details button to add the vendor address into specific fields. If you enter the address incorrectly while entering the vendor, the Edit Address Information window opens automatically, allowing you to enter the address information in the appropriate fields.

18.	**Press**	(tab) to advance to the Phone field
19.	**Type**	**(204) 459-4990**
20.	**Press**	(tab) to advance to the FAX field
21.	**Type**	**(204) 459-6889**
22.	**Press**	(tab) twice to skip the Alt. Phone field and advance to the Alt. Contact field
23.	**Type**	**Asst. Manager**
24.	**Press**	(tab) to advance to the E-mail address field
25.	**Type**	**mc@bbargains.com**

The company name is entered by default as the name that should be printed on the cheque. You can edit this name if necessary.

| 26. | **Click** | the **Address Details** button to open the Edit Address Information window: |

Figure 6-19

This screen has separated the address fields for easier editing. If you need to make changes to the address details later, it is easier to do so from this screen. The address information has been entered in the correct fields but the country is missing.

27. **Click**   the **Country/Region field**

28. **Type**   **Canada**

29. **Press**   ⌜tab⌐ to advance to the Note field. This note will be added to address labels so it should be used only for address clarification details

30. **Click**   **OK** to return to the New Vendor form. The address is now complete

31. **Click**   the **Additional Info tab**:

Notes
If you want to add a general note for the vendor, save the record and then open it for editing. A Notes button will be available in the vendor record so you can add a note to the vendor record.

Figure 6-20

Some companies assign unique account numbers to each customer and personnel numbers to employees. The account number you enter on this vendor form is the number assigned by Bulk Bargains to Just a Buck. Vendors can also be grouped by types such as region or type of business for targeted business contacts. For example, information about items needed for special contracts may be sent only to the businesses that supply those kinds of products. Account numbers and types are not used by Just a Buck so we can skip these fields.

Most businesses place limits on the amounts that a customer is allowed to purchase on credit. Once the credit limit is reached, the customer may be asked for a down payment or may be granted a limit increase. The program warns when a credit limit is exceeded by a purchase or sale. Just a Buck is allowed to make purchases on account from Bulk Bargains up to $3,000.00.

Business numbers are also frequently added to invoices for tax purposes when taxes are charged by a business. The T4A field will be checked for businesses that provide subcontracting labour and need the T4A income tax form, and the T5018 field will be checked for construction businesses to report construction subcontractor payments.

32. Click the **drop-down arrow** in the Terms field to view the payment terms already set up in the Terms list:

Figure 6-21

You can select terms from this list if one applies to the new vendor. However, the one we need is not on the list so we need to add it.

33. Type **Net 25** in the Terms field and **press** ⟨tab⟩ to view the following message screen:

Figure 6-22

34. Click **Set Up** to enter the new term information. The New Terms screen opens:

Figure 6-23

There are no discounts so we need only to enter the number of days in which net payment is due. QuickBooks uses this number to calculate the due date for bills.

35. Double click the **Net Due In ___ Days** field

36. Type **25**

37. Click **OK** or **press** ⏎ to return to the Additional Info tab

38. Type **3000** and **press** (tab) to format the credit limit field

39. Click the **Business Number field**

40. Type **345 668 299**

41. Click **OK** to save the term and return to the Vendor list

---

CORRECTING VENDOR RECORDS

Click a field to return to the error. Press (tab) to move forward from one field to the next. Highlight the incorrect information and type the correct information in the field. Press (tab) if necessary to update the information.

Click the Address Info tab or the Address Details button to return to those screens to check your work before saving the vendor record. If you need to make corrections or changes later, select the vendor name in the Vendor List, then right click and choose Edit Vendor or press (ctrl) + E to open the record for editing. Click OK to save the record and return to the Vendor List.

Entering Bills from the Vendor List

We will open the Enter Bills form from the Vendor List.

1. Highlight **Bulk Bargains** in the Vendor list, if necessary. (Bulk Bargains should already be selected from the previous exercise)

2. Click the **New Transactions button** and **select Enter Bills**:

Figure 6-24

The Enter Bills form opens with Bulk Bargains automatically entered in the Vendor field. Because Bulk Bargains was selected in the Vendor List when the Enter Bills option was selected, they are automatically selected as the vendor for the bill. You can select a different vendor if needed.

3. **Press**   ⌨`tab` to update the bill. The new vendor's terms that you just added should be displayed in the Terms field

4. **Complete**   the rest of **the invoice/bill** using the information below (you can also refer to the source document information on page 232):

     a)   **Enter 04/02/12** as the date
     b)   **Enter** the **Ref # - BB-451**
     c)   **Choose Merchandise** (Inventory) as the account
     d)   **Enter G** as the tax code
     e)   **Enter 600** as the amount
     f)   **Add** a **description** in the Memo field

5. **Click**   **Save & New**

Source Documents

Now that you have learned how to enter a purchase invoice, continue to develop your skills by entering the following source document in QuickBooks using the Enter Bills form. Use the information in this chapter as a guide if necessary.

SD4: **Purchase Invoice #MKF-72236**   **Dated April 3, 2012**

From MK Foods, $200.00 for zero-rated food inventory items and $300.00 plus $15.00 GST for taxable food inventory to be sold in store. Purchase invoice totals $515.00. Terms: Net 30 days.

Printing Cheques through the Computer

We will use the computer to generate the next two cheques. Using the information in the following three source documents, we will work through the procedures to pay the vendor bills and then print the cheques:

SD5: Cheque Copy #198

                     Dated April 3, 2012

To Universal Liquidators, $1,284.00 in payment of account. Reference invoice #UL-4001. Cheque will be printed later (choose: To be printed).

SD6: Cheque Copy #199

                     Dated April 4, 2012

To Alert Promotions, $214.00 in payment of account. Reference invoice #AP-4992. Cheque will be printed later.

SD7: Memo #1

                     Dated April 4, 2012

From Owner: Print cheques #198 and 199.

For both vendor invoices, the full amount is being paid.

SD Practice
Continue to develop your skills by entering the following source document(s).

Notes
If you are working in a classroom with a shared printer, ask your instructor if you should print the cheques.

SD Instructions
Refer to the following source document and then follow the step-by-step instructions to enter it.

1.	**Click**	the **Pay Bills icon** 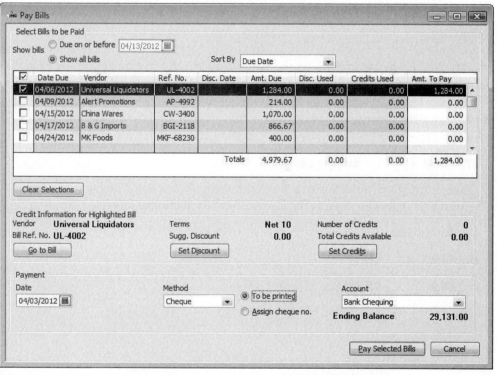 on the Icon bar or the Pay Bills Icon in the Vendor section of the Home page to open the Pay Bills form
2.	**Accept**	**Show all bills** (this is the default for this selection) to show all outstanding invoices
3.	**Click**	the **drop-down arrow** beside the Sort By field
4.	**Select**	**Due Date**
5.	**Click**	the **box beside the Universal Liquidators bill** to select it for payment. A ✓ (checkmark) will be added to the box.

Notes
This is the Pay Bills icon we added to the Icon bar.

Notes
Vendor was last selected in the Sort By field and should have been selected when you first opened the Pay Bills form. We will select Due Date in order to view all bills that are being paid.

6. The Payment Date, in the lower left-hand corner of the screen, should be correct from the previous transaction. **Enter 04/03/12** if necessary.

7.	**Click**	the **To be printed** option to select it. The Pay Bills form should look like the one shown here:

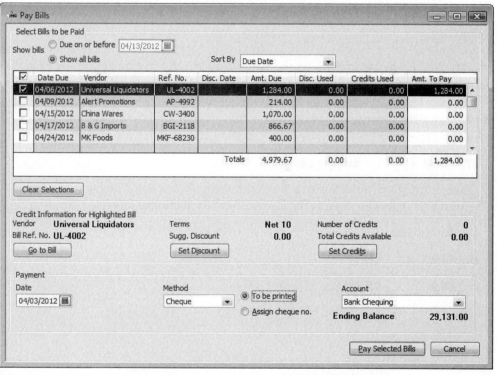

Figure 6-25

8.	**Click**	the **Pay Selected Bills** button to complete the payment
9.	**Review**	the **Payment Summary** screen and **click Done**
10.	**Open**	the **Pay Bills window** to enter the next payment
11.	**Click**	the **box beside the Alert Promotions bill** to select it for payment. A ✓ (checkmark) will be added to the box
12.	**Type**	**04/04/12** in the Payment Date field

The To be printed option should still be selected from our previous changes.

13.	**Click**	the **Pay Selected Bills** button to complete the payment

Notes
We could not enter both bill payments on the same Pay Bills screen because the Payment Date is different.

14. Review   the **Payment Summary screen** and **click Done**

15. Choose   the **File menu**, then **choose Print Forms** and **click Cheques**

16. The Select Cheques to Print window opens:

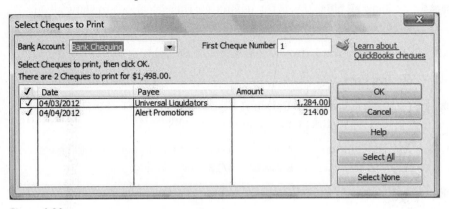

Figure 6-26

On this screen, you can edit the first cheque number, select one or more cheques for printing, or cancel the printing completely. All cheques that had the *To be printed* option selected when they were entered and have not yet been printed are automatically selected. The checkmarks are used as a toggle to select the cheque for printing. You can deselect cheques for printing by clicking the checkmark or by choosing the Select All or Select None buttons to start with the best option and toggle cheques on or off as needed. We want to print the two cheques displayed; however we need to update the starting cheque number.

17. Check   the **dates and amounts**

Make corrections if necessary before printing by editing the cheques in the Write Cheques window as described in the next section, Correcting a Cheque.

Notes
Once you enter the correct starting number for printed cheques, the cheque number will be updated automatically.

18. Double click   **1** in the First Cheque Number field

19. Type   **198**

20. Click   **OK** to open the printer form:

Figure 6-27

21. **Choose**   the **cheque style** you want

22. **Click**   **Print** to print the cheques

23. The following confirmation screen will be displayed after the cheques have printed:

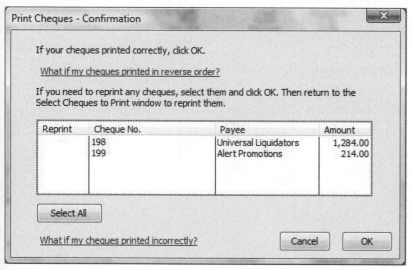

Figure 6-28

If any of the cheques did not print correctly, click on the first cheque that was not correct. A ✓ (checkmark) will be entered under the Reprint column for that cheque. Continue selecting all cheques that did not print correctly. You can use the Select All button if all the cheques did not print correctly. When you click OK, the cheques selected for re-printing will be printed.

24. **Click**   **OK** if the cheques printed correctly

Correcting a Cheque

Just as we corrected sales receipts, cheques, and General Journal entries, we can correct bill payments in QuickBooks. Cheques written in payment of Vendor invoices in the Pay Bills form can be corrected from the Write Cheques form, just like other cheques. We will correct the amount paid on the cheque to MK Foods. Refer to the following source document as we work through the steps to enter it:

SD8: Memo #2

Dated April 4, 2012

From Owner: Cheque #197 to MK Foods was entered incorrectly. The actual amount paid on the cheque was $1,045.00. Edit the cheque to make the correction.

1. **Open**   the Write Cheques form using one of the following options:

   a) **Click** the **Write Cheques icon** on the Banking section of the Home page, or

   b) **Click** the **Cheque icon** on the Icon bar (this will only be available if the icon has been added on the Icon bar), or

   c) **Press** ⌨ **+ W**, or

   d) **Choose** the **Banking menu** and **click Write Cheques**

Notes
If you are using plain paper to print the cheques, choose the Wallet style.

SD Instructions
Refer to the following source document and then follow the step-by-step instructions to enter it.

Finding a Recorded Transaction

To find the cheque we need, we could use the Previous button as we did in earlier chapters, or we can use the QuickBooks Find feature to locate the transaction we want.

2. Click   the **Find button** on the Write Cheques Icon bar as shown here:

3. The Find Cheques window is displayed:

Figure 6-29

From this window you can enter search parameters. You can choose the payee for the cheque, enter a range of dates, enter the cheque number, or enter the exact amount of the cheque to open the one you want. If there is more than one cheque for the payee or the range of dates, you can choose the one you need from the list provided from the search criteria entered.

We know that the cheque was made out to MK Foods so we will search by payee.

4. Click   the **drop-down arrow** in the Payee field to view the list of payees:

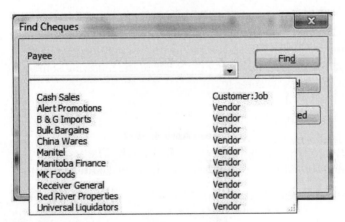

Figure 6-30

5. Click   **MK Foods** as the payee

6. Click   the **Find Button** to open the cheque that we entered to MK Foods:

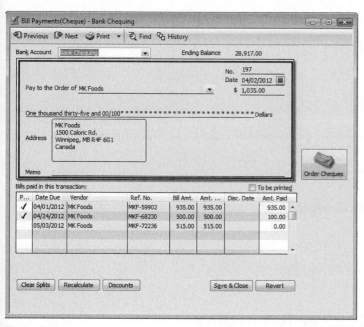

Figure 6-31

Notes
Notice that the form is renamed Bill Payments (Cheque)

Because only one payment was made to MK Foods, the cheque we need opens immediately.

With the payment displayed on the screen, you can make any necessary corrections including adding additional invoices or removing invoices from the payment. For this source document, all we need to do is edit the Amt. Paid entry on the second line.

7. **Double click**   100.00

8. **Type**   110

9. **Press**   (tab) to update the amount

10. **Click**   the **Recalculate button** at the bottom of the form to update the cheque amount if necessary

11. The completed and corrected cheque is shown below:

Notes
If there is more than one cheque for the payee, a list of cheques will open so you can select one. This secondary selection screen is similar to the one for bills in Figure 6-35 on page 245.

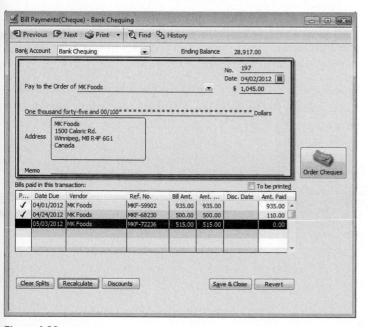

Figure 6-32

12. Check your **work** and **make** any other **necessary corrections**

13. Click **Save & Close** to record the corrected transaction

14. You will see the warning:

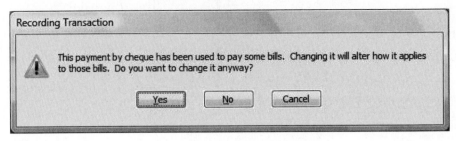

Recording Transaction

⚠ This payment by cheque has been used to pay some bills. Changing it will alter how it applies to those bills. Do you want to change it anyway?

[Yes]   [No]   [Cancel]

Figure 6-33

15. Click **Yes** to save the changes

Correcting Bills after Recording

We can make corrections to bills we entered in the same way that we make other corrections in QuickBooks. These corrections are made on the Enter Bills window. We will make a correction on the invoice entered from MK Foods. After we make the correction, we will memorize the transaction for future use so that we can enter it over and over again without having to re-enter it from scratch. Refer to the following source document as we work through the steps to enter it:

SD9: Memo #3

Dated April 5, 2012

From Owner: The invoice from MK Foods was entered incorrectly. Zero-rated food items purchased cost $250.00. Taxable food items were correctly entered. Revised invoice totalled $565.00. Terms: Net 30 days. Correct the transaction and then memorize the changed transaction because Just a Buck will be making this purchase every week beginning April 10, 2012.

SD Instructions
Refer to the following source document and then follow the step-by-step instructions to enter it.

1. Click the **Enter Bills icon** 📧 Enter Bills on the Vendors section of the Home page to open the Enter Bills form

You can look for purchase invoices or bills by clicking the Previous button as we did in the previous chapter, or you can use the Find tool to search more quickly as we did for cheques in the previous transaction. The Find tool is located on the Icon bar of the Enter Bills form.

2. Click the **Find button** on the Enter Bills Icon bar:

◀ Previous ▶ Next │ ⊜ Find ⊡ History

3. The Find Bills window is shown here:

Figure 6-34

Although the name of the window has changed to match the type of transaction we are searching for — based on the form from which we started the search — it operates the same way for all forms.

4. Click the **drop-down arrow** in the Vendor field to view the list of vendors

5. Click **MK Foods**

6. Click the **Find button** or **press** `alt` + **D**

Notes
D is the underlined letter on the Find button.

7. A list of purchases from this vendor is displayed:

Figure 6-35

8. Click the **first invoice listed** because it is the one we need to edit

The other two invoices are historical invoices that precede the starting date.

9. **Click** the **Go To button** to access the bill:

Figure 6-36

You can now make corrections to any part of the bill.

10. **Double click** **200.00** in the Amount field on the first line of the bill

11. **Type** **250**

12. **Press** tab to update the total. Notice that the amount of the cheque has not yet changed

13. **Click** the **Recalculate button** at the bottom of the form to update the cheque amount and complete the bill as shown here:

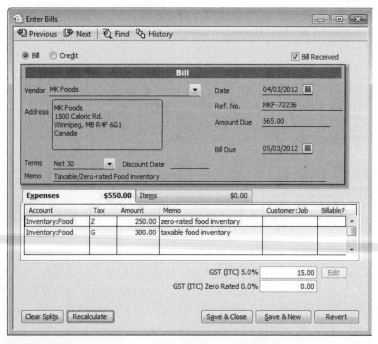

Figure 6-37

Memorizing an Unrecorded Transaction

Businesses frequently have scheduled transactions — bills that arrive on a regular basis. Supplies may be received from the same vendor every month; inventory may be purchased on a regular cycle; utility bills and rent payments are usually due at the same time each month; and insurance, loan, and mortgage payments are usually made on the same day each month. To avoid entering the same details for the bill each time it occurs, you can enter the transaction once and memorize it and then use the memorized transaction when it is needed.

We will memorize the bill from MK Foods because Just a Buck places the same order with them every week.

1. With the MK Foods bill displayed from the previous exercise, **press** ⌨ *ctrl* **+ M**, the keyboard shortcut used to memorize transactions, or **choose** the **Edit menu** and **click Memorize Bill**

2. The Memorize Transaction window opens:

Figure 6-38

You can choose a schedule for the recurring transaction, ask the program to remind you to make the entry, have it entered automatically, or enter it in a group. After you choose a schedule and then select a frequency, the entry will appear in the Memorized Transactions List with the next date that it is due to be entered.

3. **Click** the **drop-down arrow** in the How Often field to view the frequencies available:

Figure 6-39

Notes
These frequencies are available when you select the Remind Me or Automatically Enter option.

The transaction may be repeated daily, weekly, every two weeks, twice a month, every four weeks, monthly, quarterly, twice a year, or annually.

When you choose a frequency, the next due date field opens, and you should type in the next date on which you want to enter the transaction again.

You can also set the program to enter the transaction automatically according to the cycle you enter. When the computer system or current calendar date passes the transaction date, the program will enter the transaction. Of course, you can still change the schedule or edit the transaction at any time.

4.	**Choose**	**Weekly** as the frequency
5.	**Press**	⌨ *tab* to advance to the Next Date field. Your current computer system date will appear as the default date
6.	**Type**	**04/10/12**

If you choose Never as the frequency, you can still memorize the transaction and enter your own date each time you use the memorized transaction. You might use this option when the cycle is not a regular one.

7.	**Click**	**OK** to return to the Enter Bills form
8.	**Click**	**Save & New** to leave the Enter Bills form open for the next transaction
9.	**Click**	**Yes** when prompted to record the changes

Memorizing a Recorded Transaction

The next memo asks you to memorize another transaction that we have already entered. The Enter Bills form should still be open. Refer to the following source document as we work through the steps to enter it:

SD10: Memo #4

Dated April 5, 2012

From Owner: Find the invoice from Bulk Bargains and memorize the transaction with weekly reminders starting April 9, 2012. Close the transaction form.

1.	**Click**	the **Find icon** on the Enter Bills Icon bar
2.	**Click**	the **drop-down arrow** in the Vendor field
3.	**Choose**	**Bulk Bargains**
4.	**Click**	the **Find button** to open the bill from Bulk Bargains
5.	**Press**	⌨ *ctrl* + **M** to open the Memorize Transaction window
6.	**Choose**	**Weekly** from the drop-down list in the How Often field
7.	**Type**	**04/09/12** in the Next Date field
8.	**Click**	**OK** to add the bill to the memorized transaction list and return to the Enter Bills form
9.	**Click**	❌ to close the Enter Bills window without making any changes to the original invoice

Source Documents

Now that you have learned some more of the new concepts taught in this chapter, continue to develop your skills by entering the following source documents in QuickBooks. Use the information in this chapter as a guide if necessary.

SD11: Cash Purchase Invoice #HAC-6733   **Dated April 5, 2012**

From Hold All Containers (use Quick Add for the new vendor), $85.00 plus $4.25 GST and $5.95 PST for supply of bags for customer purchases. Purchase invoice total $95.20. Cheque #200 will be printed later to pay invoice in full. Memorize the transaction with reminders every two weeks beginning April 19, 2012.

SD12: Cash Purchase Invoice #RDP-4-12   **Dated April 5, 2012**

From Red River Properties, $3,000.00 plus $150.00 GST for monthly rent. Purchase invoice totals $3,150.00. Cheque #201 will be printed later to pay invoice in full. Memorize the transaction. Choose to be reminded monthly starting May 5, 2012.

Memorizing Sales Receipts

We have created a customer called Cash Sales to record sales receipts. In addition, to avoid entering a very large number of small sales, we record weekly summaries for sales. The summary cash sales involve the sale of more than one type of item to the customer. In addition, we want to memorize the receipt because each week the entry is the same, except for the amounts. We can edit the amounts each time we use the transaction and still save some data entry time. Refer to the following source document as we work through the steps to enter it:

SD13: Sales Summary Receipt #234

Dated April 7, 2012

To Cash Sales customers:

Food - Taxable	$ 500.00
Food - Non-taxable	220.00
Other merchandise	4,380.00
GST	244.00
PST	341.60
Total deposited to the Bank Chequing account;	$5,685.60

Do not print the receipt. Memorize the transaction with weekly reminders beginning April 14, 2012.

1. **Choose**   the **Customers menu** and **click Enter Sales Receipts**
2. **Choose**   **Cash Sales** as the customer
3. **Enter**   **04/07/12** as the Date
4. **Press**   (tab) to advance to the Sale No. field
5. **Type**   **234**
6. **Choose**   **Food - Taxable** as the first item
7. **Enter**   **500** in the amount field
8. **Press**   (tab) to advance to the Tax field
9. **Click**   the **drop-down arrow** and **click S** (both PST and GST are charged on this item)
10. **Click**   the **second detail line**
11. **Choose**   **Food - Non-taxable** as the second item and **enter 220** in the amount field

WARNING!
Use the Write Cheques form for cash purchases.
Do not change the default selection for **To be printed** in the Write Cheques form for the cash purchases from Hold All Containers and Red River Properties.

SD Instructions
Refer to the following source document and then follow the step-by-step instructions to enter it.

Notes
Although the sales amounts will change, the remainder of the receipt will be the same each week.

12.	**Press**	(tab) to advance to the Tax field
13.	**Click**	the **drop-down arrow** and **click E** (no taxes are charged on this item)
14.	**Click**	the **third detail line**
15.	**Choose**	**Merchandise** (Inventory) as the item and **enter 4380** in the amount field
16.	**Press**	(tab) to advance to the Tax field
17.	**Click**	the **drop-down arrow** and **click S** (both PST and GST are charged on this item)
18.	**Click**	**To be printed** to remove the ✓
19.	**Click**	the **drop-down arrow** in the Deposit To field
20.	**Click**	**Bank Chequing** (it should be the default)
21.	**Press**	(ctrl) + **M** to memorize the transaction
22.	**Choose**	**Weekly** as the frequency and **enter 04/14/2012** in the Next Date field
23.	**Click**	**OK** to return to the sales receipt
24.	**Click**	**Save & Close** or **press** (alt) + **a** to save the receipt and close the form

Notes
The procedure for memorizing transactions is the same for all types of transactions.

Source Documents

Continue to develop your skills by entering the following source documents in QuickBooks. Use the information in this chapter as a guide if necessary.

SD Practice
Continue to develop your skills by entering the following source document(s).

SD14: Memo #5   **Dated April 7, 2012**

> From Owner: Print cheques #200 and #201 to Hold All Containers and Red River Properties. (The first cheque number should be correctly entered as the default.)

SD15: Purchase Invoice #CW-4101   **Dated April 9, 2012**

> From China Wares, $520 plus $26.00 GST for houseware items (merchandise inventory) to be sold in the store. Purchase invoice totalled $546.00. Terms: Net 20 days.

Using a Memorized Transaction

When we use a memorized transaction we do not need to re-enter all the transaction details. QuickBooks adds the memorized transactions created from all forms to a single list so you can see all the memorized transactions at the same time. You can access the form for any one of these transactions directly from the list. You do not need to open the form before choosing the memorized transaction. We will enter a purchase invoice using the purchase invoice that we memorized earlier from Bulk Bargains. Refer to the following source document as we work through the steps to enter it:

SD Instructions
Refer to the following source document and then follow the step-by-step instructions to enter it.

SD16: Purchase Invoice #BB-611

                                        Dated April 9, 2012

> From Bulk Bargains, $600.00 plus $30.00 GST for merchandise inventory to be sold in the store. Purchase invoice totalled $630.00. Terms: Net 25 days. Use the memorized transaction.

1. Use one of the following options to access the memorized transaction list:
    a) **Choose** the **Lists menu** and **click Memorized Transaction List**, or
    b) **Press** `ctrl` + **T**

2. The list of all the transactions we have memorized will be displayed:

Figure 6-40

Notes
Once you open the memorized transaction list, you may want to leave it open for easy access for later transactions. Simply click the memorized transaction list from the Open Window List or the Window menu the next time you need it.

Notes
Click the Next Date column to change the order of the memorized transactions.

Notes
After changing the order of transactions, you can restore the initial order by choosing the Memorized Transaction button and clicking Re-sort List. Click OK to confirm the change.

Notes
To select the memorized transaction you want, click anywhere on the line to select it.

Initially, the list is sorted alphabetically by transaction name. To change the order of transactions, click on any of the column headings to sort by that criterion. For example, to sort by next date, you would click the Next Date column heading. Bulk Bargains is selected because it is first on the list. It is the transaction we need so we can proceed.

3. Click   the **Enter Transaction button** at the bottom of the List window to open the Enter Bills form:

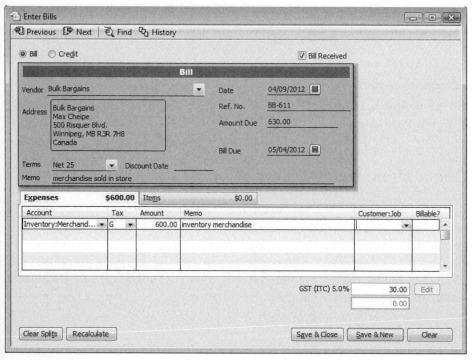

Figure 6-41

The bill is almost complete. The bill and due dates have been updated based on the information we entered when we memorized the transaction. All we need to do is add the reference number. Because this number cannot be duplicated, its field remains blank on the form.

4. **Click**   the **Ref. No. field**

5. **Type**   **BB-611**

6. **Click**   **Save & Close** to return to the Memorized Transaction List

7. **Click**   the **Next Date** column heading to sort the list by the next date. This places the transaction we need next at the top of the list (**click** the **Next Date** column heading until the purchase from MK Foods is displayed at the top of the list)

Another invoice from MK Foods has arrived so use the transaction you memorized earlier to record it. The source document is as follows:

SD17: Purchase Invoice #MKF-83100   **Dated April 10, 2012**

From MK Foods, $250.00 for zero-rated food inventory items and $300.00 plus $15.00 GST for taxable food inventory to be sold in the store. Purchase invoice totalled $565.00. Terms: Net 30 days. Use the memorized transaction.

Source Documents

Now that you have learned more of the new concepts taught in this chapter, continue to develop your skills by entering the following source documents. Use the information in this chapter as a guide if necessary.

SD18: Purchase Invoice #MT-40101   **Dated April 12, 2012**

From Manitel, $62.00 plus $3.10 GST and $4.34 PST for the store telephone. Purchase invoice totalled $69.44. Terms: Net 10 days. Memorize the transaction. Choose to be reminded every month starting May 12, 2012.

SD19: Cheque Copy #202   **Dated April 13, 2012**

To China Wares, $1,070.00 in payment of account. Reference invoice #CW-3400. The cheque will be printed later.

Editing a Memorized Transaction

Once we memorize a transaction, we can use it directly or edit it to reflect changes in the automatic entry. Sometimes using a memorized transaction for a complex entry is easier than redoing the entry each time from scratch. Because many of the details remain the same each time, all you need to do is edit the amounts. We are going to edit the memorized sales receipt that we entered earlier. Refer to the following source document as we work through the steps to enter it:

SD Practice
Continue to develop your skills by entering the following source document(s).

SD Practice
Continue to develop your skills by entering the following source document(s).

SD20: Sales Summary Receipt #235

Dated April 14, 2012

To Cash Sales customers:

Food - Taxable	$ 400.00
Food - Non-taxable	190.00
Other merchandise	3,990.00
GST	219.50
PST	307.30
Total deposited to the Bank Chequing account;	$5,106.80

Use the memorized transaction and edit the amounts.

1. **Press** $ctrl$ + **T** to open the Memorized Transaction list (or **use a method of your choice**)

2. **Click**   **Cash Sales** to select the memorized transaction

3. **Click**   the **Enter Transaction button** at the bottom of the list window or **press** alt + **T** to open the Cash Sales Receipt transaction. You can now edit the amounts.

4. **Double click**   **500.00**, the first amount

5. **Type**   **400**

6. **Press**   ▼, the down arrow key, to highlight the next amount, 220.00

7. **Type**   **190**

8. **Press**   ▼ to highlight the next amount, 4,380.00

9. **Type**   **3990**

10. **Press** tab to update the sales receipt totals and taxes

The date and Sales No. field should be correct. The date is determined by the frequency of the memorized transaction and the Sales No. field is automatically updated to the next sequential number. The Sales No. should be 235.

11. **Click**   **Save & Close** to save the transaction and return to the Memorized Transaction List

Source Documents

Now that you have learned more of the new concepts taught in this chapter, continue to develop your skills by entering the following source documents in QuickBooks. Use the information in this chapter as a guide if necessary.

SD21: Memo #6   Dated April 14, 2012

From Owner: Print cheque #202 to China Wares.

SD22: Purchase Invoice #UL-5184   Dated April 15, 2012

From Universal Liquidators, $1,100.00 plus $55.00 GST for small toys and party favours from a bankruptcy sale (merchandise inventory to be sold in store). Purchase invoice totalled $1,155.00. Terms: Net 10 days.

SD23: Purchase Invoice #BB-883　　　　　　　**Dated April 16, 2012**

> From Bulk Bargains, $600.00 plus $30.00 GST for merchandise inventory to be sold. Purchase invoice totalled $630.00. Terms: Net 25 days. Use the memorized transaction.

SD24: Cheque Copy #203　　　　　　　**Dated April 16, 2012**

> To B & G Imports, $866.67 in payment of account. Reference invoice #BGI-2118.

SD25: Purchase Invoice #MKF-96123　　　　　　　**Dated April 17, 2012**

> From MK Foods, $250.00 for zero-rated food inventory items and $300.00 plus $15.00 GST for taxable food inventory to be sold in the store. Purchase invoice totalled $565.00. Terms: Net 30 days. Use the memorized transaction.

Changing the Frequency or Next Date

Sometimes we need to change the details of a memorized transaction, such as the frequency or the next due date. We can edit these details by editing the memorized transaction from the Memorized Transaction List. We need to change the frequency of the purchase from Hold All Containers and its next due date. Refer to the following source document as we work through the steps to enter it:

SD26: Memo #7

　　　　　　　　　　　Dated April 18, 2012

> The purchase from Hold All Containers will be repeated every four weeks rather than bi-weekly. Edit the memorized transaction details to change the frequency.

1. **Open**　　　　the **Memorized Transaction List** using an option of your choice

2. **Click**　　　　**Hold All Containers** to select the memorized transaction for that vendor

3. **Click**　　　　the **Memorized Transaction button** and **choose Edit Memorized Transaction** or **press** ⌨*ctrl* + **E** to open the details of the memorized transaction:

Figure 6-42

We can now edit any information about the transaction.

4. **Click**　　　　the **drop-down arrow** in the How Often field

5. **Choose**　　　　**Every Four Weeks**

6. **Press**　　　　*tab* to advance to the Next Date

7.	**Type**	**05/03/12**
8.	**Click**	**OK** to save the changes and close the form. You will return to the Memorized Transaction List

Notes
Depending on how the list of memorized transactions is sorted, the item may have moved up or down in the list.

SD Practice
Continue to develop your skills by entering the following source document(s).

Source Documents

Using the information you have learned in this chapter and others, continue entering the following source documents in QuickBooks:

SD27: Cheque Copy #204   **Dated April 20, 2012**

To Manitel, $69.44 in payment of account. Reference invoice #MT-40101.

SD28: Sales Summary Receipt #236   **Dated April 21, 2012**

To Cash Sales customers:

Food - Taxable	$ 410.00
Food - Non-taxable	210.00
Other merchandise	5,110.00
GST	276.00
PST	386.40
Total deposited to the Bank Chequing account;	$6,392.40

Use the transaction in the memorized transactions list and edit the amounts.

SD29: Memo #8   **Dated April 21, 2012**

From Owner: Print cheques #203 and #204 to B & G Imports and Manitel.

SD30: Cheque Copy #205   **Dated April 22, 2012**

To MK Foods, $955.00 in payment of account. Reference invoices #MKF-68230 and MKF-72236.

SD31: Purchase Invoice #CL-719   **Dated April 22, 2012**

From Cards for Less (Set up the new vendor), $450.00 plus $22.50 GST for greeting cards and note cards to be sold in the store (merchandise inventory). Purchase invoice totalled $472.50. Terms: Net 15 days.

SD32: Purchase Invoice #BB-1299   **Dated April 23, 2012**

From Bulk Bargains, $600.00 plus $30.00 GST for inventory merchandise to be sold in the store. Purchase invoice totalled $630.00. Terms: Net 25 days. Use the memorized transaction.

SD33: Purchase Invoice #MKF-99011   **Dated April 24, 2012**

From MK Foods, $250.00 for zero-rated food inventory items and $300.00 plus $15.00 GST for taxable food inventory to be sold in the store. Purchase invoice totalled $565.00. Terms: Net 30 days. Use the memorized transaction.

SD34: Cheque Copy #206   **Dated April 25, 2012**

To Universal Liquidators, $1,155.00 in payment of account. Reference invoice #UL-5184.

Notes
Cards for Less
Contact: Trite Sayers
1200 Bavarder Ave., Suite 5A
Winnipeg, MB R2P 7F4
Canada
Phone: (204) 698-2301
Fax: (204) 698-3923
E-mail: ts@cardsforless.com
Terms: Net 15
Credit Limit: $2,000.00
Business No.: 488 566 302

SD35: Purchase Invoice #AL-5622   **Dated April 26, 2012**

From Alert Promotions, $800.00 plus $40.00 GST and $56.00 PST for business cards for owner and promotional flyers to distribute in the mall. Purchase invoice totalled $896.00. Terms: Net 20 days.

Deleting a Memorized Transaction

When a memorized transaction is no longer needed, the transaction should be deleted from the list. These unneeded transactions can make it harder to find the entry we need and might be used in error. Just a Buck will not be making additional purchases from Hold All Containers, so we can delete its entry from the memorized list. Refer to the following source document as we work through the steps to enter it:

SD36: Memo #9

Dated April 28, 2012

From Owner: Delete the transaction for Hold All Containers from the memorized transactions list because it is no longer needed. Another supplier was found.

1. Open   the **Memorized Transaction List** using one of the options you've learned in this chapter

2. Click   **Hold All Containers** to select the memorized transaction

3. Click   the **Memorized Transaction button** and **choose Delete Memorized Transaction** or **press** ⌨ctrl + **D** to view the warning:

Figure 6-43

4. Click   **OK** to confirm the deletion

You will return to the Memorized Transaction List. You should see that the entry for Hold All Containers has been removed.

Source Documents

Using the information you have learned in this chapter and other chapters, continue entering the following source documents in QuickBooks:

SD37: Sales Summary Receipt #237   **Dated April 28, 2012**

To Cash Sales customers:

Food - Taxable	$ 470.00
Food - Non-taxable	180.00
Other merchandise	5,330.00
GST	290.00
PST	406.00
Total deposited to the Bank Chequing account;	$6,676.00

Use the transaction in the memorized transaction list and edit the amounts.

SD Instructions
Refer to the following source document and then follow the step-by-step instructions to enter it.

Notes
When a transaction is selected on the list, you can choose the Edit menu and click Delete Memorized Transaction to remove the entry.
Pressing ⌨ctrl + D will delete the selected entry on any type of list in QuickBooks.

SD Practice
Continue to develop your skills by entering the following source document(s).

SD38: Memo #10   **Dated April 28, 2012**

From Owner: Print cheques #205 and #206 to MK Foods and Universal Liquidators.

SD39: Purchase Invoice #BB-1624   **Dated April 30, 2012**

From Bulk Bargains, $600.00 plus $30.00 GST for inventory merchandise to be sold in the store. The purchase invoice totals $630.00. Terms: Net 25 days. Use the memorized transaction. Allow the transaction to proceed and exceed the credit limit. A payment will be made immediately.

SD40: Cheque Copy #207   **Dated April 30, 2012**

To Bulk Bargains, $630.00 in payment of account. Reference invoice #BB-451. Print the cheque.

SD41: Memo #11   **Dated April 30, 2012**

From Owner: Complete adjusting entries for inventory sold during month.

Food inventory	$1,600.00
Merchandise inventory	8,200.00
Supplies (cleaning, office supplies, plastic bags)	285.00

SD42: Memo #12   **Dated April 30, 2012**

From Owner: Complete adjusting entry for $2,300.00 of expired prepaid insurance.

SD43: Bank Debit Memo DM-56621   **Dated April 30, 2012**

From MidWest Bank: Loan payment $1,140.00, consisting of $140.00 interest and $1,000.00 principal was withdrawn from the Bank Chequing account.

Vendors and Payables Reports

Vendor reports and graphs can be accessed from the Reports menu or from the Report Centre. Each report can be modified by adding or removing columns; by sorting and filtering to select only parts of the data for the report; and by changing headers, footers, fonts, and number formats. The principles for modifying and customizing vendor reports are the same as they are for the reports discussed in Chapter 4.

You can also memorize the report after modifying it, rename it, and add it to your list of memorized reports.

1. **Choose** the **Reports menu**, then **choose Vendors & Payables** as shown here to view the list of all vendor reports:

Notes
The T4A Detail Report will be covered in later chapters.

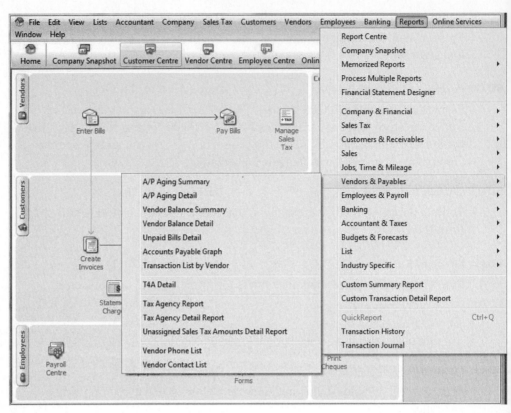

Figure 6-44

Because the Report Centre shows a sample of the report and a description of the purpose of the report, we will print reports from the Report Centre rather than selecting them from the Report menu.

2. **Click** the **Report Centre** icon on the Icon bar to open the Report Centre

3. **Click** the **Vendors & Payables** heading on the left-hand side of the screen to view the list of vendor & payables reports:

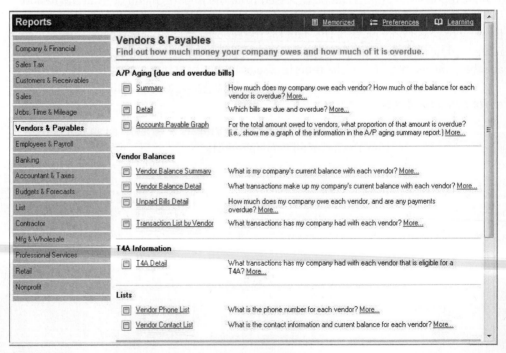

Figure 6-45

Accounts Payable Aging Reports

The Accounts Payable Aging Reports show the amounts in columns aged according to the period in which the invoices were dated. The default is to show 30-day intervals for the columns. You can view the report in Summary form with only the total amount owing to each vendor for each period, and in Detail form showing the transaction details for each invoice that is outstanding. From these reports, you can see if any invoices are overdue or plan a payment schedule.

The Accounts Payable Aging Summary Report

1. **Hover** your mouse pointer over the **icon** to the left of the Summary report link under the A/P Aging heading to view the sample report

2. **Click** the **Summary** link to open the report

3. **Double click** in the **date field**

4. **Type** 04/30/12

5. **Click** the **Refresh button** or press (tab) to update the report:

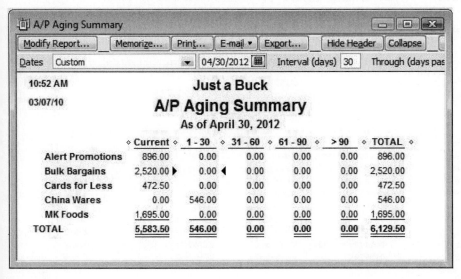

Figure 6-46

The report shows the total amount owing to each vendor. All current invoices are dated within the last 30 days and are displayed in the 1–30 days column while the historical invoices are displayed in the 31–60 days column. By default, vendors without outstanding balances are included in the report. You can sort the report by total amount or vendor (the default) from the Sort By field list. By default, the report shows aging intervals to 90 days but you can include more periods (columns) by entering a different number in the Through (Past Days Due) field. If some of your accounts are not due for 120 days, you may want to extend the reporting detail to show the accounts beyond 120 days.

To change the periods in the column heading, we can enter a different number in the Interval (Days) field. We will modify the report to show 15-day intervals instead of 30 because some vendors request payment in less than 30 days.

6. **Double click** 30 in the Interval days field

7. **Type** 15

Notes
Refer to page 84 for a review of the date fields for reports.

Notes
To access the report from the Reports menu,
- Choose the Reports menu, then choose Vendors & Payables, and click A/P Aging Summary to open the report
- Enter 04/30/12 in the Date field
- Press (tab) or click Refresh to update the report

8. **Click**   **Refresh** to change the column headings to Current, 1–15, 16–30, and so on

You can also drill down on the report to view more transaction details.

9. **Double click**   an **amount** or a total for a vendor to view the transaction details for that amount. **Double click** the **transaction detail line** to view the transaction

10. **Close**   the **report** when you have finished, unless you want to print it first

11. **Click**   **No** to indicate that you do not want to memorize the report

The Accounts Payable Aging Detail Report

1. With the Vendors & Payables heading selected in the Report Centre, **click** the **Detail link** under the A/P Aging heading to open the report

2. **Double click**   the **date field**

3. **Type**   **04/30/12**

4. **Click**   the **Refresh button** or press ⌐tab⌐ to update the report:

Notes
To access the report from the Reports menu:
• Choose the Reports menu, then choose Vendors & Payables, and click A/P Aging Detail to open the report
• Enter 04/30/12 in the Date field
• Press ⌐tab⌐ or click the Refresh button to update the report

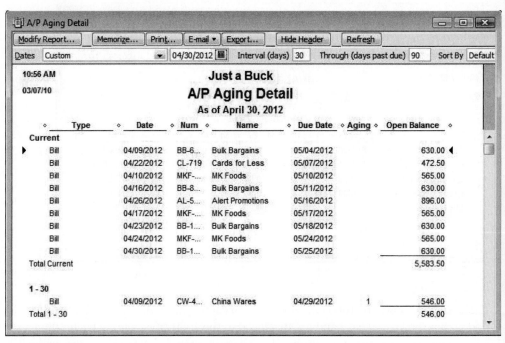

Figure 6-47

The detail report has a separate line for each transaction by vendor within each period and the due date is displayed for each invoice.

You can modify the detail report as you can the summary report. You can change the aging intervals, change the reporting through period, you can sort by vendor or total, and drill down to view more detail.

Notes
Double clicking a total amount in the A/P Aging Detail report will open the individual transaction.

5. **Double click**   a **transaction line** to drill down to the transaction

6. **Close**   the **report** when you have finished, unless you want to print it first

7. **Click**   **No** to indicate that you do not want to memorize the report, if you changed the report default settings

Vendor Balance Reports

The Vendor Balance Reports show the amounts currently owed to each vendor. The summary report shows only the total amount while the detail report shows individual transactions, both invoices and payments.

The Vendor Balance Summary Report

1. With the Vendors & Payables heading selected in the Report Centre, click the Vendor Balance Summary link under the Vendor Balances heading to open the report:

Notes
To access the report from the Reports menu:
  • Choose the Reports menu, then choose Vendors & Payables and click Vendor Balance Summary to open the report

Figure 6-48

The date for this report is entered automatically by the program as the date of the latest transaction. Totals for each vendor are shown as the default but you can add columns for different intervals, such as weeks or months, by choosing from the Columns drop-down list. You can sort the report by total amount instead of the default, by vendor.

2. **Double click** an **amount** or total for a vendor to view the transaction details for that amount

3. **Double click** a **transaction detail line** to view the original invoice or payment

4. **Close** the **report** when finished, unless you want to print it first

5. **Click** **No** to indicate that you do not want to memorize the report, if you changed the report default settings

The Vendor Balance Detail Report

Notes
To access the report from the Reports menu:
  • Choose the Reports menu, then choose Vendors & Payables, and click Vendor Balance Detail to open the report

1. With the Vendors & Payables heading selected in the Report Centre, **click** the **Vendor Balance Detail link** under the Vendor Balances heading to open the report:

Figure 6-49

The report is organized by vendor, with a line for each invoice and payment. All dates are included initially, but you can change the date range for the report in the From and To date fields.

You can sort the report by any of the column headings — Type, Date, Number, Account, and Amount — in either ascending or descending order.

2. **Double click** a **transaction line** to drill down to the transaction

3. **Close** the **report** when finished, unless you want to print it first

4. **Click** **No** to indicate that you do not want to memorize the report, if you changed the report default settings

The Unpaid Detail Report

The unpaid bills detail report shows which invoices have not been paid by a specific date, the due dates, and the age´of the invoice (number of days). Individual transactions are listed.

1. With the Vendors & Payables heading selected in the Report Centre, **click** the **UnPaid Bills Detail link** under the Vendor Balances heading to open the report

2. **Double click** the **Date field**

3. **Type** 04/30/12

Notes

To access the report from the Reports menu:
- Choose the Reports menu, then choose Vendors & Payables and click Unpaid Bills Detail to open the report
- Enter 04/30/12 in the Date field

4. The following report will be displayed:

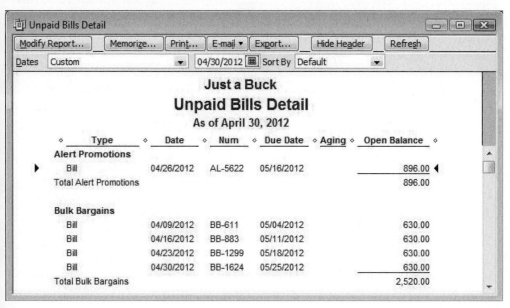

Figure 6-50

The aging column shows the number of days since the invoice was entered. You can sort the report by any of the column headings, Type, Date, Number, Due Date, Aging, and Open Balance amount, in either ascending or descending order. Sorting is done within the transactions for each vendor. You can also zoom in to more detail.

5. Double click a **transaction line** to drill down to the invoice

6. Close the **report** when finished, unless you want to print it first

7. Click **No** to indicate that you do not want to memorize the report, if you changed the report default settings

The Transaction List by Vendor Report

This is another report that shows individual transactions for all vendors for the selected report period.

1. With the Vendors & Payables heading selected in the Report Centre, **click** the **Transaction List by Vendor** link under the Vendor Balances heading to open the report

2. Double click the **From date field**

3. Type **04/01/2012**

4. Double click the **To date field**

5. Type **04/30/2012**

6. Press (tab) or **click** the **Refresh button** to update the report:

Notes
To access the report from the Reports menu:
- Choose the Reports menu, then choose Vendors & Payables and click Transaction List by Vendor to open the report
- Enter 04/01/12 as the From date
- Enter 04/30/12 as the To date
- Press (tab) or click the Refresh button to update the report

Figure 6-51

The report includes all accounts involved in a transaction. You can sort this report by any of the column headings and show the transactions in ascending or descending order. Sorting is done within the transactions for each vendor.

7. **Double click**   a **transaction line** to drill down to the transaction

8. **Close**   the **report** when finished

9. **Click**   **No** to indicate that you do not want to memorize the report, if you changed the report default settings

Vendor Lists

QuickBooks offers two lists for vendors: the phone list and the contact list. These lists allow you to check for missing details.

The Vendor Phone List

The Vendor phone list includes only the vendor's name and phone number.

1. With the Vendors & Payables heading selected in the Report Centre, **click** the **Vendor Phone List link** under the Lists heading to open the report:

Figure 6-52

Notes
If - SPLIT - appears in the Split column, it indicates that more than one account was used in the transaction.

Notes
To access the report from the Reports menu:
- Choose the Reports menu, then choose Vendors & Payables and click Vendor Phone List; or
- Choose the Reports menu, then choose List, and click Vendor Phone List

264   Chapter 6

You can sort the list by vendor name or by phone number. Sorting by phone number might be useful if you have different vendors with different area codes and want to phone all the vendors in one region.

You can double click a vendor on the report to open the vendor record and make any necessary changes.

2. Close   the **report** when finished

3. Click   **No** to indicate that you do not want to memorize the report, if you changed the report default settings

The Vendor Contact List

The contact list has the vendor's name, account number, address, contact name, phone and fax numbers, and balance owing as at the latest transaction date.

1. With the Vendors & Payables heading selected in the Report Centre, **click** the **Vendor Contact List link** under the Lists heading to open the report:

Notes
To access the report from the Reports menu:
- Choose the Reports menu, then choose Vendors & Payables and click Vendor Contact List; or
- Choose the Reports menu, then choose List and click Vendor Contact List

Vendor Contact List						
Modify Report...	Memorize...	Print...	E-mail ▾	Export...	Hide Header	Refresh	Sort By Default ▾

Just a Buck
Vendor Contact List
December 2, 2009

Vendor	Account No.	Address	Contact	Phone	Fax	Balance Total
Alert Promotions		Alert Promotions 64 Publicity Rd. Winnipeg, M...	Shawna Nues	(204) 386-1892	(204) 386-1900	896.00
B & G Imports		B & G Imports 450 Red Deer Path Winnipeg, ...		(204) 577-6875	(204) 577-9012	0.00
Bulk Bargains		Bulk Bargains Max Cheipe 500 Risquer Blvd....	Max Cheipe	(204) 459-4990	(204) 459-6889	2,520.00
Cards for Less		Cards for Less Trite Sayers 1200 Bavarder ...	Trite Sayers	(204) 698-2301	(204) 698-3923	472.50
China Wares		China Wares 510 Corelle Blvd. Winnipeg, MB...	Crystal Bowles	(204) 386-3377	(204) 386-8100	546.00
Hold All Containers		Hold All Containers				0.00
Manitel		Manitel 19 Converse Ave. Winnipeg, MB Can...	Oral Speaker	(204) 577-3481	(204) 577-3927	0.00

Figure 6-53

You can sort this report by any of the column headings and show the report lines in ascending or descending order.

You can double click a vendor on the report to open the vendor record and make any necessary changes.

2. Close   the **report** when finished

3. Click   **No** to indicate that you do not want to memorize the report, if you changed the report default settings

The Accounts Payable Graph

The final report for vendors is presented as a graph. It shows aging information as well as the total amount owing to individual vendors.

1. With the Vendors & Payables heading selected in the Report Centre, **click** the **Accounts Payable Graph link** under the A/P Aging heading to open the graph

2. Click   the **Dates button**

3. Type   **04/30/12** in the Show Aging as of field

4. Click   **OK** to view the graph:

Notes
To access the graph from the Reports menu:
- Choose the Reports menu, then choose Vendors & Payables, and click Accounts Payable Graph to open the graph
- Click the Dates button to set the date
- Enter 04/30/12 in the Show Aging as of field
- Click OK to view the report

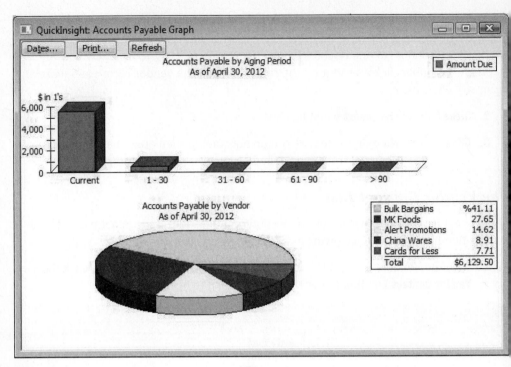

Figure 6-54

The graph has two sections: a bar graph in the upper section that shows the total amount owing for each aging interval, and a pie chart in the lower section that shows the total owing to each vendor. You can zoom down to several other reports and graphs from both sections of the graph.

Double click a bar in the bar chart in the upper section of the graph to view the pie chart breakdown of vendor amounts that make up its total. Then, double click a section of this pie chart to view the A/P Aging report for the vendor selected. Double click a transaction listed in the A/P Aging report to drill down to the transaction.

Double click a pie section in the pie chart in the lower section of the graph to view an aging bar chart for that vendor with separate bars for the total in each aging period. Then, double click a bar in this chart to view the A/P Aging report for the vendor selected. Double click a transaction listed in the A/P Aging report to drill down to the transaction.

5. **Close**   the **report** when finished

6. **Click**   **No** to indicate that you do not want to memorize the report, if you changed the report default settings

Finishing Your Session

1. **Back up**   your **company data file**

2. **Close**   the **company file**

3. **Close**   the **QuickBooks program**

Malin's Makeovers

Objectives

After completing this chapter, you should be able to:

- **enter** invoices for customer sales
- **enter** receipts from customers
- **add** complete new customer records
- **deposit** receipts in a bank account
- **print** sales invoices
- **print** mailing labels
- **enter** NSF cheques from customers
- **correct** sales invoices after recording
- **correct** receipts after recording
- **display** and **print** customer and sales reports and graphs

Company Information

Company Profile

Malin's Makeovers, located in Ottawa, Ontario, is owned and operated by Malin Andersson as a partnership. After studying hairdressing and cosmetology in Stockholm, Malin Andersson immigrated to Canada. For the next few years, she worked in some excellent salons building her reputation and skills. Before launching her own business, she completed additional courses in colour and design and in business studies. After working on her own for three years, the demand for her services led her to bring in two classmates from her course as partners, Kiera O'Sullivan and Dhaibhen Mehta. She has been operating her salon now for several years. The salon has three booth areas so that the clients always have privacy during their consultations.

 Notes
Malin's Makeovers
515 Sparks Street
Ottawa, ON K2C 8J9
Tel: (613) 753-9219
Fax: (613) 753-8003
E-mail: mm@makeover.com
Web: www.makeover.com
Business No.: 277 544 732

The consultants, affectionately known as "change artists," offer complete makeover consultations, from changes in hair styles and makeup, to dress, colour, and fashion advice. They use computer imaging, a digital camera, and specialized software to place the client in photographs with alternate styles, designs, and colours to illustrate how a change in design can be more or less flattering. The partners also advise professionals on dressing or changing their image for a new career or a special occasion. Assistance with wardrobe shopping is also available. Malin's Makeovers has helped some local politicians prepare for increased media exposure. For corporate groups, the team offers training seminars as well as individual follow-up consultation. Clients can order personalized reports after a consultation.

January and February are busy months for the salon because the consultation sessions are popular gifts for holidays and for Valentine's Day.

Individual customers pay for their services immediately, while corporate customers have accounts set up with Malin's Makeovers and carry account balances. All customers pay 13 percent HST on services in the salon, and accounts are to be settled within 15 days with no discounts for early payment. Customer cheques and cash are deposited weekly. The salon does not sell any products directly to customers.

The partners use their own vehicles for business travel and always carry their cell phones and laptop computers. In this way, they can contact each other or give client demonstrations at any time. They are reimbursed for expenses. The partners clean the salon themselves daily, but rely on professional cleaners for a thorough weekly service.

Accounts are set up with regular vendors who provide salon supplies such as cosmetics and hair care products, customized salon chairs, and hair dryers. None of these vendors offers discounts for early payment. Malin's Makeovers pays 13 percent HST on business-related purchases. Invoices are received with merchandise and paid later. Some bills are paid immediately by manually prepared cheques.

At the end of January 2012, the business converted the accounting records to QuickBooks using the following documents:

- Chart of Accounts
- Trial Balance
- Vendor List
- Customer List
- Item List
- Accounting Procedures

Chart of Accounts

Malin's Makeovers

ASSETS
Bank
  Bank Chequing
  Bank Savings

Accounts Receivable
  Accounts Receivable

Other Current Assets
  Cosmetics Supplies
  Hair Care Supplies
  Imaging Software
  Office and Computer Supplies
  Prepaid Insurance

FIXED ASSETS
  Computer Equipment:Cost
  Computer Equipment:Depreciation
  Computer Equipment:Other

Salon:Cost
Salon:Depreciation
Salon Equipment:Cost
Salon Equipment:Depreciation
Salon Furniture:Cost
Salon Furniture:Depreciation

LIABILITIES
Accounts Payable
  Accounts Payable

Other Current Liabilities
  Bank Loan
  HST Payable

Long Term Liabilities
  Long Term Loan
  Mortgage Payable

EQUITY
  Capital, Dhaibhen Mehta
  Capital, Kiera O'Sullivan
  Captial, Malin Andersson
  Drawings, Dhaibhen Mehta
  Drawings, Kiera O'Sullivan
  Drawings, Malin Andersson
  Retained Earnings

INCOME
  Other Revenue
  Revenue from Interest
  Revenue from Services

EXPENSE
  Advertising and Promotion
  Depreciation Expense
  General Expense
  Insurance Expense
  Interest Expense
  Maintenance and Cleaning
  Other Supplies Used
  Salon Supplies Used
  Telephone Expense
  Travel/Vehicle Expenses

Trial Balance

Malin's Makeovers

AS AT JANUARY 31, 2012

	Debits	Credits		Debits	Credits
Bank Chequing	$ 8,995.00		Mortgage Payable		120,000.00
Bank Savings	35,460.00		Capital, Dhaibhen Mehta		27,393.56
Accounts Receivable	5,370.70		Capital, Kiera O'Sullivan		27,393.57
Cosmetics Supplies	1,256.00		Captial, Malin Andersson		27,393.57
Hair Care Supplies	980.00		Drawings, Dhaibhen Mehta	2,000.00	
Imaging Software	4,000.00		Drawings, Kiera O'Sullivan	2,000.00	
Office and Computer Supplies	590.00		Drawings, Malin Andersson	2,000.00	
Prepaid Insurance	4,200.00		Revenue from Interest		55.00
Computer Equipment:Cost	12,000.00		Revenue from Services		27,410.00
Computer Equipment:Depreciation		$ 300.00	Advertising and Promotion	1,400.00	
Salon:Cost	180,000.00		Depreciation Expense	1,220.00	
Salon:Depreciation		750.00	General Expense	245.00	
Salon Equipment:Cost	1,400.00		Insurance Expense	2,100.00	
Salon Equipment:Depreciation		20.00	Interest Expense	1,940.00	
Salon Furniture:Cost	18,000.00		Maintenance and Cleaning	600.00	
Salon Furniture:Depreciation		150.00	Other Supplies Used	110.00	
Accounts Payable		2,506.00	Salon Supplies Used	195.00	
Bank Loan		8,000.00	Telephone Expense	285.00	
HST Payable		1,325.00	Travel/Vehicle Expenses	1,350.00	
Long Term Loan		45,000.00		$287,696.70	$287,696.70

Vendor Information

Malin's Makeovers

Vendor Name (Contact)	Address	Phone No. Fax No.	E-mail Business No.	Terms Credit Limit
Crystal Wireless Communications (Kia Noe)	399 Mobility Ave. Kanata, ON K5C 1Y5	Tel: (613) 462-3918 Fax: (613) 462-7322	kia.noe@cwc.com	net 10 $500.00
Faces Inc. (Klier Visages)	8 Foundation St. Ottawa, ON K3B 5D6	Tel: (613) 776-2938 Fax: (613) 776-2199	kv@facesinc.com 384 674 288	net 30 $3,000.00
Keep It Clean (Mollie Maydes)	25 Sanitizing St. Ottawa, ON K4B 7J1	Tel: (613) 288-1725		net 15 $1,000.00
Office Outfitters (Daye Tymer)	210 Stationery Rd. Ottawa, ON K3J 7V2	Tel: (613) 622-3456 Fax: (613) 622-3917	273 911 720	net 20 $2,000.00
Receiver General				due quarterly

Outstanding Vendor Transactions

Malin's Makeovers

Vendor Name	Date	Terms	Due Date	Invoice No./	Amount	Total Owing
Faces Inc.	01/06/2012	net 30	02/05/2012	F-4910	$805.00	$805.00
Keep It Clean	01/20/2012	net 15	02/04/2012	KC-662	$160.50	
	01/27/2012	net 15	02/11/2012	KC-688	$160.50	$321.00
Office Outfitters	01/24/2012	net 20	02/13/2012	OO-500	$1,380.00	$1,380.00
				Grand Total		$2,506.00

Malin's Makeovers

Customer Name (Contact)	Address	Phone No. Fax No.	E-mail Tax Code	Terms Credit Limit
AIM International (Purdy Lookes)	5180 Richmond St. Ottawa, ON K2H 8B4	Tel: (613) 688-3613 Fax: (613) 688-1928	plookes@AIM.com H	net 15 $5,000.00
Cash Sales			H	due on receipt
Jammers (Harde Rock)	69 Swingers Ave. Ottawa, ON K4P 1M8	Tel: (613) 527-5223 Fax: (613) 527-3813	rocke@jammers.com H	net 15 $3,000.00
ODSB (Sloe Lerner)	450 Fastrak Rd. Ottawa, ON K4B 2B6	Tel: (613) 725-4611 Fax: (613) 725-9124	slerner@odsb.on.ca H	net 15 $5,000.00
OTV News (Vanna Taye)	13 Broadcast Ave. Ottawa, ON K7G 3P8	Tel: (613) 286-3977 Fax: (613) 286-0971	vanna@otv.com H	net 15 $5,000.00

Outstanding Customer Transactions

Malin's Makeovers

Customer Name	Date	Terms	Due Date	Invoice No.	Amount	Total Owing
AIM International	01/18/2012	net 15	02/02/2012	3084	$ 588.50	
	01/28/2012	net 15	02/12/2012	3118	$1,177.00	$1,765.50
Jammers	01/19/2012	net 15	02/03/2012	3092	$ 609.90	$ 609.90
ODSB	01/24/2012	net 15	02/08/2012	3101	$ 856.00	$ 856.00
OTV News	01/21/2012	net 15	02/05/2012	3097	$2,139.30	$2,139.30
				Grand Total		$5,370.70

Item List

Malin's Makeovers

Item	Description	Price	Tax Code	Revenue Account
Clothing style consultation	Consultation on suitable clothing styles and colours	$190.00	H	Revenue from Services
Customized seminar/training	Customized training seminars and presentations	custom pricing	H	Revenue from Services
General consultation	General consultation charged on hourly basis	$110.00/hour	H	Revenue from Services
Hair consultation	Hair style consultation and cut	$150.00	H	Revenue from Services
Makeover	Complete makeover consultation: hair, makeup and clothing	$390.00	H	Revenue from Services
Makeup consultation	Consultation and demonstration of makeup techniques	$120.00	H	Revenue from Services
Report	Personalized makeover report following consultation	$90.00	H	Revenue from Services
NSF Charges	Service fee for NSF cheque	$25.00	Not Used	Other Revenue
NSF Cheque	Amount of NSF cheque	cheque amount	Not Used	Bank Chequing

Accounting Procedures

Taxes: HST

Malin's Makeovers pays HST on all goods and services that it buys and charges HST on all services it provides. It uses the regular method for remittance of the HST. HST collected from customers is recorded as a liability in the *HST Payable* account. HST paid to vendors is recorded in the *HST Payable* account as a decrease in liability to the Canada Revenue Agency. The report is filed with the Receiver General for Canada every quarter, remitting the balance owing or requesting a refund.

Account Terms

Most customers have set up accounts with Malin and are expected to settle these accounts by cheque within 15 days. One-time customers who do not order customized services pay by cash immediately at the time of the service. These cash sales are summarized and entered on a weekly basis as total sales for the week.

All cash and cheques are held in the on-site safe until they are deposited to the bank account. Bank deposits are made weekly.

Accounts are also set up with most vendors, although none presently offers discounts for early payment. Malin pays for business purchases by cheque.

Supplies

The partners count the supplies left in the salon on a monthly basis to determine the cost of materials and supplies used. Adjusting entries are then made.

Partner Expenses and Drawings

Each partner draws $2,000.00 per month in lieu of a salary. Partners are also reimbursed for their travel expenses at a rate of $0.50 per kilometre when they use their personal vehicles for business. Reimbursement is made at the end of each month.

Instructions

1. Using the Chart of Accounts, the Trial Balance, and other information, you will record entries for source documents for February 2012 using QuickBooks. You will find the source documents marked with an SD beside them and listed as you work through the chapter. The procedures for entering each new type of transaction introduced in this chapter are outlined in step-by-step instructions. Additional source documents will be provided, allowing you to have more practice entering transactions. If you have used this textbook in the past and would prefer to skip the step-by-step instructions and work only with a list of source documents, refer to the CD in the back of the textbook for the list of source documents for this chapter.

2. After you have finished making your entries, print the reports and graphs for February 2012 as indicated on the following printing form:

> **Notes**
> Instructions for customer and sales reports begin on page 315.

REPORTS FOR FEBRUARY 2012

Lists
- ☐ Account Listing
- ☐ Customer Phone List
- ☐ Customer Contact List
- ☐ Vendor Phone List
- ☐ Vendor Contact List
- ☐ Item Listing
- ☐ Item Price List

Company & Financial
- ☑ Balance Sheet Standard at Feb. 29
- ☑ Profit & Loss Standard from Feb. 1 to Feb. 29
- ☐ Expenses by Vendor
- ☐ Income by Customer

Accountant & Taxes
- ☑ Trial Balance at Feb. 29
- ☐ General Ledger
- ☑ Journal from Feb. 1 to Feb. 29
- ☐ Transaction List by Date
- ☐ Transaction Detail by Account

Other
- ☐ Custom Summary Report
- ☐ Custom Transaction Detail Report
- ☐ Transaction History
- ☐ Transaction Journal

Vendor
- ☑ A/P Aging at Feb. 29
- ☐ Vendor Balance
- ☐ Unpaid Bills
- ☐ Transaction List by Vendor

Customer
- ☑ A/R Aging at Feb. 29
- ☑ Customer Balance
- ☐ Open Invoices
- ☐ Collections Report
- ☐ Transaction List by Customer

Sales
- ☑ Sales by Customer from Feb. 1 to Feb. 29
- ☐ Sales by Item

GRAPHS
- ☐ Income and Expense
- ☐ Net Worth
- ☐ Accounts Payable
- ☑ Accounts Receivable at Feb. 29
- ☑ Sales from Feb. 1 to Feb. 29

Entering Sales Invoices

Entering sales transactions for merchandise purchased by your customers on account is similar to entering sales receipts. However, instead of entering cash sales where the payment is made by the customer at the time of invoice entry using the Enter Sales Receipts form, as you learned in Chapter 3, you enter the customer invoice, the customer pays you at a later time, and the payment must be deposited in the bank. Depending on whether the deposit is sent directly to the bank, this could result in two or three transactions in QuickBooks.

1. **Open**   the **Malin's Makeovers company file**. The QuickBooks Home page should be displayed on the screen

The first transaction that we will enter is a Sales Invoice. Refer to the following source document as we work through the steps to enter it:

SD Instructions
Refer to the following source document and then follow the step-by-step instructions to enter it.

SDI: Sales Invoice #3125

Dated February 1, 2012

To AIM International, $3,150.00 plus $409.50 HST for customized seminars on international dress standards to prepare employees for overseas assignments. Invoice total $3,559.50. Terms: Net 15 days.

Customer transactions can be entered from three different areas in QuickBooks;

a. The Customers section of the Home page:

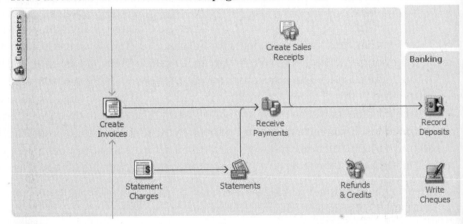

Figure 7-1

The Customers section of the Home page is organized like a flow chart that indicates the usual sequence of transactions. A portion of the Banking section has been included to show the Record Deposits icon.

For example, after entering customer invoices, the next step is to receive payments for invoices and then deposit the payments. Finance charges, customer statements, and credits or refunds may occur before payments are received. Finance charges and credits will be covered in a later chapter. We have turned off the sales orders and estimates options because they are not used by Malin's Makeovers, so the icons for them have been removed from this company file.

From the Customers section of the Home page, you can also enter Sales Receipts as you learned in Chapter 3, and you can access the Customer Centre by clicking on the Customers icon.

b.   The Customers menu:

Figure 7-2

You can use the Customers menu to access the Customer Centre, enter customer transactions, and access the item list.

c.   The Customer Centre:

Figure 7-3

The Customer Centre contains more information and it requires more explanation. On the left-hand side of the screen, you'll see two tabs: a Customers & Jobs tab and a Transactions tab.

When you click on the Customers & Jobs tab, the customer list is displayed on the left-hand side of the screen, which displays each customer's name and total balance. You can sort the customer & jobs list by customer name or total balance and by ascending or descending order by clicking on the list headings.

When you highlight a customer in the list, their customer information is displayed in the top right portion of the screen allowing you to quickly view the customer address information, click on the Edit Customer button to access the customer record where you can make changes to it, click on the QuickReport or Open Balance button to print reports for the customer, or use the Edit Notes button to add notes to the customer record. The transaction details for the customer are listed in the bottom right portion of the screen. You can use the headings across the top of the transaction details to select which type of transactions you'd like to view and filter them by a date range.

You can use the buttons across the top of the screen to add a new customer & job, enter new transactions, print customer information, export information to Excel, or print Word documents. The customer highlighted in the customers & jobs list will automatically be selected when you choose one of these options.

When you click on the Transactions tab, a list of transaction types is displayed. When you click on one of the transaction types, a list of all transactions for all customers will be displayed based on the criteria selected in the Filter By and Date fields.

As we work through this chapter, we will use various methods to access the customer transactions.

In this first transaction, we will be working with the Invoices form. As you have learned, there are a number of ways to access customer transactions, including the Invoices form, so you can choose the one you prefer.

2. **Open** the **Create Invoices form** using one of the following options:

a) **Click** the **Create Invoices icon** in the Customers section of the Home page; or

b) **Choose** the **Customers menu** and **click Create Invoices**; or

c) **Press** ctrl + I

Notes
You can also access the Create Invoices form from the Customer Centre. Highlight the customer name, click the New Transactions button, and click Invoices.

3. The Create Invoices form is displayed as shown:

Figure 7-4

Notice that this form resembles the Sales Receipt form, but the deposit and payment method details are missing because the payments are made later. Completing the invoice is also similar to entering sales receipts.

4. Click the **drop-down arrow** in the Customer:Job field to view the list of customers on file:

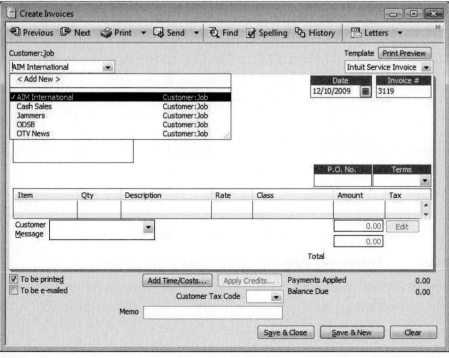

Figure 7-5

5. **Click**   **AIM International**

The customer address and payment terms (net 15 days) are added to the form from the customer record. The current calendar date is entered as the default date. As in the previous chapter, once you enter transactions, the last date used will appear as the default date until you close the program or data file.

6. **Double click**   the **date** to select it

7. **Type**   **02/01/12**

8. **Press**   (tab) to accept the transaction date and advance to the Invoice # field

The invoice number follows the last historical invoice number that was entered as part of the setup of the company file. Once we update it, it should be correct for the remaining invoices.

9. **Type**   **3125**

10. **Click**   the **Item field** to display the drop-down arrow

11. **Click**   the **drop-down arrow** in the Item field to view the list of services:

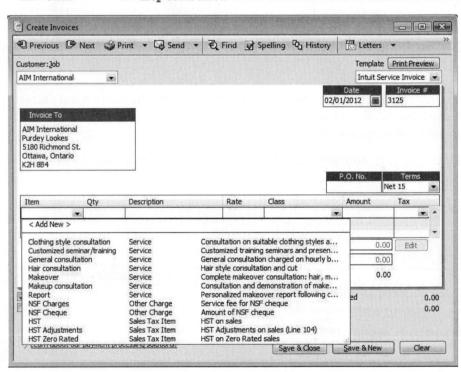

Figure 7-6

Notice the list includes two entries related to NSF cheques that are not customer services for regular sale. These will be used later in the chapter.

12. **Click**   **Customized seminar/training** to add it to the invoice

Notice that the item description is automatically displayed. This information is coming from the item record.

13. **Press**   (tab) to advance to the Quantity field (Qty)

For customized work, the quantity is one and the price is negotiated before the work is started.

14.	**Type**	1
15.	**Press**	(tab) to skip the Description field and advance to the Rate field
16.	**Type**	3150
17.	**Press**	(tab) to update the Amount and taxes
18.	**Click**	the **drop-down arrow** in the Customer Message field
19.	**Choose**	**It's been a pleasure working with you!**

We will print the invoices in batches later so the invoice is now complete as shown:

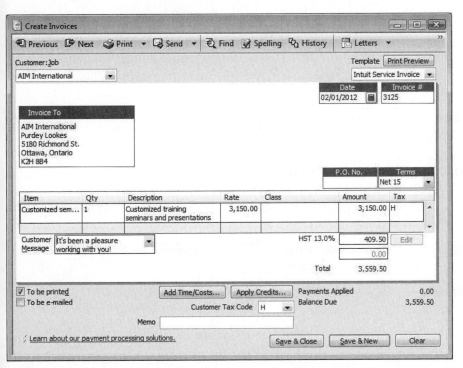

Figure 7-7

20.	**Check**	**your work** carefully before recording the invoice so you won't need to make corrections later

CORRECTING SALES INVOICES

Click the field that contains the error. You can press (tab) to move forward from one field to the next. Highlight the incorrect information and type the correct information in the field. Press (tab) if necessary to update the information.

If the incorrect information was selected from a list, click the drop-down arrow again and select the correct item. If you select a different item, you must re-enter the quantity and/or the amount. If you change the amount, press (tab) to update the taxes and totals.

Click the Clear button to start again.

We want to review the Journal Transaction so we need to save the invoice and keep the Create Invoices window open.

21. Click   **Save & New** or **press** ⟨alt⟩ **+ S** to record the invoice and leave the Create Invoices form open. You will see the following warning:

Recording Transaction

⚠️ The credit limit for AIM International is 5,000.00. The current balance, including this transaction, is 5,325.00. Continue?

[Yes]   [No]

Figure 7-8

AIM International has a credit limit of $5,000.00 and an outstanding balance. The current invoice will cause them to exceed this limit so you must choose what to do next. You can proceed with the sale or return to the invoice form and request a customer deposit or payment before continuing. We will proceed with the sale because the company has always paid its account on time.

22. Click   **Yes** to continue and record the sale

Reviewing the Transaction

To begin this exercise, a blank Invoice should be displayed on the Create Invoices form from the previous exercise.

1. Click   the **Previous button** 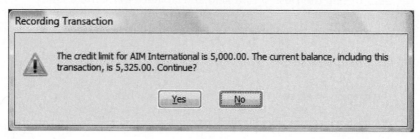 or **press** ⟨alt⟩ **+ P** to view the invoice we just completed

2. Press   ⟨ctrl⟩ **+ Y** to view the Transaction Journal report:

Malin's Makeovers
Transaction Journal
All Transactions

Date	Num	Name	Memo	Item	Item Description	Account	Sales Price	Amount
▶ 02/01/2012	3125	AIM International				Accounts Receivable		3,559.50 ◀
		AIM International	Customized ...	Custom...	Customized trainin...	Revenue from Services	3,150.00	-3,150.00
		Receiver General	HST on sales	HST	HST on sales	HST Payable	13.0%	-409.50
								0.00
								0.00

Figure 7-9

The complete journal entry is included, with all accounts properly debited and credited. QuickBooks has made the entry in the background by increasing the *Accounts Receivable* balance. The *Accounts Receivable* debit entry is matched by the negative amounts for *HST Payable* and *Revenue from Services*. The customer's account balance — amount owing — has also increased by the total amount of the sale.

3. Click   ❌ when you have finished viewing the journal entry to close the Transaction Journal report and return to the Invoice for AIM International

The next transaction that we are going to enter is a cash receipt so we will close the Create Invoices form.

4. Click   ❌ to close the Create Invoices form and return to the QuickBooks Home page

Notes
We have deleted the type, transaction number, and class columns from the transaction journal report and re-sized some of the other columns by dragging the column heading markers to the desired location in order to display all the important details on the screen.

Entering Receipts

The second transaction that we are going to enter is a cheque from AIM International that should be applied to outstanding invoices for sales before the starting date; that is, before the files were converted to QuickBooks. Refer to the following source document as we work through the steps to enter it:

SD2: Cash Receipt #249

Dated February 2, 2012

From AIM International, cheque #1285 for $1,100.00 in payment of account. Reference invoices #3084 and #3118. Cheque held for deposit.

In this transaction, one cheque has been received to partially pay the account. The first invoice is fully paid and the second invoice is partially paid. Customer receipts are entered after the invoices are recorded in the Receive Payments form.

You cannot enter receipts received for payment of invoices on the Sales Receipts form. The Sales Receipts form is used only for cash sales — sales that are accompanied by a payment.

<table>
<tr><td>1. **Click**</td><td>the **Receive Payments icon** in the Customers section of the Home page, or **choose** the **Customers menu** and **click Receive Payments** to open the Receive Payments form:</td></tr>
</table>

SD Instructions
Refer to the following source document and then follow the step-by-step instructions to enter it.

WARNING!
Do not attempt to use the Sales Receipts form for payments on account. This form is used only for cash sales – sales that are accompanied by payment.

Notes
The Icon bar does not include an icon to access the Receive Payments form directly. You can access the form from the Customers menu. We will add an icon for it on the Icon bar after entering the receipt.

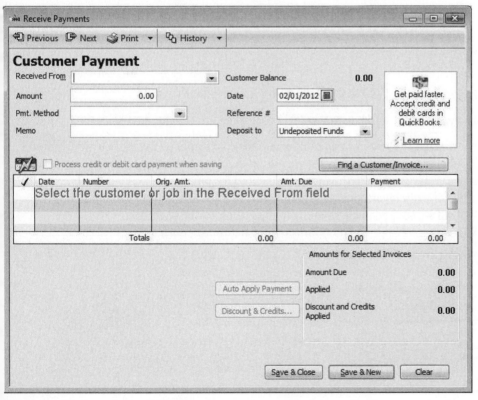

Figure 7-10

<table>
<tr><td>2. **Click**</td><td>the **drop-down arrow** in the Received From field to access the list of customers</td></tr>
<tr><td>3. **Choose**</td><td>**AIM International**</td></tr>
<tr><td>4.</td><td>All outstanding invoices for AIM International are displayed in the Receive Payments form as shown:</td></tr>
</table>

Figure 7-11

5. Press   `tab` to advance to the Amount field

6. Type   **1100** and **press** `tab` to advance to the date field

Notice that the payment amount is automatically applied first to the oldest invoice until it is fully paid. The remaining amount is then applied to the second oldest invoice, and so on. You can change the invoices selected for payment if needed by entering the payment for each invoice in its corresponding invoice line in the Payment field.

We will accept the invoices and amounts selected for payment.

We need to change the date for this transaction to February 2, 2012.

7. Click   the **Date field** calendar icon to display the calendar:

←	February - 2012	→

Su	Mo	Tu	We	Th	Fr	Sa
			1	2	3	4
5	6	7	8	9	10	11
12	13	14	15	16	17	18
19	20	21	22	23	24	25
26	27	28	29			

Figure 7-12

8. Click   **2** on the February 2012 calendar

If you closed the data file before opening the Receive Payments form, the current date will be displayed in the date field and depending on the current year, you may have to scroll through a number of months to reach the one you want. In that case, it would be easier to manually type 02/02/12 in the Date field.

9. Press   `tab` to advance to the Pmt. Method field

10. Click   the drop-down arrow to display the payment methods available on the payment method list:

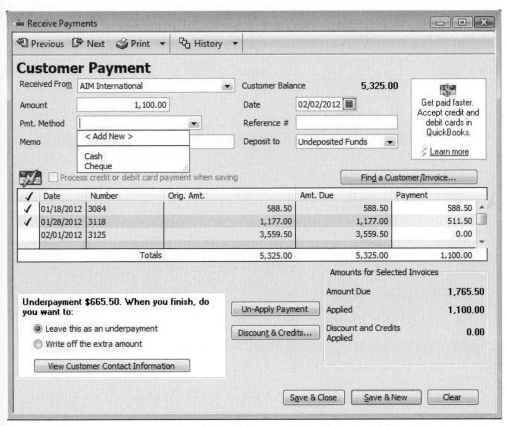

Figure 7-13

You can select a payment method in the list or create a new payment method by selecting the Add New option.

11. Select   **Cheque** and **press** `tab`

12. Type   **1285**

13. Press   `tab` to the Deposit to field

The final option that we have to select is whether the cheque is held for later deposit or deposited immediately to the bank account. In previous chapters, we deposited receipts immediately to the bank account. Malin's Makeovers holds the cheques and makes weekly deposits. Thus the Undeposited Funds account is the account to which we want to deposit this receipt.

14. Accept   the **Undeposited Funds account** (select it if necessary)

15. The completed customer payment is displayed in the Receive Payments form as shown:

Figure 7-14

In the bottom left-hand corner of the screen, the following message is displayed:

Underpayment $665.50. When you finish, do you want to:

◉ Leave this as an underpayment
○ Write off the extra amount

[View Customer Contact Information]

Figure 7-15

This message indicates that there is an underpayment of $665.50 and asks whether you want to leave the amount as an underpayment or write off the extra amount. This message is displayed because a partial payment has been made on invoice 3118. AIM International still owes you the balance of $665.50 on this invoice, so you will accept the default option and leave the amount as an underpayment.

16. **Check**   **your work** carefully before recording the sale so you won't have to make corrections later

CORRECTING CUSTOMER PAYMENTS

Click the field that contains the error. Press ⌨tab to move forward from one field to the next. Highlight the incorrect information and type the correct information in the field. Press ⌨tab if necessary to update the information.

You can also start the transaction again by clicking the Clear button.

17. **Click**   **Save & New** or **press** ⌨alt + **S** to record the payment

Reviewing the Transaction

In this exercise, we will review the journal entry that was created by the receive payments transaction. But before we do, let's review the updated outstanding payments for AIM International.

With a blank Receive Payments form displayed on the screen:

1. **Click**   the **drop-down arrow** in the Received From field and select Aim International

2. You will see that the list of outstanding invoices for AIM International has been updated:

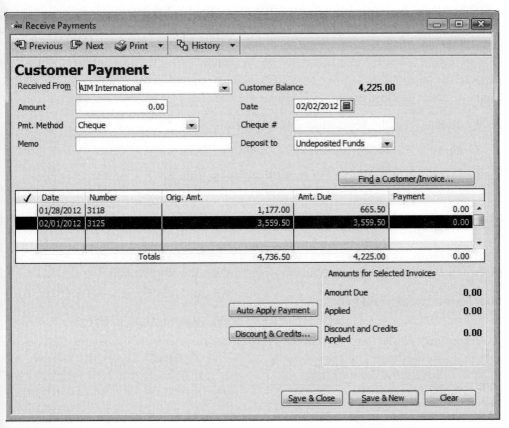

Figure 7-16

Notice that the first invoice has been removed, the Amount Due for the next invoice has been reduced by the partial payment, and the amount due is the amount you saw in Figure 7-15.

We will now look at the journal entry for the receipt we entered in the previous exercise.

3. **Click**   the **Clear button** at the bottom of the form to clear the form

4. **Click**   ⬅ Previous to view the completed customer payment

5. **Press**   ctrl + **Y** to view the transaction journal report:

Malin's Makeovers
Transaction Journal
All Transactions

Type	Date	Num	Name	Account	Debit	Credit
▶ Payment	02/02/2012	1285	AIM International	Undeposited Funds	1,100.00	◀
			AIM International	Accounts Receivable		1,100.00
					1,100.00	1,100.00
TOTAL					**1,100.00**	**1,100.00**

Figure 7-17

QuickBooks created a journal entry that debits the *Undeposited Funds* account and credits the *Accounts Receivable* account to reduce the customer's balance. QuickBooks created the *Undeposited Funds* account when we chose to deposit the funds to the *Undeposited Funds* account in the Receive Payments window. When we deposit the funds in the Make Deposits form, they will be transferred from the *Undeposited Funds* account (credit) to the *Bank Chequing* account (debit).

6. **Close**   the **Transaction Journal report**

7. **Click**   [X] to close the Receive Payments form

You should be returned to the QuickBooks Home page.

Adding a Complete Customer Record

The next transaction that we need to enter is a Sales Invoice for a new customer. Refer to the following source document as we work through the steps to enter it:

SD3: Sales Invoice #3126

Dated February 3, 2012

To Amore Bridal Party (Set up new customer)

3	Clothing style consultations	$190.00 each	$ 570.00
5	General consultations	110.00 each	550.00
3	Reports	90.00 each	270.00
	HST 13%		180.70
	Invoice total		$1,570.70
	Terms: Net 15 days		

Notes
Amore Bridal Party
Contact: Ms Lisa Amore
250 Busquer St.
Ottawa, ON K3R 2P8
Canada
Phone: (613) 769-4180
Fax: (613) 769-3829
Alt. Phone: (613) 534-9418
E-mail: l.amore@romanza.ca
Tax Code: HST
Terms: Net 15
Credit Limit: $3,000.00
Pay by: Cheque

You can add new customer records from several locations in QuickBooks. In previous chapters, we added customer names only by choosing Quick Add when we typed a new name in a Customer:Job field in a transaction form. We can also add complete customer details when entering a new name in a Customer:Job field in a transaction form by choosing Set Up instead of Quick Add when prompted.

When you type a new name in the Customer:Job field and press (tab), the following Customer:Job Not Found message is displayed:

Figure 7-18

Choosing Set Up opens the Customer record where you can enter detailed customer information, such as address details and payment terms. When you click OK after entering the customer information, you will be returned to the sales transaction form with the record details — terms and address information — added to the transaction.

You can also add customers directly on the Customers & Jobs list found in the Customer Centre. To access the Customer Centre:

Notes
You can also open the Customer Centre from the Customers menu, clicking on the Customers button in the Customer section of the Home page or by pressing `ctrl` + **J**.

1. Click the **Customer Centre icon** on the Icon bar: [Customer Centre] to open the Customer Centre:

Customer Centre: AIM International (All Transactions)			

New Customer & Job ▾   New Transactions ▾   Print ▾   Excel ▾   Word ▾

Customers & Jobs   Transactions

View Active Customers ▾

Find [ ] 🔍

Name	Balance Total
◆ AIM International	4,225.00
◆ Cash Sales	0.00
◆ Jammers	609.90
◆ ODSB	856.00
◆ OTV News	2,139.30

Customer Information   [Edit Customer...]

Customer Name: AIM International
Customer Type:
Company Name: AIM International
Billing Address: AIM International
Purdey Lookes
5180 Richmond St.
Ottawa, Ontario
K2H 8B4

Contact: Purdey Lookes
Phone: (613) 688-3613
Alt Phone:
Fax: (613) 688-1928
Email: plookes@AIM.c...
Terms: Net 15
Price Level:

Notes   [Edit Notes...]

Reports for this Customer
▪ QuickReport
▪ Open Balance

Show [All Transa... ▾]   Filter By [All ▾]   Date [All ▾]

Type	Num	Date ▾	Account	Amount
Payment	1285	02/02/2012	Undeposited Funds	1,100.00
Invoice	3125	02/01/2012	Accounts Receivable	3,559.50
Invoice	3118	01/28/2012	Accounts Receivable	1,177.00
Invoice	3084	01/18/2012	Accounts Receivable	588.50

Figure 7-19

The following methods can be used to add a new customer in the Customer Centre:

a. **Click** the **New Customers & Jobs button** at the top of the screen to add a new customer or job as shown:

New Customer & Job ▾
New Customer
Add Job

Figure 7-20

b. **Right click** the **Customers & Jobs** list to display the following menu:

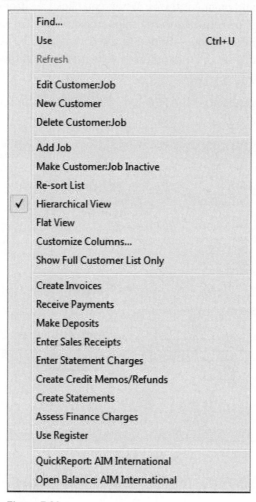

Find...	
Use	Ctrl+U
Refresh	
Edit Customer:Job	
New Customer	
Delete Customer:Job	
Add Job	
Make Customer:Job Inactive	
Re-sort List	
✓ Hierarchical View	
Flat View	
Customize Columns...	
Show Full Customer List Only	
Create Invoices	
Receive Payments	
Make Deposits	
Enter Sales Receipts	
Enter Statement Charges	
Create Credit Memos/Refunds	
Create Statements	
Assess Finance Charges	
Use Register	
QuickReport: AIM International	
Open Balance: AIM International	

Figure 7-21

From this menu you can create new customers, edit existing customer records, delete a customer record, or make an unused customer record inactive if it does not meet the deletion criteria so it does not appear in forms that access the Customers & Jobs list. You can also enter customer transactions directly from this menu.

c. **Press** *ctrl* **+ N**, the **New** keyboard shortcut

2. Click   the **New Customer & Job button** and **click New Customer** or **press** $\boxed{ctrl}$
+ N to open the New Customer record form:

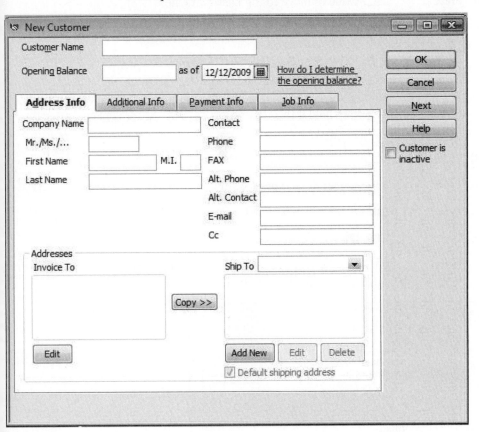

Figure 7-22

The cursor is in the Customer Name field, where you add the name of the customer.

3. Type   **Amore Bridal Party**

The historical transactions were already entered in the company file before you began entering transactions.

There is no opening balance because this is a new customer. If there were an opening balance, you would enter the opening balance in the as of field so that the opening balance could be aged correctly, according to the payment terms.

The date displayed in the as of field will be the current system date on your computer.

4. Click   the **Company Name field**

5. Type   **Amore Bridal Party**

6. Press $\boxed{tab}$ to move to the title (Mr/Ms) field

7. Type   **Ms**

8. Press $\boxed{tab}$ to move to the First Name field

📄 **Notes**
  QuickBooks allows you to add historical information (before the Start date) after you start using the program by entering an amount in the *Opening Balance* field and entering a date in the *as of* field.

📄 **Notes**
  You can copy the Customer Name field to the Company Name field.
  Highlight the name you entered in the Customer Name field to select it.
   Press $\boxed{ctrl}$ + **C** to copy it.
   Click in the Company Name field.
   Press $\boxed{ctrl}$ + **V** to paste the name in the Customer Name field to the Company Name field.

9.	**Type**	**Lisa**
10.	**Press**	(tab) twice to move to the Last Name field
11.	**Type**	**Amore**
12.	**Press**	(tab)

The company name and contact appear in the Address area under the Invoice To section, and the contact name is also added to the Contact field. You can enter a different name in the Contact field if this is appropriate. The cursor is placed after the contact name in the Address text area.

13.	**Press**	(enter) to move the cursor to the line below Lisa Amore
14.	**Type**	**250 Busquer St**. and **press** (enter)
15.	**Type**	**Ottawa, ON** and **press** (enter)
16.	**Type**	**K3R 2P8**
17.	**Press**	(tab) to select the Edit button and then **press** (enter) to open the Edit Address Information window:

WARNING!
Pressing (tab) in the Address text box will take the cursor out of the address area and select the Edit button.
Pressing (enter) in the Address text box will allow you to enter each address line; however, pressing (enter) in a field other than the Address text box will save and close the record because the OK button is selected by default.

Figure 7-23

Notes
The note entered on the Edit Address Information screen will be displayed below the customer address. To add a general note for the customer record, you must save the customer record and then edit the record and add a note. The Notes button appears after you create the customer record.

You can enter additional lines of address information on the Edit Address Information screen and correct the address details if needed. Alternatively, you could have opened the Edit Address Information screen and entered the details in here first. We will add the country information on this screen. This screen also has a field for an address note.

18.	**Correct**	the **address details** if needed
19.	**Click**	the **Country/Region field**
20.	**Type**	**Canada**
21.	**Click**	**OK** to return to the Customer Record
22.	**Click**	Copy >> to copy the invoice address to the ship to address box.

The ship to address is automatically given the name *Ship To 1*. If the customer has merchandise shipped to different locations, you can enter multiple ship to addresses by clicking on the Add New button below the Ship To address text box. Each ship to address will be given a unique name and that name can be selected on customer transactions if a template allowing ship to addresses is selected.

23.	**Click**	the **Phone field**
24.	**Type**	**(613) 769-4180**
25.	**Press**	(tab) to advance to the FAX field
26.	**Type**	**(613) 769-3829**
27.	**Press**	(tab) to advance to the Alt. Phone field. Amore has given her home number as an alternate
28.	**Type**	**(613) 534-9418**
29.	**Press**	(tab) to skip the Alt. Contact field and advance to the E-mail field
30.	**Type**	**l.amore@romanza.ca**
31.	**Click**	the **Additional Info tab**:

Notes
You must format the phone number.

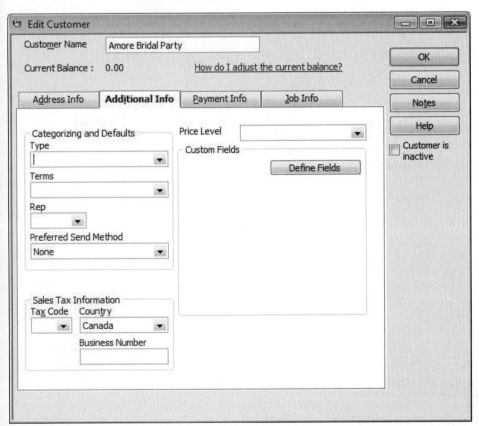

Figure 7-24

Malin's Makeovers does not use customer types, such as region, or type of business, to organize the records. It also does not keep track of customer and vendor business numbers.

The Rep field may be used to select an employee from a list if one is usually assigned to the customer. Price levels may also be set up so that different customers receive preferred discounted prices. Malin's Makeovers does not have employees or use differential pricing for customers.

32.	**Click**	the **drop-down arrow** in the Terms field to view the payment terms already set up

33. **Click**	**Net 15** to add the term to the customer record
34. **Click**	the **drop-down arrow** in the Tax Code field

The default code is H; HST at 13 percent is applied to services.

35. **Click**	**H**

The H tax code will now be added to invoices for this customer automatically but can, of course, be changed for individual items if necessary.

36. **Click**	the **Payment Info tab**:

Figure 7-25

Most businesses place limits on the amount that a customer is allowed to purchase on credit. Once the credit limit is reached, the customer may be asked for a down payment or may be granted a credit limit increase. Customer credit limits should be reviewed regularly with reference to a customer's buying and payment patterns to determine whether the limits should be raised or lowered for individual customers. As we saw on page 278, the program warns when a credit limit is exceeded by a purchase or sale. The limit for Amore-Bridal Party is $3,000.00.

37. **Click**	the **Credit Limit field**
38. **Type**	**3000**
39. **Click**	the **drop-down arrow** in the Preferred Payment Method list to view the payment methods available:

Figure 7-26

Malin's Makeovers accepts only cash and cheques in payment for services, so these are the only payment methods available.

40. Click   **Cheque**

The fourth tab, Job Info, allows you to organize the work done for customers according to specific jobs. This allows you to track the work done for customers in a more detailed way. When jobs are set up, you can choose the Customer and Job from the Customers & Jobs list. Malin's Makeovers has not set up customer jobs.

41. Check   **your work** carefully before saving the customer record

---

CORRECTING CUSTOMER RECORDS

Click the field that contains the error. You can press `tab` to move forward from one field to the next. Highlight the incorrect information and type the correct information in the field. Click the Address Info tab, Additional Info tab, and Payment Info tab to return to those tabs to review your work and make any necessary corrections.

If you need to make corrections or changes later after the customer record has been saved, open the Customer Centre and double click the customer name or press `ctrl` + E to open the customer record.

---

42. Click   **OK** to save the record and return to the Customer Centre

43. Right click   on **Amore Bridal Party** in the Customers & Jobs list

44. Choose   **Create Invoices**

The Create Invoices form opens with Amore Bridal Party entered in the Customer:Job field.

45. Press   `tab` to add the customer's address, terms, and tax code to the invoice

46. Enter   **02/03/12** as the date

47. Click   the **drop-down arrow** in the Item list field and **click Clothing style consultation**

48. Press   `tab` to advance to the Qty (quantity) field

The item description, rate and tax code are entered automatically from the item record.

49. Type   **3** and **press** `tab` to update the Amount field

50. Press   `tab` repeatedly to advance to the Item field on the second line, or **click** the **Item field on the second line**

51. Click   the **drop-down arrow** in the Item list field and **click General consultation**

52. Press   `tab`

53. Type   **5** and **press** `tab` to update the Amount

54. Click   the **Item field** on the third line

55. Click   the **drop-down arrow** in the Item list field and **click Report**. **Press** `tab`

56. Type   **3**

57. Press   `tab` to update the Amount. Your completed invoice should look like the one shown here:

Notes
You can also open the Create Invoices form by clicking the New Transactions button and selecting Invoices or by pressing `ctrl` + I.

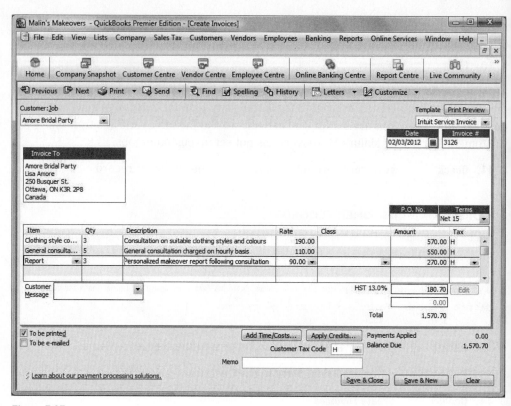

Figure 7-27

58.	**Check**	**your work** and **make corrections** if needed
59.	**Click**	**Save & Close** or **press** *alt* + **a** to return to the Customer Centre
60.	**Click**	![X] to close the Customer Centre

Printing Sales Invoices

The next source document refers to printing sales invoices. Refer to the following source document as we work through the steps to print the sales invoices:

SD4: Memo #1

Dated February 3, 2012

From Partners: Print sales invoices #3125 and #3126.

Even if you do not print the invoices and labels, you may want to work through the printing procedure in order to preview the final printed documents.

You can print or e-mail invoices individually at the time of a sale or you can print them in batches later for mailing to customers. Sometimes customers are invoiced regularly for services delivered over a period of time, items ordered for delivery, or services provided at the customer's location, such as telephone or security services. Invoices for construction or contracting work also may be sent later. The Create Invoices form window includes both a Print button ![Print] and a Send button ![Send] that is used to e-mail invoices.

These buttons allow you to print or email individual invoices or print or email batches of invoices.

SD Instructions
Refer to the following source document and then follow the step-by-step instructions to enter it.

To print a batch of invoices:

1. **Choose** the **File menu** in the desktop window, then **choose Print Forms** and **click Invoices** to view the list of invoices that have not been printed:

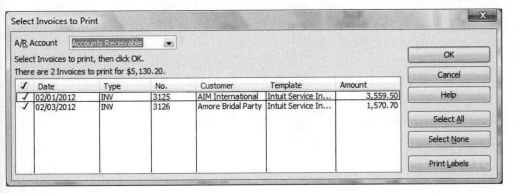

Figure 7-28

Notes
You can also print a batch of invoices from the Create Invoices form by selecting the drop-down arrow in the print button and selecting Print Batch. The same screen that you see in Figure 7-28 will be displayed.

All invoices you marked "To be printed" and have not yet been printed will be displayed on this list.

If some invoices are selected that you do not want to print, choosing the Select None button will remove all checkmarks. Choosing the Select All button will include all invoices for printing. Clicking individual invoices will toggle the checkmark on and off. Selecting all or none and changing a few selections is faster than clicking individual invoices in a long list.

The two invoices that we need to print are already selected so we can proceed.

From the Select Invoices to Print screen, you can also print mailing labels for the invoices to be printed and mailed to customers.

2. **Click** **Print Labels** to access the Select Labels to Print screen:

Figure 7-29

You can select the labels you need to print from various lists.

3. **Click** the **drop-down arrow** beside the Name field to view the choices from which you can select:

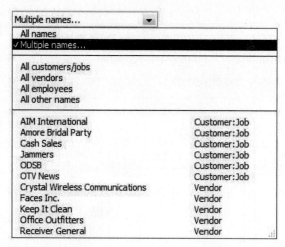

Figure 7-30

You can create labels for all names in the data file, for all customers and jobs, for all vendors, for all employees, or for all other names. You can also print the label for an individual by choosing a name from the list, or you can print labels for some of the names on the list. Sorting features are also available to further define the list of names you want.

The names on the invoices to be printed are preselected initially. You can click individual names to add them to the list of labels.

4. Click   **Multiple names** to view the list of preselected names based on the invoices that have been selected to be printed in the batch:

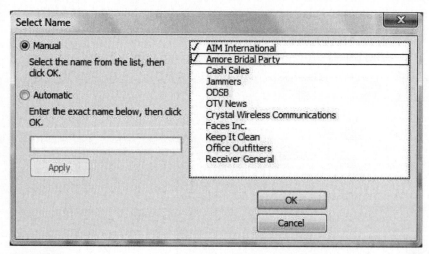

Figure 7-31

Notice that the two names selected are AIM International and Amore Bridal Party, the names of the customers for whom the invoices are going to be printed in the batch.

5. Click   **OK** to return to the Select Labels to Print screen

6. Click   **OK** again to open the Print Labels printer control window

7. Click   **Preview** to see what the printed labels will look like

8. Click   **Close** to return to the Print Labels control screen. Make changes to the setup if needed

If you do not want to print the labels, click Cancel to return to the Select Labels to Print screen. Click Cancel again to return to the Select Invoices to Print screen.

Notes
Printing from a Preview window will close the preview.

If you want to print labels, be sure that you have label forms in your printer and that the correct label format is selected in the Print Labels control screen.

9. Click   **Print** to begin printing labels (or click Cancel twice to return to the Select Invoices to Print screen)

If you printed the labels to the printer, return to the Select Invoices to Print screen.

10. Click   **OK** to view the Print Invoices printer control screen:

Figure 7-32

Make the printer control selections you need. Indicate whether you are using pre-printed forms, blank paper, or letterhead for the invoices. You can also choose whether to add lines (boxes) around each field on the invoice. This is recommended if you are using blank paper, but not if you are using preprinted forms. You can also use this screen to indicate the number of copies you want to print.

QuickBooks also provides Templates that you can use to customize your invoices. You can customize a template from the Create Invoices form or from the Templates list.

11. Click   **Blank Paper** as the Print On option

12. Click   **Preview** to see what the printed document will look like. You can print directly from the Preview screens by clicking the Print button

13. Click   **Close** to return to the Print Invoices printer control screen. Make changes to the setup if needed

14. Click   **Print** to start printing. QuickBooks will ask you whether the forms printed correctly:

Figure 7-33

For any invoices that did not print correctly, click in the box beside it under the Reprint column. A ✓will be displayed, indicating that the invoice needs to be printed again. You can then click OK to begin reprinting the necessary invoices.

We'll assume that our invoices have printed correctly.

15. Click   **OK** to continue

Correcting a Previously Recorded Receipt

The next source document that we must enter is a memo from the partners indicating that the cheque from AIM International was entered incorrectly. Refer to the following source document as we work through the steps to make the corrections to the cheque:

SD5: Memo #2

Dated February 3, 2012

From Partners: Cash Receipt #249, the cheque from AIM International, was entered incorrectly. The actual cheque amount was $1,200.00. Edit the receipt to make the correction.

SD Instructions
Refer to the following source document and then follow the step-by-step instructions to enter it.

Just as you can correct sales receipts, bills, and cheques after recording, you can correct receipts and sales invoices. The procedure is the same for all forms — display the completed form on the screen, edit it, and save the changed form.

1. Click   **the Receive Payments icon** [Receive Payments] in the Customers section of the Home page to open the Receive Payments form

The Receive Payments form does not have a Find button, so we need to use the Previous button to scroll back through payments previously entered.

2. Click   [Previous]

3. The receipt entered most recently is displayed on the screen. It is the one from AIM International that we want to edit:

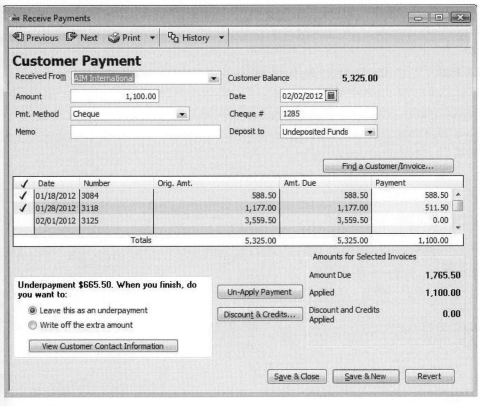

Figure 7-34

4. **Double click** **1,100.00** in the Amount field of the cheque portion to select it

5. **Type** **1200** and **press** (tab) to update the receipt form:

Figure 7-35

Notes

You can also click the ✓ for invoice #3118 and then click the 3 column again. This will remove the payment amount and enter the correction.

Or, you can double click 511.50, the Payment field amount for the invoice line, and type the amount that should be applied to this invoice, 611.50.

The revised amount has not been reallocated to invoices. In the bottom left-hand corner, you can see that QuickBooks now thinks there is a $100.00 overpayment. We need to change the amount applied to invoice #3118.

6. Click the **Un-Apply Payment button** to remove the ✓s beside the selected invoices

Notice that the Un-Apply Payment button has changed to Auto Apply Payment. Clicking this button will allow QuickBooks to allocate the payment amount to the invoices.

7. Click the **Auto Apply Payment button** to reapply the payment and update the receipt:

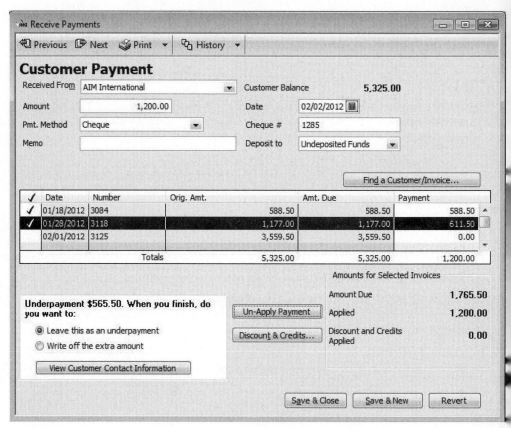

Figure 7-36

8. Click **Save & Close** or **press** ⌐alt⌐ + **a** to view the following confirmation message:

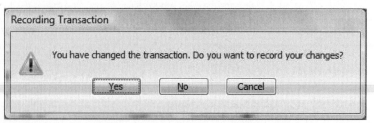

Figure 7-37

9. Click **Yes** to indicate that you want to record the changed receipt. It will replace the original transaction.

Correcting Sales Invoices

The next source document that we must enter is a memo from the partners indicating that sales invoice #3126 to Amore Bridal Party was entered incorrectly. Refer to the following source document as we work through the steps to make the corrections to the sales invoice:

SD6: Memo #3

Dated February 3, 2012

From Partners: Sales invoice #3126 was entered incorrectly. The Amore party had 3 hours of consultation, not 5. The revised invoice total is $1,322.10. Edit the invoice to make the correction and then print the corrected invoice.

Like other transactions in QuickBooks, sales invoices can be edited by displaying the recorded transaction on the screen. Use the Previous and Next buttons until the invoice you want to correct is displayed on the screen. You can also use the Find button on the invoice form to locate the invoice. For the next correction, we will use the Find button to locate the transaction that was recorded incorrectly. After correcting the invoice, we will print it in order to mail the revised copy to our customer.

1. **Click** _____ or **press** ⌨️ + **I** to open the Create Invoices form

The Find button is located on the Create Invoices Icon bar as shown here:

Figure 7-38

There are three ways to open the Find window when a QuickBooks invoice is displayed on the screen:

a) **Click** the **Find button** 🔍 Find in the Create Invoices form; or

b) **Choose** the **Edit Menu** and **click Find Invoices**; or

c) **Press** ⌨️ + **F** to open the Find Invoices window:

Figure 7-39

When you want to find a transaction but a QuickBooks form is not displayed on the screen, choose the Edit menu and click Find. Click the Simple tab, choose Invoice as the

SD Instructions
Refer to the following source document and then follow the step-by-step instructions to enter it.

Notes
You can also open the Create Invoices form directly from the Customers menu or from the shortcut menu in the Customers & Jobs list.

Notes
Because the Invoices form is open, the Edit menu will have Find Invoices as its Find option, and ⌨️ + F will open the Find Invoices form directly.

transaction type, and enter the rest of the search criteria. The Advanced tab has even more search options.

You can find all invoices for a single customer, all invoices that fall within a given range of dates, or a specific invoice. When more than one invoice results from the search, you will see a list of invoices to select from. We will enter the invoice number because we know which one we need.

2. **Click**   the **Invoice # field**

3. **Type**   **3126**

4. **Click**   🔍 **Find**   to access the invoice directly:

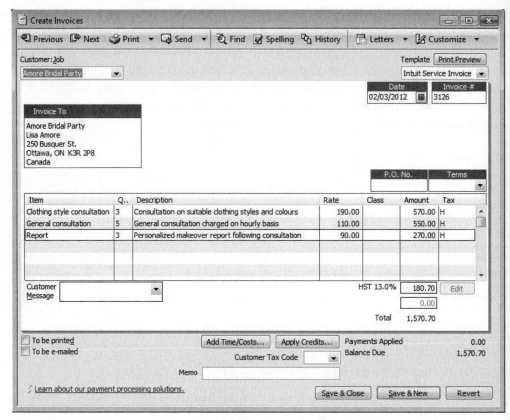

Figure 7-40

Notice that the To be printed box is not checked because we already printed this invoice in a previous exercise.

5. **Double click**   **5** in the Qty field for General consultation on the second invoice line

6. **Type**   **3**

7. **Press**   (tab) to update the tax and total amounts as shown:

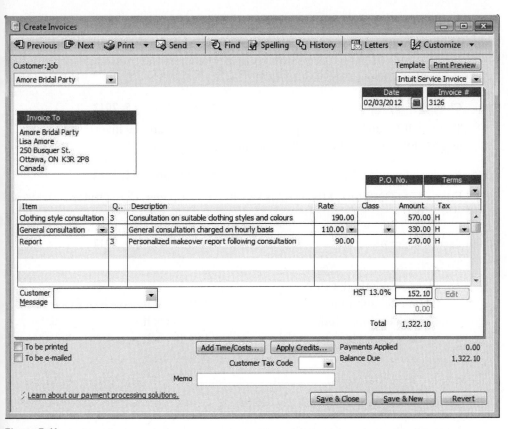

Figure 7-41

We will also add a note to the Memo field and reprint the invoice so that we can send the revised copy to the customer.

8.	**Click**	the **Memo field**
9.	**Type**	**Revised invoice**
10.	**Click**	⊜ Print ▾ to open the printer dialogue box
11.	**Click**	**Yes** when you are asked to record the changes before you print
12.	**Click**	**Print** in the Print One Invoice control screen

The next transaction that we need to enter is another invoice, so we will leave the Create Invoices form open.

| 13. | **Click** | **Save & New** or **press** (alt) + S |

Source Documents

Now that you have learned some of the new concepts introduced in this chapter, continue to develop your skills by entering the following source document in QuickBooks. Use the information in this chapter as a guide if necessary.

SD7: Sales Invoice #3127   **Dated February 5, 2012**

To ODSB, $185.00 plus $24.05 HST for a one-hour customized seminar for school staff on upcoming changes in policy concerning school dress codes and how to reinforce them in a positive manner with students. Invoice totals $209.05. Terms: Net 15 days. The seminar will be repeated in all schools over the coming months. Memorize the transaction with weekly reminders to begin February 12, 2012.

⚠ WARNING!
If you do not save the changes before printing and recording the changes, the invoice will revert to the original entry.

▢ SD Practice
Continue to develop your skills by entering the following source document(s).

SD8: **Purchase Invoice #KC-724**   **Dated February 5, 2012**

From Keep It Clean, $150.00 plus $19.50 HST for a weekly cleaning of the salon. Invoice totals $169.50. Terms: Net 15 days. Memorize the transaction with weekly reminders to begin February 12, 2012.

SD9: **Cheque Copy #388**   **Dated February 5, 2012**

To Keep It Clean, $321.00 in payment of account. Reference invoices #KC-662 and KC-688. Assign cheque #388 (do not print cheque).

SD10: **Purchase Invoice #OO-692**   **Dated February 6, 2012**

From Office Outfitters, $180.00 plus $23.40 HST for paper, CDs, printer cartridges, and other office and computer supplies. Invoice totals $203.40. Terms: Net 20 days.

Notes
For the sales receipt, accept the default to deposit to the Undeposited Funds account so the deposit can be made later.

SD11: **Sales Receipt #5**   **Dated February 6, 2012**

To Cash Sales customers

Payment Method: Cash		
2 Hair consultations	$150.00 each	$ 300.00
1 Makeup consultation	120.00 each	120.00
2 Clothing style consultations	190.00 each	380.00
2 Makeovers	390.00 each	780.00
4 Reports	90.00 each	360.00
HST	13%	252.20
Sales receipt total cash held for deposit		$2,192.20

Memorize the transaction with weekly reminders beginning February 13, 2012. The summary will be entered each week with different sales amounts.

SD12: **Cash Receipt #250**   **Dated February 6, 2012**

From OTV News, cheque #4663 for $2,139.30 in payment of account. Reference invoice #3097. Cheque held for deposit.

Making Deposits to a Bank Account

Our next source document involves depositing all cheques and cash held for weekly deposit to the Bank Chequing account. Refer to the following source document as we work through the steps to enter it:

SD Instructions
Refer to the following source document and then follow the step-by-step instructions to enter it.

SD13: Memo #4

Dated February 6, 2012

From Partners: Deposit all cheques and cash held for weekly deposit to the Bank Chequing account. Total deposit is $5,531.50.

When cheques and cash are received from customers they can be held for later deposit. QuickBooks records these items as debits in the *Undeposited Funds* account. Later, when deposits are entered, the funds from the Undeposited Funds account are transferred to the selected bank account.

When there is money in the *Undeposited Funds* account, it is ready to be deposited into a bank account. You can use the Reminders list to view various functions to be performed in QuickBooks. One of the reminders you can set is to show when money is available to be deposited. To view the Reminders list on a regular basis, you can set the Reminders List to display when you open a company file.

1. **Select**   **Company** from the menu and click Reminders:

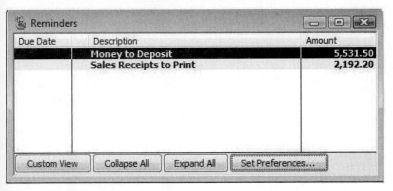

Figure 7-42

The total amount of $5,531.50 held for deposit is displayed beside the Money to Deposit heading. We will expand the list to view the details.

2. **Double click**   the **Money To Deposit** heading in the Reminders list to expand the list and show the details:

Due Date	Description	Amount
	Money to Deposit	5,531.50
02/02/2012	AIM International	1,200.00
02/06/2012	Cash Sales	2,192.20
02/06/2012	OTV News	2,139.30
	Sales Receipts to Print	2,192.20

Figure 7-43

3. **Open**   the **Payments to Deposit form** using one of the following options:

a) **Click** the **Record Deposits icon** in the Banking section of the Home page; or

b) **Choose Banking** from the menu and then **click Make Deposits**

4. The Payments to Deposit form will be displayed as shown:

Figure 7-44

The Payments to Deposit form lists the three payments that are ready to be deposited. The details for the payments include not only the amount and the date, but also the payment method. Many companies have more than one bank account — credit card bank accounts are usually separate from the chequing bank accounts.

You can select a payment method by choosing a type in the View payment method type field. By selecting a payment type from the list, one payment method can be selected for a deposit. This list makes it easy to select the payments that should be deposited to each account. By default, all payments are listed, and this is the correct selection in our case. We will deposit all the cheques and cash to the *Bank Chequing* account. In Chapter 9, we will use multiple bank accounts for deposits.

5. **Click**   the **✓ column** for each of the three payments, with Cheque or Cash as the payment method, or **click** the **Select All button**

6. **Click**   **OK** to advance to the Make Deposits form:

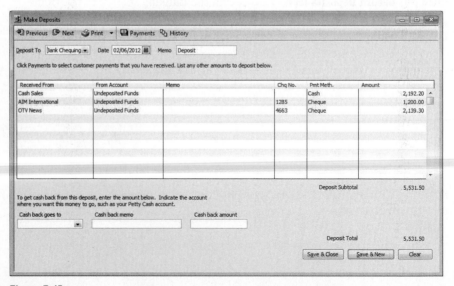

Figure 7-45

> **Notes**
> You can click anywhere on the payment line to add a ✓ for the line.

> **Notes**
> If a cheque number or Payment Method is missing on the Make Deposits form, you can enter it in the appropriate columns. Since you are changing the original transaction, select Yes when prompted to record the changes.

If you made an error when selecting the payments on the Payments to Deposit form, click the Payments button to return to the Payments to Deposit form and select or deselect the payments as necessary. When you're finished making the changes, click OK to return to the Make Deposits form. Now the transactions we selected are listed and the total deposit amount is shown at the bottom of the form. *Bank Chequing* should be selected in the Deposit to field at the top of the form. If you are depositing the funds into a different account, click the drop-down arrow in the Deposit to field and select the appropriate account. The fields at the bottom of the form allow you to record a cash withdrawal from the deposit. If part of the total payment amount is taken in the form of cash at the time of the deposit, you should complete these fields by entering the Cash back amount, a memo or explanation of the use of the funds, and the account that the cash should be credited to — often a Petty Cash account. No cash is withdrawn at this time. We should also print the deposit summary for reference.

7. **Verify**   that **Bank Chequing** is selected as the account in the Deposit to field

8. **Enter**   **02/06/12** as the date of the deposit if this is not the date already shown

9. **Check**   the **form carefully** before proceeding and **make** any **necessary corrections**

CORRECTING RECORDED DEPOSITS

The changes you can make to a recorded deposit are limited. You can change the date and you can correct the account for deposit. To do this, select the correct account in the Deposit to field.

You can delete a deposit line from the deposit form if it should not have been included in the deposit. To remove a deposit line, click the payment that you want to remove. Then choose the Edit menu and click Delete Line. After saving the deposit, repeat the deposit process to deposit the deleted payment to the correct account.

Alternatively, you can delete an entire deposit if necessary. For example, you may have selected to make the deposit to the wrong account. To delete the entire deposit, display the deposit in the Make Deposits window. Then choose the Edit menu and click Delete Deposit. After you have deleted the deposit, repeat the deposit process to deposit the payments to the correct account.

You cannot edit a customer name, account, or deposit amount on the deposit form. To change any of these, you must delete the payment from the deposit form (Edit menu, Delete line), edit the original receipt (refer to page 296) and then complete the deposit for it.

If you try to change a customer name, account, or deposit amount on the deposit form you will receive the following message:

Warning

⚠ You cannot edit payment information in a deposit transaction. 1) Delete the payment from the deposit. 2) Go to the original payment transaction to edit it. 3) Redeposit the payment.

[OK]

Figure 7-46

10. **Click**   **OK** to return to the deposit form

When the deposit form is correct, you can print the deposit slip and deposit summary. These reports are both printed from the Print button; however, how you click the Print button will depend on which menu is displayed:

a. **Click** the **drop-down arrow** on to view the options available:

Figure 7-47

b. **Click** 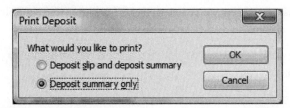 and you will see the following message:

Figure 7-48

Depending on the print option you select, you can choose to print a deposit slip, a deposit summary, or both, or order deposit slips from Intuit.

The deposit slip is printed and taken to the bank with the deposit. To print the deposit slip, you should use the proper form so that the amounts will be aligned in the correct deposit slip boxes with their labels.

The summary includes cheque numbers, payment method, customer name, memo, and amounts in columns with totals. The deposit summary can be printed on plain paper because column headings are included.

Notes
You can preview both the summary and the deposit slips before printing.

11. **Click**   and **select** Deposit slip and deposit summary to print the **Deposit slip and deposit summary**

12. **Click**   **OK**

13. **Click**   **Print**

14. **Click**   **Save & New** to save the deposit and leave the Deposits window open so you can review the journal entry created from the deposit transaction in the next exercise

Reviewing the Transaction

With a blank Make Deposits form displayed on the screen:

1. **Click**   Previous to view the deposit form that we just entered and then **click** ctrl + **Y** to view the Transaction Journal report:

Malin's Makeovers
Transaction Journal
All Transactions

Type	Date	Name	Memo	Account	Debit	Credit
▶ Deposit	02/06/2012		Deposit	Bank Chequing	5,531.50	◀
		Cash Sales	Deposit	Undeposited Funds		2,192.20
		AIM International	Deposit	Undeposited Funds		1,200.00
		OTV News	Deposit	Undeposited Funds		2,139.30
					5,531.50	5,531.50
TOTAL					**5,531.50**	**5,531.50**

Figure 7-49

Notes
We have removed the Transaction, Number, and Class columns from this Transaction Journal report.

The *Bank Chequing* account is debited for the full deposit amount of $5,531.50. All individual transactions that were deposited to the *Undeposited Funds* account are credited to reverse the original entries, and customer names are included so that the journal records of the transactions are complete.

2. Close   the **Transaction Journal report**

3. Click   [X] to close the Make Deposits form Source Documents

Now that you have learned more of the new concepts introduced in this chapter, continue to develop your skills by entering the following source document in QuickBooks. Use the information in this chapter as a guide if necessary.

SD Practice
Continue to develop your skills by entering the following source document(s).

SD14: Cheque Copy #389   **Dated February 7, 2012**

To Faces Inc., $805.00 in payment of account. Reference invoice #F-4910. Automatically assign cheque number.

SD15: Cash Receipt #251   **Dated February 9, 2012**

From ODSB, cheque #10034 for $856.00 in payment of account. Reference invoice #3101. Cheque held for deposit.

SD16: Cash Receipt #252   **Dated February 10, 2012**

From Jammers, cheque #102 for $300.00 in partial payment of account. Reference invoice #3092. Cheque held for deposit.

SD17: Sales Invoice #3128   **Dated February 12, 2012**

To ODSB $185.00 plus $24.05 HST for a one hour customized seminar for school staff on dress code policy. Invoice totals $209.05. Terms: Net 15 days. Use the memorized transaction.

SD18: Purchase Invoice #KC-779   **Dated February 12, 2012**

From Keep It Clean, $150.00 plus $19.50 HST for weekly cleaning of salon. Invoice totals $169.50. Terms: Net 15 days. Use the memorized transaction.

SD19: Sales Invoice #3129   Dated February 13, 2012

To OTV News, $780.00 plus $101.40 HST for two complete makeover consultations for newly hired news broadcasters to prepare them for regular television appearances. Invoice totals $881.40. Terms: Net 15 days.

SD20: Cash Receipt #253   Dated February 13, 2012

From AIM International, cheque #1428 for $4,125.00 in full payment of account. Reference invoices #3118 and #3125. Cheque held for deposit.

SD21: Sales Receipt #6   Dated February 13, 2012

To Cash Sales customers
Payment Method: Cash

3	Hair consultations	$150.00 each	$ 450.00
2	Makeup consultations	120.00 each	240.00
1	Clothing style consultation	190.00 each	190.00
2	Makeovers	390.00 each	780.00
3	Reports	90.00 each	270.00
	HST	13%	250.90

Sales receipt total cash held for deposit $2,180.90

Use the memorized transaction and edit the amounts.

SD22: Memo #5   Dated February 13, 2012

From Partners: Deposit all cheques and cash held for weekly deposit to the Bank Chequing account. Total deposit is $7,461.90.

SD23: Cheque Copy #390   Dated February 13, 2012

To Office Outfitters, $1,380.00 in payment of account. Reference invoice #OO-500. Automatically assign cheque number.

SD24: Purchase Invoice #F-5723   Dated February 14, 2012

From Faces Inc., $120.00 plus $15.60 HST for makeup and cosmetics supplies. Invoice totals $135.60. Terms: Net 30 days.

SD25: Cash Purchase Invoice #H-388   Dated February 15, 2012

From Heads Up (use Quick Add for new vendor), $140.00 plus $18.20 HST and for hair care products for use in salon. Invoice total of $158.20 is paid in full with cheque #391.

Recording NSF Cheques

For the next transaction, a cheque received from Jammers was returned by the bank as NSF. We will record the returned cheque and NSF charges. Refer to the following source document as we work through the steps to enter it:

SD26: Bank Debit Memo #CB-5338

Dated February 15, 2012

From Capital Bank: Cheque #102 for $300.00 from Jammers for invoice #3092 was returned as NSF. The bank charged $25.00 as the NSF fee. Create invoice #3130 to record the returned cheque and NSF charges to restore the customer's account balance. No taxes are charged on these amounts. Invoice totals $325.00.

Terms: Due on receipt.

Sometimes a cheque is drawn on an account that does not have sufficient funds to cover the amount of the cheque. When this happens, the bank will return the cheque as NSF (non-sufficient funds). Normally, the bank will charge for this service, and a business may choose to pass this cost on to its customers. Customers should be notified immediately of any outstanding amounts so that they can replace the bad cheque.

Malin has created two Other Charges items to handle the NSF cheques: one to enter the amount of the cheque and one for the administration or handling charges. Malin's Makeovers passes the bank charges on to the customer. NSF cheques are entered as sales invoices — selecting these special items for the sale.

1. **Click** from the Customers section of the Home page to open the Create Invoices form

2. **Choose** **Jammers** in the Customer:Job field

3. **Enter** **02/15/12** as the date if this date does not appear already

Several defaults for the customer are entered automatically.

4. **Choose** **NSF Cheque** as the first item

5. **Enter** **1** as the quantity and 300 as the amount

The customer's tax code is entered as the default and overrides the non-taxable code for the item so we must change it.

6. **Select** **E - Tax Exempt** as the tax code

7. **Choose** **NSF Charges** as the second item

The price and amount are entered automatically because they remain the same for all customers; however, you can override it if necessary.

8. **Enter** **1** as the quantity and **select E - Tax Exempt** as the tax code

We need to change some of the other defaults for the customer. The terms for this invoice should be set to Due On Receipt and we should add the customer's cheque number for reference as a memo for the invoice.

9. **Click** the **drop-down arrow** in the Terms field and **select Due on receipt**

10. **Click** the **Memo field**

11. **Type** **Ref: NSF Cheque #102 Re: Invoice #3092**

12. **Choose** **Please remit to above address** in the Customer Message field

13. The completed invoice will be displayed as shown:

Figure 7-50

14. Click   **Save & New**. The following message appears:

Figure 7-51

Because we changed the customer's default terms on this invoice, QuickBooks allows us to save the new terms as the default for the customer or to revert to the terms currently entered in the customer record. When an NSF cheque is received from a customer, Malin requires the customer to pay immediately for all future services. The method of payment may also be changed, so that cheques are no longer accepted from this customer. We want to change the terms.

15. Click   **Yes** to save the invoice and the new terms

Reviewing the Transaction

Let's review the journal entry for the NSF transaction.

With a blank Create Invoices form displayed on the screen:

1. **Click** **Previous** to view the invoice we just entered

2. **Press** ctrl + **Y** to view the Transaction Journal report:

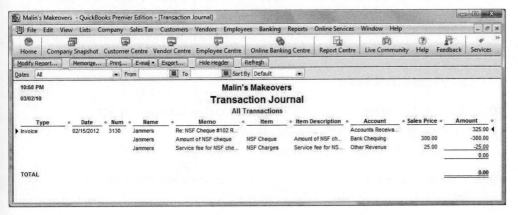

Figure 7-52

You can see that this transaction will reverse the receipt. The *Accounts Receivable* account has increased by the amount of the cheque and charges. The *Bank Chequing* account has decreased by the amount of the NSF cheque and the charges have been credited to the *Other Revenue* account. These are the default accounts assigned to the Other Charges items.

3. **Close** the **Transaction Journal** report

4. **Click** **No** to memorize the report

5. **Click** **Save & New** to save the invoice and display a blank Invoice form ready for the next sale

Notes
When you click Next, the next invoice will be displayed. When there are no invoices left to display, clicking Next displays a blank form.

Source Documents

Now that you have learned more of the new concepts introduced in this chapter, continue to develop your skills by entering the following source documents in QuickBooks. Use the information in this chapter as a guide if necessary.

SD27: Sales Invoice #3131   **Dated February 15, 2012**

To Skin Deep Inc. (set up new customer), makeup consultations for new models.

10	Makeup consultations	$120.00 each	$1,200.00
	HST	13%	156.00
	Invoice total		$1,356.00

Terms: Net 15 days.

Memorize the transaction with weekly reminders because the consultations will be repeated for different models each week beginning February 22nd.

SD Practice
Continue to develop your skills by entering the following source document(s).

Notes
Skin Deep Inc.
Budd Ng Moddles
377 Runway Rd.
Ottawa, ON K8G 3V9
Phone: (613) 677-7291
Fax: (613) 679-8229
E-mail: budd.ng@skindeep.ca
Tax code: H
Terms: Net 15
Credit limit: $3,000.00
Pay by: Cheque

SD28: Purchase Invoice #OO-904   Dated February 18, 2012

From Office Outfitters, $320.00 plus $41.60 HST for new scanner to use with computer. Invoice totals $361.60. Terms: Net 20 days. Ignore the message about fixed assets.

SD29: Purchase Invoice #KC-811   Dated February 19, 2012

From Keep It Clean, $150.00 plus $19.50 HST for weekly cleaning of salon. Invoice totals $169.50. Terms: Net 15 days. Use the memorized transaction.

SD30: Sales Invoice #3132   Dated February 19, 2012

To ODSB $185.00 plus $24.05 HST for a one hour customized seminar for school staff on dress code policy. Invoice totals $209.05. Terms: Net 15 days. Use the memorized transaction.

SD31: Cheque Copy #392   Dated February 19, 2012

To Keep It Clean, $339.00 in payment of account. Reference invoices #KC-724 and #KC-779. Automatically assign cheque number.

SD32: Cash Receipt #254   Dated February19, 2012

From Amore Bridal Party, cheque #532 for $500.00 in partial payment of account. Reference invoice #3126. Cheque held for deposit.

SD33: Cash Receipt #255   Dated February 20, 2012

From ODSB, cheque #12103 for $209.05 in payment of account. Reference invoice #3127. Cheque held for deposit.

SD34: Sales Receipt #7   Dated February 20, 2012

To Cash Sales customers. Salon visits were a popular Valentine's day gift.
Payment Method: Cash

10	Hair consultations	$150.00 each	$1,500.00
8	Makeup consultations	120.00 each	960.00
3	Clothing style consultations	190.00 each	570.00
4	Makeovers	390.00 each	1,560.00
10	Reports	90.00 each	900.00
	HST	13%	713.70
	Sales receipt total cash held for deposit		$6,203.70

Use the memorized transaction and edit the amounts.

SD35: Memo #6   Dated February 20, 2012

From Partners: Deposit all cheques and cash held for weekly deposit to the Bank Chequing account. Total deposit is $6,912.75.

SD36: **Cash Purchase Invoice #P-450**   Dated February 21, 2012

From Perfect Publicity (use Quick Add for new vendor), $2,400.00 plus $312.00 HST for series of poster ads to run for next 12 weeks. Invoice total of $2,712.00 is paid in full with cheque #393. Create new Other Current Asset account: Prepaid Advertising.

SD37: **Sales Invoice #3133**   Dated February 22, 2012

To Skin Deep Inc., makeup consultations for new models.

10	Makeup consultations	120.00 each	$1,200.00
	HST	13%	156.00
	Invoice total		$1,356.00

Terms: Net 15 days. Use the memorized the transaction.

SD38: **Sales Invoice #3134**   Dated February 26, 2012

To ODSB, $185.00 plus $24.05 HST for a one-hour customized seminar for school staff on dress code policy. Invoice totals $209.05. Terms: Net 15 days. Use the memorized transaction.

SD39: **Cash Receipt #256**   Dated February 26, 2012

From OTV News, cheque #4969 for $881.40 in payment of account. Reference invoice #3129. Cheque held for deposit.

SD40: **Sales Invoice #3135**   Dated February 26, 2012

To Sci-Tek, Inc. (use Quick Add for new customer), $390.00 plus $50.70 HST for a complete makeover consultation for member of executive team in a growing company. The team wants to take on a more professional image for presentations and meetings. Invoice totals $440.70. Terms: Net 15 days. Memorize the transaction with weekly reminders beginning March 5, 2012, because consultations will be repeated for a different member of the executive team each week.

SD41: **Purchase Invoice #KC-848**   Dated February 26, 2012

From Keep It Clean, $150.00 plus $19.50 GST for weekly cleaning of the salon. Invoice totals $169.50. Terms: Net 15 days. Use the memorized transaction.

SD42: **Cheque Copy #394**   Dated February 26, 2012

To Office Outfitters, $203.40 in payment of account. Reference invoice #OO-692. Automatically assign cheque number.

SD43: Sales Receipt #8   **Dated February 27, 2012**

To Cash Sales customers.

Payment Method: Cash

4	Hair consultations	$150.00 each	$ 600.00
2	Makeup consultations	120.00 each	240.00
2	Clothing style consultations	190.00 each	380.00
1	Makeover	390.00 each	390.00
6	Reports	90.00 each	540.00
	HST	13%	279.50
	Sales receipt total held for deposit		$2,429.50

Use the memorized transaction and edit the amounts.

SD44: Memo #7   **Dated February 27, 2012**

From Partners: Deposit all cheques and cash held for weekly deposit to the Bank Chequing account. Total deposit is $3,310.90.

SD45: Cash Purchase Invoice #FFF-216   **Dated February 28, 2012**

From Crystal Wireless Communications, $180.00 plus $23.40 HST for telephone, cell phone, and Internet service for one month. Purchase invoice totals $203.40. Write cheque #395 to pay invoice in full.

SD46: Memo #8   **Dated February 28, 2012**

Notes
Use the General Journal for the adjusting entries.
The depreciation amounts are the capital cost allowance amounts for the year divided by 12 to arrive at the amount for one month.

From Partners: Complete adjusting entries for one month of depreciation:

Computer equipment	$300.00
Salon	750.00
Salon equipment	20.00
Salon furniture	150.00

SD47: Memo #9   **Dated February 28, 2012**

From Partners: Complete adjusting entries for supplies used during February.

Cosmetics supplies	$220.00
Hair care supplies	90.00
Office and computer supplies	70.00

SD48: Memo #10   **Dated February 28, 2012**

From Partners: Complete adjusting entry for prepaid expenses expired.

Insurance	$2,100.00

SD49: Bank Debit Memo DM-56621   **Dated February 28, 2012**

From Capital Bank: Authorized withdrawals from Bank Chequing account for service charges and loan payments. Create new Expense account: Bank Charges.

Monthly bank service charges	$ 35.00
Mortgage ($1,000.00 principal; $200.00 interest)	1,200.00
Bank loan ($160.00 principal; $40.00 interest)	200.00
Long term loan ($780.00 principal; $220.00 interest)	1,000.00

SD50: Memo #11   **Dated February 28, 2012**

From Partners: Write cheques #396, #397, and #398 for partners for drawings and travel expenses for February. Use Quick Add to create the new records and choose Other as the type of record.

Partner	Cheque No.	Drawings	Travel	Total
Malin Andersson	396	$2,000.00	$120.00	$2,120.00
Kiera O'Sullivan	397	2,000.00	335.00	2,335.00
Dhaibhen Mehta	398	2,000.00	180.00	2,180.00

SD51: Bank Credit Memo CM-89211   **Dated February 28, 2012**

From Capital Bank: Interest earned on bank deposits.

Chequing account	$12.00
Savings account	35.00

Customers & Receivables Reports

You can access customer reports and graphs from the Reports menu or from the Report Centre. You can modify each report by adding or removing columns; by sorting and filtering to select only parts of the data for the report; and by changing headers, footers, fonts, and number formats. The principles for modifying and customizing customer reports are the same as they are for the reports discussed in previous chapters. After modifying reports, you can memorize, rename, and add them to your list of memorized reports.

Because the Report Centre shows a sample of the report and a description of the purpose of the report, we will print reports from the Report Centre rather than selecting them from the Reports menu.

1. **Click**   the **Report Centre icon** on the Icon bar

2. **Click**   the **Customers & Receivables** heading on the left-hand side of the screen to view the list of Customer & Receivable reports:

Notes
Refer to page 125 to review modifying reports.

Notes
Customer reports are very similar to vendor reports. A very similar set of reports are available for customers and vendors. The same options for modifying, displaying, and drilling down to more detail are also available on customer reports.

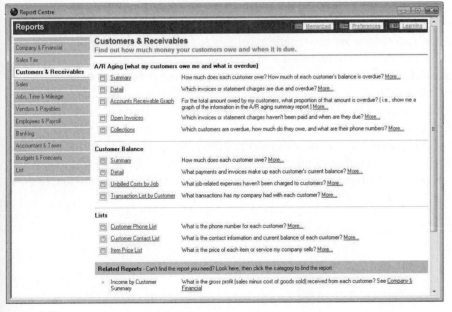

Figure 7-53

Accounts Receivable Aging Reports

The Accounts Receivable Aging Reports show the amounts owing in columns aged according to the invoice dates. The default is to show 30-day intervals for the columns. You can view the report in Summary form, with only the total amount owed by each customer for each period, or in Detail form, showing the transaction details for each outstanding invoice. From these reports, you can see if any invoices are overdue and require reminder notices to be sent to customers.

The Accounts Receivable Aging Summary Report

Notes
To access the report from the Reports menu:
• Choose the Reports menu, then choose Customers & Receivables, and click A/R Aging Summary to open the report
• Enter 02/29/12 in the Date field
• Press *tab* or click the Refresh button to update the report

Notes
There are 29 days in February 2012.

1. **Hover**   **your mouse pointer** over the icon to the left of the Summary report link under the A/R Aging heading to view the sample report

2. **Click**   the **Summary** link to open the report

3. **Double click** in the **date field**

4. **Type**   **02/29/12**

5. **Click**   the **Refresh button** or press *tab* to update the report:

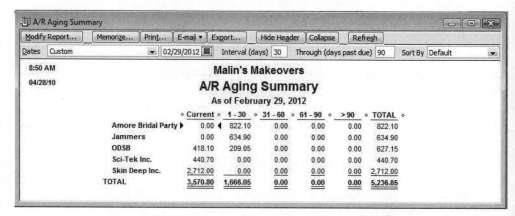

Figure 7-54

The report shows the total amount that each customer owes. All invoices are entered in the appropriate aging columns according to the invoice date. By default, customers with zero balances are included in the report.

You can sort the report by total amount or customer (the default) from the Sort By field list. By default the report shows aging intervals to 90 days, but you can include more periods (columns) by entering a different number in the Through (days past due) field. If some of your accounts are not due for 120 days, you may want to extend the reporting detail to show the accounts beyond 120 days. To change the periods in the column heading, enter a different number in the Interval (days) field. We will modify the report to show 15-day intervals because the terms for Malin's Makeovers are net 15 days.

6. **Double click**   **30** in the Interval (days) field

7. **Type**   **15**

8. **Click**   the **Refresh button** to update the report with Current, 1–15, 16–30, 31–45, etc. as the column headings

You can also drill down on the report to view more transaction details.

9. **Double click**   the **total for an aging period** to view the A/R Aging QuickZoom report which displays the transactions that make up the total amount. **Double click** a **transaction** to drill down to the transaction.

10. **Close**   the **report** when finished, unless you want to print it first

11. **Click**   **No** to indicate that you do not want to memorize the report if you changed the report default settings

The Accounts Receivable Aging Detail Report

1. **Hover**   your **mouse pointer** over the icon to the left of the Detail report link under the A/R Aging heading to view the sample report

2. **Click**   the **Detail link** to open the report

3. **Double click**   in the **date field**

4. **Type**   **02/29/12**

5. **Click**   the **Refresh button** or press (tab) to update the report:

Notes
To access the report from the Reports menu:
- Choose the Reports menu, then choose Customers & Receivables, and click A/R Aging Detail
- Enter 02/29/12 in the Date field
- Press (tab) or click the Refresh button to update the report

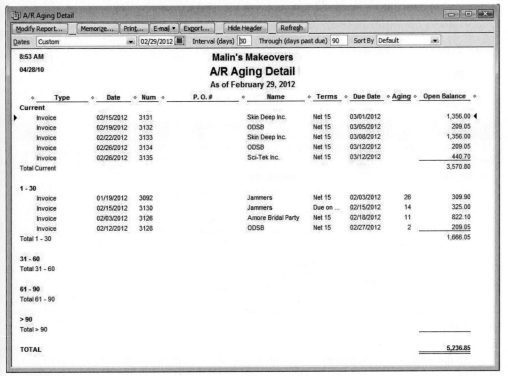

Figure 7-55

The detail report has a separate line for each transaction for each customer within each period and the due date is displayed for each invoice. You can modify the detail report as you can the summary report. You can change the aging intervals, change the reporting through period, and drill down to view more detail. You can sort by any of the column headings — Type, Date, Number, P.O. #, Name, Terms, Due Date, Aging (age of invoice), and Opening Balance — in either ascending or descending order.

Double click a transaction line to view the invoice. Double click a total for an aging period to see the Transaction Detail report for the amount.

6. **Double click**   a **transaction line** to drill down to the transaction

7. **Close**   the **report** when finished, unless you want to print it first

8. **Click**   **No** to indicate that you do not want to memorize the report, if you changed the report default settings

The Customer Balance Reports

The Customer Balance Reports show the amount each customer currently owes. The summary report shows only the total amount while the detail report shows individual transactions, both invoices and payments.

The Customer Balance Summary Report

1. **Hover**   your **mouse pointer** over the icon to the left of the Summary report link under the Customer Balance heading to view the sample report

2. **Click**   the **Summary link** to open the report

3. **Type**   **02/01/12** in the From date field

4. **Press**   ⌘tab⌘ to advance to the To date field

5. **Type**   **02/29/12** and press ⌘tab⌘ to display the report:

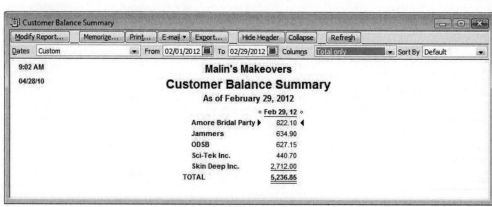

Figure 7-56

The date for this report is entered automatically by the program as the date of the latest transaction. Totals for each customer are shown as the default but you can add

Notes
To access the report from the Reports menu:
• Choose the Reports menu, then choose Customers & Receivables, and click Customer Balance Summary
• Enter 02/01/12 in the From date field
• Enter 02/29/12 in the To date field
• Press ⌘tab⌘ or click the Refresh button to update the report

columns for different intervals, such as weeks or months, by choosing from the Columns drop-down list. You can sort the report by total amount or by customer (the default).

Double click an amount or total for a customer to view the invoices and payments that make up that amount on the Customer Balance Detail report. Double click a transaction on the Customer Balance Detail report to view the original transaction.

Double click the report total on the Customer Balance Summary report to view the Customer Balance Detail Report that lists all the customer transactions that make up the report total.

6. **Close**	the **report** when finished
7. **Click**	**No** to indicate that you do not want to memorize the report, if you changed the report default settings

The Customer Balance Detail Report

1. **Hover**	your **mouse pointer** over the icon to the left of the Detail report link under the Customer Balance heading to view the sample report
2. **Click**	the **Detail link** to open the report
3. **Type**	**02/01/12** in the From Date field
4. **Press**	(tab) to advance to the To date field
5. **Type**	**02/29/12**

6. The Customer Balance Detail report will be displayed for February as shown:

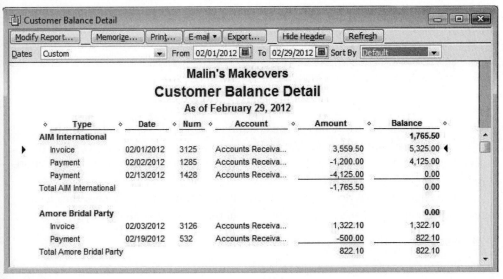

Figure 7-57

Notes
To access the report from the Reports menu:
• Choose the Reports menu, then choose Customers & Receivables, and click Customer Balance Detail
• Type 02/01/12 in the From Date field
• Type 02/29/12 in the To Date field

The report is organized by customer with a line for each invoice and payment.

You can sort the report by any of the column headings — Type, Date, Number, Account, and Amount — in either ascending or descending order.

Double click a transaction line to view the original transaction. Double click a customer total amount to view the transaction detail report for that amount.

7. **Close**	the **report** when finished
8. **Click**	**No** to indicate that you do not want to memorize the report, if you changed the report default settings

The Open Invoices Report

The Open Invoices report shows which invoices have not been paid as at a specific date and when invoices are due. The Aging column provides the number of days since the invoice was created. Individual transactions are listed.

Notes
To access the report from the Reports menu:
- Choose the Reports menu, then choose Customers & Receivables, and click Open Invoices
- Enter 02/29/12 in the Date field
- Press (tab) or click the Refresh button to view the report

1. **Hover** your **mouse pointer** over the icon to the left of the Open Invoices report link under the A/R Aging heading to view the sample report

2. **Click** the **Open Invoices** link to open the report

3. **Double click** the **Date field**

4. **Type** **02/29/12**

5. The Open Invoices report will be displayed for February as shown:

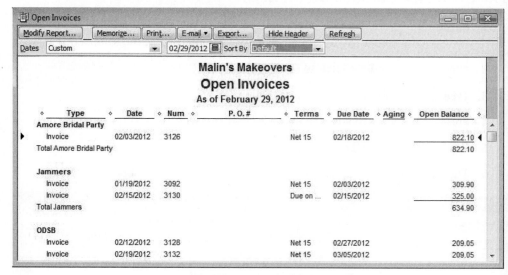

Figure 7-58

You can sort the report by any of the column headings — Type, Date, Number, P.O. #, Terms, Due Date, Aging, and Open Balance amount — in either ascending or descending order. You can also drill down on the information in the report to view more details.

Double click a transaction line to view the original transaction. Double click a customer total amount to view the transaction detail report for that amount.

6. **Close** the **report** when finished

7. **Click** **No** to indicate that you do not want to memorize the report, if you changed the report default settings

The Collections Report

The Collections Report shows invoices that have not been paid and are overdue as at a specific date. The contact name and phone number are provided so that the customers can be contacted from these reports. Individual overdue transactions are listed. You can narrow the report further by providing a different past due interval. For example, you may want to phone accounts that are at least 30 days overdue. The default is one day — any invoice at least one day overdue is included on the report by default.

1. **Hover** your **mouse pointer** over the icon to the left of the Collections report link under the A/R Aging heading to view the sample report

2. **Click** the **Collections link** to open the report

3. **Type** **02/29/12** in the Date field

4. **Click** the **Refresh button** or press ⌈tab⌋ to update the report:

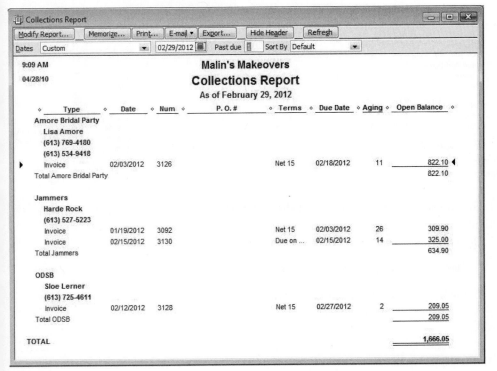

Figure 7-59

Notes
To access the report from the Reports menu:
- Choose the Reports menu, then choose Customers & Receivables, and click Collections Report
- Enter 02/29/12 in the date field
- Press ⌈tab⌋ or click the Refresh button to update the report

You can sort the report by any of the column headings — Type, Date, Number, P.O. #, Terms, Due Date, Aging, and Open Balance amount — in either ascending or descending order. You can also drill down on a transaction to view more detail.

5. **Double click** a **transaction line** to view the original transaction. **Double click** a **total amount** to view the transaction detail report for that amount.

6. **Close** the **report** when finished

7. **Click** **No** to indicate that you do not want to memorize the report, if you changed the report default settings

Transaction List by Customer Report

This report shows all individual transactions for all customers for the selected report period.

1. **Click** **Transaction List by Customer** under the Customer Balance heading

2. **Double click** the **From date field**

3. **Type** **02/01/12**

4. **Press** ⌈tab⌋ to advance to the To date field

5. **Type** **02/29/12**

Notes
To access the report from the Reports menu:
- Choose the Reports menu, then choose Customers & Receivables, and click Transaction List by Customer
- Enter 02/01/12 in the From date field
- Enter 02/29/12 in the To date field
- Press ⌈tab⌋ or click the Refresh button to update the report

6. Press [tab] or click the Refresh button to update the report:

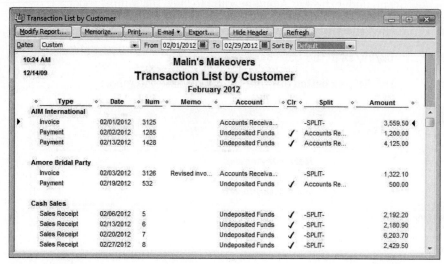

Figure 7-60

You can sort this report by any of the column headings and you can show the transactions in ascending or descending order.

Double click a transaction line to view the original transaction.

7. Close the **report** when finished

8. Click **No** to indicate that you do not want to memorize the report, if you changed the report default settings

Customer Lists

QuickBooks offers two lists for customers: the phone list and the contact list. You can use filters to select a specific group of customers on both of these lists that can be used to contact all or some customers or to check for missing data.

The Customer Phone List

The Customer phone list includes only the customer's name and phone number.

1. Hover your mouse pointer over the icon to the left of the Customer Phone List report link under the Lists heading to view the sample report

Notes
To access the report from the Reports menu:
• Choose the Reports menu, then choose Customers & Receivables, and click Customer Phone List; or
• Choose the Reports menu, then choose List, and click Customer Phone List

2. Click the Customer Phone List link to open the report:

Figure 7-61

You can sort the list by customer name or by phone number. Sorting by phone number allows you to display all customers within the same area code.

Double click a customer in the report to open the customer record. You can edit the information in the customer record if necessary.

3. **Close**   the **report** when finished

4. **Click**   **No** to indicate that you do not want to memorize the report, if you changed the report default settings

The Customer Contact List

1. **Hover**   your **mouse pointer** over the icon to the left of the Customer Contact List report link under the Lists heading to view the sample report

2. **Click**   the **Customer Contact List link** to open the report:

Notes
To access the report from the Reports menu:
- Choose the Reports menu, then choose Customers & Receivables, and click Customer Contact List; or
- Choose the Reports menu, then choose List, and click Customer Contact List

Malin's Makeovers
Customer Contact List
December 14, 2009

Customer	Invoice to	Contact	Phone	Fax	Balance Total
AIM International	AIM International Purdey Lookes 5180 Richmond S...	Purdey Lookes	(613) 688-3613	(613) 688-1928	0.00
Amore Bridal Party	Amore Bridal Party Lisa Amore 250 Busquer St. O...	Lisa Amore	(613) 769-4180	(613) 769-3829	822.10
Cash Sales					0.00
Jammers	Jammers Harde Rock 69 Swingers Ave. Ottawa, ...	Harde Rock	(613) 527-5223	(613) 527-3813	634.90
ODSB	ODSB Sloe Lerner 450 Fastrak Rd. Ottawa, Ontar...	Sloe Lerner	(613) 725-4611	(613) 725-9124	627.15
OTV News	OTV News Vanna Taye 13 Broadcast Ave. Ottaw...	Vanna Taye	(613) 286-3977	(613) 286-0971	0.00
Sci-Tek Inc.	Sci-Tek Inc.				440.70
Skin Deep Inc.	Skin Deep Inc. Budd Ng Moddles 377 Runway Rd....	Budd Ng Moddles	(613) 677-7291	(613) 679-8229	2,712.00

Figure 7-62

By default, the Customer Contact List contains the customer's name, invoice address, contact name, phone number, fax number, and balance total as of the latest transaction date. You can sort this report by any of the column headings and show the transactions in ascending or descending order. You can also modify the report to add additional customer details.

Double click a customer in the report to open the customer record. You can edit the information in the customer record if necessary.

3. **Close**   the **report** when finished

4. **Click**   **No** to indicate that you do not want to memorize the report, if you changed the report default settings

Item Price Lists

The item price list contains the item name, description, preferred vendor, and price.

1. **Hover**   your **mouse pointer** over the icon to the left of the Item Price List report link under the Lists heading to view the sample report

Notes
To access the report from the Reports menu:
- Choose the Reports menu, then choose Customers & Receivables, and click Item Price List; or
- Choose the Reports menu, then choose List, and click Item Price List

2. Click   the **Item Price List** link to open the report:

Item	Description	Preferred Vendor	Price
Clothing style consultation	Consultation on suitable clothing styles and colours		190.00
Customized seminar/training	Customized training seminars and presentations		0.00
General consultation	General consulation charged on hourly basis		110.00
Hair consultation	Hair style consultation and cut		150.00
Makeover	Complete makeover consultation: hair, makeup an...		390.00
Makeup consultation	Consultation and demonstration of makeup techniq...		120.00
Report	Personalized makeover report following consultat...		90.00
NSF Charges	Service fee for NSF cheque		25.00
NSF Cheque	Amount of NSF cheque		0.00

Malin's Makeovers
Item Price List
December 14, 2009

Figure 7-63

You can sort this report by any of the column headings and show the items in ascending or descending order, and you can modify the report to add additional details.

Double click an item to view the item record. You can edit the information in the item record if necessary.

3. Close   the **report** when finished

4. Click   **No** to indicate that you do not want to memorize the report, if you changed the report default settings

Accounts Receivable Graphs

The final report for customers is presented as a graph. It displays aging information as well as the total amount owed by individual customers.

Notes
To access the graph from the Reports menu:
- Choose the Reports menu, then choose Customers & Receivables, and click Accounts Receivable Graph
- Click the Dates button
- Enter 02/29/12 in the Show aging as of date field
- Click OK to view the graph

1. Click   **Accounts Receivable Graph** under the A/R Aging heading

2. Click   the **Dates button** in the top left-hand corner of the screen

3. Type   **02/29/12** in the Show aging as of field

4. Click   **OK** to view the graph:

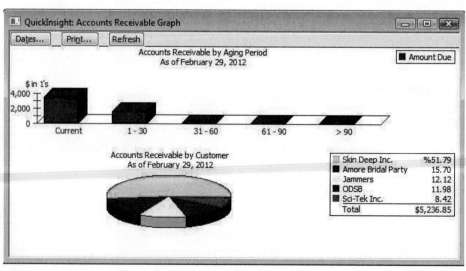

Figure 7-64

The graph has two sections: a bar graph in the upper section that shows the total amount owing for each aging interval and a pie chart in the lower section that shows the total owed by each customer. You can drill down to several other reports and graphs from both sections of the graph.

Double click a bar in the bar chart in the upper section of the graph to view the pie chart breakdown of customer amounts that make up its total. Then, double click a section of this pie chart to view the A/R Aging report for the customer selected. Double click a transaction listed in the A/R Aging report to drill down to the transaction.

Double click a pie section in the pie chart in the lower section of the graph to view an aging bar chart for that customer with separate bars for the total in each aging period. Then, double click a bar in this chart to view the A/R Aging report for the customer selected. Double click a transaction listed in the A/R Aging report to drill down to the transaction.

5. **Close**   the **report** when finished

6. **Click**   **No** to indicate that you do not want to memorize the report, if you changed the report default settings

Sales Reports

In addition to the customer reports, there are several sales reports that include customer information. Some of them display information similar to the customer reports, but they are organized by item instead of by customer.

Sales reports are accessed from the Reports Centre, by clicking on the Sales heading on the left-hand side of the screen:

Figure 7-65

Notes
The Sales by Rep reports and the Pending Sales report will be covered in a later chapter. There is no data for these reports for Malin's Makeovers.

Sales by Customer Summary Report

This report also shows the total sales for each customer during the selected period.

Notes
To access the report from the Reports menu:
- Choose the Reports menu, then choose Sales, and click Sales by Customer Summary
- Enter 02/01/12 in the From date field
- Enter 02/29/12 in the To date field
- Press (tab) or click the Refresh button to update the report

1. **Click**   **Summary** under the Sales by Customer heading

2. **Double click**   the **date** in the From field

3. **Type**   **02/01/12**

4. **Press**   (tab) to advance to the To date field

5. **Type**   **02/29/12**

6. **Press**   (tab) or **click** the **Refresh button** to update the report:

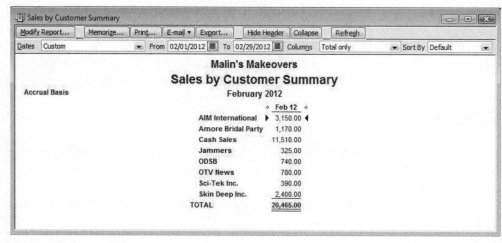

Figure 7-66

Totals for each item are displayed as the default but you can add columns for different intervals, such as weeks or months or other details, by selecting a different option from the Columns drop-down list. By default, this report is sorted by customer; however, you can also choose to sort it by total.

Double click an amount to view the individual transactions that make up the total. Double click an individual transaction line to drill down to the original transaction. Double click a customer total to drill down to the Customer Detail Report to view the details that make up the total for that customer, or double click the report total to drill down to the Customer Detail Report to view the details that make up the total for all customers.

7. **Close**   the **report** when finished

8. **Click**   **No** to indicate that you do not want to memorize the report, if you changed the report default settings

Sales by Customer Detail Report

Notes
To access the report from the Reports menu:
- Choose the Reports menu, then choose Sales, and click Sales by Customer Detail
- Enter 02/01/12 in the From date field
- Enter 02/29/12 in the To date field
- Press (tab) or click the Refresh button to update the report

This detail version of the Sales by Customer Summary Report displays individual sales transactions for each customer during the selected period.

1. **Click**   **Detail** under the Sales by Customer heading

2. **Double click**   the **date** in the From field

3. **Type**   **02/01/12**

4. **Press**   (tab) to advance to the To date field

5. **Type**   **02/29/12**

6. **Press**   (tab) or **click** the **Refresh button** to update the report:

Figure 7-67

You can sort this report by any of the report column headings — Type, Date, Number, Memo, Name, Item, Quantity, Sales Price, and Amount — in either ascending or descending order.

Double click an individual transaction line to view the original transaction. Double click a total to view the Transaction Detail Report for that amount.

7. **Close**   the **report** when finished

8. **Click**   **No** to indicate that you do not want to memorize the report, if you changed the report default settings

Sales by Item Summary Report

This report shows how many of each item or service has been sold during the selected period and displays the percentage of total sales for each item or service. The average price for each item is also displayed on this report.

1. **Hover**   your **mouse pointer** over the icon to the left of the Summary report link under the Sales by Item heading to view the sample report

2. **Click**   the **Summary report link** to open the report

3. **Double click**   the **From date field**

4. **Type**   **02/01/12**

5. **Press**   (tab) to advance to the To date field

6. **Type**   **02/29/12**

7. **Press**   (tab) or **click** the **Refresh button** to update the report:

Notes
To access the report from the Reports menu:
- Choose the Reports menu, then choose Sales, and click Sales by Item Summary
- Enter 02/01/12 in the From date field
- Enter 02/29/12 in the To date field
- Press (tab) or click the Refresh button to update the report

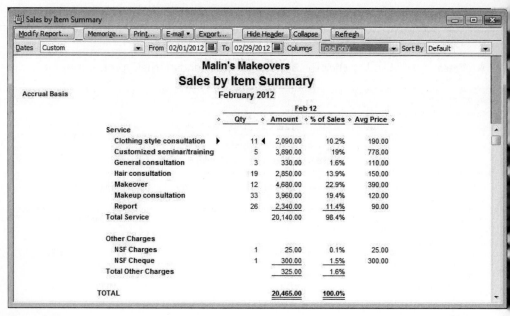

Figure 7-68

Items of the same type are grouped together in the report. You can sort this report by total or by item, the default.

Double click an item amount to view the Sales by Item Detail report that lists the individual transactions that make up the total for that item. Double click an individual transaction line to view the original transaction. Double click the report total to view the Sales by Item Detail Report that displays the transactions that make up the total amount of the report.

8. Close   the **report** when finished

9. Click   **No** to indicate that you do not want to memorize the report, if you changed the report default settings

Sales by Item Detail Report

This detail version of the Sales by Customer Summary Report shows individual transactions for each customer during the selected period.

1. Hover   your **mouse pointer** over the icon to the left of the Detail report link under the Sales by Item heading to view the sample report

2. Click   the **Detail report link** to open the report

3. Double click the **From date field**

4. Type   **02/01/12**

5. Press   (tab) to advance to the To date field

6. Type   **02/29/12**

7. Press   (tab) or **click** the **Refresh button** to view the report:

Notes
To access the report from the Reports menu:
- Choose the Reports menu, then choose Sales, and click Sales by Item Detail
- Enter 02/01/12 in the From date field
- Enter 02/29/12 in the To date field
- Press (tab) or click the Refresh button to update the report

Figure 7-69

You can sort this report by any of the report column headings — Type, Date, Number, Memo, Name, Quantity, Sales Price, and Amount — in either ascending or descending order.

Double click an individual transaction line to view the original transaction. Double click a total to view the Transaction Detail Report for the amount.

8. **Close**   the **report** when finished

9. **Click**   **No** to indicate that you do not want to memorize the report, if you changed the report default settings

Sales Graphs

The final sales report is presented in a Sales Graph. It shows aging information as well as the total amount owing to individual customers.

1. **Hover**   your **mouse pointer** over the icon to the left of the Sales Graph link under the Sales by Customer heading to view the sample report

2. **Click**   the **Sales Graph link** to open the graph

3. **Click**   the **Dates button**

4. **Double click**   the **From date field**

5. **Type**   **02/01/12**

6. **Press**   *tab* to advance to the To date field

7. **Type**   **02/29/12**

Notes
To access the graph from the Reports menu:
- Choose the Reports menu, then choose Sales, and click Sales Graph
- Click the Dates button
- Enter 02/01/12 in the From date field
- Enter 02/29/12 in the To date field
- Click OK to view the graph.

8. Click   **OK** to view the graph:

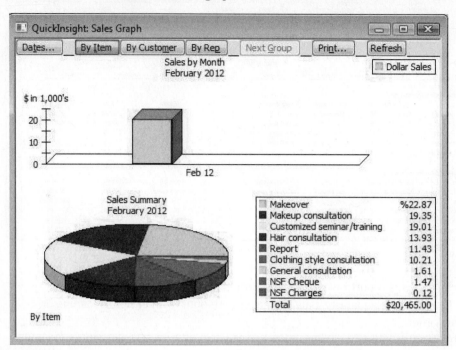

Figure 7-70

The graph has two sections: a bar graph in the upper section that shows the total amount sold in the selected period and a pie chart in the lower section that shows the total sold to each customer. You can drill down to several other reports and graphs from both sections of the graph.

Double click a bar in the bar chart in the upper section of the graph to view the pie chart breakdown of items that make up its total. Then, double click a section of this pie chart to view the individual transactions that make up the total for the item. Double click a transaction to drill down to the original transaction.

Double click a pie section in the pie chart in the lower section of the graph to view a bar chart for that item. Then, double click a bar in this chart to view the detail report with individual transactions for the item selected. Double click a transaction line in this detail report to view the original transaction.

9. Close   the **report** when finished

10. Click   **No** to indicate that you do not want to memorize the report, if you changed the report default settings

Finishing Your Session

1. Back up   the **company data file**

2. Close   the **company file**

3. Close   the **QuickBooks program**

Objectives

After completing this chapter, you should be able to:

- *apply* sales discounts to receipts from customers
- *apply* purchase discounts to payments
- *apply* sales and purchase credits and deposits
- *prepare* sales estimates for customers
- *enter* sales orders for customers
- *customize* estimate and order forms for customers
- *enter* purchase orders
- *enter* prepayments from customers
- *enter* prepayments to vendors
- *enter* credit card sales
- *enter* memorized transactions
- *enter* bills for received items
- *enter* sales invoices from orders and estimates
- *fill* purchase orders

Company Information

Company Profile

Terrific Tours in Calgary, Alberta, is owned and operated by Icharus Mannitoula. His wife, Serena, is employed by the business. Serena was working as a flight attendant and Icharus was employed in a travel agency when they met. Several years later, Icharus started his own travel agency, and his wife resigned from her job and is now employed by her husband. Planning trips for others did not fulfill their own desire to travel so Icharus

Notes
Terrific Tours
550 Journeys Rd.
Calgary SW, AB T2P 4N9
Tel: (403) 719-8029
Fax: (403) 719-7333
E-mail: info@terrifictours.com
Web: www.terrifictours.com
Business No.: 643 653 843

and Serena decided to add hosted tours to the business a few years ago. They took additional travel and hospitality courses offered by the community college to help them prepare for the tour business. The tour business has grown steadily and now employs their sons.

Because of the Mannitoulas' personal interest in education and the arts, they organize all-inclusive guided tours for school groups and seniors with themes like art, architecture, or gardens. They arrange air, hotel, meals, local transportation, local guides, and admission to local attractions to fit the tour's theme. Most tours occur throughout the school year, September to June, to avoid the peak prices and summer holiday crowds. During the summers the Mannitoulas plan the tours for the coming year.

One family member accompanies each tour as a concierge and makes local arrangements such as paying the hotel, restaurant, and admission bills; arranging emergency medical care; and troubleshooting to help trips run smoothly. All student groups travel with adult chaperones.

Theme tours are also available to individual clients — often well-educated professionals with flexible schedules that allow them to travel off-season. These customers may join in the full tour or buy only the air travel portion of the trip and make their own arrangements for hotel and local sightseeing.

Prices vary with the tour length and location, and with the variety of planned events. A 5 percent discount for groups of more than 10 allows the group chaperones to travel for half price. Individual customers pay full price for all tours. Schools and groups who have accounts with Terrific Tours receive an additional 1 percent discount if they settle their accounts within 10 days of the booking date. Deposits are requested at the time of booking because the airlines and hotels used by Terrific Tours also require deposits. Individual customers usually pay by credit card, while account customers pay by cheque. Athabaska Alumni Association, an account customer, has just confirmed a tour to Prague for the month of October and has paid the deposit.

Terrific Tours always gives their clients travel accessories as a gift: waist or neck wallets or a small carry-on tote bag. The business places special orders for these promotional items that are printed with the company name and logo, and it keeps inventory of these items on hand.

Terrific Tours has accounts with major airlines and hotel chains. Because of the volume of business, the company receives preferential prices from these vendors as well as discounts for early account settlement. Some vendors request prepayments or deposits from the tour company. Most accounts are paid by cheque but some smaller purchases are paid by credit card. Credit cards are also used for incidental expenses incurred during the tours.

Customers pay 5 percent GST on the airfare component of the tour packages. The tour component is not taxable because it occurs outside of Canada. Terrific Tours pays GST on business-related purchases. Provincial sales taxes are not levied in Alberta.

At the end of September 2012, two months into a new fiscal year, Terrific Tours converted their accounting records to QuickBooks using the following:

- Chart of Accounts
- Trial Balance
- Vendor List
- Customer List
- Item List
- Accounting Procedures

Chart of Accounts

Terrific Tours

ASSETS

Bank

    Bank Chequing
    Bank Savings
    Bank Visa

Accounts Receivable

    Accounts Receivable

Other Current Assets

    Brochures
    Office and Computer Supplies
    Prepaid Insurance
    Travel Accessories

Fixed Assets

    Business Vehicle:Cost
    Business Vehicle:Depreciation
    Computer Equipment:Cost

Computer Equipment:Depreciation
Office:Cost
Office:Depreciation
Office Furniture:Cost
Office Furniture:Depreciation

LIABILITIES

Accounts Payable

    Accounts Payable

Credit Card

    Credit Card Payable

Other Current Liabilities

    Bank Loan
    GST Payable

Long Term Liabilities

    Long Term Loan
    Mortgage Payable

EQUITY

    Capital, Icharus Mannitoula
    Drawings, Icharus Mannitoula
    Retained Earnings

NON-POSTING

    Estimates
    Purchase Orders
    Sales Orders

INCOME

    Revenue from Interest
    Revenue from Tours
    Sales Credits & Allowances
    Sales Discounts

EXPENSE

Cost of Goods Sold

    Cost of Tours:
        Air Travel Expenses

        Hotel Expenses
        Local Tours & Admissions
        Miscellaneous Expenses

Expense

    Advertising & Promotion
    Depreciation Expense
    Insurance Expense
    Interest Expense
    Maintenance & Cleaning
    Purchase Discounts
    Research Expenses
    Supplies Used
    Telephone Expense
    Travel Accessories Issued
    Travel Brochures Used
    Vehicle Expenses

Trial Balance

Terrific Tours

AS AT SEPTEMBER 30, 2012

	Debits	Credits		Debits	Credits
Bank Chequing	$ 49,895.00		Capital, Icharus Mannitoula		$102,019.40
Bank Savings	38,490.00		Drawings, Icharus Mannitoula	$ 8,600.00	
Bank Visa	3,850.00		Revenue from Interest		1,400.00
Accounts Receivable	41,940.00		Revenue from Tours		165,000.00
Brochures	4,680.00		Sales Credits & Allowances	500.00	
Office & Computer Supplies	740.00		Sales Discounts	4,500.00	
Prepaid Insurance	12,000.00		Cost of Tours:		
Travel Accessories	2,690.00		Air Travel Expenses	47,520.00	
Business Vehicle:Cost	24,000.00		Hotel Expenses	41,360.00	
Business Vehicle:Depreciation		$ 7,200.00	Local Tours & Admissions	8,910.00	
Computer Equipment:Cost	5,000.00		Miscellaneous Expenses	5,220.00	
Computer Equipment:Depreciation		750.00	Advertising & Promotion	8,900.00	
Office:Cost	120,000.00		Depreciation Expense	2,160.00	
Office:Depreciation		11,700.00	Insurance Expense	12,000.00	
Office Furniture:Cost	4,000.00		Interest Expense	1,535.00	
Office Furniture:Depreciation		1,120.00	Maintenance & Cleaning	1,440.00	
Accounts Payable		27,905.60	Purchase Discounts	3,210.00	
Credit Card Payable		1,510.00	Research Expenses	620.00	
Bank Loan		40,000.00	Supplies Used	120.00	
GST Payable		1,720.00	Telephone Expense	420.00	
Long Term Loan		30,000.00	Travel Accessories Issued	1,120.00	
Mortgage Payable		60,000.00	Travel Brochures Used	885.00	
			Vehicle Expenses	440.00	
				$453,535.00	$453,535.00

Terrific Tours

Vendor Name (Contact)	Address	Phone No. Fax No.	E-mail Business No.	Terms Credit Limit
Air Europe (Ava Winger)	334 Aviation Circle Toronto, ON M8J 2X4	Tel: (416) 238-4181 Fax: (416) 238-2619 Alt. tel: (877) 238-4000	a.winger@aireurope.com 249 498 587	net 20 $50,000.00
Capital Tours (Ona Coach)	314 Journeys Rd. Toronto, ON M2C 4F3	Tel: (800) 285-2355 Fax: (416) 285-3186	ona@capitaltours.com	1/10, n/30 $25,000.00
Foothills Communications (Ken Tellus)	44 Static St. Calgary NW, AB T5H 8P9	Tel: (403) 654-2355	tellus@foothills.com	net 10 $500.00
Heritage Hotels (Reste Fulle)	20 Rue Accommodation Montreal, QC H2J 7C5	Tel: (877) 377-1900 Fax: (514) 377-2728	rf@heritagehotels.com	1/10, n/30 $25,000.00
Parry's Printing House (Parry Papers)	109 Scanner St. Calgary NW, AB T4C 4F4	Tel: (403) 723-2302	parry@PPH.com 283 283 197	2/10, n/30 $2,000.00
Receiver General	875 Heron Rd. Ottawa, ON K2C 84G	Tel: (800) 633-1020		quarterly remittances
Travel Totes (Fanny Packes)	900 Denier Ave. Calgary SW, AB T9N 8C9	Tel: (403) 274-8125 Fax: (403) 274-1288	fp@traveltotes.com 201 501 601	2/5, n/30 $3,000.00
Universal Theatre Bookings (Plaice Booker)	133 Showcase Rd. Toronto, ON M5B 3Y4	Tel: (800) 233-SHOW Fax: (416) 233-4990	booker@universal.com	2/5, n/30 $15,000.00

Terrific Tours

Vendor Name	Date	Terms	Due Date	Cheque No.	Amount
Air Europe	Sep. 30/12	net 20	Oct. 20/12	AE-4897	$11,663.00
Foothills Communications	Sep. 21/12	net 10	Oct. 1/12	FC-10982	$128.40
Heritage Hotels	Sep. 25/12	1/10, n/30	Oct. 25/12	HH-2099	$13,910.00
Parry's Printing House	Sep. 25/12	2/10, n/30	Oct. 25/12	PPH-1800	$952.30
Travel Totes	Sep. 28/12	2/5, n/30	Oct. 28/12	TT-5001	$1,251.90
				Grand Total	$27,905.60

Terrific Tours

Customer Name (Contact)	Address	Phone No. Fax No.	E-mail Business No.	Terms Credit Limit
Athabaska Alumni Association (Olda Grads)	75 Olde Thyme Cres. Calgary, AB T3E 5R4	Tel: (403) 228-6532 Fax: (403) 229-3915	OG@athagrads.org	1/10, n/30 $50,000.00
Calgary District School Board (Zolof Tutor)	100 Highroads Ave. Calgary, AB T4G 2L9	Tel: (403) 621-6299 Fax: (403) 628-6381	ZTutor@cdsb.ab.ca 399 722 532	1/10, n/30 $50,000.00
Calgary Region Catholic School Bd. (Vader Priestly)	200 Lowrodes Ave. Calgary, AB T6V 4S3	Tel: (403) 255-7734 Fax: (403) 255-2524	VPriestly@crcsb.ab.ca 444 576 511	1/10, n/30 $50,000.00
Cash Sales				due on receipt

Terrific Tours

Customer Name (Contact)	Address	Phone No. Fax No.	E-mail Business No.	Terms Credit Limit
Foothills Academy of Art (Emmy Oscar)	45 Stage Dr. Calgary, AB T3P 7VN	Tel: (403) 754-2910 Fax: (403) 754-3926	oscar@faa.ca	1/10, n/30 $50,000.00
Rocky Mtn School for the Performing Arts	699 Limelight Cr. Calgary, AB T2H 4C8	Tel: (403) 681-6296 Fax: (403) 688-4361	499 510 294	1/10, n/30 $50.000.00
UpperCrust School for Boys (Rex Master)	RR #1 Bragg Creek, AB T3K 4H8	Tel: (403) 733-5188 Fax: (403) 732-6994	RM@ucsb.ca 502 638 566	1/10, n/30 $50,000.00

Outstanding Customer Transactions

Terrific Tours

Customer Name	Date	Terms	Due Date	Invoice No./ Cheque No.	Amount	Balance Owing
Athabaska Alumni Association	Sep. 24/12	1/10, n/30	Oct. 24/12	208	$17,120.00	
	Sep. 26/12	1/10, n/30		210	$38,520.00	
	Sep. 26/12	deposit cheque		Chq 3990	−$26,000.00	$29,640.00
Foothills Academy of Art	Sep. 1/12	1/10, n/30	Oct. 1/12	199	$18,300.00	
	Sep. 1/06	deposit cheque		Chq 487	−$9,000.00	$9,300.00
UpperCrust School for Boys	Sep. 18/12	1/10, n/30	Oct. 18/12	204	$3,000.00	$3,000.00
			Grand Total			$41,940.00

Item List

Terrific Tours

Item	Description	Account	Tax Code
Service Items			
Air Travel	Airfare component of tour	Revenue from Tours	G
Tour	Accommodation and local travel component of tour	Revenue from Tours	E
Non-Inventory Items			
Brochures & Books	Travel information booklets	Brochures	G
Local Tours & Events	Tour components arranged locally	Local Tours & Admissions	E
Travel Accessories		Travel Accessories	G

Accounting Procedures

Taxes: GST and PST

Terrific Tours pays GST on goods and services that it buys in Canada and charges GST on airfare. It uses the regular method for remittance of the Goods and Services Tax. GST collected from customers is recorded as a liability in the *GST Payable* account. GST paid to vendors is recorded in the *GST Payable* account as a decrease in liability to the Canada Revenue Agency. The report is filed with the Receiver General for Canada by the last day of the month for the previous quarter, either including the balance owing or requesting a refund.

No taxes apply to services consumed outside of Canada — hotel, tours, event admissions and local travel. The tax exempt code is used for these parts of the tour. Local taxes are included in the prices for these services, but these taxes are not recorded separately because they are not refundable and therefore are not tracked. Because airfares are taxable, they are priced separately and listed as separate items.

Alberta does not charge PST on any goods or services.

Account Terms

Organized groups set up accounts with Terrific Tours and receive a one percent discount if they settle their accounts within 10 days of confirming a tour. The full balance is required within 30 days of booking the tour or before the tour starts, whichever comes first. Most tours are booked at least six weeks in advance of the departure date.

Individual customers who join a pre-packaged tour do not receive discounts and must settle the account in full within 10 days of booking, or before travel, whichever comes first. Most of these customers pay by Visa.

Some vendors offer discounts for early payment.

Bank Deposits and Cheques

All cheques and credit card payments are deposited immediately; they are not held for later deposit. Cheques are manually prepared at the time of the transaction.

Estimates, Orders, and Deposits

Terrific Tours provides estimates for customers who request them. Terrific Tours uses purchase orders for their custom-made inventory. They also place purchase orders for the tour components that involve admissions to local events and local travel arrangements.

Customers pay 50 percent of the price of tour packages as a deposit to confirm the bookings when they accept the estimate. Some vendors also require deposits.

Drawings

The owner withdraws money from the business as needed in lieu of receiving a salary.

Instructions

1. Using the Chart of Accounts, the Trial Balance, and other information, you will record entries for source documents for October 2012 using QuickBooks. You will find the source documents marked with an SD beside them and listed as you work through the chapter. The procedures for entering each new type of transaction introduced in this chapter are outlined in step-by-step instructions. Additional source documents will be provided, allowing you to have more practice entering transactions. If you have used this textbook in the past and would prefer to skip the step-by-step instructions and work only with a list of source documents, refer to the CD in the back of the textbook for the list of source documents for this chapter.

2. After you have finished making your entries, print the reports and graphs for October 2012 as indicated on the following printing form:

REPORTS FOR OCTOBER 2012

Lists
- ☐ Account Listing
- ☐ Customer Phone List
- ☐ Customer Contact List
- ☐ Vendor Phone List
- ☐ Vendor Contact List
- ☐ Item Listing
- ☐ Item Price List

Company & Financial
- ☑ Balance Sheet Standard at Oct. 31
- ☑ Profit & Loss Standard from Oct. 1 to Oct. 31
- ☐ Expenses by Vendor
- ☐ Income by Customer

Accountant & Taxes
- ☑ Trial Balance at Oct. 31
- ☐ General Ledger
- ☑ Journal from Oct. 1 to Oct. 31

- ☐ Transaction List by Date
- ☐ Transaction Detail by Account

Other
- ☐ Custom Summary Report
- ☐ Custom Transaction Detail Report
- ☐ Transaction History
- ☐ Transaction Journal

Vendor
- ☑ A/P Aging Detail at Oct. 31
- ☐ Vendor Balance
- ☑ Unpaid Bills at Oct. 31
- ☐ Transaction List by Vendor

Purchases
- ☐ Purchases by Vendor
- ☐ Purchases by Item
- ☑ Transaction List by Vendor from Oct. 1 to Oct. 31
- ☑ Open Purchase Orders by Vendor

Customer
- ☑ A/R Aging Detail at Oct. 31
- ☐ Customer Balance
- ☑ Open Invoices at Oct. 31
- ☐ Collections Report
- ☑ Transaction List by Customer from Oct. 1 to Oct. 31

Sales
- ☑ Sales by Customer from Oct. 1 to Oct. 31
- ☐ Sales by Item
- ☑ Open Sales Orders by Customer

GRAPHS
- ☐ Income and Expense
- ☐ Net Worth
- ☐ Accounts Payable
- ☐ Accounts Receivable
- ☐ Sales

Applying Credits to Customer Accounts

Businesses frequently ask customers to pay a deposit when they make a purchase on account. Prepayments can serve several purposes: they allow the business to order and pay for items required for a job for that customer; they help to ensure that a customer will proceed with the purchase; they reduce the final amount owing by the customer so that the customer will not exceed the credit limit; and so on. The deposit creates a credit balance in the customer's receivables account. When a sales invoice is recorded, the initial credit balance reduces the amount owing from the invoice.

Terrific Tours requires a deposit of about 50 percent of the total tour package price when a customer confirms a tour, accepts a sales estimate, or places an order. After the money is received and an invoice is prepared, the deposit must be applied to the balance owing by the customer.

The first transaction that we will enter is a deposit that needs to be applied to recorded sales invoices for Athabaska Alumni Association. The deposit has already been received. Refer to the following source document as we work through the steps to enter it:

SD1: Memo #1

Dated October 1, 2012

Apply the deposit to the balance owing from Athabaska Alumni Association. Apply $8,000.00 to invoice #208 and $18,000.00 to invoice #210.

1. **Open** the **Terrific Tours** company file. The QuickBooks Home page should be displayed on the screen

Customer deposits are entered on the Receive Payments form. To open the form:

a) **Click** the **Receive Payments icon** in the Customers section of the Home page; or

b) **Choose** the **Customers menu** and then **click Receive Payments**

Notes
Accounts Receivable normally has a debit balance because the customer owes money to the business. When there is a credit balance, the business owes something to the customer, usually some goods or services.

SD Instructions
Refer to the following source document and then follow the step-by-step instructions to enter it.

Notes
Remember that you can add icons to the Icon bar for any of the forms required for these transactions. Refer to page 71.

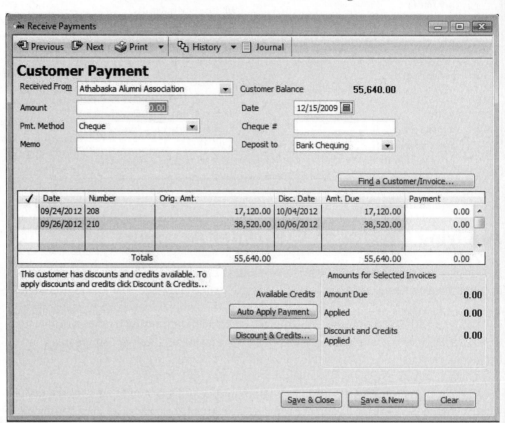

2. Click the **Receive Payments icon** in the Customers section of the Home page or **choose** the **Customers menu** and **click Receive Payments** to open the Receive Payment form

3. Click the **drop-down arrow** in the Received From field and **choose Athabaska Alumni Association** to view the outstanding invoices for the customer:

Notes
You can also type A in the Received From field to enter the customer. QuickBooks displays the full name of Athabaska Alumni Association as the default choice because it is the first customer beginning with the letter A. Press (tab) to accept the customer.

Notes
Credits can also be applied at the time the receipt is entered (when the customer pays the invoice). Applying the credits as a separate step shows the procedure more clearly.

Notes
When you click the ✓ (Applied To) column, the program shows a warning message because the amount of the payment is zero.

Figure 8-1

4. Read the **information** displayed in the bottom left-hand corner of the screen:

This customer has discounts and credits available. To apply discounts and credits click Discount & Credits...

Figure 8-2

The information in the bottom left-hand corner of the form indicates that this customer has discounts and credits available. To view the discounts and credits available, you must click on the Discount and Credits button.

5. Click the **Discount and Credit button** to open the Discount and Credits screen:

Figure 8-3

Notice that the customer has a total credit amount of $26,000.00 that can be applied to invoices. When you click the Discount and Credits button, the first invoice is selected by default. The credits applicable to that invoice are displayed on the Discount and Credits screen. We need to apply the credit so that approximately 50 percent of each invoice owed by the customer is covered by the deposit so we will not be accepting the distribution of the credits as shown on this screen.

6. Click   **Cancel** to close the Deposit and Credits screen

On the Receive Payments form, choose the invoices to apply the credit to. To select an invoice, click anywhere on the line except in the Applied To ✓ (checkmark) column.

7. Click   **208**, the invoice number in the Number field (or any invoice detail on that line) to select the first invoice if it is not already selected

8. Click   the **Discount and Credits button** to access the Discount and Credits screen

The Credits tab is selected. Notice that the date in this window is the date of the deposit cheque, September 26, 2012. The default is to apply the entire credit or the full amount of the invoice, whichever is less. In this case, the credit is greater than the balance owing on the invoice, so there would be a credit balance remaining. However, we want to apply only $8,000.00 to this invoice.

9. Double click   **16,948.80** in the Amt. To Use column to select the amount

10. Type   **8000**

11. Press   ⌨ *tab* to update the Credit Balance as shown:

Figure 8-4

Notice the remaining credit balance is $18,000.00.

12. Click   **Done** because we have finished working with the first invoice and the following warning message will be displayed:

Figure 8-5

This message indicates that QuickBooks has determined that a discount is available for this invoice based on the 1 percent within 10 days, net 30 days terms (abbreviated 1/10, n/30) that have been associated with this invoice. The invoice date is September 24th, and the date of this deposit is September 26th; therefore, QuickBooks has determined that a discount is due. However, discounts are not given on deposits.

13. Click   **OK** and the Discount tab is displayed

14. Highlight   the **amount** in the Amount of Discount field and **press** $\boxed{del}$

15. The completed Discount tab should be displayed as shown:

Figure 8-6

16. Click   Done

You will be returned to the Receive Payments window. Notice that $8,000.00 now appears in the Credits column for invoice #208. We can now apply the remaining credit to the second invoice. The first invoice line should still be selected.

17. Click   the **second invoice line**

18. Click   the **Discount and Credits button** again to view the updated Discount and Credits screen:

Figure 8-7

This time, the default amount in the Amt. To Use column is correct — the remaining amount of $18,000.00 is applied to invoice #210.

19. **Click** **Done**

20. **Highlight** the **amount** in the Amount of Discount field and **press** del

21. **Click** **Done** to return to the Receive Payments form

Notice that $18,000.00 now appears in the Credits column for invoice #210.

The current computer date may still be displayed in the date field. We need to change this date to reflect the transaction date, and we should add a memo to indicate the source of the transaction.

22. **Type** **10/01/12** in the date field

23. **Click** the **Memo field**

24. **Type** **Memo 1 - apply outstanding credit to invoices**

The transaction is now complete.

25. Your completed Receive Payments form should look like the one shown here:

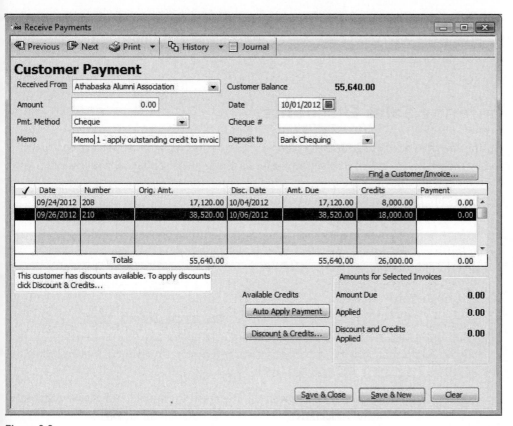

Figure 8-8

Notice that the information in the bottom left-hand corner of the screen that previously indicated that this customer had discounts and credits available has been updated to indicate that this customer only has discounts available.

26. Click the **Save & New button** so we can apply the next credit

No journal entry results from applying the credits to the customer invoices. When the deposit or prepayment cheque was originally entered, it generated a normal journal entry that debited *Bank Chequing* and credited *Accounts Receivable*. When the deposit is distributed, no journal entries are created; however, the customer's account is updated — the amounts owing for the invoices are reduced and no unused credits remain.

Source Document

> **TIP**
>
> Before entering the following source documents, you must make sure that QuickBooks has been updated to R3P or later. Press F2 from the home page to view the Product Information screen, where you can view the update version at the top of the screen. You must see Release R3P or later. If necessary, refer to the Update QuickBooks heading on page x of the Preface for instructions on updating QuickBooks.

Now that you have learned how to apply a customer deposit to an invoice, enter the deposit received from Foothills Academy of Art against a recorded sales invoice. The deposit has already been received. The source document is as follows:

SD2: Memo #2   Dated October 1, 2012

Apply the $9,000.00 deposit from Foothills Academy of Art to the balance owing on invoice #199.

Entering Sales Discounts

Businesses offer discounts for early payment of accounts as an incentive for customers to pay their bills on time. Terrific Tours offers a 1 percent discount to all account customers when they pay their invoices in full within the 10-day discount period. Discounts are not offered on partial payments.

The first payment cheque from Athabaska Alumni Association falls within the discount period and both invoices are being fully paid. The cheque should be deposited to the *Bank Chequing* account. Refer to the following source document as we work through the steps to enter it:

SD3: **Cash Receipt #345**

Dated October 2, 2012

From Athabaska Alumni Association, cheque #4038 for $29,083.60 in payment of the account, including the discount for early payment. Reference invoices #208 and #210.

1. **Click**   the **drop-down arrow** in the Received From field and **choose Athabaska Alumni Association** to display the outstanding invoices:

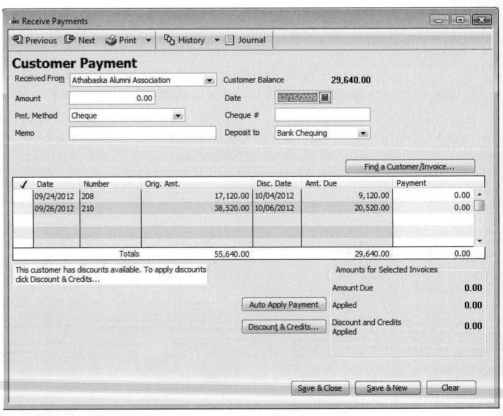

Figure 8-9

2. **Press**   (tab) to advance to the date field and **enter 10/02/12**

Notice that the amounts in the Amount Due column have been reduced to reflect the applied credits. Discounts are applied like credits — select an invoice, click the Discount & Credits button, accept or enter the discount for the invoice, select the next invoice that is paid by the same cheque, click the Discount & Credits button, accept or enter the discount, and so on.

3. Click   **208** to select the number of the first invoice, or anywhere on the line to select the invoice (do not click in the box to the left of the invoice)

4. Click   the **Discount & Credits button** to open the Discount and Credits screen:

Notes
If the discount does not show in the Discount and Credits window, check that you have entered the correct date for the payment.

Figure 8-10

The Discount tab should be displayed. The full discount amount, the suggested discount according to the payment terms, is entered in the Amount of Discount field — $171.20, which is 1 percent of the full invoice amount $17,120.00. You can change the amount to provide a different discount amount if you want. The original customer, number, date, and amount are all displayed for reference. In addition, the amount due, discount used, credit used, and balance due are also displayed. The discount date is the last date on which the discount is available, based on the terms. If the cheque date is later than the discount date, the suggested discount is removed (set at zero).

The discount amount entered by default is correct so you should accept it. We also need to select the account that the sales discount will be allocated to.

5. Click   the **drop-down arrow** in the Discount Account field

6. Click   **Sales Discounts**

7. Click   **Done** to return to the Receive Payments form

Notes
Sales Discounts is a contra-revenue account that normally has a debit balance and reduces total income.

Before applying the discount to the second invoice, we will change the transaction date to view the effect this will have.

8. **Double click**   the **date field**

9. **Type**   **10/10/12**

10. **Click**   **210**, the number of the second invoice, or anywhere on the line to select the invoice (do not click in the box to the left of the invoice)

11. **Click**   the **Discount & Credits** button to open the Discount and Credits screen:

Invoice

Customer:Job	Athabaska Alumni Association		
Number	210	Amount Due	20,520.00
Date	09/26/2012	Discount Used	**0.00**
Original Amt.	38,520.00	Credits Used	**0.00**
		Balance Due	20,520.00

Discount   Credits

Discount Date	10/06/2012
Terms	1% 10 Net 30
Suggested Discount	0.00
Amount of Discount	0.00
Discount Account	Sales Discounts

Done   Cancel   Help

Figure 8-11

Notice that the amount in the Amount of Discount field is zero because the discount period expires on October 6, 2012. If you recall, we changed the payment date to 10/10/12, and, therefore, a discount amount is not available according to the date.

12. **Click**   **Cancel** to return to the Receive Payments form so you can change the date back to October 2, 2012

13. **Double click**   the **date field**

14. **Type**   **10/02/12**

15. Invoice #210 should still be selected

16. **Click**   the **Discount & Credits button** to open the Discount and Credits screen:

Figure 8-12

Notice that the suggested discount has been restored to $385.20, that is, 1 percent of the original invoice total amount. The discount account should be entered from the previous invoice discount. If it is not, select *Sales Discounts* in the Discount Account field.

17. Click   **Done** to return to the Receive Payments form

We still need to add the cheque amount, include the cheque number for reference, and select the invoices for payment. You can enter a comment in the Memo field if you want.

The total for the amount due (Amt. Due) column should now match the cheque amount because the customer is paying the account in full.

18. Double click   **0.00** in the Amount field

19. Type   **29083.60**

20. Press   (tab)

Notice that the invoices have been selected for payment based on the cheque amount.

21. Press   (tab) to advance to the Cheque # field

22. Type   **4038**

23. Select   the **Bank Chequing** account in the Deposit to field if this is not the account selected already

24. Check   your **work** carefully. The completed payment entry should look like the one shown here:

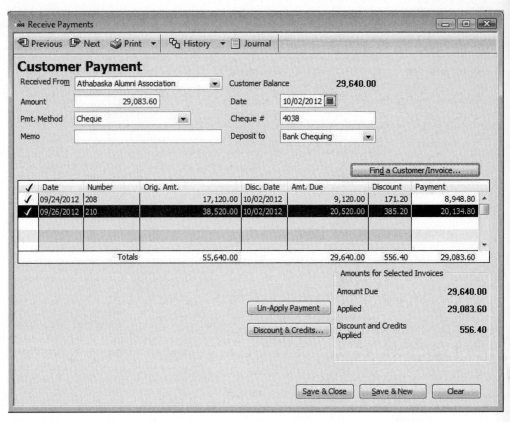

Figure 8-13

You should correct any errors before recording the payment.

CORRECTING DISCOUNTED CUSTOMER PAYMENTS

Click the field that contains the error. You can press `tab` to move forward from one field to the next. Highlight the incorrect information and type the correct information in the field. Press `tab` if necessary to update the information.

To correct a discount, select the invoice line and then click the Discount & Credits button to open the Discount & Credits screen. Edit the information as needed and click Done. Edit any other details of the Customer Payment that are incorrect just as you would correct regular customer payments (see page 282).

You can also start again by clicking the Clear button.

We want to review the Journal Transaction created from the payment transaction so we need to save the payment and keep the Create Payments window open.

25. Click   **Save & New** to record the payment

Reviewing the Transaction

With a blank Receive Payments form displayed on the screen:

1. Click   **Previous** or **press** `alt` + **P** to view the payment we just entered from Athabaska Alumni Association

2. Press   `ctrl` + **Y** to view the Transaction Journal report:

Notes
We have removed
columns from this report before
displaying it here.

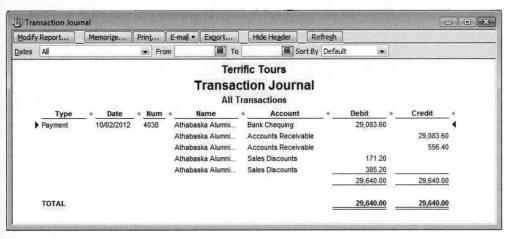

Figure 8-14

You can see that QuickBooks has debited (increased) the *Bank Chequing* account for the net amount of the cheque, after taking the discount. The discount amount is debited to the *Sales Discounts* account, a contra-revenue account that reduces total income. The *Accounts Receivable* account has been credited (reduced for both the amount of the cheque and the amount of the sales discount). As usual, the customer record is updated, and the amount owing is reduced by the full amount of the cheque and discount.

Notes
Revenue accounts usually
have a credit balance.

3. **Close**   the **Transaction Journal report**

4. **Close**   the **Receive Payments window**

Entering Purchase Discounts

The next transaction that we need to enter is a cheque to Travel Totes in payment of account. The payment is made before the early period discount date so it includes a discount. Refer to the following source document as we walk through the steps to enter it:

SD4: Cheque Copy #480

Dated October 2, 2012

To Travel Totes, $1,226.86 in payment of account, including 2 percent discount for early payment. Reference invoice #TT-5001.

SD Instructions
Refer to the following
source document and then
follow the step-by-step
instructions to enter it.

1. **Click**   the **Pay Bills icon** in the Vendors section of the Home page to open the Pay Bills form:

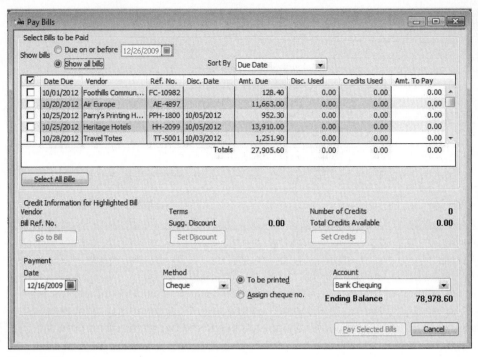

Figure 8-15

The Show All Bills option under the Select Bills to be Paid heading should be selected by default.

Notice that the Disc. Date column shows the last date that the discount will be available. No discount amounts are entered yet.

2. Enter **10/02/12** in the Payment Date field

3. Click the **pay column** — the ✓ (checkmark) column — beside invoice TT-5001 from Travel Totes (the last invoice on the list)

4. The Pay Bills form is updated as shown:

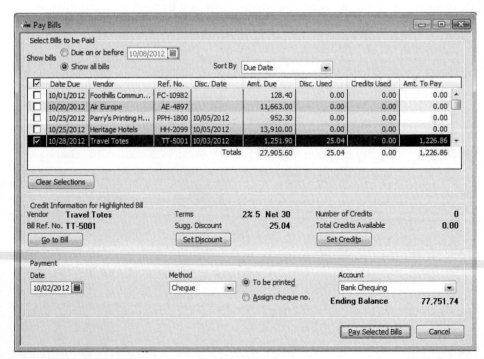

Figure 8-16

Notice that a discount amount is suggested for the selected invoice and the Set Discount button is available. An amount appears in the Disc. Used column because we selected the preference to apply credits and discounts automatically for bill payments and because the payment date is within the discount period. We can enter the credits and discounts the way we did for customer payments. If you need to edit a discount or credit amount for the invoice to which it is applied, you must choose the Set Discount or Set Credits button to access the relevant screen.

5. Click the **Set Discount button** to access the Discount and Credits screen:

Figure 8-17

The Discount tab is displayed. As for customer discounts, if the date is beyond the last discount date, the suggested discount amount will be zero. If the discount is not available, check the date entered for the payment.

All the details are correct. The suggested discount is the correct discount amount and the *Purchase Discounts* account is the correct Discount Account. You can change the discount amount and the account if necessary. The discount will be credited to this contra-expense account — the discount reduces the total expenses in the Income (Profit & Loss) Statement.

6. Click **Done** to return to the Pay Bills window

7. Click **Assign Cheque Number** to complete the Bill Payment

The form should now look like the one shown here:

Notes
If the discount is not displayed on the Discount tab, check that you have entered the correct date for the payment.

Notes
We will assign cheque numbers later.

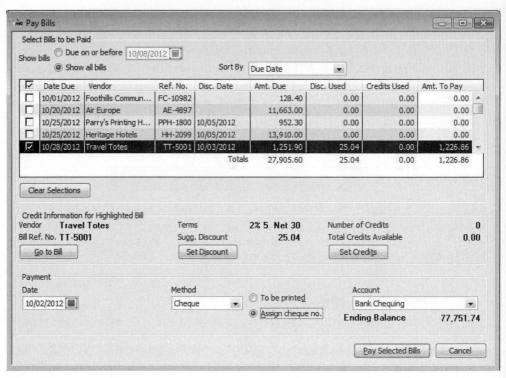

Figure 8-18

Before saving this transaction, we will record the payment of a second bill, so do not close the Pay Bills window yet.

Paying a Second Bill

We will pay the telephone bill from Foothills Communications at the same time, so we need to include it in this payment entry. Refer to the following source document as we work through the steps to enter it:

SD Instructions
Refer to the following source document and then follow the step-by-step instructions to enter it.

SD5: Cheque Copy #481

Dated October 2, 2012

To Foothills Communication, $128.40 in full payment of account. Reference invoice #FC-10982.

1. Click   the ✓ (checkmark) column beside the bill from Foothills Communications to pay this bill together with the bill from Travel Totes

Notice that this bill does not have a discount associated with it. A date is not displayed in the Disc. Date field and an amount is not displayed in the Disc. Used field.

2. Click   the **Pay Selected Bills button** to open the Assign Cheque Numbers window:

Figure 8-19

The *Let me assign the cheque numbers below* option should be selected. Both cheques are listed so we can assign numbers to both.

3. Click   the **Cheque No.** column for the cheque to Travel Totes (the second transaction line)

4. Type   **480**

5. Click   ▼ to move to the cheque for Foothills Communications

6. Type   **481**

7. Click   **OK** to complete the payment and close the Pay Bills window

8. The Payment Summary window is displayed:

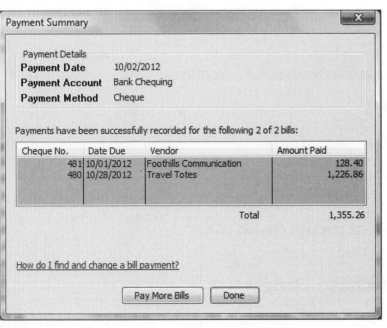

Figure 8-20

9. Click   **Done**

Now that we have assigned the starting cheque numbers, we can let QuickBooks automatically assign these numbers. For the next cheque you write, choose the *Let QuickBooks Assign Cheque Numbers* on the Assign Cheque Numbers window.

Reviewing the Transaction

We can now view the journal entry for the cheques that we just entered. The cheque for Foothills Communications is similar to the undiscounted payments that we made in previous chapters so we will view only the discounted transaction for Travel Totes. Remember that we view all cheques written in the Pay Bills window in the Write Cheques form. When the cheque is displayed on the screen, we can view the journal entry.

1. **Click**   the **Write Cheques icon** in the Banking section of the Home page

2. **Click**   Previous   to view the cheque for Foothills Communications

3. **Click**   Previous   again to view the cheque for Travel Totes

4. **Press**   ctrl + **Y** to view the Transaction Journal report:

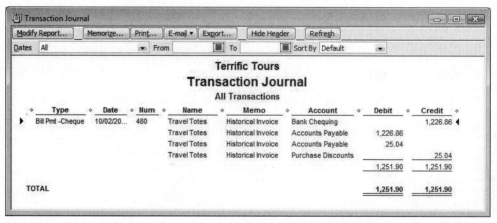

Figure 8-21

Notice that *Bank Chequing* is credited for the net amount of the cheque, after taking the discount. The remainder of the original invoice amount is credited to *Purchase Discounts*, the contra-expense account. *Accounts Payable* is debited, or reduced, by the full invoice amount — the amount of the cheque plus the amount of the discount.

5. **Close**   the **Transaction Journal report** to return to the cheque

6. **Close**   the **Bill Payments (Cheque) window**

Entering Purchase Orders

Purchase orders are used to request items from vendors for later delivery. For internal control, some businesses require authorized purchase orders for all purchases that exceed a certain dollar amount. In the next transaction, we will enter a purchase order for Travel Totes. Refer to the following source document as we work through the steps to enter it:

SD6: Purchase Order #30

Dated October 2, 2012

To Travel Totes, $900.00 plus GST for 100 tote bags and passport wallets printed with the company logo. Purchase order totals $945.00. A deposit of 50 percent is requested to confirm the order. (We will enter the purchase order now, and enter the deposit a little later in the chapter.)

Purchase orders are entered on the Create Purchase Orders form. The workflow that contains the Purchases Orders icon can be found in the Vendors section of the Home page as shown here:

Figure 8-22

SD Instructions
Refer to the following source document and then follow the step-by-step instructions to enter it.

Notes
Notice the flow or sequence of icons in the Vendors section of the Home page.

1. **Click**   the **Purchase Orders icon** in the Vendors section of the Home page, or **choose** the **Vendors menu** and **click Create Purchase Orders** to open the Create Purchase Orders form:

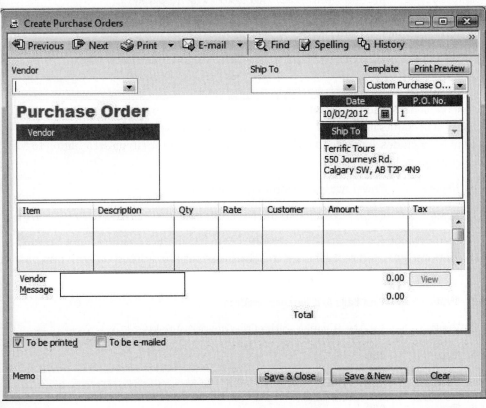

Figure 8-23

Entering a purchase order is similar to entering an invoice or bill and the form is also similar.

2. Click   the **drop-down arrow** in the Vendor field

3. Choose   **Travel Totes**

4. Press   `tab` to advance to the date field

5. Enter   **10/02/12** as the order date, if necessary

6. Press   `tab` to advance to the P.O. No. field

Purchase orders are numbered just like most other company forms. Number 1 is entered as the default because we have not entered any purchase orders yet. Terrific Tours uses pre-numbered order forms, and the next number is 30.

7. Type   **30**

8. Press   `tab` to the Item field on the first detail line

9. Click   the **drop-down arrow** to view the list of items:

Item	Description	Qty	Rate	Customer	Amount	Ta
< Add New >						
Air Travel	Service			Airfare component of tours		
Tour	Service			Accomodation and local travel componen...		
Brochures & Books	Non-inventory Part			Travel information booklets		
Local Tours & Events	Non-inventory Part			Tour components arranged locally		
Travel Accessories	Non-inventory Part					
GST (ITC)	Sales Tax Item			GST on purchases (Input Tax Credit)		
GST (ITC) Adjustments	Sales Tax Item			GST Adjustments on purchases (Line 107)		
GST (ITC) Zero Rated	Sales Tax Item			GST on Zero Rated purchases (Input Tax...		
GST Instalments	Sales Tax Item			Instalments and net tax paid (Line 110)		

Figure 8-24

To complete a purchase order, you must choose an item from the item list because the chart of accounts list is not accessible from the purchase order form. Therefore, our item list includes some frequently purchased non-inventory items in addition to the service inventory items.

10. Choose   **Travel Accessories** from the Item list

11. Press   `tab` to advance to the Description field

The description for the Travel Accessories item has not been entered as a default for the item because different kinds of travel accessories are ordered on each purchase order.

12. Type   **Tote bags and passport wallets**

13. Press   `tab` to advance to the Qty (quantity) field

14. Type   **100**

15. Press   `tab` to advance to the Amount field

16. Type   **900**

17. Press   `tab` to update the unit rate, taxes, and the total

18. Click   the **To be printed** option to remove the ✓ if you do not want to place the order in a print batch (the purchase order is selected for batch printing by default)

Notes
Normally, a business would print all estimates and purchase orders but you may not want to print all the documents. To print the purchase order immediately, click the Print button to open the Print One Purchase Order dialog box. To print the purchase order later in a batch, choose the File menu, then choose Print Forms, and click Purchase Orders.

19. Your purchase order is now complete, as shown below:

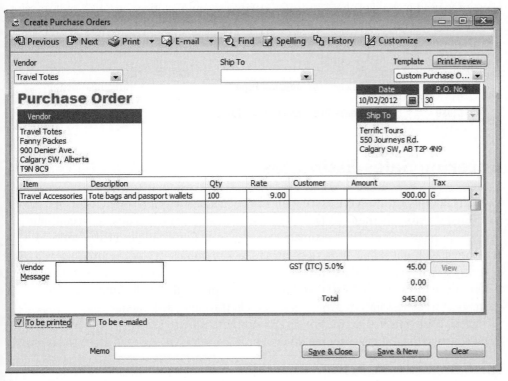

Figure 8-25

Check your work carefully and make corrections if necessary. You can make corrections to purchase orders just as you make corrections to regular vendor bills.

20. Click   **Save & New** to save the order and leave the form open to review it

Reviewing the Purchase Order

Although the purchase order does not create debit and credit entries, it does generate a transaction entry that we can review.

With a blank purchase order form displayed on the screen:

1. Click   Previous to view the purchase order to Travel Totes that we just entered

2. Press   *ctrl* + **Y** to view the Transaction Journal report:

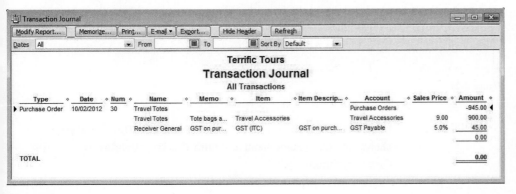

Figure 8-26

Notes
We have removed columns from this report to display it in the textbook.

This entry is the same as a regular vendor bill except that the *Purchase Orders* account is used instead of the *Accounts Payable* account. Notice too that a unit or sales price is calculated and entered for the accessories. The *Purchase Orders* account, like the *Estimates* and the *Sales Orders* accounts, is a non-postable account that appears at the end of the Chart of Accounts.

3. **Close**   the **Transaction Journal report** to return to the purchase order

4. **Close**   the **Create Purchase Orders form**

Entering Sales Estimates

Companies that provide services frequently give customers cost estimates for the service requested. Customers then can decide whether to get other estimates, or to continue with the purchase. Sometimes estimates are required. For example, a car insurance company may request one or more estimates for automobile repairs before they will cover the repair costs. Medical insurers also often ask for written estimates from doctors before procedures are completed and payment is approved. Terrific Tours provides estimates on request for any group interested in travelling with them.

In the next transaction, we will enter a sales estimate to UpperCrust School for Boys. Refer to the following source document as we work through the steps to enter it:

SD7: **Sales Estimate #21**

Dated October 2, 2012

To UpperCrust School for Boys, $16,020.00 plus GST for airfare and $28,800.00 for tour component of complete tour package for 18 senior students and adults. The price of the nine-day tour includes airfare and accommodation and will cover major galleries and museums in European capital cities. Total cost of tour including taxes is $45,621.00.

Sales Estimates are entered on the Create Estimates form. The workflow that contains the Sales Estimates icon can be found in the Customers section of the Home page as shown here:

Figure 8-27

1. **Click**   the **Estimates icon** in the Customers section of the Home page, or **choose** the **Customers menu** and **click Create Estimates** to open the Create Estimates form:

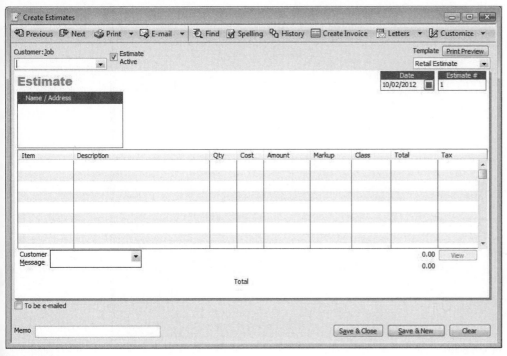

Figure 8-28

Notes
Estimates can be entered only if Estimates have been turned on in QuickBooks preferences. To turn the preference on, choose Edit from the menu, select Preferences, click the Jobs & Estimates heading, click the Company Preferences tab, and select Yes in the *Do you Create Estimates* field.

The Create Estimates form is almost the same as the Create Invoices form, and entering estimates is similar to entering invoices. However, some columns on the form are not suitable for Terrific Tours, so we will first customize the form by removing the columns that do not suit our needs.

2. Click   the **Customize button** [🖊 Customize] to open the Basic Customization form

3. Click   the **Additional Customization button** [Additional Customization...] on the bottom of the form

4. The following message will be displayed:

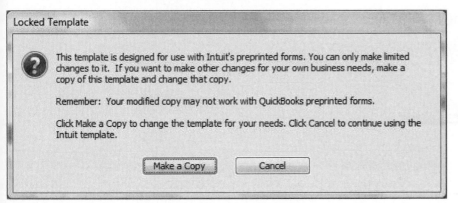

Figure 8-29

This message indicates that this template has been designed for use with Intuit's pre-printed forms and cannot be modified. In order to make modifications to this template, you must make a copy of the template and then modify the copy.

5. Click   the **Make a Copy button** [Make a Copy]

6. Click   the **Columns tab** to open the list of columns:

Figure 8-30

All items with a ✓ under the Screen column indicate that the field is displayed on the Create Estimates form. All items with a ✓ under the Print column indicate that the field is displayed on the printed estimate form. You can select which fields will be displayed on the form and which ones will be printed for the customer.

We will remove the Markup and the Cost columns on the Create Estimates form. UpperCrust school, however, requires individual cost estimates, so we will leave the Cost column on the printed copy. Accept any Layout Designer messages that you receive.

7. Click   the **check box for Markup** to remove the ✓ under the Screen column

8. Click   the **check box for Cost** to remove the ✓ under the Screen column

9. Click   **OK** to return to the Basic Customization form

10. Click   **OK** to return to the revised Create Estimates form:

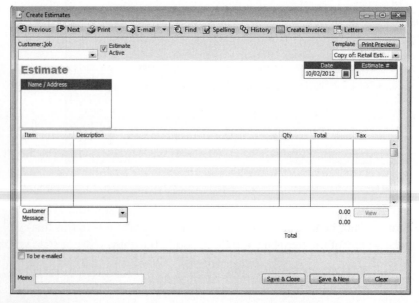

Figure 8-31

11.	**Choose**	**UpperCrust School for Boys** in the Customer:Job field
12.	**Enter**	**10/02/12** in the Date field if this is not the date displayed on your screen
13.	**Choose**	**Air Travel** as the first item on the estimate
14.	**Press**	(tab) to advance to the Qty (quantity) field

We will enter the total cost of the tours for all 18 travellers.

15.	**Type**	**18**
16.	**Press**	(tab) to advance to the Total field
17.	**Type**	**16020**
18.	**Press**	(tab) and the taxes are added to the Invoice total
19.	**Press**	(tab) again to advance to the second invoice line
20.	**Choose**	**Tour** as the second item on the estimate
21.	**Press**	(tab) twice to advance to the Qty (quantity) field
22.	**Type**	**18**
23.	**Press**	(tab) to advance to the Total field
24.	**Type**	**28800**
25.	**Press**	(tab) to update the Invoice total. Taxes are not charged for this item
26.	**Choose**	**We'll take care of you.** as the message in the Customer Message field

Estimates are prepared on pre-numbered forms, and the program updates these numbers automatically. The default initial number is 1 because no estimates have been entered yet.

27.	**Double click**	**1** in the Estimate # field beside the date field
28.	**Type**	**21**

29. The estimate is now complete as shown here:

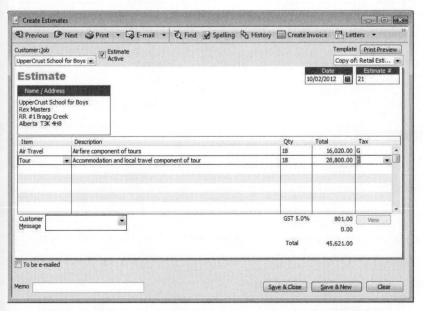

Figure 8-32

30. Review the **estimate** and **make** any **corrections** before saving it

---

CORRECTING CUSTOMER ESTIMATES

Correcting an estimate is just like correcting a sales invoice. See page 277 if you need any further assistance.

Click the field that contains the error. You can press ⟨tab⟩ to move forward from one field to the next. Highlight the incorrect information and type the correct information in the field. Press ⟨tab⟩ if necessary to update the information.

If you choose a different item, you must re-enter the quantity and total amount. Press ⟨tab⟩ to update the totals.

You can also start again by clicking the Clear button.

CORRECTING CUSTOMER ESTIMATES AFTER RECORDING

After saving the estimate, you can review it and make corrections. Open the Create Estimates form. Click the Previous button until you see the estimate you need, or use the Find button to locate the estimate. Edit the estimate as described above and save the revised form. Click Yes when prompted to save the changes.

---

31. Click **Save & Close** to record the estimate and close the Estimates form

Reviewing the Estimate

Although QuickBooks tracks estimates, it does not create a journal entry for them because no financial transactions have occurred. You can see which customers have estimates on the Customer:Job list in the Customer Centre. From the list you can view the report for the estimate.

1. Click the **Customer Centre** icon on the Icon bar

When you click on a customer, all transactions for that customer are displayed based on the date and filters selected.

2. Click **UpperCrust School for Boys** in the Customers & Jobs list:

Figure 8-33

Notice the Estimate that we entered is displayed in the transaction section of the screen.

3. Right click **UpperCrust School for Boys**

4. Select **Show Estimates** to display the Estimates by Job report as shown:

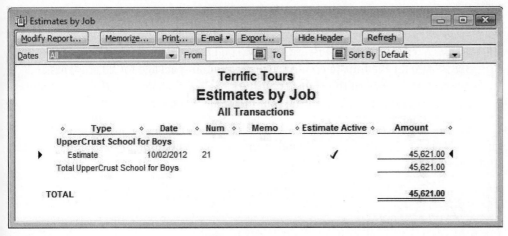

Figure 8-34

The report lists all estimates for the customer, with the estimate number and total amount. *Estimates* is a non-postable account that appears in the Chart of Accounts.

5. **Close**   the **Estimates by Job report**

6. **Click**   the **Transactions tab** and **click Estimates**:

Figure 8-35

This tab displays all transactions for the selected transaction type for all customers based on the filters and dates selected. The Estimate that we entered for UpperCrust School for Boys is also displayed on this screen.

Double clicking the estimate displayed on the Customers & Jobs tab or the Transactions tab will open the original estimate where you can edit it or use it to create an invoice.

Entering Sales Orders

Sales orders differ from estimates in that they originate with the customer. Frequently, after a company provides an estimate, the customer will place an order for the items or services in the estimate. Estimates precede the decision to buy and often influence the decision to buy. Sales orders come after the customer has decided to proceed with a purchase. Terrific Tours prepares sales orders when customers place a firm order.

In the next transaction, we will enter a sales order to Calgary District School Board. Refer to the following source document as we work through the steps to enter it:

SD8: Sales Order #6

Dated October 3, 2012

To Calgary District School Board, $16,280.00 plus GST for the airfare and $28,380.00 for the tour to create the complete tour package for 20 students and two teachers. Price of the eight-day history of England tour includes airfare and accommodation. Total cost of the tour including taxes is $45,474.00.

Sales Orders are entered on the Create Sales Orders form. The workflow that contains the Sales Orders icon can be found in the Customers section of the Home page, as shown here:

Figure 8-36

1. **Click** the **Sales Orders icon** in the Customers section of the Home page, or **choose** the **Customers menu** and **click Create Sales Orders** to open the Create Sales Orders form:

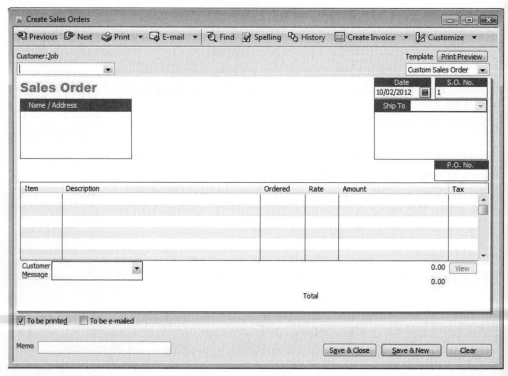

Figure 8-37

The Create Sales Order form is similar to the Create Estimates and Create Invoices form, and entering sales orders is similar to entering estimates or invoices. The Ship To fields are added because items on sales orders are frequently shipped to customers. The purchase order number (P.O. No.) is the number on the purchase order received from the customer that links to this sales order. Again, some of the columns on the form are not suitable for Terrific Tours, so we will begin by customizing the form. Accept any Layout Designer messages that you receive.

Notes
The sales order for a business is the customer's purchase order. Similarly, a purchase order for a business becomes a sales order for the vendor who receives the order.

2. **Click** to open the Basic Customization form

3. **Click** Additional Customization... on the bottom of the form

4. **Click** the **Columns tab** to open the list of columns:

Figure 8-38

All items with a checkmark under the Screen column indicate that the field is displayed on the Create Sales Orders form. All items with a checkmark under the Print column indicate that the field is displayed on the printed sales order form. You can select which fields will be displayed on the form and which ones will be printed for the customer.

We will remove the Rate column, and change the Quantity column title to Number and the Amount column title to Total.

5. **Click** **both check boxes** for Rate to remove the ✓

6. **Click** **OK** if you receive the Layout Designer message

7. **Double click** **Ordered in the Quantity Title field**

8. **Type** **Number**

9. **Double click** **Amount** in the Amount Title field

10. **Type** **Total**

11.	**Click**	**OK** to return to the Basic Customization screen
12.	**Click**	**OK** to return to the revised form
13.	**Choose**	**Calgary District School Board** as the Customer:Job for this Sales Order
14.	**Enter**	**10/03/12** as the date
15.	**Choose**	**Air Travel** as the first item on the Sales Order
16.	**Press**	tab to advance to the Number field
17.	**Type**	**22**
18.	**Press**	tab to advance to the Total field

We will enter the total cost of the tour for all 22 travellers.

19.	**Type**	**16280**
20.	**Press**	tab to add the taxes to the Invoice total and advance to the second invoice line
21.	**Choose**	**Tour** as the next item on the Sales Order
22.	**Press**	tab to advance to the Number field
23.	**Type**	**22**
24.	**Press**	tab to advance to the Total field
25.	**Type**	**28380**
26.	**Press**	tab to update the Invoice total
27.	**Choose**	**We'll take care of you.** in the Customer Message field

The program updates the Sales Order numbers automatically. The default initial number is 1 because no Sales Orders have been entered yet.

28.	**Double click**	**1** in the S.O. No. field beside the date
29.	**Type**	**6**

Click the To be printed option to remove the ✓ if you do not want to include the sales order in a batch of sales orders to be printed at a later time.

30. The sales order is now complete as shown here:

Notes

After entering a number in the S.O. No. Field, Quick-Books will update the numbers automatically.

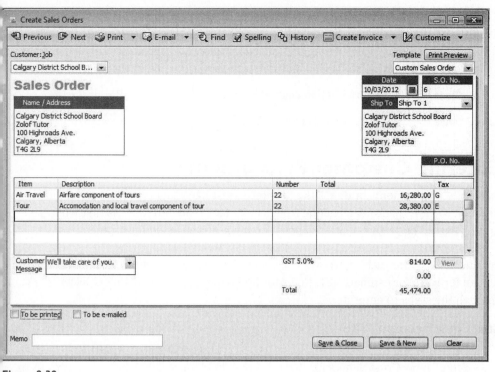

Figure 8-39

31. **Review** the **Sales Order** and **make** any **corrections** before saving it

---

CORRECTING CUSTOMER SALES ORDERS

Correcting a sales order is just like correcting a sales estimate. See page 367 if you need any further assistance.

---

32. **Click** **Save & New** to record the sales order and leave the form open to review it

Reviewing the Sales Order

Although the order does not create debit and credit entries, it does generate a transaction entry that we can review, just as we review any other transaction.

With a blank sales order form displayed on the screen:

1. **Click** ◄] Previous to view the sales order that we just entered for the Calgary District School Board

2. **Press** [ctrl] + **Y** to view the Transaction Journal report:

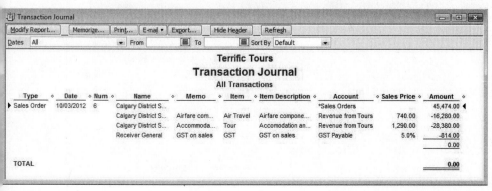

Figure 8-40

Notes
We have removed columns from the report to display it in the textbook.

The journal entry for a sales order is the same as a regular invoice entry except that the *Sales Orders* account is increased instead of the *Accounts Receivable* account. Notice too that unit or sales prices are calculated and entered for Air Travel and Tour. *Sales Orders* is a non-postable account that appears at the end of the Chart of Accounts.

3. **Close**   the **Transaction Journal report** to return to the sales order

4. **Close**   the **Create Sales Orders form**

Entering Customer Prepayments

Customer prepayments or deposits are entered just like other customer payments because you are receiving a cheque from a customer. The difference is that when you enter a customer prepayment or deposit, no invoice is selected for payment.

Prepayments are entered on the Receive Payments form.

In the next transaction, we will enter a customer prepayment from UpperCrust School for Boys for estimate #21. Refer to the following source document as we work through the steps to enter it:

SD Instructions
Refer to the following source document and then follow the step-by-step instructions to enter it.

SD9: Cash Receipt #346

Dated October 3, 2012

From UpperCrust School for Boys, cheque #698 for $25,000.00 as prepayment to accept estimate #21 and confirm the tour.

Notes
You can also access the Receive Payments form from the Customers menu.

1. **Click**   [Receive Payments] in the Customers section of the Home page to open the Receive Payments form:

2. **Choose**   **UpperCrust School for Boys** as the customer for this payment

One outstanding invoice for this customer is displayed on the Receive Payments form

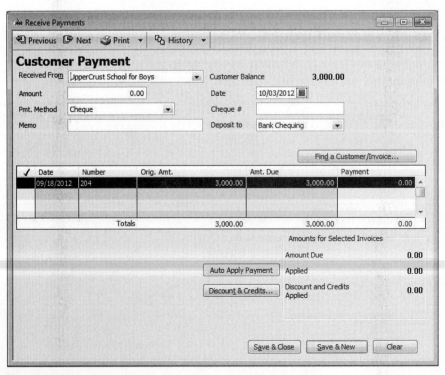

Figure 8-41

3. **Press**   (tab) to advance to the amount field

4. **Type**   **25000** and **press** (tab) to advance to the Date field

5. **Enter**   **10/03/12** as the date if necessary

6. **Click**   the **drop-down arrow** in the Pmt. Method field and **click Cheque**

7. **Press**   (tab) to the Cheque # field

8. **Type**   **698**

QuickBooks automatically applies the payment to the outstanding invoice. Any excess amount not needed to cover the invoice is entered as an Overpayment. However, this payment is a prepayment for estimate #21. The invoice for this estimate will be issued later. We must remove the ✓ beside invoice #204. We should also add a memo to link the deposit with the estimate.

9. **Click**   the **Un-Apply Payment button** or the ✓ for invoice #204 to remove the ✓

10. **Click**   the **Memo field**

11. **Type**   **Prepayment re: Estimate #21**

12. **Confirm**   that the **Bank Chequing account** is selected in the Deposit To field (select it if necessary)

13. The payment is now complete as shown:

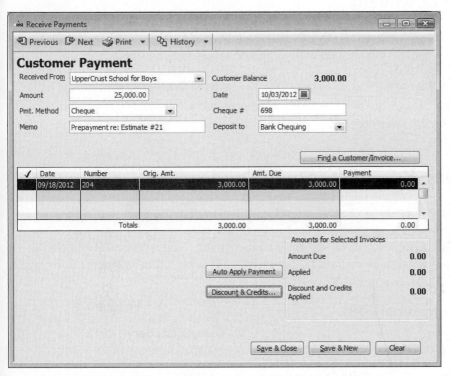

Figure 8-42

Because the payment was not applied to any invoices, the entire cheque amount is an overpayment. The transaction creates a credit balance in the customer's Accounts Receivable ledger.

14. **Check**   your **work** and **make** any necessary **corrections**

15. Click   **Save & New** to record the payment and leave the form open for the next receipt. The following warning will be displayed:

Figure 8-43

You now have the choice of printing a credit memo for the customer overpayment or saving the transaction as an overpayment. Because payments are usually applied to invoices, QuickBooks issues this warning so you can correct the transaction if necessary. In this case, the transaction is correct.

After you record the payment and until you apply the credit to an invoice, the overpayment will appear as a credit when entering payments for this customer.

16. Click   **OK** to proceed with recording the payment and return to the Receive Payments form

SD Practice
Continue to develop your skills by entering the following source document(s).

Source Document

Now that you have learned some of the new concepts introduced in this chapter, continue to develop your skills by entering the following source document in QuickBooks. Use the information in this chapter as a guide if necessary.

SD10: Cash Receipt #347   **Dated October 3, 2012**

From Calgary District School Board, cheque #3902 for $22,000.00 as prepayment to confirm sales order #6.

Notes
Because there are no outstanding invoices for Calgary District School Board, the total cheque amount is entered immediately as an overpayment.

Entering Prepayments to Vendors

Entering prepayments to vendors is just like making a cash purchase, i.e., writing a cheque, but without selecting an item for the transaction.

In the next transaction, we will enter a prepayment to our vendor Travel Totes as prepayment for purchase order #30. Refer to the following source document as we work through the steps to enter it:

SD11: Cheque Copy #482

                             Dated October 4, 2012

To Travel Totes, $500.00 as prepayment to confirm purchase order #30.

SD Instructions
Refer to the following source document and then follow the step-by-step instructions to enter it.

1. Open   the **Write Cheques form** using one of the following methods:

         a) **Choose Banking** from the menu and **click Write Cheques**; or

         b) **Click**   in the Banking section of the Home page; or

         c) **Press** `ctrl` + **W**

2. **Choose**   **Travel Totes** in the Pay to the Order of field

3. The following message will be displayed:

Open POs Exist

⚠️ Open purchase orders exist for this vendor. Do you want to receive against one or more of these orders?

[Yes]   [No]

Figure 8-44

QuickBooks recognizes that there is an outstanding order for this vendor and offers you the chance to fill the order immediately. However, we have not yet received the items so we are not filling the order yet.

4. **Click**   **No** to return to the Write Cheques form

5. **Press**   ⟨tab⟩ to advance to the Amount field

6. **Type**   **500**

7. **Click**   the **drop-down arrow** in the Account field on the Expenses tab

8. **Scroll up**   the **account list** and choose Accounts Payable

9. **Click**   the **To be printed option** to remove the ✓

10. **Click**   the **Memo field**

11. **Type**   **Deposit for PO #30**

12. **Double click**   the **date** to select it

13. **Type**   **10/04/12**

14. Your completed cheque should look like this:

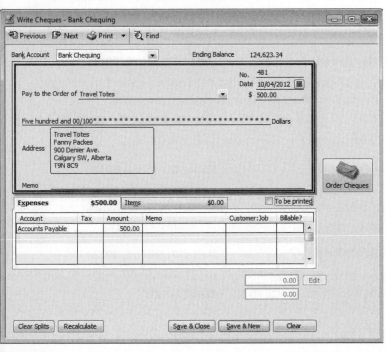

Figure 8-45

> **Notes**
> If you want to fill the order, the rest of the invoice will be completed automatically based on the purchase order information when you choose Yes on this screen.

15. **Check**   your **work** carefully and **make corrections** if necessary

16. **Click**   **Save & Close**

The default cheque number is 481. If you do not change this number, you will see the following warning when you try to save the cheque:

Notes
The cheque sequence should be incorrect because we entered cheque #481 as the first cheque number on the list and #480 as the second cheque number (on page 353).

Figure 8-46

QuickBooks does not use duplicate cheque numbers without warning you first. We chose this setting as a preference for the company file.

If you see this message,

17. **Click**   **Cancel** to return to the cheque so you can change the number

18. **Double click** **481**, the cheque number, to select it

19. **Type**   **482**

20. **Click**   **Save & Close**

Source Documents

SD Practice
Continue to develop your skills by entering the following source document(s).

Now that you have learned more of the new concepts introduced in this chapter, continue to develop your skills by entering the following source documents in QuickBooks. Use the information in this chapter as a guide if necessary.

SD12: Cheque Copy #483 and #484   **Dated October 5, 2012**

To Parry's Printing House, cheque #483 for $933.25 in payment of account, including the discount for early payment. Reference invoice #PPH-1800.

To Heritage Hotels, cheque #484 for $13,770.90 in payment of account, including the discount for early payment. Reference invoice #HH-2099.

SD13: Purchase Invoice #SC-1008   **Dated October 5, 2012**

From Spotless Cleaners (set up new vendor), $180.00 plus GST for cleaning office. Purchase invoice total, $189.00. Terms: 2/10, n/30. Memorize the transaction with weekly reminders beginning October 12, 2012.

Notes
Spotless Cleaners
(Les Spotts)
420 Vacuum Cr.
Calgary, AB T3C 8H9
Tel: (403) 388-2886
E-mail: less@spotless.com
Terms: 2/10, n/30
Credit limit: $1,000.00
Business No.: 388 477 562

SD14: Purchase Invoice #AE-5992   **Dated October 5, 2012**

From Air Europe, $12,600.00 plus GST for airfare for UpperCrust School for Boys tour. Purchase invoice total, $13,230.00. Terms: Net 20.

SD15: Purchase Invoice #HH-3956   **Dated October 6, 2012**

From Heritage Hotels, $16,300.00 including all local taxes for double hotel accommodation for 18 adults for eight nights. No Canadian taxes apply because the hotels are not in Canada. (Tax Exempt is the tax code.) Terms: 1/10, n/30.

Receiving Items from a Purchase Order

When you receive merchandise that has been entered on a purchase order, you must fill the order. Items may be shipped with the invoice, or the invoice may be mailed separately. In this example, the items arrive before the invoice so we will enter the received items first.

In the next transaction, we will receive items from purchase order #30 from Travel Totes. Refer to the following source document as we work through the steps to enter it:

SD16: Received Items: Shipment #45590

Dated October 6, 2012

Fill purchase order #30 from Travel Totes. Received 100 tote bags and wallets for $900.00 plus $45.00 GST. Invoice totals $945.00. All items were received and the bill will follow. Terms: 2/5, n/30.

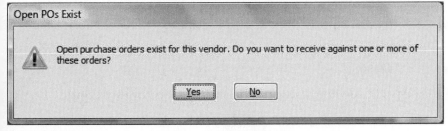

📄 **SD Instructions**
Refer to the following source document and then follow the step-by-step instructions to enter it.

Received items are entered from the Receive Inventory icon ![Receive Inventory] found in the Vendors section of the Home page. When you click the Receive Inventory icon or click on the drop-down arrow beside it, you select whether you are receiving the inventory with a bill or receiving items without a bill:

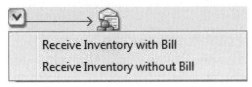

QuickBooks has separate forms for these options. You cannot enter the bill before receiving the items.

1. Click   the **Receive Inventory icon** and **click Receive Inventory without Bill**

The screen is clearly marked as an item receipt only. However, clicking the check box beside Bill Received in the upper right-hand corner of the form will change the form to an Enter Bills form. Make sure the Bill Received option is not selected for this source document.

2. Choose   **Travel Totes** in the Vendor field

3. The following message is displayed:

> **Open POs Exist**
>
> ⚠ Open purchase orders exist for this vendor. Do you want to receive against one or more of these orders?
>
> [Yes] [No]

Figure 8-47

Because we have previously placed a purchase order with Travel Totes, QuickBooks displays a message allowing us to receive items against those previously entered purchase orders. We will receive items against a previously entered purchase order for this source document.

4. Click   **Yes** to view the list of outstanding or open purchase orders placed with Travel Totes:

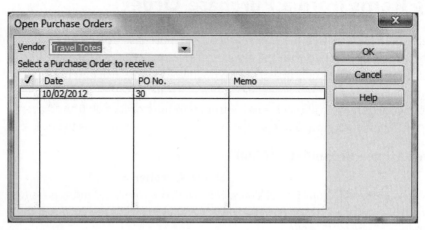

Figure 8-48

You can select purchase orders for other vendors on this screen by choosing a different vendor in the Vendor field.

The Open Purchase Orders screen displays only the single order that we entered previously for Travel Totes.

5. Click   **PO #30** (click anywhere on the line) to select it

6. Click   **OK** to add the ordered items to the form

Sometimes, a purchase order is only partially filled with a single shipment. It is important to verify that the shipped items match the number and description on the original purchase order. The purchase order will remain open until all items are marked as received.

If the bill has been received with the items, you can mark the Bill Received check box so you don't have to enter the bill separately.

If a partial shipment is received, you can change the quantity on the Receipt form and then record the receipt. When the rest of the items on the purchase order arrive, you can enter another receipt for them. The quantity on the purchase order will reflect only the items not previously entered as received.

All items have been received in this shipment and the date should be correct.

7. Press   (tab) to advance to the date field

8. Type   **10/06/12**

9. Click   the **Ref. No. field**. We will add the shipping reference number in this field.

10. Type   **45590**

11. The completed Create Item Receipts form should be displayed as shown:

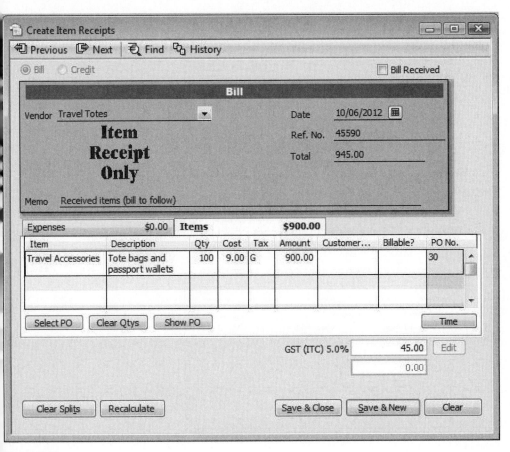

Figure 8-49

12. **Check** your **work** carefully and **make** any necessary **corrections**

13. **Click** **Save & Close**

Entering a Bill for Received Items

When a bill arrives for items that have already been received and entered on the Create Item Receipts form, it is entered by selecting the Enter Bills Against Inventory icon in the Vendors section of the Home page.

In the next transaction, we will receive a purchase invoice from Travel Totes for shipment #45590. Refer to the following source document as we work through the steps to enter it:

SD17: Receive Purchase Invoice #TT-5987

SD Instructions
Refer to the following source document and then follow the step-by-step instructions to enter it.

Dated October 6, 2012

Received a bill from Travel Totes for $900.00 plus $45.00 GST. Invoice totals $945.00. Terms: 2/5, n/30.

Enter Bills
Against
Inventory

1. **Click** the **Enter Bills Against Inventory icon** to open the Select Item Receipt screen:

Figure 8-50

> 2. **Choose**   **Travel Totes** in the Vendor field to view all shipments received without a bill from this vendor:

Figure 8-51

The item receipt that we entered in the previous exercise is displayed on the Select Item Receipt screen.

> 3. **Click**   the **Item Receipt** dated 10/06/12, Ref. No. 45590
>
> 4. **Click**   **OK** to add the Item Receipt to the bill

Figure 8-52

You can use the buttons on this form to select a purchase order, clear the quantities (edit the bill), or show the original purchase order.

Choosing Revert on the Enter Bills form will open the related Create Item Receipts form.

The form is almost complete. We should add the invoice number in the Ref. No. field and change the date if necessary. We will save the shipment reference number as well by adding it in the Memo field.

5. **Double click**   the **date** and **type 10/06/12** if necessary

6. **Press**   (tab) to advance to the Ref. No. field

7. **Type**   **TT-5987**

8. **Click**   the **Memo field** and **type Ref: Shipment #45590**

9. **Check**   your **work** carefully and **make corrections** if necessary

10. **Click**   **Save & Close** to view the warning:

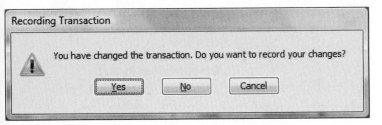

> **Recording Transaction**
>
> ⚠ You have changed the transaction. Do you want to record your changes?
>
> [Yes]   [No]   [Cancel]

Figure 8-53

> **Notes**
> The warning appears because we changed the reference number.

11. **Click**   **Yes** to record the changes and save the Bill

Source Documents

Continue to develop your skills by entering the following source document in QuickBooks. Use the information in this chapter as a guide if necessary.

SD18: Purchase Order #31   **Dated October 6, 2012**

To Parry's Printing House, $1,400.00 plus GST for printing new travel brochures to give to clients. Purchase order totals $1,470.00. A 25 percent deposit is requested to confirm order.

> **SD Practice**
> Continue to develop your skills by entering the following source document(s).

Entering Credit Card Sales

Most businesses accept credit cards in payment of an account, usually at the time of a sale. There are advantages and disadvantages to accepting credit cards. The business must pay the credit card provider company a merchant fee, usually a small percentage of each transaction amount, as the cost of using the service. The fee or rate varies from one type of business to another and from one company to another within the business type. Businesses that generate a higher volume of sales usually pay a lower fee than smaller businesses with lower sales volumes. Despite paying the fee, most companies prefer to accept credit cards in payment in order to minimize the number of NSF cheques. One NSF cheque can outweigh the fees from a number of sales. Because of the fees involved, companies that have a very small profit margin may decide not to accept credit cards, or they may accept credit cards only for sales above a specified dollar amount.

Credit card sales are entered like other cash sales because the customer pays in full at the time of the sale. The only difference is the selection of the type of payment — a credit card instead of cash or a cheque. Credit card receipts are usually deposited directly if the business has a direct terminal connection with the credit card bank account. If the business uses manual transaction charge plate slips, the receipts are held and deposited later. The card processing fee, a percentage of the sale amount, may be taken at the time of the deposit or entered as service charges on the monthly statement, depending on the arrangements with the credit card company.

QuickBooks allows a business to set up direct access to the related bank account for immediate processing of credit card receipts at the time of the transaction. In this text, the fees will be entered manually at the time of reconciling the account. This procedure is covered in Chapter 9, along with bank and account reconciliation. Terrific Tours deposits credit card receipts directly, so these receipts are not held for later deposit.

We have created a customer record named Cash Sales to enter the credit card sales in order to avoid creating a large number of individual invoices.

In the next transaction, we will enter a credit card sale from individual cash sales customers. Refer to the following source document as we work through the steps to enter it:

SD19: Cash Sales Receipt Summary #24

Dated October 7, 2012

From individual cash sales customers, $4,200.00 plus GST for flights and $3,100.00 for tours booked during the week. Sales invoice total of $7,510.00 was paid by Visa. Visa credit card receipts are deposited to Bank Visa account. Memorize the transaction with weekly reminders beginning October 14, 2012.

Create Sales Receipts

1.	**Click**	the **Create Sales Receipts icon** in the Customers section of the Home page to open the Enter Sales Receipt form
2.	**Choose**	**Cash Sales** as the customer for the transaction

We have selected Visa as the preferred or default payment method in the Cash Sales customer record so it is entered automatically when we choose Cash Sales. You can select a different payment method in the Enter Sales Receipts form if the customer pays differently for the purchase. The rest of the information is entered the same way as other sales receipts.

3.	**Enter**	**10/07/12** as the transaction date
4.	**Press**	⎯tab⎯ to advance to the Sale No. field
5.	**Type**	**24**
6.	**Choose**	**Air Travel** as the first item for the sale
7.	**Enter**	**4200** as the amount for the item. The **tax code of G** is correct
8.	**Choose**	**Tour** as the second item for the sale
9.	**Enter**	**3100** as the amount for the item. The **tax code of E** is correct
10.	**Click**	the **drop-down arrow** in the Deposit To field
11.	**Choose**	**Bank Visa** from the account list
12.	**Click**	the **Memo field**

SD Instructions
Refer to the following source document and then follow the step-by-step instructions to enter it.

Notes
Bank Chequing is set up as the default account for deposits so we need to change the account selection each time we enter a Visa sales receipt.

13. **Type**	**Weekly sales summary**
14. **Click**	the **To be printed** option to remove the ✓ (checkmark) in the box so the form will not be selected for batch printing

We do not need to choose a message because this is not a customer copy of the receipt. The form is complete as shown:

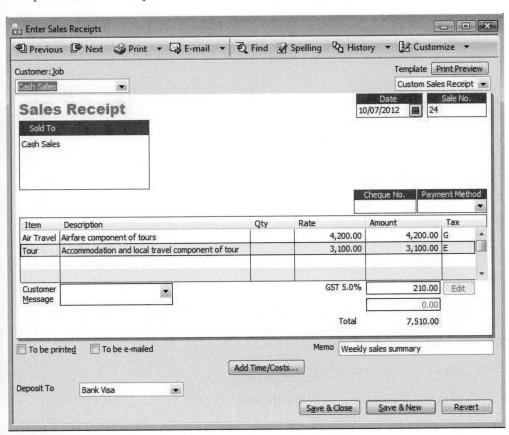

Figure 8-54

15. **Check**	your **work** carefully and **make corrections** if needed, just as you would correct any other sales receipt

If this sales receipt was for a customer, and the customer was in the store, you could print the receipt immediately by clicking the Print button on the form.

We can memorize the transaction so that we won't need to enter all the details each time the summary is entered.

Memorizing the Transaction

With the sales receipt still displayed on the screen:

1. **Right click**	and **select Memorize Sales Receipt** to open the Memorize Transaction screen
2. **Select**	**Remind Me** (this should be selected as the default)
3. **Choose**	**Weekly** as the reminder frequency
4. **Enter**	**10/14/12** as the next reminder date
5. **Click**	**OK** to save the memorized transaction details

6. **Click**   **Save & New** to leave the Enter Sales Receipt window open so we can view the journal entry that was just created from the cash sales transaction

Reviewing the Transaction

1. **Click**   ⬅ Previous   to display the cash sales receipt that we just entered

2. **Press**   ⌨ ctrl + **Y** to display the Transaction Journal report:

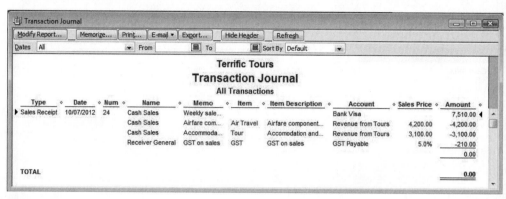

Figure 8-55

The only difference between this and other sales receipt transactions that we've entered previously is that the *Bank Visa* account is debited for the deposit instead of the *Bank Chequing* account because we selected it in the Deposit To field.

3. **Close**   the **Transaction Journal report**

4. **Close**   the **Enter Sales Receipt form**

Creating Invoices from Estimates

Once a customer accepts an estimate, you can use that estimate to create the invoice.

Estimates are converted to invoices from the Invoices icon. You can see that the Create Invoices icon follows the Estimates icon in the workflow in the Customers section of the Home page:

Figure 8-56

When you open the Create Invoices form and select a customer for whom an estimate has been entered, an available estimates screen will be displayed. From this screen, you select the estimate that you want to use for the invoice and the invoice will be created automatically from the information on the estimate.

You can also create invoices directly from the estimates form. Open the Create Estimates form, find the estimate that is being invoiced, and click the Create Invoice button on the form. The estimate details will be copied to the invoice. The Create Estimates form will close and the Create Invoices form will open where you can add, modify, or delete information on the invoice.

In the next transaction, we will create an invoice from an estimate. Refer to the following source document as we work through the steps to enter it:

SD20: Sales Invoice #212

SD Instructions
Refer to the following source document and then follow the step-by-step instructions to enter it.

Dated October 9, 2012

To UpperCrust School for Boys, based on estimate #21, $16,020.00 plus 5% GST for the airfare and $28,800.00 for the tour component in the European capital cities tour. Total cost of the tour including taxes is $45,621.00. Terms: 1/10, n/30.

1. **Click**   the **Invoices icon**, or **press** ctrl + **I** to open the Create Invoices form

2. **Choose**   **UpperCrust School for Boys** in the Customer:Job field. A list of estimates available for this customer is displayed on the Available Estimates screen:

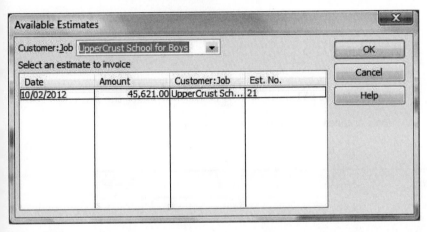

Figure 8-57

Notes
To create an invoice for a customer that is not based on an estimate, click Cancel to return to the Create Invoices screen directly.

The single estimate we entered for this customer is listed. From this screen we can choose an estimate so that the invoice will be created immediately based on the estimate.

3. **Click**   estimate number **21** to select it. You can click anywhere on the line

4. **Click**   **OK** to continue and display the related invoice:

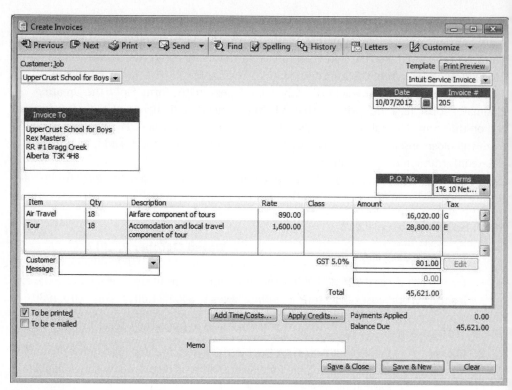

Figure 8-58

5. **Enter**   **10/09/12** as the transaction date

6. **Enter**   **212** in the Invoice field

7. **Enter**   **Ref: Estimate #21** in the Memo field to complete the invoice

8. **Click**   **Save & Close** to close the Create Invoices form

9. The following message is displayed:

Figure 8-59

This message indicates that the customer has available credits and asks if you would like to apply them to this invoice. We will not apply the credit to this invoice.

10. **Click**   **No**

Source Documents

Continue to develop your skills by entering the following source documents in QuickBooks. Use the information in this chapter as a guide if necessary:

SD Practice
Continue to develop your skills by entering the following source document(s).

SD21: Cheque Copy #485 **Dated October 9, 2012**

To Parry's Printing House, $375.00 as prepayment to confirm purchase order #31.

SD22: Purchase Invoice #CT-59927 **Dated October 9, 2012**

From Capital Tours, $8,400.00 for special local tours arranged for Athabaska Alumni Association. Terms: 1/10, n/30.

SD23: Cheque Copy #486 **Dated October 11, 2012**

To Travel Totes, $427.00 in payment of account, including the discount for early payment. Reference invoice #TT-5987.

SD24: Sales Estimate #22 **Dated October 12, 2012**

To Rocky Mountain School for the Performing Arts, $14,450.00 plus GST for the airfare and $20,060.00 for the tour component of the complete tour package for 15 students and two teachers. Price of the eight-day tour to Russia includes airfare and accommodation, and attendance at several ballet and other dance performances. Total cost of the tour including taxes is $35,232.50.

SD25: Purchase Invoice #SC-112 **Dated October 12, 2012**

From Spotless Cleaners, $180.00 plus GST for cleaning office. Purchase invoice totals $189.00. Terms: 2/10, n/30. Use the memorized transaction.

SD26: Purchase Order #32 **Dated October 13, 2012**

To Universal Theatre Bookings, $3,810.00 to arrange admissions for several tour groups. No Canadian taxes apply. Deposit requested.

Creating Invoices from Sales Orders

When a sales order is filled, you can create the invoice from the sales order directly.

In the next transaction, we will create an invoice from a sales order. Refer to the following source document as we work through the steps to enter it:

SD Instructions
Refer to the following source document and then follow the step-by-step instructions to enter it.

SD27: Sales Invoice #213

Dated October 14, 2012

To Calgary District School Board, based on sales order #6, $16,280.00 plus 5% GST for airfare and $28,380.00 for the tour in the England tour package. Total cost of the tour including taxes is $45,474.00. Terms: 1/10, n/30.

1. **Click** the **Create Invoices icon** in the Customers section of the Home page or **press** `ctrl` **+ I** to open the Create Invoices form

2. **Choose** **Calgary District School Board** in the Customer:Job field

3. A list of available sales orders for this customer is displayed:

Notes
You can also choose the Customers menu and click Create Invoices to open the Create Invoices form.

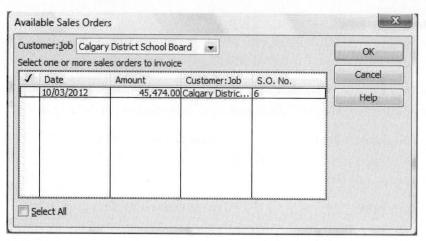

Figure 8-60

Notes

When you create an invoice from a Sales Order, this window will be displayed asking if you want to fill the entire order or not.

The single sales order that we entered previously is displayed on the Available Sales Orders screen. From this screen we can choose an order so that the invoice will be created immediately based on that order.

4. **Click**   sales order **6** to select it. You can click anywhere on the line

5. **Click**   **OK**

6. The Create Invoice Based on Sales Order(s) screen is displayed:

Figure 8-61

From this screen, you can select to create the invoice for all the sales order(s) selected or to create the invoice for selected items. If you select to create the invoice for all the sales orders (this is the option selected by default), all the items on the sales order will be transferred to the invoice. If you select to create the invoice for selected items, a screen will be displayed listing all the items on the sales order where you can enter the quantity that you will ship on the invoice.

7. **Click**   **Create invoice** for selected items option

8. **Click**   **OK** to view the Specify Invoice Quantities for Items on Sales Orders(s) screen:

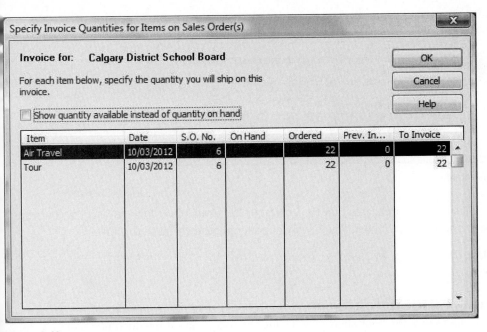

Figure 8-62

Use this screen to change the item quantities for the invoice. When you enter smaller quantities than the quantities ordered, the sales order will remain open until the complete order is filled. In this case, we want to fill the complete order so we don't need to change the quantities.

9. **Click**   **OK** to view the invoice

10. **Enter**   **10/14/12** as the invoice date

The sales order number is entered automatically for reference in the S.O. No. field and the invoice number is updated with the next available invoice number, so the form is complete as shown:

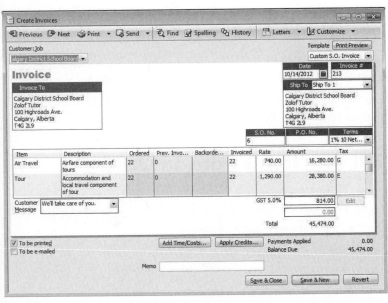

Figure 8-63

11. **Click**   **Save & Close**

12. The following message is displayed:

Figure 8-64

This message indicates that the customer has available credits and asks if you would like to apply them to this invoice. We will not apply the credit to this invoice.

13. Click   No

SD Practice
Continue to develop your skills by entering the following source document(s).

Source Documents

Continue to develop your skills by entering the following source documents in QuickBooks. Use the information in this chapter as a guide if necessary:

SD28: Purchase Order #33   Dated October 14, 2012

To Universal Theatre Bookings, $3,600.00 for admission to ballet and dance performances for members of the tour. No Canadian taxes apply. A deposit is requested to confirm order.

SD29: Cash Sales Receipt Summary #25   Dated October 14, 2012

From individual cash sales customers, $3,600.00 plus GST for flights and $1,740.00 for tours booked during the week. Sales invoices total $5,520.00 paid by Visa and deposited directly to Bank Visa account. Use the memorized transaction and edit the amounts.

Notes
Remember to select Bank Visa as the account for the deposit.

SD30: Cheque Copy #487   Dated October 15, 2012

To Spotless Cleaners, $370.80 in payment of account, including the discount for early payment. Reference invoices #SC-1008 and SC-1128.

SD31: Purchase Order #34   Dated October 15, 2012

To Travel Totes, $100.00 plus GST for luggage tags printed with Terrific Tours logo. Purchase order totals $105.00.

Receiving a Bill with Items from an Order

When ordered items arrive with the invoice, you can complete two steps at the same time — enter the items and the bill. The procedure is almost the same as filling the order without the bill, except that the starting point is different.

In the next transaction, we will receive the bill at the same time we receive the items. Refer to the following source document as we work through the steps to enter it:

SD32: Purchase Invoice #PPH-2675

SD Instructions
Refer to the following source document and then follow the step-by-step instructions to enter it.

Dated October 16, 2012

Fill purchase order #31 from Parry's Printing House, $1,400.00 plus GST for printing travel brochures. Purchase invoice totals $1,470.00. Terms: 2/10, n/30. All items received with bill.

To receive the items from purchase order #31 from Parry's Printing House and enter the invoice at the same time, we will use the Receive Items with Bill option from the Receive Inventory icon in the Vendors section of the Home page.

1. **Click** the **Receive Inventory icon** in the Vendors section of the Home page

2. **Click** the **Receive Inventory with Bill** option as shown:

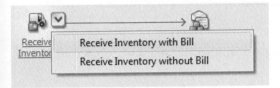

Figure 8-65

3. The Enter Bills form will be displayed as shown:

Figure 8-66

Notes
Notice the Bill Received option is selected automatically. When you select the Receive Inventory with Bill option from the Receive Inventory icon, QuickBooks knows that the Bill was received with the items. If you selected this option by mistake, you can uncheck the Bill Received option to display the Create Item Receipts form.

We can use the same approach we used earlier: select the vendor, receive the message that there are open orders, and create the invoice from those orders. However, in this example we will select the order directly before selecting the vendor.

4. Click   the **Select PO button** Select PO to access the Open Purchase
Orders window:

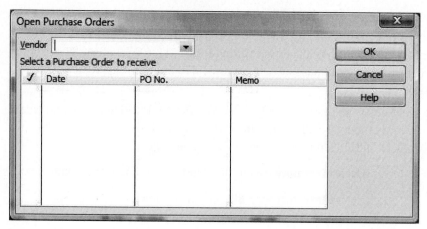

Figure 8-67

From this screen, we can select any vendor with whom we have open purchase
orders.

5. Click   the **drop-down arrow** in the Vendor field

6. Choose   **Parry's Printing House**

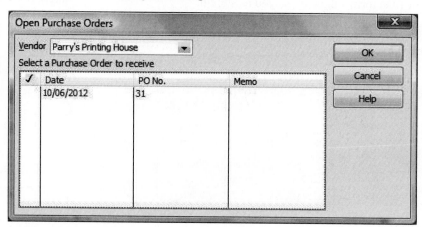

Figure 8-68

Only one order is listed but we still need to select it.

7. Click   anywhere on the line for **PO #31** to select the order. A ✓ is displayed
in the column to the left of the purchase order

8. Click   **OK** to add the information on the purchase order to the Enter Bills
form as shown:

Figure 8-69

By default, the entire quantity ordered is entered on the Enter Bills form. If only a partial shipment is received, change the quantity on the bill. The Purchase Order will remain open until the order is completely filled.

To complete the entry, we need to change the date, add the invoice reference number, and add a Memo that links the invoice to the purchase order.

9.	**Enter**	**10/16/12** the date field
10.	**Click**	the **Ref. No.** field
11.	**Type**	**PPH-2675**
12.	**Click**	the **Memo field**
13.	**Type**	**Fill PO #31**
14.	**Check**	your **work** and **make** any necessary **corrections** as you would correct any other bill
15.	**Click**	**Save & Close** to save the bill and close the form

Source Documents

Continue to develop your skills by entering the following source document in QuickBooks. Use the information in this chapter as a guide if necessary.

SD33: Sales Order #7

SD Practice
Continue to develop your skills by entering the following source document(s).

Dated October 16, 2012

To Calgary Region Catholic School Board, $8,400.00 plus GST for the airfare and $16,200.00 for the tour component of the complete tour package for 10 students and two teachers. Price of the nine-day tour to Tokyo includes airfare and accommodation, and attendance at local cultural events. Total cost of the tour including taxes is $25,020.00.

SD34: Cheque Copy #488

Dated October 16, 2012

To Universal Theatre Bookings, $3,500.00 as prepayment to confirm purchase orders #32 and #33.

SD35: Purchase Invoice #AE-8120

Dated October 16, 2012

From Air Europe, $12,040.00 plus GST for airfare for 22 adults. Purchase invoice totals $12,642.00. Terms: net 20.

SD36: Cheque Copy #489

Dated October 16, 2012

To Heritage Hotels, $16,137.00 in payment of account, including discount for early payment. Reference invoice #HH-3956.

SD37: Purchase Invoice #HH-5993

Dated October 16, 2012

From Heritage Hotels, $12,770.00, including all local taxes for hotel accommodation and some meals for seven-day tour. The students will share hotel rooms and the two adults have single rooms. No Canadian taxes apply. Terms: 1/10, n/30.

SD38: Purchase Invoice #BCC-5664

Notes
BroadCast
Communications
(Spinne Docktor)
65 Spammer Rd.
Calgary, AB T5C 7N9
E-mail: sd@bcc.com
Terms: net 20
Credit limit: $3,000.00
Business No.: 529 733 922

Dated October 17, 2012

From BroadCast Communications (Set up new vendor), $1,920.00 plus GST for advertising campaign for upcoming tours. Purchase invoice totals $2,016.00. Terms: net 20.

SD39: Cheque Copy #490

Dated October 19, 2012

To Capital Tours, $8,316.00 in payment of account, including the discount for early payment. Reference invoice #CT-59927.

SD40: Purchase Invoice #SC-1212

Dated October 19, 2012

From Spotless Cleaners, $180.00 plus GST for cleaning the office. Purchase invoice totals $189.00. Terms: 2/10, n/30. Use the memorized transaction.

SD41: Cheque Copy #491

Dated October 19, 2012

To Air Europe, $11,663.00 in payment of account. Reference invoice #AE-4897.

SD42: Purchase Invoice #UTB-390

Notes
Enter the invoice from
Universal Theatre Bookings as a
Bill with Items Received.

Dated October 20, 2012

From Universal Theatre Bookings, to fill purchase order #32, $3,810.00 to arrange admissions for several tour groups. No Canadian taxes apply. Terms: 2/5, n/30.

SD43: Sales Estimate #23

Dated October 20, 2012

To Foothills Academy of Art, $9,900.00 plus GST for the airfare and $18,000.00 for the tour component of the complete tour package for 22 students and two teachers. Price of the five-day tour to New Orleans includes airfare and accommodation, and attendance at Mardi Gras events. Total cost of the tour including taxes is $28,395.00.

SD44: Purchase Invoice #FC-14336

Dated October 20, 2012

From Foothills Communication, $120.00 plus GST for monthly telephone charges. Purchase invoice totals $126.00. Terms: Net 10.

SD45: Cash Sales Receipt Summary #26

Dated October 21, 2012

From individual cash sales customers, $4,500.00 plus GST for flights and $1,360.00 for tours booked during the week. Sales invoices total $6,085.00 paid by Visa and deposited to the Bank Visa account. Use the memorized transaction and edit the amounts.

Notes
Remember to select Bank Visa as the account for the deposit.

SD46: Purchase Invoice #CT-68342

Dated October 22, 2012

From Capital Tours, $4,980.00 for special local tours arranged for UpperCrust School for Boys. Terms: 1/10, n/30.

SD47: Cheque Copy #492

Dated October 23, 2012

To Universal Theatre Bookings, $1,933.80 in payment of account. Reference invoice #UTB-390. Apply $1,800.00 of the outstanding credits to this invoice.

Notes
To change the credits applied, choose the invoice from Universal Theatre Bookings and click the Set Credits button. Enter 1800 as the Amount to Use to replace the default amount.

SD48: Cash Receipt #348

Dated October 23, 2012

From Calgary District School Board, cheque #4988 for $23,027.40 in full payment of account, including the discount for early payment. Reference invoice #213. Apply the unused credits and discount, and then apply the cheque in payment.

SD49: Purchase Order #35

Dated October 24, 2012

To Capital Tours, $6,000.00 for bus and admissions to museums and galleries for all members of the tour group. No Canadian taxes apply. Twenty-five percent deposit was requested to confirm order.

SD50: Cheque Copy #493

Dated October 25, 2012

To Capital Tours, $1,500.00 as prepayment to confirm purchase order #35.

SD51: Cheque Copy #494

Dated October 25, 2012

To Air Europe, $13,230.00 in payment of account. Reference invoice #AE-5992.

SD52: Cheque Copy #495

Dated October 25, 2012

To Parry's Printing House, $1,067.00 in payment of account, including the discount for early payment. Reference invoice #PPH-2675.

SD53: Cash Receipt #349

Dated October 25, 2012

From Rocky Mountain School for the Performing Arts, cheque #1993 for $16,500.00 as prepayment to accept estimate #22 and confirm the tour.

SD54: Invoice #214

Dated October 25, 2012

To Rocky Mountain School for the Performing Arts, based on estimate #22, $14,450.00 plus GST for airfare and $20,060.00 for the Russia tour component. Total cost of the tour including taxes is $35,232.50. Terms: 1/10, n/30.

SD55: Purchase Invoice #AE-7824

Dated October 25, 2012

From Air Europe, $14,150.00 plus GST for the airfare for the tour to Russia. Purchase invoice totals $14,857.50. Terms: net 20.

SD56: Purchase Invoice #HH-6986

Dated October 25, 2012

From Heritage Hotels, $11,720.00 including all local taxes for hotel accommodation with breakfast for the tour group. No Canadian taxes apply. Terms: 1/10, n/30.

SD57: Cheque Copy #496

Dated October 25, 2012

To Heritage Hotels, $12,642.30 in payment of account, including the discount for early payment. Reference invoice #HH-5993.

SD58: Purchase Invoice #SC-1311

Dated October 26, 2012

From Spotless Cleaners, $180.00 plus GST for cleaning the office. Purchase invoice totals $189.00. Terms: 2/10, n/30. Use the memorized transaction.

SD59: Cash Sales Receipt Summary #27

Dated October 28, 2012

Notes

Remember to select Bank Visa as the account for the deposit.

From individual cash sales customers, $4,900.00 plus GST for flights and $1,210.00 for tours booked during the week. Sales invoices total $6,355.00 paid by Visa and deposited to Bank Visa account. Use the memorized transaction and edit the amounts.

SD60: Cash Receipt #350

Dated October 29, 2012

From Calgary Region Catholic School Board, cheque #801 for $12,500.00 as prepayment to accept sales order #7 and confirm the tour.

SD61: Cash Receipt #351

Dated October 29, 2012

From Foothills Academy of Art, cheque #546 for $14,000.00 as prepayment to accept estimate #23 and confirm the tour. Do not apply this payment to the outstanding invoice.

SD62: Sales Order #8

Dated October 29, 2012

To Athabaska Alumni Association, $14,700.00 plus GST for the airfare and $28,700.00 for the tour component of the complete tour package for 14 adults. Price of the eight-day tour to Athens includes airfare and accommodation, admission to museums and galleries, and local transportation. Total cost of the tour including taxes is $44,135.00.

SD63: Sales Order #9

Dated October 29, 2012

To Matheson College (set up new customer), $8,690.00 plus GST for the airfare and $24,200.00 for the tour component of the complete tour package for 10 students and one adult. Price of the 12-day tour to France includes airfare and accommodation, admission to museums and galleries, and local transportation. Total cost of the tour including taxes is $33,324.50.

SD64: Bank Debit Memo #DM-31188

Dated October 29, 2012

From West Hills Premium Bank: Preauthorized withdrawals were made from the Bank Chequing account. Create a new Expense account: Bank Charges.

Mortgage ($390.00 interest and $120.00 principal)	$510.00
Bank loan ($210.00 interest and $560.00 principal)	770.00
Long term loan ($140.00 interest and $130.00 principal)	270.00
Bank service charges	25.00

SD65: Cheque Copy #497

Dated October 30, 2012

To Icharus Mannitoula, $10,190.50 to reimburse the owner for expenses incurred for business and charged to personal credit card. Receipts were provided for all expenses.

Vehicle expenses	$ 210.00 plus GST
Research for upcoming tours	$3,800.00 plus GST
Miscellaneous expenses incurred on tours	$5,980.00

SD66: Memo #3

Dated October 31, 2012

From Owner: Apply unused credits for Rocky Mountain School for the Performing Arts to invoice #214.

Making Estimates Inactive

When we use an estimate to create an invoice, the estimate is still available for future use. If the estimate will not be needed again, we should make it inactive so it does not continue to pop up each time we choose that customer.

In the next transaction, we will review active estimates and make two of them inactive. Refer to the following source document as we work through the steps to enter it:

SD67: Memo #4

Dated October 31, 2012

From Owner: Make estimates #21 and #22 inactive. They have been invoiced and should not appear on customer lists.

Before we make the estimates inactive, let's view the active customer estimates:

1. **Click**   the **Customer Centre icon** on the icon bar to open the Customer Centre

2. **Click**   the **Transactions tab**

Notes

Matheson College
(SooLing Lee)
500 Classic Ave.
Calgary, AB T4T 8N9
Tel: (403) 588-1020
Fax: (403) 589-4198
E-mail: SL.Lee@
matheson.ca
Terms: 1/10, n/30
Credit Limit: $40,000.00
Payment: By cheque

Notes

Choose Other as the type of payee when you add the new record for Mannitoula. Accept the default tax codes.

SD Instructions

Refer to the following source document and then follow the step-by-step instructions to enter it.

3. Click the **Estimates heading** on the left-hand side of the screen to view all open estimates:

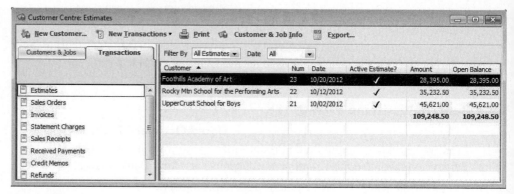

Figure 8-70

The estimates for Foothills Academy of Art, UpperCrust School for Boys, and Rocky Mountain School for the Performing Arts are still listed even though they have already been used to create invoices.

The ✓ (checkmark) under the Active Estimate column indicates that the estimate is active. As long as an estimate is active, it will be available for use when we create invoices for those customers with active estimates.

We want to make estimates #21 and # 22 inactive. We can make them inactive from this screen.

4. Double click Estimate #21 to open it on the screen as shown:

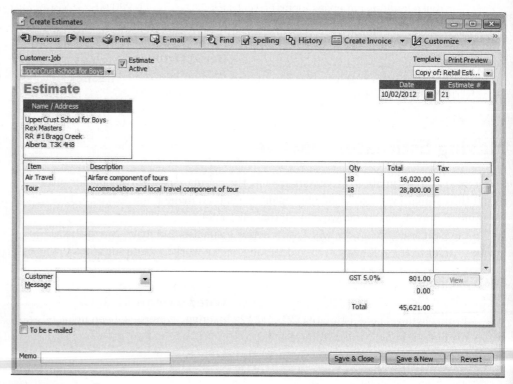

Figure 8-71

The estimate is marked as active. There is a ✓in the Estimate Active check box ☑ Estimate Active . Click the Estimate Active check box to remove the ✓and make the Estimate inactive.

5. **Click**   **Save & Close** to save the changes to Estimate #21. You will be asked if you want to record your changes:

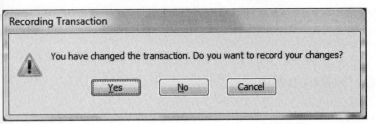

Figure 8-72

6. **Click**   **Yes** to save the changes

7. **Open**   **Estimate #22**

8. **Click**   the **Estimate Active** check box to remove the ✓

9. **Click**   **Save & Close**

10. **Click**   **Yes** to save the record the changes and close the Create Estimates form

You will be returned to the transaction tab in the Customer Centre with the Estimates heading selected.

The inactive estimates no longer have a ✓ under the Active Estimate column and they will not be available for use when we enter invoices for the customers associated with them.

To use the estimates again for future invoices, change the status back to active by clicking the Estimate Active check box.

Source Documents

Continue to develop your skills by entering the following source document in QuickBooks. Use the information in this chapter as a guide if necessary.

SD68: Memo #5   **Dated October 31, 2012**

From Owner: Complete adjusting entries for supplies and prepaid expenses used during month.

Travel brochures and magazines	$2,040.00
Travel accessories	1,990.00
Office and computer supplies	380.00
Prepaid insurance	6,000.00

SD69: Memo #6   **Dated October 31, 2012**

From Owner: Complete adjusting entries for depreciation.

Computer equipment	$160.00
Office furniture	50.00
Business vehicle	425.00
Office	450.00

SD Practice
Continue to develop your skills by entering the following source document(s).

Notes
You can ignore and close the message about fixed assets.

Open Order Reports

Two reports show the orders that are not yet filled — one for sales and one for purchases.

Open Sales Orders Reports

The Open Sales Orders by Customer Report shows a list of all customer sales orders that are not completed, filled, or invoiced as of the latest transaction date.

Notes
You can also choose the Reports menu, click Sales, and then click Open Sales Orders by Customer to access the report.

1. **Open**   the **Report Centre**

2. **Choose**   the **Sales** heading on the left-hand side of the screen

3. **Click**   the **Open Sales Orders by Customer** link under the Open Sales Order heading to view the report:

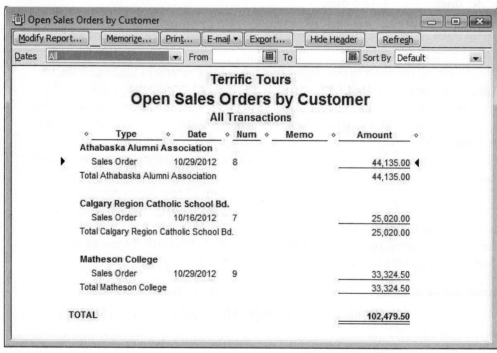

Figure 8-73

Sales orders are listed by customer as the default and include the date of the sales order, the number, a memo, and the amount. You can see that it would be helpful to have the date that the order is to be filled, or, in this case, the date of the tour. This information can be added in the Memo field so that it would be included in the report.

You can sort the report by any of the column headings in ascending or descending order.

Double click a sales order on the report to drill down to the original sales order. Double click a customer total or the report total to view the Custom Transaction Detail Report for that amount.

4. **Close**   the **report** when you have finished

Open Purchase Orders Reports

The Open Purchase Orders Report shows a list of all purchase orders that are not completely filled as of the latest transaction date.

1. **Open** the **Report Centre**

2. **Choose** the **Purchases** heading on the left-hand side of the screen

3. **Click** the **Open Purchase Orders** link under the Open Purchase Orders heading to view the report:

Notes
You can also choose the Reports menu, click Purchases, and then click Open Purchase Orders to access the report.

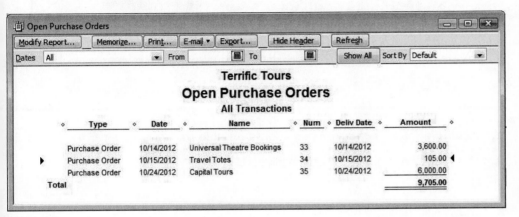

Figure 8-74

Purchase orders are listed by order date but they can be sorted by any of the column headings in ascending or descending order. By default, the order date is entered as the delivery date.

Double click a line in the report to see the original purchase order entry for that line. Double click a total amount to see the Custom Transaction Detail Report for that amount.

Double click a purchase order on the report to drill down to the original purchase order. Double click the report total to view the Custom Transaction Detail Report.

4. **Close** the **report** when you have finished

Orders and Estimates in Other Reports

Two other reports have order information added to them. The Transaction List by Customer Report (found in the Customer & Receivables heading) has a transaction line included for each estimate and sales order. The Transaction List by Vendor Report (found in the Vendors & Payables heading) has a transaction line included for each purchase order.

Finishing Your Session

1. **Back up** the **company data file**

2. **Close** the **company file**

3. **Close** the **QuickBooks program**

Objectives

After completing this chapter, you should be able to:

- **deposit** sales receipts in multiple bank accounts
- **use** account numbers
- **enter** credit card purchases
- **pay** credit card accounts
- **remit** sales taxes
- **assess** finance charges
- **transfer** funds between bank accounts
- **reconcile** bank and credit card accounts
- **make** end-of-period adjusting journal entries
- **close** the books at the end of a fiscal period
- **display** and **print** banking and tax reports
- **enter** closing date passwords
- **enter** transactions for a previous fiscal period

Company Information

Notes
Curly's Cabinets
46 Maple Cres.
Lindsay, ON K9V 2P3
Tel: (705) 618-7200
Fax: (705) 618-7281
E-mail: curly@
curlyscabinets.ca
Web: www.curlyscabinets.
com
Business No.: 844 759 309

Company Profile

Curly's Cabinets in Lindsay, Ontario, is owned and operated by Charles (Curly) Cutter in the garage attached to his home, which he converted into a spacious shop.

Curly builds custom-made wooden furniture: cabinets, bedroom suites, wall units, book shelves, plate rails, wainscotting, dressers, tables, and chairs. For new homes, he also designs built-in cabinets and shelves. He sells some smaller pieces at craft shows in Toronto. These shows provide an opportunity to promote his craftsmanship to new customers.

Woodworking was Curly's hobby in high school, and he completed a program in carpentry and small business at a community college. After a two-year apprenticeship, he started his own business. In his spare time, he volunteers at a seniors' residence, doing small repair jobs and supervising and teaching in the woodworking shop.

Curly accepts cash, cheques, and Visa for his furniture. For all his products, he uses fine wood that he buys when a customer places an order. Customer deposits pay for these purchases. All customers pay 13 percent HST on purchases.

For some business purchases, Curly uses a credit card. He also has accounts set up with local lumber supply stores. Other supplies that he purchases regularly include nails, screws, sandpaper of all grades, stains, finishing varnishes, and oils. His tools include small manual woodworking tools, as well as a variety of power saws, drills, and routers. Curly's Cabinets pays HST on all business-related purchases and on items that are not used directly to make furniture.

At the end of September 2012, Curly is ready to enter the last month of transactions for his fiscal year and close the books. He converted his accounting records to QuickBooks using the following:

- Chart of Accounts
- Trial Balance
- Vendor List
- Customer List
- Item List
- Accounting Procedures

Chart of Accounts

Curly's Cabinets

ASSETS

Bank
- 1020 Bank Chequing
- 1040 Bank Savings
- 1060 Bank Visa
- 1100 Petty Cash

Accounts Receivable
- 1200 Accounts Receivable

Other Current Assets
- 1210 Undeposited Funds
- 1260 Prepaid Insurance
- 1280 Prepaid Taxes
- 1300 Office and Computer Supplies
- 1320 Carpentry Supplies
- 1340 Lumber Inventory

Fixed Assets
- 1500 Business Truck:
- 1520 Cost

- 1540 Depreciation
- 1560 Computer Equipment:
- 1580 Cost
- 1600 Depreciation
- 1620 Carpentry Tools & Equipment:
- 1640 Cost
- 1660 Depreciation
- 1680 Shop:
- 1700 Cost
- 1720 Depreciation

LIABILITIES

Accounts Payable
- 2100 Accounts Payable

Credit Card
- 2200 Visa Payable

Other Current Liabilities
- 2260 Bank Loan
- 2300 HST Payable

Long Term Liabilities
- 2720 Long Term Loan
- 2740 Mortgage Payable

EQUITY
- 3220 Capital, Charles Cutter
- 3260 Drawings, Charles Cutter
- 3500 Retained Earnings

INCOME
- 4100 Revenue from Sales
- 4140 Sales Credits and Allowances
- 4160 Sales Discounts
- 4180 Freight Revenue
- 4200 Revenue from Interest
- 4250 Sales Tax Compensation

EXPENSE

Cost of Goods Sold
- 5040 Lumber Used
- 5060 Carpentry Supplies Used

Expense
- 5120 Advertising and Promotion
- 5140 Purchase Discounts
- 5180 Office & Computer Supplies Used
- 5200 Depreciation Expense
- 5220 Maintenance Expenses
- 5240 Insurance Expense
- 5260 Interest Expense
- 5280 Property Tax Expense
- 5340 Hydro Expense
- 5360 Telephone Expense
- 5380 Truck Expenses

Curly's Cabinets

AS AT SEPTEMBER 30, 2012

Account	Debits	Credits	Account	Debits	Credits
1020 Bank Chequing	$23,540.00		2720 Long Term Loan		$ 25,000.00
1040 Bank Savings	42,180.00		2740 Mortgage Payable		30,000.00
1060 Bank Visa	4,385.00		3220 Capital, Charles Cutter		117,203.00
1100 Petty Cash	460.00		3260 Drawings, Charles Cutter	$ 22,000.00	
1200 Accounts Receivable	4,730.00		4100 Revenue from Sales		81,410.00
1210 Undeposited Funds	14,280.00		4140 Sales Credits and Allowances	660.00	
1260 Prepaid Insurance	2,400.00		4160 Sales Discounts	720.00	
1280 Prepaid Taxes	1,260.00		4180 Freight Revenue		750.00
1300 Office and Computer Supplies	685.00		4200 Revenue from Interest		710.00
1320 Carpentry Supplies	620.00		4250 Sales Tax Compensation		320.00
1340 Lumber Inventory	1,290.00		5040 Lumber Used	3,890.00	
1520 Business Truck:Cost	18,000.00		5060 Carpentry Supplies Used	465.00	
1540 Business Truck:Depreciation		$ 5,400.00	5120 Advertising and Promotion	1,295.00	
1580 Computer Equipment:Cost	6,000.00		5140 Purchase Discounts		495.00
1600 Computer Equipment:Depreciation		1,800.00	5180 Office & Computer Supplies Used	370.00	
1640 Carpentry Tools & Equipment:Cost	30,000.00		5200 Depreciation Expense	17,200.00	
1660 Carpentry Tools & Equipment: Depreciation		6,000.00	5220 Maintenance Expenses	420.00	
1700 Shop:Cost	80,000.00		5240 Insurance Expense	6,600.00	
1720 Shop:Depreciation		4,000.00	5260 Interest Expense	4,520.00	
2100 Accounts Payable		6,420.00	5280 Property Tax Expense	880.00	
2200 Visa Payable		445.00	5340 Hydro Expense	1,320.00	
2260 Bank Loan		12,000.00	5360 Telephone Expense	1,650.00	
2300 HST Payable		2,247.00	5380 Truck Expenses	2,380.00	
				$294,200.00	$294,200.00

Vendor Information

Curly's Cabinets

Vendor Name (Contact)	Address	Phone No. Fax No.	E-mail Business No.	Terms Credit Limit
Hydro Two (N. Power)	45 Turbine St. Lindsay, ON K9F 7J9	Tel: (705) 478-2300	npower@hydro2.ca	net 10 $500.00
Kawartha Building Supplies (Markus Sanderling or Nabir)	200 Sylvan Cres., Peterborough, ON K7G 4F5	Tel: (705) 556-0987 Alt: (705) 556-3821 Fax: (705) 556-7743	msanderling@kbs.com 369 466 509	1/10, n/30 $10,000.00
Kawartha Lumber (Freya Pine)	600 Cherry St. Lindsay, ON K9C 5S8	Tel: (705) 676-2929 Alt: (705) 877-3009 Fax: (705) 676-3388	sales@kawarthalumber.com 321 354 812	net 30 $10,000.00
Lindsay's Hardware & Paint (Lindsay Painter or Joel)	155 Millwood Rd. Lindsay, ON K9F 4B9	Tel: (705) 699-8191 Fax: (705) 698-3882	lindsays@shaw.com 125 843 782	1/10, n/30 $3,000.00
Northern Telecom (Bea Hurd)	5 Digital Circle Lindsay, ON K9F 4D6	Tel: (705) 510-2355		net 15 $500.00
Otto's Autos (Otto Ford)	45 Driver Route Lindsay, ON K9B 3G9	Tel: (705) 677-4821		due on receipt
Receiver General				quarterly remittance

Outstanding Vendor Transactions

Curly's Cabinets

Vendor Name	Date	Terms	Due Date	Invoice No./ Cheque No.	Amount
Kawartha Lumber	Sep. 12/12	net 30	Oct. 12/12	KL-2339	$4,280.00
Lindsay's Hardware & Paint	Sep. 24/12	1/10, n/30	Oct. 24/12	LHP-3011	$2,140.00
				Grand Total	$6,420.00

Customer Information

Curly's Cabinets

Customer Name (Contact)	Address	Phone No. Fax No.	E-mail Preferred Payment	Terms Credit Limit
Bayler, Lucas (Lucas Bayler)	11 Router Ave. Lindsay, ON K9P 4D6	Tel: (705) 678-1391	bayler_23@hotmail.com cheque	1/5, n/30 $5,000.00
Cash Sales			cash	due on receipt
Doze, Conn (Conn Doze)	88 Walnut Grove Lindsay, ON K9N 4F7	Tel: (705) 659-3773	condoze@istar.com cheque	1/5, n/30 $5,000.00
Flatte, R. Rapindra or Jason Flatte	499 Oakwood Ave. Lindsay, ON K9G 4D2	Tel: (705) 688-7191 Fax: (705) 688-7191	rflatte@sympatico.ca cheque	1/5, n/30 $5,000.00
Frame, Alva (Alva Frame)	22 Elm St. Lindsay, ON K9N 4N4	Tel: (705) 678-3298	Aframe@inet.com cheque	1/5, n/30 $5,000.00
House, M. T. M. T. or Alan House	12 Pinecrest Dr., Lindsay, ON K9T 2B6	Tel: (705) 664-8921 Alt: (905) 884-8200	mthouse@hotmail.com credit card	due on receipt $5,000.00
Nailer, Benchley (Benchley Nailer)	25A Beech St. Lindsay, ON K9T 4D2	Tel: (705) 566-4577	bnailer@interlog.com credit card	due on receipt $5,000.00

Outstanding Customer Transactions

Curly's Cabinets

Customer Name	Date	Terms	Type	Number	Amount	Balance Owing
Cash Sales	Sep. 28/12	due on receipt	Cash sale	184	$230.00	$ 0.00
Lucas Bayler	Sep. 18/12	1/5, n/30	Invoice	448	$3,600.00	3,600.00
Conn Doze	Sep. 30/12		Deposit cheque	510	$3,000.00	−3,000.00
R. Flatte	Sep. 29/12		Deposit cheque	349	$2,000.00	
	Sep. 29/12	1/5, n/30	Invoice	456	$4,830.00	2,830.00
Alva Frame	Sep. 28/12		Deposit cheque	195	$1,000.00	
	Sep. 29/12	1/5, n/30	Invoice	457	$2,300.00	1,300.00
M. T. House	Sep. 30/12	due on receipt	Credit card sale	182	$4,600.00	0.00
Benchley Nailer	Sep. 30/12	due on receipt	Credit card sale	183	$3,450.00	0.00
					Grand Total	$4,730.00

Curly's Cabinets

Item	Description	Price	Tax Code	Account
NON-INVENTORY:				
Furniture	Custom-made wood furniture		H	4100 Revenue from Sales
Lumber	Raw lumber inventory		H	1320 Lumber Supplies (raw materials)
Hardware	Carpentry and woodworking supplies		H	1340 Carpentry Supplies (raw materials)
Advertising material			H	5120 Advertising and Promotion
OTHER CHARGES:				
Delivery	Delivery charge	$75.00	H	4180 Freight Revenue
Finance Charges	Finance Charges on Overdue Balance	18%	E	4200 Revenue from Interest
	(18% > 30 days, min. charge $25.00, grace period 5 days)			

Accounting Procedures

Taxes: HST

Curly's Cabinets pays 13 percent HST on all goods and services that it buys and charges 13 percent HST on all sales. It uses the regular method for remittance of the HST. The HST collected from customers is recorded as a liability in the *HST Payable* account. The HST paid to vendors is recorded in the *HST Payable* account as a decrease in liability to the Canada Revenue Agency. The sales tax is filed with the Receiver General for Canada by the last day of the month for the previous quarter, either including the balance owing or requesting a refund.

Account Terms

Account customers who pay by cheque receive a 1 percent discount if they settle their account within five days after completion of the work. The full balance is required within 30 days of the sale or completion of work. Finance charges at 18 percent per year are assessed when accounts are more than 30 days overdue, with a minimum charge of $25.00 and a five-day grace period. This revenue is credited to the *Revenue from Interest* account. No discount is available for credit card sales because of the fee attached to cards. Some vendors offer discounts for early payment.

Bank Deposits and Cheques

All cheques, credit card payments, and cash are held for weekly deposit. Cheques are manually prepared at the time of the transaction.

Estimates, Orders, and Deposits

Curly provides estimates on request. When customers decide to order furniture based on the estimate, they pay a 25 percent deposit so that Curly can buy the lumber needed to make the furniture. Some vendors also require deposits.

Delivery Charges

Customers can pay a flat rate of $75.00 plus HST to have their furniture delivered. Not all customers choose the delivery service. Delivery is set up as a sales item and is entered on invoices, estimates, and sales receipts just like any other item.

Supplies

At the end of each month, Curly counts the supplies left in his shop and completes adjusting entries for the cost of lumber and other supplies used. Depreciation is entered at the end of each month.

Instructions

1. Using the Chart of Accounts, the Trial Balance, and other information, you will record entries for source documents for October 2012 using QuickBooks. You will find the source documents marked with an SD beside them and listed as you work through the chapter. The procedures for entering each new type of transaction introduced in this chapter are outlined in step-by-step instructions. Additional source documents will be provided, allowing you to have more practice entering transactions. If you have used this textbook in the past and would prefer to skip the step-by-step instructions and work only with a list of source documents, refer to the CD in the back of the textbook for the list of source documents for this chapter.

2. After you have finished making your entries, **print** the **reports and graphs for October 2012** as indicated on the following printing form:.

Notes
Instructions for banking reports begin on page 452.

REPORTS FOR OCTOBER 2012

Lists
- ☐ Account Listing
- ☐ Customer Phone List
- ☐ Customer Contact List
- ☐ Vendor Phone List
- ☐ Vendor Contact List
- ☐ Item Listing
- ☐ Item Price List

Company & Financial
- ☑ Balance Sheet Standard at Oct. 31 and Nov. 01
- ☑ Profit & Loss Standard from Oct. 01 to Oct. 31
- ☐ Expenses by Vendor
- ☐ Income by Customer

Accountant & Taxes
- ☑ Trial Balance at Oct. 31 and Nov. 01
- ☐ General Ledger
- ☑ Journal from Oct. 01 to Oct. 31
- ☐ Transaction List by Date
- ☐ Transaction Detail by Account

Other
- ☐ Custom Summary Report
- ☐ Custom Transaction Detail Report
- ☐ Transaction History
- ☐ Transaction Journal

Vendor
- ☑ A/P Aging Detail at Oct. 31
- ☐ Vendor Balance
- ☐ Unpaid Bills
- ☐ Transaction List by Vendor

Purchases
- ☐ Purchases by Vendor
- ☐ Purchases by Item
- ☐ Transaction List by Vendor
- ☐ Open Purchase Orders by Vendor

Customer
- ☑ A/R Aging Detail at Oct. 31
- ☐ Customer Balance
- ☐ Open Invoices
- ☐ Collections Report
- ☐ Transaction List by Customer

Sales
- ☐ Sales by Customer
- ☐ Sales by Item
- ☐ Open Sales Orders by Customer

Banking
- ☑ Deposit Detail from Oct. 01 to Oct. 31
- ☑ Cheque Detail from Oct. 01 to Oct. 31 for 1020
- ☑ Missing Cheques for 1020
- ☐ Reconcile Discrepancy
- ☑ Previous Reconciliation for accounts 1020 and 2200

GRAPHS
- ☐ Income and Expense
- ☐ Net Worth
- ☐ Accounts Payable
- ☐ Accounts Receivable
- ☐ Sales

Making Deposits to Multiple Bank Accounts

Curly's Cabinets holds all cheques, cash, and credit card receipts from customers for later deposit. Because two bank accounts are used, you must make a separate deposit for each bank account and choose the items to be deposited to each bank account. Other than choosing the bank account, the deposit procedure is the same as the one described in Chapter 7 for a single account (see page 302).

The first transaction that we will enter is a deposit to the Bank Chequing account. Refer to the following source document as we work through the steps to enter it:

SD Instructions
Refer to the following source document and then follow the step-by-step instructions to enter it.

SD1: Memo #1

Dated October 1, 2012

Deposit the following undeposited cash and cheques to Bank Chequing account.

Cash from cash sale	$ 230.00
Cheque from Doze	3,000.00
Cheque from Flatte	2,000.00
Cheque from Frame	1,000.00
Total deposit	6,230.00
Owner withdraws cash for personal use	200.00
Net deposit	$6,030.00

You can enter deposits by selecting the Record Deposits icon in the Banking section of the Home page, or by choosing the Banking menu and then clicking Make Deposits.

1. **Start**   **QuickBooks** and **open** the **file** for Curly's Cabinets

Notes
You can also choose the Banking menu and click Make Deposits to start the deposit procedure.

2. **Click**   the **Record Deposits icon**   in the Banking section of the Home page to open the Payments to Deposit window:

Figure 9-1

Six payments are ready to be deposited. This list makes it easy to select the payments that should be deposited to each account when the business has more than one bank account. Initially, all types of payments are on the same list, but we can choose specific types of payments for the list. We will deposit the cheques and cash to the *Bank Chequing* account and the Visa payments to the *Bank Visa* account. First, we will record the *Bank Chequing* account deposits, so we will select the cheques and cash. You can click the individual items for the deposit from this all-inclusive list or choose to show only one type of payment.

3. Click   the **drop-down arrow** in the View Payment Method Type field to view the payment methods that can be selected:

Figure 9-2

Notice that cash and cheques are combined on this list because most businesses use their primary chequing account for depositing both.

4. Click   **Cash and Cheque** as the payment method to refine the list:

Payments to Deposit   ✕

Select View

View payment method type   Cash and Cheque ▼   What are payment method views?

Select Payments to Deposit

✓	Date	Time	Type	No.	Payment Method	Name	Amount
	09/28/2012		RCPT	184	Cash	Cash Sales	230.00
	09/28/2012		PMT	195	Cheque	Frame, Alva	1,000.00
	09/29/2012		PMT	349	Cheque	Flatte, R.	2,000.00
	09/30/2012		PMT	510	Cheque	Doze, Conn	3,000.00

0 of 4 payments selected for deposit   **Payments Subtotal**   0.00

Select All   Select None

OK   Cancel   Help

Figure 9-3

You can select the individual items to be deposited by clicking anywhere on a transaction line, or you can select all the items at once. We want to include all items.

5. **Click**   the **Select All button**. Checkmarks appear beside each item in the ✓ column

6. **Click**   OK to advance to the next screen:

Notes

You can remove a deposit from the Make Deposits form by selecting a receipt, then choosing the Edit menu and clicking Delete Line.

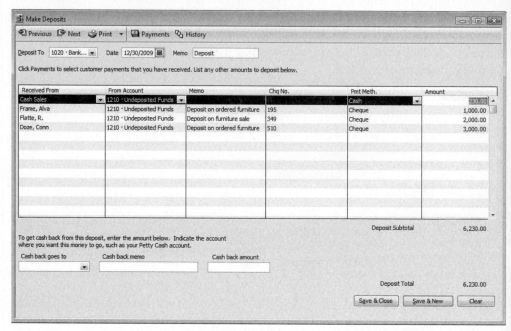

Figure 9-4

If you made an error when selecting the payments for deposit, click the Payments button to return to the Payments to Deposit form and modify the payments selected.

The four payments we selected are listed on the deposit form and the total deposit amount is shown at the bottom of the form. Account *1020 - Bank Chequing* should be selected in the Deposit To field at the top of the form. The Deposit To field is used to select the account to which you are depositing the payments. We will need to change the account for the second deposit.

The fields at the bottom of the form allow you to record a cash withdrawal from the deposit. If part of the total payment amount is taken in cash at the time of the deposit, you should complete these fields by entering the amount of cash, a memo or an explanation of the use of the funds, and the account that the cash should be credited to — often a *Petty Cash* or a *Drawings* account. The owner is withdrawing $200.00 from this deposit for personal use.

7. **Check**   that account **1020 - Bank Chequing** is selected as the Deposit To account

8. **Enter**   **10/01/12** as the date of the deposit

9. **Click**   the **drop-down arrow** in the Cash back goes to field to view the account list:

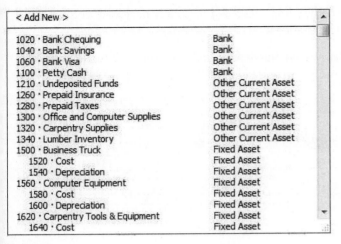

< Add New >	
1020 · Bank Chequing	Bank
1040 · Bank Savings	Bank
1060 · Bank Visa	Bank
1100 · Petty Cash	Bank
1210 · Undeposited Funds	Other Current Asset
1260 · Prepaid Insurance	Other Current Asset
1280 · Prepaid Taxes	Other Current Asset
1300 · Office and Computer Supplies	Other Current Asset
1320 · Carpentry Supplies	Other Current Asset
1340 · Lumber Inventory	Other Current Asset
1500 · Business Truck	Fixed Asset
1520 · Cost	Fixed Asset
1540 · Depreciation	Fixed Asset
1560 · Computer Equipment	Fixed Asset
1580 · Cost	Fixed Asset
1600 · Depreciation	Fixed Asset
1620 · Carpentry Tools & Equipment	Fixed Asset
1640 · Cost	Fixed Asset

Figure 9-5

Accounts are listed in numerical order as follows for Curly's Cabinets:

- 1000 Assets
- 2000 Liabilities
- 3000 Equity
- 4000 Revenue
- 5000 Expense

Notes

You can use any numbering system that you want in QuickBooks. We will use the same numbering system for all company files in this text.

10. Scroll down   the list and **select** account **3260 - Drawings, Charles Cutter**

11. Press   ⟨tab⟩ to advance to the Cash back memo field

12. Type   **Owner, personal use**

13. Press   ⟨tab⟩ to advance to the Cash back amount field

14. Type   **200**

15. Press   ⟨tab⟩ to update the Deposit Total and complete the form as shown:

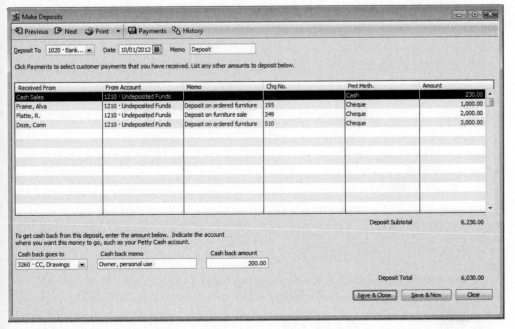

Received From	From Account	Memo	Chq No.	Pmt Meth.	Amount
Cash Sales	1210 · Undeposited Funds			Cash	230.00
Frame, Alva	1210 · Undeposited Funds	Deposit on ordered furniture	195	Cheque	1,000.00
Flatte, R.	1210 · Undeposited Funds	Deposit on furniture sale	349	Cheque	2,000.00
Doze, Conn	1210 · Undeposited Funds	Deposit on ordered furniture	510	Cheque	3,000.00

Deposit Subtotal   6,230.00

To get cash back from this deposit, enter the amount below. Indicate the account where you want this money to go, such as your Petty Cash account.

Cash back goes to	Cash back memo	Cash back amount
3260 · CC, Drawings	Owner, personal use	200.00

Deposit Total   6,030.00

Figure 9-6

Check the form carefully before proceeding and make any necessary corrections. Refer to page 305 if you need assistance with the corrections.

16. Click   **Save & New** to save the deposit and open the updated Payments to Deposit form:

Figure 9-7

Making a Second Deposit Entry

The second deposit includes the two Visa receipts, and they should be deposited to the *Bank Visa* account. These are the only two items left on the Payments to Deposit form.

Refer to the following source document as we work through the steps to enter it:

SD Practice
Continue to develop your skills by entering the following source document(s).

SD2: Memo #2

Dated October 1, 2012

Deposit all credit card receipts to the Bank Visa account.

Visa sale to House	$4,600.00
Visa sale to Nailer	3,450.00
Total deposit	$8,050.00

1. Click   the **Select All button** to select both payments and add the ✓ beside them

2. Click   **OK** to continue to the Make Deposits form

These payments need to be deposited to the *Bank Visa* account so we need to change the account in the Deposit To field.

3. Click   the **drop-down arrow** in the Deposit To field to view the accounts available to select:

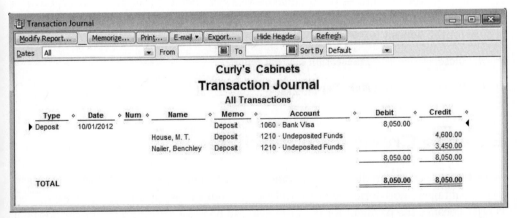

Figure 9-8

4. **Click**   **1060 - Bank Visa** to select the correct bank account

The date should be 10/01/12 from the previous deposit and no cash is taken back so the transaction is complete.

5. **Click**   **Save & New** to save the deposit and leave the Make Deposits form open

The Payments to Deposit form does not open after saving the deposit because all the payments have been deposited. Before entering the next transaction, we will look at the journal entry that QuickBooks created for the deposits.

Reviewing the Journal Entry

Let's take a look at the journal entries that we have created from the two deposits. We will review the journal entry for the Visa deposit first.

1. **Click**   the **Previous button** 🔁 Previous to view the Visa deposit

2. **Press**   ⌨ *ctrl* + **Y** to view the Transaction Journal report:

Figure 9-9

The journal entry shows the transfer of funds. QuickBooks has debited the *Bank Visa* account for the full amount of the deposit. The entries for the *Undeposited Funds* account are credits to clear the amounts from the account — the original entries were debits to the *Undeposited Funds* account (the holding account). Customer names are also included so that the journal record for the deposit is complete.

3. **Close**   the **Transaction Journal report** to return to the Make Deposits form

Let's look at the Transaction Journal report for the first deposit that we made. When you use the Previous and Next buttons on the Make Deposits form, you scroll through transactions entered for the account in the Deposit To field. To view the first deposit that we made, we need to select the Bank Chequing account in the Deposit To field before using the Previous button.

4. **Click**   the **Save & New button**

5. **Click**   the **drop-down arrow** in the Deposit To field

6. **Choose**   **1020 - Bank Chequing**

7. **Click**   **the Previous button** ⬅ Previous to view the bank deposit

8. **Press**   `ctrl` **+ Y** to view the Transaction Journal report:

Figure 9-10

The journal entry shows that the bank account has been debited for the full amount of the deposit, and *Drawings, Charles Cutter* has been debited for the amount of cash held back. The entries for the *Undeposited Funds* account are credits to clear the amounts from the account — the original entries were debits to the *Undeposited Funds* account (the holding account). Customer names are also included so that the journal record for the deposit is complete.

9. **Close**   the **Transaction Journal report**

10. **Close**   the **Make Deposits form**

Entering Credit Card Purchases

Many businesses use credit cards for some of their business purchases. This has at least two advantages: short-term credit is available without setting up an account with a vendor because the payment for the purchase can be made later, and the buyer does not need to carry cash. When the credit card bill arrives, it provides a concise summary of business transactions. For most cards, if the balance is paid in full before the due date, no additional charges are incurred. Thus, the credit card provides an interest-free short-term loan. Additional credit cards may be obtained on the same account for employees as well, making it easy for employees to cover legitimate business expenses without the need for personal reimbursement.

Credit card purchases are like cash purchases (writing cheques) because the payment is made at the time of the purchase. Credit card transactions are entered on the Enter Credit Card Charges form.

The next transaction that we will enter is a credit card purchase. Refer to the following source document as we work through the steps to enter it:

SD3: Credit Card Purchase #OA-4550

Dated October 1, 2012

To Otto's Autos, $180.00 plus $23.40 HST for gasoline, oil change, and minor repairs. Invoice totalling $203.40 was paid in full by Visa.

SD Instructions
Refer to the following source document and then follow the step-by-step instructions to enter it.

1. **Click**   the **Enter Credit Card Charges icon** ![Enter Credit Card Charges] from the Banking section of the Home page to open the Credit Card Charges form:

Notes
You can also open the Credit Card Charges form by choosing the Banking menu and then Enter Credit Card Charges.

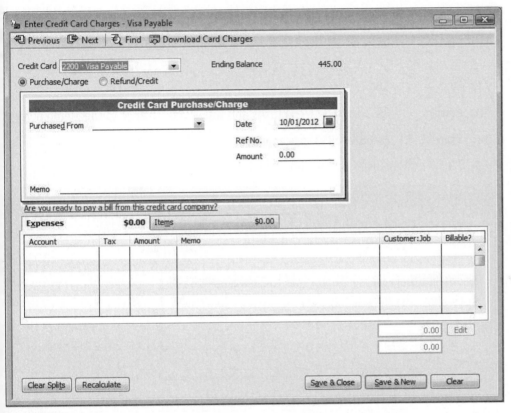

Figure 9-11

Curly's Cabinets uses only one credit card for business purchases, the Visa card, so this account is the default for credit card charges. As you add different types of credit cards, they will be available for selection from the Credit Card drop-down list, and you can add a new card from this field as well. The balance owing on the card is shown for reference.

Each type of credit card should be linked to a different liability account. The account for Visa, *Visa Payable*, is added to the title bar of the Enter Credit Card Charges form.

The form also includes the option to enter the transaction as a Purchase/Charge or a Refund/Credit. When entering Visa purchases, select the Purchase/Charge option and when entering returns or allowances, select the Refund/Credit option.

This form is the same as the Write Cheques form and the transactions are entered the same way.

Notes
When you choose Refund/Credit as the type of transaction, you will create a debit entry to the Visa Payable account and reduce the amount owing. Returns and credits are covered in Chapter 12.

2. **Click**   the **drop-down arrow** in the Purchased From field

Notice that this list includes all customers and vendors, just as the Pay to the Order of field does in the Write Cheques form. Both customers and vendors are listed because payments can be made to both customers and vendors.

3. **Choose**   **Otto's Autos**

We will add the invoice number as the reference number.

4. **Press**   (tab) to advance to the date field

5. **Type**   **10/01/12** if necessary

6. **Press**   (tab) to the Ref No. field

7. **Type**   **OA-4550**

8. **Click**   the **drop-down arrow** in the Account field

9. **Choose**   **Truck Expenses** as the expense account for the transaction

10. **Press**   (tab) twice to advance to the Amount field and skip the tax code (H should be displayed)

11. **Type**   **180**

12. **Press**   (tab) to update the taxes and totals and advance to the Memo field

13. **Type**   **gasoline, oil change, repairs**

14. The completed transaction should be displayed as shown here:

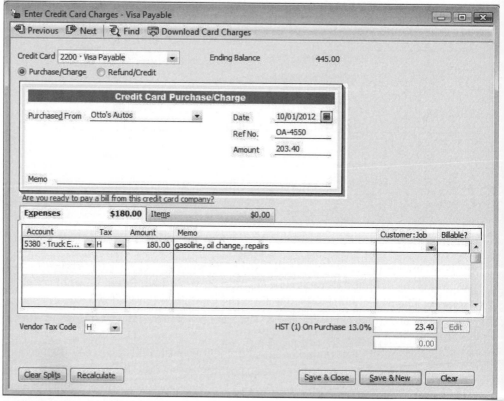

Figure 9-12

15. **Check**   your **work** and **make corrections** if necessary, just as you would correct any other cheque or cash purchase (see page 61).

16. **Click**   **Save & New**

17. **Click**   Previous to display the entry again

18. Press `ctrl` **+ Y** to view the Transaction Journal report:

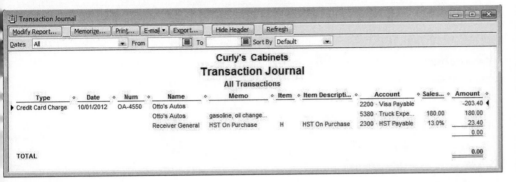

Figure 9-13

Notice that the *Visa Payable* account is credited for the total amount of the credit card charge instead of the bank account. The *expense account* and the *HST Payable account* are debited just as they would be in a cash purchase.

19. Close the **Transaction Journal report**

20. Close the **Enter Credit Card Charges form**

Paying a Credit Card Bill

When a credit card bill arrives, it should be reconciled and paid. The amounts on the credit card bill may be different from the amount in the account's register in QuickBooks. The credit card bill amount may be higher — it may include interest charges assessed on previous purchases that were not fully paid before the due date, interest charges for cash advances, or monthly or annual fees associated with the credit card. None of these amounts is known until the credit card bill is received. The bill amount can also be lower if purchases were made after the credit card's billing date. These purchases will appear on the next statement. Curly's Cabinets' bill from Visa includes an amount for interest charges for a cash advance from the previous month. The single purchase we entered was made after the credit card billing date, so it is not included in the current amount owing.

Credit card bills are paid as part of the reconciliation process. The Reconcile icon found in the Banking section of the Home page will open the Begin Reconciliation form.

The next transaction that we will enter is a credit card bill payment. Refer to the following source document as we work through the steps to enter it:

SD4: Credit Card Bill Payment

Dated October 1, 2012

To Kawartha Bank Visa (use Quick Add for new Other payee), $451.00 in payment of account, including $445.00 for purchases before September 30 and $6.00 interest charges for cash advances. The credit card bill is paid in full with cheque #502. Create a new Expense account: 5130 Credit Card Fees.

1. Click the **Reconcile icon** to open the Begin Reconciliation form shown here:

Notes
The default date for the
statement is the end of the
month before the calendar
date (your current system or
computer date).

Figure 9-14

The first bank account is shown as the default account in the Account field. Fields for interest and expenses normally associated with a bank account are displayed on the form. The opening account balance is also shown in the beginning balance field. If you were reconciling a bank statement, it would list the information required for the fields on this form. Since we are reconciling a credit card statement, we need to select the *Visa Payable* account from the account list.

2. **Click**   the **drop-down arrow** in the Account field

3. **Click**   **2200 - Visa Payable**

4. The fields displayed on the form are modified for the credit card account as shown:

Figure 9-15

The reconciliation form for a credit card account includes only the expense portion. The information required to complete this form is available from the credit card statement.

5. **Press**   ⟨tab⟩ to advance to the Statement Date field

6. **Type**   **10/01/12**

7. **Press**   ⟨tab⟩ to advance to the Ending Balance field

Enter the amount currently due according to the credit card statement in the Ending Balance field.

8. **Type**   **451**

9. **Press**   (tab) to advance to the Finance Charge field

Credit card fees may be associated with using the credit card and will vary from one credit card company or type of credit card to another. Some credit cards have no fees. Charges may also arise from interest owing on unpaid account balances or on cash advances. Curly's Cabinets has incurred an interest charge of $6.00 for a cash advance in the previous month. We need to create a new account for these charges. We can create it on-the-fly as we do in other forms.

10. **Type**   **6**

11. **Press**   (tab) to advance to the Date field

12. **Type**   **10/01/12**

13. **Press**   (tab) to advance to Account field

14. **Type**   **5130**

15. **Press**   (tab) to view the Account Not Found message:

Notes
The ending balance is $451.00 – this is $445.00 for previous purchases (the opening balance for the account) plus $6.00 in additional charges.

Notes
You can add a new account on the fly from any account field in QuickBooks.

Figure 9-16

16. **Click**   **Set Up** to add the new account:

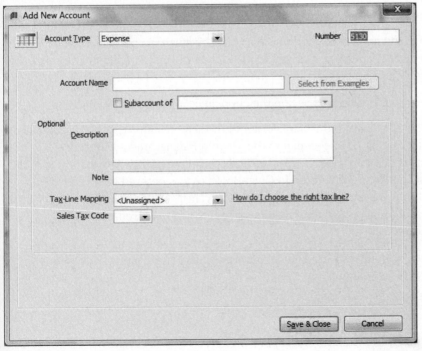

Figure 9-17

Notice that the Add New Account form has fields for account number and name. The account type is correctly selected as Expense so we do not need to change it. The account number is also entered. We need to add the account name.

17. **Click**   the **Account Name field**

18. **Type**   **Credit Card Fees**

19. **Click**   **Save & Close** to save the account and return to the Begin Reconciliation form with the account information entered

20. **Click**   **Continue** to advance to the detailed transaction listing for the account:

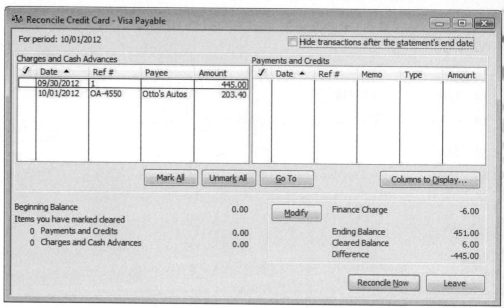

Figure 9-18

Notes
Click Leave in the Reconcile window to save the reconciliation before finishing. This allows you to return to the reconciliation where you left off and to make changes and corrections later.

Because we have not yet completed many transactions in QuickBooks, and this is the first time we are reconciling the credit card account, the transactions list is not complete. The opening balance entered on 09/30/12 for the *Visa Payable* account is displayed. The credit card charge that we just entered for Otto's Auto is also displayed; however, it is not included in the statement balance because the purchase occurred after the billing date for the credit card. It will be cleared on the next credit card statement so you should leave it unchecked.

21. **Click**   the **check box** beside the opening balance amount of $445.00

The details in the lower right-hand corner of the screen summarize the reconciliation. We have an Ending Balance equal to the Cleared Balance and a Difference of zero. If the difference is not zero, you will need to find the source of the discrepancy. It could be that a transaction was not entered in QuickBooks or was entered incorrectly. The credit card company also may have made a mistake. These errors should be followed up by checking the original credit card receipts and contacting the credit card company if necessary to correct the error.

22. **Check**   your **work** carefully and **make** any necessary **corrections** before continuing

23. Click   **Reconcile Now** to view the Make Payment screen:

Figure 9-19

You can write a cheque immediately to pay the bill or to enter the payment due as a bill. The choice you make will determine which screen you see next. We want to write a cheque for payment now so the default selection is correct.

24. Click   **OK**

25. If you see a message about online banking, **click OK** to continue

26. The Select Reconciliation Report screen is displayed:

Figure 9-20

Now you should choose what kind of report you want and whether you want to display or print it. You can choose the summary, or the detail report, or both. Both is selected as the default. We will display the Detail Report.

27. Click   **Detail** to change the report selection

28. Click   the **Display button**

Notes

You can undo the last reconciliation if necessary by selecting the Undo Last Reconciliation button on the Begin Reconciliation form.

⚠ WARNING!

You cannot make changes to the reconciliation after you click the Reconcile Now button, so check your work carefully before completing this step. You may want to make a backup copy of the file before starting the reconciliation procedure. This way, you can restore the backup file if you have made a mistake, such as clearing a transaction in error.

29. The following status message is displayed:

Figure 9-21

This status message lets you know what information will be provided in the report.

30. Click the box beside **Do not display this message in the future** option to bypass this message in the future

31. Click **OK** to view the Reconciliation Detail report:

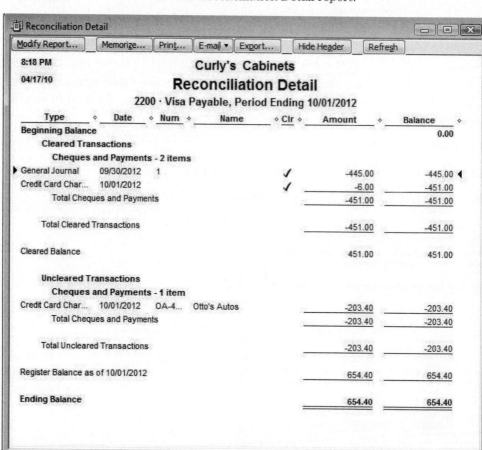

Notes
The Ending Balance amount for the Register is the balance before making the payment and includes the finance charge.

Figure 9-22

The report includes all cleared transactions — in this case, the finance charges, any uncleared transaction amounts, and the ending register balance as of 10/01/2012. Notice that the finance charges are included in the register balance. The new credit card charge is shown as an Uncleared Transaction. It will be cleared in the next reconciliation performed for this account.

The next step is to write the cheque to pay the bill.

32. Close the **Reconciliation Detail report** using ▮ ✕ ▮

33. The Write Cheques form will be displayed:

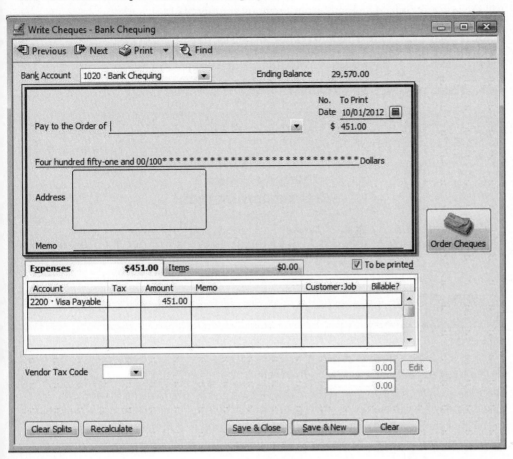

Figure 9-23

The cheque has been partially completed with the information that is already available — the date, amount and account. You can change the date or amount. QuickBooks assumes that you are paying the full amount that is due. Because this is the first reconciliation, some details are still missing. The Visa bank is not yet on the list of payees so we need to add it. We also need to add the cheque number to start the correct cheque sequence number for cheques in this company data file.

34.	**Click**	the **Pay to the Order of** field
35.	**Type**	**Kawartha Bank Visa**
36.	**Press**	(tab)
37.	**Choose**	**Quick Add** to add the name to the payee list
38.	**Choose**	**Other** to indicate that this is not a vendor, a customer, or an employee
39.	**Click**	**OK** to return to the cheque
40.	**Click**	the **check box** beside **To be printed** to turn this option off
41.	**Click**	the **No. field**
42.	**Type**	**502**

If you are making a partial payment, edit the amount in the Amount field and click the Recalculate button to update the amount in the cheque portion of the form.

When you pay a partial amount, the ending balance on the next month's statement will include any unpaid amounts from previous statements.

43. Click   **Save & New** to record the payment

44. Click   ⬅️ Previous   to view the cheque again

45. Press   ctrl + **Y** to view the Transaction Journal report:

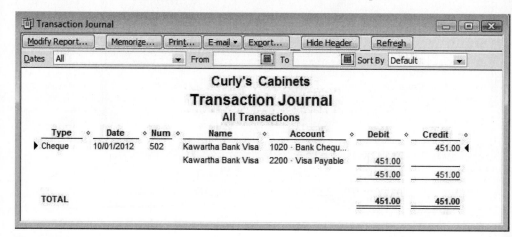

Figure 9-24

Notice that this Transaction Journal report shows only the cheque portion of the transaction because we were in the Write Cheques window when we pressed ctrl + Y. The finance charges were recorded when you clicked Reconcile Now and will appear in the Journal Report for the period they were entered and in the register and ledger reports for the *Credit Card Fees* and *Visa Payable* accounts, the relevant accounts.

46. Close   the **Transaction Journal** window

47. Close   the **Write Cheques** window

Source Documents:

Now that you have learned some of the new concepts introduced in this chapter, enter the following source documents. You may need to refer to previous chapters for additional information:

October 3 – October 7, 2012

SD5: Credit Card Sales Receipt #185

Dated October 3, 2012

To M. T. House, $1,450.00 plus $188.50 HST for a pine table and a deacon's bench. Invoice totalling $1,638.50 was paid in full by Visa and held for deposit.

SD6: Purchase Invoice #NT-582

Dated October 4, 2012

From Northern Telecom, $88.00 plus $11.44 HST for one month of telephone and Internet service. Invoice totals $99.44. Terms: Net 15 days.

SD7: Credit Card Purchase Invoice #P-7530

Dated October 4, 2012

From Papers Plus (set up new vendor), $145.00 plus $18.85 HST for computer and office supplies. Invoice totalling $163.85 was paid in full by credit card.

SD8: Cash Receipt #51

Dated October 4, 2012

From Alva Frame, cheque #215 for $1,277.00 in payment of account, including the discount for early payment. Apply credits, discount, and payment to invoice #457.

SD9: Cash Receipt #52

Dated October 4, 2012

From R. Flatte, cheque #364 for $2,781.70 in payment of account, including the discount for early payment. Apply credits, discount, and payment to invoice #456.

SD10: Cheque Copy #503

Dated October 4, 2012

To Lindsay's Hardware & Paint, $2,118.60 in payment of account, including the discount for early payment. Reference invoice #LHP-3011.

Notes
Do not print cheques. You can automatically assign cheque numbers or enter them yourself.

SD11: Purchase Invoice #KL-4811

Dated October 5, 2012

From Kawartha Lumber, $945.00 plus $122.85 HST for cherry lumber to build a bookcase and dressers. Purchase invoice totals $1,067.85. Terms: Net 30.

SD12: Sales Invoice #461

Dated October 6, 2012

To Conn Doze, $7,900.00 plus $1,027.00 HST for a maple dining room table, chairs, a buffet, and a hutch. Delivery charge is $75.00 plus HST. Invoice totals $9,011.75. Terms: 1/5, n/30. Allow customer to exceed credit limit.

Notes
Customer tax codes are not used. Customers are listed in alphabetic order by last name. Remember to reset the invoice number to start at 461.

SD13: Sales Estimate #35

Dated October 6, 2012

To M. T. House, $3,470.00 plus $451.10 HST for a custom-built walnut bedroom set, including night tables and a headboard. Estimate totals $3,921.10. Terms: 1/5, n/30 and 25 percent deposit on acceptance of estimate.

SD14: Visa Receipt #53

Dated October 6, 2012

From M. T. House, $1,000.00 as deposit on sales estimate #35, paid by credit card.

SD15: Visa Purchase Invoice #OA-6110

Dated October 6, 2012

From Otto's Autos, $50.00 plus $6.50 HST for gasoline for truck. Purchase invoice totalling $56.50 was paid in full by Visa. Memorize the transaction with weekly reminders starting 10/13/12.

SD16: Credit Card Sales #186

Dated October 7, 2012

To Mina Staples (set up a new customer), $1,800.00 plus $234.00 HST for a cherry bookcase. Delivery charge is $75.00 plus HST. Invoice totalling $2,118.75 was paid in full by Visa.

Notes
Mina Staples
33 Maple St.
Lindsay, ON K5F 7C5
Tel: (705) 798-1290
Alt: (705) 798-1220
Terms: 1/5, n/30
Credit limit: $4,000.00
Preferred payment: Visa

SD17: Cash Sales Receipt #187

Dated October 7, 2012

From cash sales customers, $540.00 plus $70.20 HST for a set of nesting tables. Invoice totalling $610.20 was paid in full by cash.

Notes
Remember to change the method of payment for the deposit from Staples.

October 8 – October 14, 2012

Notes
If your deposit amounts do not match the ones we show, check that you chose the correct method of payment for all receipts.

SD18: Memo #3

Dated October 8, 2012

From Owner: Deposit all cash and cheques to Bank Chequing account and deposit all credit card receipts to the Bank Visa account. Total deposits:

Bank Chequing	$4,668.90
Bank Visa	4,757.25

SD19: Purchase Order #18

Dated October 9, 2012

To Papers Plus, $170.00 plus $22.10 HST for business cards and promotional flyers to distribute at the craft show. Invoice totals $192.10. Terms: Due on receipt. Choose Advertising Material as the item.

SD20: Sales Estimate #36

Dated October 10, 2012

To Mina Staples, $2,600.00 plus $338.00 HST for matching cherry chests of drawers. Delivery charge is $75.00 plus HST. Estimate totals $3,022.75. Terms: 1/5, n/30 and 25 percent deposit on acceptance of estimate.

SD21: Purchase Invoice #LHP-3864

Dated October 11, 2012

From Lindsay's Hardware & Paint, $205.00 plus $26.65 HST for carpentry supplies including stains, polishes, and paints. Invoice totals $231.65. Terms: 1/10, n/30.

Notes
Remember to select the method of payment for all Cash Sales.

SD 22: Cash Receipt #54

Dated October 11, 2012

From Mina Staples, cheque #147 for $800.00 as the deposit on sales estimate #36.

SD23: Cash Receipt #55

Dated October 11, 2012

From Conn Doze, cheque #583 for $5,932.00 in payment of account, including the discount for early payment. Apply credits, discount, and payment to invoice #461.

SD24: Purchase Invoice #KL-5922

Dated October 12, 2012

From Kawartha Lumber, $1,300.00 plus $169.00 HST for lumber to build various furniture pieces. Purchase invoice totals $1,469.00. Terms: Net 30.

SD25: Visa Purchase Invoice #OA-7103

Dated October 12, 2012

From Otto's Autos, $230.00 plus $29.90 HST for truck tune-up. Purchase invoice totalling $259.90 was paid in full by Visa.

SD26: Purchase Invoice #SFE-4550

Dated October 12, 2012

From Something for Everyone (use Quick Add for new vendor), $1,300.00 plus $169.00 HST for rental of a craft show booth. Purchase invoice totals $1,469.00. Terms: Net 10. Create a new expense account: 5300 Rental Expense (tax code H).

SD27: Cheque Copy #504

Dated October 12, 2012

To Kawartha Lumber, $4,280.00 in payment of account. Reference invoice #KL-2339.

SD28: Visa Purchase Invoice #OA-7218

Dated October 13, 2012

From Otto's Autos, $50.00 plus $6.50 HST for gasoline. Purchase invoice totalling $56.50 was paid in full by Visa. Use the memorized transaction.

SD29: Cash Sales Receipt #188

Dated October 14, 2012

From cash sales customer, $470.00 plus $61.10 HST for a pair of end tables. Invoice totalling $531.10 was paid in full by cash.

SD30: Credit Card Sales Receipt #189

Dated October 14, 2012

From cash sales customer, $275.00 plus $35.75 HST for a pair of night tables. Invoice totalling $310.75 was paid in full by Visa.

SD31: Purchase Invoice #KBS-1003

Dated October 14, 2012

From Kawartha Building Supplies, $550.00 for lumber and $90.00 for hardware plus $83.20 HST to build an entertainment wall unit. Purchase invoice totals $723.20. Terms: 1/10, n/30.

October 15 – October 21, 2012

SD32: Memo #4

Dated October 15, 2012

From Owner: Deposit all cash and cheques to Bank Chequing account and deposit all credit card receipts to Bank Visa account. Total deposits:

Bank Chequing	$7,263.10
Bank Visa	310.75

SD33: Purchase Order #19

Dated October 16, 2012

To Kawartha Building Supplies, $1,200.00 plus $156.00 HST for a special order of lumber. Order totals $1,356.00. Terms: 1/10, n/30.

SD34: Sales Invoice #462

Dated October 16, 2012

To M. T. House, to fill estimate #35, $3,470.00 plus $451.10 HST for a custom-built walnut bedroom set including night tables and headboard. Invoice totals $3,921.10. Terms: 1/5, n/30. Change the customer's terms but do not save the changes (the new terms should not appear next time).

SD35: Credit Card Purchase Invoice #P-9321

Dated October 18, 2012

From Papers Plus, to fill purchase order #18, $170.00 plus $22.10 HST for business cards and promotional flyers to distribute at the craft show. Invoice totalling $192.10 was paid in full by Visa.

SD36: Purchase Invoice #HT-49901

Dated October 18, 2012

From Hydro Two, $120.00 plus $15.60 HST for hydro service for the shop for two months. Purchase invoice totals $135.60. Terms: Net 10.

> **Notes**
> Use the Carpentry Supplies account for the hardware purchase.

SD37: Cash Receipt #56

Dated October 19, 2012

From M. T. House, cheque #92 for $2,886.40, including the discount for early payment. Apply credits, discount, and payment to invoice #462. Remember to change the payment method.

SD38: Cheque Copy #505

Dated October 19, 2012

To Lindsay's Hardware & Paint, $229.60 in payment of account, including the discount for early payment. Reference invoice #LHP-3864.

SD39: Cheque Copy #506

Dated October 19, 2012

To Northern Telecom, $99.44 in payment of account. Reference invoice #NT-582.

SD40: Credit Card Sales Receipt #190

Dated October 20, 2012

From cash sales customer, $510.00 plus $66.30 HST for small bookshelves. Invoice totalling $576.30 was paid in full by Visa.

SD41: Visa Purchase Invoice #OA-7840

Dated October 20, 2012

From Otto's Autos, $50.00 plus $6.50 HST for gasoline. Purchase invoice totalling $56.50 was paid in full by Visa. Use the memorized transaction.

SD42: Sales Invoice #463

Dated October 21, 2012

To Mina Staples, to fill estimate #36, $2,600.00 plus $338.00 HST for a set of cherry chests of drawers. Delivery charge is $75.00 plus HST. Invoice totals $3,022.75. Terms: 1/5, n/30.

October 22 – October 28, 2012

SD43: Memo #5

Dated October 22, 2012

From Owner: Deposit all credit card receipts to the Bank Visa account. Total deposit:

Bank Chequing	$2,886.40
Bank Visa	576.30

SD44: Purchase Invoice #KBS-2191

Dated October 22, 2012

From Kawartha Building Supplies, to fill purchase order #19, $1,200.00 plus $156.00 HST for lumber. Purchase invoice totals $1,356.00. Terms: 1/10, n/30.

SD45: Cheque Copy #507

Dated October 22, 2012

To Something for Everyone, $1,469.00 in payment of the account. Reference invoice #SFE-4550.

SD46: Cheque Copy #508

Dated October 23, 2012

To Kawartha Building Supplies, $716.80 in payment of the account, including the discount for early payment. Reference invoice #KBS-1003.

SD47: Cheque Copy #509

Dated October 24, 2012

To Hydro Two, $135.60 in payment of the account. Reference invoice #HT-49901.

SD48: Cash Receipt #57

Dated October 24, 2012

From Mina Staples, cheque #159 for $2,196.00 in payment of the account, including the discount for early payment. Apply credits, discount, and payment to invoice #463. Remember to change the payment method.

SD49: Credit Card Sales Receipt #191–193

Dated October 25, 2012

From cash sales customers at the craft show for pre-made furniture items.
File cabinet: $410.00 plus $53.30 HST. Invoice totals $463.30.
Wall unit: $3,100.00 plus $403.00 HST. Invoice totals $3,503.00.
Book shelves: $1,650.00 plus $214.50 HST. Invoice totals $1,864.50.

All sales paid by Visa.

Notes
Enter the three credit card sales receipts as separate sales.

SD50: Cash Sales Receipts #194–196

Dated October 25, 2012

From cash sales customers at the craft show for pre-made furniture items.
Coffee table: $400.00 plus $52.00 HST. Invoice totals $452.00.
End table: $90.00 plus $11.70 HST. Invoice totals $101.70.
TV stand: $250.00 plus $32.50 HST. Invoice totals $282.50.

All sales paid by cash.

Notes
Enter the three cash sales receipts as separate sales.

SD51: Visa Purchase Invoice #OA-8223

Dated October 27, 2012

From Otto's Autos, $50.00 plus $6.50 HST for gasoline. Purchase invoice totalling $56.50 was paid in full by Visa. Use the memorized transaction.

SD52: Visa Purchase Invoice #OA-8229

Dated October 28, 2012

From Otto's Autos, $70.00 for emergency towing and $600.00 for truck battery plus $87.10 HST. Purchase invoice totalling $757.10 was paid in full by Visa.

October 29 – October 30, 2012

SD53: Memo #6

Dated October 30, 2012

From Owner: Deposit all cash and cheques to the Bank Chequing account and deposit all credit card receipts to the Bank Visa account. Total deposits:

Bank Chequing	$3,032.20
Owner withdraws Petty Cash for postage	50.00
Net deposit to Bank Chequing	$2,982.20
Bank Visa	$5,830.80

SD54: Cheque Copy #510

Dated October 30, 2012

To Kawartha Building Supplies, $1,344.00 in payment of account, including discount for early payment. Reference invoice #KBS-2191.

Dated October 30, 2012

From Woodworkers Credit Union, Preauthorized withdrawals were made for:

Mortgage ($45.00 principal and $205.00 interest)	$250.00
Bank loan ($140.00 principal and $90.00 interest)	230.00
Long term loan ($225.00 principal and $180.00 interest)	405.00

SD56: **Memo #7**

Dated October 30, 2012

From Owner: Complete adjusting entries for depreciation for October.

Business truck	$ 315.00
Computer equipment	105.00
Carpentry tools & equipment	400.00
Shop	315.00

SD57: **Memo #8**

Dated October 30, 2012

From Owner: Complete adjusting entries for supplies used during month.

Office and computer supplies	$ 140.00
Carpentry supplies	505.00
Lumber	2,800.00

Assessing Finance Charges

When customers fail to pay their accounts within the due date period, they may be charged interest on the overdue amounts. Curly's Cabinets charges 18 percent interest per year on accounts past the 30-day period. Interest charges are assessed at the end of each month. Lucas Bayler has an outstanding overdue account.

Although you can display or print various reports to find the overdue accounts, you can use the Finance Charges feature in QuickBooks to find overdue accounts directly.

The next transaction that we will enter is a finance charge on an overdue account. Refer to the following source document as we work through the steps to enter it:

SD58: **Memo #9**

Dated October 31, 2012

From Owner, Assess Finance charges on Bayler's overdue account.

Interest on overdue accounts is entered from the Finance Charges icon in the Customer section of the Home page.

1. **Click** the **Finance Charges icon** to open the Assess Finance Charges form:

Notes

The Collections Report, Open Invoices Report, and A/R Aging Reports will all show overdue accounts.

SD Instructions

Refer to the following source document and then follow the step-by-step instructions to enter it.

Notes

Overdue accounts are charged 18 percent interest, assessed from the invoice date. A minimum charge of $25.00 is applied to cover administrative costs.

Curly's Cabinets allows a five-day grace period after the due date before charging interest. This is entered as 35 days in the Finance Charges settings to allow the grace period to pass the original due date by five days.

Figure 9-25

If the date displayed in the Assessment Date field is earlier than the due date for all invoices, then there will be no invoices subject to finance charges displayed on the form. The date is selected so you can change it.

2. Type   **10/31/12**

3. Press   (tab) to refresh the information on the form

The finance charge of $76.34 on an overdue balance of $3,600.00 for Bayler is displayed on the form. He is charged interest for the period after the invoice date, September 18, as shown here:

Figure 9-26

You can change the finance amount charged if you want.

Practice entering different dates to view the effect on the finance charge. Try entering October 20, 2012 and October 24, 2012 to view the grace period expiration. Press ⓣⓐⓑ after entering a new date to update the calculations. Enter October 31, 2012 again before completing the next step.

4. Click   the **Assess Charges** button to complete the finance charge

The form will close and you will return to the Home page. QuickBooks has created an invoice for the finance charge and the amount is added to the customer's account. To view the effect of assessing the finance charges, you can look at the customer's outstanding invoices in the Receive Payments window.

5. Click   the **Receive Payments** icon

6. Choose   **Bayler, Lucas** to view the customer's outstanding invoices:

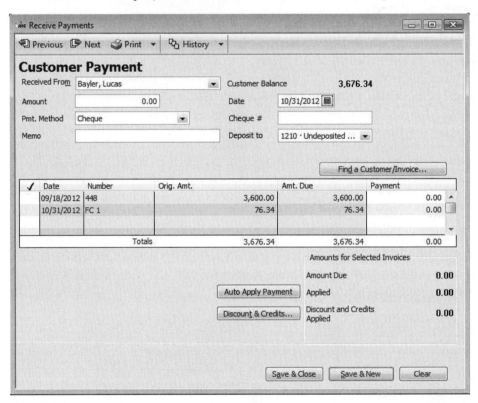

Figure 9-27

Notice that the second invoice represents the Finance Charge and has been given an invoice number of FC 1 automatically by QuickBooks.

When a customer pays their account, payments should be credited first to the finance charge and then to the invoice balance.

7. Click   the **Clear button** to remove the customer's information from the form

8. Close   the **Receive Payments** form

Let's take a look at the effect on the finance charges if Lucas Baylor does not pay his account.

9. Click   the **Finance Charges** icon again

10. Enter   **11/30/12** as the date

11. Press   ⓣⓐⓑ to update the information in the Access Finance Charges form:

Figure 9-28

A finance charge for the current month is added for Lucas Baylor and the date of the previous finance charge is displayed in the last finance charge column. Interest is not assessed on the previous interest charges.

12. **Click**   **Cancel** to close the Access Finance Charges form

Making Tax Remittances

After a business registers to collect taxes from customers, it must report on and remit these collections to the government on a regular basis. Depending on the size of the business, the reports may be required monthly, quarterly, or annually. With annual reporting, quarterly installments may be required as well. Curly's Cabinets files federal HST tax returns quarterly with the Receiver General of Canada.

You cannot return to the tax remittance forms after filing the tax return, so make a backup copy of your company file before starting and proceed carefully. You can make corrections only in the registers for the relevant accounts and adjust later tax returns if errors are made when filing previous tax returns.

Next, we will prepare the HST return. Refer to the following source document as we work through the steps to enter it:

SD59: Memo #10

Dated October 31, 2012

Prepare the HST return and write cheque #511 in remittance to the Receiver General for HST payable as of October 31, 2012.

1. **Back up**   your **company data file**

2. **Print**   the **General Ledger Report** for **HST Payable** for the remittance period
for reference purposes

> **Notes**
> For further information on sales taxes, refer to Chapter 2. You should also always consult the latest federal and provincial regulations about taxes in your region.

> **SD Instructions**
> Refer to the following source document and then follow the step-by-step instructions to enter it.

> **Notes**
> Refer to page 135 for assistance with displaying and printing General Ledger Reports.

Tax Reports

Notes
You can also access the Sales Tax reports from the Sales Tax and Vendors & Payables menu options from the Reports menu.

Tax reports can be accessed from the Sales Tax report heading or from the Vendors & Payables heading in the Report Centre. These reports can be viewed only before the taxes are remitted, so we will view them before completing the returns.

Tax Agency Reports

There are two tax agency reports available in QuickBooks.

The Tax Agency Detail Report lists the transactions for each box number on the sales tax return. The Tax Agency Report lists the information for each line on the sales tax return. Use this report to help you file your sales tax return to the appropriate sales tax agency. You can click any amount in this report to drill down to the Tax Agency Detail report.

1. **Click** the **Report Centre icon** on the Icon bar

2. **Click** the **Sales Tax heading** on the left-hand side of the screen

3. **Click** the **Tax Agency report**

4. **Click** the **drop-down arrow** in the Tax Agency field

5. **Select** **Receiver General**

6. **Enter** **08/01/12** in the From date field

7. **Enter** **10/31/12** in the To date field

8. **Press** (tab) or **click Refresh** to update the report:

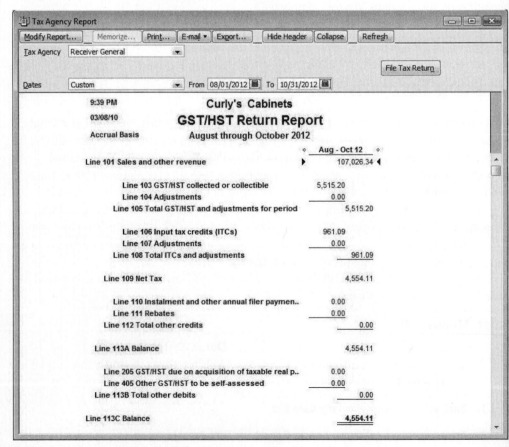

Figure 9-29

You can double click an amount to view the individual amounts that make up that total. These amounts will be displayed on the Tax Agency Detail report. Then double click an amount on the Tax Agency Detail report to view the original transaction.

9. **Double click** the **Tax Collected** amount to drill down to the details that make up the amount on the Tax Agency Detail report

10. **Double click** an **amount** to drill down to the original transaction

11. **Close** the **report** when you have finished viewing it

Notes
The Tax Agency Detail report can also be selected directly from the Sales Tax heading in the Report Centre or from the Manage Sales Tax window.

Making an HST Remittance

QuickBooks automatically creates a vendor record for the Receiver General when you set up the company files. The completion of the HST tax return is largely automatic and based on the transactions for the relevant period. Taxes are filed from the Manage Sales Tax window, which can be opened using one of the following methods:

a) **Click** the **Manage Sales Tax icon** in the Vendors section of the Home page; or

b) **Click Sales Tax** from the menu and then **click Manage Sales Tax**

1. **Open** the **Manage Sales Tax window** using one of the methods listed above:

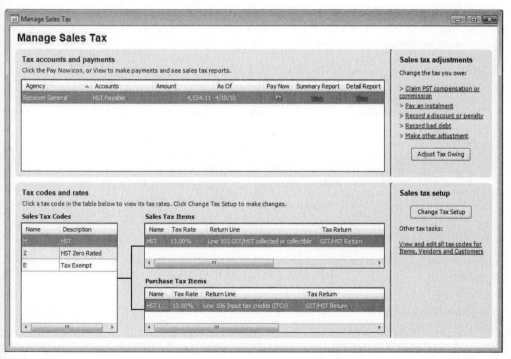

Figure 9-30

You can see that detailed information for each Tax Agency is displayed on one line. For example, you can see that as of today's date, you owe the Receiver General $4,554.11.

Click the Pay Now icon to file the HST Sales Tax return, click the View link under the Summary Report heading to view the Tax Agency Report, and click the View link under the Detail Report heading to view the Tax Agency Detail report.

2. Click   the **Pay Now** icon beside the Receiver General to open the File Sales Tax form

The Receiver General should already be selected in the Tax Agency field. Curly's pays HST on a quarterly basis. The current quarter is between August 1, 2012, and October 31, 2012. We need to change the dates to reflect our remittance period.

3. Type   **08/01/12** in the From date field

4. Type   **10/31/12** in the To date field

5. Press   (tab) to update the File Sales Tax form:

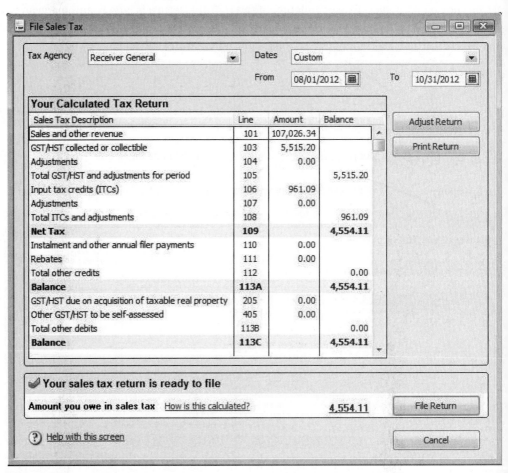

Figure 9-31

The amounts for the sales and other revenue are displayed for the period, together with the HST collected, any adjustments, and input tax credits. The Balance equals the HST collected minus the Input tax credits. If a refund is due (when HST paid is greater than the HST collected), the balance will be in brackets; otherwise an amount is owed to the tax agency.

You can drill down on any of the balances that are displayed on the Sales Tax form and continue to drill down until the original transaction is displayed.

You can make Sales Tax Adjustments from this window by clicking on the Adjust Return button.

Notes

Curly's pays HST on a quarterly basis. The current quarter is August through October, 2012.

6. Click the **Adjust Return** button to display the Sales Tax Adjustment form:

Figure 9-32

Use the Sales Tax Adjustment form to enter an adjustment to your sales tax liability if necessary. Adjustments may be required for sales returns, credits, discounts, or bad debts for which tax was not recorded. Sales credits will reduce the tax owing, so a negative amount will be entered. Purchase credits will increase the tax owing. Adjustment accounts can be created at this point if you do not already have them. QuickBooks will create a General Journal entry from the adjustment you enter here.

7. Click **Cancel** to return to the File Sales Tax form

Use the Print Return button to print the GST/HST Return report before filing the return.

QuickBooks completes the return based on the journal transaction details.

To make corrections later, you must make a journal entry for the adjustment. If you have not yet made a backup of the file, you should click Cancel and make the backup before proceeding.

For Curly's Cabinets, the amounts entered on the Files Sales Tax form are correct so we can accept them and continue.

8. Click the **File Return button** when you are ready to file the return

9. The following message will be displayed:

Figure 9-33

⚠️ **WARNING!**
You cannot return to the tax remittance forms after filing the tax return, so make a backup copy of your company file before starting and proceed carefully. You can make corrections only in the registers for the relevant accounts and adjust later tax returns if errors are made when filing previous tax returns.

QuickBooks allows you to file your return online or manually.

10. Click the **Paper or filing method option** to file the return manually

11. Click   **Continue**

12. The following message will be displayed:

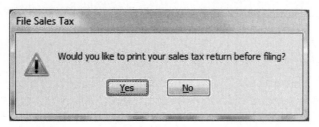

Figure 9-34

13. Click   **No**. The following message will be displayed:

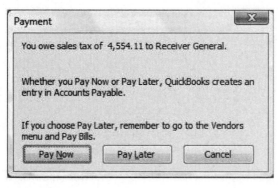

Figure 9-35

This message indicates that you owe the Receiver General $4,554.11. If you select Pay Now, a general journal entry will automatically be created and the Pay Bills form will automatically be displayed, allowing you to make the payment to the Receiver General in the Pay Bills form. If you select Pay Later, a journal entry will automatically be created and you will have to pay the bill at a later time. If you click Cancel, the return will not be filed and you will be returned to the File Sales Tax form.

14. Select   **Pay Now** and the following message will be displayed:

Figure 9-36

15. Click   **OK** and the Pay Bills form will be displayed:

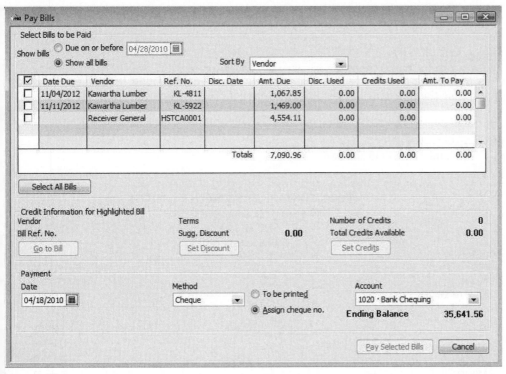

Figure 9-37

Notice that because you selected the Pay Now option, the general journal entry has already been created and all you have to do is select it for payment in the Enter Bills form.

16. Click   the **check box** beside the Receiver General

Most of the default selections on the Enter Bills form are correct because they have been set for the other cheques we wrote. The default bank account is correct and cheque is correct as the method of payment. In addition, we want to assign the cheque number and prepare the cheque manually, so this selection is also correct.

17. Click   the **Payment Date field**

18. Type   **10/31/12**, if necessary

19. Click   the **Pay Selected Bills** button

20. Type   **511** in the Cheque field

21. Click   **OK**

22. Click   **Done** in the Payment Summary window

Reconciling a Bank Account

Reconciling a bank account statement against the computer files is an important step in verifying the accuracy of your records. The bank statement may be different from the ledger for the bank account in QuickBooks for many reasons: cheques written on the account may not have been cashed; a deposit may not be recorded if it was made at the end of the banking day before the statement was prepared; bank charges and interest paid appear on the bank statement but not in the ledger record; and deposits or cheques may have been recorded incorrectly by you or by the bank. Reconciliation is the process of resolving, or accounting for, all these differences between two sets of records.

Next, we will reconcile the Bank Chequing account. Refer to the following source document as we work through the steps to enter it:

SD 60: Memo #11

Dated October 31, 2012

Use the following bank statement to reconcile the Bank Chequing account.

To begin the reconciliation, you should compare the bank statement with the bank register in QuickBooks.

The bank statement follows:

Curly's Cabinets			October 31/12
46 Maple Cres.			Chequing Account
Lindsay, ON K9V 2P3			42045 774990

Date	Item	Deposits	Withdrawals	Balance
	Balance Forward			23,540.00
10/01/2012	Deposit	6,030.00		29,570.00
10/04/2012	502		451.00	29,119.00
10/05/2012	503		2,118.60	27,000.40
10/08/2012	Deposit	4,668.90		31,669.30
10/14/2012	504		4,280.00	27,389.30
10/15/2012	Deposit	7,263.10		34,652.40
10/20/2012	505		229.60	34,422.80
	506		99.44	34,323.36
10/22/2012	Deposit	2,886.40		37,209.76
10/23/2012	507		1,469.00	35,740.76
10/23/2012	508		716.80	35,023.96
10/24/2012	509		135.60	34,888.36
10/28/2012	510		1,344.00	33,544.36
10/30/2012	Debit Memo: mortgage		250.00	33,294.36
	Debit Memo: loan		230.00	33,064.36
	Debit Memo: loan		405.00	32,659.36
10/30/2012	Deposit	2,982.20		35,641.56
	Interest		25.00	35,666.56
	Service fee		35.00	35,631.56
	Closing Balance			35,631.56
			Total Deposits: 5	23,830.60
			Total Withdrawals: 10	11,729.04

Next, you should print the ledger record for the bank account for reference. You can use the General Ledger Report or the Custom Transaction Detail report. The General Ledger Report includes all accounts so you should modify it and apply Account as the filter. The Custom Transaction Detail Report must also be filtered for the account we want.

1. **Click**   the **Report Centre icon** from the Icon bar
2. **Click**   the **Accountant & Taxes heading** on the left-hand side of the screen
3. **Click**   the **General Ledger** link
4. **Type**   **10/01/12** in the From date field

SD Instructions
Refer to the following source document and then follow the step-by-step instructions to enter it.

Notes
To print the transaction report, choose the Reports menu and click Custom Transaction Detail Report. Enter 9/30/12 and 10/31/12 as the report dates in Modify Report window.

Or, to print the General Ledger Report, choose the Reports menu, then choose Accountant & Taxes, and click General Ledger. Enter 10/1/12 and 10/31/12 as the report dates. Press (tab) and click Modify Report.

For either report, click the Modify Report button, then the Filters tab, and select Account as the filter. Choose the Bank Chequing account from the list of accounts. Click OK to return to the report. Click the Print button.

Close the report window. Refer to page 126 for assistance with filtering reports.

5. **Type** 10/31/12 in the To date field

6. The report will be displayed for the *Bank - Chequing* account as shown:

Curly's Cabinets
General Ledger
As of October 31, 2012

11:46 AM
04/18/10
Accrual Basis

Type	Date	Num	Name	Memo	Split	Amount	Balance
1020 · Bank Chequing							23,540.00
Deposit	10/01/2012			Deposit	-SPLIT-	6,030.00	29,570.00
Cheque	10/01/2012	502	Kawartha Bank Visa		2200 · Visa P...	-451.00	29,119.00
Bill Pmt -Cheque	10/04/2012	503	Lindsay's Hardwa...		-SPLIT-	-2,118.60	27,000.40
Deposit	10/08/2012			Deposit	-SPLIT-	4,668.90	31,669.30
Bill Pmt -Cheque	10/12/2012	504	Kawartha Lumber	Historical Inv...	2100 · Accou...	-4,280.00	27,389.30
Deposit	10/15/2012			Deposit	-SPLIT-	7,263.10	34,652.40
Bill Pmt -Cheque	10/19/2012	505	Lindsay's Hardwa...	stains, polis...	-SPLIT-	-229.60	34,422.80
Bill Pmt -Cheque	10/19/2012	506	Northern Telecom		2100 · Accou...	-99.44	34,323.36
Deposit	10/22/2012			Deposit	1210 · Undep...	2,886.40	37,209.76
Bill Pmt -Cheque	10/22/2012	507	Something for Eve...	Rental for cr...	2100 · Accou...	-1,469.00	35,740.76
Bill Pmt -Cheque	10/23/2012	508	Kawartha Building...	to build ente...	-SPLIT-	-716.80	35,023.96
Bill Pmt -Cheque	10/24/2012	509	Hydro Two	Hydro servic...	2100 · Accou...	-135.60	34,888.36
Deposit	10/30/2012			Deposit	-SPLIT-	2,982.20	37,870.56
Bill Pmt -Cheque	10/30/2012	510	Kawartha Building...		-SPLIT-	-1,344.00	36,526.56
General Journal	10/30/2012	4		DM-31188	5260 · Interes...	-885.00	35,641.56
Bill Pmt -Cheque	10/31/2012	511	Receiver General		2100 · Accou...	-4,554.11	31,087.45
Total 1020 · Bank Chequing						7,547.45	31,087.45

Figure 9-38

Notice the differences between the account register and the bank statement:

- a cheque written on October 31 does not appear on the bank statement
- The mortgage payable, bank loan, and interest expenses are posted in detail on the bank statement; however, they are lumped together as one payment of $885.00 in the QuickBooks ledger
- interest income and service charges appear on the bank statement but not in the ledger report
- the dates for the cheques and deposits do not match the dates in the ledger report

We are now ready to reconcile the bank account so that the two reports match.

1. **Click** the **Reconcile icon** on the Banking section of the Home page to open the Begin Reconciliation form:

This is the same screen we used earlier to reconcile the *Visa Payable* account, and *Visa Payable* is still selected because it was the account we last reconciled. We need to select the *Bank Chequing* account.

2. **Click** the **drop-down arrow** in the account field and **select Bank Chequing** to open the Begin Reconciliation form for this account as shown:

Notes
If you closed the Curly data file after reconciling the Visa Payable account, the Bank Chequing account will be displayed in the Account field.

Notes
All Balance Sheet accounts are available for selection in the Account field on the Begin Reconciliation form. In theory, you could receive statements for any asset, liability, or equity account for reconciliation.

Figure 9-39

The opening balance is shown for the account in the beginning balance field. This is the balance from the end of the last reconciliation, or in this case, the historical balance we entered to set up the company data files. It should be the opening balance in the ledger record and on the bank statement.

The Ending Balance is the closing balance or ending balance on the bank statement.

3. Type   **10/31/12** in the Statement Date field

4. Press   (tab) to advance to the Ending Balance field

5. Type   **35632.31**

6. Press   (tab) to advance to the Service Charge field.

This field is used for any fees that the bank has charged, including monthly service fees, NSF fees, and so on. You can add all the fees together and enter a single amount.

A single entry appears on the statement for fees, the entry on October 31st for $35.00.

7. Type   **35**

8. Press   (tab) to advance to the Date field

As elsewhere, the calendar date appears as the default date.

9. Type   **10/31/12**

10. Press   (tab) to advance to the Account field

When you click on the drop-down arrow in the Account field, you will see that you do not have an account called *Bank Charges*, so it needs to be created.

11. Type   **5080**

12. Press   (tab) to display the Account Not Found message

13. Click   **Set Up**

Notice the expense account type has automatically been selected for this account.

14. Click   the **Account Name** field

15. Type   **Bank Charges**

16. Click   **Save & Close** to return to the Begin Reconciliation form

Notes
The default Statement Date is the last day of the month before your current calendar month (according to your computer system date).

Notes
If you want to enter different kinds of charges for different accounts, you should make individual General Journal entries for them on the dates they occurred and then clear them with the other transactions in the next step.

The cursor is now in the Interest Earned field.

17. **Type**   **25**

18. **Press**   ⬚tab⬚ to move to the Date field

19. **Type**   **10/31/12**

20. **Press**   ⬚tab⬚

21. **Click**   the **drop-down arrow** in the Account field

22. **Choose**   **4200 Revenue** from Interest

23. The Begin Reconciliation form is now complete as shown:

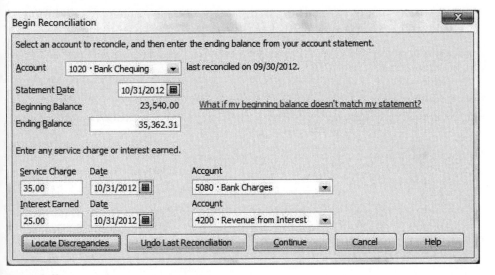

Figure 9-40

24. **Check**   your **work** and **make** any necessary **corrections**

25. **Click**   the **Continue** button to proceed to the next screen:

Figure 9-41

Notes

If you are reconciling for more than one month at a time, you may want to show the transactions before the statement date (click the check box at the top of the Reconcile window beside the Hide transactions after the statement's end date option) so that only the transactions that will be cleared from that statement are displayed on the screen.

Notes

You can click on any part of a transaction to add a ✓ or to remove a ✓.

Notes

If the difference is not zero when you click Reconcile Now, QuickBooks will ask you if you want to return to the Reconcile window (now or later) to make corrections or allow QuickBooks to make an adjustment for the difference. If you allow QuickBooks to make an adjustment, the adjusting journal entry will be made to the bank and capital accounts.

This screen shows all transactions for the account for the relevant period. Most of these transactions also appear on the bank statement. We need to indicate which of these transactions have been cleared on the bank statement. The ✓ column is used to mark the cleared transactions. We can mark each transaction individually, or mark them all and deselect the ones that do not appear on the statement. Most of the transactions have cleared the bank so we will mark all of them first, then unmark the last two cheques that have not cleared the bank.

26. **Click**   the **Mark All** button

A checkmark is displayed in the ✓ column for all transactions.

27. **Click**   the ✓ **column** for Receiver General, cheque #514 to remove the ✓

The Difference amount should be zero because we have accounted for all the differences already. Your complete Reconcile form should look like the following:

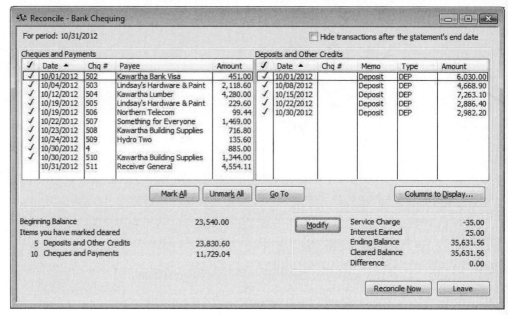

Figure 9-42

28. **Check**   your **work** carefully and **make corrections** before proceeding.

Once you choose Reconcile Now, you cannot return to this window for these dates. You can, however, undo the reconciliation and start over again if necessary. Transactions remain cleared but you can edit the service charge or interest amounts in the bank account's register.

Once you are sure that the information is correct, you can save the reconciliation.

29. Click   **Reconcile Now** to open the report screen.

30. Click   **Display or Print** to view the Reconciliation Summary report:

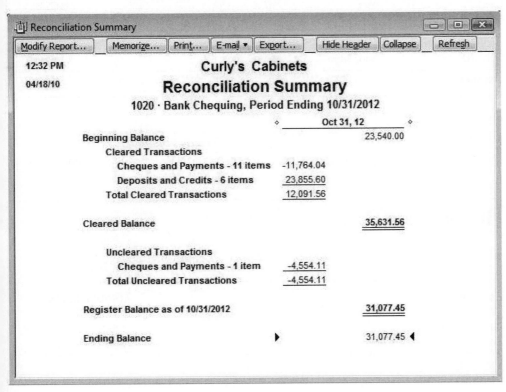

Figure 9-43

Source Documents

Now that you have learned some of the new concepts introduced in this chapter, enter the following source documents. Refer to the information in this chapter for help if necessary.

SD Practice

Continue to develop your skills by entering the following source document(s).

Notes

The transaction fees are 2.3 percent of the total sales amount. Enter this charge as a Service Charge. Choose Credit Card Fees as the account for the charge.

SD61: Memo #12

Dated October 31, 2012

Use the following bank statement to reconcile the Bank Visa account.

Kawartha Bank

www.kbfg.ca
29 Moneysworth St.
Lindsay, ON K6B 5F9
(705) 644-8409

ACCOUNT
Visa Deposit Account
3499 6003340
October 31/12

ACCOUNT HOLDER
Curly's Cabinets
46 Maple Cres.
Lindsay, ON K9V 2P3

	Balance Forward			$ 4,385.00
10/01/12	Deposit	$8,050.00		12,435.00
10/08/12	Deposit	4,757.25		17,192.25
10/15/12	Deposit	310.75		17,503.00
10/22/12	Deposit	576.30		18,079.30
10/30/12	Deposit	5,830.80		23,910.10
10/30/12	Transaction Fees		$640.50	23,269.60
10/31/12	Closing Balance			$23,269.60

SUMMARY   Deposits $19,525.10   Withdrawals $640.50

SD62: Memo #13

Dated October 31, 2012

Use the following bank statement to reconcile the Visa Payable account. Write cheque #512 for $1,060.25 to pay the full balance owing.

Kawartha Bank

Visa Statement

www.kbfg.ca
29 Moneysworth St.
Lindsay, ON K6B 5F9
(705) 644-8409

ACCOUNT
Visa Account
4505 7499 6558 6443
October 31/12

ACCOUNT HOLDER
Curly's Cabinets
46 Maple Cres.
Lindsay, ON K9V 2P3

10/01/2012	Otto's Autos	$203.40
10/02/2012	Payment - thank you	−451.00
10/04/2012	Papers Plus	163.85
10/06/2012	Otto's Autos	56.50
10/12/2012	Otto's Autos	259.90
10/13/2012	Otto's Autos	56.50
10/18/2012	Papers Plus	192.10
10/20/2012	Otto's Autos	56.50
10/27/2012	Otto's Autos	56.50
10/29/2012	Annual Fee	15.00

STATEMENT SUMMARY

Previous Balance	$ 451.00	
New Charges	1,060.25	
Total Credits	451.00	
Balance Owing	1,060.25	
Minimum Payment	$110.00	by Nov 12, 2012

Transferring Funds between Bank Accounts

Companies frequently need to transfer funds from one account to another to cover cheques or to move excess funds to a savings or investment account that earns a higher rate of interest. Curly's Cabinets does not need to keep a large balance in the *Bank Visa* account because this account is not used to write cheques.

The next transaction that we will enter is a transfer of funds from the *Bank Visa* to the *Bank Savings* account. Refer to the following source document as we work through the steps to enter it:

SD63: Memo #14

SD Instructions
Refer to the following source document and then follow the step-by-step instructions to enter it.

Dated October 31, 2012

Transfer $15,000.00 from the Bank Visa account to the Bank Savings account.

1. **Choose**   the **Banking menu** and **click Transfer Funds** to open the Transfer Funds Between Accounts form:

Figure 9-44

This form is very easy to use. All you need to do is choose the two bank accounts involved in the transfer and enter the date and amount of the transfer. The *Bank Chequing* account is selected as the default, so we need to change it. The current account balance for the *Bank Chequing* account is displayed on the form. The date should be correct from previous entries.

2. **Type**   **10/31/12** as the date if necessary

3. **Click**   the **drop-down arrow** in the Transfer Funds From field

4. **Choose**   **1060 Bank Visa**. The *Bank Visa* account balance replaces the *Bank Chequing* balance.

5. **Click**   the **drop-down arrow** in the Transfer Funds To field

6. **Choose**   **1040 Bank Savings**. The Bank Savings account balance is displayed.

7. **Press**   (tab) to advance to the Transfer Amount field

8. **Type**   **15000**

9. **Press**   (tab) to advance to the Memo field

"Transfer Funds" is entered in the memo field as the default memo, and we will accept the default memo. The account balances will be updated when we save the transfer so the form is complete as shown:

Figure 9-45

Check the form carefully and make any necessary corrections. Choose the correct account from the drop-down list and correct the amount or date if necessary. Highlight an incorrect field and retype the correct information.

We can now review the journal entry so we will save the form without closing.

10. **Click**   **Save & New**

11. **Click**   ◄ Previous to view the transfer you just entered

Notice that the account balances have now been updated by the transferred amount.

12. **Press**   (ctrl) + **Y** to display the Transaction Journal report:

Notes
We have removed columns from the report to display it in the textbook.

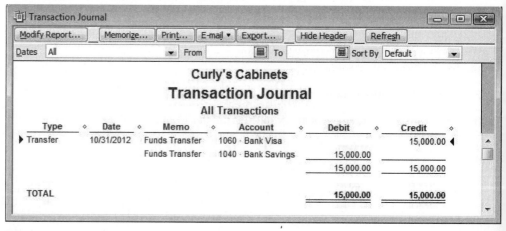

Figure 9-46

The entry shows a credit to the *Bank Visa* account and a debit entry for to the *Bank Savings* account, just as it would if we had used the General Journal to complete the transaction.

13. **Close**   the **Transaction Journal** report

14. **Close**   the **Transfer Funds Between Accounts** form

Ending a Fiscal Period

At the end of a fiscal period, a business normally closes its books. In accrual-based accounting, this procedure involves completing all adjusting entries so that all revenue and expenses have been recorded for the appropriate period. Income and expense accounts are then closed to the appropriate capital accounts so that the next period can begin with zero balances for these accounts. We have already completed the adjustments for depreciation, supplies used, and expired prepaid expenses. Except for these adjusting entries, QuickBooks completes most of the closing steps automatically when you define the end date for a fiscal period.

Next, we will work through the necessary steps to close the books as of October 31, 2012. Refer to the following source document as we work through the steps to close the books:

SD64: Memo #15

Dated October 31, 2012

Close the books as of October 31, 2012. Transfer the Retained Earnings balance to the Capital account.

SD Instructions
Refer to the following source document and then follow the step-by-step instructions to enter it.

Defining the Fiscal End Date

The first step in closing the books is the selection of a date for closing the books that will define the end of the fiscal period. Normally a business will choose one year as its fiscal period, but shorter periods may also be used.

However, before we close the books, we should make a backup copy of the data file so that we can return to the pre-closing period if necessary.

1. **Back up**   the **data file** to a new CD or other backup medium

2. **Label**   the **CD** "Pre-closing Data for Curly" and **store** the **CD** in a safe place

Now we will select a closing date for the fiscal period.

3. **Choose**   the **Edit menu** and **click Preferences**

4. **Click**   the **Accounting heading** on the left-hand side of the screen

5. **Click** the **Company Preferences** tab:

Figure 9-47

6. **Click** the **Set Date/Password** button on the bottom of the screen to open the Set Closing Date and Password form

7. **Click** the **Closing Date** field (the Date through which the books are closed)

8. **Type** **10/31/12**

9. **Press** (tab) to advance to the Closing Date Password field

The closing date password you set here applies only to transactions dated on or before the closing date: October 31, 2012. Although you can enter this password at any time, it is advised to set it at the time of setting the closing date.

This password will prevent unauthorized access to the transactions dated on or before the closing date. For security purposes, in an ongoing business, you should set a password after setting the closing date. The password will also help ensure that transaction dates for the previous fiscal period are not entered in error.

For practice, choose a password that is easy to remember, such as your first name. In an ongoing business, you should choose a password that is easy for you to remember but unknown to anyone else (and cannot be guessed). The cursor is in the Password field. You must enter the same code twice. This ensures you typed the password that you intended, without making a mistake that you cannot duplicate later.

10. **Type** **curly** in the Closing Date Password field

11. **Press** (tab) to advance to the Confirm Password field

For added security, the characters you type do not appear on the screen.

12. **Type** **curly** in the Confirm Password field

13. The completed Set Closing Date and Password form is displayed as shown:

Figure 9-48

While working in QuickBooks, if you try to save a transaction dated October 31, 2012, or earlier, you will be prompted for the closing password. If the transaction date is correct, and it should be completed, enter the password to continue with the transaction. Otherwise, choose Cancel and correct the transaction date.

14. Click **OK** to continue

15. The following message will be displayed:

Figure 9-49

In an ongoing company, it is important to set an administration password and select a challenge question that no one can guess. This will protect your QuickBooks company file from being viewed by people who should not be able to view it.

16. Click the box beside the **Do not display this message in the future** option

17. Click **Yes**

18. The User List is displayed:

Figure 9-50

To set up the Administration password:

19. Click   the **Edit User button** to display the Change user password and access form as shown:

Figure 9-51

20. Press   `tab` to advance to the Password field

Type a password that no one can guess. For this company file, we will use "curly" as the password.

21. Type   **curly**

22. Press   `tab` to advance to the Confirm Password field

23. Type   **curly**

24. Click   the **drop-down list** in the Challenge Question field

25. Select   a **Challenge Question** that no one will guess

> **Notes**
> Select a Challenge Question that you can easily remember.

26. Press `tab` to advance to the Challenge Answer field

27. Type the **answer** to your challenge question

If you forget the company file password and can answer your challenge question, you will be able to re-set your password for the company file.

28. Click **Next** to display the following message:

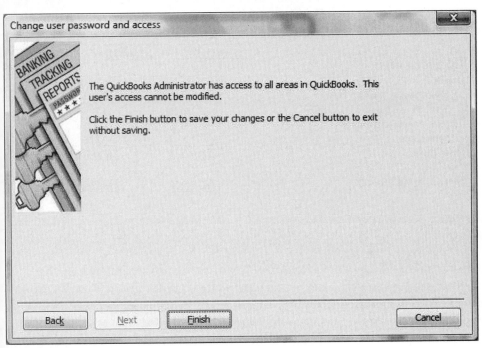

Figure 9-52

29. Click **Finish**

30. Close the **User List**

From now on, when you open the Curly company data file, you will have to enter the admin password.

Closing the Books

When you enter a date in QuickBooks within the new year (after the closing date), QuickBooks automatically transfers the income and expense balances to the *Retained Earnings* account. Income and expense account balances are reset to zero to begin a new fiscal period.

We can see the effect of entering a date in the new year (after the set closing date) when we examine the equity section of the Balance Sheet for the last day of the previous fiscal period and the first day of the current period.

Notes
To show the comparative Balance Sheet:
- Open the Report Centre
- Choose the Company & Financial heading on the left-hand side of the screen
- Click the Standard link under the Balance Sheet and Net Worth heading
- Enter 11/01/12 as the date for the statement
- Press (tab) or click the Refresh button
- Click the Modify Report button
- Click Previous Period in the Add Subcolumns For section
- Click OK

The equity section of the comparative statement is shown here:

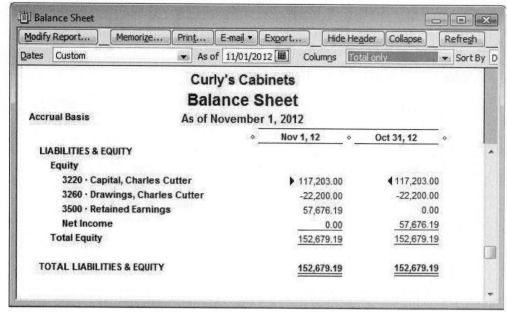

Figure 9-53

Some businesses maintain the *Retained Earnings* balance separately from the invested capital. Many small businesses do not maintain this distinction. Curly's Cabinets does not keep these balances separately. Therefore, we should make a final General Journal entry to transfer the balance from *Retained Earnings* to *Capital, Charles Cutter* to finish closing the books. The Balance Sheet on the previous page shows the amount that we must transfer, $57,676.19.

1. **Make** the **General Journal entry** to debit (reduce) Retained Earnings and credit (increase) Capital, Charles Cutter for $57,676.19 as shown here:

Figure 9-54

2. **Click**   **Save & Close** to display the screen that requires the closing date password before proceeding with the transaction:

Figure 9-55

Normally, once you have closed the books, you won't make entries to the previous period. Sometimes, you need to make entries after closing the books because the information for the adjusting entries isn't available until after the closing date. As long as you set the closing date and password, this screen will be displayed requesting the closing date password in order to allow you to save the transaction.

3. **Type**   curly

4. **Click**   **OK**

If you enter a closing date but do not enter a closing date password, the following warning will be displayed when you try to save a transaction dated on or before the closing date:

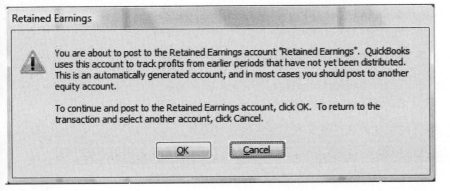

Figure 9-56

5. **Click**   **OK** to continue

When you review the equity section of the Balance Sheet for November 1 after transferring the balance from *Retained Earnings* to *Capital, Charles Cutter* you will see that the entry for *Retained Earnings* has been removed and *Capital, Charles Cutter* has been increased as shown here.

Figure 9-57

Banking Reports

The banking reports show detailed records of cheques, deposits, and reconciliations. You can view these reports from the Reports menu or from the Report Centre. We will view the reports from the Report Centre as we have in previous chapters.

1. **Click**   the **Reports Centre icon** from the Icon bar

2. **Click**   the **Banking heading** on the left-hand side of the screen to view the Banking reports available:

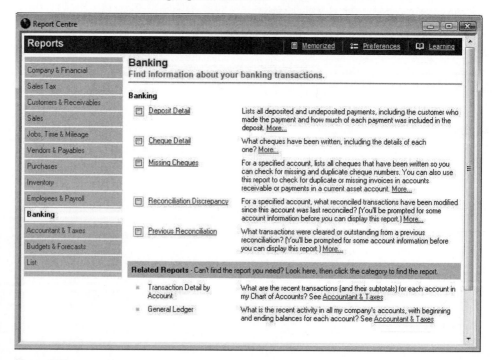

Figure 9-58

The Deposit Detail Report

The Deposit Detail Report includes a list of all deposits to all accounts that have been used in a Deposit To field in the journals and the customers who made the payments.

1. **Click**   the **Deposit Detail** link under the Banking heading

2. **Type**   10/01/12 in the From date field

3. **Type**   10/31/12 in the To date field

4. **Press**   (tab) or **click** the **Refresh button** to update the report:

Notes
To access the report from the Reports menu:
- Choose the Reports menu, then choose Banking, and click Deposit Detail to open the report
- Enter 10/01/12 as the From date
- Enter 10/31/12 as the To date
- Press (tab) or click the Refresh button to update the report

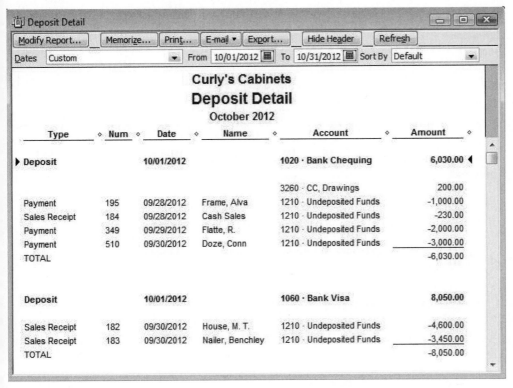

Figure 9-59

Each deposit shows the individual receipts that were part of that deposit. Undeposited receipts, if there are any, will be shown separately in the report. The report can be sorted by any of the column headings.

5. **Double click**   any detail to view the original transaction

6. **Close**   the **report** when you have finished viewing it

The Cheque Detail Report

The Cheque Detail Report includes a list of all cheques written from bank accounts during the selected period and the vendors and accounts involved in the payment. General Journal transactions that involve the Bank accounts are also listed.

1. **Click**   the **Cheque Detail link** under the Banking heading

2. **Type**   10/01/12 in the From date field

3. **Type**   10/31/12 in the To date field

Notes
To access the report from the Reports menu:
- Choose the Reports menu, then choose Banking and click Cheque Detail to open the report
- Enter 10/01/12 in the From date
- Enter 10/31/12 in the To date
- Press (tab) or click the Refresh button to update the report

4. Press ⌨tab⌨ or **click** the **Refresh button** to view the report:

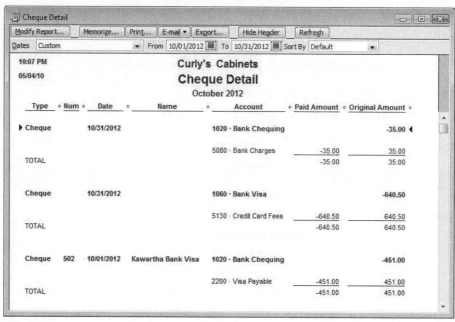

Figure 9-60

You can sort the report by any of the column headings.
Double click any detail to view the original transaction.

5. Close the **report** when you have finished viewing it

The Missing Cheques Report

The Missing Cheques Report includes a list of all cheques written from the selected bank account so you can see whether a cheque number is missing from the sequence.

1. Click the **Missing Cheques** link under the Banking heading

2. Click the **drop-down arrow** beside the Specify Account field to view the accounts available for selection:

Notes
To access the report from the Reports menu:
• Choose the Reports menu, then choose Banking and click Missing Cheques
• Select the account from the drop-down list and click OK

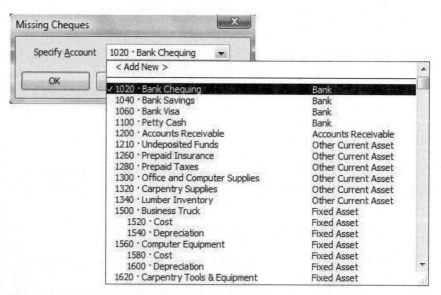

Figure 9-61

All bank and asset accounts are available for selection.

Reports are created for each account separately because each account has its own numbering sequence. Select the account from the drop-down list for which you want to view the report. The account we want — *1020 - Bank Chequing* — is already selected so we can continue.

3. Click   **1020 - Bank Chequing**

4. Click   **OK** to view the report:

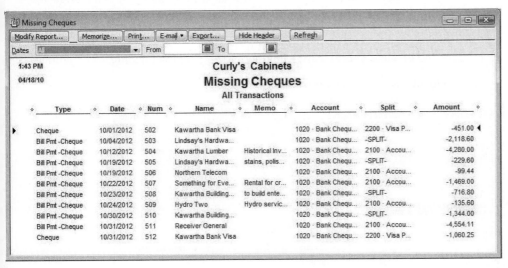

Figure 9-62

All the details you need to trace a cheque are included on the Missing Cheques report: type of transaction, date, cheque number, payee, invoice number (provided you entered the invoice number in the memo field on the payment form), account, other accounts involved, and the cheque amount. If more than one account was involved with the transaction, SPLIT appears in the Split column.

5. Double click   any **detail line** to drill down to the original transaction

6. Close   the **report** when you have finished viewing it

The Reconcile Discrepancy Report

The Reconcile Discrepancy Report lists reconciled transactions that have been modified since the account was last reconciled.

1. Click   the **Reconciliation Discrepancy** link under the Banking heading

2. Select   **1020 - Bank Chequing** and **click OK**

3. The Previous Reconciliation Discrepancy Report will be displayed as shown:

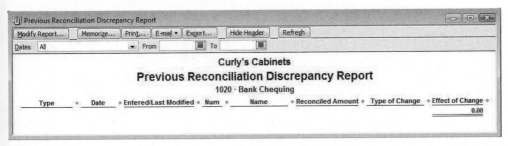

Figure 9-63

Notes
To access the report from the Reports menu:
• Choose the Reports menu, then choose Banking and click Reconciliation Discrepancy to open the account selection window

Notes
You can enter a range of dates for the report or you can choose to show modified transactions for all periods.

The report has no data because no changes were made to reconciled transactions. The column headings give you a good idea of the report's purpose.

4. Close the **report window** when you have finished viewing it

The Previous Reconciliation Report

The Previous Reconciliation Report shows you what transactions were cleared or which ones were outstanding from a previous reconciliation. This is the same report that you can print when you complete a reconciliation. It is available in summary and detail form.

Notes
To access the report from the Reports menu:
• Choose the Reports menu, then choose Banking and click Previous Reconciliation to open the account selection window

1. Click the **Previous Reconciliation link** under the Banking heading

2. The following screen will be displayed:

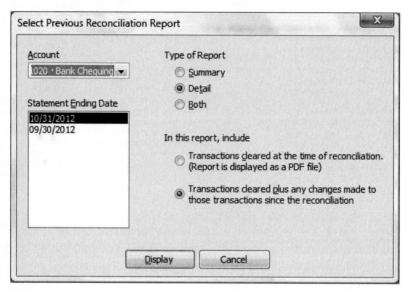

Figure 9-64

For each account selected, you can choose to print the summary or detail report or both. You can include only the transactions that were cleared at the time of reconciliation or include transactions cleared at the time of reconciliation plus any changes made to those transactions since the reconciliation (the default selection).

3. Choose **1020-Bank Chequing** in the Account field

4. Choose **Summary** as the type of report and leave the final selection to include transactions and changes

The Statement Ending date of 10/31/2012 should be highlighted. As you perform more reconciliations for this account, they will also be available for selection.

5. Click   Display to continue and display the report:

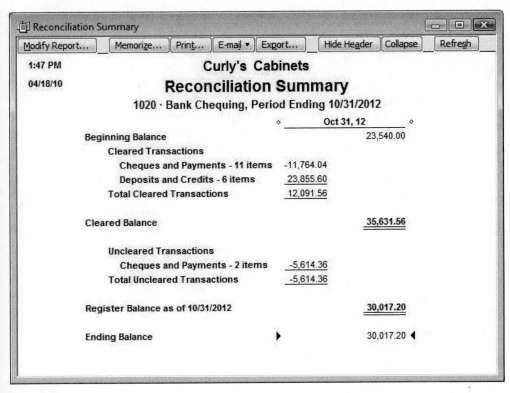

Figure 9-65

The Summary Report shows the total amount of cleared transactions for both cheques and deposits, the total of uncleared transactions, and the ending balance.

The Reconciliation Detail Report shows the individual transactions that make up the totals on the Summary Report.

6. Double click   the **ending balance amount** on the Summary Report to drill down to the Detail Report

7. Double click   **any detail on the Detail Report** to drill down to the original transaction

8. Close   all **open reports** when you have finished viewing them

Finishing Your Session

1. Back up   the **company data file**

2. Close   the **Company file**

3. Close   the **QuickBooks program**

CHAPTER TEN

Darya's Dance Studio

Objectives

After completing this chapter, you should be able to:

- **set up** new company files from manual accounting records
- **convert** manual accounting records to QuickBooks
- **create** a Chart of Accounts with opening balances
- **understand** and **use** different account types
- **enter** opening balances for income and expense accounts
- **create** customer records with opening balances
- **create** vendor records with opening balances
- **customize** QuickBooks preferences for a company
- **set up** taxes for a company
- **create** items
- **set up** and **edit** account terms for vendors and customers
- **understand** and **use** different types of items
- **set up** finance charges for customers

Company Information

▶ **Notes**
Darya's Dance Studio
11 Nutcracker St.
Regina, SK S3G 2P6
Tel: (306) 224-8632
Fax: (306) 224-3918
E-mail: lessons@
daryasdance.com
Web: www.daryasdance.
com
Business No.: 577499299

Company Profile

Darya's Dance Studio in Regina, Saskatchewan, is owned and operated by Darya Danovich. Darya retired from professional dancing several years ago and has been teaching ever since. Now she runs a variety of dance classes for all ages, as well as general stretch and conditioning classes. Darya offers classical ballroom, basic ballet, and jazz dance classes, so they attract single adults, couples, and children. Sometimes entire families enroll for the different classes.

Most students enroll in 15-week program sessions, and many attend more than one class per week. The stretch and conditioning classes are available on a drop-in or pay-as-you-go basis. Those students who register and pay for three classes per week may attend as many additional classes as they want.

Members of a family who enroll for several sessions can set up accounts with Darya's Studio. Groups requesting custom-designed programs can also set up accounts. For example, Darya taught dance routines to gymnastics students and provided coordination and balance training to Olympic athletes to promote teamwork. She also designs special short programs for schools.

The Studio accepts cash, cheques, and credit cards in payment. For purchases, Darya has a business credit card and accounts set up with some vendors.

Darya owns a studio, piano, and sound system. Her studio consists of two classrooms and two change rooms with washrooms — one for men and one for women. The instructors are paid monthly by cheque according to their contracts for the number of classes they teach. They are not on payroll so there are no payroll deductions. The pianist is also paid on a contractual basis. Most classes use live music to teach the basic dance steps but also rely on recordings for longer routines and some performances. Darya herself withdraws money from the business periodically in lieu of a regular salary.

Customers pay 5 percent GST for all classes, but PST is not applied to the services offered by the Studio. Darya's Dance Studio pays both PST and GST on all business-related purchases.

No classes are held in August, though some students have already enrolled for the session beginning in September. August is used to plan for the coming year and to close the business records for the previous fiscal period. At the end of August 2012, the following information is available for converting the accounting records to QuickBooks:

- Chart of Accounts
- Trial Balance
- Vendor List
- Customer List
- Item List
- Accounting Procedures

Chart of Accounts

Darya's Dance Studio

ASSETS
Bank
  1050 Bank - Chequing
  1080 Bank - Savings
  1100 Bank - Credit Card

Accounts Receivable
  1200 Accounts Receivable

Other Current Assets
  1260 Music Inventory
  1280 Prepaid Insurance
  1300 Office and Computer Supplies
  1450 Undeposited Funds

Fixed Assets
  1500 Computers [P]
  1520 Computers:Cost [S]
  1540 Computers:Depreciation [S]
  1560 Piano [P]
  1580 Piano:Cost [S]
  1600 Piano:Depreciation [S]

1620 Stereo Equipment [P]
1640 Stereo Equipment:Cost [S]
1660 Stereo Equipment: Depreciation [S]
1700 Studio [P]
1720 Studio:Cost [S]
1740 Studio:Depreciation [S]
1760 Vehicle [P]
1780 Vehicle:Cost [S]
1800 Vehicle:Depreciation [S]

LIABILITIES
Accounts Payable
  2100 Accounts Payable

Credit Card
  2150 Visa Payable

Other Current Liabilities
  2260 Bank Loan
  2460 GST Payable

Long Term Liabilities
  2720 Long Term Loan
  2740 Mortgage Payable

EQUITY
  3200 Capital, Darya Danovich
  3260 Drawings, Darya Danovich
  3400 Retained Earnings

INCOME
  4100 Revenue from Lessons
  4160 Sales Discounts
  4200 Revenue from Interest
  4250 Other Revenue

EXPENSE
  5020 Advertising and Promotion
  5060 Office and Computer Supplies Used
  5080 Music Inventory Expenses

5100 Depreciation Expense
5120 Maintenance Expenses
5140 Insurance Expense
5160 Interest Expense
5180 Printing and Copying
5200 Property Tax Expense
5220 Purchase Discounts
5240 Hydro Expense
5260 Telephone Expense
5280 Vehicle Expenses
5300 Wages Expenses

Non-posting Accounts
  6000 Estimates
  6050 Purchase Orders

[P] Parent account
[S] Subaccount

Darya's Dance Studio

AS AT AUGUST 31, 2012

	Debits	Credits		Debits	Credits
1050 Bank - Chequing	$ 8,860.00		2720 Long Term Loan		$ 22,000.00
1080 Bank - Savings	14,900.00		2740 Mortgage Payable		30,000.00
1100 Bank - Credit Card	6,400.00		3200 Capital, Darya Danovich		96,165.00
1200 Accounts Receivable	1,445.00		3260 Drawings, Darya Danovich	$ 7,400.00	
1260 Music Inventory	1,460.00		4100 Revenue from Lessons		3,800.00
1280 Prepaid Insurance	4,500.00		4160 Sales Discounts	30.00	
1300 Office and Computer Supplies	480.00		4200 Revenue from Interest		20.00
1520 Computers:Cost	4,500.00		5020 Advertising and Promotion	2,100.00	
1540 Computers:Depreciation		$ 1,820.00	5060 Office and Computer Supplies Used	185.00	
1580 Piano:Cost	10,000.00		5080 Music Inventory Expenses	45.00	
1600 Piano:Depreciation		1,450.00	5100 Depreciation Expense	1,000.00	
1640 Stereo Equipment:Cost	6,000.00		5120 Maintenance Expenses	220.00	
1660 Stereo Equipment:Depreciation		2,430.00	5140 Insurance Expense	3,250.00	
1720 Studio:Cost	90,000.00		5160 Interest Expense	420.00	
1740 Studio:Depreciation		6,000.00	5180 Printing and Copying	560.00	
1780 Vehicle:Cost	24,000.00		5200 Property Tax Expense	120.00	
1800 Vehicle:Depreciation		9,720.00	5220 Purchase Discounts		95.00
2100 Accounts Payable		1,455.00	5240 Hydro Expense	85.00	
2150 Visa Payable		875.00	5260 Telephone Expense	120.00	
2260 Bank Loan		11,500.00	5280 Vehicle Expenses	240.00	
2460 GST Payable		990.00		$188,320.00	$188,320.00

Darya's Dance Studio

Vendor Name (Contact or Alternate)	Address	Phone No. Fax No.	E-mail Business No.	Terms Credit Limit
Foley's (Jane Foley or Robin)	122 Baryshnikov St. Regina, SK S3P 7N5	Tel: (306) 224-4632 Fax: (306) 225-6722	JF@foleys.com 398446722	1/5 n/30 $300.00
Fox Trotte, Instructor T4A eligible	18 Tango Circle Regina, SK S3K 4T2	Tel: (306) 238-4916	FTrotte@hotmail.com	due on receipt
Mimi Pascoe, Pianist T4A eligible	88 Keyes Blvd. Regina, SK S4N 2H5	Tel: (306) 296-2991	mpascoe@yahoo.ca	due on receipt
Prairie Energy Corp. (Business Accounts Dept.)	55 Windmill Rd. Regina, SK S3V 4C2	Tel: (306) 229-5166 Fax: (306) 229-6019	accounts@pec.sk.ca	net 10 $500.00
Prime Contacts (Tokk Toomee)	200 Cellular Way Regina, SK S2S 4G4	Tel: (306) 278-7835 Fax: (306) 278-2815	toomee@prime.ca	net 15 $500.00
Receiver General	4 Legislate Dr. Regina, SK S4B 3P5	Tel: (800) 959-2019		quarterly reports
Sounds Inc. (Dylan or Bob)	69 Acoustic Rd. Regina, SK S2R 1B7	Tel: (306) 257-4994 Fax: (306) 257-5181	dylan@sounds.com 277344598	2/10, n/30 $1,000.00
Treble & Bass (Ken Fiddler)	5 Kettledrum Way Regina, SK S3F 6K8	Tel: (306) 256-6388 Fax: (306) 255-7188	fiddler@treble&bass.com 471639672	1/10, n/30 $5,000.00
Wendy Groen, RMT	100 Healer St. Regina, SK S3K 7C5	Tel: (306) 277-3997	w.groen@sympatico.ca	net 10 $500.00

Darya's Dance Studio

Vendor Name	Date	Terms	Due Date	Opening Balance
Foley's	Aug. 28/12	1/5, n/10	Sep. 9/12	$115.00
Sounds Inc.	Aug. 24/12	2/10, n/30	Sep. 23/12	$510.00
Treble & Bass	Aug. 29/12	1/10, n/30	Sep. 28/12	$380.00
Wendy Groen, RMT	Aug. 25/12	net 10	Sep. 4/12	$450.00
			Grand Total	$1,455.00

Customer Information

Darya's Dance Studio

Customer Name (Contact)	Address	Phone No. Fax No.	E-mail Preferred Payment	Terms Credit Limit
Canadian Sledder (Pers Johansson)	189 Bobsled Hill Rd. Regina, SK S3T 7E8	Tel: (306) 299-8644 Fax: (306) 298-6219	thefastest@yahoo.ca cheque	1/10, n/30 $2,000.00
Minuet Family (Ron or Lynda)	2 Steppe Rd. Regina, SK S3R 3W1	Tel: (306) 246-5643	r.minuet@shaw.ca cheque	1/10, n/30 $2,000.00
Saskie Gliders (Korinne)	42 Skaters Ave. Regina, SK S4B 2C8	Tel: (306) 341-7299 Fax: (306) 342-2915	korinne@gliders.com cheque	1/10, n/30 $8,000.00
Waltzer Family (Lee)	3 Fourtime Cr. Regina, SK S3M 4B9	Tel: (306) 284-3882 Fax: (306) 284-4290	lee.w.57@hotmail.com cheque	1/10, n/30 $2,000.00
Wheatfields Academy (F. Astaire)	90 Granery Rd. Regina, SK S4C 5F7	Tel: (306) 248-1920 Fax: (306) 246-4837	fastaire@wheatfields.ca cheque	1/10, n/30 $9,000.00
Cash Sales			Cash	due on receipt
Visa Sales			Visa	due on receipt

Customer Opening Balances

Darya's Dance Studio

Customer Name	Date	Terms	Due Date	Opening Balance
Canadian Sledders	Aug. 10/12	1/10, n/30	Sep. 20/12	$400.00
Minuet Family	Aug. 5/12	1/10, n/30	Sep. 4/12	$310.00
Saskie Gliders	Aug. 29/12	1/10, n/30	Sep. 28/12	$735.00
			Grand Total	$1,445.00

Darya's Dance Studio

Item	Description	Price	Tax Code	Account
Service Items				
Class - Single	Single dance or exercise class	$ 25.00	G	4100 Revenue from Lessons
Classes - Month	One month of classes	75.00	G	4100 Revenue from Lessons
Classes - Session	Four month seasonal session	220.00	G	4100 Revenue from Lessons
Non-inventory Part Items				
Music Inventory	CDs and sheet music	varies	S	1260 Music Inventory
Supplies	Office and computer supplies	varies	S	1300 Office and Computer Supplies
Other Charge Items				
Admin Charge	Handling charge for NSF cheque	$30.00		4250 Other Revenue
NSF Cheque	Amount of NSF Cheque	varies		1050 Bank - Chequing
Finance Charge	Interest Charges on Overdue Balance	15%		4200 Revenue from Interest
(enter from Preferences)	over 30 days, 5 days' grace, $10.00 minimum			

Accounting Procedures

Taxes: GST and PST

Darya's Dance Studio pays 5 percent GST and 5 percent PST on all goods and services that it buys, and charges GST on all lessons. PST is not charged on any of the lessons offered by Darya's Dance Studio. The business uses the regular method for remittance of the Goods and Services Tax. GST collected from customers is recorded as a liability in the *GST Payable* account. GST paid to vendors is recorded in the *GST Payable* account as a decrease in liability to the Canada Revenue Agency. The report is filed with the Receiver General for Canada by the last day of the month for the previous quarter, either including the balance owing or requesting a refund.

Account Terms

> **Notes**
> A five-day grace period becomes 35 days past the invoice date before charges are assessed.

Account customers (families and groups) receive a discount of 1 percent if they settle their accounts within 10 days after signing up for classes. The full balance is required within 30 days of the start of classes. Individual students pay in full at the start of a session or individual class. Finance charges are applied to overdue accounts at 15 percent per year starting after the due date, but there is a five-day grace period before interest charges are applied. A minimum charge of $10.00 applies to overdue accounts to cover administration costs. Some vendors also offer discounts for early payment.

Deposits and Cheques

All cheques, credit card payments, and cash are held for deposit. Cheques are hand printed at the time of the transaction.

Estimates, Orders, and Prepayments

Estimates are provided for custom-designed programs. When customers decide to proceed with these classes, they pay a 50 percent deposit. Darya's Dance Studio also places purchase orders with regular suppliers who may require deposits.

Account Numbers

Darya's Dance Studio uses account numbers for all accounts.

Instructions

1. Using the Chart of Accounts, the Trial Balance, and other information, set up the company files for Darya's Dance Studio. Detailed keystroke instructions for the setup follow.

2. After completing the setup, record entries for the source documents for September 2012 in QuickBooks. The source documents begin on page 519, following the instructions for setup.

3. After you have finished making your entries, print the reports and graphs for September 2012 indicated on the following printing form.

REPORTS FOR SEPTEMBER 2012

Lists	Other	Sales
☐ Account Listing	☐ Transaction List by Date	☐ Open Invoices
☐ Customer Phone List	☐ Transaction Detail by Account	☐ Collections Report
☐ Customer Contact List		☐ Transaction List by Customer
☐ Vendor Phone List	☐ Custom Summary Report	
☐ Vendor Contact List	☐ Custom Transaction Detail Report	☐ Sales by Customer
☐ Item Listing	☐ Transaction History	☐ Sales by Item
☐ Item Price List	☐ Transaction Journal	☐ Open Sales Orders by Customer
☐ Tax Code		
☐ Terms List	Vendor	Banking

Lists

- ☐ Account Listing
- ☐ Customer Phone List
- ☐ Customer Contact List
- ☐ Vendor Phone List
- ☐ Vendor Contact List
- ☐ Item Listing
- ☐ Item Price List
- ☐ Tax Code
- ☐ Terms List

Company & Financial

- ☑ Balance Sheet Standard at Sep. 30
- ☑ Profit & Loss Standard from Sep. 01 to Sep. 30
- ☐ Expenses by Vendor
- ☐ Income by Customer

Accountant & Taxes

- ☑ Trial Balance at Sep. 30
- ☐ General Ledger
- ☑ Journal from Sep. 01 to Sep. 30

Other

- ☐ Transaction List by Date
- ☐ Transaction Detail by Account

- ☐ Custom Summary Report
- ☐ Custom Transaction Detail Report
- ☐ Transaction History
- ☐ Transaction Journal

Vendor

- ☑ A/P Aging Detail at Sep. 30
- ☐ Vendor Balance
- ☐ Unpaid Bills
- ☐ Transaction List by Vendor

Purchases

- ☐ Purchases by Vendor
- ☐ Purchases by Item
- ☐ Transaction List by Vendor
- ☐ Open Purchase Orders by Vendor

Customer

- ☑ A/R Aging Detail at Sep 30
- ☐ Customer Balance

- ☐ Open Invoices
- ☐ Collections Report
- ☐ Transaction List by Customer

Sales

- ☐ Sales by Customer
- ☐ Sales by Item
- ☐ Open Sales Orders by Customer

Banking

- ☐ Deposit Detail
- ☐ Cheque Detail
- ☑ Missing Cheques for 1050
- ☐ Reconcile Discrepancy
- ☐ Previous Reconciliation

GRAPHS

- ☐ Income and Expense
- ☐ Net Worth
- ☐ Accounts Payable
- ☐ Accounts Receivable
- ☐ Sales

Creating a New Company

We will create a set of files from scratch for Darya's Dance Studio rather than use the EasyStep Interview. We will review the setup steps from Chapter 5 as we use them in the setup and provide complete detail for any aspects that are new.

If you would prefer to skip the setup and work through the source documents only, open the Darya file in the Setup folder on the CD.

Refer to the setup instructions in Chapter 5 for more details and to review any of the setup steps.

1. **Start**   the **QuickBooks** program

2. **Choose**   the **File** menu and **click Close Company**

The files you worked with most recently are displayed in the central **No Company Open window**. We need to select the option to create a new company.

3. **Click**   the **Create a new company button** or **choose** the **File** menu and **click New Company**

The EasyStep Interview welcome screen appears:

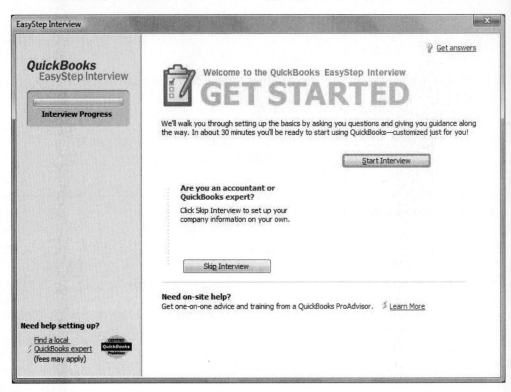

Figure 10-1

We must create the new file within the EasyStep Interview; however, we can leave the EasyStep Interview after we have saved the company file.

4. **Click**   **Skip Interview** to begin the setup of the company file and to open the Company Information window

The cursor is in the Company Name field. Darya's Dance Studio uses the legal name as the company name.

5. **Type**   **Darya's Dance Studio**

6. **Press**   (*tab*) to copy the company name to the Legal name field

7. **Press**   (*tab*) to advance to the first line of the Street address field

8. **Type**   **11 Nutcracker St.**

9. **Press**   (*tab*) to advance to the City field

10. **Type**   **Regina**

11. **Press**   (*tab*) to the Province field

12. **Click**   on the **drop-down arrow** in the Province field and **select SK**

13. **Press**   (*tab*) to the Postal Code field and **type S3G 2P6**

14. **Press**   (*tab*) to the Country field and **accept Canada**

15. **Press**   (*tab*) to the Phone field and **type (306) 224-8632**

16. **Press**   (*tab*) to advance to the FAX field and **type (306) 224-3918**

Notes
You can also enter or edit company information after creating the company file by choosing the Company menu and clicking Company Information.

Notes
You must format the phone and fax numbers in these fields the way you want them to appear in QuickBooks.

17.	**Press**	(tab) to advance to the E-mail address field
18.	**Type**	**lessons@daryasdance.com**
19.	**Press**	(tab) to advance to the Web site field
20.	**Type**	**www.daryasdance.com**

21. The completed Company Information screen should be displayed as shown here:

Figure 10-2

22.	**Click**	**Next** to open the next window in the EasyStep Interview where you indicate how your company is organized
23.	**Select**	**Sole Proprietorship**
24.	**Click**	**Next** to open the next window in the EasyStep Interview where the company's fiscal year is defined

Darya's Dance Studio begins its fiscal year and its income tax year in August.

25.	**Choose**	**August** from the drop-down list in the My fiscal year starts in field
26.	**Click**	**Next** to view the selection of industries available to choose from

Click some of the different industries on the list to view the preset accounts that QuickBooks will create for you when you choose that industry. These lists all include many accounts that we will not need. We will choose Other/None to start with only a few preset accounts.

27.	**Select**	**Other/None** as the industry (you will have to scroll down to the bottom of the list)
28.	**Click**	**Next** to continue to the Create your company file window

Notes
To close the books, the first month of the fiscal year must be 12 months before the closing date. You can change this month as needed if you want to close the books more frequently.

WARNING!
You cannot change the type of industry so you must choose carefully.

This screen indicates that your QuickBooks information will be stored in a company file. When you click the Finish button, you must select the file name and location to store your company file.

29. Click   **Finish** to continue to the File name for New Company screen

Now you must enter a file name and location for the data files. The name you entered for the company is the default file name and it is selected. We will name the file Dance. QuickBooks will add the appropriate file extension.

30. Type   **Dance** in the File name field

31. Change   the **location of the file** if necessary by selecting another location from the Save In field. **Click** the **drop-down arrow** in the Save In field to change folders or drives

32. Click   **Save**

Be patient while QuickBooks creates the file based on the information you have provided.

33. QuickBooks opens with the Home page displayed, and the Live Community tab opens by default

QuickBooks has created the new company file with some default settings that control how the program works; a preliminary set of taxes and codes for the province you selected for the business; and a set of payment terms, payment methods, and messages. The Chart of Accounts includes only some basic QuickBooks accounts. We will modify these defaults or preferences to suit Darya's Dance Studio. Then we will create the Chart of Accounts, the vendor and customer records, and the list of items. We also need to add historical information for accounts, customers, and vendors to create the opening balances for accounts and the outstanding balances for vendors and customers.

Setting Preferences

One of the first steps in setting up new company files is the creation of new accounts. However, before we can create the new accounts, we should select some preferences that will influence how the accounts are set up.

Other preferences include choosing default accounts, such as the accounts used for writing cheques or entering discounts and finance charges. We will set these preferences after creating the Chart of Accounts.

Refer to the sections in Chapter 5 beginning on pages 155, 179, and 200 to review QuickBooks Preferences.

1. Choose   the **Edit menu** and **click Preferences**

2. Click   the **Help button** to update the information displayed in the Help tab

The Preferences window opens at the My Preferences tab for General Preferences.

The General Preferences do not affect the financial aspects of the program, so you should decide how you want to interact with the program by choosing your settings. In our data files we have used the default settings for all QuickBooks preferences except the beep for entering transactions.

3. Click   the **Company Preferences tab**

The preferences on this tab affect the date and time formats for the data files. You can accept the default settings for dates. You can also decide whether changes you make to customer or vendor information in transactions will update the customer or vendor records permanently, and whether transactions should be saved before they are printed.

We will accept the default settings for the preferences on this tab.

4. Click the **Desktop View** preferences to view the Desktop View preferences

The settings on the Company Preferences tab allow you to select which features you use in QuickBooks. Depending on the features you select, the icons will be displayed on the Home page.

5. Click the **My Preferences tab**

Again, we have not changed the default settings that control the appearance of open windows in QuickBooks. You may select your own preferences if you want.

6. Click the **Payroll & Employees** heading to view the Payroll preferences

7. Click the **Company Preferences tab**

The preferences on the Company Preferences tab allow you to turn payroll on or off (assuming you have subscribed to QuickBooks payroll), and then set various payroll preferences. The QuickBooks student software includes payroll, so we will turn it off for this company file.

8. Select **No Payroll**

9. Click the **Reminders** preference heading to view the Reminder preferences

10. Click **Yes** to save the Payroll preferences.

On the My Preferences tab in the Reminders preference, you can select to show the Reminders List when opening the company file.

11. Click the **Company Preferences tab**

If you use reminders in the program, you should choose to show them and then indicate how you want to show them and how many days before the item is due that the reminder should be displayed on the Reminders list. We have not changed these settings for any of our data files. Use the Help button to provide more detail if needed.

12. Click the **Reports & Graphs** heading to view the Reports & Graphs preferences

13. Click **Yes** if you made any changes to the Reminders preferences and want to save them

The Company Preferences tab should be displayed.

14. Click the **Age From Transaction Date** under the Aging Reports heading to select it

15. Click the **My Preferences tab**

16. Choose the **Reports & Graphs** options you want for your data file on this tab

17. Click the **Spelling** heading to view the Spelling preferences

18. Click **Yes** to save the changes you made to the Reports & Graphs preferences

The My Preferences tab should be displayed.

19. Choose the **Spelling** options you want for your company data file

Before we create the accounts for the data file, we should define the accounting preference settings.

Notes
If you make changes to any of the QuickBooks preferences, you will be prompted to save your changes when you move to the next preference heading.

Changing Accounting Preferences

Preferences on the Company Preferences tab for all QuickBooks preferences can only be changed by the administrator of the company file. Other users cannot change these settings. If the file has only one user, then that user is the Administrator.

Most of the Accounting preferences are found on the Company Preferences tab for the Accounting preference, which means that only the Administrator can change the accounting preferences.

1. Click   the **Accounting** heading to view the Accounting preferences

2. Click   **Yes** to save any changes you made to the Spelling preferences

On the My Preferences tab, you can select to autofill the memo field in general journal entries. This means that when you enter general journal entries, the memo that you enter on the first line of the transaction will automatically be displayed for all other transaction lines in the journal entry.

3. Click   the **Company Preferences tab**:

Figure 10-3

One preference that affects accounts is the option to use account numbers. In some of our earlier applications, we did not use account numbers and accounts were listed in alphabetic order within their account type. When account numbers are used, the accounts are listed in numerical order within their account type. Although you can use any numbering system you want, it is best to use a logical sequence of account numbers. We will use the following numbering sequence for accounts:

- 1000–1999 Assets
- 2000–2999 Liabilities
- 3000–3999 Equity
- 4000–4999 Income
- 5000–5999 Expense

The default account setting is not to use account numbers, but Darya's Dance Studio uses account numbers. By changing this setting before we create accounts, we can add numbers at the start instead of editing all accounts later to add the numbers.

4. Click   **Use account numbers**

Notes
This numbering sequence is consistent with the GIFI codes used by CRA for online tax reporting by companies.

We will show all accounts — parent accounts as well as subaccounts — so that we can easily select the correct account when names are similar; therefore, we want to leave the Show lowest subaccount only option turned off. For example, *Depreciation* applies to more than one fixed asset account. When we display a depreciation account, we want to see which fixed asset account it belongs to. The only way to see this is to leave the Show lowest subaccount only option turned off. If we turn this option on, we would only see the depreciation account and may select the wrong one.

We will leave the Require accounts option selected so that income and expenses will be assigned to the appropriate income and expense accounts. If we turn this option off and do not enter an account during transaction entry, QuickBooks will post the income or expense account to the *Uncategorized Income* or *Uncategorized Expense* account.

QuickBooks will automatically assign numbers to journal entries. You have the option to be warned when we post transactions to the *Retained Earnings* account and when transactions are entered 90 days in the past or 30 days in the future. The number of days entered in these fields can also be modified. When we are ready to close the books, we can add the closing date and password. The password for this field prevents unauthorized changes to historical records.

Notes
Journal entry numbers are not assigned to other types of transactions.

Since the transactions in this textbook are in the year 2012 and are likely more than 30 days in the future in relation to your current computer date, we will turn off the *Warn if transactions are 30 days in the future* option so we do not receive a warning message each time we enter a transaction. In a work environment, you should keep this option selected to ensure proper dates are entered on your transactions.

5. **Click**   the **check box** beside the Warn if transactions are 30 days in the future option to turn this option off

Notes
If you are using this text in 2012 or later, turn off the *Warn if transactions are 90 days in the past* option.

Changing Sales Tax Preferences

Sales tax preferences are located on the Sales Tax Preferences screen.

1. **Click**   the **Sales Tax** preference heading

2. **Click**   **Yes** to save the Accounting Preferences changes

3. **Click**   the **Company Preferences tab**:

Figure 10-4

Most of the default settings are already correct. Darya's is registered for GST, so we must indicate that we charge sales taxes. The default selection for the Do you charge sales tax option should be set to "yes."

In the next section, you indicate whether you want to use customer and vendor tax codes. If you choose to use customer or vendor tax codes, a field will be available in each customer and vendor record, allowing you to select a tax code. If selected, QuickBooks will use the customer and vendor tax codes during transaction entry and they will over-ride item tax codes. Tax codes can always be changed during transaction entry. Although we won't be using customer and vendor tax codes, we will leave the Use Customer Tax Codes option selected so you can see the tax code field when setting up customers.

Customers pay GST on lessons, but no taxes on finance or NSF charges. In this scenario, it would be best to turn off the Use Customer Tax Codes option and use the taxes assigned to items and not customers, since all items use the same tax code. However, we will leave the Use Customer Tax Codes option selected so you can view the tax code field displayed in the customer records.

Under the Assign Sales Tax Codes heading, you enter the tax codes that you use most often for taxable and non-taxable items. These tax codes will be used as the default when setting up items and services. Taxable items are charged GST Only and non-taxable items are tax exempt.

4. **Leave**   the **checkmark** in the Allow Customer Tax Codes box displayed in order to leave this option selected

Although we won't be using customer sales tax codes, leave this option selected to view the sales tax code field displayed in customer records.

5. **Click**   the **drop-down arrow** in the Taxable Items field

6. **Click**   **G - GST Only** from the tax code list

For non-taxable items, E - Exempt is already selected and this is the tax code that we want to use by default for non-taxable items.

7. **Click**   **OK** to save the changes

Entering the Company Business Number

The Company business number is entered on the Company Information screen.

1. **Choose**   **Company** from the menu and **click Company Information:**

Figure 10-5

You can make the necessary changes to the information on this screen.

2. **Click**   the **CRA Business Number** field

3. **Type**   **577499299**

4. **Click**   **OK**

5. **Click**   the **Continue Anyway button** when the Invalid Business Number message is displayed

Notes
When you're setting up your own company file, you will have a valid business number to enter.

Creating the Chart of Accounts

It is not necessary to enter all the required accounts in the Chart of Accounts before using QuickBooks on a daily basis because they can be created from any account field on the fly; however, we will create them first so that we can choose the default accounts for the other setup steps as they are needed. We can also monitor the creation of the accounts in a logical order when we set them up first.

In this chapter, we will show the New Account screens for the types of accounts and features that were not covered in Chapter 5. For a review of how to create new accounts, refer to page 162.

New accounts are created from the Chart of Accounts list.

1. **Click**   the **Chart of Accounts** icon   in the Company section of the Home page to open the Chart of Accounts:

Notes
You can also choose the Lists menu and click Chart of Accounts or press _ctrl_ + **A** to open the Chart of Accounts.

Figure 10-6

As you can see, some accounts are set up in the Chart of Accounts by default even though we selected Other/None as the industry in the EasyStep Interview. We will use some of these default accounts, rename others, and delete or make other accounts inactive.

Also notice that each default account has been given an account number. These numbers do not match the account numbering system that we are using, so they will have to be modified.

<table>
<tr><td>2. **Click**</td><td>the **Account button** to view the list menu and **click New**, or **press** <kbd>ctrl</kbd> + **N**</td></tr>
</table>

Notes

When you create accounts on the fly from an account field, the account type that is most commonly used for that field will be selected as the default.

When you create accounts directly from the Chart of Accounts list, the account type for the new account is blank.

Entering Bank Accounts

<table>
<tr><td>1. **Select**</td><td>**Bank** as the account type and **click Continue** to display the Add New Account form:</td></tr>
</table>

Figure 10-7

Because we chose to use account numbers, a Number field is added to all Account forms. The bank account is not a subaccount. We are not using online banking so we don't need to add the name of the bank and account number. We also are not using pre-printed cheques so we can leave those fields blank as well.

We need to add the opening account balance. We will enter the balance as of August 31, 2012, the day before we begin to use the program for current transactions. By using this opening date, we can produce complete reports for current entries beginning in September without including the historical transactions.

We need to enter three bank accounts:

Number	Name	Opening Balance	Date
1050	Bank - Chequing	$ 8,860.00	August 31/12
1080	Bank - Savings	14,900.00	August 31/12
1100	Bank - Credit Card	6,400.00	August 31/12

2. Press (tab) or **click** the **Number field**

3. Type **1050**

4. Press (tab) to advance to the Account Name field

5. Type **Bank - Chequing**

6. Click the **Enter Opening Balance** button to display the Enter Opening Balance screen:

Notes
Remember that we cannot use colons in account names. Colons are reserved for subaccounts and are added automatically by the program.

Figure 10-8

7. Type **8860** in the Statement Ending Balance field

8. Press (tab)

9. Type **08/31/12** in the Statement Ending Date field

Because you will need the same opening balance date for all accounts, you can copy it so you can easily paste it in the rest of the accounts and you don't have to type it each time.

10. Double click the **date** and **press** (ctrl) + **C** to copy the date to the Windows Clipboard

When you enter the next account and reach the Statement Ending Date field, press (ctrl) + **V** to paste the date.

11. Click **OK**

Notes
Remember that you can also use spaces or other characters as separators in the date field. For example:
Type 8 31 12 (or)
Type 8.31.12

Before we create more accounts, let's return to the Chart of Accounts.

12. Click   **Save & Close** to save the account and return to the Chart of Accounts

13. Click   **No** when prompted to set up online services

Notice that QuickBooks has created an *Opening Balance Equity* account. The account currently has a credit balance of $8,860.00 — the same amount as the *Bank Chequing* account. The *Opening Balance Equity* account is used as the offsetting account when setting up opening balances. We will rename this account later and make adjustments to the amount as needed.

We will continue adding the rest of the account in the Chart of Accounts.

14. Press   ⌃ctrl + **N** to open the Add New Account form

If a message is displayed about pre-printed cheques, click Do not display this message in the future and click No (we are not using pre-printed cheques).

15. Create   the **Bank - Savings** account. Refer to the list on page 460.

16. Click   **Save & New** or **press** ⌥alt + **N** to save the account and open a blank Add New Account form

The *Bank - Credit Card* account, used for deposits from customer credit card receipts, is also a bank account. Do not select the Credit Card account type for this account. The Credit Card account type applies to credit cards used by the business and creates a credit card payable account, a liability account. The Credit Card account type cannot be used for credit cards accepted in payment from customers.

17. Enter   the **Bank - Credit Card** account. Refer to the list on page 460.

18. Click   **Save & New** or **press** ⌥alt + **N** to open another blank Add New Account form

Entering Accounts Receivable Accounts

1. Click   the **drop-down arrow** in the Type field and **click Accounts Receivable** (or **type a**) to change the Add New Account form:

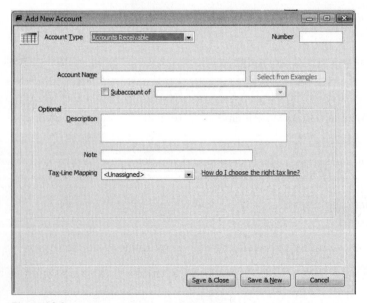

> **Notes**
> When you type a or A in the Type field, Accounts Receivable will be selected as the type because it is the next account type in the list whose initial letter is A. Accounts Payable appears later in the list so it would not be selected. If you type A again, or type A from an Accounts Receivable form, Accounts Payable will be displayed because it is the next type in the list that begins with the letter A.
>
> Keyboard shortcuts are not case sensitive so you can type A or a.

Figure 10-9

Fields that apply to bank accounts have been removed. When Accounts Receivable is selected as the account type, the form does not have an Enter Opening Balance button because its balance is created automatically by QuickBooks as the sum of all amounts owed by customers. The balance is increased from the sales invoices and opening balances you enter for customers. Customer payments reduce the *Accounts Receivable* balance. We will enter these amounts when we create the customer records.

2.	**Press**	(tab) to advance to the Number field
3.	**Type**	**1200**. **Press** (tab) to advance to the Account Name field
4.	**Type**	**Accounts Receivable**
5.	**Click**	**Save & New** or **press** (alt) + **N** to save the account and open a blank Add New Account form

Entering Other Current Asset Accounts

The next accounts are also current assets but they are neither bank nor accounts receivable accounts. This group is called Other Current Assets. When you clicked Save & New to open an Add New Account form, the previous account type you used remains selected as the default.

6.	**Click**	the **drop-down arrow** in the Type field and **select Other Current Asset** as the account type (or **type o**) to change the Add New Account form

Notes
Typing o will advance to the next account type on the list that begins with the letter o. In this case, if you start from Accounts Receivable, you will advance to Other Current Asset.

Fields that apply only to bank accounts are not included but the Enter Opening Balance button is available. The bank account number field remains because assets like treasury bills or investments are current assets that may be linked to a bank account.

For this group of accounts you must enter the account number, account name, opening balance, and date. The remaining fields, including the description, are optional.

The three other current asset accounts are listed here, with the descriptions in brackets:

Number	Name	Opening Balance	Date
1260	Music Inventory (CDs and sheet music)	$1,460.00	08/31/12
1280	Prepaid Insurance	4,500.00	08/31/12
1300	Office and Computer Supplies	480.00	08/31/12

7.	**Press**	(tab) to advance to the Number field
8.	**Type**	**1260**
9.	**Press**	(tab) to advance to the Account Name field
10.	**Type**	**Music Inventory**
11.	**Click**	the **Description field**
12.	**Type**	**CDs and sheet music**
13.	**Click**	the **Enter Opening Balance button**
14.	**Type**	**1460** in the Opening Balance field
15.	**Press**	(tab) to select the as of date field
16.	**Press**	(ctrl) + **V** to paste the date if you copied it earlier (or type 08/31/12)

| 17. | **Click** | **OK** |
| 18. | **Click** | **Save & New** or **press** (alt) **+ N** |

Enter the two Other Current Asset accounts and then click Save & New to open a blank Add New Account form.

Entering Fixed Asset Accounts

Notes
You can also create items for fixed assets and enter the purchase date and cost to help track these assets. You can enter these special items when you purchase or order fixed assets.

Darya's Dance Studio's fixed assets are grouped into parent (heading) and subaccounts for each type of asset. This structure allows us to view the net asset value or subaccount total (cost minus accumulated depreciation) in the parent account balance.

Other Current Asset is still selected as the type.

| 1. | **Click** | the **drop-down arrow** in the Account Type field and **select Fixed Asset** as the account type (or **type f**) to change the Add New Account form |

Fixed asset account forms also allow you to add a note.

Notes
The account type for a subaccount must be the same as the account type for its parent account.

For parent accounts, you must enter the account number and account name. For subaccounts you must enter the number, name, opening balance, and date; indicate that the account is a subaccount; and choose the parent account from the list. The other fields are optional. For parent accounts, the balance is calculated automatically by the program as the sum of its subaccount balances.

Depreciation accounts are contra-asset accounts. Their credit balances are entered as negative amounts, so they reduce the total asset value.

The complete list of fixed assets is displayed in the following chart:

No.	Name	Subaccount of	Description	Opening Balance	Date
1500	Computers	[Parent account]			
1520	Cost	1500 Computers	Original cost of computers	$4,500.00	08/31/12
1540	Depreciation	1500 Computers	Accum deprec on computers	−1,820.00	08/31/12
1560	Piano	[Parent account]			
1580	Cost	1560 Piano	Original cost of piano	$10,000.00	08/31/12
1600	Depreciation	1560 Piano	Accum deprec on piano	−1,450.00	08/31/12
1620	Stereo Equipment	[Parent account]			
1640	Cost	1620 Stereo Equipment	Original cost of stereo equip	$6,000.00	08/31/12
1660	Depreciation	1620 Stereo Equipment	Accum deprec on stereo equip	−2,430.00	08/31/12
1700	Studio	[Parent account]			
1720	Cost	1700 Studio	Original cost of studio	$90,000.00	08/31/12
1740	Depreciation	1700 Studio	Accum deprec on studio	−6,000.00	08/31/12
1760	Vehicle	[Parent account]			
1780	Cost	1760 Vehicle	Original cost of vehicle	$24,000.00	08/31/12
1800	Depreciation	1760 Vehicle	Accum deprec on vehicle	−9,720.00	08/31/12

2.	**Press**	(tab) to advance to the Number field
3.	**Type**	**1500**
4.	**Press**	(tab) to advance to the Account Name field
5.	**Type**	**Computers**

You do not need to define an account as a parent account. QuickBooks defines a parent account automatically when you identify a subaccount for it. QuickBooks also calculates its opening balance as the sum of all its subaccount balances.

| 6. | **Click** | **Save & New** or **press** (alt) **+ N** |

7.	**Press**	(tab) to advance to the Number field
8.	**Type**	**1520**
9.	**Press**	(tab) to advance to the Account Name field
10.	**Type**	**Cost**
11.	**Click**	the **box** beside the Subaccount of field to display a ✓ in the box
12.	**Press**	(tab)
13.	**Click**	the **drop-down arrow** in the subaccount name field
14.	**Choose**	account **1500 - Computers**
15.	**Press**	(tab) to advance to the Description field
16.	**Type**	**Original cost of computers**
17.	**Click**	the **Enter Opening Balance** button
18.	**Type**	**4500** in the Opening Balance field
19.	**Press**	(tab) to advance to the as of field
20.	**Press**	(ctrl) + **V** to paste the date (or **type 08/31/12**)
21.	**Click**	**Save & New** or **press** (alt) + **N**
22.	**Enter**	the **remaining Fixed Asset accounts** in the chart on page 476.

Depreciation accounts are contra-asset accounts with a credit balance that reduces the total asset value on the Balance Sheet. Therefore, you must enter negative opening balance amounts (add a minus sign) for these accounts.

23.	**Click**	**Save & Close** or **press** (alt) + **a** after adding account 1800 to save and close the Add New Accounts form and return to the Chart of Accounts

We have now completed entering all of the assets accounts for Darya's Dance Studio.

Entering Liability Accounts

Liability accounts are the next group of accounts that we will enter. As with assets, there are several types of liability accounts. *Accounts Payable* is the first type of QuickBooks liability account — it appears before other liability accounts on the Balance Sheet; however, it was automatically entered when we created the company file. We do not have to enter the *Accounts Payable* account; however, we do need to change the account number assigned automatically by QuickBooks.

1.	**Right click**	the **Accounts Payable account**
2.	**Click**	**Edit Account**

Your cursor should be in the Number field. Notice the number automatically assigned by QuickBooks to this account is 20000. This number does not fit in with our account numbers so we will have to change it.

3.	**Type**	**2100**

The Accounts Payable account has no opening balance because the balance is created automatically by the program as the sum of all amounts owing to vendors. The

Notes
QuickBooks has some helpful shortcuts on the Add New Account form. From the Name field, press (tab) to advance to the Subaccount field. Press the Space bar to select the subaccount option. The space bar will also toggle the subaccount option off. Press (tab) to move to the Subaccount name field. Type c— the first letter in the Computers account name and press (tab) to continue. Computers is the first account on the Chart of Accounts beginning with the letter c, so it is entered as the default. If it was not the first account on the Chart of Accounts beginning with the letter c, all accounts beginning with the letter c would be displayed where you can then highlight the account you want to use.

Notes
Enter negative amounts for depreciation accounts by adding a minus sign in the Opening Balance field.

balance is updated each time you enter a purchase invoice, a bill, or an opening balance amount for a vendor.

    4. Click   **Save & Close** to save the account and return to the Chart of Accounts list

Entering Credit Card Accounts

Credit Card accounts appear next in order on the Balance Sheet. This account type is reserved for credit cards that the business uses for purchases. Darya's uses one credit card for business and has a single account for it.

    1. Press   ⌐ctrl⌐ **+ N** to open the Add New Account form

    2. Choose   **Credit Card** as the account type and **click Continue**

Figure 10-10

    The Credit Card form has a field for the credit card number. This field is optional. For security reasons, you may not want to include the card number in your data files.

    3. Type   **2150** in the Number field

    4. Press   ⌐tab⌐ to advance to the Account Name field

    5. Type   **Visa Payable**

    6. Click   the **Enter Opening Balance** button

    7. Type   **875** in the Statement Ending Balance field

    8. Press   ⌐tab⌐ to advance to the Statement Ending Date

    9. Press   ⌐ctrl⌐ **+ V** to paste the date (or type 08/31/12)

    10. Click   **OK**

    11. Click   **Save & New** or **press** ⌐alt⌐ **+ N** to open a new blank Add New Account form

Entering Other Current Liability Accounts

The next group of liability accounts are other current liabilities. QuickBooks has already created four accounts in this group — *GST/HST Payable, GST/QST Payable, Payroll Liabilities,* and *PST Payable (SK).* We need to add one other current liability account type, the *Bank Loan* account.

    1. Choose   **Other Current Liability** as the account type (or **type o**)

    This form has the same input fields as the Other Current Asset type. Refer to page 475 for assistance if needed.

    2. Enter   the **account number, name, opening balance, and date** for the Bank Loan account

Number	Name	Opening Balance	Date
2260	Bank Loan	$11,500.00	08/31/12

    3. Click   **Save & New** or **press** `alt` + **N** to open a blank Add New Account form

Entering Long Term Liability Accounts

Long Term Liabilities form the final group of liability accounts. They are not due within the next year and therefore appear after Current Liabilities on the Balance Sheet.

    1. Choose   **Long Term Liability** as the account type (or **type l**) to enter the next group of accounts

    This form has the same fields as Other Current Assets and Other Current Liabilities (see page 475).

    2. Add   the **two long term liability accounts** by entering the account number, name, opening balance, and date.

Number	Name	Opening Balance	Date
2720	Long Term Loan	$22,000.00	08/31/12
2740	Mortgage Payable	$30,000.00	08/31/12

    3. Click   **Save & New** or **press** `ctrl` + **N** to save the account and open a blank Add New Account form

Entering Equity Accounts

QuickBooks has already created three equity accounts: *Opening Balance Equity, Owners Draw,* and *Owners Equity.* We will modify these accounts. The *Opening Balance Equity* account will be renamed *Capital, Darya Danovich.* The *Owners Equity* account will be deleted and the *Owners Draw* account will be renamed *Drawings, Darya Danovich.* We will edit the accounts later in the Deleting and Making Accounts Inactive and the Editing Accounts section to match the Equity section in our Chart of Accounts shown on page 459.

Entering Income Accounts

After adding all the Balance Sheet accounts, we must create Income Statement accounts. Darya's Dance Studio has only regular income accounts.

1. Choose   **Income** as the account type (or **type i**) to change the Add New Account form

    The balance for income accounts is generated automatically from the transactions for the account. We will add the year-to-date income balances in a ledger entry for the *Opening Balance Equity* account (decreasing equity balance) after creating all accounts.

2. Create   the **following income accounts**. **Enter account numbers and names**:

Number	Name
4100	Revenue from Lessons
4160	Sales Discounts
4200	Revenue from Interest
4250	Other Revenue

3. Click   **Save & New** or **press** ⌨ctrl + **N** to save the account and open a blank Add New Account form

Entering Expense Accounts

QuickBooks has two types of expense accounts: Cost of Goods Sold to calculate Gross Profit, and other expenses to determine Net Income. Service businesses like Darya's have no Cost of Goods Sold accounts so we will only enter the expense accounts.

1. Choose   **Expense** as the account type (or **type e**) to change the Add New Account form

    Like income accounts, the expense account balance is generated by the program from transactions for the account. We will make the adjusting entry for the opening balance (year-to-date expenses) later.

    Expense accounts are listed in the following chart:

Notes
If Bank is selected as the account Type, type e to select Equity and then type e again to select Expense.

Number	Name	Tax Code	Number	Name	Tax Code
5020	Advertising and Promotion	S	5180	Printing and Copying	S
5060	Office and Computer Supplies Used		5200	Property Tax Expense	
5080	Music Inventory Expenses		5220	Purchase Discounts	
5100	Depreciation Expense		5240	Hydro Expense	G
5120	Maintenance Expenses	G	5260	Telephone Expense	S
5140	Insurance Expense	P	5280	Vehicle Expenses	S
5160	Interest Expense		5300	Wages Expenses	

2. Create   the **expense accounts**. For each account, **enter** the **account number, name, and tax code**, if there is one

3. Click   **Save & Close** instead of Save & New to save the account and close the Add New Account form after adding the Wages Expenses account

Notes
Two other account types are not used by Darya's. These are the Other Income and Other Expense account types. These accounts would be used for one-time events in the business, such as losses or gains from the sale of assets.

You will be returned to the Chart of Accounts. You should notice several changes. All the new accounts you created have been added with balances, if you entered them. The following accounts need some adjustments:

a. The *GST/HST Payable* account needs to be renumbered and renamed to GST Payable (Saskatchewan does not collect HST) and it does not have a balance yet. The balance will be entered when the historical invoices, which include GST, are entered

b. The *GST/QST Payable* account is not needed and needs to be removed. This account is associated with a sales tax agency vendor, so we will make both the GST/QST Payable account and the associated sales tax agency inactive.

c. The *PST Payable (SK)* account is not needed and needs to be removed. This account is associated with a sales tax agency vendor, so we will make both the PST Payable (SK) account and the associated sales tax agency inactive.

d. The *Opening Balance Equity* account balance has changed. Every time you entered an account balance, the program added an offsetting amount to the *Opening Balance Equity* account. If the account you created had a debit balance, the *Opening Balance Equity* account was credited by the same amount. If you added a credit balance, a debit amount was entered for the *Opening Balance Equity* account. This ensures that the Trial Balance remains balanced. We will renumber and rename this account to *3200 Capital, Darya Danovich* and correct the balance by adding outstanding historical income and expense amounts.

e. The *Owners Draw* account needs to be renumbered and renamed to *3260 Drawings, Darya Danovich*.

f. The *Owners Equity* account is not needed and needs to be removed.

g. The *Uncategorized Expenses* account is not needed and needs to be removed.

h. The *Payroll Liabilities* and *Payroll Expenses* accounts are not needed. These accounts are used in payroll items that have been set up by default; therefore, they cannot be deleted so we'll make these accounts inactive.

Always check the account balances with the amounts in the reports used to enter the setup information.

4. **Compare** the **Chart of Accounts** on the screen with the information on pages 459 and 460, and **mark** the **accounts** that require corrections.

We will now make the necessary corrections to the Chart of Accounts.

Deleting and Making Accounts Inactive

QuickBooks automatically creates accounts when you create a new company. You may want to delete some of those accounts to match your own Chart of Accounts. Accounts with a balance, linked to other items in QuickBooks or those that have been used in journal transactions, cannot be deleted.

If an account cannot be deleted, you can make it inactive to remove it from the Chart of Accounts. For example, you will see that some of the accounts in this exercise cannot be deleted from the Chart of Accounts because they are linked to other QuickBooks items. You will have to make them inactive in order to remove them from the Chart of Accounts.

> **WARNING!**
> The Opening Balance Equity amount may still be incorrect if you entered an incorrect amount for any account or you omitted an account balance.

The Chart of Accounts includes six accounts that are not needed for this company: *GST/QST Payable, PST Payable (SK), Owners Equity, Uncategorized Expenses, Payroll Liabilities*, and the *Payroll Expenses* accounts. The Chart of Accounts should still be open.

1. **Highlight**   the **GST/QST Payable account**

2. **Press**   *ctrl* + **D** to delete the account and the following warning will be displayed:

Figure 10-11

The warning indicates that you cannot delete this account because it is associated with a sales tax agency, the Ministère du Revenu. We will make the account and the sales tax agency inactive.

First, we will make the *GST/QST Payable* account inactive.

3. **Click**   **OK** to close the warning

4. **Right click**   the **GST/QST Payable** account

5. **Select**   **Make Account Inactive**

Notice that the *GST/QST Payable* account is removed from the Chart of Accounts.

Next, we will remove the sales tax agency, the Ministère du Revenu, from the Vendors list.

6. **Click**   the **Vendor Centre icon** on the Icon bar

7. **Highlight**   the **Ministère du Revenu**

8. **Press**   *ctrl* + **D**

9. The following warning will be displayed:

Figure 10-12

The warning indicates that you cannot delete this vendor because it is used in the "Payable to" field in a payroll item. We will make the sales tax agency inactive.

10. **Click**   **OK** to close the warning

11. **Right click**   on **Ministère du Revenu**

12. **Select**   **Make Vendor Inactive**

The vendor's name is no longer displayed by default on the Vendor list and cannot be selected from Vendor fields in QuickBooks forms.

You can restore a vendor record (make it active) at any time. Click the drop-down arrow in the View field and select All Vendors. All active and inactive vendors will be displayed in the Vendor list. The inactive vendors will be marked with an X displayed in the column to the left. To make an inactive vendor active, right click an inactive vendor and choose Make Vendor Active. You can also click the X displayed in the column to the left, which will remove the X and automatically make the vendor active.

Notice the Ministère du Revenu is removed from the Vendors list.

13. **Close**   the **Vendor Centre**

14. **Return**   to the **Chart of Accounts**

15. **Highlight**   the **PST Payable (SK)** account

16. **Press**   ⌷ctrl⌷ + **D**

17. **Click**   **OK** to accept the warning

Just like with the *GST/QST Payable* account, you receive a warning that the *PST Payable (SK)* account cannot be deleted because it is associated with the Saskatchewan Finance sales tax agency. We need to make the account and the sales tax agency inactive.

18. **Make**   the **PST Payable (SK)** account inactive

19. **Make**   the **Saskatchewan Finance sales tax agency** inactive

20. **Return**   to the **Chart of Accounts**

We will now delete the *Owners Equity* account.

21. **Right click** the **Owners Equity account**

22. **Press**   ⌷ctrl⌷ + **D**

23. The following message will be displayed:

Figure 10-13

This message is displayed if the account can be deleted from the Chart of Accounts.

24. **Click**   **OK** to delete the account

We will now delete the *Uncategorized Expenses* account.

25. **Right click** the **Uncategorized Expenses account**

26. **Press**   ⌷ctrl⌷ + **D**

27. **Click**   **OK** to delete the account

Notes
Follow the same steps used to make the GST/QST Payable account and the Ministère du Revenu sales tax agency inactive.

We will remove the *Payroll Liabilities* and *Payroll Expenses* accounts.

28. Highlight   the **Payroll Liabilities account**

29. Press   (ctrl) + **D** to delete the account and the following warning will be displayed:

Figure 10-14

This warning indicates that the account is used on a payroll item and cannot be deleted. We will make the account inactive.

30. Click   **OK** to close the warning

31. Right click   the **Payroll Liabilities** account

32. Click   **Make Account Inactive**

The *Payroll Liabilities* account is now removed from the Chart of Accounts.

33. Right click   the **Payroll Expenses** account

34. Press   (ctrl) + **D**

Just like with the *Payroll Liabilities* account, you receive a warning that the account cannot be deleted because it is used on a payroll item. We need to make the account inactive.

35. Right click   the **Payroll Expenses** account

36. Click   **Make Account Inactive**

The *Payroll Expenses* account is now removed from the Chart of Accounts.

Editing Accounts

When you review the Chart of Accounts, you may find that some of the accounts were entered incorrectly. You can easily correct an account number or name at this stage by opening the account record. To correct an opening balance or date, you must change the amount in the ledger for the account. As soon as you save a new account, the Opening Balance field is no longer available in the record.

Editing Account Names and Numbers

The accounts created by QuickBooks do not match the accounts on our Chart of Accounts so we need to edit them. We need to edit the *GST/HST Payable* account and the equity accounts. The *GST/HST Payable* account name and number are incorrect, and the equity account names and numbers require the changes shown in the following chart:

Number	Name	Changes to	Number	Name
25500	GST/HST Payable		2460	GST Payable
30000	Opening Balance Equity		3200	Capital, Darya Danovich
30800	Owners Draw		3260	Drawings, Darya Danovich

1. **Open**   the **Chart of Accounts**

2. **Click**   **25500 GST/HST Payable**

3. **Press**   `ctrl` + **E**, or **choose** the **Account** button and **click Edit Account**

Notes
You can also edit an account by choosing the Edit menu and clicking Edit Account when the account is highlighted.

The Edit Account form appears for the selected account:

Figure 10-15

Notice that the Enter Opening Balance button has been removed for the *Other Current Liability* account. The account type is dimmed. Some account types cannot be changed. (Refer to page 488 for assistance with correcting account types.) The *GST Payable* account is linked to the GST tax setup so its type cannot be changed. The *Opening Balance Equity* account is also a special linked account, so its type cannot be changed. To edit an account balance, we need to edit the ledger for the account. The account number is highlighted so we can change it.

4. **Type**   **2460** to replace the account number

5. **Press**   `tab` to advance to the account name

6. **Type**   **GST Payable**

7. **Click**   **Save & Close** to save the change and return to the Chart of Accounts

8. **Highlight**   **30000 Opening Balance Equity**

9. **Press**   `ctrl` + **E**

10.	**Type**	**3200** to replace the account number
11.	**Press**	(tab) to advance to the account name
12.	**Type**	**Capital, Darya Danovich**
13.	**Click**	**Save & Close** to save the changes and return to the Chart of Accounts
14.	**Highlight**	**30800 Owners Draw**
15.	**Press**	(ctrl) + **E**
16.	**Type**	**3260** to replace the account number
17.	**Press**	(tab) to advance to the account name
18.	**Type**	**Drawings, Darya Danovich**
19.	**Click**	**Enter Opening Balance** button
20.	**Type**	**7400**
21.	**Press**	(tab) to advance to the as of field
22.	**Type**	**08/31/12**
23.	**Click**	**OK**
24.	**Click**	**Save & Close** to save the changes and return to the Chart of Accounts

Editing Opening Balances and Dates

As soon as you save a new account with its opening balance, the opening balance field is closed. To edit the balance, or the opening balance date, you must edit the ledger entry.

We need to add $990.00 as the opening balance for *GST Payable* on Aug. 31, 2012. The balance will also be added to *Capital, Darya Danovich*. Because the opening balance field is not available, we have to create a journal entry to add the account balance.

The Chart of Accounts should still be open.

1. **Double click 2460 GST Payable** to open the account's register

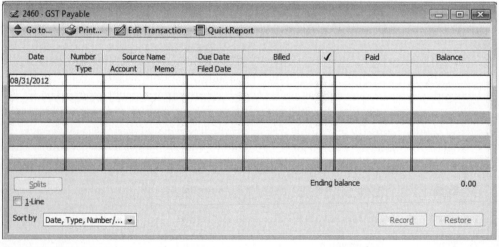

Figure 10-16

The last date you used for opening balances should be entered. However, when you try to enter information in any of the fields, you will find that the fields are locked. We need to enter the opening balance as a General Journal entry.

2. **Double click**   the **date** or **double click any field** in the first register entry to view the message that QuickBooks automatically assigns numbers to journal entries

3. **Click**   the **Do not display this message in the future option** and then **click OK** to close the message

4. The Make General Journal Entries form is displayed

The *GST Payable* account is different from other General Ledger accounts because of its link to the tax report. The journal entry form has an extra Tax Item column for this account. In this column, you must choose the tax item that the amount is associated with. To connect the *GST Payable* opening balance to the correct lines on the GST return, we will enter the GST on purchases separately from the GST collected on sales. That is, we will enter two separate detail lines on the journal entry so that we can select the correct tax item for each line. The *Capital, Darya Danovich* account will be used as the offsetting account. For Darya's Dance Studio, these tax amounts are shown below:

Tax Account	GST Paid on Purchases	GST Collected on Sales	GST Payable
2460 GST Payable	$640.00	$1,630.00	$990.00

Notes
As a liability account, GST Payable normally has a credit entry. GST collected on sales increases the liability so a credit amount is entered. GST paid on purchases reduces the liability so it requires a debit entry. Refer to Chapter 2 for additional information on GST.

5. **Enter**   **08/31/12** as the date if this is not the date shown for the entry

6. **Click**   the **Debit field** on the first line of the journal entry

7. **Type**   **640**

8. **Press**   (tab) to advance to the Memo field

9. **Type**   **Opening account balance**

10. **Press**   (tab) to advance to the Tax Item field

11. **Click**   the **drop-down arrow** in the field to view the tax items available:

Tax Item		
< Add New >		
GST	Sales Tax Item	GST on sales
GST (ITC)	Sales Tax Item	GST on purchases (Input Tax Credit)
GST (ITC) Adjustments	Sales Tax Item	GST Adjustments on purchases (Input Ta...
GST (ITC) Zero Rated	Sales Tax Item	GST on Zero Rated purchases (Input Tax...
GST Adjustments	Sales Tax Item	GST Adjustments on sales
GST Instalments	Sales Tax Item	GST Instalments and net tax paid
GST Zero Rated	Sales Tax Item	GST on Zero Rated sales

Figure 10-17

12. **Click**   **GST (ITC) - GST on purchases (Input Tax Credit)**

13. **Press**   (tab) to the second line on the journal entry

14. **Click**   the **drop-down arrow** in the Account field

15. **Choose**   **2460 - GST Payable** from the account list

16. **Click**   the **Credit field**

17. **Type**   **1630**

18. **Press**   (tab) to advance to the Tax Item field

19. **Click**   the **drop-down arrow** in the field

20. **Click**   **GST - GST on sales**

Notes
Typing a negative amount in the Debit field also generates a credit entry.

21. Press   tab to the third line on the journal entry

22. Click   the **drop-down arrow** in the Account field

23. Choose   **Capital, Darya Danovich**

The debit entry is correct.

24. The completed journal entry should be displayed as shown:

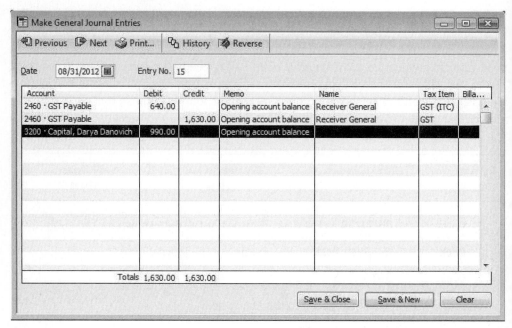

Figure 10-18

25. Click   **Save & Close** to save the transaction and return to the *GST Payable* Register

Both entries to the *GST Payable* account have been added to the register, and the final balance of $990.00 as shown in the bottom right-hand corner of the register is correct.

26. Close   the **GST Payable** register to return to the Chart of Accounts.

The *GST Payable* balance is now displayed in the Chart of Accounts.

⚠️ **WARNING!** Do not change account types except to make corrections. An account's position in the Balance Sheet and Income statement is linked to the account type.

CORRECTING BALANCE SHEET ACCOUNT OPENING BALANCES

To edit other amounts or dates for other Balance Sheet accounts, open the Chart of Accounts. Double click an account name to open the account register. Highlight the date or amount that is incorrect. Type the correction. Click Record and then click Yes to confirm the change.

CORRECTING AN ACCOUNT TYPE

To edit the account type, click the account type list and select the correct type. However, some account types cannot be changed; you cannot change an account type to or from Accounts Receivable or Accounts Payable, and parent and subaccounts must be of the same type. QuickBooks will display a warning message when you try to make one of these changes. If the account type is dimmed, as it is for the GST Payable account and the Capital, Darya Danovich account, you cannot change the account type.

If you cannot change the account type, you must delete the account. If the account has been used in journal entries, you must delete the journal entry (the opening balance) before you can delete the account. Entering an opening balance creates a journal entry. To delete an opening balance, open the account register and highlight the journal entry. Choose the Edit menu and click Delete Journal. Click Yes to confirm. Close the register and then delete the account (press ctrl + D). Click Yes to confirm. Create the account again and choose the account type carefully.

Entering Opening Income and Expense Account Balances

The ideal time for a business to convert its accounting records to QuickBooks is after closing the books or at the start of a new fiscal period. At that time, all the income and expense accounts have zero balances. But you can convert the files after the start of the fiscal period. You have two options at this point: to add all the transactions for the fiscal period up to the starting date, or to enter historical outstanding amounts as summaries.

When adding income and expense accounts, the Add New Account form does not include the Enter Opening Balance button, which allows the opening balance to be entered for an account. Assuming that you do not want to enter all the transactions for the fiscal period up to the starting date, the opening balances for income and expense accounts can be entered either as journal entries on the Make General Journal Entries form or as transactions in the offsetting account register — the capital account. We will enter one transaction for income and one transaction for expenses in the capital account register. We cannot access the registers for income or expense accounts, which is why we must add the appropriate amounts for these accounts to the *Capital, Darya Danovich* account.

1. **Double click** the **Capital, Darya Danovich** account to open the account register:

Figure 10-19

Notice that each opening balance appears as an individual entry in the register. We could enter the historical income and expense amounts individually as well but it is faster to enter them together as a split transaction. A split transaction indicates that the transaction is split across different accounts.

The date is correct — 08/31/2012. This date is entered because our General Preferences included the option to use the last transaction date as the default, and we used this date for the *GST Payable* entry.

2. **Click** the **Splits button** [Splits] in the lower left-hand corner of the screen

A warning will be displayed indicating that you cannot use registers to enter transactions with sales taxes.

3. **Click** the **box** beside Do not display this message in the future

4. **Click** **OK** to accept the warning

> **Notes**
> You can access revenue and income accounts from the Make General Journal Entries form, but the account registers are not available for these accounts.

> **Notes**
> You could also make a General Journal entry as we did for GST Payable.

5. The split area is displayed as shown here:

Figure 10-20

The income amounts we need to add are summarized in the following chart:

Number	Name	Amount
4100	Revenue from Lessons	$3,800.00
4160	Sales Discounts	−30.00
4200	Revenue from Interest	20.00

Notes

Sales Discounts is a contra-revenue account. Since this balance reduces the total revenue, you must enter it as a negative amount.

6.	**Click**	the **drop-down arrow** in the account field on the first line in the transaction
7.	**Choose**	**4100 Revenue from Lessons**
8.	**Press**	⌨ *tab* to advance to the Amount field
9.	**Type**	**3800**
10.	**Click**	the **drop-down arrow** in the account field on the second line in the transaction
11.	**Choose**	**4160 Sales Discounts**
12.	**Press**	⌨ *tab* to advance to the Amount field
13.	**Type**	**−30**
14.	**Click**	the drop-down arrow in the account field on the third line in the transaction
15.	**Choose**	**4200 Revenue from Interest**
16.	**Press**	⌨ *tab*
17.	**Type**	**20**
18.	**Click**	the **Memo field** beside **-split-** in the Ledger section of the transaction
19.	**Type**	**Opening income balance**

Notice that QuickBooks enters the total income amount of $3,790.00 automatically in the Decrease column in the *Capital, Darya Danovich* account register.

20.	**Check**	the **amounts** carefully and **make corrections** if necessary

21. The completed transaction should look like the one below:

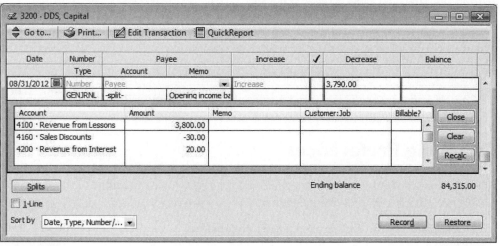

Figure 10-21

22. Click   **Record** to save the transaction and update the *Capital, Darya Danovich* account balance

23. Click   the **Splits button** again to prepare for entering the expense balances

24. The expense amounts we need to add are summarized in the following chart:

Number	Name	Amount	Number	Name	Amount
5020	Advertising and Promotion	$2,100.00	5180	Printing and Copying	$560.00
5060	Office & Computer Supplies Used	185.00	5200	Property Tax Expense	120.00
5080	Music Inventory Expenses	45.00	5220	Purchase Discounts	−95.00
5100	Depreciation Expense	1,000.00	5240	Hydro Expense	85.00
5120	Maintenance Expenses	220.00	5260	Telephone Expense	120.00
5140	Insurance Expense	3,250.00	5280	Vehicle Expenses	240.00
5160	Interest Expense	420.00			

> **Notes**
> Purchase Discounts is a contra-expense account. It normally has a credit balance and reduces the total expenses. Enter its balance as a negative amount.

25. Enter   the **expense accounts and balances**

26. Click   the **Memo field** beside **-split-** in the Ledger section of the transaction

27. Type   **Opening expenses balance**

28. Check   the **amounts** carefully and **make corrections**, if necessary

29. Click   **Record** to save the entry

30. Click   **Record** to save the transaction and update the *Capital, Darya Danovich* account balance

31. Close   the **Capital, Darya Danovich** register and return to the Chart of Accounts

32. Close   the **Chart of Accounts**

Changing Preferences

Now that we have created all the accounts, we are ready to change some of the preferences that we did not change earlier.

1.	**Choose**	the **Edit menu** and **click Preferences**

The preference that you last used will be displayed on the screen.

Changing Preferences for Chequing

Notes
Refer to page 201 for more information on chequing preferences.

1.	**Click**	the **Chequing** heading on the left-hand side of the screen
2.	**Click**	the **My Preferences tab** if it is not already selected

On this tab you can enter the default account for writing cheques, paying bills, and making deposits. Darya's uses the *Bank - Chequing* account as the default account for all these QuickBooks transactions.

Notes
You can also type 1050, the account number, in the Account field to choose the account.

3.	**Click**	the **check box** beside Open the Write Cheques option to add a ✓
4.	**Choose**	**1050 Bank - Chequing** in the account field
5.	**Click**	the **check box** for Open the Pay Bills and Open the Make Deposits options and **choose 1050 Bank - Chequing** as the default account for both types of transactions

Changing Company Preferences for Chequing

1.	**Click**	the **Company Preferences tab**

The company preferences affect all users and can only be changed by the administrator of the company file.

The warning about duplicate cheque numbers is on by default and you should leave it on. We are not using payroll so we don't need to select accounts for any of the payroll options. Do not select the option to change cheque dates when cheques are printed. This will ensure that the transactions you enter will match the exercises in the textbook. For the other settings you can choose your own preferences.

Changing Company Preferences for Finance Charges

QuickBooks will create an item record named Fin Chg automatically when you add details about the finance charges in the Preference settings.

1.	**Click**	the **Finance Charge** heading on the left-hand side of the screen

2. **Click**	**Yes** to save the Chequing preferences and to view the Finance Charge preference options:
3. **Click**	the **Company Preferences tab** if necessary:

Figure 10-22

Use the options on this tab to define the interest charges on overdue customer accounts. Darya charges 15 percent interest on accounts after the 30-day account period. A minimum charge of $10.00 is applied as an administrative fee and charges are cumulative — that is, interest is charged on previous overdue interest amounts. Darya's allows a five-day grace period after the 30 days before charging interest. That means interest charges are assessed starting 35 days after the transaction date. The overdue period is assessed from the invoice or billing date rather than the due date. Interest revenue is credited to the *Revenue from Interest* account.

The default settings are set to charge no interest. Zero is entered in the default Annual Interest Rate field.

4. **Press**	_tab_ to select 0.0% in the Annual Interest Rate field
5. **Type**	**15**
6. **Press**	_tab_ to advance to the Minimum Finance Charge field
7. **Type**	**10**
8. **Press**	_tab_ to advance to the Grace Period (days) field
9. **Type**	**35**
10. **Press**	_tab_ to advance to the Finance Charge Account field
11. **Type**	**4200**
12. **Press**	_tab_ to advance to the Assess finance charges on overdue finance charges field

13. Press the **Space bar** or **click** in the **check box** to select this option and see the warning:

Warning

⚠ Laws vary as to whether you can assess finance charges on finance charges. Please confirm with the appropriate jurisdiction that you are in compliance with that jurisdiction's lending laws.

OK

Figure 10-23

Notes
In some regions it may be illegal to charge interest on previous interest charges.

14. Click **OK** to indicate that we can legally select this option

15. Click **invoice/billed date** to change the starting date from which the charges are calculated

16. Click the **check box** for **Mark finance charge invoices "To be printed"** if you want the finance charge invoices to be available for batch printing

There are no personal preferences for finance charges.

Once you have set up preferences for finance charges, an item called Fin Chg is automatically added to the Item list. You can edit finance charges either from the Finance Charge preferences, or by editing the Fin Chg item on the Item List. Depending on the changes you need to make, you may need to make the changes to the item in the Item list or in the Finance Charge preferences.

Notes
You can edit some aspects of the finance charges settings from the item record – the name, description, rate (amount), tax code, and account. To change the setting for calculating charges from the due date or transaction date, or for assessing charges on previous charge amounts, you must access the Finance Charge Preferences.

Changing Company Preferences for Jobs & Estimates

1. Click the **Jobs & Estimates** heading on the left-hand side of the screen

2. Click **Yes** to save the changes made to the Finance Charges preferences

3. Click the **Company Preferences** tab if necessary:

Figure 10-24

Use the options on this tab to indicate whether the business uses estimates for customer jobs or services and to assign names to the different stages of a job in progress. Progress invoicing is also enabled from this tab. Progress invoicing allows you to invoice customers regularly for work in progress. Again, a warning about duplicate estimate numbers is switched on as the default, and you should leave this warning turned on.

All the default settings for Jobs & Estimates are correct for Darya's: estimates are used and progress invoicing is not, so we do not need to make any changes to these preferences.

There are no personal preferences for jobs and estimates.

Changing Company Preferences for Items & Inventory

1. **Click**   the **Items & Inventory** heading on the left-hand side of the screen

2. **Click**   the **Company Preferences tab** if necessary:

Figure 10-25

Many of the settings on this tab apply to inventory and Darya's does not use inventory. However, inventory and purchase orders are activated together and Darya's does use purchase orders.

3. **Click**   the **box** beside **Inventory and purchase orders are active** to select this option

By selecting this option, the purchase orders icon will be displayed in the Vendors section of the Home page and all the related menu options will be available from the Vendors menu. The warning about duplicate purchase order numbers should remain selected. The next two options are related to inventory so we can ignore these settings.

Changing Company Preferences for Bills

1. **Click**   the **Bills** heading on the left-hand side of the screen

2. **Click**   **Yes** to save the changes made to the Items & Inventory preferences

3. Click   the **Company Preferences tab** if necessary:

Figure 10-26

Use the options on this tab to determine when bills are due and whether discounts and credits are automatically applied. By default, bills are due 10 days after receipt when no other terms are entered for a bill, and you will be warned when entering duplicate vendor invoice numbers.

The final part of the screen allows you to apply discounts and credits automatically when they are available and to choose a default discount account. We want to use this option.

4. Click   **Automatically use discounts and credits** to add a ✓ to the check box

5. Click   the **drop-down arrow** in the Default Discount Account field

6. Choose   **5220 Purchase Discounts** as the default account

There are no personal preferences for Bills.

Changing Company Preferences for Reports & Graphs

1. Click   the **Reports & Graphs** heading on the left-hand side of the screen

2. Click   **Yes** to save the changes made to the Bills preferences

3. Click   on the **Company Preferences tab** if necessary:

Figure 10-27

Darya's uses the accrual basis so the setting for the Summary Reports Basis is correct. We want to use account names only in reports because we have not used descriptions for all accounts. If you want, you can add both names and descriptions to reports. We want aging periods in reports to be based on the transaction date rather than the due date so the Aging Reports setting is correct.

The format button allows you to choose a standard format for reports — what headings to include, date format, fonts, etc. — the Classify Cash button allows you to decide how accounts should be classified for cash flow reports.

You may want to change the standard format for reports. For example, you can add your name as a report footer to make it easier to identify your work.

4. Click   the **Format button** and review the formatting settings that you can modify for reports and **make** any **changes** you want for your reports

5. Click   **OK** to save any changes that you made

6. Click   the **My Preferences tab**:

Figure 10-28

From this tab, you can decide whether to display the Modify Report window automatically when you select a report. You can also choose whether reports should be refreshed automatically when you make a change to any of the settings or data. Graphs can be drawn in two or three dimensions and with or without patterns.

7. Click   **Refresh Automatically** under the Reports and Graphs heading

8. Change   **other settings** to suit the way you want to work with the program

Changing Company Preferences for Sales & Customers

1. Click   the **Sales & Customers** heading on the left-hand side of the screen

2. Click   **Yes** to save the changes made to the Reports and Graphs preferences

3. Click   the **My Preferences tab** if it isn't already selected:

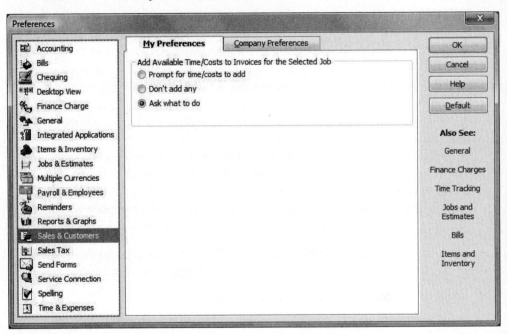

Figure 10-29

If you record billable time and costs that will be charged to customers, use this tab to determine how the costs are added to customer invoices.

4. Click   the **Company Preferences tab**:

Figure 10-30

Many of these settings refer to businesses that sell inventory. These fields can be skipped for Darya's. Shipping does not apply to Darya's and neither does markup or pricing levels. Duplicate invoice numbers should prompt a warning, sales orders should be enabled, and zero amounts should not be included on forms. These default settings are correct.

We want QuickBooks to automatically apply customer payments to invoices when we enter customer payments, so we leave the Automatically Apply Payments option selected. We also want QuickBooks to automatically enter the amount in the Amount Received field as we select customer invoices that have been paid so we will leave the Calculate Payments option selected. Darya's holds all cheques and deposits before taking them to the bank, so we will leave the Use Undeposited Funds as a default deposit to account option selected.

5. **Click**   **Use Price Levels** to remove the ✓ in the check box

6. **Click**   **OK** to save the final preference changes to the preferences

7. **Click**   **OK** if a message is displayed indicating that QuickBooks must close all its open windows to change the preferences

> **Notes**
> Depending on the changes made to the preferences, QuickBooks may need to close all open windows before the changes are accepted. Once this is completed, a blank screen will be displayed. Click the Home icon on the Icon bar to return to the Home page.

Creating Customer Accounts

As we have seen in earlier chapters, customer records can be entered from any customer field in a QuickBooks form. Although we can add customers on the fly as needed, it is more efficient to start with a list of existing customers. As with many other activities in QuickBooks, customers can be added in many ways. Other than starting in a Customer:Job field on a form, all methods begin from the Customer:Job list. This list can only be accessed from the Customer Centre.

To access the Customer Centre:

a. **Click**   the **Customer Centre** icon on the icon bar; or

b. **Choose** **Customers** from the menu and **click Customer Centre;** or

c. **Click**   the **Customers button** in the Customers section of the Home page; or

d. **Press**   `ctrl` + **J**

1. **Open**   the **Customer Centre** using one of the methods described above

2. **Open**   the **New Customer** form by performing one of the following options:
   a) **Right click** in the **Customers & Jobs list** and **select New Customer**; or
   b) **Click the New Customer & Job button and click New Customer**; or
   c) **Choose Edit from the menu and click New Customer:Job**; or
   d) **Click** `ctrl` **+ N**

3. The New Customer form will be displayed:

Figure 10-31

This is the same record form we used earlier when we added customer records from the Customer:Job field for River Run and Malin's Makeovers. This time we will add the opening balances for customers — the outstanding invoice amounts.

Use the customer information chart on page 461 to create customer records.

4. **Type**   **Canadian Sledders**

5. **Press**   `tab` to advance to the Opening Balance field

6. **Type**   **400**

7. **Press**   `tab` to advance to the Date field

The date applies to the invoice date. Entering this date correctly will allow the correct calculation of discounts, due dates, and finance charges.

8. **Type**   **08/10/12**

9. **Press**   `tab` to advance to the Company Name field

10. **Type**   **Canadian Sledders**

11.	**Press**	[tab] twice to move to the First Name field
12.	**Type**	**Pers**
13.	**Press**	[tab] twice to move to the Last Name field
14.	**Type**	**Johansson**
15.	**Press**	[tab]

The company name and contact appear in the Address text area, and the name we entered is added to the Contact field. You can enter a different name in the Contact field if this is appropriate. The cursor is in the Address text box beside the contact.

16.	**Press**	[enter] to move to the next line in the Addresses Invoice To text box
17.	**Type**	**189 Bobsled Hill Rd.**
18.	**Press**	[enter]
19.	**Type**	**Regina, Saskatchewan**
20.	**Press**	[enter]
21.	**Type**	**S3T 7E8**
22.	**Click**	the **Edit button** to check the information and add the Country
23.	**Correct**	the **address details** if needed
24.	**Click**	the **Country/Region** field
25.	**Type**	**Canada**
26.	**Click**	**OK** to return to the Customer Record

Notes
Information entered in the Note field on the Edit Address Information screen will appear in the Address field on invoices and forms for the customer.

If the customer has merchandise shipped, you should enter the shipping address by clicking the Copy To button or by entering a different address as the ship to address. Both addresses will appear on invoices. The shipping address is not used by Darya's Dance Studio because no items are shipped to customers.

27.	**Click**	the **Phone field**
28.	**Type**	**(306) 299-8644**
29.	**Press**	[tab] to advance to the FAX field
30.	**Type**	**(306) 298-6219**

There is no Alternate phone number or contact so we can skip these fields.

31.	**Click**	the **E-mail address** field
32.	**Type**	**thefastest@yahoo.ca**
33.	**Click**	the **Additional Info tab**:

Figure 10-32

Darya's Dance Studio does not use customer types and sales reps are not used. A number of payment terms are set up automatically by QuickBooks, and we can add more if needed. We will edit the list of terms later.

The Tax Code field is displayed only because we chose to leave the Use Customer Tax Codes option selected in the Sales Tax preferences. If a sales tax code is entered in this field in the customer record, it will be used when entering sales taxes on sales transactions for the customer and it will override item tax codes. Darya's does not use customer tax codes, which means that the item tax codes will be used as the default tax codes on sales transactions. The sales tax codes are correct for all customers. The tax codes can be changed on invoices for individual invoice items if needed.

34. **Click**   the **drop-down arrow** in the Terms field to view the payment terms set up by default

35. **Click**   **1% 10 Net 30** to add the terms to the customer record

36. **Click**   the **Payment Info tab**:

Figure 10-33

Most businesses place limits on the amount a customer is allowed to purchase on credit. Once the credit limit is reached, the customer may be asked for a down payment or may be granted a limit increase. Customer credit limits should be reviewed regularly with reference to a customer's buying and payment patterns to determine whether the limits should be raised or lowered for individual customers. As we saw on page 278, the program warns when a credit limit is exceeded by a purchase or sale. The limit for Canadian Sledders is $2,000.00.

37. Click   the **Credit Limit** field

38. Type   2000

39. Click   the **drop-down arrow** in the Preferred Payment Method list to view the options available for selection

These payment methods were created automatically by QuickBooks. We will edit the list later. The Sledding team pays by cheque.

40. Click   **Cheque**

The fourth tab, the Job Info tab, allows you to organize the work done for customers according to specific jobs. This allows you to track the work done for customers in a more detailed way. When jobs are set up, you can choose the Customer and Job from the customer name lists. Customer jobs do not apply to Darya's Dance Studio.

41. Check   your **work** carefully before **saving** the **customer record**

Notes
To edit a selected customer, you can also choose the Edit menu and click Edit Customer:Job.

CORRECTING CUSTOMER RECORDS

Before Saving the Record

To correct a record while you are creating it, just return to the field that has the error and type the correction. Click the Address Info, Additional Info, or Payment Info tab to return to those screens to check your work. To change the terms or payment method, select the correct terms or payment method from the drop-down list.

After Saving the Record

If you need to make corrections or changes later, open the Customer Centre to access the Customers & Jobs list. Right click a customer name, then click Edit Customer:Job (or press _ctrl_ + E). With the customer record displayed, highlight the incorrect details, and type the correction. Click OK to save the changes and return to the Customers & Jobs list.

42. **Click Next** to save the record and open another blank customer record form

43. **Enter** the **remaining customer records** on page 461

44. **Close** the **Customer Centre** when you have finished entering the customers

Entering Opening Balances as Invoices

When we entered the Canadian Sledders customer record, we added the opening balance for this customer in the Opening Balance field. When entering a balance in the opening balance field, you can enter only the as of date and you cannot add invoice details; however, once the customer record is recorded, you can open the invoice created in the Create Invoices form and add an invoice number giving the transaction more detail. If you use the opening balance field, only one invoice is created for the customer.

If your customers have multiple outstanding invoices, you can add opening balances for customers and vendors as ordinary invoices in the same way you would enter a current invoice. This allows you to track more information for the sales, such as the invoice number, customer's cheque number for prepayments, and so on.

Sometimes a customer has more than one outstanding invoice. The sales probably occurred on different dates and therefore have different due dates. Entering them as a single opening balance with one date will make it impossible to apply discounts correctly for early payments. If there is more than one outstanding invoice for a customer, and you want to track each invoice separately, you must add them as separate invoices. This method will allow you to record payments and apply discounts to specific invoices.

Notes
When we used this approach in earlier chapters, we created a special item called History and used it when entering the historical invoices. The History item was linked to the Uncategorized Income account.

Creating Vendor Records

As we have seen in earlier chapters, vendor records can be entered from any vendor field in a QuickBooks forms.

Although we can add vendors on the fly as needed, it is more efficient to start with a list of existing vendors. As with many other activities in QuickBooks, vendors can be added in many ways. Other than starting in a Vendor field on a form, all methods begin from the Vendors List. This list can only be accessed from the Vendor Centre.

To access the Vendor Centre:

a. **Click** the **Vendor Centre icon** on the icon bar; or

b. **Choose Vendors** from the menu and **click Vendor Centre**; or

c. **Click** the **Vendors button** in the Vendors section of the Home page

1. **Open** the **Vendor Centre**, using one of the methods described above

2. **Open** the **New Vendor** form by performing one of the following options:

   a) **Right click** in the **Vendors list** and **select New Vendor**; or

   b) **Click** the **New Vendor button**; or

   c) **Choose Edit** from the menu and **click New Vendor**; or

   d) **Click** ⌨ctrl + **N**

3. The New Vendor form will be displayed:

Figure 10-34

QuickBooks has automatically created vendor records for the Receiver General and Saskatchewan Finance, the tax agencies for the collection of sales taxes. You cannot remove these records even if you do not collect taxes. We will edit the record for the Receiver General to add the address details, and we will make the Saskatchewan Finance record inactive so it will not appear on our lists.

This is the same New Vendor form we used earlier when we added complete vendor records. This time, we will add opening invoice balance amounts for the new vendors.

4. **Type** **Foley's** in the Vendor Name field

5. **Press** ⌨tab to move to the Opening Balance field

6. **Type** **115**

7. **Press** ⌨tab to move to the as of date field

The date applies to the invoice date. Entering this date correctly will allow the correct calculation of discounts and due dates.

8.	**Type**	**08/28/12**
9.	**Press**	(tab) to advance to the Company Name field
10.	**Type**	**Foley's**
11.	**Press**	(tab) twice to move to the First Name field
12.	**Type**	**Jane**
13.	**Press**	(tab) twice to move to the Last Name field
14.	**Type**	**Foley**
15.	**Press**	(tab)

The company name and contact appear in the Address text area, and the name we entered is added to the Contact field. You can enter a different name in the Contact field if this is appropriate. The cursor is in the Address field text box.

16.	**Press**	(enter) to move the next blank line in the Address text box
17.	**Type**	**122 Baryshnikov St.**
18.	**Press**	(enter)
19.	**Type**	**Regina, Saskatchewan**
20.	**Press**	(enter)
21.	**Type**	**S3P 7N5**

There are no more lines for address information. We will complete the fields on this screen before adding address details. The vendor has only one phone number.

22.	**Click**	the **Phone Field**
23.	**Type**	**(306) 224-4632**
24.	**Press**	(tab) to advance to the FAX field
25.	**Type**	**(306) 225-6722**
26.	**Press**	(tab) twice to advance to the Alt. Contact field
27.	**Type**	**Robin**
28.	**Press**	(tab) to advance to the E-mail address field
29.	**Type**	**jf@foleys.com**

The company name is entered by default as the name that should appear on the cheque. You can edit this name if necessary.

30.	**Click**	the **Address Details** button to open the Edit Address Information window

This screen has the address fields separated for easier editing. If you need to make changes to the address details later, it is easier to do so from this screen. The address information has been entered in the correct fields already but the country is missing.

31.	**Click**	the **Country/Region** field
32.	**Type**	**Canada**
33.	**Click**	**OK** to return to the New Vendor form. This tab is now complete

34. Click   the **Additional Info tab**:

New Vendor

Vendor Name	Foley's
Opening Balance	115.00 as of 08/28/2012 How do I determine the opening balance?

Buttons: OK, Cancel, Next, Help

Tabs: Address Info | **Additional Info** | Account Prefill

Account No. |

Categorizing and Defaults

Type [▼]

Terms [▼]

Credit Limit [ ]

Sales Tax Information

Country [Canada ▼]

Business Number [ ]

Custom Fields

[Define Fields]

☐ Vendor is inactive
☐ Vendor is a Sales Tax Agency

☐ Vendor eligible for T4A

Figure 10-35

Companies can assign unique vendor numbers to each vendor to make it easier to organize the vendor records in reports. Vendors can also be grouped by types, such as region or type of business for targeted business contacts. For example, information about items needed for special contracts may be sent only to the businesses that supply those kinds of products. Vendor account numbers and vendor types are not used by Darya's vendors so we can skip these fields.

Most vendors place limits on the amount that a customer is allowed to purchase on credit. Once the credit limit is reached, the customer may be asked for a down payment or may be granted a credit limit increase. The program warns when a credit limit is exceeded by a purchase or sale; Darya's is allowed to carry an account balance of $300.00 with Foley's.

Business numbers are also frequently added to invoices for tax purposes when taxes are charged by a business. The T4A field will be checked for vendors who provide subcontracted labour and need the T4A income tax form. Both the pianist and the instructor who work with Darya's need T4A forms.

35. Click   the **drop-down arrow** in the Terms field to view the terms set up by default. Add the term 1/5, n/30 (1% 5 Net 30) for Foley's

36. Click   **Add New** at the top of the terms list as shown:

Terms

< Add New >

1% 10 Net 30
2% 10 Net 30
Consignment
Due on receipt
Net 15
Net 30
Net 60

Figure 10-36

37. The New Terms form opens:

Figure 10-37

The cursor is in the Terms field. The 1% 5, Net 30 term is a standard term rather than a Date Driven term. Payments due at the end of a month or on the 15th of each month are Date Driven terms.

38. Type	**1% 5 Net 30** in the Terms field
39. Double click	the **Net due in ___ days** field
40. Type	**30**
41. Press	(tab) to advance to the Discount Percentage Is field
42. Type	**1**
43. Press	(tab) to advance to the Discount if paid within __ days field
44. Type	**5**
45. Click	**OK** to return to the Additional Info tab of the New Vendor form

The new terms code is automatically displayed in the Terms field.

46. Click	the **Credit Limit** field
47. Type	**300**
48. Press	(tab) to advance to the Business Number field
49. Type	**398446722**
50. Click	the **Account Prefill tab**

This tab is used to enter up to three expense accounts that will automatically be entered when you create a bill or write a cheque to the vendor, making data entry easier to accurately track expenses. The accounts can be changed during transaction entry.

Darya's will not be entering expense accounts for vendors on this tab.

51. **Click**   **Next** to save the record and open a new blank vendor input form

52. **Enter**   the **remaining vendor records** on pages 460–461

53. **Click**   **OK** to save the last new vendor and to return to the Vendor List in the Vendor Centre (**Click Cancel** if you have a blank vendor form open on the screen)

Editing Vendor Records

1. **Highlight**   the **Receiver General** on the Vendor List

2. **Press**   ⌃ctrl + **E** to open the incomplete vendor record

3. **Complete**   the **record** by entering the address and phone number shown on page 460

4. **Click**   **OK** to save the changes and return to the Vendor Centre

5. **Close**   the **Vendor Centre**

> **Notes**
> You can also edit a selected vendor by right clicking in the Vendors list and choosing Edit from the menu, or choosing the Edit menu and clicking Edit Vendor.

Creating Items

We have seen that QuickBooks processes all sales, estimates, and orders by selling items. Revenue accounts are linked to items. Therefore you must create items to use the program. You cannot access revenue accounts from any of the customer sales forms.

Perhaps because items are central to the way the program operates, you can add records for items from many different places. Just as you can add other types of records on the fly during transaction entry from their respective fields in the forms, you can add items on the fly from any Item field in any form in QuickBooks. You can also set up records for items from the Item List, and you can access this list in several ways.

> **Notes**
> Any account can be linked to any item but normally a revenue account is selected for items and services you sell. For merchandise you purchase, you would normally use an asset account.

1. **Open**   the **Item List** using one of the following methods:

a) **Click the Items & Services icon** found in the Company section of the Home page; or

b) **Click Lists** from the menu and select Item List; or

c) **Click Sales Tax** from the menu and **select Item List**; or

d) **Click Customers** from the menu and **select Item List**; or

e) **Click Vendors** from the menu and **select Item List**

2. The Item List is displayed as shown:

Figure 10-38

The list window includes taxes that are automatically set up for the province selected in the EasyStep Interview and the item QuickBooks created for finance charges, based on the preference setting we entered.

3. Press <kbd>ctrl</kbd> + **N** to open a New Item form:

Figure 10-39

Creating Service Items

Service is the item type selected as the default, and it is the one we use first. The dance and exercise classes offered by Darya's Dance Studio are service items. They are associated only with an income account for tracking purposes. For each service item, you can indicate the item name and/or number, whether the account is a subitem of another item, whether the service is performed by a subcontractor, the item description, a default rate, the tax code, and the account. You can change the tax code and rate for individual sales at any time during transaction entry, but you cannot change the income account associated with the item.

Darya does not use item numbers or subitems, and no services are provided by sub-contractors. By de°fault, the item list will appear in alphabetical order when selected in forms, so we will have to keep that in mind when entering item names.

The first service item we will enter is Class - Single, first on the Item list on page 462.

4. Press <kbd>tab</kbd> to select Service and advance to the Item Name/Number field

5. Type **Class - Single**

> **Notes**
> You cannot use colons in item names because colons are used to identify subitem relationships.

6.	Click	the **Description** field
7.	**Type**	**Single dance or exercise class**
8.	**Press**	(tab) to advance to the Rate field
9.	**Type**	**25**
10.	**Press**	(tab) to advance to the Sales Tax Code field

Services are subject to GST but not to PST, so the correct code is G. This sales tax code charges GST only at 5%.

11.	**Accept**	**G** as the sales tax code

G should already be displayed as the sales tax code because it was selected as the sales tax code used most often for taxable items in the Sales Tax preferences.

12.	**Press**	(tab) to advance to the Account field
13.	**Click**	the **drop-down arrow** in the Account field to view the chart of accounts

Notice that the Chart of Accounts list is displayed, beginning with the Income accounts.

14.	**Select**	**4100 Revenue from Lessons**

If the account you need is not on the list, type the account number in the account field and press (tab) to add the account. Click Set Up to open the New Account form. Income will be selected correctly as the account type for the service.

CORRECTING ITEM RECORDS

To correct a record while you are creating it, return to the field that has the error, highlight the incorrect details, and type the correction. To correct the item type, tax code, or account, select the correct type, tax code, or account from the drop-down lists.

If you need to make corrections or changes later, after saving the item record, refer to page 514.

15.	**Click**	**Next** to save the item and open a blank New Item form

Notice that the default tax code and account number from the previous item are still displayed.

16.	**Enter**	the **remaining service items** on page 462.
17.	**Click**	**Next** after entering the last service item to leave a blank New Item form displayed on the screen

Creating Non-inventory Part Items

In addition to services, Darya's will create items for some assets it buys or places on purchase orders because purchase orders require you to select an item. The type most appropriate for these purchases is Non-inventory Part. The Non-inventory Part type is used for items, such as supplies or materials, for specific customer jobs that are later charged to a customer.

Notes
In previous chapters, we selected Non-inventory Part for items, sold to customers, that were not tracked as inventory.

1.	**Click**	the **drop-down arrow** in the Type field
2.	**Click**	**Non-inventory Part** to change the selection and the New Item form

Notice that the default tax code and account number from the previous entry are still displayed, even though the type is different. Refer to the list on page 462.

3.	**Press**	〔tab〕 to advance to the Item Name/Number field
4.	**Type**	**Music Inventory**
5.	**Click**	the **Description** field
6.	**Type**	**CDs and sheet music**

Do not enter a price because prices will change with each purchase or order.

7.	**Click**	the **drop-down arrow** in the Tax Code field
8.	**Choose**	**S**, which will calculate both GST and PST at 5%
9.	**Click**	the **drop-down arrow** in the Account field
10.	**Choose**	**1260 Music Inventory**
11.	**Click**	**Next**
12.	**Enter**	**Supplies**, the second Non-inventory Part item as shown on page 462
13.	**Click**	**Next** after entering the last Non-inventory Part item to leave a blank New Item form displayed on the screen

Creating Other Charge Items

Darya's also requires items for charges relating to NSF cheques. We used these items to record NSF charges for Terrific Tours' customers. Items of this type are entered as Other Charges in QuickBooks. The Fin Chg (finance charge) item is already entered. Again, refer to the list on page 462.

1.	**Click**	the **drop-down arrow** in the Type field
2.	**Click**	**Other Charge** to change the selection and the New Item form:

Figure 10-40

Read the description displayed for this type of item.

Notice that the default tax code and account number from the previous entry are displayed, even though the type is different.

3.	**Press**	(tab) to advance to the Item Name/Number field
4.	**Type**	**Admin Charge**
5.	**Click**	the **Description** field
6.	**Type**	**Handling charge for NSF cheque**
7.	**Press**	(tab) to advance to the **Amount or % field**
8.	**Type**	**30**
9.	**Press**	(tab) to advance to the Sales Tax Code field
10.	**Press**	(del) to remove the sales tax code. Sales Taxes do not apply on NSF charges
11.	**Press**	(tab) to advance to the Account field
12.	**Choose**	**4250 Other Revenue** as the account
13.	**Click**	**Next**
14.	**Enter**	**NSF Cheque** as the final Other Charge. Refer to page 462
15.	**Click**	**OK** to save the item and return to the Item List
16.	Notice that the Item list now includes all the items we have created	

Editing the Finance Charge Item

We will now edit the item for finance charges created when we set up the Finance Charge preferences to match our item list. We will change the name and terms of the finance charge. Darya has decided not to charge interest on previous interest amounts. The Item List should still be open.

1. **Double click** **Fin Chg** to open the item record:

Figure 10-41

Notes
You can edit only some of the finance charge settings from the Item List – the name, description, rate (amount), tax code, and account. To change the annual interest rate, minimum finance charge, grace period, finance charge account, or to determine how finance charges are calculated, you must access the Finance Charge Preferences screen.

2.	**Type**	**Interest Charge** to replace the default name of Fin Chg
3.	**Double click**	**Finance** in the Description field (select only the single word)
4.	**Type**	**Interest**

5.	**Click**	the **drop-down arrow** in the Account field
6.	**Accept**	**4200 - Revenue from Interest**
7.	**Click**	**OK** to save the changes and close the item record

We must return to the Finance Charge preferences screen to change the assessment of charges on previous charge amounts.

8.	**Choose**	the **Edit** menu and **click Preferences**
9.	**Click**	the **Finance Charge** heading on the left-hand side of the screen
10.	**Click**	the **Company Preferences tab**
11.	**Click**	**Assess finance charges on overdue finance charges** to remove the ✓

12. The completed Finance Charge should be displayed as shown:

Figure 10-42

13.	**Click**	**OK** to save the changes

CORRECTING ITEMS AFTER THEY HAVE BEEN SAVED

To correct items, open the Item List. Double click the item that you want to edit. With the item displayed in the Edit Item form, highlight the text that you want to change and type the correct information to replace it. Select a different tax code or account from the drop-down lists for those fields. When you select a different account for an item, QuickBooks will ask if you want all previous transactions for the item to use the new account. Choose Yes to change prior transactions, No to leave the previous account, or click Cancel to return to the item record.

You cannot change the item type, even if you haven't used the item in transactions. To change the item type for a service item, you must create a new item. If the incorrect item has not been used in transactions, you can delete it. You can change subitem links after creating an item. You can change the item type to Service from Non-inventory Part or from Other Charge, but these changes cannot be reversed.

You cannot use the same item name for different items, even if their types are different.

Adjusting Opening Balances

Now that we have entered opening balances for all customers and vendors, the *Accounts Payable* and *Accounts Receivable* balances should be correct. All vendor balances have been debited to the *Uncategorized Expense* account — the account QuickBooks created for this purpose. All customer balances have been credited to the *Uncategorized Income* account — the account QuickBooks created for this purpose. QuickBooks created these accounts automatically when we entered an amount in the Opening Balance field in customer and vendor records. If the *Accounts Receivable* and *Accounts Payable* amounts do not match the balances shown in the Trial Balance on page 460, one or more of the entries may be incorrect, and they can be edited just as any other bill or sales invoice would be edited.

1.	**Print**	the **A/R Aging Detail Report and the A/P Aging Detail Report at August 31, 2012**, to check the opening balance entries for customers and vendors
2.	**Compare**	these **reports** with the charts on pages 460–461
3.	**Make**	**corrections** if necessary using the information in the Correcting Opening Balances paragraph before completing the next step

CORRECTING OPENING BALANCES

You can correct vendor bills from the Enter Bills form. With the Enter Bills form open, find the bill by using the Find tool or by clicking the Previous and Next buttons to review the entries and locate the error. Refer to page 244 for assistance if needed.

Correct customer invoices from the Create Invoices form. With the Create Invoices form open, use the Find tool or click the Previous and Next buttons to review the entries and locate the error. Refer to page 299 for assistance if needed.

After making all the corrections to the customer and vendor opening balances, the final adjustment that remains is to transfer the amounts in the *Uncategorized Expense* and *Uncategorized Income* amounts to the *Capital, Darya Danovich* account, the equity account. We need to complete this step because these amounts have been entered twice — once in the original expense and revenue entries (page 489) and once in the opening balances for vendors and customers. We need to add back the revenue to the capital account and subtract the expenses. Originally, we created the opening revenue balances by subtracting them from capital because they are still part of current income.

First, we will record the adjustment for the revenue amount entered from the customer opening balances.

> **Notes**
> You can access revenue accounts from the General Journal but you cannot open the register for revenue accounts.

1.	**Open**	the **Chart of Accounts**
2.	**Double click**	the **Capital, Darya Danovich** account to open the account register
3.	**Enter**	**08/31/12** as the date for the transaction
4.	**Choose**	**49900 - Uncategorized Income** as the account in the Account field
5.	**Type**	**Adjust opening income** in the Memo field
6.	**Enter**	**1445** (the amount of the customer opening balances) as the amount in the Increase column
7.	**Click**	**Record** to record the transaction and update the account register

Next, we will record the adjustment for the expense amount entered from the vendor opening balances.

8.	**Accept**	the **date** of 08/31/12 for the next transaction
9.	**Choose**	**69800 - Uncategorized Expenses** as the account in the Account field
10.	**Type**	**Adjust opening expenses** in the Memo field
11.	**Enter**	**1455** (the amount of the vendor opening balances) as the amount in the Decrease column
12.	**Click**	**Record** to record the transaction and update the account register

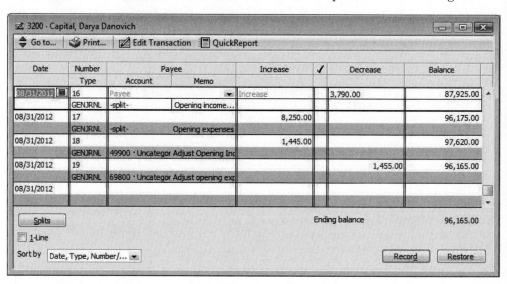

Figure 10-43

| 13. | **Close** | the **ledger** to return to the Chart of Accounts |

Making Accounts Inactive

Now that we have entered our customer and vendor opening balances and transferred the amounts in the Uncategorized Income and Uncategorized Expenses accounts, we no longer need these accounts. We cannot delete them because they were used in transactions; however, we can make them inactive so they are not included in account lists.

1.	**Click**	the **Uncategorized Income** account to select it
2.	**Click**	the **Account button** and then **click Make Account Inactive**
3.	**Click**	the **Uncategorized Expense** account to select it
4.	**Click**	the **Account button** and then **click Make Account Inactive**

These two accounts are now inactive and are not displayed in the Chart of Accounts. You can restore these accounts (make them active) at any time. Choose the Account button and click Show Inactive Accounts. The inactive accounts will be marked with an X displayed in the column to the left. Click the account you want to change. Choose the Account button and click Make Active to make the account active.

| 5. | **Close** | the **Chart of Accounts** |

Notes

To make a selected account inactive, you can also right click in the Chart of Account window and choose Make Inactive from the menu, or choose the Edit menu and click Make Account Inactive.

Editing Lists

When we chose terms and payment methods for vendors and customers, we saw that QuickBooks created a number of terms automatically. We don't need all these terms so we should delete the ones that we won't be using.

Editing Terms

1. **Choose** the **Lists** menu, then **choose Customer & Vendor Profile Lists** and **click Terms List** to open the Terms List:

Figure 10-44

The Terms List is just like any other list in QuickBooks. From this window, you can create new terms, edit or delete terms, make terms inactive, display a number of reports, and so on. The keyboard shortcut commands are the same as the commands for other lists.

Although we are not using all these terms, we can retain most of them in case we need them later. We will delete the Net 60 days term.

2. **Click** **Net 60**

3. **Click** the **Terms** button and **click Delete Terms** or **press** `ctrl` + **D** to view the warning message

4. **Click** **OK** to delete the terms code

5. **Close** the **Terms List**

Editing Payment Methods

1. **Choose** the **Lists** menu, then **choose Customer & Vendor Profile Lists**, and **click Payment Method List** to open the Payment Method List:

Figure 10-45

We can delete most of the payment methods on the list. Darya's Dance Studio accepts cash, cheques, and Visa for payment so we will keep these payment methods.

2. **Click**   **American Express**

3. **Click**   the **Payment Method** button and **click Delete Payment Method** or **press**
                  $\boxed{ctrl}$ **+ D** to view the warning message

4. **Click**   **OK** to delete the payment method

5. **Repeat**   the **above steps** to **delete MasterCard, Direct Payment, and Interac Debit**

6. **Close**   the **Payment Method List**

Editing Customer Messages

1. **Choose**   the **Lists** menu, then **choose Customer & Vendor Profile Lists**, and **click Customer Message List** to open the Customer Message List:

Figure 10-46

We can keep most of the messages on the list. We don't need the first customer message because it applies to customized service or contract work that is not applicable to Darya's.

2. **Click**   the **All work is complete!** customer message

3. **Click**   the **Customer Message** button and **click Delete Customer Message** or
                  press $\boxed{ctrl}$ **+ D** to view the warning message

4. **Click**   **OK** to delete the customer message

5. **Close**   the **Customer Message List**

Checking the Setup

You should check all the information you entered to verify the accuracy of your work. Although you can make corrections at any time, you should attempt to have a data file that is error free before entering current year transactions. To check your work,

1. **Print**   or display the **following reports**:
   a) **Trial Balance** as of August 31, 2012
   b) **Customer Contact List: Add columns** for Terms, E-mail, and Credit Limit to the list
   c) **Vendor Contact List: Add columns** for Terms, E-mail, Credit Limit, and Business Number to the list

Notes
To add columns of additional information on reports, display the report, and click the Modify Report button. Click the Display tab. Then click each field that you want to add to the list. Click OK to return to the revised list.

d) **A/R Aging Detail Report** as of August 31, 2012
e) **A/P Aging Detail Report** as of August 31, 2012
f) **Item Price List:** Add columns for Account and Sales Tax Code

Source Documents

Now that you have set up the company file, enter the following source documents. You may need to refer to previous chapters for additional information.

SD Practice
Continue to develop your skills by entering the following source document(s).

September 1 – September 7, 2012

SD1: Sales Invoice #115

Dated September 1, 2012

To Waltzer Family, two classes per week for three family members for a 15-week session (6 sessions of classes) at $220.00 each plus GST. Invoice totals $1,386.00. Terms: 1/10, n/30.

SD2: Visa Purchase Invoice #GP-30012

Dated September 1, 2012

From The Grand Papery (set up new vendor), $130.00 plus $6.50 GST and $6.50 PST for copying dance class schedules and pamphlets for a new session. Invoice totalling $143.00 was paid in full by Visa.

Notes
The Grand Papery
(Greeting Card)
33 Woodpulp St.
Regina, SK S3V 6F6
Terms: Due on receipt
Credit Limit: $1,000.00

SD3: Cheque Copy #591

Dated September 2, 2012

To Foley's, $113.85 in payment of account, including the discount for early payment. Reference invoice #F-445.

SD4: Cheque Copy #592

Dated September 3, 2012

To Sounds Inc., $499.80 in payment of account, including the discount for early payment. Reference invoice #SI-390.

SD5: Visa Purchase Invoice #WG-209

Dated September 3, 2012

From Wendy Groen, RMT, $85.00 plus $4.25 GST for a weekly one-hour massage. Invoice totalling $89.25 was paid in full by Visa. Create new Expense account: 5170 Massage Therapy Expense (tax code G, GST only). Memorize the transaction with weekly reminders beginning Sep. 10, 2012.

Notes
Close the message about outstanding invoices.
Enter Wendy Groen, RMT as the name for the memorized transaction if necessary.

SD6: Cash Receipt #40

Dated September 4, 2012

From Minuet Family, cheque #204 for $310.00 in payment of account. Reference invoice #92. Group all deposits with other undeposited funds.

Notes
The first time you enter a sales receipt or receive a customer payment in QuickBooks, an Undeposited Funds account is automatically created in the Chart of Accounts. Renumber it to account number 1450.

SD7: Cheque Copy #593

Dated September 4, 2012

To Wendy Groen, RMT, $450.00 in payment of account. Reference invoice #WG-103.

SD8: Visa Purchase Invoice #P-7107

Dated September 5, 2012

From Petra's Petrol (use Quick Add for new vendor), $30.00 plus $1.50 GST and $1.50 PST for the weekly gasoline purchase for the business vehicle. Invoice totalling $33.00 was paid in full by Visa. Memorize the transaction with weekly reminders beginning Sep. 12, 2012.

SD9: Cash Receipt #41

Dated September 6, 2012

From Saskie Gliders, cheque #1098 for $727.65 in payment of account, including the discount for early payment. Reference invoice #102.

SD10: Purchase Invoice #LT-199

Dated September 6, 2012

From Les Toyle (use Quick Add for new vendor), $220.00 plus $11.00 GST for the weekly cleaning bill. Invoice totals $231.00. Terms: Net 15. Memorize the transaction with weekly reminders beginning September 13, 2012. Save the new terms.

SD11: Sales Estimate #11

Dated September 6, 2012

To Saskie Gliders, $220.00 each plus GST for teaching a dance routine to the eight-member skating team. Classes to begin in two weeks. Estimate totals $1,848.00. Terms: 1/10, n/30. Deposit of 50 percent required on acceptance of estimate.

    Create new Service item (price varies; do not enter an item price):
        Item Name: Customized Program
        Description: Classes created for customer
        Tax code: G
        Account: 4100 Revenue from Lessons

SD12: Memo #1

Dated September 6, 2012

From Owner: Customize the Estimates form by removing the Markup column.

SD13: Visa Sales Receipt Summary #420

Dated September 6, 2012

To Visa Sales customers:

100	Classes - Session	$220.00 each	$22,000.00
12	Classes - Month	75.00 each	900.00
12	Classes - Single	25.00 each	300.00
	GST	5%	1,160.00
	Total receipts held for deposit:		$24,360.00

Memorize the transaction with weekly reminders to begin September 13, 2012.

SD14: Cash Sales Receipt Summary #421

Dated September 7, 2012

To Cash Sales customers

1	Classes - Session	$220.00 each	$ 220.00
8	Classes - Month	75.00 each	600.00
10	Classes - Single	25.00 each	250.00
	GST	5%	53.50
	Total cash receipts held for deposit		$1,123.50

Memorize the transaction with weekly reminders to begin September 14, 2012.

SD15: Memo #2

Dated September 7, 2012

From Owner: Deposit $2,161.15 to chequing and $24,360.00 to the Visa account.

SD16: Cheque Copy #594

Dated September 7, 2012

To Treble & Bass, $376.20 in payment of account, including the discount for early payment. Reference invoice #TB-2918.

September 8 – September 14, 2006

SD17: Sales Invoice #116

Dated September 8, 2012

To Minuet Family, two classes per week for three children and two adults for a 15-week session (10 sessions of classes) at $220.00 each plus GST. Invoice totals $2,310.00. Terms: 1/10, n/30. Allow customer to exceed credit limit.

SD18: Bank Debit Memo #29901

Dated September 8, 2012

Cheque #204 from Minuet Family for $310.00 in payment of invoice #92 was returned as NSF. Create invoice #117 to charge the $310.00 NSF cheque amount to the Minuet Family and add the $30.00 Admin Charges. No taxes apply to these amounts. Invoice totals $340.00. Terms: Due on receipt. Do not save the new terms.

SD19: Visa Purchase Invoice #GP-30891

Dated September 9, 2012

From The Grand Papery, $75.00 plus $3.75 GST and $3.75 PST for computer and office supplies. Invoice totalling $82.50 was paid in full by Visa.

SD20: Cash Receipt #42

Dated September 9, 2012

From Saskie Gliders, cheque #1203 for $900.00 as deposit on sales estimate #11.

SD21: Cash Receipt #43

Dated September 9, 2012

From Waltzer Family, cheque #235 for $1,372.80 in payment of account, including the discount for early payment. Taxes are not included in the discount. Reference invoice #115.

Notes

If some payments do not show in the Cash and Cheque list, select items for deposit individually from the list of all Payments to Deposit.

SD22: Cash Receipt #44

Dated September 10, 2012

From Minuet Family, certified cheque #RB-204 for $340.00 in full payment of account. Reference invoice #117.

SD23: Visa Purchase Invoice #WG-264

Dated September 10, 2012

From Wendy Groen, RMT, $85.00 plus $4.25 GST for the weekly one-hour massage. Invoice totalling $84.25 was paid in full by Visa. Use memorized transaction.

SD24: Purchase Order #102

Dated September 10, 2012

To Sounds Inc., $900.00 plus $45.00 GST and $45.00 PST for specialized choreography software. Invoice totals $990.00. Terms: 2/10, n/30.

SD25: Purchase Invoice #PC-4911

Dated September 11, 2012

From Prime Contacts, $245.00 plus $12.25 GST and $12.25 PST for business telephone service. Invoice totals $269.50. Terms: Net 15 days.

SD26: Sales Estimate #12

Dated September 11, 2012

To Canadian Sledders, $220.00 each plus GST for specialized rhythm and stretch classes for the six-member bobsled team (6 sessions of classes). Estimate totals $1,386.00. Terms: 1/10, n/30. A 50 percent deposit is required on accepting the estimate.

SD27: Visa Purchase Invoice #P-7865

Dated September 12, 2012

From Petra's Petrol, $30.00 plus $1.50 GST and $1.50 PST for the weekly gasoline purchase for the business vehicle. Invoice totalling $33.00 was paid in full by Visa. Use memorized transaction.

SD28: Cash Receipt #45

Dated September 13, 2012

From Canadian Sledders, cheque #85 for $700.00 as deposit on sales estimate #12.

SD29: Purchase Invoice #LT-235

Dated September 13, 2012

From Les Toyle, $220.00 plus $11.00 GST for the weekly cleaning bill. Invoice totals $231.00. Terms: Net 15. Use memorized transaction.

SD30: Sales Invoice #118

Dated September 13, 2012

To Polka Family (use Quick Add for new customer), three classes per week for two children for the entire 15-week session (6 sessions of classes) at $220.00 each plus GST. Invoice totals $1,386.00. Terms: 1/10, n/30. Save the new terms.

Notes
A non-posting Purchase Orders account is automatically added to the Chart of Accounts the first time you enter a purchase order in QuickBooks. This non-posting account does not affect your Balance Sheet or Income Statement. Change its account number to 6050.

Notes
Do not apply the receipt from Canadian Sledders to the outstanding invoice.

SD31: Visa Sales Receipt Summary #422

Dated September 13, 2012

To Visa Sales customers:

80	Classes - Session	$220.00 each	$17,600.00
19	Classes - Month	75.00 each	1,425.00
8	Classes - Single	25.00 each	200.00
	GST	5%	961.25
	Total receipts held for deposit:		$20,186.25

Use the memorized transaction and edit the quantities.

SD32: Cash Sales Receipt Summary #423

Dated September 14, 2012

To Cash Sales customers:

2	Classes - Session	$220.00 each	$ 440.00
4	Classes - Month	75.00 each	300.00
11	Classes - Single	25.00 each	275.00
	GST	5%	50.75
	Total cash receipts held for deposit:		$1,065.75

Use the memorized transaction and edit the quantities.

SD33: Sales Estimate #13

Dated September 14, 2012

To Wheatfields Academy, $220.00 each plus GST for special classes in ballroom dancing to prepare for the New Year's Eve dance gala. Classes will be open to 30 students in total. Estimate totals $6,930.00. Terms: 1/10, n/30. Classes will be offered only if fully enrolled.

SD34: Memo #3

Dated September 14. 2012

From Owner: Deposit $4,378.55 to chequing and $20,186.25 to the Visa account.

September 15 – September 21, 2012

SD35: Purchase Order #103

Dated September 17, 2012

To The Grand Papery, $210.00 plus $10.50 GST and $10.50 PST for printing customized receipt forms and invoices. Invoice totals $231.00. Terms: Due on receipt.

SD36: Visa Purchase Invoice #WG-291

Dated September 17, 2012

From Wendy Groen, RMT, $85.00 plus $4.25 GST for the weekly one-hour massage. Invoice totalling $89.25 was paid in full by Visa. Use memorized transaction.

SD37: Sales Invoice #119

Dated September 18, 2012

To Canadian Sledders, to fill estimate #12, $220.00 each plus GST for specialized rhythm and stretch classes for the six-member bobsled team (6 sessions of classes). Invoice totals $1,386.00. Terms: 1/10, n/30.

SD38: Purchase Invoice #PEC-9182

Dated September 18, 2012

From Prairie Energy Corp., $80.00 plus $4.00 GST for one month of hydro service for studio. Purchase invoice totals $84.00. Terms: Net 10.

SD39: Visa Purchase Invoice #P-8120

Dated September 19, 2012

From Petra's Petrol, $30.00 plus $1.50 GST and $1.50 PST for weekly gasoline purchase for business vehicle. Invoice totalling $33.00 was paid in full by Visa. Use memorized transaction.

SD40: Sales Invoice #120

Dated September 19, 2012

To Wheatfields Academy, to fill estimate #13, $220.00 each plus GST for special classes in ballroom dancing to prepare for the New Year's Eve dance gala. 30 students enrolled. Invoice totals $6,930.00. Terms: 1/10, n/30.

SD41: Purchase Invoice #TB-3449

Dated September 20, 2012

From Treble & Bass, $8,500.00 plus $425.00 GST and $425.00 PST for upright grand Yamaha piano. Invoice totals $9,350.00. Terms: 1/10, n/30.

SD42: Visa Sales Receipt Summary #424

Dated September 20, 2012

To Visa Sales customers:

6	Classes - Session	$220.00 each	$1,320.00
6	Classes - Month	75.00 each	450.00
9	Classes - Single	25.00 each	225.00
	GST	5%	99.75
	Total receipts held for deposit:		$2,094.75

Use the memorized transaction and edit the quantities.

SD43: Purchase Invoice #LT-259

Dated September 20, 2012

From Les Toyle, $220.00 plus $11.00 GST for the weekly cleaning bill. Invoice totals $231.00. Terms: Net 15. Use memorized transaction.

SD44: Sales Invoice #121

Dated September 21, 2012

To Saskie Gliders, to fill estimate #11, $220.00 each plus GST for teaching dance routine to the eight-member skating team. Invoice totals $1,848.00. Terms: 1/10, n/30.

SD45: Cheque Copy #595

Dated September 21, 2012

To Les Toyle, $462.00 in payment of account. Reference invoices #LT-199 and #LT-235.

SD46: Cash Purchase #GP-37212

Dated September 21, 2012

From The Grand Papery, to fill purchase order #103, $210.00 plus $10.50 GST and $10.50 PST for printing customized receipt forms and invoices. Invoice totalling $231.00 is paid by cheque #596.

Notes
Do not create a fixed asset item for the piano. Enter 1580 Piano:Cost account.

Allow the purchase from Treble & Bass to exceed the credit limit.

SD47: Cash Sales Receipt Summary #425

Dated September 21, 2012

To Cash Sales customers:

6	Classes - Session	$220.00 each	$1 320.00
2	Classes - Month	75.00 each	150.00
20	Classes - Single	25.00 each	500.00
	GST	5%	98.50
	Total cash receipts held for deposit:		$2,068.50

Use the memorized transaction and edit the quantities.

SD48: Memo #4

Dated September 21, 2012

From Owner: Deposit $1,868.50 to chequing and $2,094.75 to the Visa account. Owner held back $200.00 cash from the Bank Chequing deposit for personal use.

September 22 – September 30, 2006

SD49: Sales Estimate #14

Dated September 22, 2012

To Wheatfields Academy, $1,500.00 flat rate plus GST for special dance instruction for a performance in a school fundraising event. Estimate totals $1,575.00. Terms:

1/10, n/30. A deposit of $500.00 is required on acceptance of estimate.

SD50: Visa Purchase Invoice #WG-325

Dated September 24, 2012

From Wendy Groen, RMT, $85.00 plus $4.25 GST for the weekly one-hour massage. Invoice totalling $89.25 was paid in full by Visa. Use memorized transaction.

SD51: Visa Purchase Invoice #P-8921

Dated September 26, 2012

From Petra's Petrol, $30.00 plus $1.50 GST and $1.50 PST for the weekly gasoline purchase for the business vehicle. Invoice totalling $33.00 was paid in full by Visa. Use memorized transaction.

SD52: Cash Receipt #46

Dated September 26, 2012

From Wheatfields Academy, cheque #277 for $500.00 in acceptance of estimate #14.

SD53: Purchase Invoice #S-3002

Dated September 26, 2012

From Sounds Inc., to fill purchase order #102, $900.00 plus $45.00 GST and $45.00 PST for specialized choreography software. Invoice totals $990.00. Terms: 2/10, n/30.

SD54: Cheque Copy #597

Dated September 26, 2012

To Prime Contacts, $269.50 in payment of account. Reference invoice #PC-4911.

SD55: Cheque Copy #598

Dated September 26, 2012

To Prairie Energy Corp, $84.00 in payment of account. Reference invoice #PEC-9182.

> **Notes**
> Do not apply the receipt from Wheatfields to the outstanding invoice.

SD56: Cash Receipt #47

Dated September 26, 2012

From Wheatfields Academy, cheque #276 for $6,864.00 in payment of account, including the discount for early payment. Taxes are not included in the discount. Reference invoice #120. Do not apply used credits.

SD57: Purchase Invoice #LT-274

Dated September 27, 2012

From Les Toyle, $220.00 plus $11.00 GST for the weekly cleaning bill. Invoice totals $231.00. Terms: Net 15. Use memorized transaction.

SD58: Visa Sales Receipt Summary #426

Dated September 27, 2012

To Visa Sales customers:

4	Classes - Session	$220.00 each	$ 880.00
10	Classes - Month	75.00 each	750.00
10	Classes - Single	25.00 each	250.00
	GST	5%	94.00
	Total receipts held for deposit:		$1,974.00

Use the memorized transaction and edit the quantities.

SD59: Cash Sales Receipt Summary #427

Dated September 28, 2012

To Cash Sales customers:

3	Classes - Session	$220.00 each	$ 660.00
6	Classes - Month	75.00 each	450.00
8	Classes - Single	25.00 each	200.00
	GST	5%	65.50
	Total cash receipts held for deposit:		$1,375.50

Use the memorized transaction and edit the quantities.

SD60: Cheque Copy #599

Dated September 28, 2012

To Treble & Bass, $9,265.00 in payment of account, including the discount for early payment. Reference invoice #TB-3499.

SD61: Cash Receipt #48

Dated September 28, 2012

From Saskie Gliders, cheque #1401 for $930.40 in payment of account. Reference invoice #121. Apply credits, discount, and payment.

SD62: Memo #5

Dated September 28, 2012

From Owner: Deposit $9,669.90 to chequing and $1,974.00 to Visa account.

SD63: Cash Purchase Invoice #MP-39

Dated September 29, 2012

From Mimi Pascoe, Pianist, $2,000.00 fee for accompanying dance classes for four weeks, as per contract. Invoice total is paid by cheque #600.

SD64: **Cash Purchase Invoice #FT-9-4**

Dated September 29, 2012

From Fox Trotte, Instructor, $1,500.00 fee for instructing dance classes for four weeks, as per contract. Invoice total was paid by cheque #601.

SD65: **Memo #6**

Dated September 30, 2012

From Owner: Transfer funds to cover scheduled end-of-month payments.
Transfer $15,000.00 from Bank - Credit Card to Bank - Chequing.
Transfer $30,000.00 from Bank - Credit Card to Bank - Savings.

SD66: **Memo #7**

Dated September 30, 2012

Pay GST owing as of September 30, 2006. Write cheque #602 for $3,725.25 in payment.

SD67: **Bank Debit Memo #38103**

Dated September 30, 2012

From Mid-Prairies Trust, preauthorized withdrawals from chequing account for September:

Bank loan ($690.00 principal and $110.00 interest)	$800.00
Mortgage ($120.00 principal and $180.00 interest)	300.00
Long term loan ($180.00 principal and $130.00 interest)	310.00

SD68: **Visa Payment**

Dated September 30, 2012

Reconcile Visa Payable account. The following transactions appeared on the statement.

Date	Transaction Details	Amount
Sep. 27	Ending balance	$1,484.25
Aug. 31	Balance forward from previous statement	875.00
Sep. 1	The Grand Papery	−143.00
Sep. 3	Wendy Groen, RMT	89.25
Sep. 5	Petra's Petrol	−33.00
Sep. 9	The Grand Papery	82.50
Sep. 10	Wendy Groen, RMT	89.25
Sep. 12	Petra's Petrol	33.00
Sep. 17	Wendy Groen, RMT	89.25
Sep. 19	Petra's Petrol	33.00
Sep. 27	Interest charges	17.00

Create a new Expense account for the interest charge: 5010 Credit Card Expenses.
Write cheque #603 for $1,484.25 in full payment, payable to Artists' Credit Union Visa (use Quick Add to create new Other payee).

SD69: **Memo #8**

Dated September 30, 2012

Assess finance charges for overdue accounts.

SD70: Memo #9

Dated September 30, 2012

Prepare adjusting entries for supplies and prepaid expenses for September:

Office and computer supplies	$ 155.00
CDs and sheet music damaged	90.00
Prepaid insurance expired	3,250.00

SD71: Memo #10

Dated September 30, 2012

From Owner: Enter depreciation for the month of September as follows:

Computers	$ 65.00
Piano	140.00
Stereo equipment	90.00
Studio	345.00
Vehicle	360.00

Finishing Your Session

1. **Back up**   your **company data file**

2. **Close**   the **company file**

3. **Close**   the **QuickBooks program**

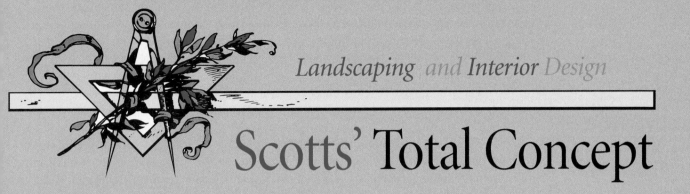

CHAPTER ELEVEN

Landscaping and Interior Design

Scotts' Total Concept

Objectives

After completing this chapter, you should be able to:

■ *prepare* paycheques for hourly and salaried employees

■ *enter* time taken for employee sick leave

■ *release* accrued vacation pay and time

■ *pay* and *recover* advances to employees

■ *pay* payroll liabilities

■ *edit* and *review* payroll transactions

■ *record* sales reps on invoices to track commissions

■ *correct* payroll journal entries after saving

■ *understand* automatic payroll deductions

■ *pay* sales commissions to employees

■ *display* and *print* payroll reports

Company Information

Company Profile

Scotts' Total Concept in Victoria, British Columbia, is owned and operated by Jennifer and Heather Scott. After completing their degrees in interior design and landscape architecture, respectively, the sisters started their business together. They offer complete interior home and garden design work, from concept design to completed project. Although some customers use only one part of the business, either interior design or landscaping, many, especially buyers of new homes, take advantage of both services Scotts' can provide.

▷ Notes
Scotts' Total Concept
28 Artistic Cres.
Victoria, BC V9V 1K7
Tel: (250) 484-9026
Fax: (250) 484-2991
E-mail: scott@
totalconcept.ca
Web: www.totalconcept.
com
Business No.: 247 561 550

Scotts' interior design work might include consulting on fabric colour and design, regular indoor painting or murals, choosing and hanging wallpaper, reupholstering furniture, and making drapes. Scotts' can also design complete period restorations.

Scotts' landscape design work often includes installing stone work; selecting and planting trees, shrubs, and perennials; and designing and building waterfalls and ponds. By emphasizing native plants, Scotts' often creates lower-maintenance gardens.

The sisters have recently purchased office and work space, but they still use their own garages to store the two vans and most of the landscaping equipment. Most of the landscaping tools are stored in the vans.

The moderate Victoria climate makes it possible to continue outdoor garden work into late fall. Scotts' business late in the year is a bit slower than during the spring and summer months, so employees take most of their vacation time in late fall and winter. No employees have taken vacation time yet this year.

Scotts' Total Concept accepts cash, cheques, and Visa in payment, with discounts for early payment and finance charges for overdue accounts. Accounts set up with regular vendors often have favourable payment terms because of the volume of business supplied by Scotts'. A credit card is used for some business purchases.

Customers pay 12 percent HST on all purchases and Scotts' pays HST on all business-related purchases.

At the end of September 2012, Scotts' is ready to enter transactions in QuickBooks after using the following information to convert their manual accounting records:

- Chart of Accounts
- Trial Balance
- Vendor List
- Customer List
- Item List
- Employee Information
- Accounting Procedures

NOTE: We are using a QuickBooks sample file while working in this chapter in order to keep the payroll taxes the same no matter what year you are working with this file.

Chart of Accounts

Scotts' Total Concept

ASSETS

Bank
- 1020 Bank Chequing
- 1040 Bank Savings
- 1060 Bank Visa

Accounts Receivable
- 1200 Accounts Receivable

Other Current Assets
- 1210 Undeposited Funds
- 1220 Employee Advances
- 1260 Prepaid Insurance
- 1280 Prepaid Taxes
- 1300 Office and Computer Supplies
- 1320 Decorating Supplies & Material
- 1350 Landscaping Supplies & Material
- 1380 Lawn Signs

Fixed Assets
- 1520 Design Software
- 1580 Computer Equipment
- 1640 Sewing Machines & Sergers
- 1660 Landscaping Tools
- 1680 Landscaping Equipment
- 1700 Vans
- 1740 Office

LIABILITIES

Accounts Payable
- 2100 Accounts Payable

Credit Card
- 2200 Visa Payable

Other Current Liabilities
- 2260 Bank Loan
- 2300 HST Payable
- 2400 Payroll Liabilities

Long Term Liabilities
- 2720 Long Term Loan
- 2740 Mortgage Payable

EQUITY
- 3220 Capital, Jennifer Scott
- 3240 Capital, Heather Scott
- 3260 Drawings, Jennifer Scott
- 3280 Drawings, Heather Scott
- 3600 Retained Earnings

INCOME
- 4100 Revenue from Design
- 4120 Revenue from Landscaping
- 4160 Sales Discounts
- 4200 Revenue from Interest
- 4300 Other Revenue

EXPENSE

Cost of Goods Sold
- 5040 Decorating Materials Used
- 5050 Decorating Supplies Used
- 5060 Landscaping Material Used

Expense
- 5080 Bank Service Charges
- 5100 Credit Card Fees
- 5120 Advertising and Promotion
- 5140 Purchase Discounts
- 5180 Office & Computer Supplies Used
- 5220 Maintenance Expenses
- 5240 Insurance Expense
- 5260 Interest Expense
- 5280 Property Tax Expense
- 5340 Hydro Expense
- 5360 Telephone Expense
- 5380 Vehicle Operating Expenses
- 5510 Payroll Expenses

Scotts' Total Concept

AS AT SEPTEMBER 30, 2012

	Debits	Credits			Debits	Credits
1020 Bank Chequing	$ 28,320.00		3220 Capital, Jennifer Scott			39,171.68
1040 Bank Savings	55,450.00		3240 Capital, Heather Scott			39,171.68
1060 Bank Visa	3,680.00		3260 Drawings, Jennifer Scott		7,000.00	
1200 Accounts Receivable	29,556.00		3280 Drawings, Heather Scott		7,000.00	
1210 Undeposited Funds	8,000.00		4100 Revenue from Design			308,500.00
1260 Prepaid Insurance	2,940.00		4120 Revenue from Landscaping			270,000.00
1280 Prepaid Taxes	810.00		4160 Sales Discounts		4,200.00	
1300 Office and Computer Supplies	370.00		4200 Revenue from Interest			510.00
1320 Decorating Supplies & Material	1,650.00		4300 Other Revenue			50.00
1350 Landscaping Supplies & Material	2,120.00		5040 Decorating Materials Used		74,000.00	
1380 Lawn Signs	890.00		5050 Decorating Supplies Used		4,900.00	
1520 Design Software	8,500.00		5060 Landscaping Material Used		80,000.00	
1580 Computer Equipment	9,800.00		5080 Bank Service Charges		380.00	
1640 Sewing Machines & Sergers	3,100.00		5100 Credit Card Fees		285.00	
1660 Landscaping Tools	2,200.00		5120 Advertising and Promotion		9,900.00	
1680 Landscaping Equipment	24,500.00		5140 Purchase Discounts			1,400.00
1700 Vans	41,000.00		5180 Office & Computer Supplies Used		290.00	
1740 Office	160,000.00		5220 Maintenance Expenses		10,600.00	
2100 Accounts Payable		$ 11,363.00	5240 Insurance Expense		8,700.00	
2200 Visa Payable		390.00	5260 Interest Expense		5,340.00	
2260 Bank Loan		12,000.00	5280 Property Tax Expense		3,200.00	
2300 HST Payable		3,500.00	5340 Hydro Expense		950.00	
2400 Payroll Liabilities		17,770.19	5360 Telephone Expense		1,830.00	
2720 Long Term Loan		40,000.00	5380 Vehicle Operating Expenses		6,500.00	
2740 Mortgage Payable		80,000.00	5510 Payroll Expenses		215,865.55	
					$823,826.55	$823,826.55

Vendor Information

Scotts' Total Concept

Vendor Name (Contact)	Address	Phone No. Fax No.	E-mail Business No.	Terms Credit Limit
BC Energy Group (Mo Turbine)	500 Generator St. Victoria, BC V6D 3L9	Tel: (250) 487-2100	m.turbine@bceg.com	net 10 $500.00
Celine's Service Centre (Celine)	48 Motor Way Victoria, BC V5D 3P8	Tel: (250) 337-2819 Fax: (250) 339-2016		net 20 $2,000.00
Freya's Home Interiors (Freya Brocade, or Belle Chintz)	188 Silkworm Rd. Victoria, BC V6G 3P5	Tel: (250) 866-8201 Fax: (250) 866-1010	freya@freyas.com 364 577 409	2/5, n/30 $10,000.00
Groen's Greens (Sherri Groen)	386 Blooming Way Victoria, BC V8T 3R5	Tel: (250) 484-1726	sherri@groensgreens.com 478 265 253	1/15, n/30 $10,000.00
Haida Investments Inc. (Penny Money)	200 Totem Cres. Victoria, BC V7E 3F5	Tel: (250) 778-2983 Alt: (800) 498-2314 Fax: (250) 778-4821	money@haida.inv.com	end-of-month
Minister of Finance	100 Legislature Rd. Vancouver, BC V2D 8J9	Tel: (800) 288-6217		end-of-month

Scotts' Total Concept

Vendor Name (Contact)	Address	Phone No. Fax No.	E-mail Business No.	Terms Credit Limit
Primus Communications (Dyal Tone)	33 Synergic Rd. Victoria, BC V3B 2J8	Tel: (250) 508-7108	accounts@primus.ca	net 15 $500.00
Receiver General	1050 Federal Lane Vancouver, BC V2P 7E8	Tel: (800) 926-3917		end-of-month
Stonewall Inc. (Rocky Plaices)	79 Flagstone Ave. Victoria, BC V6D 2L9	Tel: (250) 481-4956 Fax: (250) 488-1927	Rocky@stonewall.ca 289 367 455	1/10, n/30 $9,000.00
Workers' Compensation Board of BC	10 Protectorate Cres. Vancouver, BC V1B 5G5	Tel: (604) 526-3828 Alt: (800) 466-1927		end-of-month

Outstanding Vendor Transactions

Scotts' Total Concept

Vendor Name	Date	Terms	Due Date	Invoice No./ Cheque No.	Amount
Celine's Service Centre	Sep. 15/12	net 20	Oct. 5/12	CSC-3324	$286.00
Freya's Home Interiors	Sep. 28/12	2/5, n/30	Oct. 28/12	FHI-4801	$2,675.00
Groen's Greens	Sep. 22/12	1/15, n/30	Oct. 22/12	GG-559	$912.00
Stonewall Inc.	Sep. 23/12	1/10, n/30	Oct. 23/12	SI-3981	$4,280.00
	Sep. 26/12	1/10, n/30	Oct. 26/12	SI-3998	$3,210.00
				Balance Owing	$7,490.00
				Grand Total	$11,363.00

Customer Information

Scotts' Total Concept

Customer Name (Contact)	Address	Phone No. Fax No.	E-mail Preferred Payment	Terms Credit Limit
Everwood, Ashby	114 Bluegrass Rd. Victoria, BC V7N 4B1	Tel: (250) 489-1514	everwoods@shaw.ca cheque	1/5, n/30 $25,000.00
Planter, Flora	67 Peony Rd. Victoria, BC V6N 9J7	Tel: (250) 487-6673	flora67@yahoo.ca cheque	1/5, n/30 $25,000.00
Schleger, Marie Rose	200 Fescue St. Victoria, BC V8G 5G2	Tel: (250) 904-6229 Fax: (250) 905-2619	marie.rose@sympatico.ca cheque	1/5, n/30 $25,000.00
Toussieng, Nina	711 Oceanview Rd. Victoria, BC V8T 4B9	Tel: (250) 766-4928	nina9@hotmail.com cheque	1/5, n/30 $25,000.00
Woodslea, Nedaa	528 Hedgerow Blvd. Victoria, BC V7T 2M5	Tel: (250) 779-2561 Alt: (250) 720-8380	Woodslea@firstcontact.ca cheque	1/5, n/30 $25,000.00

Outstanding Customer Transactions

Scotts' Total Concept

Customer Name	Date	Terms	Type	Invoice No./ Cheque No.	Amount	Balance Owing
Ashby Everwood	Sep. 22/12	1/5, n/30	Invoice	351	$9,160.00	
	Sep. 24/12		Cheque	128	$3,000.00	$6,160.00
Flora Planter	Sep. 14/12	1/5, n/30	Invoice	345	$16,946.00	
	Sep. 21/12		Cheque	1888	$5,000.00	$11,946.00
Marie Rose Schleger	Sep. 28/12	1/5, n/30	Invoice	359	$11,450.00	$11,450.00
			Grand Total			$29,556.00

Item List

Scotts' Total Concept

Item	Description	Price	Tax Code	Account
SERVICES				
Design	Interior design and decorating		H	4100 Revenue from Design
Landscaping	Garden landscaping		H	4120 Revenue from Landscaping
OTHER CHARGES				
Finance Charges	Finance Charges on Overdue Balance	18%	not used	4200 Revenue from Interest
	18% > 30 days, $25.00 min., 5-day grace period			
NSF Cheque	Amount of NSF cheque from customer		not used	1020 Bank Chequing
NSF Fee	Administrative charge for NSF cheque	$25.00	not used	4300 Other Revenue
NON-INVENTORY				
Decorating Material	Paint, paper, etc.		H	1320 Decorating Supplies & Material
Decorating Supplies	Paintbrushes, cleaning products, etc.		H	1320 Decorating Supplies & Material
Landscaping Material	Stones, tiles, plants, soil		H	1350 Landscaping Supplies & Material
Landscaping Tools	Shovels, hoes, rakes, etc.		H	1660 Landscaping Tools

Employee Information

Scotts' Total Concept

Employee	**Dee Zijner**	**Vijay Gardner**	**Stone Kutter**	**Nicolai Digger**	**Mita Paynter**	**Serge Draper**
Position	Interior Designer	Landscaper	Stoneworker	Gardener	Decorator	Upholsterer
Address	55 Windswept Pl.	350 Treeline Ave.	498 Marble Court	1040 Paradise Rd.	18 Chartreuse Cr.	299 Velveteen Dr.
	Victoria, BC	Victoria, BC	Victoria, BC	Victoria, BC	Victoria, BC	Victoria, BC
	V3Y 9K9	V6S 2D1	V5P 1B1	V4R 1J2	V7M 3B3	V6B 3W8
Telephone	(250) 455-7162	(250) 728-2910	(250) 522-3954	(250) 613-7029	(250) 279-9115	(250) 274-3714
Alt. Telephone	(250) 587-7399		(250) 633-1098		(250) 832-8711	(250) 485-8109
SIN	129 632 774	428 161 020	563 444 868	931 216 550	148 196 835	406 529 420
Employee Number	1177	1389	1328	1499	1023	1239
Date of Birth (mm-dd-yy)	07-13-78	12-16-69	04-29-63	09-19-79	02-27-72	10-31-74
Date of Hire (mm-dd-yy)	05-01-02	06-15-04	01-01-04	04-01-05	03-01-00	10-15-03
Earnings						
Regular Wage Rate			$24.00/hour	$14.00/hour	$18.00/hour	$14.00/hour
Overtime Wage Rate			$36.00/hour	$21.00/hour	$27.00/hour	$21.00/hour
Regular Annual Salary	$42,600.00	$42,600.00	—	—	—	—
Commission	2%	2%	—	—	—	—
	(design revenue)	(landscaping revenue)				

Scotts' Total Concept

Employee	Dee Zijner	Vijay Gardner	Stone Kutter	Nicolai Digger	Mita Paynter	Serge Draper
Pay Period	monthly	monthly	semi-monthly	weekly	semi-monthly	weekly
Hours per Period	160	160	80	40	80	40
WCB Rate	6.94%	4.7%	4.7%	3.07%	6.94%	6.94%
Deductions each pay period						
Medical - Employee (limit)	$48.00 (576)	$27.00 (324)	$13.50 (324)	$6.25 (324)	$27.00 (648)	$6.25 (324)
RRSP	$400.00	$200.00	$150.00	$25.00	$150.00	$25.00
CSB	$200.00	$200.00	$50.00	–	$50.00	–
Income Tax, EI, and CPP	Amounts and calculations built in to QuickBooks program					
Federal (BC) Claim - TD1						
Personal	$10,382.00 (11,000.00)	$10,382.00 (11,000.00)	$10,382.00 (11,000.00)	$10,382.00 (11,000.00)	$10,382.00 (11,000.00)	$10,382.00 (11,000.00)
Spousal/Equivalent	$10,382.00 (9,653.00)	–	–	–	$10,382.00 (9,653.00)	–
Education	–	–	–	$ 2,850.00 (2,250.00)	–	–
Other (Age)	–	–	–	–	$ 4,223.00 (4,118.00)	–
Total Claim	$20,764.00 (20,653.00)	$10,382.00 (11,000.00)	$10,382.00 (11,000.00)	$13,332.00 (13,250.00)	$24,987.00 (24,771.00)	$10,382.00 (11,000.00)
Vacation	4 weeks	4 weeks	8% retained	6% retained	8% retained	6% retained
Sick Pay Rate	same as regular hourly or salary rate					
Accrued Vacation	$3,550.00	$3,550.00	$3,075.84	$1,506.96	$2,350.08	$1,408.68
Accrued Sick Leave Time	80 hours	70 hours	80 hours	40 hours	80 hours	40 hours

PAYROLL LIABILITY	AMOUNT	PAYABLE TO
Medical - Employee	$ 206.00	Minister of Finance
Medical - Company	206.00	Minister of Finance
RRSP	1,400.00	Haida Investments Inc.
CSB Plan	600.00	Haida Investments Inc.
Income Tax	3,167.39	Receiver General
EI - Employee	391.64	Receiver General
EI - Company	548.32	Receiver General
CPP - Employee	894.73	Receiver General
CPP - Company	894.73	Receiver General
WCB	1,119.82	Workers' Compensation Board of BC
Total	$9,428.63	

Employee Profiles and TD1 Information

All employees receive vacation and sick leave benefits. Gardner and Zijner, the salaried employees, are allowed four weeks' vacation each year. Kutter and Paynter, the senior employees, receive 8 percent of their pay as vacation pay (about four weeks), and this amount is retained until they take their time off. Digger and Draper, the junior employees, receive 6 percent vacation pay (about three weeks) and this amount is also retained. Employees are encouraged to take their time off during the late fall and winter months because the company is less busy at this time of year. No employee has taken vacation time yet this year. All employees are entitled to 10 days' leave per year for illness and can carry forward two extra days.

Gardner and Zijner are set up as sales representatives so the program will track their sales for the purpose of calculating sales commissions.

Occasionally, the Scotts will grant employees small advances on future paycheques. These amounts are paid back from future paycheques at an agreed rate.

Through an investment company, Scotts' allows payroll deductions for Canada Savings Bond (CSB) purchases and contributions to Registered Retirement Savings Plans (RRSPs).

As required, Scotts' pays 50 percent of the provincial medical premiums for employees and the compulsory contributions for Employment Insurance (EI), Canada Pension Plan (CPP), and Workers' Compensation Board (WCB).

Dee Zijner is the head designer and sales rep for all design projects. She works with Jenn Scott to design interiors and supervise the completion of tasks by Paynter and Draper. She earns a monthly salary of $3,550.00, or $42,600.00 per year, plus a sales commission of 2 percent of the revenue from design. She fully supports her spouse who is a full-time student, and therefore claims the spousal amount for tax purposes and pays the provincial medical insurance for a couple. She has elected to purchase a CSB and contribute to her RRSP through regular salary deductions.

Vijay Gardner is the head landscaper and the sales rep for all landscaping projects. He works with Heather Scott to plan the garden projects, supervise Kutter and Digger, and order materials. His annual salary of $42,600.00 per year is paid monthly at the rate of $3,550.00. He also earns a sales commission of 2 percent of the revenue from landscaping work. Gardner is single, so he claims the single tax amount and pays the single medical premium. He also contributes to both his RRSP and his CSB plan.

Stone Kutter works on the landscaping tasks and specializes in cutting and laying stones and tiles. He is paid twice per month at a rate of $24.00 per hour for 40 hours per week. He earns $36.00 per hour for any overtime hours. As a single individual, he claims the single tax amounts and pays single medical premiums. Kutter has elected to participate in both the CSB purchase and the RRSP.

Nicolai Digger performs a variety of gardening and landscaping tasks under Kutter's supervision. He receives his pay every week at a rate of $14.00 per hour for the first 40 hours and $21.00 per hour for additional time worked beyond 40 hours. As a part-time student, Digger has a tax claim amount for education and tuition in addition to the single claim amount. His medical premiums are also deducted at the single rate. Part of his weekly pay is withheld as an RRSP contribution.

Mita Paynter works under the direction of Zijner on the interior decorating parts of the projects. A skilled decorator herself, she can work independently at the customer's home as needed. Paynter is paid twice each month at a rate of $18.00 per hour for a 40-hour week and $27.00 per hour for additional time worked. As a single parent who supports her elderly infirm mother, Paynter is allowed to claim the spousal equivalent and caregiver amounts for income tax purposes. She pays the family rate for medical premiums and participates in both RRSP and CSB programs.

Serge Draper performs a variety of decorating tasks under Paynter's supervision. He receives his weekly pay at a rate of $14.00 per hour for 40 hours and $21.00 per hour for additional time worked. He is single and therefore claims the single amount for income tax purposes and pays the single rate for medical premiums. He makes regular RRSP contributions through payroll but does not participate in the CSB purchase.

Accounting Procedures

Taxes: HST

Scotts' Total Concept pays HST on all goods and services that it buys and charges HST on all services. HST collected from customers is recorded as a liability in the *HST Payable* account. HST paid to vendors is recorded in the *HST Payable* account as a

Most provinces have a medical plan that covers all residents in the province. In Alberta, the premiums for these are shared between employees and employers. In Ontario, employers contribute to the provincial medical program through the Employer Health Tax and individuals pay a health tax that is combined with their income taxes.

These plans are different from optional private health insurance plans that usually supplement the basic provincial coverage, such as for drug or dental care. These private plans may be offered as company-paid employee benefits or as employee-paid programs.

decrease in liability to the Canada Revenue Agency. The report is filed with the Receiver General for Canada by the last day of each month for the previous month, either including the balance owing or requesting a refund.

Scotts' Total Concept pays 12 percent HST on all taxable purchases.

Account Terms

All customers receive a 1 percent discount if they settle their account within five days after completion of the work. The full balance is required within 30 days of completion of the work. Customers with small jobs often pay by credit card and receive no discount.

For overdue accounts, customers pay finance charges of 18 percent per year after 30 days from the invoice date and a minimum charge of $25.00 for administration expenses. A five-day grace period results in charges being applied 35 days after the invoice date and credited to the *Revenue from Interest* account.

Customers whose cheques are returned as NSF are notified of their outstanding account balance and are assessed a handing charge of $25.00 to cover the fee charged by the bank.

Some vendors offer discounts for early payment.

Deposits and Cheques

All cheques, credit card payments, and cash are held for deposit. Cheques are hand printed at the time of the transaction.

Estimates, Orders, and Deposits

Scotts' Total Concept prepares estimates on request. When customers decide to proceed with a project, they pay a deposit of 25 percent so that Scotts' can buy the materials or items needed for the project.

Scotts' Total Concept also places purchase orders with regular suppliers and sometimes pays a deposit on these orders.

Supplies

At the end of each month, Scotts' counts supplies and materials remaining to determine costs and prepare adjusting entries for these and other prepaid expenses. Depreciation will be entered at the end of the fiscal year.

Instructions

1. Using the Chart of Accounts, the Trial Balance, and other information, you will record entries for source documents marked with an SD beside them and for October 2012 using QuickBooks. You will find the source documents listed as you work through the chapter. The procedures for entering each new type of transaction introduced in this chapter are outlined in step-by-step instructions. Additional source documents will be provided, allowing you to have more practice entering transactions. If you have used this textbook in the past and would prefer to skip the step-by-step instructions and work only with a list of source documents, refer to the CD in the back of the textbook for the list of source documents for this chapter.

Notes
Instructions for Payroll Reports begin on page 573.

2. After you have finished making your entries, print the **reports and graphs** for October 2012 as indicated on the following printing form:.

REPORTS FOR OCTOBER 2012

Lists

- ☐ Account Listing
- ☐ Customer Phone List
- ☐ Customer Contact List
- ☐ Vendor Phone List
- ☐ Vendor Contact List
- ☐ Employee Contact List
- ☐ Item Listing
- ☐ Item Price List
- ☐ Payroll Item List

Company & Financial

- ☑ Balance Sheet Standard at Oct. 31
- ☑ Profit & Loss Standard from Oct. 1 to Oct. 31
- ☐ Expenses by Vendor
- ☐ Income by Customer

Accountant & Taxes

- ☑ Trial Balance at Oct. 31
- ☐ General Ledger
- ☑ Journal from Oct. 1 to Oct. 31
- ☐ Transaction List by Date
- ☐ Transaction Detail by Account

Other

- ☐ Custom Summary Report
- ☐ Custom Transaction Detail Report
- ☐ Transaction History
- ☐ Transaction Journal

Vendor

- ☑ A/P Aging Detail at Oct. 31
- ☐ Vendor Balance
- ☐ Unpaid Bills
- ☐ Transaction List by Vendor

Purchases

- ☐ Purchases by Vendor
- ☐ Purchases by Item
- ☐ Transaction List by Vendor
- ☐ Open Purchase Orders by Vendor

Customer

- ☑ A/R Aging Detail at Oct. 31
- ☐ Customer Balance
- ☐ Open Invoices
- ☐ Collections Report
- ☐ Transaction List by Customer

Sales

- ☐ Sales by Customer
- ☐ Sales by Item
- ☐ Open Sales Orders by Customer
- ☑ Sales by Rep from Oct. 1 to Oct. 31

Employees & Payroll

- ☑ Payroll Summary from Oct. 1 to Oct. 31
- ☐ Payroll Item Detail from Oct. 1 to Oct. 31
- ☐ Payroll Detail Review
- ☑ Employee Earnings Summary from Oct. 1 to Oct. 31

- ☑ Payroll Transactions by Payee from Oct. 1 to Oct. 31
- ☐ Payroll Transaction Detail
- ☐ Payroll Liability Balances
- ☐ Employee Withholding
- ☐ TD1 Review List
- ☐ T4 Summary
- ☐ PD7A Summary
- ☐ Record of Employment

Banking

- ☐ Deposit Detail
- ☑ Cheque Detail from Oct. 1 to Oct. 31
- ☐ Missing Cheques
- ☐ Reconcile Discrepancy
- ☐ Previous Reconciliation

GRAPHS

- ☐ Income and Expense
- ☐ Net Worth
- ☐ Accounts Payable
- ☐ Accounts Receivable
- ☐ Sales

Paying Hourly Wage Employees

Preparing paycheques in QuickBooks is similar to entering other transactions — we enter the information on forms that look like payroll cheques and stubs.

1. **Start**   the **QuickBooks program**

2. **Open**   the **Scott company file**. The QuickBooks Home page should be displayed on the screen

IMPORTANT: This file has been converted to a Sample file so that you can enter payroll information for dates outside the current payroll tax table period. This is important for learning purposes. No matter what QuickBooks tax table you have installed, the payroll information in the print screens in the textbook will be the same as yours as long as you use the sample file. The sample data file is set up so that December 15, 2007, is the current date displayed when entering forms. You will change the dates, using the year 2012 as you work through the textbook.

3. The following message will be displayed:

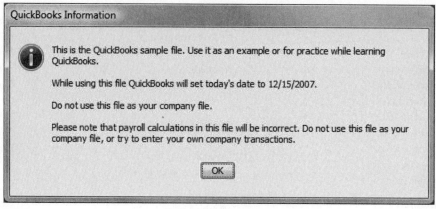

Figure 11-1

4. Click   **OK** to continue

The first transaction that we will enter is a payroll for two hourly employees. Refer to the following source document as we work through the steps to enter it:

SD Instructions
Refer to the following source document and then follow the step-by-step instructions to enter it.

SD1:

EMPLOYEE TIME SUMMARY SHEET #1

Date: October 1, 2012 (for the pay period ending September 27, 2012)

Name of Employee	Regular Hours	Overtime Hours	Sick Leave Hours	Vacation Pay	Advances Received/ Advances Repaid
Nicolai Digger	40	2	—	—	—
Serge Draper	32	4	8	—	$200

a. Using Employee Time Summary Sheet #1 and the Employee Information Sheet, complete payroll for weekly paid employees

b. Issue a $200.00 advance to Serge Draper and recover $50.00 from each of the following four paycheques

c. Manually prepare cheques #521 and #522 (do not use computer generated cheques)

Payroll functions are performed from the Payroll Centre.

5. Open   the **Payroll Centre** using one of the following methods:

a) **Click** the **Payroll Centre icon** in the Employees section of the Home page; or

b) **Choose Employees** from the menu and **click Payroll Centre**

Figure 11-2

The Payroll Centre is part of the Employee Centre. Notice the tab currently displayed is the Payroll tab. All activities connected with payroll can be accessed from the Payroll tab: paying employees, submitting payroll liabilities, preparing Records of Employment (ROEs) and T4s (or RL-1s for Quebec), and managing payroll items.

The Employees tab contains the Employees list, which includes contact information and payroll transactions for each of your employees, and the transactions tab allows you to view all payroll transactions.

Payroll Dates

Because this is a specially prepared file, you are allowed to enter dates outside of the dates covered by the current tax tables. In other company files, you must work with dates that fall within the range of the current tax tables. Most tables allow you to go back a few months, but you cannot go forward into the next calendar year. To see the tax table expiry date for your program, choose the Help menu and click My Licence Information.

To pay employees, you select either the Unscheduled Payroll icon or the Scheduled Payroll icon in the Pay Employees section of the Payroll Centre. A scheduled payroll is a payroll that has been set up to occur on a regular frequency and an unscheduled payroll can be run at any time. You don't need to set up a scheduled payroll in order to pay your employees. We will be using the unscheduled payroll option.

6. **Click**   the **Unscheduled Payroll icon**   , or **choose** the **Employees menu**, **click Pay Employees**, and then **click Unscheduled Payroll**:

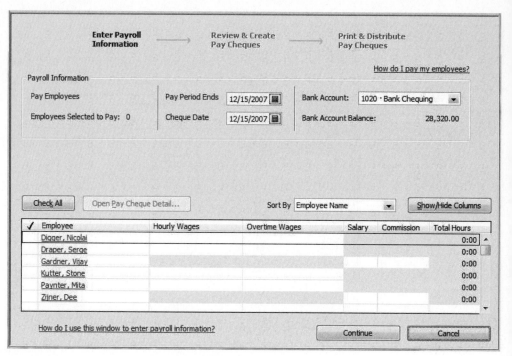

Figure 11-3

All employees are listed. Two dates appear on the form: the date that defines the end of the pay period and the cheque date. Often these dates are different. Hourly paid employees must usually complete their work period before the number of hours is known, so the pay period date usually precedes the cheque date. Salaried employees are paid on a schedule that is not based on hours worked so their pay period end dates often match and may even follow the cheque date. Cheques are manually prepared.

You can select one or more employees from the list for each payroll run. We are paying the two weekly paid hourly employees for the week ended September 29th.

7.	**Click**	the ✓ **(pay) column for Digger** to add a ✓ beside her name
8.	**Click**	the ✓ **(pay) column for Draper** to add a ✓ beside his name
9.	**Double click**	the **Pay Period Ends date**
10.	**Type**	**09/27/12** (12/15/07 is the sample file current date)
11.	**Press**	⌜tab⌟ to advance to the Cheque Date field
12.	**Type**	**10/01/12**
13.	**Click**	the **drop-down arrow** in the Bank Account field to view the accounts available
14.	**Click**	**1020 Bank Chequing**

If all amounts are the same from one pay period to the next, you can create the cheque directly, but previewing the cheque gives you a chance to verify the amounts before printing.

| 15. | **Click** | the **Open Pay Cheque Detail button** to open the Review or Change Pay Cheque window for the first employee: |

Notes

The default dates for the sample file are 2007. You will be changing them as you work through the transactions.

Review Or Change Pay Cheque

Digger, Nicolai   Pay Period 09/21/2012 - 09/27/2012

☐ Use Direct Deposit

Earnings

Item Name	Rate	Hours	Customer:Job
Hourly Wages	14.00		
Overtime Wages	21.00		

Adv. Pay Bal. ($)   0.00

Sick Hours Avail.   40:00
Vacation Avail. ($)   1,506.96
Sick Hours Acc.   0:00
Vac. Accrued ($)   0.00
☐ Do not accrue

Total Hours: 0:00

Other Payroll Items

Item Name	Rate	Quantity
Medical - Company	6.25	
Medical - Employee	-6.25	
RRSP	-25.00	
WCB	3.07%	

Employee Summary

Item Name	Amount	YTD
Hourly Wages	0.00	21,840.00
Overtime Wages	0.00	3,276.00
Medical - Employee	-6.25	-250.00
RRSP	-25.00	-1,000.00
Advances	0.00	0.00
Advances Repayment	0.00	0.00
CPP - Employee	0.00	-1,113.45
EI - Employee	0.00	-497.75
Federal Income Tax	0.00	-3,414.06

Company Summary

Item Name	Amount	YTD
Medical - Company	6.25	250.00
WCB	0.00	771.06
CPP - Company	0.00	1,113.45
EI - Company	0.00	696.15

Cheque Amount: -31.25

[Clear all] [Save & Previous] [Save & Next]   [Save & Close]   [Cancel] [Help]

Figure 11-4

Just as sales in QuickBooks are based on selecting items, all payroll amounts are entered by selecting Payroll Items. Each item is set up with a number of defaults, including a linked account. Items usually selected for an employee are already entered in the employee record as defaults. Some of these items have an amount or rate predefined and some do not. Each type of income is defined as an item. Thus we have items for hourly wages, overtime wages, salary, sick leave, vacation, and so on.

For hourly employees, we need to enter the number of hours worked so that the program can calculate the total wages and deduction amounts based on wages: federal income tax, CPP, EI, WCB premiums, and so on. Both employee and employer contributions are calculated and entered. Other deductions, such as medical premiums or contributions to a savings plan, may be fixed amounts per pay period. Payroll items are also created for these deductions.

The employer's contribution to EI is 1.4 times the amount of employee's contribution. The employer's contribution to CPP equals the employee's contribution. WCB is paid entirely by the employer, and the rate is based on the type of work, and the industry's safety record. Medical premiums in BC are divided equally between employer and employee. Some deductions, such as RRSP and income tax, are paid only by the employee. Employer contributions are entered as *Payroll Expenses* and increase *Payroll Liabilities*. Employee deductions also increase *Payroll Liabilities* and reduce the net pay amount taken from the *Bank Chequing* account.

The program also tracks and reports on year-to-date amounts for the employee. Opening values are entered for the employee, and the amounts are updated with each paycheque. Some items have annual amount limits, so the program will stop making deductions when the limit is reached.

Accumulated sick leave and vacation pay are also reported on the Review Or Change Pay Cheque screen. These are shown in Sick Hours Avail. and Vacation Avail. When an employee takes sick leave or vacation, these amounts will be reduced.

For Digger, we need to enter only the number of regular and overtime wage hours worked during the week. The cursor should be in the Hours column for the hourly wages.

Notes
Limits for EI and CPP are built into the tax tables. Other items may have limits defined by the employer, such as advances, or by the employee, such as RRSP contributions.

16. Click   the **Hours column** beside Hourly Wages if necessary

17. Type   **40** and **press** (tab)

The program automatically enters amounts in the Employee Summary and the Company Summary Amount columns. The vacation accrued is also entered — Digger receives 6 percent of his wages as vacation pay. This amount is held until he takes vacation time or leaves the company, at which time, the accrued amount will be released.

18. Click   the **Hours column** beside Overtime Wages

19. Type   **2** and **press** (tab) to update the totals and deductions

The program automatically updates all Employee and Company Summary amounts and accrued vacation for the additional income.

Notice too that the program has automatically entered a one-week pay period for the paycheque in the top right-hand corner of the screen for the week ending September 27th, the pay period end date we entered.

20. The paycheque is complete as shown:

Figure 11-5

21. Check   your **work** carefully

CORRECTING A PAYCHEQUE

Return to the field you need to change. To correct a date or amount, double click the current entry to select it, highlight the amount or date, and type the correct information. Press (tab) to update the wage and deduction amounts.

If you have selected the wrong employee, or do not want to complete the paycheque, click Cancel to begin again.

---

22. Click   **Save & Next** to record the paycheque and open the preview screen for Draper, the second employee we selected for payment

We will need to work through the following three topics: entering other payroll items, entering sick leave taken, and entering payroll advances, in order to enter the information in Draper's paycheque.

Entering Other Payroll Items

Paycheques are often different from one period to the next. Employees may work a different number of hours or take time off for vacation or illness. Some employers offer coverage for illness, payroll advances, or other benefits, such as payment of tuition fees. You would set up items for each of these.

Draper received a payroll advance with this cheque, and he took one day of sick leave (8 hours). We will enter these other payroll items on his paycheque. First, we will add the regular and overtime hours as we did for Digger's paycheque.

1. **Click**   the **Hours field** beside Hourly Wages

2. **Type**   **32**

3. **Press**   ⊥ to place the cursor in the Overtime Hours field

4. **Type**   **4**

5. **Press**   ⌐tab⌐ to update the amounts

Entering Sick Leave Taken

We are now ready to enter the information for sick leave and advances. Digger has 40 hours of sick leave available to him. He has taken one day off this week and a normal work day is 8 hours. The Scotts pay their employees the regular wage rate when they are ill, to a maximum of 10 days per year. Thus, sick leave is entered as an income item to which regular taxes and deductions apply.

6. **Click**   the **line below Overtime Wages** in the Item Name field under the Earnings heading to display the drop-down arrow

7. **Click**   the **drop-down arrow** to view the income items available:

Figure 11-6

Notice that the items for sick leave and vacation are separated for hourly and salaried workers, because the pay base is different for these employees. Hourly workers are paid hourly wages for sick leave time. Salaried workers have their regular work hours

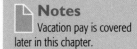

Notes
Vacation pay is covered later in this chapter.

reduced for the month, that is, some of their regular salary is assigned to sick leave instead of working hours but total pay is not affected by the number of hours.

We need to select the item and then enter the number of hours taken.

<table>
<tbody>
</tbody>
</table>

8. Click   **Sick Hourly Rate** to select the item. The regular hourly rate has automatically been entered for the item

9. Press   `tab` twice to advance to the Hours field

10. Type   **8** and **press** `tab` to update the paycheque amounts and deductions

The number in the Sick Hours Avail. field displayed on the right-hand side of the screen has been reduced from 40 to 32. All regular taxes and deductions apply to this amount. These defaults are set up for the sick hourly rate item. The actual amount paid for sick leave is recorded separately from wages in the Employee Summary.

Entering Payroll Advances

Payroll advances may be issued to an employee occasionally for personal reasons. These amounts are given at the owners' discretion and limits may be set on the amount advanced at one time, for the entire year, or for the employee's entire term of employment. Frequent requests for advances may suggest that financial counselling is advisable. Employees pay back the advance over a prearranged number of paycheques.

Two items are created for advances, one for the advance and one for the repayment. The advance — a short-term interest-free loan — is an addition to payroll, while the repayment — a repayment of the loan — is a deduction. Both items are linked to the *Employee Advances* account, an asset account. Advances and repayments are not taxable items — they do not affect income tax or other deduction amounts.

Advances are added as default items for all employees but no amounts are entered as defaults. When the item is not part of the employee record, QuickBooks will ask if you want to make it a regular payroll item for this employee, that is, add it to the record as a default.

Draper has been authorized to receive an advance of $200.00 with this paycheque, and he will pay back $50.00 on each of his next four paycheques.

Advances and Advances Repayment are listed in the Other Payroll Items section of the paycheque.

1. Use   the **scroll bar** in the Other Payroll Items section to view the Advances item

2. Click   the **Rate column** beside Advances (below WCB in the Other Payroll Items section)

3. Type   **200** and **press** `tab` to update and complete the paycheque as shown:

Notes You can edit the rate for sick leave, but permanent changes should be entered in the employee record.

Notes You might choose not to add an item to an employee record if it is an extraordinary item that you do not want to appear on each paycheque.

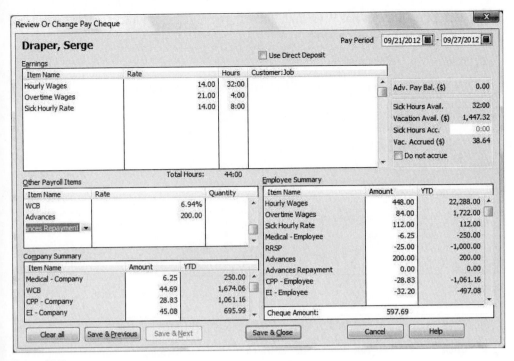

Figure 11-7

Notice that the advance is entered separately in the Employee Summary section. The Cheque Amount below the Employee Summary is updated, and the tax amounts did not change when the Advance was added to the paycheque.

4. **Check** your **work** carefully and **make corrections** before you record the pay-cheque

5. **Click** **Save & Close** to save the paycheque and return to the Enter Payroll Information screen:

Notes
  To see that the taxes and deduction amounts have not changed, you can observe the summary amounts carefully as you make changes. Delete the amount for advances and press (tab). Then enter the amount again and press (tab).

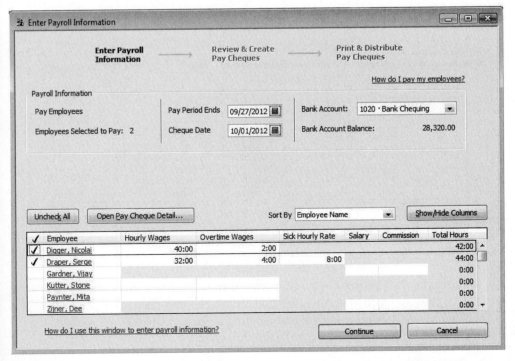

Figure 11-8

The list of employees has been updated with the number of hours for the payroll and the latest pay date has been added.

6. **Click**   **Continue**

7. The following message will be displayed about the Sample file:

Figure 11-9

8. **Read**   the **Warning**

9. **Click**   the **box** beside the Do not display this message in the future option

10. **Click**   **OK**

11. The Review and Create Pay Cheques window is updated with the payroll information as shown:

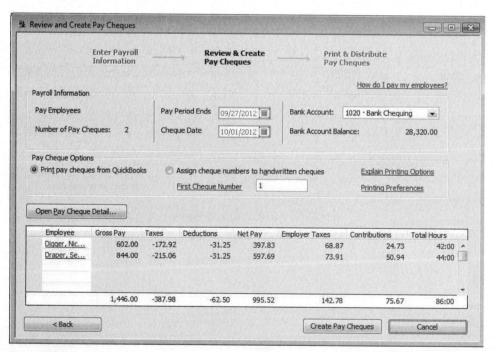

Figure 11-10

Because you can prepare cheques for several employees in a single session, the first number for the payroll cheque run is entered. This is the first cheque we are preparing in QuickBooks, so we need to start the numbering sequence. QuickBooks updates this number automatically once you enter the first number.

12. **Double click** 1 in the First Cheque Number field

13. **Type**   521

14. Click the **Create Pay Cheques button** to display the confirmation window:

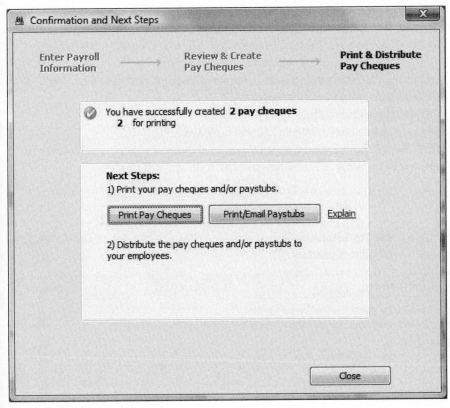

Figure 11-11

From this screen, you can print the paycheques or print and e-mail the paystubs. We will not be printing the paycheques at this time. Ask your instructor if you are required to print them.

15. Click **Close**

Paying Payroll Liabilities

Most businesses with employees have payroll liabilities with a number of different agencies and organizations. The business withholds taxes from employees and also contributes taxes. Payroll taxes remitted to the Receiver General consist of income tax, EI premiums, and CPP premiums withheld from employee income, as well as the employer's contribution to EI and the CPP. The federal government collects both provincial and federal income taxes in all provinces except Quebec. Employer expenses for WCB are submitted to the provincial Workers' Compensation Board, and medical premiums or taxes are sent to the provincial Minister of Finance. In addition, there may be company-specific payroll benefits and plans that employees and employers pay into, such as union dues, insurance plans, and savings plans.

QuickBooks tracks all these payroll taxes and liabilities. just as it tracks sales taxes and summarizes them to make remittances easier.

In the next transactions, we will pay all payroll liabilities. Refer to the following source document as we work through the steps to enter it:

Notes
The CPP employer amounts equal the CPP employee amounts. The EI employer amounts are 1.4 times the employee amounts.

SD Instructions
Refer to the following source document and then follow the step-by-step instructions to enter it.

Notes
QuickBooks uses a single default account for all payroll liabilities but tracks the amounts for each payroll item separately.

Notes
Remember, the default year in the sample company is 2007. It is displayed by default on all transactions and all reports.

Notes
Year-to-date payroll liabilities were entered as total amounts for each item for January 1 to September 30. Year-to-date payments were entered as total payments for each item on August 31.

Notes
Notice that the default date in the Through field is November 30, the end of the month before December 15, the Sample file's preset current date.

SD2: Memo #10-1

Dated October 2, 2012

From Owners: Pay all payroll liabilities outstanding from January 1 to September 30.
To Receiver General: Federal Income Tax, EI - Company, EI - Employee, CPP - Company, CPP - Employee
To Minister of Finance: Medical - Company, Medical - Employee
To Workers' Compensation Board: WCB
To Haida Investments Inc.: CSB Plan, RRSP
Issue cheques #523 to #526 to these agencies in payment.

The Payroll Centre should still be open. Payroll liabilities are paid by selecting the Pay Liabilities icon in the Payroll Liabilities section in the Payroll Centre.

1. **Click** the **Pay Liabilities icon** to open the Select Date Range for Liabilities window:

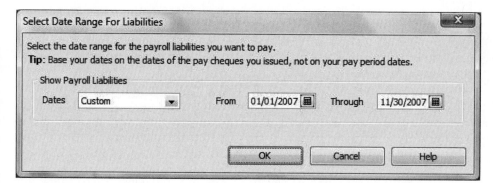

Figure 11-12

The date range for the liabilities is usually the oldest date on record for outstanding amounts to the end of the month before the current month. The default year in the sample company is 2007.

The Scotts have paid the liabilities from the beginning of the year through to August 31. The balances remaining for September have been entered as historical amounts. Custom is selected as the type of date range. We need to enter our own date range so Custom is the correct selection.

From the drop-down list in the Dates field, you can choose a time interval, such as month, week, quarter, and so on. QuickBooks will enter the corresponding date range.

2. **Press** (tab) to advance to the From date field

3. **Type** 01/01/12

4. **Press** (tab) to advance to the Through date field

5. **Type** 09/30/12

6. **Click** **OK** to advance to the Pay Liabilities window:

Figure 11-13

Notes
The liabilities list is in alphabetic order by agency (Payable To).

Outstanding amounts for all liabilities are entered. For each, the agency that collects the money is listed along with the total amount owing. You may choose to pay the total or some lesser amount. We will pay all outstanding amounts to all agencies. The Sample file date (December 15, 2007) is entered as the default payment date, so we need to change it. Also, we are not printing cheques so we will deselect this option. We want to preview all cheques before sending them, and this option is correctly selected by default.

7. Double click the **Payment Date** field

8. Type 10/02/12

Now we need to select the items we are paying. When you click in the pay column to the left of an item, a checkmark will be displayed indicating that it has been selected for payment.

9. Click the **column to the left of the CSB Plan** item to add a ✓ beside it

The amount in the Amt. Due column is added to the Amt. To Pay column. You can change this amount in order to pay more or less than the amount due. Usually, the full amount is paid because the date range selected is for the current amount due.

10. Click the **column to the left of the RRSP** item to add a ✓ beside it

11. Click the **column to the left of the other items** to add a ✓ beside them (you may have to scroll down the screen to select all items)

When you click beside CPP Company, all the items payable to the Receiver General are selected at the same time.

Check your work carefully before proceeding — you cannot go back to these amounts or this screen once you choose Create.

12. To remove an item from the pay column, **click** the ✓ in the column to remove it

13. Your completed Pay Liabilities list should look like the following one:

Figure 11-14

14. **Click** **Create** to continue to the cheque review for the first payee:

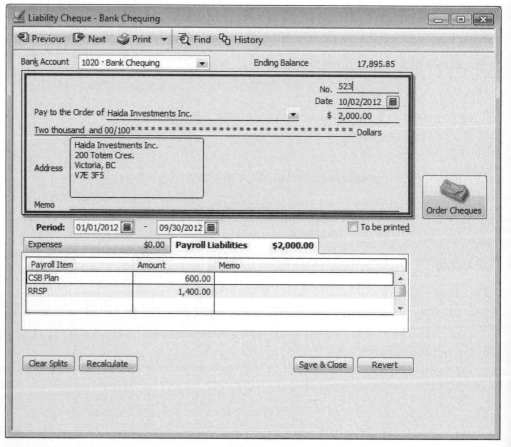

Figure 11-15

Notice that the cheque number follows our last payroll cheque number.

15. To view the journal entry for this cheque, press ⌷ctrl⌷ **+ Y:**

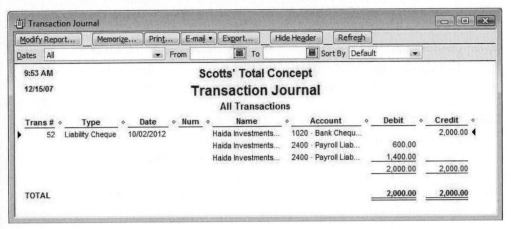

Figure 11-16

16.	**Close**	the **Transaction Journal report** when you're finished viewing it
17.	**Click**	☞ Next to review or edit the next payments. The cheque for the Minister of Finance should be displayed on the screen
18.	**Click**	**Yes** to save the changes.
19.	**Click**	☞ Next again to view the cheque issued to the Receiver General
20.	**Click**	☞ Next again to view the final payment, the one to the Workers' Compensation Board

There are times when you may need to edit a cheque. For example, you may need to add an amount for a late payment or an interest penalty. You can edit a liability cheque just like any other cheque. When you save the cheque, click Yes when asked to save the changes.

| 21. | **Close** | the **Liability Cheque window** when you have finished viewing the cheques |

Source Documents

Enter the following source documents for this company. You may need to refer to previous chapters for additional information:

SD3: **Memo #10-2**   **Dated October 2, 2012**

From Owners: Deposit $8,000.00 in outstanding receipts to chequing account.

SD4: **Sales Estimate #38**   **Dated October 2, 2012**

To Nedaa Woodslea, $6,900.00 plus $828.00 HST for redecorating living room, including painting, reupholstering furniture, and balloon-style valance with drapes. Invoice totals $7,728.00.

SD5: **Credit Card Bill Payment**   **Dated October 2, 2012**

To Pacific Coast Visa (use Quick Add for new Other payee), $500.00 in payment of account, including $390.00 for purchases before September 25 and a $110.00 annual card fee. Reconcile and pay credit card bill in full with cheque #527.

SD6: **Cash Receipt #68**   **Dated October 2, 2012**

From Marie Rose Schleger, cheque #206 for $11,335.50 in payment of account, including the discount for early payment. Apply the discount and payment to invoice #359.

SD7: **Cheque Copy #528**   **Dated October 2, 2012**

To Stonewall Inc., $7,415.10 in payment of account, including the discount for early payment. Reference invoices #SI-3981 and #SI-3998.

SD8: **Cheque Copy #529**   **Dated October 2, 2012**

To Freya's Home Interiors, $2,621.50 in payment of account, including the discount for early payment. Reference invoice #FHI-4801.

SD9: **Cheque Copy #530**   **Dated October 3, 2012**

To Groen's Greens, $902.88 in payment of account including discount for early payment. Reference invoice #GG-559.

Reviewing and Correcting Payroll Entries

There is no Previous button on the payroll forms. But we have written a cheque to the employee, so we can review and correct paycheques from the Write Cheques form.

In the next transaction, we will correct the paycheque created for Draper. Refer to the following source document as we work through the steps to correct it:

SD10: Memo #10-3

Dated October 3, 2012

From Owners: Correct the paycheque for Draper. It should have included 7.5 hours overtime. Draper has returned the incorrect cheque #522.

SD Instructions
Refer to the following source document and then follow the step-by-step instructions to enter it.

1. **Click**   the **Write Cheques icon** in the Banking section of the Home page to open the Write Cheques form

2. **Press**   ⌈ctrl⌉ + **F** to open the Find Cheques window

3. **Choose**   **Draper** from the Payee list

4. **Click**   the **Find button** to view the paycheque for Draper:

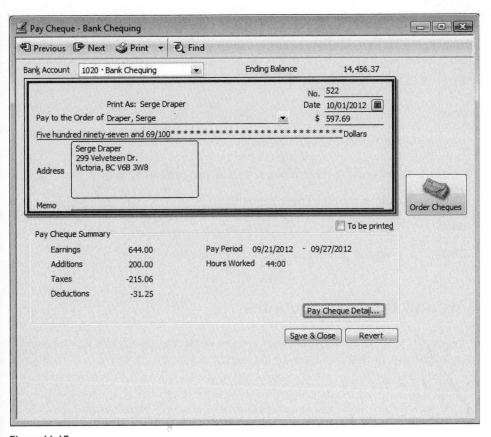

Figure 11-17

Notes
Notice that the name of the form has changed to Pay Cheque to reflect the way the cheque was created.

The cheque shows a summary of the paycheque items.

We can edit the paycheque just as we edit other transactions after saving them.

The Pay Cheque Detail button allows you to access the Preview screen with all paycheque details that we created for the entry. We will use this screen to correct the paycheque transaction.

5. Click the **Pay Cheque Detail button** to open the Review window:

Figure 11-18

Notes
Note the change in title for the screen from Preview to Review.

6. **Double click** **4:00** in the Hours column beside Overtime Wages

You can enter fractions for hours as decimals or as the number of hours and minutes separated by a colon.

7. **Type** **7.5** or **type 7:30**

8. **Press** [tab] to update all totals and deductions

If you typed 7.5, the program changes this entry to 7:30. We indicated in our preferences that this is how we want time to be entered and displayed.

You can edit the cheque number if you are using pre-printed forms.

9. **Click** **OK** to return to the cheque form

10. **Click** **Save & Close** to save the changes

11. **Click** **Yes** to confirm that you want to save the changes

Voiding and Deleting Cheques

If your cheques are pre-printed, you cannot use the same cheque number for the replacement cheque. In this case, you should void or delete the old cheque and issue a new one. Voiding a paycheque will keep a record of the cheque in the register but mark it as void. All payroll information for the employee is retained. A new cheque can be issued with the corrections for the same amount so that year-to-date payroll information will be correct, but it may be difficult to correct the year-to-date information afterwards. Therefore, you might choose this option to correct a cheque date or an incorrectly spelled name when none of the payroll amounts on the revised cheque were changed.

INSTRUCTIONS FOR VOIDING CHEQUES

I. Display a paycheque on the screen.

2. Choose the Edit menu and click Void Pay Cheque. You will see a warning message:

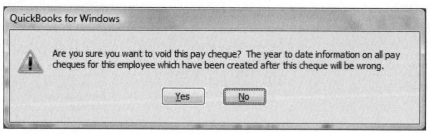

Figure 11-19

The message warns about the implications for employee history data.

3. Click Yes to confirm your decision if you want to void the pay cheque and click No to cancel.

Deleting a cheque will undo or remove the entire payroll transaction from the record, so this option is preferred when you need to revise payroll amounts.

Notes
Formats for entering and displaying time are set up on the Company Preferences tab for the General preferences.

Notes
If the incorrect cheque is not returned, remember to notify the bank to cancel the cheque.

INSTRUCTIONS FOR DELETING CHEQUES

1. Display a paycheque on the screen.

2. Choose the Edit menu and click Delete Pay Cheque. The familiar confirmation request for deleting information is displayed:

Figure 11-20

3. Click OK to confirm your decision and then re-enter the payroll information from scratch. The cheque number will be retained so you can use the next number if you use pre-printed cheques. The audit trail will list the deleted transaction with the date and time it was deleted.

Source Documents

Enter the following source documents for this company. You may need to refer to previous chapters for additional information:

SD Practice
Continue to develop your skills by entering the following source document(s).

SD11: Sales Estimate #39   **Dated October 4, 2012**

To Nina Toussieng, $15,900.00 plus $1,908.00 HST for terracing and landscaping a ravine lot with stone retaining walls and appropriate shrubs and groundcover plants. Invoice totals $17,808.00.

SD12: Cash Receipt #69   **Dated October 4, 2012**

From Nedaa Woodslea, cheque #376 for $2,000.00 as prepayment for acceptance of estimate #38.

SD13: Sales Estimate #40   **Dated October 4, 2012**

To Casa Blanca Estates (Set up new customer), $15,500.00 for design work plus $3,900.00 for landscaping plus $2,328.00 HST on model suite in new condo. Project includes designing and furnishing the suite, laying terrazzo tiles, and arranging plants and small shrubs on the balcony. Invoice totals $21,728.00.

SD14: Purchase Invoice #P-699   **Dated October 5, 2012**

From Primus Communications, $210.00 plus $25.20 HST for one month of telephone, pager, cell phone, and Internet service. Invoice totals $235.20. Terms: Net 15 days.

SD15: Cash Receipt #70   **Dated October 5, 2012**

From Nina Toussieng, cheque #48 for $4,500.00 as prepayment for acceptance of estimate #39.

 Notes
Casa Blanca Estates
Contact: Whipple Peduto
49 Wildginger Way
Victoria, BC V8T 4D7
Tel: (250) 488-7383
Terms: 1/5, n/30
Payment: Cheque
Credit Limit: $25,000.00

Entering Sales Reps on Invoices

Gardner and Zijner are paid commissions on sales. If we enter their names on invoices, the program will track their sales in order to calculate commissions. Any employee can be identified as a sales representative, and these employee names will be available in the REP field on invoices. When we fill the estimate for Nedaa Woodslea, we will add Zijner as the sales rep.

Refer to the following source document as we work through the steps to enter it:

SD16: Sales Invoice #362

Dated October 5, 2012

To Nedaa Woodslea, to fill estimate #38, $6,900.00 plus $828.00 HST for redecorating living room, including painting, reupholstering furniture, and providing balloon-style valance with drapes. Invoice totals $7,728.00. Sales Rep: Zijner. Terms: 1/5, n/30.

1. Open   the **Create Invoices form**

The service invoice does not include a field for Sales Rep so we will customize the form template before filling the estimate. The Intuit Service Invoice should be selected as the template for this invoice. If it isn't, click the drop-down arrow in the template field and select it.

2. Click   the **Customize button** on the form Icon bar

The Customize Template screen opens. We need to create a new template because we cannot add a field to the Intuit Service Invoice form.

3. Click   the **Manage Templates button**

4. Highlight   the **Intuit Service Invoice** if necessary in the Select Template box

5. Click   **Copy**

A new template called Copy of: Intuit Service Invoice is now displayed and highlighted in the Select Template box.

We need to name the new invoice template.

6. Highlight   the **template name** on the right-hand side of the screen

7. Type   **Scotts**

8. Click   **OK** to display the Basic Customization screen

9. Click   the **Additional Customization button**

10. Click   the ✓ box under the Screen column for the REP field to add a ✓ to complete the customization as shown:

Figure 11-21

11. **Click**   **OK**

12. The following message will be displayed:

Figure 11-22

This message indicates that you may have to use the Layout Designer to reposition the new field we added to the invoice template.

13. **Click**   the **box** beside Do not display this message in the future

14. **Click**   **OK**

15. **Click**   **OK** to return to the Basic Customization screen

Notes
Remember, the default
date for the sample file is
12/15/2007.

16. Click   **OK** to return to the revised invoice:

Figure 11-23

Scotts' now appears in the Template field and a Rep field is now displayed beside the Terms field. Once we save the invoice, this template will open as the default invoice. It will also appear on the drop-down list in the Template field so you can select it later if you have used another invoice template.

17. Choose   **Woodslea, Nedaa** from the Customer Name field drop-down list

18. The Available Estimates screen is displayed:

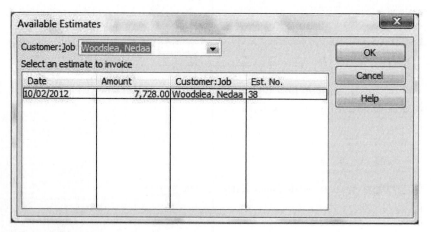

Figure 11-24

19. Click   **estimate number 38** to select it

20. Click   **OK** to add the estimate details to the invoice

21. Enter   **10/05/12** as the date if necessary

22. **Enter**   **362** as the Invoice Number

23. **Click**   the **REP field** drop-down list arrow to view the two employees desig-
                       nated as sales reps:

Figure 11-25

24. **Click**   **DZ-Zijner, Dee** to add her name as the sales rep to the invoice

25. **Click**   **Save & Close** to record the invoice. The following message pops up:

> **Name Information Changed**
>
> ⚠ You have changed: Woodslea, Nedaa
>
> Rep
>
> Would you like to have this new information appear next time?
>
> [Yes]   [No]   [Cancel]

Figure 11-26

Scotts' customers frequently work with both sales reps so we do not want a default
name attached to the customer.

26. **Click**   **No** to continue

27. **Click**   **No** when prompted that the customer has available credits that can
                       be applied to the invoice

Enter the following source documents for this company. You may need to refer to
previous chapters for additional information:

Source Documents

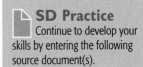

SD Practice
Continue to develop your
skills by entering the following
source document(s).

SD17: Credit Card Purchase Invoice #CSC-4530   Dated October 5, 2012

From Celine's Service Centre, $120.00 plus $14.40 HST for gasoline for the
business vans and gas-powered landscaping equipment. Invoice totalling $134.40
was paid in full by credit card. Memorize the transaction to recur every two weeks
beginning October 19, 2012.

SD18: Purchase Invoice #FHI-5628   Dated October 5, 2012

From Freya's Home Interiors, $1,050.00 plus $126.00 HST for upholstery and
drapery fabrics and notions. Purchase invoice totals $1,176.00. Terms: 2/5, n/30.

SD19: Purchase Invoice #SI-4811   Dated October 6, 2012

From Stonewall Inc., $2,100.00 plus $252.00 HST for tiles, paving stones, sand,
and screening for garden and patio area. Purchase invoice totals $2,352.00.
Terms: 1/10, n/30.

SD20: Purchase Invoice #GG-692   Dated October 6, 2012

From Groen's Greens, $1,800.00 plus $216.00 HST for perennials, shrubs, and soil
for a garden project. Purchase invoice totals $2,016.00. Terms: 1/15, n/30.

To Nina Toussieng, to fill estimate #39, $15,900.00 plus $1,908.00 HST for terracing and landscaping a ravine lot with stone retaining walls and appropriate shrubs and groundcover plants. Invoice totals $17,808.00. Sales Rep: Gardner. Terms: 1/5, n/30.

Paying Vacation Pay

Vacation items are also separated for hourly and salaried workers because vacation pay is allotted and paid out differently. Salaried workers receive regular pay during their vacation — their usual hours are allocated to vacation time instead of salary but the total pay is unchanged. Hourly paid workers receive some of the accrued vacation pay that has been held for them in addition to pay for any hours they worked in that period. They can receive the regular number of hours as vacation pay.

The following source document is available for the pay period ending October 4, 2012. Refer to the following source document as we walk through the steps to enter it:

SD Instructions
Refer to the following source document and then follow the step-by-step instructions to enter it.

SD22:

EMPLOYEE TIME SUMMARY SHEET #2

Date: October 8, 2012 (for the pay period ending October 4, 2012)

Name of Employee	Regular Hours	Overtime Hours	Sick Leave Hours	Vacation Hours	Advances Received/ Advances Repaid
Nicolai Digger	40	8	—	—	$100.00
Serge Draper	8	—	—	32	−$ 50.00

a. Using Employee Time Summary Sheet #2 and the Employee Information Sheet, complete payroll for weekly paid employees
b. Recover $50.00 advance from Serge Draper
c. Draper will take one week of vacation. Pay Draper four days of vacation pay. He worked one day before starting his vacation
d. Manually prepare cheques #531 and #532

1. **Open**   the **Payroll Centre** and **click** the **Unscheduled Payroll** icon, or **choose** the **Employees** menu and **click Pay Employees, Start Unscheduled Payroll**

2. October 4 should be displayed in the Pay Period Ends field by default (if it is not displayed, enter it)

3. **Enter**   **October 8, 2012**, as the Cheque date

4. **Select**   **Digger and Draper** for payment in this period

The Enter Payroll Information screen displays the hours from the previous period entered as defaults.

5. **Click**   **Continue to display** the Review and Create Pay Cheques form

The Review and Create Pay Cheques form shows the calculated payroll based on the hours from the previous period. If the payroll is correct, you can click the Create Pay Cheques button to create the payroll. If you need to make any changes, you must click on the Open Pay Cheque Detail button to access each individual pay cheque.

6. **Click**   the **Open Pay Cheque Detail button** to display the payroll for Digger

7. **Edit**   the **Hours for Overtime Wages** (**enter 8**) and **enter 100.00** for Advances in the Other Payroll Items section

Notes
Remember, 12/15/2007 is displayed by default in the sample file.

Notes
Entering the hours from the previous period is a company preference that can be set for the Payroll & Employees preferences.

8. **Click**   **Save & Next** to record the Digger's paycheque and display Draper's paycheque

9. The Preview Pay Cheque screen for Draper should now be displayed on the screen:

Figure 11-27

The hours worked from the previous period are entered. Notice that only the regular and overtime hours are entered; previous amounts for sickness or advances are not considered as regular occurrences and are not set up as defaults for the employee.

10. **Type**   **8** in the Hours column beside Hourly Wages

11. **Press**   ⬇ to advance to the overtime hours field

12. **Press**   _del_ to delete the number of hours currently displayed in the field

13. **Press**   _tab_ to update all amounts

14. **Click**   the **field below Overtime Wages** to display the drop-down arrow

15. **Click**   the **drop-down arrow** in the Overtime Wages field to view the Earnings available for selection:

Figure 11-28

Notes

The rate of vacation pay for the weekly paid employees is 6 percent of wages earned, or about three weeks of regular pay.

Notes

Because vacation pay is also paid on overtime wages, 6 percent vacation pay may be more than three weeks of regular wages. There may be an accrued vacation amount remaining at the end of the year.

Notes

Because the Other Payroll Items section is too small to show all the items, you can press (tab) repeatedly from the Advances item to advance to the next item in this section or to a blank field with a drop-down list arrow. Or you can press ⊕ , the down arrow, to move to the next field in the Item Name column.

Two items on the list relate to vacation pay paid to hourly employees. If the entire amount of vacation accrued is paid out, you can choose VacPay-Accrual Paid Out and enter the amount in the Rate field. The accrued vacation pay available is shown in the summary area in the upper-right corner of the Review and Create Pay Cheques screen. If the employee receives regular hourly pay while on vacation, you can choose Vacation Hourly Rate and enter the number of vacation hours for the pay period. Both entries will reduce the amount of vacation pay available. Draper worked for 8 hours and took 4 days (32 hours) of vacation time. He will be on vacation next week as well. We will enter these hours.

16. **Click**   **Vacation Hourly Rate**. The regular hourly wage rate is entered automatically.

17. **Press**   (tab) twice to advance to the Hours field

18. **Type**   **32**

19. **Press**   (tab) to update the totals and taxes

The Vacation Avail. ($) amount field is reduced by $448.00. Now we need to enter the first repayment of the advance received on a previous paycheque.

20. **Click**   **Advances** in the Other Payroll Items section (Item Name column)

21. **Press**   ⊕ to select the next item, Advances Repayment

22. **Press**   (tab) to advance to the Rate field

23. **Type**   **50**

24. **Press**   (tab) to update the totals as shown:

Figure 11-29

Advances is set up as an Addition item, so the amount is added to the net pay amount. Advances Repayment is set up as a Deduction item so its amount is deducted from net pay. No taxes or other deductions apply to either amount. The Employee Summary section tracks the amount still owing on the advance.

25.	**Click**	**Save & Close**
26.	**Check**	your **work** carefully before creating the paycheques
27.	**Click**	**Create Pay Cheques** to create the paycheques for Digger and Draper
28.	**Click**	**Close Leave** to close the Confirmation and Next Steps window

Source Documents

Enter the following source documents for this company. You may need to refer to previous chapters for additional information:

SD23: Memo #10-4   **Dated October 8, 2012**

From Owners: Deposit $17,835.50 in outstanding receipts to chequing account.

SD24: Cash Receipt #71   **Dated October 10, 2012**

From Casa Blanca Estates, cheque #1998 for $5,000.00 as prepayment for acceptance of estimate #40.

SD25: Cheque Copy #533   **Dated October 10, 2012**

To Celine's Service Centre, $286.00 in payment of account. Reference invoice #CSC-3324.

SD26: Cheque Copy #534   **Dated October 10, 2012**

To Freya's Home Interiors, $1,155.00 in payment of account, including the discount for early payment. Reference invoice #FHI-5628.

Notes
You can click on the Open Pay Cheque Detail button to review the paycheques.

SD Practice
Continue to develop your skills by entering the following source document(s).

SD27: Cash Receipt #72   **Dated October 11, 2012**

From Nina Toussieng, cheque #59 for $13,149.00 in payment of invoice #363. Apply the discount and the credit.

SD28: Cheque Copy #535   **Dated October 13, 2012**

To Stonewall Inc., $2,331.00 in payment of account, including the discount for early payment. Reference invoice #SI-4811.

SD29: Cash Receipt #73   **Dated October 14, 2012**

From Flora Planter, cheque #1925 for $11,946.00 in payment of invoice #345.

SD30: Purchase Invoice #FHI-6721   **Dated October 14, 2012**

From Freya's Home Interiors, $3,250.00 plus $390.00 HST for decorating fabrics and notions. Purchase invoice totals $3,640.00.
Terms: 2/5, n/30.

SD31: Purchase Invoice #SI-5622   **Dated October 14, 2012**

From Stonewall Inc., $1,600.00 plus $192.00 HST for tiles and paving stones for a garden and patio area. Purchase invoice total $1,792.00. Terms: 1/10, n/30.

SD32:

EMPLOYEE TIME SUMMARY SHEET #3

Date: October 15, 2012 (for the pay period ending October 13, 2012)

Name of Employee	Regular Hours	Overtime Hours	Sick Leave Hours	Vacation Hours	Advances Received/ Advances Repaid
Nicolai Digger	36	–	4	–	–$25.00
Serge Draper	–	–	–	40	–$50.00
Stone Kutter	40	–	–	40	–
Mita Paynter	80	4	–	–	–

a. Using Employee Time Summary Sheet #3 and the Employee Information Sheet, complete payroll for weekly paid and semi-monthly paid employees
b. Recover $25.00 advance from Digger and $50.00 advance from Draper
c. Release 40 hours vacation pay for Draper. He is taking his second week of vacation
d. Release 40 hours of accrued vacation pay for Kutter
e. Manually prepare cheques #536 through #539

SD33: Memo #10-5   **Dated October 15, 2012**

From Owners: Deposit $30,095.00 in outstanding receipts to the chequing account.

SD34: Purchase Invoice #GG-801   **Dated October 15, 2012**

From Groen's Greens, $1,200.00 plus $144.00 GST for perennials and shrubs for a garden project. Purchase invoice totals $1,344.00. Terms: 1/15, n/30.

SD35: Purchase Invoice #VG-1100   **Dated October 15, 2012**

From Village Galleries (set up new vendor), $5,800.00 plus $696.00 HST for a living room suite for Casa Blanca Estates project. Purchase invoice totals $6,496.00. Terms: 2/10, n/30.

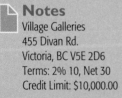
Notes
Village Galleries
455 Divan Rd.
Victoria, BC V5E 2D6
Terms: 2% 10, Net 30
Credit Limit: $10,000.00

SD36: Sales Estimate #41   **Dated October 15, 2012**

To Dawn Knight (set up new customer), $7,800.00 for interior design and $17,000.00 for landscaping plus $2,976.00 HST for consultation and period restoration of living room, dining room and garden. Invoice totals $27,776.00.

SD37: Bank Debit Memo #PC-63392   **Dated October 16, 2012**

From Pacific Coast Bank: Cheque #1925 for $11,946.00 from Flora Planter in payment of invoice #345 was returned as NSF. Create invoice #364 to record the returned cheque and NSF charges. Invoice totals $11,971.00. Terms: Due on receipt.

SD38: Cheque Copy #540   **Dated October 16, 2012**

To Primus Communications, $235.20 in full payment of account. Reference invoice #P-699.

SD39: Cash Receipt #74   **Dated October 16, 2012**

From Dawn Knight, cheque #108 for $6,000.00 as prepayment for acceptance of estimate #44.

Creating Two Invoices from One Estimate

Some estimates include both design and landscaping projects. However, the invoice form allows for only one sales rep. Because these two types of work are connected with different sales reps, we need to fill the estimate as two separate invoices. The invoice for Casa Blanca Estates needs to be separated in this way.

Refer to the following source document as we work through the steps to enter it:

SD40: Sales Invoices #365 & #366

Dated October 16, 2012

To Casa Blanca Estates, to fill estimate #40, $15,500.00 for design work plus $3,900.00 for landscaping work plus $2,328.00 HST on model suite and balcony in new condo building. Invoice totals $21,728.00. Sales Reps: Zijner for design project and Gardner for landscaping work. Terms: 1/5, n/30.

1. **Open**   the **Create Invoices form** and **choose Casa Blanca Estates** as the customer

2. **Choose**   **estimate #40** and **click OK** to add the details to the invoice

3. **Click**   **Landscaping** on the second line of the invoice.

4. **Choose**   the **Edit** menu and **click Delete Line** or **press** ⌨ **+ D**.

5. **Choose**   **DZ, Zijner, Dee** as the sales rep

6. **Enter**   **10/16/12** in the date field if necessary

7. **Click**   **Save & New** to save the invoice

8. **Click**   **No** so you do not save this employee as the customer's sales rep

Notes
Dawn Knight
198 Crestview Blvd.
Victoria, BC V6B 2C9
Tel: (250) 399-2019
Terms: 1% 10, Net 30
Credit Limit: $25,000.00
Payment: By cheque

SD Instructions
Refer to the following source document and then follow the step-by-step instructions to enter it.

Notes
The Scotts' template should be displayed in the Template field. If it isn't displayed, select it.

9. The Available Credits screen is displayed. **Click No** to not apply the Customer's credits at this time

10. **Choose**   **Casa Blanca Estates** as the customer for the next invoice

11. **Choose**   **estimate #40** and **click OK** to add the details to the invoice

12. **Click**   **Design** on the first line of the invoice

13. **Choose**   the **Edit menu** and **click Delete Line** or **press** ⌨ `ctrl` **+ D**

14. **Choose**   **VG, Gardner, Vijay** as the sales rep

15. **Click**   **Save & Close** to save the invoice

16. **Click**   **No** so you do not save this employee as the customer's sales rep

📄 **SD Practice**
Continue to develop your skills by entering the following source document(s).

📄 **Notes**
Digby Shack
200 Pacific Blvd.
Victoria, BC V8M 3C4
Tel: (250) 488-4660
Terms: 1% 10, Net 30
Credit Limit: $25,000.00
Payment: By cheque

Source Documents

Enter the following source documents for this company. You may need to refer to previous chapters for additional information:

SD41: Sales Estimate #42

                                    Dated October 17, 2012

To Digby Shack (set up new customer), $12,000.00 plus $1,440.00 HST for designing and painting murals in nursery and family rooms. Invoice totals $13,440.00.

SD42: Cheque Copy #541

                                      Dated October 18, 2012

To Groen's Greens, $1,998.00 in payment of account, including the discount for early payment. Reference invoice #GG-692.

SD43: Cash Receipt #75

                                      Dated October 18, 2012

From Digby Shack, cheque #544 for $3,000.00 as prepayment for acceptance of estimate #42.

SD44: Credit Card Purchase Invoice #CSC-6993

                                      Dated October 19, 2012

From Celine's Service Centre, $120.00 plus $14.40 HST for gasoline for vans and gas-powered landscaping equipment. Invoice totalling $134.40 was paid in full by credit card. Use the memorized transaction.

SD45: Credit Card Purchase Invoice #OS-2113

                                      Dated October 19, 2012

From Office Suppliers (use Quick Add for new vendor), $220.00 plus $26.40 HST for pre-printed forms. Invoice totalling $246.40 was paid in full by credit card.

SD46: Cash Receipt #76

                                      Dated October 19, 2012

From Flora Planter, certified cheque #31 for $11,971.00 in payment of invoice #364.

SD47: Cheque Copy #542

                                      Dated October 19, 2012

To Freya's Home Interiors, $3,575.00 in payment of account, including the discount for early payment. Reference invoice #FHI-6721.

SD48: Cheque Copy #543

Dated October 20, 2012

To Village Galleries, $6,380.00 in payment of account, including the discount for early payment. Reference invoice #VG-1100.

SD49: Sales Estimate #43

Dated October 21, 2012

To Siobhan Marble (set up new customer), $15,400.00 plus $1,848.00 HST for consultation and landscaping of a front garden and creation of a new backyard design with swimming pool. Invoice totals $17,248.00.

SD50: Sales Invoice #367

Dated October 21, 2012

To Digby Shack to fill estimate #42, $12,000.00 plus $1,440.00 HST for murals in nursery and family rooms. Invoice totals $13,440.00. Sales Rep: Zijner. Terms: 1/5, n/30.

Notes
Siobhan Marble
122 Glistening Way
Victoria, BC V7V 3E3
Tel: (250) 498-1920
Terms: 1% 10, Net 30
Credit Limit: $25,000.00
Payment: By cheque

SD51:

EMPLOYEE TIME SUMMARY SHEET #4

Date: October 22, 2012 (for the pay period ending October 18, 2012)

Name of Employee	Regular Hours	Overtime Hours	Sick Leave	Vacation Hours	Advances Received/ Advances Repaid
Nicolai Digger	40	2	–	–	–$25.00
Serge Draper	40	4	–	–	–$50.00

a. Using Employee Time Summary Sheet #4 and the Employee Information Sheet, complete payroll for weekly paid employees
b. Recover $25.00 advance from Digger and $50.00 advance from Draper
c. Manually prepare cheques #544 and #545

SD52: Memo #10-6

Dated October 22, 2012

From Owners: Deposit $20,971.00 in outstanding receipts to chequing account.

SD53: Cheque Copy #546

Dated October 23, 2012

To Stonewall Inc., $1,776.00 in payment of account, including the discount for early payment. Reference invoice #SI-5622.

SD54: Purchase Invoice #FHI-8102

Dated October 25, 2012

From Freya's Home Interiors, $2,800.00 plus $336.00 HST for upholstery and drapery fabrics and notions. Purchase invoice totals $3,136.00. Terms: 2/5, n/30.

SD55: Purchase Invoice #SI-7006

Dated October 25, 2012

From Stonewall Inc., $1,920.00 plus $230.40 HST for large rocks and interlocking paving stones for garden area. Purchase invoice totals $2,150.40. Terms: 1/10, n/30.

SD56: Purchase Invoice #GG-831

Dated October 25, 2012

From Groen's Greens, $840.00 plus $100.80 HST for flowers and shrubs for a garden project. Purchase invoice totals $940.80. Terms: 1/15, n/30.

Sales Invoices #368 & #369

Dated October 28, 2012

To Dawn Knight, to fill estimate #41, $7,800.00 for design and $17,000.00 for landscape work plus $2,976.00 HST for period restoration. Invoice totals $27,776.00. Sales Reps: Zijner for design and Gardner for landscaping work. Terms: 1/5, n/30.

SD58: **Cheque Copy #547**

Dated October 28, 2012

To Freya's Home Interiors, $3,080.00 in payment of account, including the discount for early payment. Reference invoice #FHI-8102.

SD59: **Cash Receipt #77**

Dated October 28, 2012

From Siobhan Marble, cheque #236 for $4,000.00 as prepayment for acceptance of estimate #43.

SD60:

EMPLOYEE TIME SUMMARY SHEET #5

Date: October 29, 2012 (for the pay period ending October 25, 2012)

Name of Employee	Regular Hours	Overtime Hours	Sick Leave	Vacation Hours	Advances Received/ Advances Repaid
Nicolai Digger	40	2	–	–	–$25.00
Serge Draper	40	4	–	–	–$50.00

a. Using Employee Time Summary Sheet #5 and the Employee Information Sheet, complete payroll for weekly paid employees
b. Recover $25.00 advance from Digger and $50.00 advance from Draper
c. Manually prepare cheques #548 and #549

SD61: **Memo #10-7**

Dated October 29, 2012

From Owners: Deposit $4,000.00 in outstanding receipts to chequing account.

SD62: **Sales Invoice #370**

Dated October 30, 2012

To Siobhan Marble to fill estimate #43, $15,400.00 plus $1,848.00 HST for garden landscaping. Invoice totals $17,248.00. Sales Rep: Gardner. Terms: 1/5, n/30.

Paying Salaried Employees

The procedure for paying salaried employees is similar to that for hourly employees. Although you select different items, you still enter the number of hours for each item. Scotts' pays salaried employees a commission based on sales. Before creating the paycheque, we need to find the sales amounts on which the commissions are based. We can find these amounts in the Sales by Rep Summary Report for the pay period. You cannot display this report while creating the paycheque so we will review the report first.

Refer to the following source document as we work through the steps to enter it:

SD63:

SD Instructions
Refer to the following source document and then follow the step-by-step instructions to enter it.

Displaying the Sales by Rep Summary Report

1. **Choose**   the **Reports menu**, then **click Sales** and **choose Sales by Rep Summary**

2. **Enter**   **10/01/12** in the From date field **and 10/31/12** in the To date field

3. **Click**   the **Refresh** button to update the report:

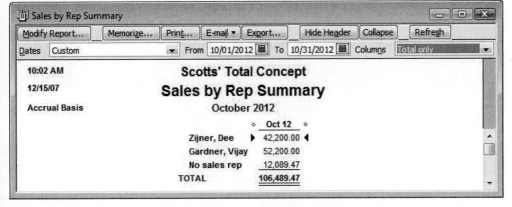

Figure 11-30

Notes
You can also find the revenue amounts in the Profit & Loss Standard Report from October 1 to October 31, 2012.

Notes
The Sales Rep by Detail Report shows all transactions that make up the total sales amount in the Summary Report.

Notes
The amount beside No sales rep represents the NSF cheque and NSF fee to Flora Planter and the finance charge to Ashby Everwood.

4. **Write**   down the **sales amounts** for Zijner and Gardner

5. **Close**   the **report**. **Do not save** the **changes**

Entering the Hours Worked

1. **Open**   the **Payroll Centre**

2. **Click**   the **Unscheduled Payroll icon** _____, or **choose** the **Employees menu**, click **Pay Employees**, and **click Start Unscheduled Payroll**

3. **Enter**   **10/29/12** in the Pay Period Ends field, if necessary

4. **Enter**   **10/31/12** in the Cheque Date field

5. **Select**   the **four employees** who are being paid (refer to SD63 above)

6. Click   **Continue** to open the Review or Change Pay Cheque screen:

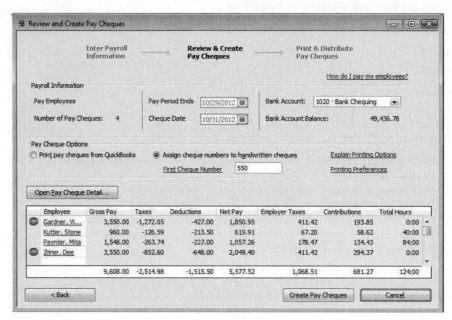

Figure 11-31

A Stop button is displayed beside Gardner and Zinger. This indicates that there is a problem with their payroll information.

7. Click   the **Open Pay Cheque Detail button** to open the Review or Change Pay Cheque screen for Gardner

8. The following warning message is displayed:

Figure 11-32

This warning indicates that we have not recorded the hours worked for Gardner and Vijay. Canada Revenue Agency requires the number of insurable hours worked for the Record of Employment.

9. Click   **OK** to close the warning and display the Review or Change Pay Cheque form for Gardner

One notable difference between the Review or Change Pay Cheque form for the salaried employees and the hourly employees is the addition of a Quantity column. This column is used to enter a base for the calculation of a commission, either a revenue amount or the number of items sold, depending on how the extra pay is calculated.

Gardner has taken one week's vacation and one day's sick leave this month. We need to enter the hours for each of these items as well as the number of regular hours worked and the revenue amount that forms the basis for the 2 percent commission. The number of hours is used to determine eligibility for EI benefits, not to calculate pay. The pay amount is fixed for the month.

First we will enter the number of hours for each item.

10. **Click**   the **Hours column** beside Salary if necessary

11. **Type**   **112** and **press** (tab)

Notice that the Salary amount in the Employee Summary section does not change.

12. **Click**   the **Item Name field** below Commission to display the item list arrow

For salaried workers, we must choose the sick leave payroll item created for them.

13. **Choose**   **Sick Salary** from the Item Name drop-down list

14. **Press**   (tab) twice to advance to the Hours field

15. **Type**   **8**

16. **Press**   (tab) to update the form

Notice that the amount in the Rate field for Salary has decreased proportionately so that eight hours' worth of the regular salary amount is allocated to sick leave. The number of hours of sick leave available is reduced by eight hours.

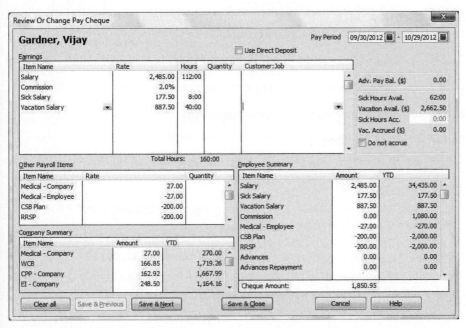

Paying Vacation Pay to Salaried Employees

For salaried workers, we choose a different payroll item for vacation than the one used for hourly paid employees.

17. **Press**   (tab) again to advance to the Item Name field

18. **Choose**   **Vacation Salary** from the drop-down list

19. **Press**   (tab) twice to advance to the Hours field

20. **Type**   **40**

21. **Press**   (tab) to update the amounts

The regular total salary amount is now divided among salary, sick leave, and vacation in proportion to the number of hours for each, as shown:

> **Notes**
> The payroll item for sick leave for salaried workers is different from the one for hourly paid employees.
> The payroll item for vacation pay leave for salaried workers is also different from the one for hourly paid employees.

Review Or Change Pay Cheque

Gardner, Vijay   Pay Period 09/30/2012 ▦ - 10/29/2012 ▦

☐ Use Direct Deposit

Earnings

Item Name	Rate	Hours	Quantity	Customer:Job
Salary	2,485.00	112:00		
Commission	2.0%			
Sick Salary	177.50	8:00		
Vacation Salary ▾	887.50	40:00		

Adv. Pay Bal. ($)   0.00

Sick Hours Avail.   62:00
Vacation Avail. ($)   2,662.50
Sick Hours Acc.   0:00
Vac. Accrued ($)   0.00
☐ Do not accrue

Total Hours: 160:00

Other Payroll Items

Item Name	Rate	Quantity
Medical - Company	27.00	
Medical - Employee	-27.00	
CSB Plan	-200.00	
RRSP	-200.00	

Company Summary

Item Name	Amount	YTD
Medical - Company	27.00	270.00
WCB	166.85	1,719.26
CPP - Company	162.92	1,667.99
EI - Company	248.50	1,164.16

Employee Summary

Item Name	Amount	YTD
Salary	2,485.00	34,435.00
Sick Salary	177.50	177.50
Vacation Salary	887.50	887.50
Commission	0.00	1,080.00
Medical - Employee	-27.00	-270.00
CSB Plan	-200.00	-2,000.00
RRSP	-200.00	-2,000.00
Advances	0.00	0.00
Advances Repayment	0.00	0.00

Cheque Amount: 1,850.95

Clear all   Save & Previous   Save & Next   Save & Close   Cancel   Help

Figure 11-33

The Vacation Available amount has decreased by the vacation amount taken. Gardner has about three weeks' vacation remaining. Again, net pay has not changed.

Paying Sales Commissions

We are now ready to enter the commission. The rate is entered as 2 percent, the default set up for the employee. We need to enter the revenue amount that this rate is based on.

1. **Click**   the **Quantity** field for Commission

2. **Type**   **52200**

3. **Press**   `tab` to update and complete the paycheque:

Figure 11-34

The commission amount is entered in the Employee Summary section and added to the gross pay amount. The commission is fully taxable so all tax amounts are increased.

4. **Check**   your **work** carefully and **make corrections** before continuing

5. **Click**   **Save & Next** to save the paycheque and open the next paycheque

6. **Enter**   the **remaining three paycheques** in SD63

7. **Create**   the **Pay Cheques**

Source Documents

SD Practice
Continue to develop your skills by entering the following source document(s).

Enter the following source documents for this company. You may need to refer to previous chapters for additional information:

SD64: Memo #10-8   **Dated October 31, 2012**

Assess finance charges on Ashby Everwood's overdue account. Apply the unused credits to the invoice before assessing interest charges.

SD65: Bank Debit Memo #42291   **Dated October 31, 2012**

From Pacific Bank, preauthorized bank service charges and loan and mortgage payments were taken from the chequing account as follows:

Bank service charges	$ 55.00
Mortgage ($350.00 interest and $100.00 principal)	$450.00
Bank loan ($60.00 interest and $880.00 principal)	$940.00
Long term loan ($180.00 interest and $540.00 principal)	$720.00

SD66: Memo #10-9   **Dated October 31, 2012**

From Owners: Pay all payroll liabilities outstanding from October 1 to October 31. Issue cheques #554 to #557 in payment.

To Receiver General: Federal Income Tax, EI - Company, EI - Employee, CPP - Company, CPP - Employee

To Minister of Finance: Medical - Company, Medical - Employee

To Workers' Compensation Board: WCB

To Haida Investments Inc.: CSB Plan, RRSP

SD67: Memo #10-10   **Dated October 31, 2012**

Make remittance to the Receiver General for HST payable as of October 31. Issue cheque #558 in payment.

SD68: Memo #10-11   **Dated October 31, 2012**

From Owner: Complete adjusting entries for supplies and inventory used in October and for prepaid expenses expired.

Decorating supplies	$ 1,200.00
Decorating materials	$13,400.00
Landscaping materials	$11,350.00
Office & computer supplies	$305.00
Prepaid insurance	$970.00
Prepaid taxes	$270.00

SD69: Credit Card Bill Payment   **Dated October 31, 2012**

To Pacific Coast Visa, $515.20 in full payment of account for purchases before October 25. Reconcile and pay credit card bill in full with cheque #559. The statement included the following entries:

Date	Description	Amount
Oct. 2/12	Payment Received	$–390.00
Oct. 5/12	Celine's Service Centre	$134.40
Oct. 19/12	Celine's Service Centre	$134.40
Oct. 19/12	Office Suppliers Inc.	$246.40
Oct. 25/12	Ending Balance (Total owing)	$515.20

Payroll Reports

Like other reports, the group of payroll reports can be displayed from the Report Centre or the Reports menu. We'll use the Report Centre to view the payroll reports.

1. **Click**   the **Report Centre** icon on the Icon bar

> **Notes**
> The procedures for sorting, filtering, and customizing the reports are the same as for other reports.

Notes

The Reports menu has one report that is not in the Report Centre: the Record of Employment Report.

2. **Click**   the **Employees & Payroll** heading on the left-hand side of the screen to view the reports available under this heading:

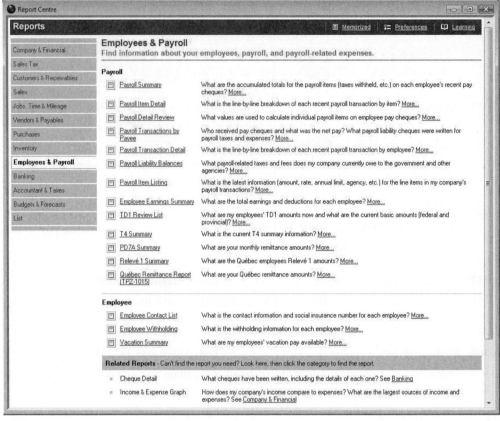

Figure 11-35

When we are displaying the payroll reports in this chapter, it is assumed that you are beginning from the Report Centre with the Employees & Payroll heading selected.

The Payroll Summary Report

The Payroll Summary Report shows the total for each payroll item for each employee for any period you select.

Notes

To access the report from the Reports menu:
- Choose the Reports menu, then choose Employees & Payroll and click Payroll Summary to open the report.
- Enter 10/01/12 in the From date field
- Enter 10/31/12 in the To date field
- Press *tab* or click the Refresh button to update the report

1. **Click**   **Payroll Summary** under the Payroll heading

2. **Double click**   the **date** in the From date field

3. **Type**   **10/01/12**

4. **Press**   *tab* to advance the To date field

5. **Type**   **10/31/12**

6. **Press**   *tab* or **click** the **Refresh button** to update the report:

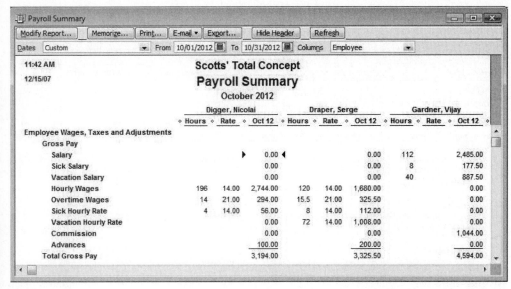

Figure 11-36

Each item — earnings items, additions to income, deductions, and accruals — is listed separately and the number of hours for each type of income is included. Gross and net pay amounts are also provided on the reports.

You can add several columns to the report — different payroll details and different time intervals — by selecting from the Columns drop-down list.

Double click an amount to see the transactions by payroll item report. Double click any transaction detail to see the original paycheque.

7. **Close** the **displayed report** when finished. Choose not to memorize the changes if you made any

The Payroll Item Detail Report

This report organizes payroll details by item. A line is added for each payroll transaction that uses the item, along with the totals for each item in the selected period.

1. **Click** **Payroll Item Detail** under the Payroll heading

2. **Double click** the **date** in the From date field

3. **Type** **10/01/12**

4. **Press** ⌷tab⌷ to advance the To date field

5. **Type** **10/31/12**

> **Notes**
> To access the report from the Reports menu:
> - Choose the Reports menu, then choose Employees & Payroll, and click Payroll Item Detail to open the report
> - Enter 10/01/12 in the From date field
> - Enter 10/31/12 in the To date field
> - Press ⌷tab⌷ or click the Refresh button to update the report

6. Press ⸤tab⸥ or **click** the **Refresh button** to update the report:

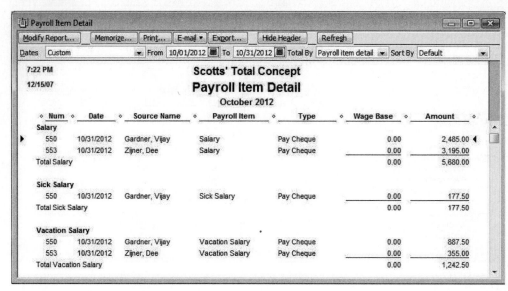

Figure 11-37

You can sort the report by any of the column headings. You can organize the report to show total amounts differently by selecting a different total from the Total By drop-down list. For example, you can show totals by account instead of the default, by Payroll Item Detail.

Double click any transaction detail to view the original paycheque.

7. Close the **displayed report** when finished. Choose not to memorize the changes if you made any

The Payroll Detail Review Report

The Payroll Detail Review Report provides a detailed listing of each item and amount that was used to calculate the payroll cheques. It also has an "audit" column indicating whether the transaction was modified after the original entry. The default dates are for year-to-date amounts so that all transactions for each item are listed for each employee.

1. Click **Payroll Detail Review** under the Payroll heading

2. Double click the **date** in the From date field

3. Type **10/01/12**

4. Press ⸤tab⸥ to advance the To date field

5. Type **10/31/12**

6. Press ⸤tab⸥ or **click** the **Refresh button** to update the report:

Notes
To access the report from the Reports menu:
- Choose the Reports menu, then choose Employees & Payroll, and click Payroll Detail Review to open the report
- Enter 10/01/12 in the From date field
- Enter 10/31/12 in the To date field
- Press ⸤tab⸥ or click the Refresh button to update the report

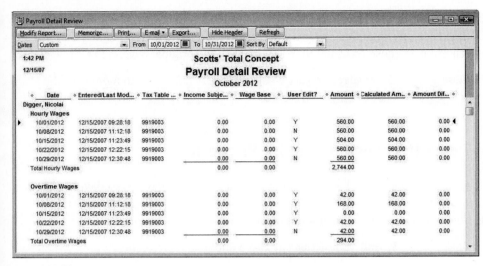

Figure 11-38

You can sort the report by transaction number, date, or the date/time the transaction was entered or modified. Double click any transaction detail to view the original paycheque.

7. Close the **displayed report** when finished. Choose not to memorize the changes if you made any

The Employee Earnings Summary Report

The Employee Earnings Summary Report shows the total for each payroll item for each employee for the selected period. Totals for each item for all employees are included.

1. Click **Employee Earnings Summary** under the Payroll heading

2. Double click the **date** in the From date field

3. Type **10/01/12**

4. Press ⌨(tab) to advance the To date field

5. Type **10/31/12**

6. Press ⌨(tab) or **click** the **Refresh button** to update the report:

Notes
To access the report from the Reports menu:
- Choose the Reports menu, then choose Employees & Payroll, and click Employee Earnings Summary to open the report
- Enter 10/01/12 in the From date field
- Enter 10/31/12 in the To date field
- Press ⌨(tab) or click the Refresh button to update the report

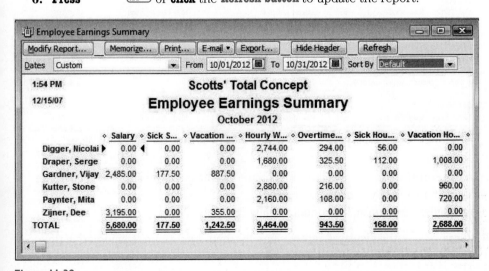

Figure 11-39

You can sort the report by total.

Double click any amount to view the individual transactions that formed that total. Double click any of these transaction details to view the original paycheque.

7. Close   the **displayed report** when finished. Choose not to memorize the changes if you made any

The Payroll Transactions by Payee Report

The Payroll Transactions by Payee Reports lists all payees who received payroll-related cheques — employees as well as agencies to whom payroll liability remittances were made. For each payee, the total amount of each cheque is provided.

1. Click   **Payroll Transactions by Payee** under the Payroll heading

2. Double click   the **date** in the From date field

3. Type   **10/01/12**

4. Press   ⎡tab⎤ to advance the To date field

5. Type   **10/31/12**

6. Press   ⎡tab⎤ or **click** the **Refresh button** to update the report:

Notes

To access the report from the Reports menu:
- Choose the Reports menu, then choose Employees & Payroll, and click Payroll Transactions by Payee to open the report
- Enter 10/01/12 in the From date field
- Enter 10/31/12 in the To date field
- Press ⎡tab⎤ or click the Refresh button to update the report

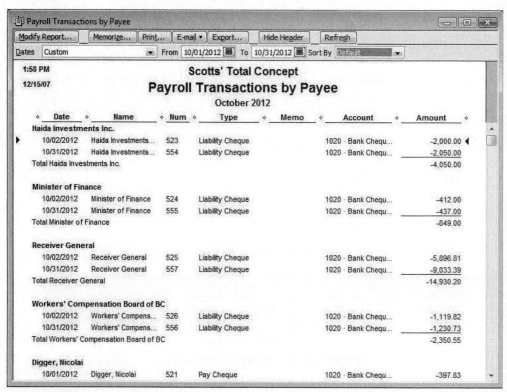

Figure 11-40

You can sort the report by any of the column headings. If you sort the report, the transactions for each payee name are sorted.

Double click any transaction detail to view the original paycheque.

7. Close   the **displayed report** when finished. Choose not to memorize the changes if you made any

The Payroll Transaction Detail Report

The Payroll Transaction Detail Report shows the item amounts that make up each payroll transaction. Both liability payments and employee paycheques are included.

1. **Click**   **Payroll Transactions Detail** under the Payroll heading

2. **Double click**   the **date** in the From date field

3. **Type**   **10/01/12**

4. **Press**   *(tab)* to advance the To date field

5. **Type**   **10/31/12**

6. **Press**   *(tab)* or **click** the **Refresh button** to update the report:

Notes
To access the report from the Reports menu:
- Choose the Reports menu, then choose Employees & Payroll, and click Payroll Transaction Detail to open the report
- Enter 10/01/12 in the From date field
- Enter 10/31/12 in the To date field
- Press *(tab)* or click the Refresh button to update the report

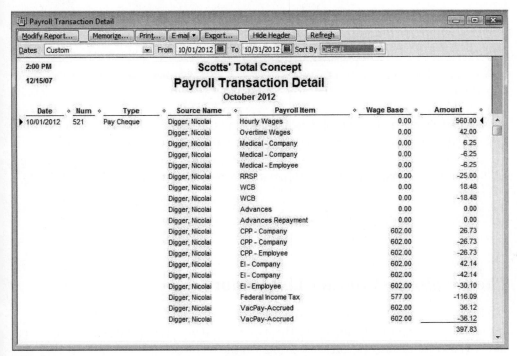

Figure 11-41

You can sort the report by any of the column headings.

Double click any transaction detail to view the original paycheque or liability cheque.

Close the displayed report when finished. Choose not to memorize the changes if you made any.

The Payroll Liability Balances Report

The Payroll Liability Balances Report shows the monthly totals owing for each payroll item.

1. **Click**   **Payroll Liability Balances** under the Payroll heading

2. **Double click**   the **date** in the From date field

3. **Type**   **10/01/12**

4. **Press**   *(tab)* to advance the To date field

Notes
To access the report from the Reports menu:
- Choose the Reports menu, then choose Employees & Payroll, and click Payroll Liability Balances to open the report
- Enter 10/01/12 in the From date field
- Enter 10/31/12 in the To date field
- Press *(tab)* or click the Refresh button to update the report

5. **Type**   10/31/12

6. **Press**   `tab` or **click** the **Refresh button** to update the report:

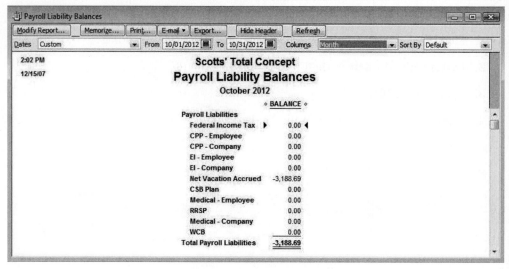

Figure 11-42

Notes
You must display this report before paying the liabilities. If you have paid the liabilities, the amounts in the report will be zero. However, you can still zoom down to the detail report by double clicking a zero entry.

You can choose additional columns for the report from the Columns drop-down list, including different time intervals. You can sort by total amount.

Double click any amount in the report to view the individual transactions that make up the total. Double click any transaction detail to view the original paycheque or liability screen.

7. **Close**   the **displayed report** when finished. Choose not to memorize the changes if you made any

The Employee Contact List Report

The Employee Contact List provides the name, address, phone number, and social insurance number for each employee. The list forms an easy base for mailing or phoning employees or for identifying information gaps in the records.

1. **Click**   **Employee Contact List** under the Employee heading to view the report:

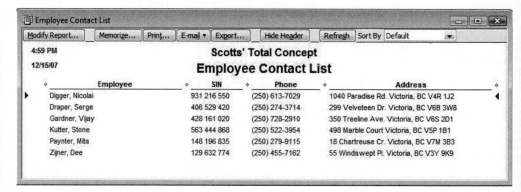

Figure 11-43

Notes
To access the report from the Reports menu:
• Choose the Reports menu, then choose Employees & Payroll, and click Employee Contact List to open the report; or
• Choose the Reports menu, then choose List, and click Employee Contact List to open the report

You can sort the list by any of the column headings.

Double click any employee to open the employee record for editing.

2. **Close**   the **displayed report** when finished. Choose not to memorize the changes if you made any

The Employee Withholding Report

The Employee Withholding Report shows the TD1 federal tax claim amounts and EI factor for each employee. The employee's social insurance number and date of birth and whether the employee pays income tax are also in the report.

1. Click   **Employee Withholding** under the Employee heading to view the report:

Notes
To access the report from the Reports menu:
- Choose the Reports menu, then choose Employees & Payroll and click Employee Withholding to open the report

Employee	SIN	Payroll Province	Birth Da...	Fed TD1	EI Factor	Fed. In...
Digger, Nicolai	931 216 550	BC	09/19/19...	13,332.00	1.4	Yes
Draper, Serge	406 529 420	BC	10/31/19...	10,382.00	1.4	Yes
Gardner, Vijay	428 161 020	BC	12/16/19...	10,382.00	1.4	Yes
Kutter, Stone	563 444 868	BC	04/29/19...	10,382.00	1.4	Yes
Paynter, Mita	148 196 835	BC	02/27/19...	24,987.00	1.4	Yes
Zijner, Dee	129 632 774	BC	07/13/19...	20,764.00	1.4	Yes

Figure 11-44

Notes
An EI factor of 1.4 means that the employer's share of EI premiums is 1.4 times the amount of the employee's share.

You can sort the report by any of the column headings.
Double click any employee to open the employee record for editing.

2. Close   the **displayed report** when finished. Choose not to memorize the changes if you made any

The Payroll Item Listing Report

The Payroll Item Listing Report shows the item record details: item type, Record of Employment information, default amounts and limits, default accounts, and the box used for the item on T4 statements.

1. Click   **Payroll Item Listing** under the Payroll heading to view the report:

Notes
To access the report from the Reports menu:
- Choose the Reports menu, then choose Employees & Payroll, and click Payroll Item Listing to open the report; or
- Choose the Reports menu then choose List, and click Payroll Item Listing to open the report

Payroll Item	Type	ROE Ear...	ROE Hours	ROE Period	Amount	Limit	Expense Account	Liability Account
Salary	Yearly Salary	Yes	Yes	For which is p...			5510 · Payroll Expenses	
Sick Salary	Yearly Salary	Yes	Yes	For which is p...			5510 · Payroll Expenses	
Vacation Salary	Yearly Salary	Yes	Yes	For which is p...				2400 · Payroll Liabilities
Hourly Wages	Hourly Wage	Yes	Yes	For which is p...			5510 · Payroll Expenses	
Overtime Wages	Hourly Wage	Yes	Yes	For which is p...			5510 · Payroll Expenses	
Sick Hourly Rate	Hourly Wage	Yes	Yes	For which is p...			5510 · Payroll Expenses	
Vacation Hourly Rate	Hourly Wage	Yes	Yes	For which is p...				2400 · Payroll Liabilities
Commission	Commission	Yes	No	For which is p...	2.0%		5510 · Payroll Expenses	
VacPay-Accrual Pa...	Vacation Pay	Yes	Yes	For which is p...				2400 · Payroll Liabilities
Advance	Advance	Yes	No	For which is p...			5510 · Payroll Expenses	
Advances	Addition	No	No	In which is paid			1220 · Employee Adva...	

Figure 11-45

You can sort the report by any of the column headings.
Double click any item detail to open the wizard for editing the item.

2. Close   the **displayed report** when finished. Choose not to memorize the changes if you made any

The Employee TD1 Review List Report

The Employee TD1 Review List Report shows the province of taxation and federal and provincial TD1 amounts for each employee. This report also shows whether the employee's claim amounts are base amounts or include claims for other deductions (custom amounts).

Notes

To access the report from the Reports menu:
- Choose the Reports menu, then choose Employees & Payroll, and click Employee TD1 Review List to open the report

1. **Click**   **Employee TD1 Review List** under the Payroll heading to view the report:

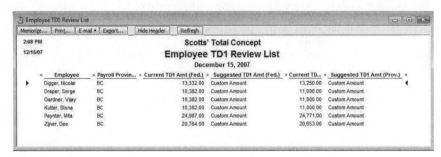

Figure 11-46

Notes

The default date for the TD1 Review List is the current computer date. You are working in a sample file, so the current date is 12/15/2007.

You cannot sort or modify this list.

2. **Close**   the **displayed report** when finished

The T4 Summary Report

The T4 Summary Report shows the totals for all employees in the company for the items on the T4 statements for the current year. The number of T4 slips already printed for this tax year is included.

Notes

T4 slips are usually prepared at the beginning of a new year in preparation for employees filing their personal income tax returns before April 30.

1. **Click**   **T4 Summary** under the Payroll heading to view the report:

Notes

To access the report from the Reports menu:
- Choose the Reports menu, then choose Employees & Payroll, and click T4 Summary to open the report

Notes

You can select this calendar year or the last calendar year for this report. The current year in the sample company file is 2007, even though our transactions have been entered in 2012. You cannot change the date to 2012; therefore, this report is blank because there were no payroll transactions in 2007.

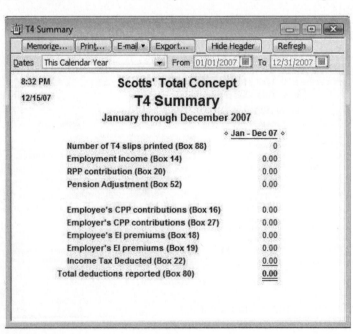

Figure 11-47

You cannot sort or modify this report.

2. **Close** the **displayed report** when finished

The PD7A Summary Report

The PD7A Report shows the total monthly payroll tax liabilities for federal taxes (income tax, CPP, and EI employer and employee amounts).

1. **Click** **PD7A Summary** under the Payroll heading

2. **Double click** the **date** in the From date field

3. **Type** **10/01/12**

4. **Press** (tab) to advance the To date field

5. **Type** **10/31/12**

6. **Press** (tab) or **click** the **Refresh button** to update the report:

Notes
To access the report from the Reports menu:
- Choose the Reports menu, then choose Employees & Payroll, and click PD7A Report to open the report
- Enter 10/01/12 in the From date field
- Enter 10/31/12 in the To date field
- Press (tab) or click the Refresh button to update the report

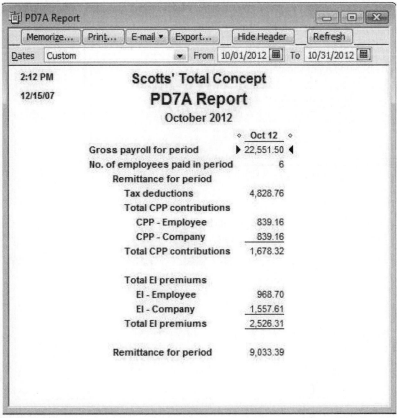

Figure 11-48

You cannot sort or modify this report, though you can change the date range from the date fields inside the report window. The report always shows the totals for the selected period.

7. Close   the **displayed report** when finished

The Record of Employment Report

Notes
You cannot display a record of employment unless an employee has left the company.

The Record of Employment Report is prepared for employees who have terminated their employment with the company. It shows the number of hours worked, the date of hire, the date of termination, and the reason for termination (to assess the employee's eligibility for EI benefits).

The Record of Employment report can be displayed only from the Reports menu.

1. Choose   the **Reports menu**, then **choose Employees & Payroll**, and **click Record Of Employment**. The following message will be displayed:

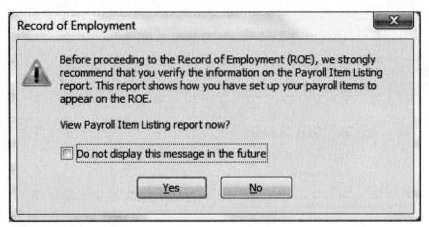

Record of Employment

Before proceeding to the Record of Employment (ROE), we strongly recommend that you verify the information on the Payroll Item Listing report. This report shows how you have set up your payroll items to appear on the ROE.

View Payroll Item Listing report now?

☐ Do not display this message in the future

[Yes]   [No]

Figure 11-49

2. Click   **No** to skip the Payroll Item Listing

The Payroll Item Listing Report shows the Record of Employment status for each payroll item. The following screen will be displayed where you select the employee for whom you want to generate a Record of Employment:

Figure 11-50

Before you can generate the report, the date of hire, termination date, and reason for leaving work must be entered in the employee record.

3. **Choose**   the **employee** who has left the company

4. **Click**   **OK** to view the report.

5. **Close**   the **displayed report** when finished

Finishing Your Session

1. **Back up**   your **company data file**

2. **Close**   the **Company file**

3. **Close**   the **QuickBooks program**

SPARKLES

Objectives

After completing this chapter, you should be able to:

- **sell** inventory items
- **purchase** and **order** inventory items
- **enter** sales returns and credits
- **enter** purchase returns and credits
- **enter** returns for credit card sales and purchases
- **adjust** inventory for losses
- **assemble** inventory items
- **apply** discounts to invoice subtotal amounts
- **handle** transactions for insufficient inventory
- **display** and print inventory reports

Company Information

Company Profile

Notes
Sparkles
55 Glittering Way
Toronto, ON M3T 5F9
Tel: (416) 889-3918
Fax: (416) 887-4112
E-mail: sales@sparkles.
com
Web: www.sparkles.com
Business No.: 233 495 851

Sparkles, located in Toronto, Ontario, is owned and run by Rubie Dimond. The jewellery store sells diamond jewellery in unique gold settings and also makes customized settings for the precious gem.

As a child, Dimond experimented with many media. She created original and interesting jewellery with ceramics and modelling clay. But the sparkle of diamonds always held the most interest for her, so she completed a jewellery making and design program at community college. There she learned how to work with gems and to make original gold settings. She makes many of the pieces she sells now, but she also carries a number of standard chains and bracelets to which she can attach her custom-designed pendants.

Dimond employs two assistants — one works exclusively on sales and one assists with making jewellery and sales. Dimond herself also works in the store regularly because she enjoys interacting with customers, and learning more about their tastes and preferences helps her plan her future designs.

The store accepts cash, cheques, and Visa in payment and has a credit card for some business purchases. Many customers have also set up accounts and these customers receive a discount for early payment as well as a volume sales discount of 10 percent when they buy multiple pieces of jewellery. For custom-designed pieces, customers pay a deposit on accepting an estimate or placing an order. Dimond has also arranged discounts with some of her vendors and has accounts set up for regular purchases.

Customers pay 13 percent HST on all purchases. Sparkles pays HST on all business-related non-inventory purchases.

Dimond will use the inventory features of QuickBooks to help track inventory costs and sales. At the beginning of January 2012, she is ready to enter the first month of transactions in QuickBooks after closing the books at the end of 2011 and submitting all payroll and tax liabilities. Her sales assistant converted the accounting records to QuickBooks using the following:

- Chart of Accounts
- Post-closing Trial Balance
- Vendor Information
- Customer Information
- Item Lists
- Employee Information List
- Accounting Procedures

NOTE: We are using a QuickBooks sample file while working in this chapter in order to keep the payroll taxes the same no matter what year you are working with this file.

Chart of Accounts

Sparkles

ASSETS

Bank
  1020 Bank Chequing
  1040 Bank Savings
  1060 Bank Visa

Accounts Receivable
  1200 Accounts Receivable

Other Current Assets
  1220 Employee Advances
  1300 Jewellery Boxes and Bags
  1320 Jewellery Parts Inventory
  1340 Office & Computer Supplies
  1360 Other Supplies
  1400 Inventory [Parent account]
  1410 Bracelets
  1420 Diamonds
  1430 Earrings
  1440 Necklaces
  1450 Pendants
  1460 Rings

Fixed Assets
  1520 Computer Equipment
  1540 Display Cabinets & Fixtures
  1550 Equipment and Tools
  1560 Safe
  1580 Store

LIABILITIES

Accounts Payable
  2100 Accounts Payable

Credit Card
  2200 Visa Payable

Other Current Liabilities
  2260 Bank Loan
  2300 HST Payable
  2360 Payroll Liabilities

Long Term Liabilities
  2740 Mortgage Payable

Equity
  3220 Capital, Rubie Dimond
  3260 Drawings, Rubie Dimond
  3600 Retained Earnings

INCOME
  4100 Revenue from Sales
  4120 Revenue from Services
  4140 Sales Discounts
  4200 Revenue from Interest
  4250 Sales Tax Compensation
  4300 Other Revenue

EXPENSE
Cost of Goods Sold
  5040 Cost of Inventory Sold
  5060 Jewellery Parts Used

Expense
  5120 Advertising and Promotion
  5130 Bank Charges
  5140 Credit Card Fees
  5160 Purchase Discounts
  5170 Boxes and Bags Used
  5180 Office & Computer Supplies Used
  5190 Other Supplies Used
  5220 Maintenance Expenses
  5240 Insurance Expense
  5260 Interest Expense
  5280 Property Tax Expense
  5340 Hydro Expense
  5360 Telephone Expense
  5600 Payroll Expenses

Post-closing Trial Balance

Sparkles

AS AT JANUARY 1, 2012

	Debits	Credits		Debits	Credits
1020 Bank Chequing	$ 33,460.00		1520 Computer Equipment	$ 9,400.00	
1040 Bank Savings	60,000.00		1540 Display Cabinets & Fixtures	18,000.00	
1060 Bank Visa	2,180.00		1550 Equipment and Tools	12,000.00	
1200 Accounts Receivable	9,350.00		1560 Safe	6,500.00	
1300 Jewellery Boxes and Bags	3,400.00		1580 Store	160,000.00	
1320 Jewellery Parts Inventory	4,900.00		2100 Accounts Payable		$ 10,700.00
1340 Office & Computer Supplies	585.00		2200 Visa Payable		210.00
1360 Other Supplies	280.00		2260 Bank Loan		25,000.00
1400 Inventory: 1410 Bracelets	8,775.00		2300 HST Payable		210.00
1400 Inventory: 1420 Diamonds	42,800.00		2740 Mortgage Payable		95,000.00
1400 Inventory: 1430 Earrings	2,100.00		3220 Capital, Rubie Dimond		337,920.00
1400 Inventory: 1440 Necklaces	26,270.00		3260 Drawings, Rubie Dimond	8,400.00	
1400 Inventory: 1450 Pendants	6,360.00			$469,040.00	$469,040.00
1400 Inventory: 1460 Rings	54,280.00				

Vendor Information

Sparkles

Vendor Name (Contact)	Address	Phone No. Fax No.	E-mail Business No.	Terms Credit Limit
Faithful Insurers				monthly
Goldcrest Inc. (Troy Waytes)	200 Crystal Cres. Markham, ON L4G 4F5	Tel: (905) 388-2819 Alt: (905) 769-2928	twaytes@goldcrest.com	1/10, n/30 $15,000.00
Hydro One (N. U. Kleer)	50 Bloor St. W. Toronto, ON M5K 2B4	Tel: (416) 524-2345	nukleer@hydroone.ca	net 10 $500.00
Kimberley Mines (Silver Minor)	600 Starlight Rd. North York, ON M4C 8B2	Tel: (416) 292-4910 Fax: (416) 292-3991	minor@kimberleymines.com	net 30 $20,000.00
Sprint Canada (Ena Tellus)	5 Satellite Circle Toronto, ON M2M 5C3	Tel: (416) 2SP-RINT		net 15 $500.00
Trevor's Treasures (Trevor)	45 Findings Lane Oakville, ON L9M 3G9	Tel: (905) 687-9812		2/10, n/30 $5,000.00
Receiver General				monthly
Workplace Safety and Insurance Board				monthly

Outstanding Vendor Transactions

Sparkles

Vendor Name	Date	Terms	Due Date	Invoice No./ Cheque No.	Amount
Goldcrest Inc.	Dec. 27/11	1/10, n/30	Jan. 26/12	GI-2018	$6,420.00
Trevor's Treasures	Dec. 29/11	2/10, n/30	Jan. 28/12	TT-3170	$4,280.00
				Grand Total	$10,700.00

Customer Information

Sparkles

Customer Name (Contact)	Address	Phone No. Fax No.	E-mail Preferred Payment	Terms Credit Limit
Cash Sales			credit card	due on receipt
Carat, Goldie	103 Sheen Ave. Toronto, ON M9T 4D2	Tel: (905) 498-1820	gcarat@sympatico.ca cheque	1/5, n/30 $10,000.00
Glitters, Jem	12 Opal Ave. Toronto, ON M4V 5C2	Tel: (416) 893-1021 Alt: (416) 884-4991	jglitters@google.ca cheque	1/5, n/30 $10,000.00
Goldwyn, William	33 Nugget Court Oak Ridges, ON L3B 7N9	Tel: (905) 372-3001	goldwyn7@rogers.ca cheque	1/5, n/30 $10,000.00
Perley, Bess	23 Tinsel Grove Toronto, ON M4J 4J3	Tel: (416) 387-1098	bperley@yahoo.ca cheque	1/5, n/30 $10,000.00
Saffire, Wanda	499 Cluster Ave. Burlington, ON L9G 4D2	Tel: (905) 458-7331 Fax: (905) 458-4301	wsaffire@sympatico.ca cheque	1/5, n/30 $10,000.00

Outstanding Customer Transactions

Sparkles

Customer Name	Date	Terms	Type	Invoice No./ Cheque No.	Amount	Balance Owing
Glitters, Jem	Dec. 10/11		Deposit cheque	192	−$1,000.00	
	Dec. 16/11	1/5, n/30	Invoice	278	$3,450.00	$2,450.00
Goldwyn, William	Dec. 24/11	1/5, n/30	Invoice	297	$4,600.00	$4,600.00
Perley, Bess	Dec. 30/11	1/5, n/30	Invoice	315	$2,300.00	$2,300.00
			Grand Total			$9,350.00

Non-inventory Item List

Sparkles

Item	Description	Price	Tax Code	Account
NON-INVENTORY PARTS				
Gold	Gold used to make and repair jewellery	$604.00/ounce	H	1320 Jewellery Parts Inventory
Jewellery Parts	Repair parts, findings, etc.	Variable	H	1320 Jewellery Parts Inventory
OTHER CHARGES				
Finance Charges	Finance Charges on Overdue Balance (18% > 30 days, min. charge $30.00, grace period 5 days)	18%		4200 Revenue from Interest
NSF Cheque	Amount of NSF Cheque	Variable		1020 Bank Chequing
NSF Fees	NSF cheque handling charge	$30.00		4300 Other Revenue
SUBTOTALS				
Subtotal - pretax	Invoice subtotal for discount application			
DISCOUNTS				
Discount	Sales discount on pretax subtotal	10%	H	4140 Sales Discounts

Inventory Item List

Sparkles

Item Name/Number	Description	Selling Price	Sales Tax Code	Purchase Tax Code	Reorder Point	Number on Hand	Total Value
INVENTORY PARTS							
BRACELETS (Revenue Account: 4100 Revenue from Sales; Asset Account: 1410 Bracelets; Cost of Goods Sold Account: 5040 Cost of Inventory Sold)							
B101 Bracelet	14 Kt bangle plain	$590.00	H	H	3	6	$1,770.00
B102 Bracelet	14 Kt bangle solitaire setting	510.00	H	H	3	6	1,530.00
B103 Bracelet	14 Kt bangle 3 stone setting	625.00	H	H	3	6	1,875.00
B104 Bracelet	14 Kt link plain	400.00	H	H	3	6	1,200.00
B105 Bracelet	14 Kt link solitaire setting	370.00	H	H	3	6	1,110.00
B106 Bracelet	14 Kt link 3 stone setting	430.00	H	H	3	6	1,290.00
					Total		$8,775.00
DIAMONDS (Revenue Account: 4100 Revenue from Sales; Asset Account: 1420 Diamonds; Cost of Goods Sold Account: 5040 Cost of Inventory Sold)							
D101 Diamond	0.10 ct diamond	$ 400.00	H	H	50	60	$12,000.00
D102 Diamond	0.25 ct diamond	1,000.00	H	H	10	14	7,000.00
D103 Diamond	0.50 ct diamond	2,500.00	H	H	4	8	10,000.00
D104 Diamond	1.0 ct diamond	6,900.00	H	H	2	4	13,800.00
					Total		$42,800.00
EARRINGS (Revenue Account: 4100 Revenue from Sales; Asset Account: 1430 Earrings; Cost of Goods Sold Account: 5040 Cost of Inventory Sold)							
E101 Earrings	18 Kt drop setting	$140.00	H	H	10	14	$ 980.00
E102 Earrings	18 Kt stud setting	80.00	H	H	10	14	560.00
E103 Earrings	18 Kt studs	80.00	H	H	10	14	560.00
					Total		$2,100.00
NECKLACES (Revenue Account: 4100 Revenue from Sales; Asset Account: 1440 Necklaces; Cost of Goods Sold Account: 5040 Cost of Inventory Sold)							
N101 Necklace	16 inch feather chain 18 Kt	$600.00	H	H	10	14	$4,200.00
N102 Necklace	16 inch box chain 18 Kt	550.00	H	H	10	12	3,300.00
N103 Necklace	16 inch wire chain 18 Kt	480.00	H	H	10	16	3,840.00
N104 Necklace	18 inch feather chain 18 Kt	800.00	H	H	10	12	4,800.00
N105 Necklace	18 inch box chain 18 Kt	750.00	H	H	10	14	5,250.00
N106 Necklace	18 inch wire chain 18 Kt	610.00	H	H	10	16	4,880.00
					Total		$26,270.00
PENDANTS (Revenue Account: 4100 Revenue from Sales; Asset Account: 1450 Pendants; Cost of Goods Sold Account: 5040 Cost of Inventory Sold)							
P101 Pendant	18 Kt gold small setting	$110.00	H	H	8	12	$ 660.00
P102 Pendant	18 Kt gold medium setting	320.00	H	H	6	12	1,920.00
P103 Pendant	18 Kt gold large setting	630.00	H	H	4	12	3,780.00
					Total		$6,360.00
RINGS (Revenue Account: 4100 Revenue from Sales; Asset Account: 1460 Rings; Cost of Goods Sold Account: 5040 Cost of Inventory Sold)							
R101 Ring	18 Kt engagement solitaire setting	$1,000.00	H	H	4	8	$ 4,000.00
R102 Ring	18 Kt engagement 3 stone setting	900.00	H	H	4	8	3,600.00
R103 Ring	18 Kt band narrow plain	375.00	H	H	6	8	1,500.00
R104 Ring	18 Kt band wide plain	570.00	H	H	6	8	2,280.00
R105 Ring	18 Kt band narrow 3 stone setting 0.25 ct	1,050.00	H	H	4	8	4,200.00
R106 Ring	18 Kt band wide 3 stone setting 0.25 ct	1,500.00	H	H	3	8	6,000.00
R107 Ring	18 Kt band narrow 5 stone setting 0.65 ct	2,000.00	H	H	3	6	6,000.00
R108 Ring	18 Kt band wide 5 stone setting 0.65 ct	2,500.00	H	H	3	6	7,500.00
R109 Ring	18 Kt diamond band 0.25 ct total	1,200.00	H	H	5	8	4,800.00
R110 Ring	18 Kt diamond band 0.50 ct total	1,900.00	H	H	3	6	5,700.00
R111 Ring	18 Kt diamond band 0.75 ct total	2,900.00	H	H	2	6	8,700.00
					Total		$54,280.00
SERVICES (Revenue Account: 4120 Revenue from Services)							
C101 Design	Custom design and setting	Custom pricing	H				
R100 Repairs	Jewellery repairs	Custom pricing	H				

Sparkles

EMPLOYEE	GARNET Y. AMARALD	JADINE R. AMETHYST
Position	Jeweller	Salesperson
Address	55 Windswept Pl.	350 Treeline Ave.
	Toronto, ON	Toronto, ON
	M3P 4J1	M6S 3H8
Telephone	(416) 461-6125	(416) 300-8210
Alt. Telephone	(416) 529-1725	
SIN	852 364 272	312 589 120
Date of Birth (mm-dd-yy)	12-01-72	03-02-80
Date of Hire (mm-dd-yy)	05-01-04	06-15-05
Earnings		
Regular Wage Rate	—	$16.00/hour
Overtime Wage Rate	—	$24.00/hour
Regular Annual Salary	$48,600.00	—
Commission	0.5% Net Revenue from Sales	0.5% Net Revenue from Sales
	5% Revenue from Services	
Pay Period	semi-monthly	semi-monthly
Hours per Period	85	85
WSIB Rate	2.58%	1.00%
Deductions Each Pay Period		
Group Insurance	$20.00	$10.00
Income Tax, EI, and CPP	Amounts and calculations built into QuickBooks program	
Federal (Ontario) Claim — TD1		
Personal	$10,382.00 (8,943.00)	$10,382.00 (8,943.00)
Spousal/Equivalent	$10,382.00 (7,594.00)	
Education		$ 7,200.00 (7,464.00)
Total Claim	$20,764.00 (16,537.00)	$17,582.00 (16,407.00)
Vacation	3 weeks	6% retained
Sick Pay Rate	same as regular hourly or salary rate	
Accrued Vacation	$2,850.00	$1,920.00
Accrued Sick Leave Time	40 hours	40 hours

Employee Profiles and TD1 Information

Garnet Y. Amarald works as an assistant to Dimond in all aspects of the business, including making and repairing jewellery. Amarald is paid twice every month based on an annual salary of $48,600.00. In addition, he receives a commission of 5 percent of all revenue from services and 0.5 percent of the sales revenue (net of the 10 percent sales discount), and he can take three weeks' vacation each year. He is married and claims the spousal amount for income tax purposes in addition to the base personal claim amount. His only paycheque deduction in addition to regular taxes is a contribution to a group insurance plan. At the beginning of January, he has 40 hours of sick leave accrued and three weeks of vacation time, the allowances for one year.

Jadine R. Amethyst works primarily as the salesperson, but she also assists with the bookkeeping for the business. She is paid $16.00 per hour for the first 40 hours each week and $24.00 per hour for additional hours. She also earns a sales commission of 0.5 percent of the sales revenue (net of the 10 percent sales discount). As a single part-time student, she is allowed an education deduction in addition to the personal tax claim

Notes

The Workplace Safety and Insurance Board (WSIB) is the name for the Workers' Compensation Board in Ontario.

Organizations in Ontario that have total payroll greater than $400,000.00 must pay EHT (Employer Health Tax) to pay for health insurance coverage for Ontario residents.

When used, EHT is set up as an employer-paid payroll tax, similar to WSIB/WCB.

amount. Her vacation pay is calculated at the rate of 6 percent of her pay and is retained until she takes time off. She also makes contributions to the group insurance plan and has vacation and sick leave entitlements accrued for the coming year.

Accounting Procedures

Taxes: HST

Sparkles pays HST on all goods and services that it buys and charges HST on all sales. HST collected from customers is recorded as a liability in the *HST Payable* account. HST paid to vendors is recorded in the *HST Payable* account as a decrease in liability to the Canada Revenue Agency. The report is filed with the Receiver General for Canada by the last day of the month for the previous quarter, either including the balance owing or requesting a refund. The next remittance is due at the end of January.

Account Terms

All customers receive a 1 percent discount if they settle their accounts within five days after a purchase. The full balance is required within 30 days of a sale or on completion of a special order. Finance charges of 18 percent per year apply after 30 days from the invoice date, with a minimum charge of $30.00 and a five-day grace period. No discount is allowed on credit card sales because of the fee attached to cards.

Customers receive additional discounts of 10 percent when they purchase more than one piece of jewellery, not counting the diamonds for a setting. The data file includes items to calculate the pretax subtotal and discount in order to include them on invoices.

Some vendors offer discounts for early payment.

Deposits and Cheques

Cheques, credit card receipts, and cash are not held for deposit. Cheques are hand printed at the time of the transaction.

Estimates, Orders, and Deposits

For special orders, Sparkles prepares sales estimates. When customers proceed with an estimate, they pay a deposit of at least 30 percent of the finished jewellery. Some customers also place sales orders with Sparkles. These also require a deposit of about 30 percent.

Sparkles regularly places purchase orders with suppliers of premade jewellery items, special parts, and gold used to make and repair jewellery.

Supplies

At the end of each month the staff assess the quantity of supplies left in the store to determine the cost of the gold and parts used. They then make adjusting entries in QuickBooks for these costs. Depreciation will be entered at the end of each quarter.

Account Numbers

The store assigns account numbers to accounts: 1000s for asset, 2000s for liability, 3000s for equity, 4000s for income and 5000s for expense accounts. Account numbers are not used for customers, vendors or employees.

Instructions

1. Using the Chart of Accounts, the Trial Balance, and other information, you will **record entries for source documents** for January 2012 using QuickBooks. You will find the source documents marked with an SD beside them and listed as you work through the chapter. The procedures for entering each new type of transaction introduced in this chapter are outlined in step-by-step instructions. Additional source documents will be provided, allowing you to have more practice entering transactions. If you have used this textbook in the past and would prefer to skip the step-by-step instructions and work only with a list of source documents, refer to the CD in the back of the textbook for the list of source documents for this chapter.

2. After you have finished making your entries, **print** the **reports and graphs** for January 2012 as indicated on the following printing form:

> **Notes**
> Instructions for inventory reports begin on page 639.

REPORTS FOR JANUARY 2012

Lists
- ☐ Account Listing
- ☐ Customer Phone List
- ☐ Customer Contact List
- ☐ Vendor Phone List
- ☐ Vendor Contact List
- ☐ Employee Contact List
- ☑ Item Listing
- ☑ Item Price List
- ☐ Payroll Item List

Company & Financial
- ☑ Balance Sheet Standard at Jan. 31
- ☑ Profit & Loss Standard from Jan. 1 to Jan. 31
- ☐ Expenses by Vendor
- ☐ Income by Customer

Accountant & Taxes
- ☑ Trial Balance at Jan. 31
- ☐ General Ledger
- ☑ Journal from Jan. 1 to Jan. 31
- ☐ Transaction List by Date
- ☐ Transaction Detail by Account

Banking
- ☐ Deposit Detail
- ☐ Cheque Detail
- ☐ Missing Cheques
- ☐ Reconcile Discrepancy
- ☐ Previous Reconciliation

Vendor
- ☑ A/P Aging Detail at Jan. 31
- ☐ Vendor Balance
- ☐ Unpaid Bills
- ☐ Transaction List by Vendor

Purchases
- ☐ Purchases by Vendor
- ☐ Purchases by Item
- ☐ Transaction List by Vendor
- ☐ Open Purchase Orders by Vendor

Customer
- ☑ A/R Aging Detail at Jan. 31
- ☐ Customer Balance
- ☐ Open Invoices
- ☐ Collections Report
- ☐ Transaction List by Customer

Sales
- ☐ Sales by Customer
- ☑ Sales by Item Summary from Jan. 1 to Jan. 31
- ☐ Sales Pending
- ☐ Open Sales Orders by Customer
- ☐ Open Sales Orders by Item
- ☐ Sales by Rep

Employees & Payroll
- ☐ Payroll Summary
- ☐ Payroll Item Detail
- ☐ Payroll Detail Review
- ☑ Employee Earnings Summary from Jan. 1 to Jan. 31

- ☐ Payroll Transactions by Payee
- ☐ Payroll Transaction Detail
- ☐ Payroll Liability Balances
- ☐ Employee Withholding
- ☐ TD1 Review List
- ☐ T4 Summary
- ☐ PD7A Summary
- ☐ Record of Employment

Inventory
- ☐ Inventory Valuation Summary
- ☑ Inventory Valuation Detail from Jan. 1 to Jan. 31
- ☑ Inventory Stock Status by Item at Jan. 31
- ☐ Inventory Stock Status by Vendor
- ☐ Physical Inventory Worksheet
- ☐ Pending Builds

Other
- ☐ Custom Summary Report
- ☐ Custom Transaction Detail Report
- ☐ Transaction History
- ☐ Transaction Journal

GRAPHS
- ☐ Income and Expense
- ☐ Net Worth
- ☐ Accounts Payable
- ☐ Accounts Receivable
- ☑ Sales from Jan. 1 to Jan. 31

Opening the Sample Data File

1. **Start**   the **QuickBooks program**

2. **Open**   the **file** for Sparkles. You will see the following Sample file reminder:

Figure 12-1

3. **Click**   **OK** to continue

> **IMPORTANT:**
>
> This file has been converted to a Sample file so that you can enter payroll information for dates outside of the current payroll tax table period. This is important for learning purposes. No matter what QuickBooks tax table you have installed, the payroll information in the print screens in the textbook, will be the same as yours as long as you use the sample file. The sample data file is set up so that December 15, 2007 is the current date displayed when entering forms. You will override this date as you're working in the chapter.

Entering Inventory Sales

Inventory sales are not entered differently from other sales in QuickBooks because items are used for all sales transactions. Inventory items have more accounts linked to them, but these items are set up in the item record and are used by the program to create the appropriate journal entries and update the necessary ledger records.

The first transaction that we will enter is a sales invoice that includes a pre tax subtotal and a 10 percent discount. Refer to the following source document as we work through the steps to enter it:

SD1: Sales Invoice #321

Dated January 2, 2012

To Wanda Saffire

1	E101 Earrings	18 Kt drop setting	$ 140.00	$ 140.00
1	N101 Necklace	16 inch feather chain 18 Kt	600.00	600.00
1	P102 Pendant	18 Kt gold medium setting	320.00	320.00
2	D101 Diamonds	0.10 ct diamond	400.00 ea.	800.00
1	D103 Diamond	0.50 ct diamond	2,500.00	2 500.00
	Subtotal - pretax			$4,360.00
	Discount		10%	−436.00
	HST		13%	510.12
	Sales total			$4,434.12

Terms: 1/5, n/30.

Notes (margin)

1. **Click** the **Create Invoices icon** 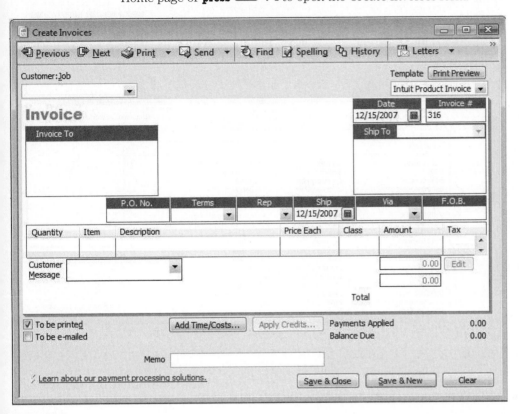 in the Customers section on the Home page or **press** ⌷ctrl⌷ **+ I** to open the Create Invoices form:

Figure 12-2

December 15, 2007, is preset as the default date for the Sample file, as it was for Scotts' Total Concept. The product invoice form is similar to ones we used previously, but it includes fields commonly used for inventory items, such as shipping details, sales rep, and purchase order number. The Quantity field comes before the Item field.

2. **Choose** **Saffire, Wanda** from the Customer: Job drop-down list

3. **Double click** the **date** field

4. **Type** **01/02/12**

5. **Press** ⌷tab⌷ to advance to the Invoice # field

6. **Type** **321**

7. **Click** **To be printed box** to remove the ✓.
   We will not print the invoices

8. **Click** the **Quantity** field in the first detail line of the invoice

9. **Type** **1**

10. **Press** ⌷tab⌷ to move to the Item field

Notes
You can customize your invoice by copying the Intuit Product Invoice template and adding, removing, or rearranging columns.

Notes
The default date for the sample company is 12/15/2007 and will be displayed by default on all forms.

11. Click   the **Item field** list arrow to view the item list:

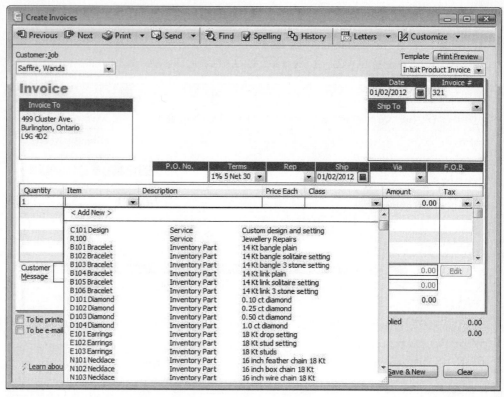

Figure 12-3

The list is just like the previous lists of items (except that we have more items).

12. Click   **E101 Earrings** as the first item

The remaining details for the line are added automatically based on the information in the item record.

You can change any of the default information if necessary. Just select the text you want to change and type the new information. You can change the price or the description, but not the item name/number.

13. Click   the **Quantity field** on the second detail line of the invoice

14. Type   1

15. Press   _tab_ to move to the Item field

16. Type   n

QuickBooks fills in the name based on what you type. If you keep typing, the program will continue to match your entry with the items on record. When a mismatch occurs, the program assumes the item is new and will offer you the chance to create it. In this case, we want the first item beginning with _n_ so we can accept the default.

17. Press   _tab_ to add the remaining item information

18. Click   the **Quantity field** on the next detail line

19. Type   1

20. Press   _tab_ to move to the Item field

21. Type   **P102** or **choose P102 Pendant** from the item list

22.	**Click**	the **Quantity field** on the next invoice detail line
23.	**Type**	**2**
24.	**Press**	⌧ *tab* to move to the Item field
25.	**Type**	**D**
26.	**Press**	⌧ *tab* to enter the remaining item details for D101
27.	**Type**	**1** in the Quantity field on the next line
28.	**Press**	⌧ *tab*
29.	**Type**	**D103** or **choose D103 Diamond** from the item list

Notes
As soon as you click a different field, the program fills in the details for the item.

Notes
D101 is the first item starting with D, and it is the item we want so we need to enter only the first letter.

Sparkles gives a 10 percent discount when customers buy more than one item, excluding the diamonds for a setting. Therefore, we need to calculate the amount on which the discount is based. The next two items we will use are special types. The first creates a subtotal amount for the invoice by adding together all amounts above the subtotal line that follow another subtotal item, if there was one. The second item calculates a discount for the amount on the previous line. We want the discount to be calculated on the subtotal amount.

30.	**Click**	the **drop-down arrow** in the Item field on the next invoice detail line
31.	**Choose**	**Subtotal - pretax** to update the invoice as shown:

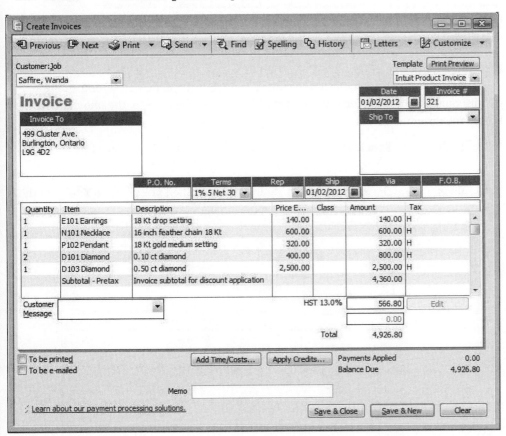

Figure 12-4

A subtotal entry is added in the Amount column. You cannot edit this amount.

32. Choose **Discount** from the Item field list on the next invoice detail line to add the 10 percent discount and complete the invoice as shown:

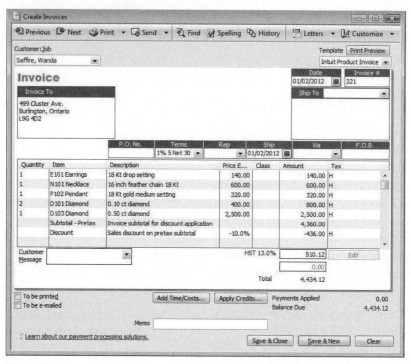

Figure 12-5

You can see the effect of changing the tax code by removing the H tax code for Discount and then re-entering it.

The discount is 10 percent of the subtotal amount. If you do not enter a subtotal, the discount will be taken on only the previous item on the invoice, the one immediately before the discount entry.

33. Click **Save & New** to save the deposit and leave the Invoice form open to review the journal entry

34. Click the **Previous button** ⟨Previous⟩ and then **press** ⟨ctrl⟩ + **Y** to view the Transaction Journal report for the transaction:

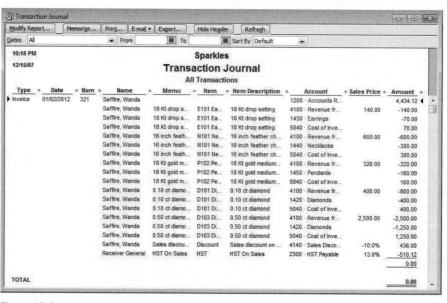

Figure 12-6

Notes
The discount is taxable so the final taxes will be based on the discounted amount and not on the subtotal before discounts.

Notes
You can create separate discount items for different percentages and apply them to individual items on a line-by-line basis.

Notes
The Trans # and Class columns have been removed from this report.

When inventory items are tracked, more accounts are involved in transactions because inventory is continually updated. For each item sold, QuickBooks has credited (increased) the *Revenue from Sales* account for the full sales price before discounts; the inventory asset account is credited (decreased) and the *Cost of Inventory Sold* account is debited (increased) for the cost of the item. The discount is debited to *Discounts*, a contra-revenue account that decreases overall revenue. The sales tax liabilities are also updated (increased). And finally, *Accounts Receivable* is debited (increased) by the net sale amount. The inventory records are updated to reduce the quantity on hand, and the customer's outstanding balance is increased.

Notes
In previous chapters, we did not track inventory — a General Journal adjusting entry was made periodically to update the inventory accounts. Even when the program tracks inventory, the business must periodically check the stock on hand against the computer records (see Physical Inventory Worksheet, page 643).

35. **Close**   the **Transaction Journal report** and then close the Create Invoices form

Entering Purchase Orders for Inventory Items

The next transaction is the entry of a purchase order for tracked inventory items. Again, the procedure is similar to that for non-inventory transactions. Refer to the following source document as we work through the steps to enter it:

SD Instructions
Refer to the following source document and then follow the step-by-step instructions to enter it.

SD2: Purchase Order #125

Dated January 3, 2012

To Goldcrest Inc.

10	N101 Necklaces	16 inch feather chain 18 Kt	$ 3,000.00
10	N102 Necklaces	16 inch box chain 18 Kt	2,750.00
10	N104 Necklaces	18 inch feather chain 18 Kt	4,000.00
10	N105 Necklaces	18 inch box chain 18 Kt	1,750.00
	HST @ 13%		1,495.00
	Purchase order total		$12,995.00

1. **Choose**   the **Vendors menu** and **click Create Purchase Orders**:

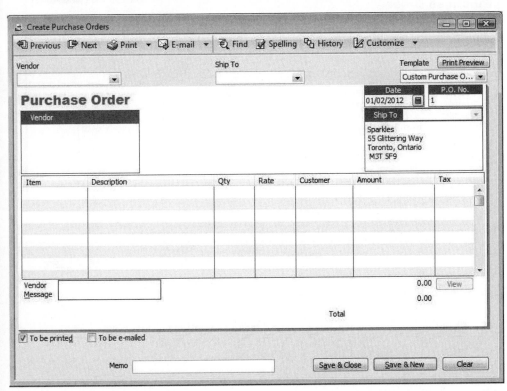

Figure 12-7

The purchase order form is unchanged.

2. **Choose**   **Goldcrest Inc.** from the Vendor drop-down list

3. **Enter**   **01/03/12** in the order date field

4. **Enter**   **125** in the P.O. No. field

5. **Click**   the **To be printed** box to remove the ✓.
We are not printing purchase orders

6. **Choose**   **N101 Necklace** from the Item field list, or **type n** and **press** (tab)

The description, cost (Rate field), and tax code are entered from the item record details. The cost is based on previous purchases of the item.

Notes
QuickBooks uses the average cost method for inventory valuation so the costs are continually updated with each transaction.

7. **Click**   the **Qty field**

8. **Type**   **10**

9. **Enter**   the **remaining items** on the purchase order as listed in SD2 on page 599

The cost for N105 has changed so we need to edit it.

10. **Double click**   **3750.00** in the Amount column (the total cost for N105)

11. **Type**   **1750**

12. **Press**   (tab) to complete the order as shown:

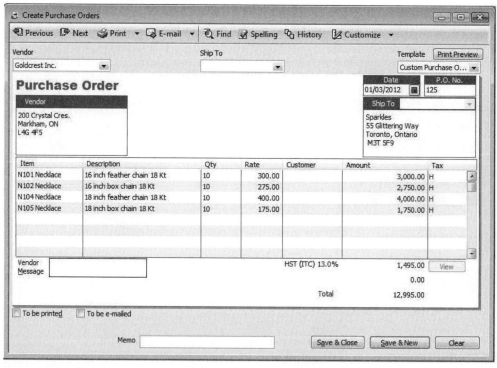

Figure 12-8

13. **Check**   your **work** carefully and **make corrections** if necessary

14. **Click**   **Save & Close** to record the order.

Entering Sales Returns

Customers frequently return items because they are not satisfied in some way: the colour or size may be wrong or the wrong item was purchased. Stores vary in their returns policies. Some stores do not allow returns, some have time limits, and some charge a handling fee. Like most jewellery stores, Sparkles does not allow earrings to be returned for health reasons, but gives refunds for other items returned within 15 days. Sapphire is returning a necklace.

Refer to the following source document as we work through the steps to enter it:

SD3: **Sales Return #321-R**

SD Instructions
Refer to the following source document and then follow the step-by-step instructions to enter it.

Dated January 4, 2012

Wanda Saffire returned the 16 inch necklace (N101) because she wanted a longer chain for her pendant. Create a credit invoice to enter the return.

1	N101 Necklace	16 inch feather chain 18 Kt*	$600	$600.00
	Discount		10%	−60.00
	HST		13%	70.20
	Sales Credit Total			$610.20

Sales returns are entered as credits for the customer when the invoice has an outstanding balance.

Notes
Cash and credit card refunds are shown later in this chapter on page 612.

1. **Click**   the **Refunds and Credits icon** 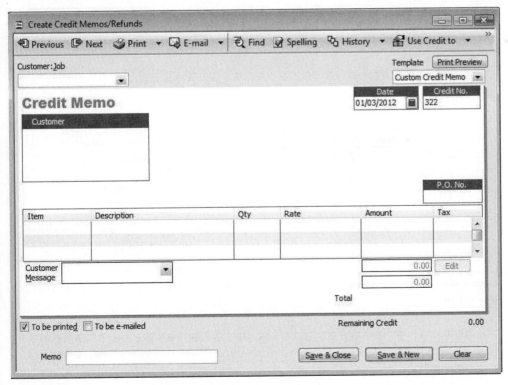 from the Customers section of the Home page to open the Create Credit Memos/Refunds form:

Notes
You can also choose the Customers menu and click Create Credit Memos/Refunds to open the Credit Memos form.

Notes
The *Use Credit to* drop-down list at the top of the screen allows you to change the credit memo into an immediate refund or apply the credit memo to an invoice. See page 613.

Figure 12-9

This form is like an invoice form, and we complete it in the same way. However, QuickBooks automatically reverses the usual sales journal entry to create the credit.

2. **Choose**   **Saffire, Wanda** from the Customer:Job field list

3. **Enter**   **01/04/12** as the credit memo date

4. **Enter**   **321-R** as the Credit No.

Adding *R* to the number will identify the form as a credit instead of an invoice.

5. **Click**   the **To be printed** box to remove the ✓

6. **Click**   the **drop-down arrow** in the Item field

7. **Click**   **N101 Necklace** to select the item

8. **Click**   the **Qty field** so we can enter the number of items

9. **Type**   1

10. **Press**   (tab)

We also need to reverse the discount for the item. This time there is only one item line so we do not need to create a subtotal.

11. **Choose**   **Discount** from the Item field list

12. **Press**   (tab) to update and complete the form as shown:

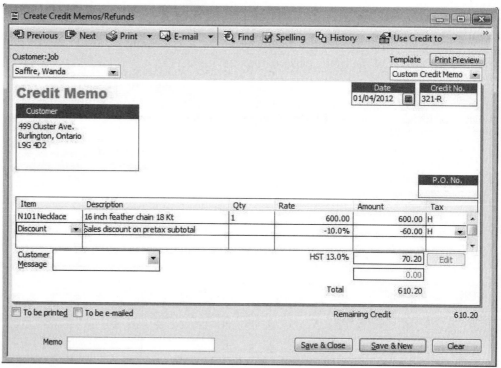

Figure 12-10

Although all the amounts entered are positive, the journal entry reverses the original amounts because we are using the credit form. We will see this effect when we review the journal entry.

13. **Check**   your **work** carefully and **make corrections** if necessary

14. **Click**   **Save & New** to record the entry and leave the form open

15. The Available Credit screen is displayed:

Figure 12-11

Use this screen to indicate what you want to do with the credit memo. You can retain it as an available credit on your customer's account, give your customer a refund, or apply it to an invoice. We will retain it as an available credit.

16. Click **Retain as an available credit** (this should be selected as the default)

17. Click **OK**

18. Click ⬅ **Previous** and then **press** `ctrl` **+ Y** to view the Transaction Journal report:

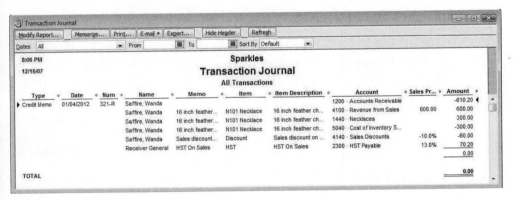

Figure 12-12

Notes
Columns have been removed from this report to display it in the textbook.

You can see that amounts that were positive for the original invoice, *Accounts Receivable*, *Cost of Inventory Sold*, and *Sales Discounts* (see Figure 12-6, page 598), are now negative. Amounts that were negative, *Revenue from Sales*, *Inventory:Necklaces*, and tax amounts, are now positive. The customer has unused credits that can be applied to the outstanding invoice, and the inventory quantity has been restored.

19. Close the **Transaction Journal report** and the **Credit Memo window**

Source Documents

Enter the following source documents for this company. You may need to refer to previous chapters for additional information:

SD Practice

Continue to develop your skills by entering the following source document(s).

Notes

Cash receipts are deposited directly to Bank Chequing and are not held for later deposit.

SD4: Cash Receipt #7-1

Dated January 4, 2012

From B. Perley, cheque #175 for $2,277.00 in payment of account, including the discount for early payment. Reference invoice #315.

SD5: Cheque Copy #1124

Dated January 4, 2012

To Goldcrest Inc., $6,355.80 in payment of account, including the discount for early payment. Reference invoice #GI-2018.

SD6: Cheque Copy #1125

Dated January 6, 2012

To Trevor's Treasures, $4,194.40 in payment of account, including the discount for early payment. Reference invoice #TT-3170.

SD7: Purchase Invoice #SSS-10082

Dated January 6, 2012

From Secure Security Services (use Quick Add for new vendor), $2,500.00 for alarm system plus HST and $1,200.00 plus HST for six months of monitoring service. Purchase invoice totals $4,181.00. Terms: Net 10.

Create new Fixed Asset account: 1500 Alarm System.

Create new Other Current Asset account: 1240 Prepaid Security Services.

SD8: Sales Estimate #35

Dated January 6, 2012

To William Goldwyn for engagement ring with matching wedding bands

	C101 Design	Custom design and setting		$ 3,000.00
6	D102 Diamond	0.25 ct diamond	$1,000.00 ea.	6,000.00
1	D103 Diamond	0.50 ct diamond	2,500.00	2,500.00
	Subtotal - pretax	$11,500.00		
	Discount		10%	−1,150.00
	HST		13%	1,345.50
	Estimate total			$11,695.50

SD9: Cash Receipt #7-2

Dated January 7, 2012

From Wanda Sapphire, cheque #123 for $3,790.08 in payment of account. Apply the credit from the return and then apply the discount and payment to invoice #321.

Adjusting Inventory for Losses

Inventory losses can occur when items are stolen by customers or employees, damaged beyond recovery, or just misplaced. The computer records should reflect the actual stock on hand so customers who make inquiries about availability can be given accurate answers. You can make inventory adjustments on an ongoing basis whenever an item is discovered missing or damaged, as well as periodically when complete inventory stock is taken.

Refer to the following source document as we work through the steps to enter it:

SD10: Memo #1-1

Dated January 8, 2012

From Owner: One 18 inch feather chain 18 Kt necklace (item N104 Necklace) is missing. Adjust inventory for the lost necklace. To record the loss, create a new Expense account: 5200 Inventory Losses. The Adjust Quantity on Hand icon can be accessed from the Company section of the Home page.

SD Instructions
Refer to the following source document and then follow the step-by-step instructions to enter it.

1. **Click** the **Adjust Quantity On Hand icon** in the Company section of the Home page or **choose** the **Vendors menu**, then **choose Inventory Activities,** and **click Adjust Quantity/Value On Hand**

2. The Adjust Quantity/Value on Hand form will be displayed:

Figure 12-13

Notes
Inventory revaluation might be done when stock is damaged but can still be sold, or when the stock is out of date and prices must be marked down. Reducing the asset value will split the expenses for the sale between the cost of goods sold accounts and the account for inventory losses.

From this form you can make adjustments to one or more inventory items based on known quantities or values.

To change the value of inventory, click the Value Adjustment check box in the lower left-hand corner of the form. The default column entries will change to dollar amounts that you can edit.

3. **Enter** **01/08/12** as the date

4. **Press** (tab) to move to the Ref. No. field. We will enter the memo number

5. **Type** **1-1**, then **press** (tab) to move to the Adjustment Account field

6. **Type** **5200 Inventory Losses**, then **press** (tab)

7. **Click** **Set Up** when the Account Not Found message is displayed

8. **Click** the **drop-down arrow** beside the Account Type field

9. **Select** **Expense**

The rest of the default information is correct.

10. **Click**   **Save & Close** to save the new account and return to the form window

11. **Click**   the **scroll bar** to move down the list until item N104 is displayed on the screen

12. **Click**   **N104 Necklace** to select the item (This will ensure that we are working on the correct line)

You can make adjustments by typing the new quantity on hand or by entering the quantity difference if that is known. We know one item is lost so we will enter the difference. Because an item is missing, we need to enter a negative number to reduce inventory.

13. **Press**   (tab) to move the cursor to the Qty Difference column

14. **Type**   **-1**. **Press** (tab) to update the form as shown:

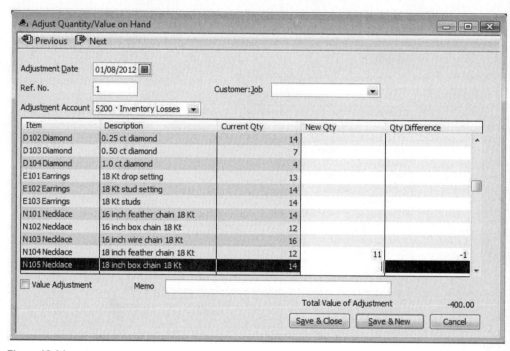

Figure 12-14

The new amount, 11, is now displayed in the New Qty field.

15. **Click**   the **Memo field** so we can add an explanation for the adjustment

16. **Type**   **Item missing**

17. **Check**   your **work** carefully and **make corrections** if necessary

18. **Click**   **Save & Close** to record the adjustment

Source Documents

Enter the following source document for this company. You may need to refer to previous chapters for additional information:

Notes
If a missing item is later recovered, enter an adjustment with a positive number as the difference. Use the same account.

Notes
To make corrections after recording an adjustment, complete another adjustment to reverse the incorrect number and use the same account (e.g., enter 1 in the Qty Different column to reverse this entry).

SDII: **Credit Card Sales Receipt #1001**

Dated January 8, 2012

To Cash Sales customers

1	B101 Bracelet	14 Kt bangle plain	$ 590.00	$ 590.00
3	D101 Diamonds	0.10 ct diamond	400.00 ea.	1,200.00
1	E103 Earrings	18 Kt studs	80.00	80.00
2	N101 Necklaces	16 inch feather chain 18 Kt	600.00 ea.	1,200.00
3	P101 Pendants	18 Kt gold small setting	110.00 ea.	330.00
1	R101 Ring	18 Kt engage. solitaire setting	1,000.00	1,000.00
1	R110 Ring	18 Kt diamond band 0.50 ct total	1,900.00	1,900.00
	R100 Repairs	Jewellery repairs		50.00
	HST		13%	825.50
	Total deposited to Bank Visa account			$7,175.50

Filling a Purchase Order for Inventory Items

When you receive inventory items from a purchase order, you must fill the order in the same way you fill orders for other items.

Refer to the following source document as we work through the steps to enter it:

SDI2: **Purchase Invoice #GI-2819**

Dated January 9, 2012

From Goldcrest Inc., to fill purchase order #125

10	N101 Necklaces	16 inch feather chain 18 Kt	$ 3,000.00
10	N102 Necklaces	16 inch box chain 18 Kt	2,750.00
10	N104 Necklaces	18 inch feather chain 18 Kt	4,000.00
10	N105 Necklaces	18 inch box chain 18 Kt	1,750.00
	HST @ 13%		1,495.00
	Invoice total		$12,995.00

Terms: 1/10, n/30

1. **Click**   the **drop-down arrow** beside the Receive Inventory Icon in the Vendors section of the Home page to view the choices available:

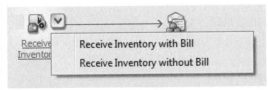

Figure 12-15

2. **Click**   **Receive Inventory with Bill**

3. The Enter Bills form will be displayed:

Notes
The date on the Enter Bills form will be 01/08/2012 unless you have closed the Company file. If you closed it, the date will be 12/15/2007, the current date in the Starter file.

Figure 12-16

4.	**Choose**	**Goldcrest Inc.** from the Vendor field drop-down list
5.	**Click**	**Yes** on the Open PO's Exist message
6.	**Click**	**PO No. 125** to select it
7.	**Click**	**OK** to add the order details to the invoice

If some of the merchandise has not arrived, you can edit the quantity (Qty field) for the item involved. You can also edit prices if they have changed since the order was placed.

8.	**Press**	*tab* to advance to the date field
9.	**Type**	**01/09/12**
10.	**Click**	the **Ref. No. field** and **type GI-2819**

11. The invoice is now complete as shown here:

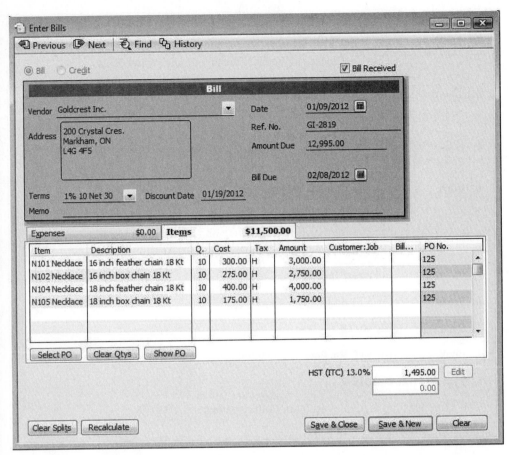

Figure 12-17

12. Check your **work** carefully and **make corrections** if necessary

13. Click **Save & Close** to record the invoice

Returning Purchased Inventory

Purchase returns are normal activities for most businesses. Once the bill is entered, you can enter the return as a credit, as we did for sales returns. As for sales returns, using a credit form causes QuickBooks to reverse the normal purchase debit and credit entries.

Refer to the following source document as we work through the steps to enter it:

SD13: Purchase Return #GI-2819-R

SD Instructions
Refer to the following source document and then follow the step-by-step instructions to enter it.

Dated January 10, 2012

To Goldcrest Inc., 10 Kt chains were delivered instead of 18 Kt chains.

10	N105 Necklaces	18 inch box chain 18 Kt	$1,750.00
	HST @ 13%		227.50
	Purchase return total credit		$1,977.50

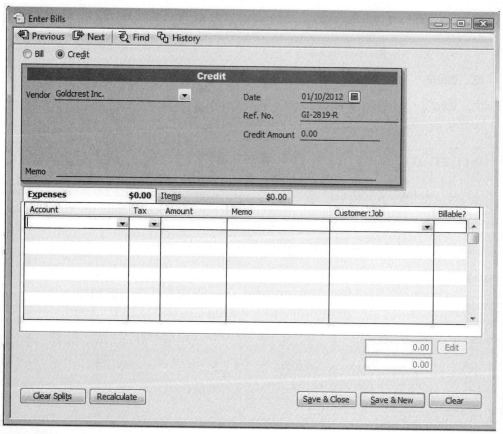

1. **Click** the **Enter Bills icon** in the Vendors section of the Home page or **choose** the **Vendors menu** and **click Enter Bills**

2. The two buttons at the top of the Enter Bills form (below the tool buttons), as shown here ⦿ Bill ○ Credit , control the option of entering a bill or a credit

3. Bill is selected as the default, and we used this option previously. Now we need to enter a credit

4. **Click** the **Credit radio button**

Notice the changes on the form. The heading across the top of the form has changed from Bill to Credit. The Bill Received box and the vendor address section have been removed, and the Amount Due field has changed to Credit Amount.

5. **Choose** **Goldcrest Inc.** as the Vendor

6. **Press** `tab` to move to the date field

7. **Type** **01/10/12**

8. **Click** the **Ref. No. field**. We will link the credit to the original invoice number

9. **Type** **GI-2819-R**

The Expenses tab is displayed by default as shown:

Figure 12-18

The Expenses tab does not allow us to enter inventory items, so we must select the Items tab.

10. Click   the **Items tab** as shown:

Figure 12-19

Item and Quantity fields are now available. The rest of the transaction is entered the same way as purchases and bills are entered.

11. Click   the **drop-down arrow** in the Item field list

12. Choose   **N105 Necklace** to add the item to the bill

13. Press   (tab) twice to advance to the Qty field

14. Type   **10**

The cost from the inventory record is entered. It is not the price we paid, so we need to edit it. We will enter the total cost and let QuickBooks calculate the unit cost. Then we will add the reason for the return as a memo.

15. Press   (tab) until you advance to the Amount field and highlight the amount

16. Type   **1750**

17. Press   (tab) to update the taxes and totals

18. Click   the **Memo field**

19. Type   **10 Kt chains delivered in error**

Notes
Because we are using the credit form, we can enter positive quantities for the return.

20. This completes the credit invoice as shown:

Figure 12-20

Although this looks like an ordinary purchase entry, choosing Credit instead of Bill automatically reverses all amounts.

21. Check your **work** carefully and **make corrections** if necessary

22. Click **Save & Close** to record the credit

Source Documents

Enter the following source documents for this company. You may need to refer to previous chapters for additional information.

SD14: Cash Receipt #7-3 **Dated January 10, 2012**

From William Goldwyn, cheque #2003 for $3,500.00 as the deposit to accept estimate #35 for custom-designed rings. Do not apply to outstanding invoice.

SD15: Credit Card Purchase Invoice #S-4253 **Dated January 10, 2012**

From Stationers (use Quick Add for new vendor), $140.00 plus $18.20 HST for computer and office supplies. Invoice total $158.20 paid in full by credit card.

Entering Credit Card Sales Returns

When a customer returns merchandise and receives a refund, the refund uses the same method of payment as the original purchase. Thus, credit notes are issued for invoices, payments by cheque or cash are usually refunded in cash, and credit card sales returns have a credit applied to the credit card. The procedure is similar for all credits, with the added step of issuing cash or a credit card credit for the refund.

Refer to the following source document as we work through the steps to enter it:

SD16: Credit Card Sales Return #1001-R

Dated January 11, 2012

One Cash Sales customer returned a pendant. Issue a credit card refund.

1	P101 Pendant	18 Kt gold small setting	$110.00	$110.00
1	D101 Diamond	0.10 ct diamond	400.00	400.00
	HST		13%	66.30
	Total credit card refund			$576.30

1. **Click**   the **Refunds & Credits icon**   or **choose** the **Customers menu** and **click Create Credit Memos/Refunds**

The Create Credit Memos/Refunds form opens. Refer to Saffire's return (see page 601) for information on entering the credit memo.

2. **Choose**   **Cash Sales** as the Customer (Normally, you would enter a customer name on this form)

3. **Enter**   **01/11/12** as the date

4. **Enter**   **1001-R** in the Credit No. field

5. **Choose**   **P101 Pendants** as the first item

6. **Enter**   **1** as the quantity

7. **Choose**   **D101 Diamond** as the second item

8. **Enter**   **1** as the quantity

Now we must indicate that we are providing a refund rather than a credit memo. The Use Credit to button   🏠 Use Credit to ▼   is located at the right end of the tool bar and is used to determine how we will process the credit.

9. **Click**   the **drop-down arrow** beside the Use Credit to button to view the choices available:

🏠 Use Credit to ▼

    Give refund

    Apply to invoice

Figure 12-21

10. Click   the **Give Refund** option to open the Issue a Refund form:

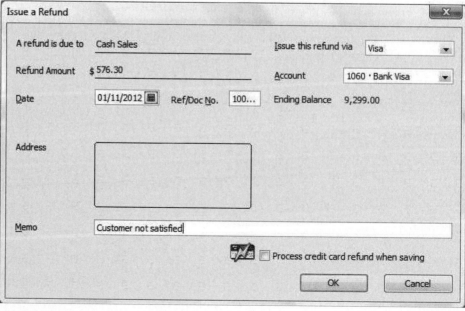

Figure 12-22

The default bank account is selected for the refund cheque. However, we are issuing a credit card refund so we need to select the bank account that credit card receipts are deposited to, *1060 Bank Visa*. *Accounts Receivable* is entered as the default account that will be debited for the refund. Because the credit memo uses *Accounts Receivable* as the default account as well, we need to reverse that entry (refer to the Journal Report in Figure 12-26 on page 616).

11. Click   the **drop-down arrow** in the Account field

12. Click   **1160 Bank Visa**

13. Enter   **1001-R** as the number in the Ref/Doc No. field

14. Enter   an **appropriate memo** to complete the transaction as shown:

Figure 12-23

15. Check your **work** carefully and **make corrections** if necessary

16. Click **OK** to display the updated Create Credit Memos/Refund form:

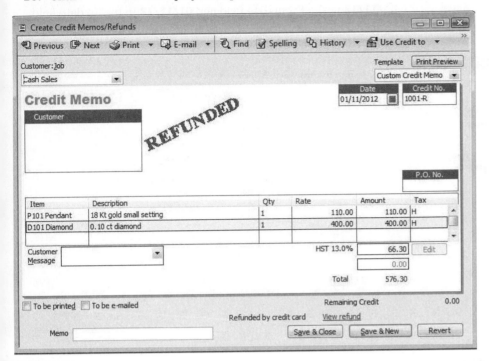

Figure 12-24

Notice that the Credit memo now has "Refunded" stamped across it. To view the refund, click the View Refund link on the bottom right-hand corner of the form.

17. Click **Save & New** to record the refund

18. Click [Previous] and **display** the **credit memo** we just entered

19. Press [ctrl] + **Y** to view the Transaction Journal:

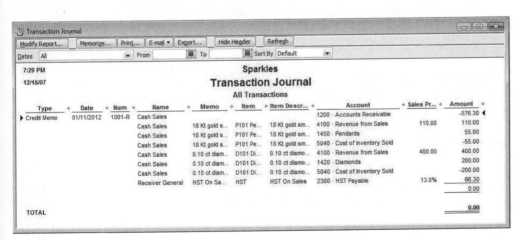

Figure 12-25

Notes
The Trans # and Class columns have been removed from the report.

This screen shows the journal entry for the credit memo.

20. Close the **Transaction Journal Report**

QuickBooks actually created two journal entries. One transaction is created for the credit memo and the other transaction is created for the credit card refund. We will look at the Journal Report for January 11 to view both transactions.

21.	**Choose**	the **Reports menu**, then **choose Accountant & Taxes**, and **click Journal** to open the report
22.	**Enter**	**01/11/12** in the From date field and **01/11/12** in the To date field
23.	**Press**	`tab` or **click Refresh button** to view the two entries:

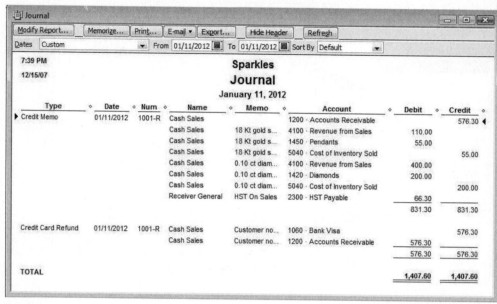

Figure 12-26

In the first entry, created by the credit memo, QuickBooks has credited (decreased) the *Accounts Receivable* account and debited (decreased) the *Revenue from Sales* account to reverse the original sale. The *Cost of Inventory Sold* account is also reduced and the inventory assets accounts have increased because the inventory was restored. The quantity on hand for these items is also increased. This part of the transaction by itself would leave the *Accounts Receivable* account with a credit balance. The cheque in the second entry, created by the refund, reverses this by debiting *Accounts Receivable* and crediting (reducing) the appropriate bank account instead.

24.	**Close**	the Journal Report

Source Documents

Enter the following source document for this company. You may have to refer to other chapters for additional information:

SD17: Sales Invoice #322   **Dated January 11, 2012**

To Sadie Hawkings (QuickAdd new customer). Edit the invoice number.

1	E102 Earrings	18 Kt stud setting	$ 80.00	$ 80.00
2	D101 Diamonds	0.10 ct diamond	400.00 ea.	800.00
	HST		13%	114.40
	Sales total			$994.40

Terms: 1/5, n/30.

Entering Credit Card Purchase Returns

Returns of items purchased on a credit card are entered on the credit card charge form, just as returns on account were entered on the Enter Bills form. Refer to the following source document as we work through the steps to enter it:

SD18: **Credit Card Purchase Return #S-4253-R**

Dated January 12, 2012

Return to Stationers, business forms costing $40.00 plus $5.20 HST (the form size does not fit store printer). Total credit $45.20 applied to credit card.

1. **Click** the **Enter Credit Card Charges icon** in the Banking section of the Home page or **choose** the **Banking menu** and **click Enter Credit Card Charges**

The default setting is to enter a Purchase/Charge, as we have done for all previous credit card transactions. Now we need to enter a credit.

2. The buttons on the Enter Credit Card Charges form, as shown here, will allow us to make this change: ⦿ Purchase/Charge ⦾ Refund/Credit

3. **Click** **Refund/Credit** to change the form

The Refund/Credit radio button is now selected and the heading on the cheque portion of the form has changed colour and has changed from Credit Card Purchase/Charge to Credit Card Refund/Credit. QuickBooks will now reverse all the usual entries when entering a transaction on this form.

4. **Choose** **Stationers** as the Vendor

5. **Enter** **01/12/12** as the transaction date

6. **Enter** **S-4253-R** as the reference number to connect this to the earlier purchase

7. **Choose** **1340 Office & Computer Supplies** from the Account field list (it should already be displayed as the default)

8. **Press** (tab) to advance to the Tax field

9. **Type** **H**

10. **Press** (tab) to advance to the Amount field

11. **Type** **40**

12. **Click** the **Memo field** so we can enter the reason for the return

13. **Type** **Incorrect form size for printer**

14. This completes the return as shown:

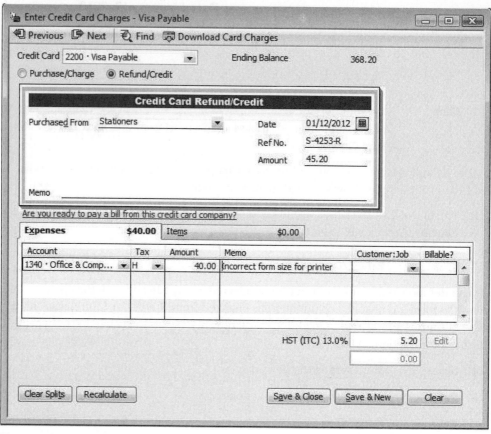

Figure 12-27

15. Check your **work** carefully and **make corrections** if necessary

16. Click **Save & New** to record the return and prepare to review the Transaction Journal report

17. Click **Previous** and **press** `ctrl` **+ Y** to view the transaction journal report:

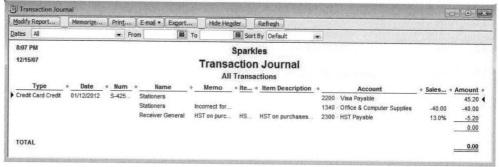

Figure 12-28

Notes
Columns have been removed from this report.

The Transaction Journal report shows that all original amounts have been reversed. The *Visa Payable* account has been debited to reduce the liability, the *HST Payable* account has been credited to increase the liability, and the *Office & Computer Supplies* account has been credited to decrease the asset account balance.

18. Close the **Transaction Journal report**

19. Close the **Enter Credit Card Charges** form

Building Inventory Items

The next transaction requires us to create a new inventory item that is made up of other items. Then we can use this definition to build the new item as required. Refer to the following source document as we work through the steps to enter it:

SD19: Assembly #A-01

SD Instructions
Refer to the following source document and then follow the step-by-step instructions to enter it.

Dated January 12, 2012

The store will sell some items as sets for discounted prices. The sets include a necklace with a diamond pendant and matching diamond earrings. Create new Inventory Assembly item: S101.00 Gift Sets (Necklace, pendant, and earrings).

3	D102 Diamonds	0.25 ct diamond
1	E102 Earrings	18 Kt stud setting
1	N101 Necklace	16 inch feather chain 18 Kt
1	P102 Pendant	18 Kt gold medium setting

Selling price for the set will be $3,500.00.
Cost of Goods Sold account: 5040 Cost of Inventory Sold
Revenue account: 4100 Revenue from Sales
Sales Tax Code: H
Asset account: Create new Other Asset subaccount: 1480 Sets
   (Sets is a subaccount of 1400 Inventory.)
Build point: 0
Assemble two Gift Sets using these component items.

First we must create the new item.

Creating Assembly Items

Notes
Item descriptions are shown in parentheses after the item number and name.

1. **Click**   the **Items & Services icon** in the Company Section of the Home page to open the Item List

You can also access the Item List in other ways:

a) **Choose** the **Lists menu** and **click Item List**; or,

b) **Choose** the **Sales Tax menu** and **click Item List**; or,

c) **Choose** the **Customers menu** and **click Item List**; or,

d) **Choose** the **Vendors menu** and **click Item List**

We are now ready to create a new item.

2. **Click**   the **Item** button and **click New** or **press** [ctrl] **+ N**

3. The New Item form opens with the item Type list displayed:

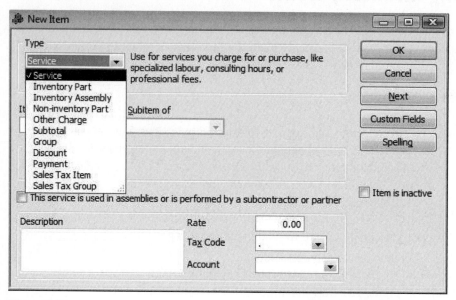

Notes

Notice that Payment is listed as an item type. You can set up this type of item to enter customer down payments directly on the invoice form.

Figure 12-29

Because we are using inventory in this company file, the Type list has been expanded from the ones we saw in previous chapters. We are creating an Inventory Assembly item.

4. Click   **Inventory Assembly**

5. The New Item form changes to the one displayed here when this type is selected:

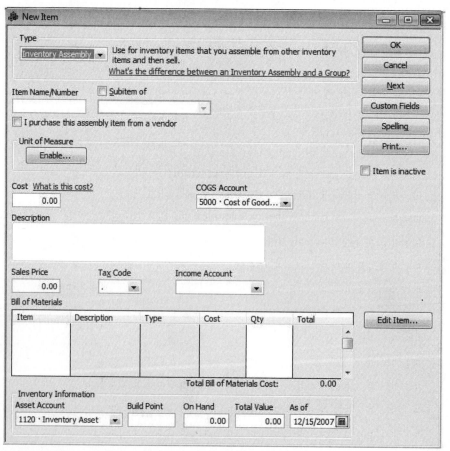

Notes

The *As of* field in a new inventory part item defaults to 12/15/2007 in the sample file.

Figure 12-30

On this form, we define how we want to create the new item, that is, what components are needed and how many of each. We also designate the default asset and cost of goods sold accounts. QuickBooks has created default accounts already, but we will change them to match our Chart of Accounts.

6. **Click**   *(tab)* to advance to the Item Name/Number field

7. **Type**   **S101 Gift Sets**

The item is not purchased so we should leave the *I purchase this assembly item from a vendor* option unchecked. We need to enter the COGS (cost of goods sold) Account. This expense account is increased each time we sell the item.

The cost field is used to enter the total cost of the assembly. It can either be the total cost of the components that you enter in the Bill of Materials table, or it can include a mark-up and other costs not listed in the Bill of Materials table. As you enter items in the Bill of Materials table, the total cost of the components will be calculated by QuickBooks. You may want to wait until the amount is calculated before entering the cost in this field. We will leave this field blank for now.

8. **Click**   the **drop-down arrow** in the COGS Account field

9. **Choose**   **5040 Cost of Inventory Sold** to add this as the default expense account

10. **Press**   *(tab)* to advance to the Description field

11. **Type**   **Necklace, pendant, and earrings**

12. **Press**   *(tab)* to advance to the Sales Price field

13. **Type**   **3500**

14. **Press**   *(tab)* to advance to the Sales Tax Code field

15. **Type**   **H**

16. **Press**   *(tab)* to advance to the Income Account field

17. **Choose**   **4100 Revenue from Sales** from the drop-down list

18. **Press**   *(tab)* to advance to the Item field in the Bill of Materials section

This section will list the inventory part items that make up the set, along with the number or quantity of each item that is required.

19. **Click**   the **drop-down arrow** in the Item field so we can select the first component item

20. **Choose**   **D102 Diamond** to add the item to the list

21. **Press**   *(tab)* to advance to the Qty field

22. **Type**   **3**

23. **Press**   *(tab)* to advance to the next Item field line

24. **Choose**   **E102 Earrings**

25. **Press**   *(tab)* to advance to the Qty field

26. **Type**   **1**

27. **Press**   *(tab)* to move to the next item line

28. **Choose**   **N101 Necklace**

Notes

QuickBooks creates the Cost of Goods Sold and Inventory Asset accounts automatically when we choose Inventory Part or Inventory Assembly as the item type. And it enters these as default accounts for the item, so you need to change the selections.

You can delete these accounts because they are not used, but QuickBooks will create them again as soon as you create another Inventory item.

29.	**Press**	(tab) to advance to the Qty field
30.	**Type**	1
31.	**Press**	(tab) to advance to the next Item field line
32.	**Choose**	**P102 Pendant**
33.	**Press**	(tab) to advance to the Qty field
34.	**Type**	1

Now we must enter the default asset account. We will create a new account for the items we sell as sets. This asset account is increased when we buy (create) the item and reduced when we sell the item.

35.	**Click**	the **drop-down arrow** in the Asset Account field. Scroll up and **click** the <**Add New**> option
36.		Other Current Asset is correctly selected as the Account Type
37.	**Press**	(tab) to advance to the Number field
38.	**Type**	**1480**
39.	**Press**	(tab) to advance to the Account Name field
40.	**Type**	**Sets**
41.	**Click**	the **box** beside the Subaccount of field to add a ✓
42.	**Choose**	**1400 Inventory** from the account list as the parent account
43.	**Click**	**Save & Close** to return to the New Item form

Notes
The program does not mark the item for "re-ordering" or building on reports if the build point is zero.

The next field, Build Point, defines the minimum quantity for the item. Once the item reaches this level, the program displays a reminder in the Reminders List that we need to build or assemble more items. Inventory reports also flag items that are low in stock. We can assemble these sets at any time so we do not need to keep extra sets on hand.

Notice that the total bill of materials cost is displayed directly below the table. We will enter this amount in the Cost field.

44.	**Click**	the **Cost field**
45.	**Enter**	**2000**

The remaining fields will be updated when we build and sell the items, so the form is complete as shown:

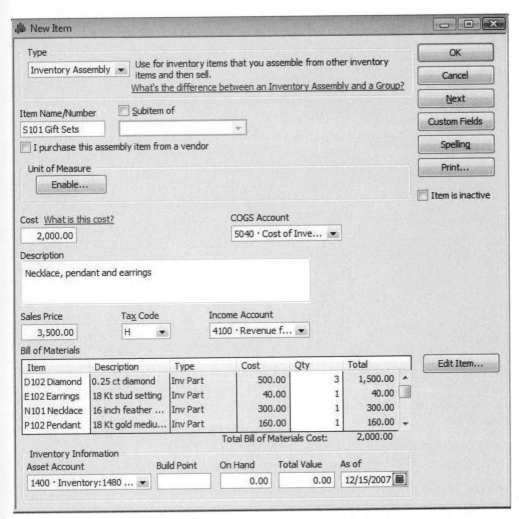

Figure 12-31

We need to complete this definition part of the build process only once for an item.

46. Check your **work** carefully and **make corrections** if necessary

47. Click **OK** to save the new inventory assembly item

48. Close the **Item List**

Building Assembly Items

Once we have defined the assembly item, we can proceed to the build process.

1. Click the **Build Assemblies icon** in the Company Section of the Home page or **choose** the **Vendors menu**, then **choose Inventory Activities**, and **click Build Assemblies** to open the Build Assemblies form:

Notes
You can also open the Build Assemblies form from the Item List window. Click the Activities button at the bottom of the Item List window, and then click Build Assemblies.
Or, open the Build Assemblies form by choosing Vendors from the menu, clicking Inventory Activities, and then clicking Build Assemblies.

Figure 12-32

2. Click   the **drop-down arrow** in the Assembly Item field

The Gift Sets Assembly Item we created is displayed on the list.

3. Click   **S101 Gift Sets** to add the item to the form

To complete the form, we must define the number of items we are building. We will enter this quantity next.

4. Click   in the **Quantity to Build** field below the list of components

5. Type   **2**

6. Press   (tab) to update the form:

The quantities for each component have been added to the form based on the amount entered in the Quantity to Build field. The date should be correct from the previous transaction. We will add a reference number and comment (memo) to complete the form.

7. Enter   **01/12/12** in the Date field if necessary

8. Click   the **Build Ref. No.** field

9. Type   **A-01**

10. Press   (tab) to advance to the Memo field

11. Type   **Create gift sets**

12. The Build Assemblies form is now complete as shown here:

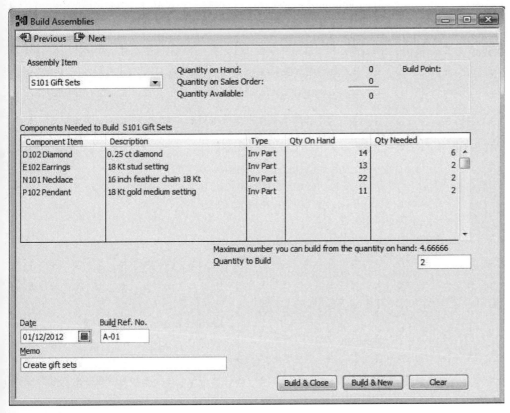

Figure 12-33

13. Check your **work** carefully and **make corrections** if necessary

14. Click **Build & Close** to create the next assembly item

Look at the Journal report to view how QuickBooks has entered the transaction. The journal entry is displayed here:

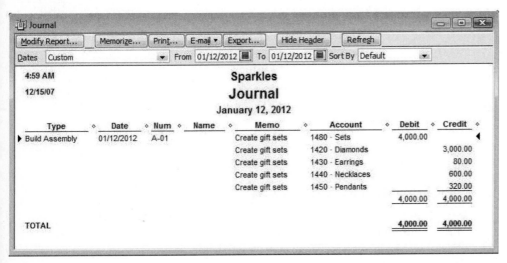

Figure 12-34

Notes
To display this Journal Report, choose the Reports menu, then choose Accountant & Taxes, and click Journal. Enter 01/12/12 in the From and To date fields for the report.

The asset values have been transferred from the components to the new item. The inventory quantities have also been updated.

Source Documents

Enter the following source documents for this company. You may need to refer to previous chapters for additional information:

SD20: **Assembly #A-02**

Dated January 12, 2012

Create new Inventory Assembly item for S102 Wedding Band Sets (Matching wedding bands).

1	R103 Ring	18 Kt band narrow plain
1	R104 Ring	18 Kt band wide plain

Selling price for the set will be $750.00.
Cost of Goods Sold account: 5040 Cost of Inventory Sold
Revenue account: 4100 Revenue from Sales
Sales Tax Code: H
Asset account: 1480 Sets
Build point: 0
Assemble two Wedding Band Sets using these component items.

SD21: **Purchase Order #126**

Dated January 13, 2012

To Trevor's Treasures

Jewellery Parts	$800.00
HST @ 13%	104.00
Purchase order total	$904.00

SD22: Sales Invoice #323

Dated January 14, 2012

To Bess Perley

1	B105 Bracelet	14 Kt link solitaire setting	$ 370.00	$ 370.00
1	N104 Necklace	18 inch feather chain 18 Kt	800.00	800.00
1	E102 Earrings	18 Kt stud setting	80.00	80.00
2	D102 Diamonds	0.25 ct diamond	1,000.00	2,000.00
	Subtotal - pretax			$3,250.00
	Discount		10%	−325.00
	HST		13%	380.25
	Sales total			$3,305.25

Terms: 1/5, n/30.

SD23: Purchase Invoice #SC-38105

Dated January 14, 2012

From Sprint Canada, $120.00 plus $15.60 HST for one month of telephone and Internet service. Invoice totals $135.60. Terms: Net 15 days.

SD24: **Purchase Invoice #FI-2012-34**

Dated January 14, 2012

From Faithful Insurers, $4,800.00 plus $624.00 HST for six months of prepaid insurance. Invoice totals $5,424.00. Create a new Other Current Asset account: 1260 Prepaid Insurance. Terms: Net 15 days. Save the new terms.

SD25: **Cheque Copy #1126**

Dated January 15, 2012

To Secure Security Services, $4,181.00 in payment of invoice #SSS-10082.

SD26:

EMPLOYEE TIME SUMMARY SHEET #2012-1

Date: January 15, 2012 (for the pay period ending January 15, 2012)

Name of Employee	Regular Hours	Overtime Hours	Sick Leave Hours	Vacation Hours	Advances Received/ Advances Repaid
Garnet Y. Amarald	75	–	–	8	–
Jadine R. Amethyst	74	6	8	–	–

a. Using Employee Time Summary Sheet #2012-1 and the Employee Information Sheet, complete payroll for two employees.

b. Amarald took one day of vacation and Amethyst took one day of sick leave.

c. Manually prepare cheques #1127 and #1128.

SD27: Sales Invoice #324

Dated January 15, 2012

To Goldie Carat

1	R101 Ring	18 Kt engage. solitaire setting	$1,000.00	$1,000.00
1	D104 Diamond	1.0 ct diamond	6,900.00	6,900.00
	HST		13%	1,027.00
●	Sales total			$8,927.00

Terms: 1/5, n/30.

SD28: Credit Card Sales Receipt #1002

Dated January 15, 2012

To Cash Sales customers

1	B106 Bracelet	14 Kt link 3 stone setting	$ 430.00	$ 430.00
6	D101 Diamonds	0.10 ct diamond	400.00 ea.	2,400.00
2	D102 Diamonds	0.25 ct diamond	1,000.00 ea.	2,000.00
1	E101 Earrings	18 Kt drop setting	140.00	140.00
1	E102 Earrings	18 Kt stud setting	80.00	80.00
1	N101 Necklace	16 inch feather chain 18 Kt	600.00	600.00
1	N102 Necklace	16 inch box chain 18 Kt	550.00	550.00
2	P102 Pendants	18 Kt gold medium setting	320.00 ea.	640.00
1	R101 Ring	18 Kt engage. solitaire setting	1,000.00	1,000.00
1	R104 Ring	18 Kt band wide plain	570.00	570.00
1	R105 Ring	18 Kt band narrow 3 st. 0.25 ct	1,050.00	1,050.00
1	S101 Gift Set	Necklace, pendant and earrings	3,500.00	3,500.00
	R100 Repairs	Jewellery repairs		90.00
	HST		13%	1,696.50

Total deposited to Bank Visa account $14,746.50

Notes
Remember to change the default account for the Visa sales deposit.

SD29: Cheque Copy #1129

Dated January 18, 2012

To Goldcrest Inc., $10,920.00 in payment of account, including the discount and credit. Change the discount amount to $97.50. Reference invoice #GI-2819.

Notes
The discount needs to be reduced because of the credit for the return.
Click the Set Discount button and edit the discount amount.

SD30: Purchase Order #127

Dated January 18, 2012

To Goldcrest Inc.

10	E101 Earrings	18 Kt drop setting	$ 700.00
10	E102 Earrings	18 Kt stud setting	400.00
10	E103 Earrings	18 Kt studs	400.00
10	N105 Necklaces	18 inch box chain 18 Kt	3,750.00
	HST @ 13%		682.50
Purchase order total			$5,932.50

SD31: Purchase Invoice #TT-4821

Dated January 19, 2012

To Trevor's Treasures, to fill purchase order #126

Jewellery Parts	$800.00
HST @ 13%	104.00
Purchase invoice total	$904.00

Terms: 2/10, n/30.

SD32: Credit Card Purchase Invoice #HSS-8002

Dated January 19, 2012

From Hardware Surplus Supplies (use Quick Add for new vendor), $45.00 plus $5.85 HST for glass and other cleaning products. Invoice totalling $50.85 was paid in full by credit card.

SD33: Cash Receipt #7-4

Dated January 19, 2012

From Bess Perley, cheque #204 for $3,276.00 in payment of account, including the discount for early payment. Reference invoice #323.

SD34: Cash Receipt #7-5

Dated January 20, 2012

From William Goldwyn, cheque #2108 for $4,600.00 in payment of invoice #297.

SD35: Cash Receipt #7-6

Dated January 20, 2012

From Goldie Carat, cheque #13 for $8,848.00 in payment of account, including the discount for early payment. Reference invoice #324.

SD36: Sales Order #25

Dated January 21, 2012

From Goldie Carat, including customization of some pieces

1	E101 Earrings	18 Kt drop setting	$ 140.00	$ 140.00
2	D102 Diamonds	0.25 ct diamond	1,000.00 ea.	2,000.00
1	D103 Diamond	0.50 ct diamond	2,500.00	2,500.00
1	P102 Pendant	18 Kt gold medium setting	320.00	320.00
1	N101 Necklace	16 inch feather chain 18 Kt	600.00	600.00
	C101 Design	Custom design and setting		500.00
	Subtotal - pretax			$6,060.00
	Discount		10%	−606.00
	HST		13%	709.02
	Sales Total			$6,163.02

SD37: Credit Card Sales Receipt #1003

Dated January 22, 2012

To Cash Sales customers

1	B104 Bracelet	14 Kt link plain	$ 400.00	$ 400.00
8	D101 Diamonds	0.10 ct diamond	400.00 ea.	3,200.00
2	D102 Diamonds	0.25 ct diamond	1,000.00 ea.	2,000.00
1	E101 Earrings	18 Kt drop setting	140.00	140.00
2	E102 Earrings	18 Kt stud setting	80.00/pr.	160.00
2	N106 Necklaces	18 inch wire chain 18 Kt	610.00 ea.	1,220.00
2	P101 Pendants	18 Kt gold small setting	110.00 ea.	220.00
1	R103 Ring	18 Kt band narrow plain	375.00	375.00
1	R104 Ring	18 Kt band wide plain	570.00	570.00
1	S102 Wed. Bd St	Matching wedding bands	750.00	750.00
	R100 Repairs	Jewellery repairs		50.00
	HST		13%	1,181.05
	Total deposited to Bank Visa account			$10,266.05

SD38: Memo #1-2

Dated January 23, 2012

From Owner: One 18 Kt gold medium setting pendant (item P102 Pendant) was damaged beyond repair. Adjust inventory for the damaged item.

SD39: Credit Card Purchase Invoice #GE-6161

Dated January 23, 2012

From Glass Experts (use Quick Add for new vendor), $300.00 plus $39.00 HST for replacing display cabinet glass. Invoice totalling $339.00 was paid in full by credit card. Use the Maintenance Expenses account.

SD40: Cheque Copy #1130

Dated January 24, 2012

To Trevor's Treasures, $888.00 in payment of account, including the discount for early payment. Reference invoice #TT-4821.

SD41: Purchase Order #128

Dated January 24, 2012

To Kimberley Mines

10	D102 Diamonds	0.25 ct diamond	$5,000.00
6 oz	Gold		3,624.00
	HST @ 13%		1,121.12
	Purchase order total		$9,745.12

Handling Out-of-Stock Inventory Items

Sometimes the items needed for a sale are out of stock. When the item your customer wants to buy is out of stock, you can enter a sales order for the customer for the outstanding items. QuickBooks provides a warning like the following whenever you enter a quantity on a sales receipt or invoice that is greater than the amount on hand:

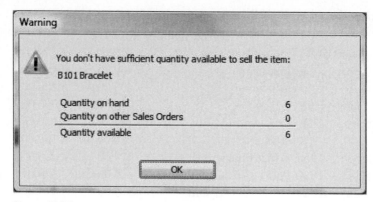

Figure 12-35

The specific wording of the warning will vary with the starting point (the form you are using and the stage in the transaction), as we will see in the following examples.

> **IMPORTANT:**
>
> In QuickBooks Premier, this warning will not stop you from completing the sale and thus entering into negative inventory. Since this is not proper accounting practice, you should review the Inventory Stock Status by Item report and determine how many items you have available to sell before continuing. If you have physically received the inventory, but have not received it in QuickBooks, you should receive it in QuickBooks first, before continuing with the sale.

Selling Out-of-Stock Inventory

SD Instructions
Refer to the following source document and then follow the step-by-step instructions to enter it.

Refer to the following source document as we work through the steps to enter it:

SD42: Sales Invoice #325

Dated January 24, 2012

To William Goldwyn for ring set, to partially fill estimate #35. Some diamonds were out of stock. Create sales order #26 for the items not available.

	C101 Design	Custom design and setting		$ 3,000.00
6	D102 Diamonds	0.25 ct diamond	$1,000.00 ea.	6,000.00
1	D103 Diamond	0.50 ct diamond	2,500.00	2,500.00
	Discount		10%	−1,150.00
	Taxable subtotal			10,350.00
	HST		13%	1,345.50
	Sales total			$11,695.50

Terms: 1/5, n/30.

1. **Open**   the **Create Invoices** form
2. **Select**   **William Goldwyn** as the customer
3. **Click**   on **Estimate 35** to bring the items into the invoice
4. The following warning is displayed:

Notes
QuickBooks Premier will still allow you to proceed with the sale of these items even though you do not have sufficient quantity on hand to sell. You should be very careful of this because this will create negative inventory in QuickBooks. This warning should prompt you to stop the transaction and review the inventory stock status report.

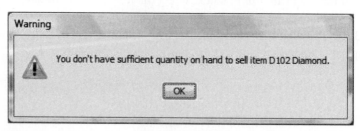

Figure 12-36

5. **Click**   **OK** to continue and the invoice is displayed on the screen with all inventory items (including the one out of stock) invoiced:

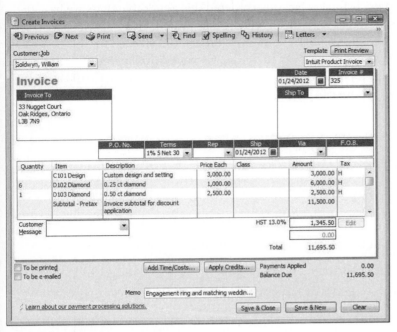

Figure 12-37

Before we enter this item, we will stop and look at the Inventory Stock Status report (which will be reviewed in more detail later in this chapter) to view how many items are actually available for sale. We'll leave the invoice open on the screen while reviewing the report.

6. **Choose**   **Reports** from the menu

7. **Click**   **Inventory** and then **click Inventory Stock Status by Item**

The date displayed on the report reflects the current date. Remember the current date in the sample company is 12/15/2007. We'll change the date to the current date of the invoice so we can see the inventory status as of the day we're entering the invoice.

8. **Type**   **01/24/12** in the From field

9. **Press**   (tab)

10. **Type**   **01/24/12** in the To field

11. **Press**   (tab) or **click** the **Refresh button** to update the report:

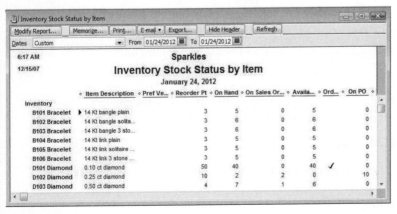

Figure 12-38

If you refer to Figure 12-37, you'll see that the customer has ordered 6 of item D102 and 1 of item D103. In Figure 12-38, you can see that we have 2 of item D102 on hand, 2 on sales orders (other customers have also ordered this item); therefore, we have 0 available. We can also see that we have 10 on purchase order and are waiting for a shipment of these items from our vendor. We have 7 of item D103 on hand but 1 is on a sales order, making 6 of these items available; therefore, we have 1 available for this invoice.

After reviewing this report, we have determined that we have only 1 D103 available to sell on this invoice, and we can also invoice for the custom design and setting service charge.

12.	**Close**	the **Inventory Stock Status by Item** report and **return** to the **invoice**
13.	**Type**	**01/24/12** as the invoice date
14.	**Type**	**1** in the quantity field for item C101 Design
15.	**Type**	**0** in the quanity field for item D102 Diamond
16.	**Accept**	**1** in the quantity field for item D103 Diamond
17.	**Press**	⌨tab to update the information
18.	The updated invoice is displayed as shown:

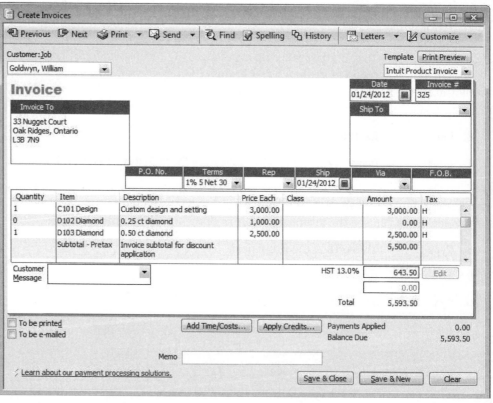

Figure 12-39

To keep track of items your customers want to purchase, you create sales orders. Create a sales order for William Goldwyn for 6 of item D102.

19.	**Click**	**Save & Close**
20.	**Open**	the **Create Sales Orders** form and **enter** the following **sales order**:

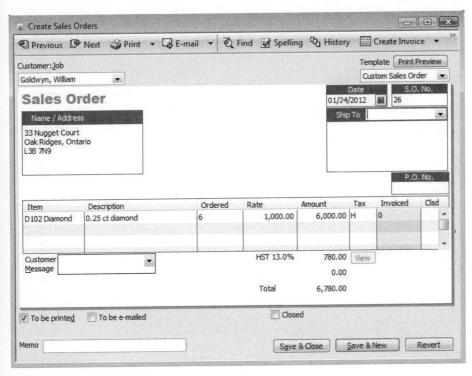

Figure 12-40

21. **Click**   **Save & Close**

Assembling Items with Insufficient Stock

Refer to the following source document as you process the next assembly:

SD43: **Assembly #A-03**

Dated January 25, 2012

Assemble three S101 Gift Sets. Delay assembly because of insufficient stock.

1. When we enter the quantity to build for the assembly of Gift Sets, we are presented with the following warning:

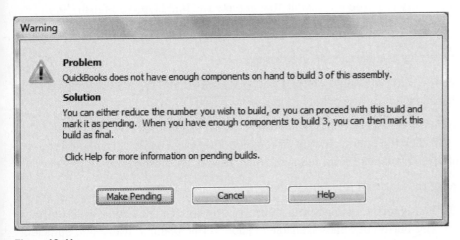

Figure 12-41

SD Instructions
Refer to the following source document and then follow the step-by-step instructions to enter it.

Notes
The Build Assemblies form window always includes a field to insert the Maximum number that you can build from the quantity on hand. Entering a value in this field will also let you know whether you can complete the assembly you want.

Again, QuickBooks recognizes that the items needed are not available. We can cancel and return to the transaction to enter a different quantity, or proceed and mark the build as pending. We will proceed.

2. Click the **Make Pending** button to return to the Build Assemblies form:

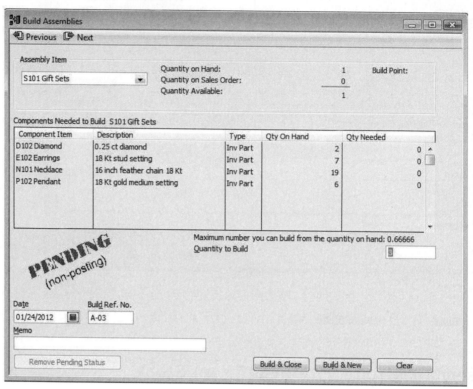

Figure 12-42

The Build Assemblies form is now stamped with the note PENDING (non-posting) to let you know that this transaction is not complete.

3. Click **Build & New** to build the next assembly item

Completing the Pending Assembly

When the inventory required is available to complete the build, you can finish the transaction. Display the Build Assemblies transaction that is pending to the screen and then change its status.

You can display the transaction in two ways:

- Open the Build Assemblies form. Click Previous until the transaction you want is displayed on the screen; or

- Choose the Reports menu, then choose Inventory, and click Pending Builds. Double click the build you want to complete (see page 643). This method is preferred if you have recorded many build assembly transactions.

To change the status of the transaction,

- Click the Remove Pending Status button on the bottom left-hand corner of the form. This button becomes available as soon as the quantity available is sufficient to complete the build; or

- Choose the Edit Menu and click Mark Build as Final.

- Click Build & Close to record the assembly.

Source Documents

Enter the following source documents for this company. You may need to refer to previous chapters for additional information:

SD Practice
Continue to develop your skills by entering the following source document(s).

SD44: Assembly #A-04

Dated January 25, 2012

Assemble three S102 Wedding Band Sets using defined component items.

SD45: Cash Receipt #7-7

Dated January 25, 2012

From Sadie Hawkings, cheque #1778 for $994.40 in full payment of invoice #322.

SD46: Purchase Invoice #HO-500834

Dated January 25, 2012

From Hydro One, $155.00 plus $20.15 HST for one month of hydro and heating service. Invoice totals $175.15. Terms: Net 10 days.

SD47: Cheque Copy #1131

Dated January 25, 2012

To Faithful Insurers, $5,424.00 in payment of invoice #FI-2012-34.

SD48: Cheque Copy #1132

Dated January 26, 2012

To Sprint Canada, $135.60 in payment of invoice #SC-38105.

SD49: Sales Invoice #326

Dated January 28, 2012

To Pearl Black (set up new customer)

1	N104 Necklace	18 inch feather chain 18 Kt	$ 800.00	$ 800.00
1	D102 Diamond	0.25 ct diamond	1,000.00	1,000.00
1	P101 Pendant	18 Kt gold small setting	110.00	110.00
	HST		13%	248.30
	Sales total			$2,158.30

Terms: 1/5, n/30.

Notes
Pearl Black
2333 Onyx Rd. #408
Toronto, ON M6D 2L9
Tel: (647) 499-1019
Credit limit: $4,000.00
Terms: 1/5, n/30

SD50: Bank Debit Memo #GT-54328

Dated January 28, 2012

From Golddiggers Trust, cheque #1778 from Sadie Hawkings for $994.40 was returned as NSF. Create sales invoice #327 for the amount of the NSF cheque and the $30.00 administrative charge. Invoice totals $1,024.40. Terms: Due on receipt.

SD51: Purchase Invoice #GI-3622

Dated January 28, 2012

From Goldcrest Inc., to fill purchase order #127

10	E101 Earrings	18 Kt drop setting	$ 700.00
10	E102 Earrings	18 Kt stud setting	400.00
10	E103 Earrings	18 Kt studs	400.00
10	N105 Necklaces	18 inch box chain 18 Kt	3,750.00
	HST @ 7%		682.50
	Purchase invoice total		$5,932.50

Terms: 1/10, n/30.

SD52: Credit Card Sales Receipt #1004

Dated January 29, 2012

To Cash Sales customers

1	B103 Bracelet	14 Kt bangle 3 stone setting	$ 625.00	$ 625.00
1	B105 Bracelet	14 Kt link solitaire setting	370.00	370.00
10	D101 Diamonds	0.10 ct diamond	400.00 ea.	4,000.00
4	E101 Earrings	18 Kt drop setting	140.00/pr.	560.00
3	E102 Earrings	18 Kt stud setting	80.00/pr.	240.00
2	N106 Necklaces	18 inch wire chain 18 Kt	610.00 ea.	1,220.00
3	P101 Pendants	18 Kt gold small setting	110.00 ea.	330.00
1	P102 Pendant	18 Kt gold medium setting	320.00	320.00
1	P103 Pendant	18 Kt gold large setting	630.00	630.00
1	R103 Ring	18 Kt band narrow plain	375.00	375.00
1	R104 Ring	18 Kt band wide plain	570.00	570.00
1	R109 Ring	18 Kt diamond band 0.25 ct	1,200.00	1,200.00
1	S101 Gift Set	Necklace, pendant, and earrings	3,500.00	3,500.00
1	S102 Wed. Bd St	Matching wedding bands	750.00	750.00
	R100 Repairs	Jewellery repairs		160.00
	HST		13%	1,930.50

Total deposited to Bank Visa account $16,780.50

SD53: Cheque Copy #1133

Dated January 29, 2012

To Hydro One, $175.15 in payment of invoice #HO-500834.

SD54: Bank Credit Memo #GT-819788

Dated January 30, 2012

From Golddiggers Trust: Preauthorized withdrawals from the chequing account for

Mortgage ($155.00 principal and $405.00 interest) $560.00

Bank loan ($210.00 principal and $80.00 interest)   290.00

Notes
Net Revenue from Sales for January was $61,424.00 (i.e., revenue less 10 percent volume discount = 62,675.00 − 1,251.00).

Revenue from Services for January was $3,350.00.

SD55:

EMPLOYEE TIME SUMMARY SHEET #2012-2

Date: January 31, 2012 (for the pay period ending January 31, 2012)

Name of Employee	Regular Hours	Overtime Hours	Sick Leave Hours	Vacation Hours	Advances Received/ Advances Repaid
Garnet Y. Amarald	85	—	—	—	—
Jadine R. Amethyst	85	10	—	—	$200.00

a. Using Employee Time Summary Sheet #2012-2 and the Employee Information Sheet, complete payroll for two employees

b. Amethyst will receive an advance of $200.00 and repay $50.00 over each of the next four paycheques

c. Pay commissions: 5% of $3,350.00 and 0.5% of $61,424.00 to Amarald and 0.5% of $61,424.00 to Amethyst

d. Manually prepare cheques #1134 and #1135

SD56: Memo #1-3

Dated January 31, 2012

From Owner: Assess finance charges on overdue account from Glitters as of January 31, 2012. Apply unused credits before assessing interest charges.

SD57: Memo #1-4

Dated January 31, 2012

From Owner: Complete adjusting entries for supplies and prepaid expenses for January. Create new Expense account: 5380 Security Expenses.

Prepaid security services	$ 200.00
Prepaid insurance	800.00
Jewellery boxes and bags	120.00
Office and computer supplies	140.00
Jewellery parts and gold	2,390.00

SD58: Memo #1-5

Dated January 31, 2012

From Owner: Make remittance to the Receiver General for HST Payable as of January 31. Issue cheque #1136.

SD59: Memo #1-7

Dated January 31, 2012

From Owner: Pay all payroll liabilities through to January 31, 2012, to the following agencies. Issue cheques #1137 to #1139.
To Receiver General: EI, CPP, and income tax
To Workplace Safety and Insurance Board: WSIB
To Faithful Insurers: Insurance

SD60: Memo #1-8

Dated January 31, 2012

Use the following bank statement to reconcile the Bank Chequing account.

Golddiggers Trust		www.golddiggers.com 200 Spenders Rd. Toronto, ON M2G 4D5 (416) 464-7111		
ACCOUNT January 31/12 Chequing Account 27765 43100		**ACCOUNT HOLDER** Sparkles 55 Glittering Way Toronto, Ontario M3T 5F9		
Date	Item	Deposits	Withdrawals	Balance
	Balance Forward			$32,460.00
01/02/2012	Deposit	$ 1,000.00		$33,460.00
01/04/2012	Deposit	2,277.00		35,737.00
01/04/2012	Cheque 1124		6,355.80	29,381.20
01/06/2012	Cheque 1125		4,194.40	25,186.80
01/07/2012	Deposit	3,790.08		28,976.88
01/10/2012	Deposit	3,500.00		32,476.88
01/15/2012	Cheque 1126		4,181.00	28,295.88
01/15/2012	Cheque 1127		1,356.83	26,939.05
01/15/2012	Cheque 1128		1,041.14	25,897.91
01/18/2012	Cheque 1129		10,920.00	14,977.91
01/19/2012	Deposit	3,276.00		18,253.91
01/20/2012	Deposit	4,600.00		22,853.91
01/20/2012	Deposit	8,848.00		31,701.91
01/24/2012	Cheque 1130		888.00	30,813.91
01/25/2012	Deposit	994.40		31,808.31
01/25/2012	Cheque 1131		5,424.00	26,384.31
01/26/2012	Cheque 1132		135.60	26,248.71
01/28/2012	NSF Cheque		994.40	25,254.31
	NSF Fee		30.00	25,224.31
	Debit Memo		560.00	24,664.31
01/30/2012	Debit Memo		290.00	24,374.31
	Service Fee		30.00	24,344.31
	Interest	50.00		24,394.31
	Closing Balance			$24,394.31
		Total Deposits: 8		$28,335.48
		Total Withdrawals: 14		$36,401.17

Dated January 31, 2012

Use the following bank statement to reconcile the Bank Visa account.

Golddiggers Trust			www.golddiggers.com 200 Spenders Rd. Toronto, ON M2G 4D5 (416) 464-7111	
ACCOUNT			**ACCOUNT HOLDER**	
Visa Deposit Account			Sparkles	
January 31/12			55 Glittering Way	
27765 89971			Toronto, Ontario M3T 5F9	

Date	Item	Deposits	Withdrawals	Balance
	Balance Forward			$ 2,180.00
01/08/2012	Deposit	$ 7,175.50		9,355.50
01/11/2012	Payment		$576.30	8,779.20
01/15/2012	Deposit	14,746.50		23,525.70
01/22/2012	Deposit	10,266.05		33,791.75
01/29/2012	Deposit	16,780.50		50,572.25
01/30/2012	2% transaction fee		967.85	51,540.10
01/31/2012	Closing Balance	$51,540.10		

SUMMARY			
	5 Deposits	$48,968.55	
	2 Withdrawals	$ 1,544.15	

SD62: Memo #1-10

Dated January 31, 2012

Use the following Visa statement to reconcile the Visa Payable account. Write cheque #1140 to Golddiggers Trust Visa (use Quick Add for new Other payee) to pay the full balance.

Golddiggers Trust		www.golddiggers.com 200 Spenders Rd. Toronto, ON M2G 4D5 (416) 464-7111

Visa Statement

ACCOUNT		**ACCOUNT HOLDER**
Visa Account 4550 3948 7449 7171		Sparkles
January 31/12		55 Glittering Way
27765 89971		Toronto, Ontario M3T 5F9

12/30/2011	Marcie's Gifts	$210.00
01/11/2012	Stationers	158.20
01/13/2012	Stationers (credit)	−45.20
01/20/2012	Hardware Surplus Supplies	50.85
01/23/2012	Glass Experts	339.00
01/29/2012	Annual fee	25.00

STATEMENT SUMMARY

New Charges	$548.05	
Credits	$ 45.20	
Balance Owing	$737.85	
Minimum Payment	$ 75.00	by Feb. 12, 2012

SD63: Memo #1-11

Dated January 31, 2012

Transfer $45,000.00 from the Bank Visa account to the Bank Savings account.

Inventory Reports

We saw some reports for inventory items in previous chapters: Sales by Item Summary Report, Sales by Item Detail Report, Item List, and Item Price. The Sales Graph also provides inventory sales information. Refer to Chapter 7 for a review of these reports. The Inventory Sales reports are reviewed on page 645. The Inventory group of reports provides inventory control information for a company.

As with other groups of reports, you can access inventory reports from the Reports menu or from the Report Centre.

We will continue to use the Report Centre because of its report preview feature. To access the same reports from the Report Centre,

1. **Click** the **Report Centre icon** on the Icon bar and **click Inventory** on the left-hand side of the screen to view the list of Inventory reports:

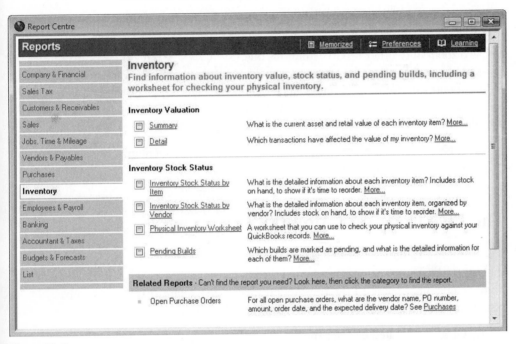

Figure 12-43

The Inventory Valuation Summary Report

The Inventory Valuation Summary Report shows the current totals for all Inventory Part and Inventory Assembly items, the items that have costs and asset values. For each item, the quantity on hand, the total asset value and the retail value based on sales prices are shown. Separate columns show the percentage of the total for each item and value.

1. **Click** **Summary** under the Inventory Valuation heading

2. **Double click** the **date field**

3. **Type** **01/31/12**

> **WARNING!**
> Remember that payroll tax amounts for the Sample file will not be correct for tax reporting purposes.

> **Notes**
> For access from the Reports menu, choose the Reports menu, then choose Inventory, and click the inventory report you want.

> **Notes**
> To access the report from the Reports menu:
> * Choose the Reports menu, then choose Inventory, and click Inventory Valuation Summary to open the report
> * Enter 01/31/12 in the date field
> * Press *tab* or click the Refresh button to update the report

Figure 12-44

The report shows the inventory value on a specific date. You cannot sort this report and the only modification you can make is to select a different date for the valuation. You can also zoom in to other reports from this one.

Double click the summary information for any item to view the Inventory Valuation Detail Report for that item. You may need to edit the date range for the Detail Report if there are no transactions for the individual item on the day of the report. Double click any of the information in the Detail Report to view the original transaction for that detail.

5. **Close** the **report** when finished. Choose not to memorize the changes if you made any

The Inventory Valuation Detail Report

The Inventory Valuation Detail Report includes all transactions for each item during the selected period. The opening value is given, as well as the type of transaction, date, number, customer name (if the transaction was a sale), quantity of items involved, remaining quantity, asset value, and average cost for the item.

1. **Click** **Detail** under the Inventory Valuation heading

2. **Double click** the **From date field**

3. **Type** **01/01/12**

4. **Press** (tab) to select the **To date field**

5. **Type** **01/31/12**

6. **Press** (tab) or click the Refresh button to update the report:

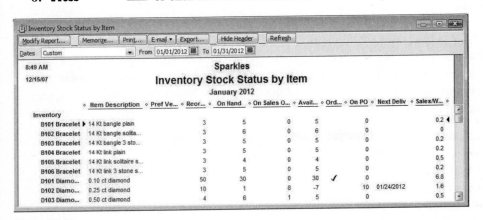

Figure 12-45

You can sort this report by any of the column headings.
You can double click any detail to view the original transaction for that detail.

7. **Close**   the **displayed report** when finished. Choose not to memorize the report if you made any changes.

The Inventory Stock Status by Item Report

The Inventory Stock Status By Item Report is a quantity report. For each item, you will see the preferred vendor for the item, the reorder point, the number currently on order from customers, the number actually in stock, the number on purchase orders, the order date (delivery date), and the average number sold each week during the selected period. In addition, an Order column shows whether the item needs to be ordered because its stock has fallen below the reorder point, so you could use this report to prepare purchase orders.

1. **Click**   **Inventory Stock Status By Item** under the Inventory Stock Status heading

2. **Double click**   the **From** date field

3. **Type**   **01/01/12**

4. **Press**   (tab) to select the To date field

5. **Type**   **01/31/12**

6. **Press**   (tab) or **click** the **Refresh** button to view the report:

Notes
To access the report from the Reports menu:
- Choose the Reports menu, then choose Inventory, and click Inventory Stock Status by Item to open the report
- Enter 01/01/12 in the From date field
- Enter 01/31/12 in the To date field
- Press (tab) or click the Refresh button to update the report

Figure 12-46

The ✓ in the Order column indicates that the item needs to be reordered.

You can modify this report only by entering a different date range.

You can double click any item detail to view the Inventory Valuation Detail Report for that item. Double click any of the information in the Detail Report to view the original transaction for that detail.

7. Close the **displayed report** when finished. Choose not to memorize the changes if you made any.

The Inventory Stock Status by Vendor Report

The Inventory Stock Status by Vendor Report is the Inventory Stock Status By Item Report organized by preferred vendor. For each vendor, the items are listed with the same details as the Item Report. If no vendors are entered, as in our data file, the two reports are the same.

Notes
To access the report from the Reports menu:
- Choose the Reports menu, then choose Inventory, and click Inventory Stock Status by Vendor to open the report
- Enter 01/01/12 in the From date field
- Enter 01/31/12 in the To date field
- Press (tab) or click the Refresh button to update the report

1. Click **Inventory Stock Status by Vendor** under the Inventory Stock Status heading

2. Double click the **From** date field

3. Type **01/01/12**

4. Press (tab) to select the To date field

5. Type **01/31/12**

6. Press (tab) or **click** the **Refresh** button to view the report:

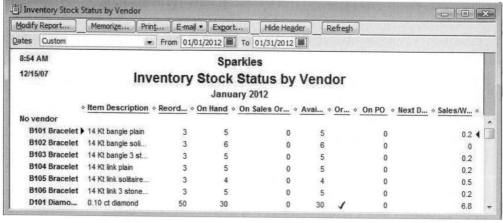

Figure 12-47

The ✓ in the Order column indicates that the item needs to be reordered.

You can modify this report only by entering a different date range.

You can double click any item detail to view the Inventory Valuation Detail Report for that item. Double click any of the information in the Detail Report to view the original transaction for that detail.

7. Close the **displayed report** when finished. Choose not to memorize the report if you made any changes

The Physical Inventory Worksheet

The Physical Inventory Worksheet is a form that you can use for taking inventory in a business. It includes the quantity on hand for each item and a space for entering the actual number found in stock, based on a physical count, i.e., a worksheet. You can handle discrepancies by adjusting the quantity on hand.

1. **Click**   **Physical Inventory Worksheet** under the Inventory Stock Status heading to view the report:

Notes
To access the worksheet from the Reports menu:
- Choose the Reports menu, then choose Inventory, and click Physical Inventory Worksheet to open the worksheet; or
- Choose the Vendors menu, and then choose Inventory Activities, and click Physical Inventory Worksheet to open the worksheet

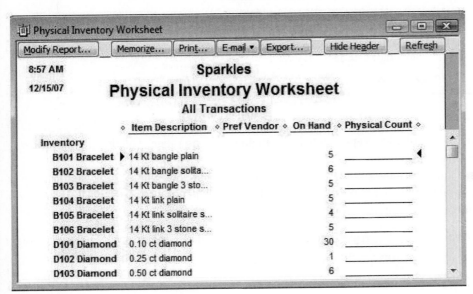

Figure 12-48

You cannot modify or filter this report.

You can double click any item detail to view the Inventory Valuation Detail Report for that item. Double click any of the information in the Detail Report to view the original transaction for that detail.

2. **Close**   the **report** when finished. Choose not to memorize the report if you made any changes

The Pending Builds Report

The Pending Builds Report shows any items that you tried to assemble with insufficient quantities and chose to mark as pending. From the report you can open the form to complete a build.

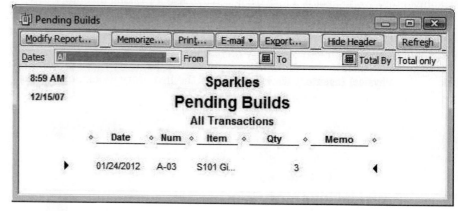

1. **Click**   **Pending Builds** under the Inventory Stock Status heading to view the report:

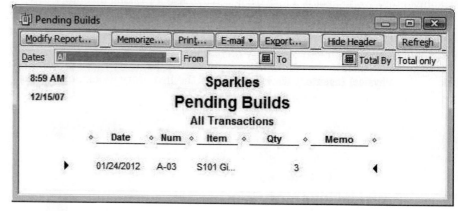

Figure 12-49

You can modify this report only by changing the date range. The default is to show all pending transactions.

You can double click any detail in the report to view the Build Assemblies form for that transaction so that you can complete the build. The form will open with all the information you entered before you marked it as pending.

2. **Close**   the **report** when finished. Choose not to memorize the report if you made any changes

Inventory Reminders

The Reminders list can include a reminder to reorder inventory that has fallen below the minimum or reorder point if the preference is selected in the Reminders preferences. The Reminders list is shown here:

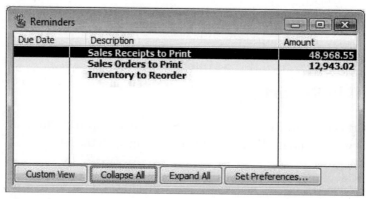

Figure 12-50

1. **Double click** **Inventory to Reorder** to open the list of reminder details:

Due Date	Description	Amount
	Sales Receipts to Print	48,968.55
	Sales Orders to Print	12,943.02
	Inventory to Reorder	
	D101 Diamond	
	P101 Pendant	
	P102 Pendant	
	R103 Ring	
	R104 Ring	

[Custom View] [Collapse All] [Expand All] [Set Preferences...]

Figure 12-51

Notes
The Gift Sets that we need to build do not appear on the Reminders list because the build point was marked as zero.

Assemblies to Build would be added as a separate line when the build point is greater than zero and the number on hand has fallen below the build point.

Sales Reports for Inventory

When the data file includes inventory (inventory part or assembly items), some sales reports have additional information. The zoom-in reports, modifying and filtering features remain unchanged. Refer to Chapter 7 for more information on sales reports.

Sales by Item Summary Report

The Sales by Item Summary Report has different information for different types of items as shown in the following report:

Sales by Item Summary

[Modify Report...] [Memorize...] [Print...] [E-mail ▾] [Export...] [Hide Header] [Collapse] [Refresh]

Dates: Custom From 01/01/2012 To 01/31/2012 Columns: Total only Sort By: Default

9:04 AM
12/15/07
Accrual Basis

Sparkles
Sales by Item Summary
January 2012

	Qty	Amount	% of Sales	Avg Price	COGS	Avg COGS	Gross M...	Gross M...
Inventory								
B101 Bracelet	1	590.00	0.9%	590.00	295.00	295.00	295.00	50.0%
B103 Bracelet	1	625.00	0.9%	625.00	312.50	312.50	312.50	50.0%
B104 Bracelet	1	400.00	0.6%	400.00	200.00	200.00	200.00	50.0%
B105 Bracelet	2	740.00	1.1%	370.00	370.00	185.00	370.00	50.0%
B106 Bracelet	1	430.00	0.7%	430.00	215.00	215.00	215.00	50.0%
D101 Diamo...	30	12,000.00	18.2%	400.00	6,000.00	200.00	6,000.00	50.0%
D102 Diamo...	7	7,000.00	10.6%	1,000.00	3,500.00	500.00	3,500.00	50.0%
D103 Diamo...	2	5,000.00	7.6%	2,500.00	2,500.00	1,250.00	2,500.00	50.0%
D104 Diamo...	1	6,900.00	10.5%	6,900.00	3,450.00	3,450.00	3,450.00	50.0%
E101 Earrings	7	980.00	1.5%	140.00	490.00	70.00	490.00	50.0%
E102 Earrings	8	640.00	1%	80.00	320.00	40.00	320.00	50.0%
E103 Earrings	1	80.00	0.1%	80.00	40.00	40.00	40.00	50.0%
N101 Neckla...	3	1,800.00	2.7%	600.00	900.00	300.00	900.00	50.0%
N102 Neckla...	1	550.00	0.8%	550.00	275.00	275.00	275.00	50.0%

Figure 12-52

Notes
To view the report,
- Open the Report Centre
- Click the Sales heading on the left-hand side of the screen
- Choose Summary under the Sales By Item heading
- Enter 01/01/12 in the From date field
- Press *tab*
- Enter 01/31/12 in the To date field

For the Inventory Part and Inventory Assembly items, the cost of goods sold, the average cost of goods sold, the gross margin and the percentage margin are added to the details provided for other items. For Discount items, only the total and the percentage of total sales is provided.

Pending Sales Report

The Pending Sales report shows the transactions that we marked as pending. In this company file, only one pending build transaction was created. The report is shown here:

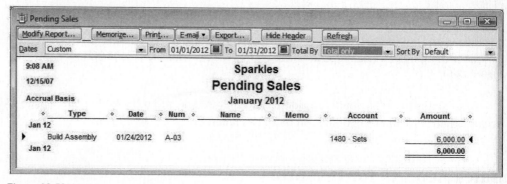

Figure 12-53

You can double click on a pending sale on the report to open the Build Assemblies form to complete the assembly. The Build Assemblies form will open with all the information you entered before you marked it as pending.

Finishing Your Session

1. **Back up**   your **Company data file**

2. **Close**   the **Company file**

3. **Close**   the **QuickBooks program**

Chapter 13 Contre Le Vent: Payroll & Inventory Setup

Chapter 14 Melody's Music Centre: Practice Application

Chapter 13 and Chapter 14 can be found on the CD that accompanies this text.

Note: Page references to "CD" indicate material in Chapters 13 and 14, which can be found on the CD accompanying the text.

"AS IS" LICENSE AGREEMENT AND LIMITED WARRANTY

READ THIS LICENSE CAREFULLY BEFORE OPENING THIS PACKAGE. BY OPENING THIS PACKAGE, YOU ARE AGREEING TO THE TERMS AND CONDITIONS OF THIS LICENSE. IF YOU DO NOT AGREE, DO NOT OPEN THE PACKAGE. PROMPTLY RETURN THE UNOPENED PACKAGE AND ALL ACCOMPANYING ITEMS TO THE PLACE YOU OBTAINED THEM. THESE TERMS APPLY TO ALL LICENSED SOFTWARE ON THE DISK EXCEPT THAT THE TERMS FOR USE OF ANY SHAREWARE OR FREEWARE ON THE DISKETTES ARE AS SET FORTH IN THE ELECTRONIC LICENSE LOCATED ON THE DISK:

1. GRANT OF LICENSE and OWNERSHIP: The enclosed computer programs and any data ("Software") are licensed, not sold, to you by Pearson Canada Inc. ("We" or the "Company") in consideration of your adoption of the accompanying Company textbooks and/or other materials, and your agreement to these terms. You own only the disk(s) but we and/or our licensors own the Software itself. This license allows instructors and students enrolled in the course using the Company textbook that accompanies this Software (the "Course") to use and display the enclosed copy of the Software for academic use only, so long as you comply with the terms of this Agreement. You may make one copy for back up only. We reserve any rights not granted to you.

2. USE RESTRICTIONS: You may not sell or license copies of the Software or the Documentation to others. You may not transfer, distribute or make available the Software or the Documentation, except to instructors and students in your school who are users of the adopted Company textbook that accompanies this Software in connection with the course for which the textbook was adopted. You may not reverse engineer, disassemble, decompile, modify, adapt, translate or create derivative works based on the Software or the Documentation. You may be held legally responsible for any copying or copyright infringement that is caused by your failure to abide by the terms of these restrictions.

3. TERMINATION: This license is effective until terminated. This license will terminate automatically without notice from the Company if you fail to comply with any provisions or limitations of this license. Upon termination, you shall destroy the Documentation and all copies of the Software. All provisions of this Agreement as to limitation and disclaimer of warranties, limitation of liability, remedies or damages, and our ownership rights shall survive termination.

4. DISCLAIMER OF WARRANTY: THE COMPANY AND ITS LICENSORS MAKE NO WARRANTIES ABOUT THE SOFTWARE, WHICH IS PROVIDED "AS-IS." IF THE DISK IS DEFECTIVE IN MATERIALS OR WORKMANSHIP, YOUR ONLY REMEDY IS TO RETURN IT TO THE COMPANY WITHIN 30 DAYS FOR REPLACEMENT UNLESS THE COMPANY DETERMINES IN GOOD FAITH THAT THE DISK HAS BEEN MISUSED OR IMPROPERLY INSTALLED, REPAIRED, ALTERED OR DAMAGED. THE COMPANY DISCLAIMS ALL WARRANTIES, EXPRESS OR IMPLIED, INCLUDING WITHOUT LIMITATION, THE IMPLIED WARRANTIES OF MERCHANTABILITY AND FITNESS FOR A PARTICULAR PURPOSE. THE COMPANY DOES NOT WARRANT, GUARANTEE OR MAKE ANY REPRESENTATION REGARDING THE ACCURACY, RELIABILITY, CURRENTNESS, USE, OR RESULTS OF USE, OF THE SOFTWARE.

5. LIMITATION OF REMEDIES AND DAMAGES: IN NO EVENT, SHALL THE COMPANY OR ITS EMPLOYEES, AGENTS, LICENSORS OR CONTRACTORS BE LIABLE FOR ANY INCIDENTAL, INDIRECT, SPECIAL OR CONSEQUENTIAL DAMAGES ARISING OUT OF OR IN CONNECTION WITH THIS LICENSE OR THE SOFTWARE, INCLUDING, WITHOUT LIMITATION, LOSS OF USE, LOSS OF DATA, LOSS OF INCOME OR PROFIT, OR OTHER LOSSES SUSTAINED AS A RESULT OF INJURY TO ANY PERSON, OR LOSS OF OR DAMAGE TO PROPERTY, OR CLAIMS OF THIRD PARTIES, EVEN IF THE COMPANY OR AN AUTHORIZED REPRESENTATIVE OF THE COMPANY HAS BEEN ADVISED OF THE POSSIBILITY OF SUCH DAMAGES. SOME JURISDICTIONS DO NOT ALLOW THE LIMITATION OF DAMAGES IN CERTAIN CIRCUMSTANCES, SO THE ABOVE LIMITATIONS MAY NOT ALWAYS APPLY.

6. GENERAL: THIS AGREEMENT SHALL BE CONSTRUED AND INTERPRETED ACCORDING TO THE LAWS OF THE PROVINCE OF ONTARIO. This Agreement is the complete and exclusive statement of the agreement between you and the Company and supersedes all proposals, prior agreements, oral or written, and any other communications between you and the company or any of its representatives relating to the subject matter.

Should you have any questions concerning this agreement or if you wish to contact the Company for any reason, please contact in writing: Permissions, Pearson Canada Inc., 26 Prince Andrew Place, Toronto, Ontario M3C 2T8.